AF352679

THE PAPERS OF

FREDERICK LAW OLMSTED

THE PAPERS OF
FREDERICK LAW OLMSTED

SUPPLEMENTARY SERIES
VOLUME I

WRITINGS ON PUBLIC PARKS, PARKWAYS, AND PARK SYSTEMS

CHARLES E. BEVERIDGE

CAROLYN F. HOFFMAN

Editors

THE JOHNS HOPKINS UNIVERSITY PRESS
Baltimore and London

This book has been brought to publication with the generous assistance of the National Historical Publications and Records Commission.

The Johns Hopkins University Press
2715 North Charles Street
Baltimore, Maryland 21218-4319
The Johns Hopkins University Press, Ltd., London

Library of Congress Cataloging-in-Publication Data
(Revised for vol. 6)

Olmsted, Frederick Law, 1822–1903.
  The papers of Frederick Law Olmsted.

  Includes bibliographical references and indexes.
  Contents: v. 1. The formative years, 1822–1852 — v. 2.
Slavery and the South, 1852–1857 — v. 3. Creating Central
Park, 1857–1861 — v. 4. Defending the Union, 1861–1863 —
v. 5. The California frontier, 1863–1865 — v. 6. The years of
Olmstead, Vaux & Company, 1865–1874.
  1. Olmsted, Frederick, 1822–1903. 2. Landscape
architects — United States — Correspondence. 3. Landscape
architects — United States — Biography. I. McLaughlin,
Charles Capen. II. Beveridge, Charles E. III. Title.
SB470.05A2 1977   712   77-741
ISBN 0-8018-1798-6 (v. 1)   ISBN 0-8018-3885-1 (v. 5)
ISBN 0-8018-2242-4 (v. 2)   ISBN 0-8018-4198-4 (v. 6)
ISBN 0-8018-2751-5 (v. 3)   ISBN 0-8018-5532-2 (suppl. ser. v. 1)
ISBN 0-8018-3067-2 (v. 4)

A catalog record of this book is available from the British
Library.

CONTENTS

CONTENTS

ILLUSTRATIONS

ACKNOWLEDGMENTS

The editors wish to give special thanks to the National Endowment for the Humanities, the National Historical Publications and Records Commission, and the Andrew W. Mellon Foundation for their longtime support of the Olmsted Papers and the contributions they made to the preparation of this volume. We also wish to express our gratitude to the Henry Luce Foundation and the Gaylord and Dorothy Donnelley Foundation for their contribution to the funding of this volume.

We wish to thank the many members of the staff of The American University, our sponsoring institution, who assisted in processing the grant proposals and administering the grants that made preparation of this volume possible. Special thanks are due to Professor Roger H. Brown for his strong support of the Olmsted Papers project during his time as chairman of the History Department.

Numerous research assistants contributed welcome energy and perseverance to the process of finding the necessary sources for identifying and explaining Olmsted's statements in the text of this volume. Kevin Corbitt, Susan Hines, Jennifer Altenhofel and Cindi Smith provided this assistance while holding the Olmsted Research Fellowship in the Department of History, funded by the Andrew W. Mellon Foundation. Significant contributions were made as well by Kenneth W. Stringer, Jr., Julie Berebitsky, and Jodi Allison-Bunnell.

Tina Raheem made a major contribution to the volume by transcribing the texts. Former associate editors of the project David Schuyler and Jane Turner Censer made valuable suggestions for improving the introduction and annotation. We very much appreciate the time spent by Charles C.

McLaughlin and other members of the advisory board in reviewing the introduction and other sections of the volume.

Other assistance has come from many different places. Tina Hummel provided us with information concerning Olmsted and Birkenhead Park, while information on Olmsted's partnership with John C. Olmsted was provided by Arleyn A. Levee.

We wish also to acknowledge the assistance provided us by the staff members of numerous institutions, including Kurtzie Gonzales of the Cincinnati Park Board Library, Julia Sniderman of the Chicago Park District, Sara Cedar Miller of the Central Park Conservancy, and the staff of the Archives Municipales of Montreal. A special tribute is due to Rex Wasserman, landscape architect and archivist in the office of the Administrator of Prospect Park in Brooklyn: his enthusiasm for the historical record of the park was always encouraging, and we will greatly miss his help as we work on future volumes.

We have benefitted from the assistance and good will of many persons for gathering the illustrations published in this volume. Once again we have been most fortunate to have Herbert Mitchell make available to us his collection of visual materials for the New York and Brooklyn parks. Important help was provided us by the staff of the Municipal Archives of the City of New York, and the Prints and Photographs Division and Geography and Map Division of the Library of Congress.

Finally, our work would not be possible without access to the Frederick Law Olmsted National Historic Site, maintained by the National Park Service in Brookline, Mass., and the Library of Congress in Washington, D.C. To Rolf Diamant, superintendent of the Olmsted Site, we wish to express our appreciation for his dedication to preserving and making available the rich archive of material in his charge. We are particularly grateful for the assistance for our research at the site provided by Joyce Connolly and Linda Genovese. We owe a debt of gratitude to the Research Facilities of the Library of Congress for supplying us with a research carrel over many years, and to the staff of the Manuscript Division for the assistance they give for our research in the papers of Olmsted and his firm that are in their holdings.

EDITORIAL POLICY

The purpose of the Frederick Law Olmsted Papers project is to publish, in annotated form, the most significant of Olmsted's letters, unpublished writings, professional reports, and articles for newspapers and periodicals. The letterpress edition will consist of twelve volumes: ten volumes arranged chronologically, one volume containing major documents on park design and city planning, and one large-format volume of plans and views of landscape designs.

Document Selection   Although the process is to some extent subjective, the editors require every document published to meet at least one of three criteria: that it provide insight into Olmsted's character, present valuable commentary on his times, or contain an important statement on landscape design.

Annotation   The editors believe that it is their responsibility to make clear the context within which Olmsted wrote the documents selected and to explain the significance of certain statements that readers not expert in the field might otherwise not adequately comprehend. They believe also that part of their function is to identify the persons, places, and events Olmsted mentions, and to explain his relation to them. The annotation in these volumes is fuller than it would be in a complete edition of Olmsted's papers, where the documents would more frequently annotate one another. In order to supply background information and provide continuity within each volume, the editors make use of volume introductions, biographical directories, and chapter headnotes, as well as chronologies, itineraries, genealogies, and other aids for the reader.

Treatment of Text   The intent of the editors is to provide a text as close to the original as possible without causing undue difficulty for the reader. In some instances we alter the original text in the interest of clarity: in such cases, we furnish guides to our alterations that permit recovery of the original text.

The complete existing text of each document is published. All of the words that Olmsted wrote and did not cross out are presented, with the exception of inadvertently repeated words. The treatment of illegible and missing words is as follows:

> {. . .} indicates illegible words or words missing because of mutilation of the manuscript.
>
> {*italic*} indicates the editor's reading of partially missing words.
>
> {roman} indicates a word supplied by the editors.

Where needed, these braces are supplemented by an explanatory endnote.

In the occasional instance where a passage does not make sense without substitution of a word or words for those in the original version, the editors make the needed substitution and supply the original wording in an endnote. When the word that Olmsted wrote appears not to be the one he meant to write and the correct word cannot be discerned, the editors suggest, in an endnote, an alternative word or phrase that seems closer to Olmsted's meaning. Where the document is not in Olmsted's hand and what appears to be incorrect wording may be due to the error of a transcriber or typesetter, one of these two approaches is used as well.

The published texts include words and phrases deleted by Olmsted only when they add material that does not appear at some other point in the document. If they are integral to the document, such deleted words are presented in the text in italics and in braces. If the deleted words are less directly relevant to the theme of the document, they are given in an endnote.

The principles of transcription stated here are applied by the editors to all kinds of documents, including drafts of articles and lectures that exist in "fair copy" as well as fragmentary drafts. When preparing a text from manuscript fragments that have no clear order, the editors construct a text, adding such indications as microfilm reel and frame numbers, extra spaces between lines of text, dividing lines, ellipses, and endnotes, to mark the transition from one segment of the original text to another. When a document exists in both printed and manuscript form, and Olmsted wrote the document for publication (as, for instance, with park reports), the most complete version is used as the basic text. If the other version or versions contain significant variations from that text, the differences are described and quoted in notes added at the appropriate places in the document. The first, unnumbered, endnote to the document explains the textual treatment in such cases.

For manuscripts that were published at a later date, the original version is used as the basic text. Differences between the two versions that appear to be printer's or transcriber's errors are noted in endnotes, as are changes apparently made by Olmsted for the published version; obvious typographical errors, such as incorrect, missing, or transposed letters, are silently corrected when a published version of a document is being used as the text.

At the end of this volume the editors provide a list of textual alterations, giving the original form of texts or quoted material where a change has not been indicated in endnotes or by braces in the text. The list indicates the original form of contractions that have been expanded. It gives each deleted or altered punctuation mark with the word preceding and the word following it, and indicates added punctuation by giving the words preceding and following it. The list indicates the original form of misspelled words that have been corrected in the text, except as noted below.

Spelling   Olmsted consistently misspelled words with double consonants (as "dissapoint" for "disappoint"). He frequently misspelled words with double vowels (consistently writing "lose" as "loose"), and he misspelled words with the diphthong "ie" (as "cheif" for "chief"). The editors silently correct these three kinds of Olmsted's misspellings. All other misspelled words are presented in the text as Olmsted wrote them. If the misspelling makes a word particularly difficult to interpret, however, it is corrected and its misspelled form is presented in the list of textual alterations. Terms such as "can not" and "no where" have been silently corrected to their modern-day forms "cannot" and "nowhere."

Paragraphing   The editors follow Olmsted's indications of internal paragraphing. Where he indicated a paragraph by a long dash or a large space between sentences, we silently make a new paragraph. We do the same where he inserted a paragraph symbol or where a change in subject matter between two pages of manuscript indicates that he used the page change as a paragraph. Sections of conversations are silently rendered as paragraphs. Other paragraphing introduced by the editors is indicated in the list of textual alterations.

Contractions   The editors present the original form of abbreviations and contractions. Superscripts are reproduced. Apostrophes are silently added if they are missing from the contraction "nt" (for "not"), from conjugations of the verb "to be," and from possessives. Particularly awkward or unclear contractions are expanded and the original form is indicated in the list of textual alterations.

Punctuation   The editors do not regularize Olmsted's punctuation or make it consistently grammatical; but we do make changes in his punctuation when it would be difficult for the reader to work out the meaning of a passage in its original form. In long and convoluted sentences, or where the original text is likely to cause the reader to misread phrases, the editors alter punctuation. We occasionally delete punctuation where it unnecessarily complicates already difficult passages, and we add punctuation in order to clarify basic sentence structure. These changes are not indicated in the text itself by braces or other symbols, since that would introduce new distractions and complexity at the very place where they would be most troublesome. Instead, the changes are given in the list of textual alterations. We silently supply periods where the end of a line served for Olmsted as the end of a sentence.

Marginalia   Material that Olmsted added in the margins is presented at the point where he indicated that it belongs. If such material has no clear place within the text, it is printed at the end of the document with an explanatory note. Notes or jottings on a document by other persons are not included in the text, but if informative are given in an endnote. Olmsted's infrequent footnotes are presented at the bottom of the page.

Place and Date of Documents   Dates for documents are given as they appear in the original. If that information is partial, incorrect, or missing, the probable date or time period is supplied in brackets, with an explanatory endnote if needed. Printed letterheads that are misleading are not reproduced but are noted in the first, unnumbered, endnote of the letter.

Arrangement of Documents   Documents are presented in chronological order except for occasional pieces such as autobiographical fragments or reminiscences written at a later time than the period covered in the volume. Such pieces are presented with the documents from the period they describe.

Citation of Sources   Full bibliographical information is provided in the first citation of a source in each chapter, except for sources that appear in a volume's list of "Short Titles Used in Citations." The latter are cited consistently by short title throughout the volume. A full listing of sources about an individual is given in the note accompanying the first mention of that person in the documents of a volume. In subsequent references, sources are given only for additional information supplied. Birth and death dates for persons mentioned in the text of the documents are given in the first note identifying them and, for selected persons, in the index.

If no repository is given for a manuscript, this means that it may be found in the Frederick Law Olmsted Papers, Manuscript Division, Library of Congress, Washington, D.C.

SHORT TITLES
USED IN CITATIONS

1. Correspondents' Names

BCCP	Board of Commissioners of the Central Park
BCPP	Board of Commissioners of Prospect Park
BPC	Brooklyn Park Commission
CV	Calvert Vaux
DPP	Department of Public Parks
FLO	Frederick Law Olmsted
FLO, Jr.	Frederick Law Olmsted, Jr.
JCO	John Charles Olmsted
MPO	Mary Perkins Olmsted
OVC	Olmsted, Vaux & Company

2. Standard References

DAB	*Dictionary of American Biography*
DNB	*Dictionary of National Biography*
EB	*Encyclopaedia Britannica*
NCAB	*National Cyclopaedia of American Biography*
OED	*Oxford English Dictionary*

3. Books by Frederick Law Olmsted

Walks and Talks   *Walks and Talks of an American Farmer in England*, 2 vols. in 1 (New York, 1852).

4. Other Published Works

Appleton's Cyc. Am. Biog.   *Appleton's Cyclopedia of American Biography,*
ed. James G. Wilson and John Fiske (New York, 1887–89).

BCCP, _______ *Annual Report* [18–]   New York City, Board of Commissioners of the Central Park, *Annual Report* (New York, 1858–70). Each annual report covers the calendar year preceding the year of publication.

BCCP, *Minutes*   New York City, Board of Commissioners of the Central Park, *Minutes of Proceedings of the Board of Commissioners of the Central Park* (New York, 1858–69).

BCPP, _______ *Annual Report* [18–]   Board of Commissioners of Prospect Park, *Annual Report* (Brooklyn, 1866–68).

BPC, *Annual Reports, 1861–1873*   Brooklyn, Park Commissioners, *Annual Reports of the Brooklyn Park Commissioners, 1861–1873* (Brooklyn, 1873).

BPC, _______ *Annual Report* [18–]   Brooklyn Park Commission, *Annual Report* (Brooklyn, 1869–1886).

DPP, _______ *Annual Report* [18–]   New York (City), Department of Public Parks, *Annual Report* (New York, 1871– 72). Each annual report covers the calender year preceding the year of publication.

DPP, *Minutes*   New York (City), Department of Public Parks, *Minutes* (New York, 1870–74).

Forty Years   Frederick Law Olmsted, Jr., and Theodora Kimball, eds., *Frederick Law Olmsted, Landscape Architect, 1822–1903 (Forty Years of Landscape Architecture),* 2 vols. (New York, 1922–28).

Papers of FLO   *The Papers of Frederick Law Olmsted,* ed. Charles C. McLaughlin et al. (Baltimore, 1977–).

5. Unpublished Sources

OAR/LC   Olmsted Associates Records, Library of Congress, Washington, D.C. Citations give box or volume number, followed by (respectively) folder or page number (i.e., A21: 624 for volume A21, page 624, or B74: #1032 for Box B74, folder number 1032). The folder number is the same as the job number assigned a given project by the Olmsted firm — in this case project 1032 is Leland Stanford, Jr., University.

THE PAPERS OF
FREDERICK LAW OLMSTED

INTRODUCTION

Although Frederick Law Olmsted spent much of his career planning public parks and recreation grounds, and explaining the purpose of his designs to his clients, he wrote no treatise on the subject. Instead, he provided partial statements as he faced particular tasks or presented general discussions in occasional lectures and articles. This volume draws together eighteen of Olmsted's most cogent statements on the subject. The documents range through his entire career — from his first experience of a public park at Birkenhead in England to an attempt in the year before his retirement to explain the purpose of parks to the Cincinnati park commission. They reveal many aspects of the special landscape qualities and social functions of the public park as he defined it.

The documents include descriptions of the two other major elements of public design that Olmsted and his partner Calvert Vaux developed during a collaboration that spanned the years 1857 to 1874. One of these was the "parkway," most thoroughly described in their report of 1868 to the commissioners of Prospect Park and further elaborated in the 1868 Buffalo report. Both of these documents indicate how the parkway was to structure the expanding city, supplying arterial routes through newly settled areas and extending green recreation space beyond the parks themselves. The other element was the park system, which Olmsted and Vaux first developed in a comprehensive way in Buffalo, New York, in 1868, and which Olmsted and his stepson and partner, John C. Olmsted, expanded further in that city in 1888. This, too, had important implications for planning the growth of cities.

All of the material presented here was part of Olmsted's attempt to explain to the American public his purpose as a landscape architect. His earlier career as a writer had given him the discipline to write even under adverse conditions such as he encountered on his voyage to China as a ship's boy in 1843–44, his six-month walking tour of Britain and the Continent in 1850, during the twelve months that he spent touring the American South by steamboat, stagecoach, and on horseback in 1852–54. In those travel writings Olmsted demonstrated an observant eye and a keen ear for nuances of speech. They suggest that writing narrative and description came easily to him. But setting forth abstract concepts of the art of landscape design was a much more demanding task, and Olmsted's prose often reflected the difficulty he experienced. He was trying to express what he considered to be original views and could turn only occasionally to more felicitous writers for help. In those writings for which early drafts survive, as with the Niagara Reservation report of 1887, it is clear that he struggled over his work, writing and rewriting crucial sections until he finally produced a draft that was acceptable to him.

The importance that Olmsted attached to the very considerable writing that he managed to do amidst the pressure of design work is indicated by the numerous times that he paid to publish writings for which he wanted a wider audience than the one for which he originally wrote them. In 1865–66, for instance, he published in New York a version of his report on the campus and community of the College of California at Berkeley before it was published in San Francisco. During the same period he expanded his report on the campus of the University of Massachusetts at Amherst and published it as *A Few Things to be Thought of before Proceeding to Plan Buildings for the National Agricultural Colleges.*[1]

He also published two reports concerning his proposals for Belle Isle in Detroit in an effort to create support for carrying out his plan for that Detroit park. The first of these, *The Park for Detroit* of 1882[2] described his plan, while *Belle Isle: After One Year* of 1884, printed below, focused on his efforts to secure construction of the remarkable shingle-style wharf and shelter that he designed for the island. He paid for the publication of other documents in this volume as well. In 1880 he published *A Consideration of the Justifying Value of a Public Park* after finding that the version printed in the *Journal of Social Science* contained many errors. A year later he published his long report on Mount Royal when it became clear that the park commissioners of Montreal did not intend to do so.

The early 1880s, as Olmsted was establishing his new residence and office in Brookline, Massachusetts, was an especially active period for his self-publishing: in 1882 he also published *The Spoils of the Park. With a Few Leaves from the Deep-Laden Note-Books of "A Wholly Unpractical Man,"* a memoir of the mismanagement of Central Park in New York. He continued the practice of publishing writings that were especially important to him until late in his career, issuing *Observations on the Treatment of Public Plantations, More Especially Relating to The Use of the Axe*[3] in 1889 and *Governmental*

Preservation of Natural Scenery, in response to a controversy over the management of the Yosemite reservation, in 1890.

Several key themes run through the documents in this volume. In them Olmsted explored the qualities of scenery desirable in a park and analyzed the psychological effect of such scenery. He also explored the problem of reconciling the need, on the one hand, for preparing the park site for the presence of large numbers of people and, on the other, of creating extended passages of landscape. He discussed the kind of management program needed and the relationship between the park commission, the landscape architect, and the park-using public. The report of 1873 on the Central Park keepers demonstrates the great importance he attached to developing a cadre of park police who could educate the public in the proper use of the park while creating an atmosphere of safety by their vigilant manner and military bearing.

Elsewhere there are classic statements on the art of park design. An outstanding example occurs in the 1872 reports on Central Park. There Olmsted observed that while no one had proposed to use the chambers of the recently erected New York County courthouse for restaurants and other nonjudicial purposes, proposals equally inappropriate and disruptive were constantly being made for Central Park. After providing a long list of incongruous uses that had been urged for the park, he declared,

> The only solid ground of resistance to dangers of this class will be found to rest in the conviction that the Park throughout is a single work of art, and as such, subject to the primary law of every work of art, namely, that it shall be framed upon a single, noble motive, to which the design of all its parts, in some more or less subtle way, shall be confluent and helpful.[4]

The importance of unity of design, with subordination of all parts to the unity of the whole, is a continuous theme in Olmsted's writing about parks.

Another theme that became increasingly important for him is the nature and purpose of parks. That single issue was central to his public design work, though little understood by his contemporaries. The issue provided the focus for "A Consideration of the Justifying Value of a Public Park," written in 1880, and remained a concern as late as his report to the Cincinnati park commission of 1894. One of the great ills of modern society, he argued, is a nervous disability caused by the stress of urban life and exacerbated by the artificiality of the city environment. The most effective antidote to this sickness, he was convinced, was a certain kind of scenery. The purpose of the urban park (as opposed to the whole range of other kinds of public recreation grounds that he designed) was to provide the scenery that most effectively counteracts and cures this nervous affliction. Anything in a park that strengthens the therapeutic action of scenery increases the value of the expenditure for the park; anything that reduces or degrades the effect of the scenery is both an economic waste and psychological misfortune. To enable parks to serve the purpose for which they were created, continuity of management with those particular purposes in mind is essential.

Accordingly, Olmsted devoted much attention to promoting a form of park management by independent commissions under the close guidance of landscape architects. This arrangement offered protection from demands to use parks for activities that would lessen their value for the one purpose that justified their existence. His desire to foster public recognition of the single, true purpose of the urban park, and of the system of management that would sustain that conception, provided the chief impetus for Olmsted's frequent publications on the subject of parks and their use.

The writings in this volume also demonstrate the importance to Olmsted of collaboration with professionals in other fields, particularly engineering and architecture. Frequently the problems he had to solve involved city-planning issues that required comprehensive sanitary engineering. At the same time, he often found that engineers were not sufficiently aware of aesthetic considerations. A prime illustration was the transformation of the Back Bay Fens, where Olmsted's concern for landscape led to a result far different from those previously developed as a solution to similar problems. Moreover, his inclusion of the architect Henry Hobson Richardson in the designing of bridges for the Fens marked an important stage in the remarkable collaboration between the two men that took place in the early 1880s.

"The People's Park at Birkenhead, near Liverpool," 1851

This article, from A. J. Downing's journal the *Horticulturist*, was Olmsted's first published writing on parks. It describes his response to the first designed park that he had the opportunity to examine. He visited Birkenhead Park in the summer of 1850 as he began a six-month walking tour of the British Isles and the Continent with his brother John Hull Olmsted and close friend Charles Loring Brace. At that time Olmsted was operating his own farm on Staten Island and was actively involved with the agricultural society there. Much of the book he wrote describing the first part of his journey with his friends, from Liverpool to the Isle of Wight and then on to London, contains descriptions of British farming practices, as befitted a book entitled *Walks and Talks of an American Farmer in England*. He recorded his enthusiastic appreciation of English scenery as well. Moreover, he admired the various communal institutions that he found in the suburban town of Birkenhead, on the Mersey River across from Liverpool. Laid out in the early 1840s, the suburb had developed in conjunction with the rise of the great Laird shipyards on the Wirral peninsula.[5] The 125-acre park was impressive to Olmsted both because it was the first "freely accessible public park" to be authorized by Parliament and because of the skill of its designer, the architect and landscape gardener Sir Joseph Paxton, who later designed the Crystal Palace for the Exposition of 1851 in London. "We passed through winding paths, over acres and acres, with a constant varying surface," Olmsted related, "where on all sides were growing every variety of shrubs and flowers, with more than natural grace, all set in borders of greenest, closest turf, and all kept with most consummate neatness." He testified that "five minutes of admiration, and a few more spent in studying the manner in which art had been employed to obtain from nature so much beauty, and I was ready to admit that in democratic America, there was nothing to be thought of as comparable with this People's Garden."[6]

Both elements made a deep impression on him — the fact that such a work of art was a communal institution open without charge to all classes, and the particular means taken by the designer to make the park such a success. Although Paxton planted in a less naturalistic way than Olmsted would come to do when he created profuse masses of shrubs along winding paths on steep ground — as in the Ramble in Central Park — and although Paxton's walks and drives followed simpler curves than would the sinuous and subtly varied ways in Olmsted's parks, there was much that Olmsted could, and apparently did, learn from the designer of Birkenhead Park. In his encyclopedia article "Park," included in this volume, Olmsted stated that Birkenhead Park was "one of the most instructive to study in Europe." The park contained the same dense planting on steep slopes and open lawn-like treatment of level areas that Olmsted consistently created in his own work in later decades, producing the same separation of the picturesque and pastoral landscape styles. Paxton's park, like Olmsted's, had paths with easy grades and gentle curves. And, as Olmsted noted at some length in his article, the walks and drives were carefully designed to provide a smooth and well-drained surface for park users. Olmsted incorporated all of these elements into his first park design, that of Central Park in 1858. Birkenhead Park provided his first demonstration of the contribution a public park could make to a community. No other park that he saw in England or on the Continent provided him with so many lessons concerning landscape composition and engineering.

As indicated by the comment that A. J. Downing added at the end of the piece, the editor of the *Horticulturist* welcomed Olmsted's article as a contribution to the campaign for creating a large park for New York City that was occurring at the time. Ever since founding the *Horticulturist* in 1846, Downing had occasionally urged the importance of creating parks in American towns and cities. Then, in the summer of 1850, he visited England for the first time. After his return to the United States in the fall, he published several letters on his travels in England. Meantime, the pressure to create a New York City park increased, and in the fall elections of 1850 the victorious mayoral candidate, Ambrose Kingsland, embraced the cause. He had not acted on his campaign promise when Downing published Olmsted's article on Birkenhead Park, but during that same month of May 1851, Kingsland called on the New York Common Council to create a 160-acre park on the East River site known as Jones Wood. Olmsted's article of May 1851 became the first of three articles that Downing published in the *Horticulturist* in a four-month period addressing the issue of a park in New York City. In June he published an article enthusiastically describing the parks of London that he had visited the previous summer. Two months after that, in the August 1851 issue of the *Horticulturist,* Downing published his most cogent statement, entitled "The New-York Park," calling for a larger park than the Jones Wood site would provide, and describing the variety of features that the park should contain.[7]

Olmsted's Early Park Designs, 1858–1866

The principal documents relating to Olmsted's early park designs, covering his work in Manhattan and the San Francisco Bay area between 1857 and 1866, have been published in volumes 3 and 5 of the Olmsted Papers series. They chronicle the evolution of the Central Park design as it changed during the years of construction. The most striking change from the original "Greensward" plan was Olmsted and Vaux's proposal of 1858–59 to expand the innovative separation of traffic ways that their competition design of 1858 had provided for crosstown traffic by means of four sunken transverse roads. They proposed as well to separate the three interior circulation systems — walks, bridle paths, and drives — from each other. The commissioners approved the new plan and much of the system of ways in the lower park was constructed by the summer of 1861.[8]

During his stay in California from 1863 to 1865, Olmsted began to evolve a style of landscape design appropriate for the semiarid American West. Since he felt that creation of broad landscape effects in the California climate was undesirable and that the irrigation to sustain them would be too costly, he designed no parks for that region. The main feature of the system of "public pleasure grounds" that he proposed for San Francisco was a wide, sunken "General Promenade" with separate ways for carriages, equestrians, and pedestrians that would run a four-mile course from the harbor along the line of Van Ness Street and on to the vicinity of present-day Buena Vista Park. Along the promenade Olmsted proposed a series of decorative plantings and scientific displays that were a far cry from the rigid subordination of all elements to overall landscape effect that he insisted on in his parks. The linear alameda of Spain, and not the pastoral park of England, was the model for his system of recreation grounds for a metropolis in the semiarid West.[9]

Other significant aspects of Olmsted's later design work also appeared during his projects of 1864–66 for California sites. His first effort to preserve a streamway in an urban area was for Strawberry Creek in Berkeley, which he proposed to retain as part of the campus of the College of California, with its upper reaches above the campus serving as a public recreation area. His first plan for a scenic carriageway, moreover, was for Piedmont Way, which was to run along the hills from Berkeley to eastern Oakland.[10]

During his years in California in the 1860s, Olmsted also continued to develop his views of the psychological effect of scenery. In his San Francisco report he stressed the importance of the relaxing and reviving effect of the public spaces he designed. The stress of business was particularly debilitating in San Francisco, he observed: "Cases of death, or of unwilling withdrawal from active business, compelled by premature failure of the vigor of the brain, are more common in San Francisco than anywhere else . . ." Daily access to public recreation grounds would be the best antidote.[11]

In his report of 1865 as chairman of the commission in charge of the Yosemite grant, Olmsted also analyzed the nature of the effect of scenery. The experience of natural scenery contrasted with the "severe and excessive exercise of the mind" demanded by close pursuit of details leading to future goals:

> In the interest which natural scenery inspires there is the strongest contrast to this. It is for itself and at the moment it is enjoyed. The attention is aroused and the mind occupied without purpose, without a continuation of the common process of relating the present action, thought or perception to some future end. There is little else that has this quality so purely. There are few enjoyments with which regard for something outside and beyond the enjoyment of the moment can ordinarily be so little mixed. . . . It therefore results that the enjoyment of scenery employs the mind without fatigue and yet exercises it, tranquilizes it and yet enlivens it; and thus, through the influence of the mind over the body, gives the effect of refreshing rest and reinvigoration to the whole system.[12]

The Yosemite report also contains Olmsted's most comprehensive statement on the importance of reserving areas of great scenic beauty for enjoyment by all members of society.

"Preliminary Report to the Commissioners for Laying Out a Park in Brooklyn, New York," 1866

With his return to New York City in the fall of 1865 and his professional reunion with Calvert Vaux, Olmsted focused his attention on the first public park whose site was at all suitable for creating truly park-like scenery. The site as originally selected had serious shortcomings, since it was bisected by Flatbush Avenue and had no section that would permit the breadth of landscape treatment that was the most important element in a park. Vaux had resolved this problem while Olmsted was still in California, prevailing on the commissioners to abandon the section north of Flatbush Avenue and to acquire additional land to the south and west that permitted creation of the Long Meadow and Prospect Lake. To secure land for what became the Long Meadow, Vaux proposed in his report of February 4, 1865, to extend the park along Ninth Avenue from 3rd Street to 14th Street. This created an extension three blocks deep between 9th and 12th streets, but left intact the Quaker cemetery that lay southeast of Eleventh Avenue between 11th and 14th streets. (See Vaux's plan on page 82 below.) By the time that Olmsted and Vaux drew up their plan a year later, they had further extended the park to 15th Street, absorbing and removing the cemetery. An important purpose of their report was to show the significance of securing adequate "range" of pastoral scenery in the Green, later called the Long Meadow.

In Prospect Park, Olmsted and Vaux carried out their most notable passage of scenery in the "pastoral" style. As they explained in a report published below,

> Civilized men, while they are gaining ground against certain acute forms of disease, are growing more and more subject to other and more insidious enemies to their health and happiness, and against these the remedy and preventive cannot be found in medicine or in athletic recreation but only in sunlight and such forms of gentle exercise as are calculated to equalize the circulation and relieve the brain.

Olmsted and Vaux taught that "*a sense of enlarged freedom* is to all, at all times, the most certain and the most valuable gratification afforded by a park."[13] Scenery that made this experience possible was the most desirable to secure. In their reports on Prospect Park Olmsted and his partner offered a clear statement of the psychological effect of park scenery and its relation to the rationale for creating parks. Based on this analysis, Olmsted drew conclusions that he would often repeat in the years to come:

> A park is a work of art, designed to produce certain effects upon the mind of men. There should be nothing in it, absolutely nothing, which does not represent study, design, a sagacious consideration & application of known laws of cause & effect with reference to that end.[14]

At the same time, the designers clearly defined the social purpose that underlay that psychological purpose. In California, while chronicling the development of the Mariposa Estate, Olmsted had concluded that the most important quality in members of society was what he termed "communitiveness." This was a combination of qualities that enabled people "to serve others and to be served by others in the most intimate, complete and extended degree imaginable."[15] Olmsted's goal for society was to make that exchange of service as effective as possible. An important purpose of his parkplanning was to restore the energy that people expended in the exercise of their duties. Much of his landscape design work was dedicated to promoting the values of community in one fashion or another, and none was more important than fostering "communitiveness." Accordingly, as he explained in the Prospect Park report of 1866, the "recuperation and recreation of force" that had been expended in exchange of service was the prime purpose of a park.

To illustrate this concept, he referred to an old story about Aesop.

According to this fable, one day when Aesop was playing games with some children an Athenian chastised him for such frivolous activity. In response he took a bow and bent it, observing that if not soon unbent it would lose all spring and flexibility. People must also "unbend" occasionally or suffer a similar fate.[16] In daily life, this was best achieved by "occupation of the imagination with objects and reflections of a quite different character from those which are associated with their bent condition." The scenery that best served this purpose would provide the most complete contrast to the conditions of the daily workplace. Resorting to another image, Olmsted described this scenery by invoking the Twenty-third Psalm with its rhapsodic phrases: "He maketh me to lie down in green pastures; he leadeth me beside the still waters. He restoreth my soul."

The report also explains how Olmsted and Vaux designed their parks so as to give the visitor a sense of space that extended well beyond the field of view at any given time, appearing to reach far beyond the actual borders of the park. The 1866 Prospect Park report includes a detailed description of the way they arranged such an experience for visitors entering Central Park from present-day Columbus Circle.

Despite the importance of scenery in a park, however, Olmsted's purpose was not simply to imitate nature. Rather, he proposed to bring together in a coherent and harmonious way the several highest ideals of the scenic character of a site. The report clearly shows this to be another of his basic precepts of landscape design. Accomplishment of this goal, while providing necessary architectural elements, was what constituted the art of landscape architecture.[17]

While the report emphasizes the value of extended passages of pastoral scenery in a park, it also recognizes the need to provide for large numbers of visitors. Both considerations were important, and they could not be fully harmonized. It was necessary to construct walks and drives sufficiently wide that visitors need not worry about the danger of collision. Yet these artificial elements must also order and enhance the experience of the landscape, and so must fit into it — though not at the expense of the engineering needed to make them usable in all weather conditions.[18] Moreover, the park must be equipped to serve large numbers of visitors at the same time. "Men must come together, and must be seen coming together, in carriages, on horseback and on foot, and the concourse of animated life which will thus be formed, must in itself be made, if possible, an attractive and diverting spectacle."[19] Olmsted and Vaux achieved this goal in Prospect Park through the liberal dimensions of the music grove area and outlook concourse, and, a few years later, in the "promenade" area along the southern edge of Prospect Lake.[20] The large refectory and series of terraces and boat landings that they proposed for the northern shore of the lake (but never constructed) were planned to meet further social needs of visitors. All of these features were intended to enrich the experience of the park. The only other facility proposed was a menagerie along Ninth Avenue in the vicinity of Litchfield Mansion, in a space the designers viewed as ancillary to the park landscape. Similar considerations led to placing the children's play area and boat pond (later named the Vale of Cashmere) on the edge of the park near Flatbush Avenue. On the opposite side of Flatbush Avenue, Olmsted and Vaux proposed to locate various institutions of popular education that the city needed but that would be intrusive and destructive to the park if placed within it. The area eventually became part of the Brooklyn Botanic Garden, and both the Brooklyn Public Library and the Brooklyn Museum were sited nearby.

Report on Parkways
to the Brooklyn Park Commission, 1868

With a treatise of 1868 to the commissioners of Prospect Park, the third report in this volume, Olmsted turned to creation of a coherent system of parks and public spaces in a city. In the process, he wrote an extended commentary on the history of city planning and street design. He believed strongly that the closely built commercial and industrial city of the early nineteenth century, as epitomized by New York, represented the persistence of anachronistic habits that were harmful both to amenity and to health. His solution was to create a "more openly built" city whose sections devoted to manufacture and trade were separate from residential areas of low density that provided healthful conditions and access to sunlight and fresh air. To plan otherwise was to perpetuate a tradition by which the dead hand of the medieval city, constructed for defense, would blight the lives of modern-day city dwellers. Olmsted would further develop this theme of anachronism in his 1879 article "The Future of New-York," in which he asserted that the city's row houses represented "a confession that it is impossible to build a convenient and tasteful residence in New-York, adapted to the ordinary civilized requirements of a single family, except at a cost which even rich men find generally prohibitory." The plan of the row house, he declared, was "more nearly that of a light house built upon a wave-lashed rock, than of a civilized family home."[21]

To illustrate the persistence of anachronistic ways of planning streets and cities, he constructed a description of the history of "street arrangements" prior to his time. Such a detailed historical analysis was unusual for Olmsted, and may in this case have been a response to a recently published report by Andrew Haswell Green, the controller and most powerful member of the Central Park commission. Green's report, describing the commission's street plans for Manhattan, included an historical section that referred to the streets of ancient Athens and Rome and seventeenth-century London.[22] Olmsted was probably annoyed that he and Vaux were not being consulted in the preparation of the new uptown avenues and boulevards in Manhattan and surely

12

resented Green's characterization of green medians in wide streets as "fanciful arrangements."[23]

Olmsted's solution for the modern city was construction of wide "parkways" that would extend the recreation grounds of cities while at the same time structuring their growth. In Brooklyn he envisioned parkways radiating from Prospect Park and providing easy access to the park while creating a series of "parkway neighborhoods" that would realize the great potential of the city as a place of residences. The parkways would extend from Fort Hamilton on New York Bay to Ravenswood on the East River opposite the Central Park section of Manhattan, and from Prospect Park to the ocean at Concy Island.

The key innovation of the parkway that Olmsted and Vaux first described in this report, and first saw constructed in Brooklyn, was the separation of ways of transit that it introduced. The highest development of urban streets thus far, in Olmsted's view, had been the Avenue Unter den Linden in Berlin and the Avenue de l'Imperatrice in Paris. Both were exceptionally wide streets with some separation of ways and wide strips of grass and trees. Olmsted and Vaux's proposed Brooklyn parkway was 270 feet wide from house to house and 210 feet between the rows of trees along the sidewalks on either side. Inside of these were four medians, each 7.5 feet wide with a single row of trees, separating the other traffic routes. These were two side roads for wagons and service to the houses, two pedestrian paths, and, in the center, the "Park Way," 65 feet wide with smooth pavement and intended for the exclusive use of private carriages. By this arrangement, private conveyances could quickly and easily move through the city without the impediment of the carts of commerce or the jolting of cobblestone streets. The creation of such separate ways was in keeping with Olmsted's longstanding desire for division of labor within cities, whereby individuals served others with specific kinds of expertise and wherein each physical arrangement realized as fully as possible the same kind of fine-tuned meeting of particular needs. Olmsted and Vaux utilized both the concept of the parkway and the term in their later urban planning. In the twentieth century this concept has seen extensive application in the form of the automobile parkway, providing a pleasant greenway for private cars separate from trucks and other commercial vehicles.

While the separate, central "park way" for carriages was the key element of Olmsted and Vaux's innovation, the parkway was also an important part of the city's park system. It extended to many sections of the city the amenity of green open space found in the park itself, and so served the needs of citizens when they lacked the means or the time to visit the park. This extension of the amenity of park-like space was crucially important, for, as Olmsted asserted once again in this report, "there is no doubt that the more intense intellectual activity, which prevails equally in the library, the work shop, and the counting-room, makes tranquilizing recreation more essential to continued health and strength than until lately it generally has been."[24] This was true in all the great cities where he worked — San Francisco, New York, Brooklyn, Chicago, or Boston.

"Address to the Prospect Park
Scientific Association," 1868

Olmsted elaborated further on the nature and effect of the pastoral scenery he wanted in parks in the fourth document in this volume. It stands as his most complete discussion of the issue. The document expresses Olmsted's belief that pastoral scenery had a universal appeal that went far deeper than did the sources of fashion. Park scenery was particularly well suited for satisfying certain propensities "which are part of human nature and which the progress of civilization does not affect, as it does mere manners & customs." That scenery was "a combination of elements which shall invite and stimulate the simplest, purest and most primeval action of the poetic element of human nature." For Olmsted, the qualities of grace and ease were the essential elements of pastoral park scenery. His purpose was to create a space that "invites, encourages & facilitates movement." His aim in designing a park, therefore, was "to make gracefully beautiful in combination with a purpose to make interesting and inviting, or hospitable, by the offer of a succession of simple, natural pleasures as a result of easy movements."[25]

Olmsted described his own experience of the universal quality of such landscape during the journey that he and his brother made across the plains of Texas in 1853. He showed how the campsites they chose offered easy access to wood and water while providing sheltering trees in places with distant views. He felt that such landscape had been specially valued by humankind ever since our emergence onto open savannahs at the dawn of the herding culture. This lecture also anticipates by a century the concept set forth by Jay Appleton in *The Experience of Landscape* that the aesthetic appeal of landscape stems from its ability to satisfy biological needs and that the key element in such a landscape is its provision of shelter and prospect.[26]

Proposal for the Buffalo Park System, 1868

Soon after the 1868 Brooklyn parkways report and before construction of Eastern Parkway and Ocean Parkway in that city began, Olmsted visited the city of Buffalo and took steps toward planning the first unified system of parks and parkways that he and Vaux were to design. The group of leading citizens who were promoting creation of a park system guided Olmsted on a hurried examination of three sites under consideration: one on the shore of Lake Erie near the entrance to the Erie Canal, one on the height of land in the eastern part of the city, and one along Scajaquada Creek to the north. In his first report, addressed to William Dorsheimer, Olmsted urged them to

14

make use of all three sites, damming the creek to form a lake and including level farm land adjoining it that became the 120-acre "meadow park" section of Delaware Park.

The city followed Olmsted's advice, although the final configuration of the system was somewhat different from the one that he proposed in this report and that the park commission and city council authorized during the last five months of 1869. Sometime after the bill authorizing creation of the park system was introduced into the state legislature, a clause was added to the bill requiring that one-fifth of the 500 acres of parks and parkways be located east of Jefferson Street. Since none of the system that Olmsted proposed, as described in the report published below, had extended east of that street, considerable changes had to be made. The original site for the Parade had been in the vicinity of present-day Masten Place and the parkway route between the Parade and Delaware Park was to have been along Jefferson Street.

To meet the new requirements of the authorizing legislation, the Parade was moved several blocks to the east and north; it was connected to Delaware Park by Humboldt Parkway, instead of following the course of existing streets as originally planned. A major reconfiguration of Delaware Park was also required. The wide meadow section of the park had to be moved eastward, while the borders of the western section of the park were drastically narrowed. As Olmsted later stated, "after pinching the ground on the north side of the water as much as possible without abandoning the design, it was still necessary . . . to throw out some ten acres of land on the south side of the water previously intended to be included in the Park and which for many years to come would be more valuable than any other." Eventually, in part as a result of Olmsted's repeated urging, the picnic grove south of the lake was added to the park in the mid-1880s.

Moreover, it was not possible to make the park crescent-shaped with parkways extending from each end toward the city as Olmsted proposed in his report of 1868. On the west side of the park this resulted from selection in November 1869 of land near the park for the site of the Buffalo State Asylum: that 200-acre tract included the route Olmsted had proposed for the last half-mile of the western parkway. Instead, he and Vaux designed three short parkway sections radiating out from Soldiers Place.[27]

The multiple elements of the Buffalo park system served three distinct purposes. First, the Parade and the "Front" on the lakeside site provided for activities other than the quiet enjoyment of scenery to which Olmsted and Vaux dedicated Delaware Park. The Parade had space for military maneuvers and gathering of crowds for civic events. It also contained a large refectory and a children's playground similar to the facility that Olmsted and Vaux had designed for Prospect Park in 1868. In addition, the design of the Front included space for team sports and concerts. This was the first time that Olmsted had the opportunity to design several recreation grounds in a city at one time, knowing that space was available outside the landscape park for potentially intrusive uses. In consequence, Delaware Park had fewer structures and facilities than any other major park that he designed prior to his last two park systems in Rochester and Louisville, beginning in 1888. By contrast, his park planning in New York City, which included Central, Riverside, and Morningside parks and Union and Tompkins squares, took place over a fifteen-year period. Planning of the four parks and two parkways he and Vaux designed for Brooklyn extended over the period 1865 to 1870. His next opportunity to plan a coherent park system would not come until the 1880s with the Boston park system.

Olmsted was also anxious to have public recreation grounds quickly accessible from the densely settled parts of a city. Existing Delaware Avenue connected the center of Buffalo with the principal park, but areas to the northwest and northeast were not similarly served. The Front and Parade were to act as neighborhood parks while at the same time providing some all-city recreational facilities.

The final element of the Buffalo system was the parkways and streets that connected the Front and Parade with Delaware Park. Most impressive was two-mile-long Humboldt Parkway. With eight parallel rows of trees and a width of 200 feet, it exceeded most of the famous boulevards of Paris in both respects. The three-spoked parkway system south of the western end of Delaware Park, with Soldiers Place as the hub, created a parkway neighborhood similar in concept—though different in configuration—to that proposed in 1868 for Brooklyn. Connection of these parkways to the Front was achieved by widening and planting trees along existing city streets. In this way, Olmsted achieved the extension of park-like grounds for which he gave the classic description found in this report:

> Thus, at no great distance from any point of the town, a pleasure ground will have been provided for, suitable for a short stroll, for a playground for children and an airing ground for invalids, and a route of access to the large common park of the whole city, of such a character that most of the steps on the way to it would be taken in the midst of a scene of sylvan beauty, and with the sounds and sites of the ordinary town business, if not wholly shut out, removed to some distance and placed in obscurity. The way itself would thus be more park-like than town-like.[28]

During the early 1870s, Olmsted witnessed construction of the system that he and Vaux had developed in 1868–69. Coupled with the original city plan of 1804 by Joseph Ellicott, he believed the system made Buffalo "the best planned city, as to its streets, public places and grounds, in the United States if not in the world."[29] He drew up an illustrated plan of the city portraying these qualities and displayed it at the Centennial Exhibition in Philadelphia in 1876. It was then displayed at the Universal Exhibition of 1878 in Paris, where it received honorable mention. In addition to the public facilities, the exhibit showed the residential subdivision, Parkside, that

Olmsted and engineer George Kent Radford planned in the mid-1870s on the northern side of Delaware Park. (This area was eventually laid out for residences, but not to any significant degree according to any of the surviving plans that Olmsted created for it, either in the 1870s or during a second phase of planning in 1886.)[30] The exhibit that Olmsted prepared also showed how Forest Lawn Cemetery south of the park and the Buffalo Asylum grounds west of it increased the area of greenspace in the city.

"Public Parks and the Enlargement of Towns," 1870

Olmsted's lecture at the Lowell Institute in Boston in February 1870, part of a series sponsored by the American Social Science Association, took place amidst spirited debate in that city about creation of a park. It would be six years before Olmsted became involved in creating Boston's park system, but at this time numerous participants in the debate sought to enlist his support. In mid-October 1869 a group of Boston citizens petitioned the city council to create a series of parks, and during the next month public hearings were held on the subject. One of the leading park proponents, James Haughton, urged Olmsted to testify before the state legislative committee considering the park bill; Robert Morris Copeland, author of one of the proposals, asked him to secure notices in the New York press; Edward Everett Hale delivered sermons and published articles drawing from Olmsted's writings on parks; and at the suggestion of James Haughton, James T. Fields, editor of the *Atlantic Monthly*, urged Olmsted to write a short article on parks. Within three weeks of receiving Fields's request, Olmsted sent him a long article that was probably close in subject and length to the address published here. Fields returned the manuscript, finding it too long, too much an "essay on social science," and "not of general interest." Olmsted seems never to have submitted the short article on the advantages of public parks that Fields desired.[31]

The same day that Fields returned the manuscript, Henry Villard, secretary of the American Social Science Association in Boston, wrote Olmsted proposing that he deliver a lecture on parks in the association's February–April lecture series at the Lowell Institute.[32] The timing of this letter and the short period it gave Olmsted to prepare his presentation suggests that Fields had informed Villard of the existence of Olmsted's manuscript.

Olmsted's Lowell Institute lecture stands as his clearest assertion of the advantages of urban life. In the first section he developed his theme that cities were improving in quality while the countryside languished. The largest cities were growing ever larger and would continue to do so. For Olmsted, this "townward movement of population" and the concurrent "suburban tendency" were developments of great promise. Nineteenth-century engineering had solved the health problems that had plagued the previous period of urbanization. If city dwellers would abandon anachronistic crowding of population into tenements and row houses and live instead in spacious suburbs open to sunshine and fresh air, cities could grow to great size while improving the living conditions of their residents. At this time, Olmsted and Vaux were developing at Riverside, Illinois, an example of what he believed the residential community of the future should be.[33]

While the separation of place of work from place of residence solved the major sanitary problems of earlier cities, the psychological toll of urban life had also to be reckoned with. Most troubling was the impersonal and heart-hardening daily contact of persons engaged in competitive business activities. The result, Olmsted observed, was that people raised in cities displayed "a peculiarly hard sort of selfishness. Every day of their lives they have seen thousands of their fellow-men, have met them face to face, have brushed against them, and yet have had no experience of anything in common with them."[34] The most promising institutions for countering this influence were public recreation grounds such as Olmsted and Vaux were developing in New York, Brooklyn, Buffalo, and Chicago. There needed to be formally arranged promenades for "gregarious" recreation, where large numbers of a city's residents could gather and see and be seen — "*congregated human life* under glorious and necessarily artificial conditions," as Olmsted called it. There should also be spacious parks where smaller "neighborly" gatherings of family and friends could take place.

In his discussion of needed urban improvements, Olmsted also stressed the importance of tree-lined avenues and parkways as a complementary element to the promenades and parks he sought for "receptive" recreation and the playing fields needed for "exertive" activities. These were significant themes for a New England audience, and within the next year and a half he would be involved in park and parkway planning for Hartford and New Britain, Connecticut, and Springfield and Fall River, Massachusetts.[35]

Olmsted made no reference to the Boston park movement in his Lowell Institute address, however, and took no sides in the debate over park sites. Instead, he limited himself to an examination of the beneficial effect that his oldest and best-known park, Central Park in Manhattan, had had on the residents of New York City. In so doing, he recalled what has become the most famous of the predictions of the park's opponents in the mid-1850s, the editorial from the *New York Herald* declaring that the city's ruffians would drive away respectable citizens and that "the great Central Park will be nothing but a great bear-garden for the lowest denizens of the city, of which we shall yet pray litanies to be delivered."[36] Quite the reverse had taken place, Olmsted assured his listeners: gentlemen and their families visited the park in large numbers, frequenting it "more than they do the opera or the church."[37]

Such a development would not have been possible, he pointed out, had not control of the park been in the hands of an independent board of commissioners. The Central Park commission had provided continuity of administration, with virtually no change in membership from its creation in

1857 to its dissolution by the Tweed Ring in 1870. He also emphasized the importance of an efficient corps of park police who would both protect visitors and instruct them in the proper use of the park. These two themes, the proper roles of commissioners and of park keepers, would recur many times in Olmsted's writings on parks during the next twenty-five years.

The Boston press enthusiastically reviewed Olmsted's talk, but given the general tenor of his remarks it is unclear what influence he had on the course of the city's park movement. The state legislature was considering the park bill when he spoke and passed it three months later; but the voters of Boston failed to provide the necessary two-thirds vote of approval in elections the next fall. Not until 1875 did Boston's park supporters secure creation of a park commission and begin the process of park-planning that would involve Olmsted and his firm for more than three decades.

"Report Accompanying Plan
for Laying Out the South Park," 1871

During the period of his partnership with Calvert Vaux, Olmsted found in the city of Chicago a challenging opportunity to plan the development of a great metropolis. The 1,600-acre village of Riverside, which he began to plan in 1868, was the most extensive and fully realized of any of his community designs. And the 1,000-acre South Park that he and Vaux designed in 1871 was to be the great metropolitan park of Chicago. Olmsted intended it to have a preeminence in its area even greater than that of Central Park in the New York City region.

Olmsted had been intrigued for several years with the opportunity for park-building that Chicago offered. Visiting the city in 1863 on U.S. Sanitary Commission business, he had investigated the possibility of constructing a privately owned and operated park. The scheme came to naught, but his host during that visit, the lawyer Ezra B. McCagg, was to be one of the leaders in the Chicago park movement.[38] Olmsted's contacts increased during his time in California. William Bross, senior editor of the *Chicago Tribune*, was a member of the party led by Speaker of the House of Representatives Schuyler Colfax that was in Yosemite Valley in the summer of 1865 when Olmsted presented his report on the management of the Yosemite grant to the Yosemite commission. Olmsted returned to San Francisco with the Colfax party. According to Bross, a prime subject of conversation during that trip was Central Park in New York. He recalled that "both Colfax and Olmsted agreed with me that nothing was needed to make Chicago the principal city of the Union but a great public improvement of similarly gigantic character."[39]

When park advocates in Chicago finally secured enabling legislation from the state in 1867–69, Olmsted could well have anticipated that he would plan the whole park system, despite its division into three administrative areas, north, south, and west, with independent commissions and sepa-

19

rate funding. The leading parks advocate, physician and sanitary reformer John Rauch, wrote Olmsted indicating his intention to see this occur, and Olmsted's friend McCagg was head of the North Park Commission. Soon after his appointment he wrote Olmsted on behalf of the commission, asking him to prepare a design for Lincoln Park. As early as October 1869 Olmsted and Vaux were also discussing terms of engagement with the South Park commissioners. In the end, only the South Park system came within Olmsted's sphere. There is no evidence that he made a plan for Lincoln Park, and Swain Nelson, a Swedish gardener who had done the first designs for Lincoln Park around 1865, continued as its designer through the 1870s. Moreover, the planning of the three West Parks—Central (later Garfield), Humboldt, and Douglas—went to the engineer William Le Baron Jenney, whom Olmsted had brought to Chicago to work on Riverside. One aspect of Jenney's West Parks was the reiteration of the same general plan and set of features in each park, rather than the creation of a distinctive plan for each project that was the hallmark of work of Olmsted and Vaux.[40] Their plan for the South Park Commission emphasized this difference in design approach, as shown in the differing character of the lakeside park and the inland park (later named Jackson and Washington parks).

The site for the parkland under the control of the South Park Commission consisted of two large areas, one of 593 acres on the lake and one inland of 372 acres, and a narrow, mile-long connecting strip. Part of Olmsted and Vaux's reason for treating this area as a single park was very likely because it would be distinctly the largest park in the Chicago system and thus better able to claim preeminence and truly metropolitan character. This remained Olmsted's intention through the rest of his career. When his firm undertook to provide a revised plan for Jackson Park following the World's Columbian Exposition of 1893, he reiterated his belief that it could be "the finest domestic boating park in the world."[41]

The features that Olmsted and Vaux included in their original plan demonstrate how complex and comprehensive they intended the park's recreational facilities to be. The inland section (later named Washington Park) was to have the "Southopen Green" for sports and gatherings, with an adjoining "pavilion ground" with a pavilion and refectory, courts, gardens, galleries, and carriage concourse. There was also to be a quarter-mile-long mall and four areas for picnics, a mounded and densely planted Ramble,[42] a deer paddock with its Farmstead Close structures, and a pond with boat landings. The narrow Midway Plaisance connected the two larger sections of the park: it contained formal bodies of water flanked by walks, drives, and rows of trees. The lakeside section, later called Jackson Park, had a concourse where the Midway met the Lagoon, a long pier on the lakeshore with adjoining concourse (one of five carriage concourses of two acres each planned for the park), and the Belvedere refectory with its large enclosed lawn. At the inner end of that lawn was an extensive promenade and concert grove, with an island for the band or orchestra, as in Prospect Park.

The 165-acre Lagoon that was the principal landscape feature of this section of the park had at least a dozen boat landings with structures of various sizes. In addition, some of the islands in the lagoon were to be refuges for wild birds, serving as part of what the designers envisioned as the finest living ornithological collection in the world. This might, they suggested, be connected with a natural history museum in the park that could include such appropriate species of animals as bison, elk, bears, seals, and sea lions. In addition, they proposed a large area for boating south of the lagoon that would be sheltered from the wind and directly accessible from the lake, its entrance protected by the 1,000-foot pier. Since the South Park was to function as a park system in itself, the designers took special pains to secure certain sections that were to be kept open and lighted at night for social gatherings and athletic activities. These were the Southopen Ground (including the Southopen Green), the Lakeopen Ground (including the Lakeopen Green) and Parkhaven Green. They were to consist of greensward and scattered trees and would have little understory or shrub planting. These areas encompassed a total of 460 acres. The three "plaisance" areas, which were to be more densely planted and so more difficult to maintain and secure, would be surrounded by fences and closed at night: they consisted of the southern section of Washington Park, the Midway Plaisance, and the lagoon area of Jackson Park, totaling 547 acres (see map on p. 220).

The circulation system of the South Park was ambitious as well. There were to be fourteen miles of interior drives and thirty miles of paths, exceeding the systems of nine and twenty miles, respectively, in New York's Central Park.[43]

This proliferation of spaces and structures stands in marked contrast to the plan that Olmsted and Vaux had drawn up two years earlier for Delaware Park in Buffalo. In that city they had the option of placing most recreational facilities in the Parade and Front, leaving the park itself with only one large public building, the boathouse-refectory on the lake. Of all the parks that Olmsted designed, only Central Park had a multiplicity of areas, structures, and activities comparable to Chicago's South Park, and several of those features had been stipulated in the original Central Park competition rules of 1857.[44]

While the South Park plan contained many "artificial" elements that met a variety of recreational needs, its central purpose was to provide passages of scenery for the enjoyment of Chicagoans. According to Olmsted's theories, the kind of landscape to be provided there should have been drawn from the "genius of the place," involving a perceptive realization of ideal forms of the kinds of scenery found on the site. But Olmsted found the soggy, windblown prairie section unappealing and later referred to the marshy area back of the lakeshore dunes as "a swamp without beauty."[45] There was only one element of the local scenery that he truly appreciated. This was Lake Michigan itself. The grandeur of the lake, he asserted, would compensate for the lack of varied terrain on the site. He was delighted to have the lake as a scenic adjunct and way of access to the park, but admitted that no artistic means could make it more grand. Still, if the artist's hand could not improve the sublime, such a feature as the lake could add immeasurably to the park. Indeed, this was the only instance in his career of urban park design where he was able to associate passages of scenery of his favorite styles of park landscape, the pastoral and the picturesque, with an expanse of the sublime. Only the Chicago South Park would bring together the three distinct styles of natural scenery that he recognized in his professional thought and work.

As Olmsted had made clear in his earlier park reports, pastoral scenery was the most valuable kind for counteracting the debilitating influences of the city. The flat prairie of the South Park offered no barrier to creating such passages of scenery, although Olmsted felt little assurance that the wet, cold soil could ever produce splendid specimens of shade trees. The inland section was particularly well suited to pastoral landscapes, which became the key for that 370-acre area. The 100-acre Southopen Green was, moreover, one of the largest open spaces of meadow he ever designed.[46] It was not, however, a prairie, or a landscape inspired by prairie conditions, that he planned for Washington Park. Rather, it was a version of the universal park-like scenery that he had traced far back in human history and considered an essential part of any urban park.[47]

Still, it was not meadow scenery but water — the water of Lake Michigan extended — that provided the unifying element of the South Park design. The Mere of Washington Park connected to the formal waterway of the Midway Plaisance, which flowed into the Lagoon of Jackson Park, which connected to the Parkhaven harbor and thence to Lake Michigan. It was in the water section of the park — the Jackson Park Lagoon — that Olmsted found the most exciting opportunity for creating scenery.

Turning to an analysis he often used, that of basing a landscape design on the actions of nature in producing scenic effects, Olmsted observed that if geologic and climatic conditions had been somewhat different, a landscape would have developed behind the lakeshore dunes that was "of a most interesting and fascinating character, that, namely, of the wooded lagoons of the tropics."[48] Olmsted proposed to make the whole 165-acre lagoon of islands and sinuous waterways of this character. His inspiration was not the swamps of the Lake Michigan shore but rather the lush bayous of the Gulf Coast and the rainforest waterways of Panama that had so impressed him in his travels. He had experienced the awe, the sense of profusion and of mystery, provoked by tropical landscapes, the "profuse careless utterance of Nature," in those southern places.[49] Olmsted welcomed the opportunity to evoke the same elemental response in this northern site, through the use of different plant materials, as he had previously welcomed a similar opportunity in Central Park. As he summed up the case in the South Park report:

> You certainly cannot set the madrepore or the mangrove at work on the banks of Lake Michigan, you cannot naturalize bamboo or papyrus, aspiring palm or waving parasites, but you *can* set firm barriers to the violence of winds and waves, and make shores as intricate, as arborescent and as densely overhung with foliage as any. You can have placid and limpid water within these shores that will mirror and double all above it as truly as any, and thus, if you cannot reproduce the tropical forest in all its mysterious depths of shade and visionary reflections of light, you can secure a combination of the fresh and healthy nature of the North with the restful, dreamy nature of the South that would in our judgment be admirably fitted to the general purposes of any park, and which certainly could nowhere be more grateful than in the borders of your city, not only on account of the present intensely wide-awake character of its people, but because of the special quality of the scenery about Chicago in which flat and treeless prairie and limitless expanse of lake are such prominent characteristics.[50]

Olmsted's concept was not realized during the first two decades of construction of the park, but selection of Jackson Park and the Midway Plaisance as the site of the 1893 Exposition breathed new life into the scheme. As he set out to plan the Exposition, he revived the concept of a lagoon with wild, profuse plantings on its verge.[51] By that time he had successfully carried out a similar project in Boston's Back Bay Fens, but had been disappointed in his attempts to realize such a plan on the Great Lakes in the Buffalo South Park project of 1888. Even so, the Wooded Island and Lagoon of the Exposition constituted the first fully realized demonstration of a kind of landscape, called the "prairie river," that became so important an icon for landscape architects in the Chicago region, most notably Jens Jensen and O. C. Simonds, in the following years. Olmsted's demonstration was impressive for its size, as well as for its extensive use of native plants gathered from nearby swamps.[52]

Even the simpler concept of greensward, groves, and ponds in Washington Park, ably carried out under the supervision of H. W. S. Cleveland in the early 1870s, had been botched in the 1880s by the banal plant-sculptures of a later superintendent. The popularity of this artificial garden art led Cleveland to conclude grudgingly, "we need two systems of parks—one for the comparatively few who really want seclusion and the beauty of nature—another for the multitude who can only enjoy solitude in crowds—to whom any work is artistic in proportion as it is artificial."[53] Neither Olmsted nor his successors had much occasion to recover the original concept for Washington Park, but the firm's thorough redesign of Jackson Park following the World's Columbian Exposition of 1893 led to the realization of much that Olmsted had wished for many years to achieve on the site.

"A Review of Recent Changes, and Changes which have been Projected, in the Plans of the Central Park," 1872

At the time they were drawing up their plan for the Chicago South Park, Olmsted and Vaux were receiving another lesson in the politics of park design from the park commission of Boss Tweed in New York. Although the designers of Central Park were nominally landscape architects advisory to the new board of the Department of Public Parks that in 1870 replaced the Central Park board that had administered the park since the design competition of 1857, their protests went unheeded. The new regime was unsympathetic to the naturalistic design of the park: it trimmed up shade trees, removing the lower limbs and treated them like street trees. It also cleared out profuse undergrowth and shrubs in the interest of neatness and "free circulation of air." In other places the park staff removed the dense border plantations that Olmsted and Vaux had carefully made in order to heighten the rural atmosphere of the park. They began construction of an extensive menagerie on the upper meadows, and built an expensive and ornamental "Sheep Fold" west of the Sheep Meadow, in a position that ruined the intended landscape effect of the area and that was accessible from within the park only by crossing the bridle path at a dangerous curve. Thus the Tweed Ring wreaked havoc on the three major landscape elements of the park that had been the focus of the dozen years of construction under Olmsted and Vaux's nominal direction. These were the border plantations, the open stretches of greensward, and the densely planted hillsides that had been planned for "picturesque sylvan scenery."

Following the overthrow of the Tweed Ring in 1871, the new park board requested Olmsted and Vaux to comment on the results of the Ring's policies and to propose a program of recovery. Their response is contained in the two letters of 1872 published as the eighth document in this volume. The letters contain some of the designers' most specific descriptions of design intent for the park. They spell out in particular the intended character of the Dairy area, which Olmsted and Vaux had planned as a secluded section for children and convalescents.

The letters also explain how Olmsted and Vaux planned extensive views northward across the playground and Sheep Meadow. They examine specifically the kinds of scenery that produced the atmosphere the designers wished the park to have, and analyze their psychological effect. There was the effect of picturesque scenery: "A cluster of hornbeams and hemlocks, the trunks of some twisting over a crannied rock, the face of the rock brightened by lichens, and half veiled by tresses of vines growing over it from the rear, and its base lost in a tangle of ground pine, mosses and ferns"; or, more beneficial, there were pastoral scenes consisting of "a broad stretch of slightly undulating meadow without defined edge, its turf lost in a haze of the shadows of scattered trees under the branches of which the eye would range."[54]

Equally significant is the discussion of the lack of public understanding of the design of Central Park. As the Tweed Ring's policies demonstrated, there were many who were willing to see the park become a great metropolitan fair ground, "a desultory collocation of miscellaneous entertainments." In a striking analogy, Olmsted and Vaux illustrated the difference between the public's understanding of architecture in contrast to its awareness of landscape design:

> The new Court House has been a great deal discussed during the last few years, but, in all that has been written, a demand has probably not been made that certain of its rooms should be fitted up with billiard tables or suitably for religious services or public demonstrations in anatomy; the lack of a convenient carriage way to the roof or to the lunch-counter has not been complained of, nor has it been proposed to remedy the present cramped, inconvenient and unattractive arrangements for refreshments by devoting the more spacious of the court rooms to this purpose. . . . But propositions quite as fantastic are not unfrequently made with earnestness in regard to the Park.[55]

The purpose of the park was to provide scenery that would counteract the psychological stress of urban life. The authors demonstrate how the three fundamental elements of the park — the border plantings, the open pastoral landscapes, and the profusely planted passages of picturesque sylvan scenery — produced the desired psychological effect. In the process, they show how even the numerous arches that they introduced to provide separation of ways intruded less upon the landscape than the traffic in the park without them would have done.

"General Order for the Organization and Routine of Duty of the Keepers' Service of the Central Park," 1873

Olmsted and Vaux carefully designed Central Park so that people engaged in different activities and traveling by different means would intrude as little as possible on the enjoyment of other park users. But careful design, however successfully carried out, would not by itself guarantee the success of the park. That success was most important to Olmsted. In 1858, as construction commenced under his supervision as architect-in-chief, he declared to his friend Parke Godwin, "it is of great importance as the first real park made in this country — a democratic development of the highest significance & on the success of which, in my opinion, much of the progress of art & esthetic culture in this country is dependent."[56] When, fifteen years later, he wrote the document on the Central Park keepers force published in this volume, he still believed that Central Park would provide the first demonstration in the country of the beneficial effect that a park could have, but regretted that "the demonstration of experience is lacking."[57] Part of the reason for this failure was that planting of the park was never completed under Olmsted's direction, a shortcoming he tried repeatedly to rectify during the 1870s. Compounding this problem was the extensive planting and maintenance work that the Tweed Ring board had done in a manner at cross-purposes with the intent of the designers. Since the advent of the Tweed Ring the park had also lacked an adequate keepers force. The importance to Olmsted of an effective force is indicated by his statement in 1873 that from the beginning he and Vaux expected the park to have a much more efficient keepers force than it ever had, and that "not a line of the Park would otherwise have been laid where it is, not a tree planted where trees now stand."[58] In the early days of the movement for the park, its opponents had expressed strong doubts that a successful public park could be created in the city. The classic dissent by James Gordon Bennett, editor of the influential *New York Herald* declared that the rowdy element of the city, epitomized by "Sam the Five-Pointer" from the dissolute area of Five Points, would overwhelm the respectable park users:

> when we open a public park, Sam will air himself in it. . . . He will enjoy himself there, whether by having a muss, or a drink at the corner groggery opposite the great gate. He will run races with his new horse in the carriage way. He will knock any better dressed man down who remonstrates with him. He will talk and sing, and fill his share of the bench, and flirt with the nursery girls in his own coarse way. Now, we ask what chance have William B. Astor and Edward Everett against this fellow-citizen of theirs?"[59]

But it was not only, or even primarily, Sam the Five-Pointer and his like that concerned Olmsted. The delicacy of the plantings on which the park's scenic beauty depended made it necessary to prevent visitors from going where they would and doing what they wished in the park. Great numbers of respectable men and women and their children were potentially capable of doing greater damage to the essential elements of the park than were loiterers and ruffians. Virtually all park users needed instruction in use of the park if it were to be a success, and it was the responsibility of the keepers to offer that instruction.

Accordingly, Olmsted wished from the beginning to form a keepers force that was very different in training and purpose from the metropolitan police. He set up the force in early 1858 with twenty-two keepers and remained in charge of it until he left the park for service with the U.S. Sanitary Commission in June 1861. By that time the number of keepers had increased to fifty-five. Olmsted did not regain authority over the keepers until May 1872. At that time he also began a five-month term as temporary president of the park board. He found his system still in place, though working poorly. By then the new park board had fired the fifty keepers that the Tweed Ring board had added for patronage purposes.[60] Even so, a physician who examined the remaining ninety-nine keepers declared a third of them to be in "decidedly unsound condition," with nineteen "positively unfit for duty."[61] In October 1872 the board authorized Olmsted to reorganize the keepers force and reduce its expense of operation. His task was made more difficult by the dissipation of discipline that had taken place during the year and a half of Tweed Ring rule in 1870–71. In addition, city employees were now subject to an eight-hour law. (Previously, keepers had been on duty at times for eighteen hours a day and gatekeepers had been required to be at their posts eleven to twelve hours every day of the week, a situation against which Olmsted had protested.)[62]

Olmsted had long wished to supplement the uniformed keepers force with a group of "extra-keepers" who would wear less formal uniforms and whose responsibilities would be maintenance of the park and assistance of visitors. He now instituted such a category of keepers. While this met the need for economy, he still faced the problem of making the formally uniformed "patrol-keepers" more effective. Most of them had been assigned to "beats" consisting of large sections of the park, ranging from fifty to one hundred acres. Surveillance of them by the eight officers responsible for the task was difficult and they could easily avoid observation for hours at a time.[63] Olmsted's solution was to create four "all-day beats" and supplement them with two "rounds." Each round was a seven-mile circuit of the park, during which a keeper observed all the gates and gatekeepers between 59th Street and 102nd Street. As a result, these keepers, being primarily on the drives, were far more visible than before. They also recorded their position eight times during each round as they performed "close inspection" of gatekeepers on their route. Olmsted scheduled the rounds to take two hours and forty minutes and allowed the keepers a ten-minute rest period between rounds. On a given day, sixteen of the thirty-six "patrol keepers" were to make three rounds, for a total of twenty-one miles, the others making two rounds. He later defended this rigorous regime by citing authorities who calculated that a walk of thirty miles was the equivalent of a day's work for a laborer, and referring to the opinion of U.S. Army officers and surgeons during the Civil War that their soldiers improved in health when marching twenty miles a day.[64]

In drawing up the new keepers' regulations, Olmsted also instituted a strict discipline that, among other things, forbade casual conversation between keepers and required military bearing at all times. In the thirty-point "Revised and Additional Rules for the Conduct of Patrol and Post Keepers" that are part of the keepers report published in this volume, he sought to anticipate every situation that might reduce that discipline, even to the point (rule number 20) of directing the course to be pursued if two keepers came abreast of each other while walking in the same direction.[65]

Olmsted's new keepers' regime was short-lived. From the time he instituted it, he met with hostility and recalcitrance from many of the keepers, as well as continual opposition from the captain in charge. Within a month of its commencement the *New-York Daily Tribune* published and endorsed a letter attacking the "Olmsted Chain-Gang System." Because of it, the author claimed, visitors could no longer find pleasure or safety in the park. Olmsted had transformed the keepers into "human velocipedes" who would hardly stop to suppress any crime short of murder, intent as they were on completing their rounds on time. While the keepers struggled on their course, young ruffians stole flowers and stoned visitors, libertines roamed the park "insulting unescorted ladies with practical impunity," and break-neck horsemen threatened life and limb. Olmsted published a rejoinder asserting that the new system had secured good order in the park and that he had simply restored the old keepers system that the *Tribune* had considered a success.[66]

However much Olmsted might protest, the newspaper controversy embarrassed him at a crucial time. A new city charter went into effect on June 1, 1873, leading to the appointment of three new park commissioners to the board. They soon proposed a reorganization of the park that stripped Olmsted of most of his authority. As a result, Henry G. Stebbins, perennial president of the board and an important supporter of Olmsted's, resigned the presidency and Olmsted himself submitted his resignation. A complete rift was averted, but Olmsted testified that thereafter the new commissioners, though outwardly respectful, treated every proposal of his as though it was "in imminent danger of being used for disseminating a pestilence." In late September the board abolished Olmsted's round system and authorized the keepers to carry clubs. It would be a year and a half before he again exerted significant influence on the maintenance and keeping of Central Park.[67]

While the larger part of the keepers document published below represents Olmsted's attempt to meet the particular problems posed by the topography and politics of Central Park, the final section of "general observations" presents his more general concept of the purpose of a park keepers force. In this section he argued that vigorous enforcement of regulations by accosting and upbraiding park visitors would be counterproductive. There was, in fact, no way that the keepers could even keep the whole park under surveillance at a given time. The purpose for the rigorous discipline that he demanded was of another sort. Rapid movement and military bearing could heighten the impression that keepers might come in sight at any moment, but the larger effect of their bearing and discipline was to work by a more subtle process. By their actions the keepers must enlist the self-respect and civic pride of the park users. They must demonstrate that there was a continuous and consistent system designed to protect the users in the park, meet their needs, answer their questions, and lead them to consider the rights of others using the park. The keepers must, in all their dealings with the public, employ "a manner of studied official respect." For, Olmsted explained, "this impression will be valuable for the purpose in proportion as it is uniform, and as it manifests systematic vigilance, order, discipline, considerateness and courtesy."

Such a regime would lead park users to recognize the legitimacy of the authority of the keepers, and would dispose the public to support the enforcement of regulations. This would support the authority of government in the matter. In his analysis Olmsted was drawing on the issues of loyalty and authority in a republic that had been a recurring concern for him during the years of secession and Civil War.[68] He observed that protection of the park rested "almost wholly on the loyal disposition of the great body of visitors to side with the keepers in discountenancing its misuse." The way they expressed that disposition would be not so much by strong actions as by a general, pervasive attitude and setting of example. In this area, as in his aesthetic thought, Olmsted emphasized the importance of the "silent and unconscious influence" of people on each other. Just as the unconscious influence of scenery was the most powerful way by which the park exerted its tranquilizing effect, so the same kind of influence, exerted by its visitors, would be the most reliable means of ensuring its proper use.

Olmsted realized that most of the keepers would not understand this, since they were disposed "in common with mankind in general, to have too little respect for or faith in influences which operate quietly and graciously, and to magnify the importance of acts of which the results are direct and obvious."[69] Thus, the complex system that he sought to establish was not directed toward enforcement of regulations by the keepers, but rather toward creation of an atmosphere, a sentiment, and a tradition, that would lead park users to respect the design purposes of the park and the rights of the other users without requiring direct intervention by the keepers themselves.

These issues of civic responsibility and unconscious influence were central to Olmsted's thought: they emerged in his planning for the park keepers in yet another of the myriad ways they infused his career. The keepers' regulations also express the crucial concept, which he frequently reiterated, that the purpose of a park was to have a beneficial effect on the health of its users, exerting a tranquilizing and restorative effect through the experience of scenery. Once again he asserted that any structure or activity that lessens that psychological effect is detrimental to the park and its prime reason for existence. The principal value of a park stems from its psychological influence: "the insensible advantage which is gained in this way by thousands who visit it without this purpose definitely in view, but whose strength and power of usefulness are thus increased, and whose lives thus prolonged, constitutes its chief value." It therefore followed that *any conduct which tends on the whole to restrict this value* is a misuse of the Park."[70] This theme would become more important as Olmsted continued to educate the American public concerning the true and universal value of parks.

"Park," 1875

One medium for this instruction was the *New American Cyclopædia*, for which Olmsted wrote an article entitled "Park" in 1861, a discussion that he revised for the new edition in 1875. In 1861 he offered an extended description of parks in Europe, the British Isles, and America, including a history of changes in gardening styles since ancient times. The value of his commentary stemmed in large part from his personal observation of many of these public parks and recreation grounds during his three trips to England and Europe in the 1850s. By 1875 his emphasis had changed; he focused more directly on what constituted a park and on situations where park-like treatment of landscape was desirable. His first step was to differentiate the park, as historically defined, from the garden and the wood. He also proposed more precise terminology for public recreation grounds that would differentiate between "parks," "places," "place parks," and "parkways." He added an original discussion, based in part on his and Vaux's plan of 1868 for Tompkins Square in Brooklyn, concerning the way that public squares and small "places" in cities should be designed.[71] As he had done in earlier writings, he emphasized the paramount importance of the park-like landscape:

> Other forms of natural scenery stir the observer to warmer admiration, but it is doubtful if any . . . are equally soothing and refreshing; equally adapted to stimulate simple, natural, and wholesome tastes and fancies, and thus to draw the mind from absorption in the interests of an intensely artificial habit of life.[72]

In the article Olmsted offered one of his clearest statements of why the picturesque style on steep and broken ground was less valuable for the purposes of a public park than was pastoral scenery. He also emphasized, as he had in the 1866 Prospect Park report, the difficulty of reaching a satisfactory compromise between scenic values and provision for intensive use of a park. This difficulty, he repeated, made it all the more desirable to exclude from a park any activities or institutions "which have nothing in common with that of tranquillizing rest and exercise, and to which the element of landscape beauty is not essential."

Olmsted also addressed the problem of creating park-like scenery in areas of inadequate rainfall. The issue had recently been recalled to his attention when he reviewed William Hammond Hall's plan for Golden Gate Park in San Francisco. Olmsted did not address the specific problem of semiarid landscape design but rather discussed the desirable approach for regions of only moderate rainfall. He recommended use of woods and water, rather than greensward, as the principal scenic features of public grounds in such places and illustrated his discussion with examples from French design practice.[73]

Following his discussion of these general themes, Olmsted added a shortened and much revised version of the commentary on contemporary parks that he had included in his 1861 article. He expanded his discussion of the park movement in America and gave a more comprehensive view of the public spaces of London and Paris. He also moderated some of the praise he had offered fourteen years earlier for Birkenhead Park and Phoenix Park and the English Garden in Munich.[74]

"A Consideration of the Justifying Value
of a Public Park," 1880

In 1880, at a meeting of the American Social Science Association in Saratoga Springs, New York, Olmsted found the opportunity to make his most extended statement on the nature of the park movement and the park. His talk was published in the association's journal, but with many errors. He was anxious that an accurate version be available to the public, and so published at his own expense the text of his speech "A Consideration of the Justifying Value of a Public Park," presented below. The problem, as he defined it in the introductory section of the article, was the lack of clarity in public understanding of what a park should be. This was aggravated by lack of continuity in administration of parks and too frequent application of "practical commonsense" standards that evaluated parks according to commercial value rather than their value as places of "mental relaxation" for the public.

Olmsted noted that the park movement was a recent phenomenon: nearly all the significant public parks in Europe and America had been constructed since 1850. The term park and the concept of what was park-like was much older, yet even this historical element added confusion to the issue. Old game-parks like Windsor Great Park or Richmond Park near London, though gradually transformed from royal hunting grounds to places of public recreation, continued to be managed for their commercial value in timber and game. Compounding this confusion was the great variety of features in public parks constructed during the nineteenth century. The extent of agreement on the definition of a public park seemed to be that it was "a ground appropriated to public recreation." In his article Olmsted illustrated the remarkable number and variety of features that had been included in parks under that broad definition. He observed that "usage accounts for nothing" in identifying the special qualities unique to a park. Many of these features need not be in a park at all and could better be placed in their own spaces, scattered throughout a city. Still other features, requiring more space, could best be placed in a long public promenade devoted solely to what Olmsted called "gregarious" activities.

Examining developments that had paralleled the park movement in order to find a clearer explanation of the role of the park, Olmsted identified "a great enlargement of towns and development of urban habits" that was attended by psychological stress, depression, and exhaustion. He cited with approval John Ruskin's commentary that "this is an age in which we grow more and more artificial day by day, and see less and less worthiness in those pleasures which bring with them no marked excitement; in knowledge which affords no opportunity for display." The parallel movement that took place in response to these problems was an increased appreciation of nature "in the *broad combining way of scenery*" as evidenced by the amount of time and money expended on tourism to areas of strikingly beautiful natural scenery.

In this propensity Olmsted saw a "self-preserving instinct of civilization" rather than a passing fad or fashion.

These facts provided the key to the justifying value of a public park, which was "the cultivation of beauty of natural scenery." The problem of a park was continuity of administration that sustained "the reconciliation of adequate beauty of nature in scenery with adequate means in artificial constructions of protecting the conditions of such beauty, and holding it available to the use, in a convenient and orderly way, of those needing it." Properly pursued, these aims would succeed in making a park "steadily gainful of that quality of beauty which comes only with age."[75]

"Mount Royal, Montreal," 1881

In the fall of 1874 Olmsted began work on Mount Royal in Montreal, the first park that he designed after the end of his partnership with Calvert Vaux. At this time he was utilizing the architectural skills of Thomas Wisedell on the U.S. Capitol grounds in Washington and collaborating with the engineer George Radford in planning Parkside, a subdivision adjoining Delaware Park in Buffalo. He would make use of the talents of both men in his work on Mount Royal.

Mount Royal was the first park that Olmsted designed whose commissioners were a committee of the City Council rather than an independent, appointed body. While the leading members of the Mount Royal commission seem to have respected Olmsted and approved his general concept, he encountered a series of discouraging instances where public demand forced actions that he viewed as precipitous and unwise. The report of 1881 published in this volume chronicles both his concept for the park and the difficulties he encountered in carrying it out. It is a revised version of two public lectures that Olmsted delivered when he unveiled his plan for the park to the public in September 1877.

By the end of his first visit to inspect the proposed park site in November 1874, Olmsted had identified the principal elements of the design. These were: a road up the mountain from its north and northeast sides that would have gradual grades permitting easy movement of carriages and making the ascent of the mountain a pleasure even for convalescent patients; enhancement, by planting and pruning, of the wild forest character of most of the site; and an extent of open, park-like scenery on the higher elevations of the southern part of the mountain. He spelled out these ideas to the park commissioners in a report of November 21, 1874. In it he praised the site as offering "a larger measure than any other place equally near so large a population" for the two key elements of value for a park. These were "the change of air afforded" and "the power of their scenery to counteract conditions which tend to nervous depressions or irritability."[76]

Olmsted then awaited completion of a topographical map on which to base his plan. But the city was in the throes of hard times following the Panic of 1873, and the City Council was impatient to begin the hiring of unemployed workers that park construction would make possible. By April 1875 the council was anxious to begin constructing the approach road. The topographical map for that section of the mountain was not completed until August, and in the interim Olmsted refused to produce a plan based on inadequate information. Within two weeks of receiving the map, however, he visited the site and by early October had completed his plan for the first two-mile section of the drive.

Construction began in early November and, despite bitter cold and heavy snow, was completed by early February. To celebrate this event a fleet of 106 sleighs containing the park commissioners and invited guests toured the new road and then went on by temporary roads to the top of the mountain.

From Olmsted's point of view the whole procedure was a disaster. As he later complained, those directing the work failed to consult his detailed instructions and produced a road that "any boy who had been a year with a surveying party might have laid out & any intelligent farmer might have constructed. The opportunity of making such an attractive way up the mountain as I had designed," he mourned, "has been lost forever."[77] In particular, the builders ignored his plan to limit the road's lateral intrusion into the surrounding landscape, which he proposed to achieve by constructing walls along the uphill side of the road and steep embankments on the downhill side. They did not contour the drive as Olmsted proposed, and failed to construct the sidewalk and row of shrubbery on the outer edge that would have given a clear definition to the sides of the drive, producing the graceful sinuosity that was the hallmark of his drives in other parks. "Had it been desirable to display barrenness on its borders, and to make the fact apparent that the road was a rude and hasty construction, made with no regard to . . . considerations for local and foreground scenery . . . ," he lamented, "the same amount of labor could hardly have been better applied to the object."[78] In a March 1877 letter to Horatio A. Nelson, president of the park commission, he made an offer (which he then crossed out) to contribute $1,000 to rebuilding that section of road, "so mortifying it is to me."[79]

Another disappointment soon followed the loss of the road up the mountain as an element of scenery. A major reason for Olmsted's approval of the site on his first visit was the discovery of a large area on the upper mountain suitable for a passage of pastoral scenery. He envisioned a lake of four or five acres in the midst of "a piece of truly park-like ground, broad, simple, quiet and of a rich sylvan and pastoral character," that would form "a harmonious, natural foreground to the view over the western valley" that would appear "in striking contrast to the ruggedness of the mountain proper." Much to his chagrin, the city decided to place a twenty-acre reservoir in this area, (the site of present-day Lac au Castors, designed in the 1930s). Olmsted accepted the decision and prepared a design for a geometrically shaped reservoir of seven acres. He proposed that it serve as the site for a promenade, with separate ways for carriages, equestrians, and pedestrians. He made it clear that nonetheless the reservoir would not be a part of the park experience, but was rather an "interpolation." Still, this change enabled him to abandon a plan for a promenade near the top of the mountain, simplifying the system of ways in that section of the park and retaining a wilder quality in the landscape.[80]

Through 1876 Olmsted was besieged by requests to proceed with various features on the mountain before he had completed his plan. The commissioners were anxious to continue their road-building to the mountain top, although Olmsted cautioned, "unless you can look further ahead and lay out your work with reference to its ultimate ends, instead of to the immediate gratification of the public, the work of properly improving the mountain will cost too much and will never be done."[81] He refused to plan the road to the top until it was definitely established that the reservoir would occupy the space intended. The commissioners also pressed for a temporary structure at the top of the mountain. Olmsted acceded to this proposal a year and a half before he finally presented his full plan. In April 1876 he supplied plans by Wisedell for a shingle-style structure with a metal-clad tower that would appear from a distance as the "crown of the mountain."[82] The following year he was distressed to learn that he must select a site for a new small-pox hospital in the park. He also warned against a plan to place a monument on the mountain, saying that all artificial objects in the park should be as inconspicuous as possible and should serve the single purpose of enjoyment of natural scenery.[83]

The major barrier to completion of the plan seems to have been the question of land acquisition. In October 1876 Olmsted forwarded a general plan to the park commissioners, stating that further questions about boundaries and approaches must be settled before he could draw up a final plan.[84] In early November 1876 he was baffled to learn that property essential to his plan for the northern end of the mountain, which he had understood to be in the possession of the city, had not been acquired and would not be. This affected the area where he intended to create residential lots along two access routes to the mountain — one along Bleury Street (present-day Park Avenue) and the other entering where present-day Pine Avenue meets University Street. "Had I received the information you now give me," he wrote Nelson, "my whole design for laying out the mountain would have been very different. . . ."[85] Then, in early 1877, the worsening hard times caused the City Council to halt all construction on the park and make plans for selling off all property not absolutely necessary to it. By early summer Olmsted had completed his plan, which included the property at the northern end of the park that the city had not acquired but that he considered essential.

Olmsted did what he could to gain a favorable hearing from the

Montreal public. He offered to give two public lectures to accompany the unveiling of the plan, recommending that they take place after the summer vacation period. The commissioners agreed, but their reluctance to spend money greatly limited the effectiveness of his presentation. To reduce the cost, they issued invitations only to government officials and placed no advertisements in the newspapers. To secure the meeting hall at the cheapest rates, they scheduled the lectures at three P.M. — "a time," one newspaper observed, "when our citizens cannot possibly attend." Indeed, the audience for the first lecture, on the general topic of public parks, consisted of only thirty or forty persons. Only one newspaper carried an extensive account, which Olmsted described as "very injudicious & misprinted selections" from his manuscript. The audience was larger the next day, a Saturday, for the lecture detailing the Mount Royal plan, but the newspapers took no notice of it. There was little prospect that this effort would produce the groundswell of public support for completion of the park according to his plan that Olmsted had hoped for. But he took some comfort from the fact that the plan would be publicly displayed at the City Hall and that the commissioners intended to publish the lectures.[86]

However, it would be three years before he completed revision of those lectures and saw them published. This was due in part to the agitation that he felt whenever he turned to the subject of Montreal and its park. In explaining his recalcitrance to Nelson in late 1879, he claimed that "whenever I have attempted to revise my discourse as you requested I have had a return of the symptoms which I first felt when engaged in its preparation and I have been obliged in consequence to defer the undertaking."[87] This debility was apparently similar to the "pen sickness" that had beset him following the intense two years of administration and letter-writing when he was general secretary of the U.S. Sanitary Commission during the Civil War.[88] Events in his professional life that occurred soon after his lectures in Montreal added to this problem. Barely three months after those lectures, Olmsted was fired from his position as landscape architect with the New York City park board, bringing abruptly and painfully to an end a nearly continuous involvement of twenty years with the design and supervision of Central Park. He left immediately on an already-planned trip to Europe and during that time, as he reported to Nelson in December 1879, "fell into a nervous illness from which I have never fully recovered." Only after making the move from New York to Brookline, Massachusetts, and securing the opportunity to plan the Boston park system does Olmsted seem to have recovered his optimism and composure. "You can have no idea what a drag life had been to me for three years or more," he wrote his friend Charles Loring Brace in March 1882, "I did not appreciate it myself until I began last summer to get better. The turning point appears to have been our abandonment of New York."[89]

Olmsted attempted to secure final payment from the Mount Royal commissioners without the painful rewriting of his 1877 lectures, but Nelson assured him that the commissioners would hold him to the task of submitting a final report. Olmsted finally completed the report during the summer of 1881, but it was very different from his lecture of three years previous. While he seems to have made few changes in his second lecture, which describes his plan for Mount Royal and appears in the published report as the Appendix, he apparently threw out most of his first lecture and wrote new material for the body of the published report. His first lecture of 1877, as described in the local newspaper article based on his manuscript, had dealt primarily with erroneous concepts of what a park should be. In the final report he omitted such "argument against specific propositions adverse to the motive of the adopted design."[90]

In the first section of the report, Olmsted reviewed his involvement with the Montreal park and demonstrated the waste and inefficiency caused by the form of park board the city had created. This is the section that his brother-in-law William Woodruff Niles, Episcopal Bishop of New Hampshire, referred to as his "effective 'showing up' of the management" of the park. Sagely, Niles observed that this might "so wound the self-esteem of those having matters in charge as to set them against your wishes whatever may be their convictions." Niles cautioned, "It is said, you know, that 'tis hard to forgive one who has injured us, but harder far to forgive one *whom we have injured*. I hope they won't find it so with you."[91] Olmsted's pressing of this issue must also have stemmed from his desire to warn the public about the danger of vacillating park administrations that failed to benefit from the professional advice of trained landscape architects. The following spring he would publish *The Spoils of the Park*, an impassioned indictment of the policies of the park board of New York City.

Still, Olmsted had another and more important task to accomplish in his final report on Mount Royal. This was to make a convincing case for his vision of the park. Economic recovery was finally underway in Montreal, which had made virtually no progress in constructing the park since the end of 1876. It was crucially important that he revive public support and direct it by the only means left to him. As he reminded the "owners of Mount Royal" in the concluding part of section V of his report, "the opportunities and advantages for producing certain charms of natural scenery which you hold as yet *inert and unproductive* in the mountain, are such as are possessed by no other city in any ground held for a public park."[92]

In the rest of the report, Olmsted spelled out for the citizens of Montreal how they could develop the charms of natural scenery of their mountain to the fullest extent. The true economy, he reiterated, was *"economy in the ultimate development of resources of poetic charm of scenery."*[93] His proposal presents many remarkable ideas and contains some of his most passionate statements concerning the power of scenery. Section VI is a particularly concentrated explication of the psychological effect of landscape. The diversity of ways that Olmsted found to increase variety in the landscape experience of the mountain testifies to the fertility of his imagination.

At the same time, the report demonstrates how he managed to achieve the fundamental purposes of a park even on a site so different from the pastoral meadows he preferred. Particularly telling is the way he proposed to make the mountain beneficial to the sick and weak, even to the point of creating a full circuit of the mountain, bottom to top, that was accessible by wheelchair. For, as he observed, it was important "to cultivate the habit of thoughtful attention to the feebler sort of folk." This meant asking, for instance, "can this or that be made easier and more grateful to an old woman or a sick child, without, on the whole, additional expense, except in thoughtfulness?" If so, he urged, "ten to one, the little improvement will simply be that refinement of judgment which is the larger part of the difference between good and poor art, and the enjoyment of every man will be increased by it, though he may not know just how."[94]

To make sure that the report reached at least the influential citizens of Montreal, Olmsted had one hundred copies printed at his expense, for free distribution. He sent fifty copies to men suggested by Niles, and requested the Montreal bookseller Samuel C. Dawson to distribute the others. He stereotyped the report and offered free use of the plates to the park commissioners for publication of the report as a public document for broader distribution.[95] The commissioners did not accept his offer for use of the plates, and Olmsted's formal involvement with the park of Mount Royal came to an end.

"Belle Isle: After One Year," 1884

Just as he was ending his seven-year relation with the Montreal park commissioners, an opportunity developed for Olmsted to plan a park on Belle Isle in Detroit. The city had recently acquired the island, and after several contretemps a board of commissioners was appointed. Its chairman was James McMillan who, two decades later as a U.S. senator, would preside over the revival of the L'Enfant plan for the city of Washington and the ambitious park system conceived by Olmsted's son and namesake, Frederick Law Olmsted, Jr. In November 1881 McMillan approached Olmsted about planning Belle Isle, but when the commissioners proposed in December that he design only one-third of the park for them, he emphatically refused.[96] Nor did he respond favorably at first to McMillan's request that he examine the site and advise the commissioners concerning it free of charge. McMillan soon persuaded him to relent, however, and in February Olmsted visited the park, charging only for his expenses.[97] The tactic was successful, and in April he received a contract to plan the park for $7,000 and to superintend work on the park for three years.[98] The usual difficulties of securing an accurate topographical map delayed the design process, but by summer's end he had the necessary information and began the work. It soon became clear, however, that unless he could secure broad support for his plan, there was little prospect that it would be realized and maintained. This was due in part to the dependence of the park commission on the city's Common Council, which had to approve every significant action of the commission. Moreover, the mayor and many others opposed financing the park through bonds or other dedicated sources of funding, which meant that progress of the work had to depend on annual appropriations by the Common Council. Strong suspicions also existed among the aldermen that Olmsted's plan would be extravagantly expensive. To allay these fears and lay a solid groundwork of support, he wrote a long report concerning his concept for the park. In early December 1882 he offered the commissioners the chance to publish the report, but they did not act on the proposal.[99] He then published one hundred copies of the fifty-eight-page report, entitled *The Park for Detroit*, at his own expense and distributed them to influential citizens.

Seeking to reassure the people of Detroit, he offered a simple and inexpensive scheme for the park. Most of it would consist of woods and meadows that would be kept open by the grazing of flocks of sheep. The landscape effect would be similar to that of Windsor Great Park in England. In addition to the woodland, he proposed to make an eighty-acre meadow on the east side of the island that would be the largest and best parade ground in any American city. "You must have a few simple, distinct objects in view, and must provide for these in a liberal, strong, quiet and thoroughly satisfying way," he counseled, "guarding with all possible care against inconsistencies and discords."[100] In fact, consistency of policy was the best guarantee that the park would not be unduly expensive. In order to sustain simplicity of treatment in most of the park, Olmsted proposed to create a "City Fair" area with structures for a variety of activities at the end of the island closest to the city. Since much of the island was low and ill-drained, he proposed to dig a series of canals or "rigolets" into which a sunken drainage system would flow, and which would provide protected passage for small boats.

Having set forth the rationale for his treatment of the island, Olmsted went ahead in early 1883 to elaborate his plan. He further developed the proposed system of canals, using a "loop canal" to separate the City Fair section from the area of the park to be grazed, and adding a straight, mile-long avenue with a canal on either side. The most important feature that he added in his plan was the remarkable 1,600-foot pier and "gallery" that he proposed for the southern end of the island and which he described fully in *Belle Isle: After One Year*. It was to function as a two-level pier for access to steamboats, a shaded colonnade overlooking the bathing beach, a roofed viewing stand for athletic events, and a shelter from sudden storms. With its great size, multiplicity of uses, and sinuously flowing roofline, it was one of the most remarkable shingle-style structures designed in the decade when American architects, most notably his friend and collaborator H. H. Richardson, were achieving such noted results in that idiom.[101]

Upon completing his preliminary plan, Olmsted took it to Detroit, displayed it at the city hall, and (so he claimed) stood by it for two weeks answering questions. He also explained the plan to the park commissioners and to relevant committees of the Common Council.[102] During the visit he did his best to convince the park commission and city engineer that the City Fair section and its boundary canal should be completed during the next working season. Work did begin, but he was greatly disappointed by how little was accomplished with the appropriated funds, meager though they were.[103]

Olmsted spent the next winter attempting to secure construction of the pier and gallery. He realized that until all activities requiring structures could be concentrated at the southern end of the island the park commissioners would be constantly tempted to make permanent the temporary structures that had been set up in other parts of the park while construction of the City Fair facilities took place. He was also concerned that the Common Council's process of doling out annual appropriations for park construction would prevent the building of the whole gallery structure. In this his fears proved correct.

By September 1883 the working plan for the pier and gallery was finished, and the next month Olmsted took the plans and drawings to Detroit.[104] As discussion began concerning the amount to be appropriated for the working season of 1884, he had his apprentice Charles Eliot redraw a bird's-eye view and then had an "architectural painter" in New York produce a large-scale version of it for exhibition in Detroit. He then spent some two weeks in the city in early March 1884, attempting to rally support for the $40,000 needed to construct the pier and gallery. But opposition began to develop in some local newspapers, with one editor condemning the gallery as a "colossal folly."[105] In response, Olmsted carefully explained to the park commission the importance of building the gallery in the coming year.

Opposition still persisted, especially in claims that the water was too shallow for steamboats to reach the pier. At the end of May, therefore, Olmsted felt compelled to demonstrate the inaccuracy of those reports. On a windy day he directed the largest of the Windsor Line's steamers to a buoy marking the end of the pier and demonstrated with a lead line that he concocted that the water was twice as deep as necessary and that the bottom was not sandy, as critics had insisted, and would not need constant dredging to keep the pier approachable. He then met with the commissioners and after an intense, hour-long presentation led the president to respond, laughing, "I guess we shall have to build the pier, gentlemen, and the gallery also, but not this year." The Belle Isle park commission then authorized their engineer to move ahead on construction of the pier section of the structure: but the future of the gallery remained uncertain.[106]

In order to prove the viability of the gallery to the public, and to explain once again its crucial importance to his plan for the park, Olmsted wrote and published his second pamphlet on Belle Isle, entitled *Belle Isle: After One Year.* He reviewed the debate over the plan during the previous two years and offered an extended rationale for having a shelter like the gallery in the place he proposed. Work on the 400-foot pier at the western end of the gallery began in the fall and was completed early in 1885.[107] But the superb design for the gallery was never carried out, and Olmsted's plan of restricting buildings to the area south of the loop canal was soon abandoned. Nor was his canal system constructed. The mile-long avenue was built, but instead of running along it, the canals that were built connect three lakes placed in the lowest parts of the island where Olmsted had instead proposed to have meadows.

By April 1885 Olmsted no longer had an official relation with Detroit and Belle Isle. His infrequent later correspondence on the subject consisted of defending his plan against a widespread belief that it would have been outrageously expensive to carry out and that his fees had been too high. Much of this he attributed to the fact that the real grounds for hostility between the Common Council and the park commission — disagreements over fees, privileges, and patronage — could not be admitted. It was much safer, he observed, to blame an interloper from out of town. To queries from the new president of the board in 1887, he responded:

> I have no connection with the park at Detroit, know nothing definitely about its history since my engagement with the Commissioners ended and . . . I wish to have nothing to do, directly or indirectly, with any public discussion of the matter, having at the outset seen the danger of just such difficulties as have since arisen, given warning of them not only to the commissioners but most strenuously, by carefully prepared publications, and by personal interviews with editors and others for the purpose, and in every way proper for me to employ, done my best to prevent work from being started except on a design the leading motives and conditions of success of which should be intelligently realized, accepted and approved, not only by the commissioners but by the people.[108]

"Paper on the Back Bay Problem and its Solution," 1886

The Back Bay Fens was the first section of the Boston park system that Olmsted designed. He began the work in 1878 after the city's park commissioners had held a design competition and awarded the prize to an amateur who had no professional stake in the carrying out of his design. Olmsted had refused to play any role in the competition, either as competitor or as judge. He had, however, reviewed the sites that the commissioners proposed to include in a park system for the city. But as they prepared their report of 1876 they gave him no more creative role. "I have given you no complete service as yet," he wrote the chairman as the commission was completing its work of selection, "in fact I have not felt sure that you regarded my visits thus far as 'business.'"[109] Only after the fiasco of the design competition for the Back Bay park did the commissioners finally make Olmsted their professional advisor.

The 100-acre site lay just beyond the fashionable section of Back Bay that was growing up on land filled beginning in the late 1850s. From the outset Olmsted had to contend with popular expectations that the site would become an expensively maintained floral display like the Boston Public Garden. Indeed, much of his work in Boston was an attempt to wean Bostonians from the artificialities of the Public Garden style of planting. During this period he also criticized the Public Garden for its cost of upkeep: in his first report on Belle Isle he pointed out that the cost per acre of maintaining the Boston Public Garden was twenty-seven times greater than that for the upkeep of the simple landscape that he and Vaux had created in Buffalo's Delaware Park.[110] He was also distressed to find many of his smaller public grounds in Boston described as parks when both their size and treatment were not park-like. He eventually succeeded in applying the name Back Bay Fens to that project, instead of Back Bay Park, but in other instances he failed to convince even the park commissioners. A prime example is the site on Boston Harbor that they insisted on calling Marine Park, instead of Pleasure Bay, as Olmsted preferred. Of all the public grounds he designed in Boston, only 500-acre Franklin Park qualified in his view as a park.

The basis of Olmsted's opposition to the idea of an elegant, well-kept "park" on the Back Bay site was that any plan for it had to take into account the sanitary engineering issues to be solved. The site was a natural drainage basin for two major streams running through the backcountry of Boston — a basin consisting of mud flats at low tide and subject to flooding after heavy rains. The streams were open sewers, and the stench from the flats penetrated the surrounding residential area. As he indicated in the lecture published below, Olmsted believed that a tidal gate must be constructed that would allow water to cover the flats at all times. He was also convinced that only the restoration of salt marsh conditions within the basin would control destructive surf during floods while at the same time providing an attractive shoreline. His first step was to consult with Boston City Engineer Joseph P. Davis, with whom he had worked in 1866–67 when Davis was chief engineer of Prospect Park in Brooklyn. Davis agreed that the park commissioners had ignored essential preconditions for dealing with the area. During the next two years he worked closely with Olmsted to devise a workable solution.

Olmsted justified his design as a "natural" one that met all the city's needs in the place better than the artificiality of the Public Garden would have done. He asserted that it was

a direct development of the original conditions of the locality in adaptation to the needs of a dense community. So regarded, it will be found to be, in the artistic sense of the word, natural, and possibly to suggest a modest poetic sentiment more grateful to town-weary minds than an elaborate and elegant garden-like work would have yielded.[111]

In his work in Boston, Olmsted often found some precondition of the site that made it ill-suited for decorative gardening. When he came to plan Charlesbank, a promenade with gymnastic facilities along the bank of the Charles River below the Fens, he assured the commissioners that the site was too bleak and exposed to permit successful flower gardening.[112] When he outlined the preferred maintenance practices for the one true park in the system, he counseled that in Franklin Park "the urban elegance generally desired in a small public or private pleasure ground ... be methodically guarded against."[113] In the same fashion, he criticized the desire to call Back Bay a park as an ill-considered bit of real estate "puffery" that would lead to constant dissatisfaction and criticism of the wild and natural appearance of his proposed design.[114]

Olmsted believed that his method of design met both engineering requirements and psychological needs more effectively than did floral displays and exotic plants. His approach to the Back Bay Fens was similar to what he and Vaux had proposed seven years earlier for the marshy terrain of Jackson Park in Chicago. He proposed creating islands as bird sanctuaries, as he had in Chicago, and went on to consider including an aquatic collection within the basin as well. He considered having small steamboats make a three-mile circuit of the basin with pleasure parties — a precursor of the system of electric launches he developed for the Lagoon in Jackson Park during the Columbian Exposition of 1893.[115]

While Olmsted's collaboration with the city of Boston's engineers was an important element of his planning, involvement of an architect in the process was also crucial. When he found City Engineer Davis undisposed to use an architect, he warned Charles Dalton, chairman of the park commission, that Davis's views on such issues as the shape and materials of bridges would be unsatisfactory, "not intentionally or consciously but from the habitual drift of the engineering mind." For, as he observed, "to an Engineer bridges are engineering works."[116] He therefore asked to plan the Boylston Street bridge crossing of the basin with his friend and close professional ally H. H. Richardson. "It is the first thing you have to do as a Commission in which striking success, giving artistic people confidence in your ability to lead the city, is practicable," he told Dalton. The wildness of the landscape called for boulders or rough brick as the material for the bridge: "A natty, formal elegant structure would put all the rural elements of the Bay out of countenance," he warned, "it would be a discord." Instead, the bridge should "have a rustic quality and be picturesque *in material* as well as in outlines and shadows."[117] Richardson heartily adopted Olmsted's concept, as he so frequently did in their collaborations. Richardson's first plan was for "a very picturesque structure of fieldstone" that satisfied Olmsted's desire for a rugged and rustic effect. But this approach was too unusual for Boston's engineers and park commissioners. So prominent a structure, according to the canons of taste of the day, needed to be more dignified and finished in appearance. Accordingly, Richardson's final plan used cut blocks of granite and had a more elegant form. Olmsted regretted the change in design, believing that the bridge would have fitted the setting better "if it had not been quite so nice."[118] The commissioners did permit several boulder bridges at less conspicuous places, most notably Agassiz Bridge crossing the middle of the Fens.[119]

The Back Bay project, with its solution of sanitary engineering problems through creation of a naturalistic landscape, marked the first step in the reconstruction and preservation of a whole stream valley for public recreation purposes. As Olmsted indicated at the end of the lecture published below, he went on to design the Riverway and other sections of the Muddy River between the Back Bay Fens and Jamaica Pond. Such preservation of watercourses and use of them as greenways had been a major concern of his since he proposed such treatment of Strawberry Creek in Berkeley, California, in 1865.[120] Typically, in order to make sure that Public Garden–style decorative plantings were neither expected nor allowed in Boston's Riverway, Olmsted insisted on calling the project the Muddy River Sanitary Improvement.

At the time that Olmsted delivered the lecture on Back Bay published below, construction of Richardson's Boylston Street bridge had been completed. In addition, most of the dredging of the channel in Back Bay and much of the filling had also been done.[121] Olmsted felt that the results belied the fears of those critics who had said that the salt marsh landscape he was creating would be "lamentably prosaic if not worse," and that the Fens would be a prolific source of mosquitoes.[122] The system had also withstood its first severe test in the storm and floods of February 1886. Equally important, Olmsted was gratified that the park commission had stood behind him even when his plans stirred up controversy. This was a welcome contrast to his recent experience in Montreal and Detroit.[123] Olmsted's ingenious engineering scheme and the landscape he created to accompany it continued to function and flourish until 1915, when the Charles River dam further downstream did away with the salt water and tidal action on which he premised his plan.

"Notes on the Plan of Franklin Park
and Related Matters," 1886

The single great scenic park of the Boston system was 500-acre Franklin Park in West Roxbury. Olmsted's official role in its creation began in September 1884, when the park board authorized him to prepare a design for the park for the sum of $5,000. By April 1885 he had drawn up a preliminary plan, but the commissioners to whom he made his presentation were about to be replaced. The election season of late 1884 that produced the first Democratic president of the United States in nearly twenty-four years also transformed Boston politics. In December 1884 Bostonians elected their first Irish mayor, Hugh O'Brien, and Yankee Boston feared the worst. Olmsted's patrician friend Charles Eliot Norton predicted a dark future. "The Irish dynasty has fairly settled itself on the throne in Boston," he mourned, "the old Boston has disappeared." The new park board appointed by O'Brien, which included the city's most powerful Democratic boss, Patrick Maguire, took office on May 1, 1885. It immediately rescinded Olmsted's contract but then quickly reinstated him on terms similar to his contract with the old park board. His relations with it thereafter were cordial, and at the end of O'Brien's time as mayor he gave strong testimony that he had found the park commissioners during his tenure to be intelligent, concerned, and disinterested men.[124]

The problems with making progress on Franklin Park came not from O'Brien, who had been a strong supporter of parks from his days as an alderman, but rather from his Republican opponents. Through the rest of 1885 and all of 1886 the Common Council refused to appropriate funds for construction of Franklin Park and the rest of the proposed park system.[125] A possible alternative was issuance of long-term bonds by the city. A bill to authorize such a bond issue was before the legislature in early February 1886, when Olmsted successfully presented his plan for Franklin Park to the mayor and park board. "The plan is accepted without a murmur," he wrote Charles Eliot, "but the fact is neither the commissioners nor the public look at it or take any intelligent interest in it."[126] Within a month the commissioners published his report, *Notes on the Plan of Franklin Park and Related Matters*.

Olmsted realized that once again he must educate both public and officials if his plan were to be realized. Part of his task was to spell out the long-term benefit of a park in order to justify the legislature's authorization of fifty-year park bonds. "You will see that my paper is indirectly all an argument for its doing so," he wrote Harvard president Charles W. Eliot.[127] He was also concerned that even many of Boston's well-informed citizens were convinced that other cities had "been led into the most reckless extravagance & to add enormously to their burdens of taxation by their park enterprises."[128] Part of his purpose in writing the report was to demonstrate the true conservatism of park-making and the great social benefits a park could confer on a city. He also emphasized how inexpensively a park could be constructed and maintained. He illustrated this by the history of the Buffalo parks and by his description of the simplicity of his design for Franklin Park. Finally, he needed to describe his plan for the park in a way that would win informed public support.

In the section of the report describing that plan, Olmsted took simplicity of treatment as the key to his discourse. As with Back Bay, he cited the natural conditions as reason enough for avoiding decoration or any attempt at elegant treatment. The soil was thin and rocky and could not sustain, except at great expense, either fancy gardening or turf thick enough to withstand athletic sports. This justified devoting the largest portion of the space to what he called the Country Park, a term Mayor O'Brien had used to describe the West Roxbury park in one of his early speeches. Little more than the clearing of rocks and planting of scattered trees would be needed to achieve the landscape he envisioned, Olmsted assured the people of Boston.

The structures in the Country Park section would also reflect his theme of rustic simplicity. He conceived them as having "the general aspect of the simplest style of English rural cottages." This meant that eventually he desired thatched roofs instead of the tile roofs he describes in the 1886 report.[129] A shelter near Ellicottdale was to have rough stone walls, while the nearby pedestrian entrance under the carriage drive would be faced with large boulders that were partially covered by shrubs and vines. On Schoolmaster Hill he designed rough stone picnic bays sheltered by simple wooden arbors. Next to these was a dairy building of field stone for which he planned a thatched roof of eccentric shape ("curve and quiddle, twist, undulation, hog's back, dormers, gable and pent," as he described it).[130] Olmsted extended this rusticity of structures to the Playstead area, which with the adjacent Greeting served the same purpose as the "plaisances" of the Chicago South Park fifteen years previous — that is, areas that were to be kept open and lighted at night and provided for activities that would have been intrusive in the open landscape of the park. The Valley Gate separating the Playstead from the Country Park consisted of metal gates separated by small fieldstone lodges with tile roofs. Overlooking the Playstead's thirty acres of playing fields was a carriage concourse faced with boulders that covered an area 500 by 300 feet. At one end of the concourse stood the Playstead Overlook shelter, a remarkable structure for whose design Olmsted was primarily responsible. Measuring 120 by 60 feet, it served as a locker room, shelter, and restaurant for the athletes using the Playstead and for spectators. The walls were of fieldstone and shingle, creating a varied texture that, combined with the shadows cast by overhanging dormers and roof, produced a constantly changing camouflage effect. Over the whole structure rose the shingle roof that park commissioner Sylvester Baxter described as "quiet and gray in tone like a huge rock, and with gentle convex curves."[131]

From the Back Bay Fens to the Country Park and Playstead of West Roxbury, the Boston park spaces that Olmsted designed were passages of naturalistic landscape, with no provision for active recreation, children's entertainment, or formal promenading. Charlesbank eventually provided some of these elements, but it was an exposed site next to a working-class section of the city. Olmsted decided that he must plan a section of the Franklin Park for these activities, as he had done in the Chicago South Park and at Belle Isle. The Greeting that he proposed was near the main entrance of the park, at the point closest to town and with direct access from the city by carriages and horsecars. The area he selected was a long, narrow upland that connected at its far end with the Playstead and was separated from the Country Park by a steep, thickly wooded hillside. Visitors to the Country Park would not be aware of its existence. On that tableland he planned a Promenade half a mile long—nearly twice the length of the pedestrian Mall in Central Park—and 300 feet wide. It had a central carriage drive flanked on each side by a walk and a bridle path. A deer park and small athletic field took up the space between the Greeting and the park boundary, while along the other side ranged the Little Folks' Fair and the Music Court. Near the end of the Greeting farthest from the Playstead was the Refectory, set on a massive boulder foundation and surveying the open valley of Nazingdale. Olmsted planned to abandon his rustic architectural style for the building itself, envisioning a story-and-a-half structure reminiscent of the simple antecedents of Moorish architecture, with much of the terrace being taken up by a trellis on terracotta columns. As constructed, following plans by the Boston architectural firm of Hartwell and Richardson, this building had instead the kind of finished and elegant quality that Olmsted had hoped at all costs to avoid in Franklin Park.[132] Most of the other structures, however, were close to his concept. His plan was carried out for the most part, except that the Greeting was not constructed. (The park commissioners planned to finance it with the long-awaited windfall when Benjamin Franklin's bequest to the city of Boston matured after a century in 1891, but the funds were not made available to them.) Moreover, the park was constructed according to a revised plan by the Olmsted firm of 1891 that added several ponds in the lower section of the Country Park.[133]

"General Plan for the Improvement
of the Niagara Reservation," 1887

In 1887 Olmsted collaborated with his old partner Calvert Vaux in preparing a report and plan for the state reservation at Niagara Falls. Nearly a decade of agitation, in which Olmsted played a leading role, preceded this event. His interest in creating a reservation at Niagara dated back even further, to at least August 1869. In that month he had visited the falls with H. H. Richardson and William Dorsheimer while engaged with them on projects in Buffalo. During a walk on Goat Island, in the Niagara River between the Canadian and American falls, he raised the question of creating a public scenic reservation in the area of the falls. That evening the discussion expanded to include several men active in the campaign for the Buffalo park system who were also visiting Niagara. The group concluded that the state government was not prepared to use its resources for such a purpose, but they agreed that those assembled would work for creation of a reservation if a serious threat to the integrity of the scenery near the falls should develop.[134]

Olmsted's interest stemmed in part from his recent involvement with the federal grant to the state of California of the Yosemite Valley and Mariposa Big Tree Grove. In the summer of 1865, while serving as chairman of the commission that administered the grant, he had drawn up a comprehen-

46

sive report concerning the scenic value of the grant and the facilities that should be constructed for the convenience of its visitors. His official connection with Yosemite had lapsed after he returned to New York in the fall of 1865, but as recently as June 1868 he had circulated petitions opposing a bill passed by the U.S. House of Representatives that approved a California law permitting private ownership of several hundred acres in Yosemite Valley. At that time he also wrote a letter to the *New York Evening Post* repeating the statements in his 1865 report emphasizing the transcendent beauty of the valley and the importance of keeping it in public ownership.[135]

The central element of Olmsted's appreciation of Yosemite was not the granite peaks and towering sequoias alone. He emphasized the botanical diversity of the area and urged that scientists be officially involved in oversight of the grant. Even more important to him was the unique ensemble of landscape elements that made up the special scenic quality of Yosemite Valley. He praised the pastoral beauty of the valley, calling it such a place as Shakespeare delighted in. Amidst the dry Sierra foothills in autumn, the quietly flowing Merced and its green meadows seemed like an oasis, strongly reminding him of England. It was no single feature, no particular peak or tree, that constituted the special beauty of Yosemite, but rather the totality of the landscape experience it provided.

This analysis, characteristic of Olmsted's approach to scenic reservations, was consistent with his general aesthetic theory. In the same way that he avoided specimen plantings and intrusive structures while designing public parks, he sought in scenic reservations to draw attention away from spectacular individual elements—such as El Capitan, Half Dome, or Yosemite Falls at Yosemite. Indeed, the notebooks in which he recorded his early experience of Yosemite testify to his preference for views of the Yosemite peaks when they were partially obscured by fog or smoke. At such times they possessed the "obscurity of detail" of distant forms that he considered an essential element of scenery. As with his urban parks, it was immersion in the landscape, letting it work by an unconscious process, that was the most valuable experience. "I felt the charm of Yosemite much more at the end of a week than at the end of a day," he testified, "much more after six weeks when the cascades were nearly dry, than after one week, and when, after having been in it, off and on, several months, I was going out, I said, 'I have not yet half taken it in.'"[136]

Olmsted returned to these themes when he came to deal with Niagara. The great falls were only one element of the "distinctive charms" of the place. They were specimen-objects that awed the viewer, but the most rewarding experience of Niagara came from immersion in the scenery of the rapids and islands in the half-mile stretch above the falls. The vegetation of the islands was remarkable: the mist from the falls fostered a profusion of plants, while the ice that formed on them in winter pruned them to an unusual density of foliage. Botanists testified that Goat Island, the large island between the falls, had a greater variety of vegetation than any equal space of ground in Europe or in America east of the Sierra Nevada. The Englishman William Robinson, whose concept of the "wild garden" Olmsted admired, wrote that "the noblest of nature's gardens that I have yet seen is that of the surroundings and neighborhood of the Falls of Niagara."[137] "All these distinctive qualities," Olmsted concluded, "the great variety of the indigenous perennials and annuals, the rare beauty of the old woods, and the exceeding loveliness of the rock foliage, — I believe to be a direct effect of the Falls, and as much a part of its majesty as the mist-cloud and the rainbow."[138]

The raging rapids on either side of Goat Island formed an accompaniment to the vegetation and were a remarkable scenic element in their own right. Olmsted approvingly quoted the description by the Duke of Argyle of the view of the rapids from the edge of the falls:

> No indication of land is visible — nothing to express the fact that we are looking at a river. The crests of the breakers, the leaping and the rushing of the waters, are still seen against the clouds, as they are seen in the ocean, when the ship from which we look is in the trough of the sea. It is impossible to resist the effect on the imagination. It is as if the fountains of the deep were being broken up, and that a new deluge were coming on the world.[139]

It was the totality of these elements of scenery that made up the Niagara that Olmsted wished its visitors to experience — not simply the falls, but also the scenery of Goat Island and the shores of the American rapids, an expanse that made it possible to wander for hours at a time enveloped by the lush foliage, the sound of cascading water, and the mist-like spray from the falls.

Olmsted made his first public statement on these matters in 1880 as part of a report on preservation of the scenery of Niagara Falls that he drew up for the New York State Survey in collaboration with its director, James T. Gardner. This development came as part of a campaign that began in 1878 when Lord Dufferin, governor-general of Canada, made a public appeal for creation of an international park at the falls. He pressed the idea on New York governor Lucius Robinson, who responded by urging protection of the falls in his last annual message in January 1879. The New York legislature in turn authorized the State Survey commissioners to report on the measures needed to carry out the governor's proposals. The survey board directed Gardner to work with Olmsted in preparing a report assessing the effect of private land ownership on the scenic resources of Niagara and indicating the steps the government should take to protect the scenery there. The two men had already worked together on a scenic reservation, since in 1864 Olmsted had hired Gardner to prepare a map of the Yosemite grant.

In the report they submitted in March of 1880, Gardner wrote a strong condemnation of the desecration of scenery at Niagara that private profit-seeking had caused. He described the unsightly mills that covered Bath Island in the American Rapids and the miscellaneous hostelries that lined the American shore. Further, he warned that the one pristine feature of the New York area of the falls, Goat Island, would soon be sold and devoted to other incongruous and intrusive activities. He supplemented his diatribe with a series of photographs of the "disfigured banks" of Niagara. In a short separate statement, Olmsted offered an analysis of the "distinctive charms" of Niagara scenery. He quoted the landscape gardener William Robinson on the beauty and delicacy of the vegetation near the falls, the botanists Joseph Hooker and Asa Gray on the variety of that vegetation, and the Duke of Argyle on the powerful impression created by the rapids.[140]

In their report Olmsted and Gardner also described the area that should be taken for public ownership in order to restore and preserve the scenic beauty of Niagara. They proposed a seventy-seven-acre reservation, consisting of Goat and Bath islands and the other small islets in the American rapids, and a strip 100 feet wide along the mainland bank, where seventeen structures would be demolished, the shore replanted, and a barrier of trees introduced between the river and the city of Niagara Falls. Moreover, a large area at Prospect Point on the mainland edge of the American Fall would be used for shelter and preparation of visitors for their visit to the reservation. In addition, Olmsted and Gardner proposed that the state secure the right to maintain a narrow belt of trees along the top of the gorge for at least a mile below the falls.[141] Preparation of the report challenged Olmsted to consider how a public reservation could be managed so as to make the scenery accessible to large numbers of visitors without destroying it in the process. To Gardner he confided, "I feel as I get nearer to it and the likelihood of its becoming real increases that if not the most difficult problem in landscape architecture to do justice to, it is the most serious — the furthest above shop work — that the world has yet had."[142]

Not content with presenting the statements and proposals in their report, the two men submitted to the governor a lengthy petition, signed by 172 dignitaries from the United States, Canada, and Great Britain, calling for creation of public reservations on both sides of the falls. Included were the names of the vice president of the United States, the chief justice of the U.S. Supreme Court and seven associate justices, leading American literary figures, including Emerson, Longfellow, Whittier, James Russell Lowell, Francis Parkman, and Oliver Wendell Holmes, and the two English writers Olmsted revered most, Thomas Carlyle and John Ruskin. This petition marked the resumption of a collaboration between Olmsted and Charles Eliot Norton, professor of fine arts at Harvard University, that had begun during the Civil War years with mutual involvement in Reconstruction programs and the founding of the *Nation* magazine.[143] Over the next few years Olmsted and Norton played a leading role in the campaign that led in 1883 to creation of a state reservation at Niagara. Norton, in particular, secured the support of many leading figures in Great Britain. A parallel movement in Canada bore fruit in the form of a provincial reservation at the same time.

The report and petition campaign of 1880 promised well at first. The New York Assembly passed a bill to create a reservation at Niagara in April, with Olmsted listed as one of the commissioners. The bill failed in the senate, however, and the outspoken opposition of Governor Ezra Cornell doomed the attempt in any case. By the next year, Norton was contemplating creation of a private joint-stock company to acquire the property near the falls and so protect it without the complexities of politics. Instead, he worked with Olmsted to hire journalists Henry Norman and Jonathan B. Harrison to write articles for the press exposing the current state of affairs and urging creation of a public reservation. The situation improved markedly in November 1882, when Grover Cleveland was elected governor of New York. In preparation for a new legislative campaign, Olmsted and Norton helped in January 1883 to form the Niagara Falls Association, which led the successful campaign of the following months. That April a bill to create the reservation passed the legislature and was signed by Governor Cleveland.[144] Assessment of the value of land to be acquired began, but the hurdle of authorizing funds for land purchase and construction still remained. Powerful opposition soon developed, since purchase of the necessary property required issuing one million dollars worth of bonds — nearly equal to the entire debt that the state could legally assume. The supporters of the reservation prevailed, and on April 30, 1885, the legislature authorized the bond issue and the new governor, David B. Hill, signed the bill into law.

By this time, however, Olmsted's role had been considerably reduced. New problems developed even amidst the victory of 1883. He was acutely embarrassed by the fact that one of the five commissioners of the reservation appointed by Governor Cleveland was his old antagonist on Central Park, Andrew H. Green. As the meticulously cost-conscious controller of the park before the Civil War, Green had constantly restricted Olmsted's freedom of action. When negotiations were under way after the war for Olmsted and Vaux to resume their position as landscape architects to the Central Park commissioners, Green was very reluctant to accept Olmsted's return. As Vaux described it, he "shyed of course at the idea of countenancing the return of that overwhelming personality FLO." (Conversely, when during his time in California Olmsted leafed through his correspondence books from the early construction period of Central Park, he confided to Vaux that "it made me boil with indignation to see how cruelly and meanly Green had managed me . . . and what a systematic small tyranny, measured exactly by the limit of my endurance, he exercised over me. It was slow murder.")[145]

Olmsted feared in 1883 that Green would immediately move to gain control of the Niagara commission. In particular, he would oppose any involvement by Olmsted in the design and construction of the reservation.

Green was doubly dangerous because he was a law partner of Samuel Tilden, still a powerful figure in the New York Democratic party even after his narrow defeat in the presidential campaign of 1876. Olmsted realized that Tilden could turn the legislature against the commission and the reservation if Green wished him to do so. Accordingly, Olmsted abruptly dropped all involvement with the reservation. He even declined an invitation to join the commissioners on their first examination of the scenery at Niagara — saying, lamely, that he had to be present at the opening of bids on the U.S. Capitol terraces in Washington.[146] His friends were dismayed by this turn of events and sought to allay his fears concerning Green's involvement. Norton partially understood Olmsted's position but was unwilling to forego his counsel. "You cannot 'escape from your interest' in the matter," he declared, "although you may decline all further responsibility."[147]

Green's first action was to oppose adoption of the boundaries of the reservation proposed by Olmsted and Gardner. He pressed instead for acquisition of the gorge below the falls at least as far as the Devil's Whirlpool. The other commissioners, unwilling to endorse the increased expenditure required, adopted Olmsted and Gardner's report, "Green protesting and being 'ugly' to the last."[148]

There followed a power struggle within the commission between Andrew H. Green and Olmsted's longtime friend and ally William Dorsheimer over the question of planning the reservation. Green wanted to award the planning of the reservation to Calvert Vaux, whom he had supported in previous years as landscape architect to the New York City parks department. He had also presumably played a role in securing for Vaux the commission to remodel Samuel Tilden's house on Gramercy Park in Manhattan. Green and Dorsheimer were the only commissioners who felt the need for the expertise of a landscape architect, which made the situation even more difficult. As early as May 1883, Vaux's partner, the engineer George Radford, had queried Olmsted on his willingness to have the firm of Vaux & Radford plan the reservation, given the danger that Green posed for the whole undertaking should Olmsted be put forward. Olmsted responded simply that he would accept no remunerative position from the commission.

The issue became more pressing after authorization of the bond issue in May 1885. Dorsheimer's first proposal as chairman of the commission was that Olmsted, Gardner, and Vaux should collaborate on a plan for laying out the reservation; but Green rejected the idea, observing that Olmsted "was a man particularly offensive to him."[149] There was no resolution of the issue during the next year. As the commissioners' meeting of June 1886 came near, Vaux informed Olmsted that Green had informally approached him concerning his terms, to which he had replied that he would prefer to have his firm carry out the work, but that he wished to have Olmsted join him as "Consulting Landscape Architect." This was the sort of subordinate position that Vaux had endured during the early years of Central Park, when Olmsted was architect-in-chief and Vaux was merely consulting architect. Olmsted remained noncommittal, saying that he had consistently distanced himself from the question of planning the reservation. "It seems to me a very big affair," he stated, "and unless I am called to I don't want to spend any more of myself upon it." The maneuvering continued for several more months, with Green attempting at every stage to hire Vaux alone. Finally on November 3, 1886, the other four commissioners overrode Green's objections and voted to employ Olmsted and Vaux together to prepare the plan for the reservation.[150]

Although Olmsted appears to have assumed primary responsibility for writing the report, Vaux was an active participant in the process. Olmsted testified that "in the Niagara report he helped me and I helped him and at some points each of us crowded the other out a little." The work began quickly, and before the end of November Olmsted had sent Vaux a considerable portion of text and Vaux had returned the first section with some stylistic changes. They continued to exchange text and comments through the next three months, and by the end of February 1887 Vaux apparently was reassured that he could in good conscience co-sign the report with Olmsted. The Olmsted Papers collection in the Library of Congress contains numerous undated exchanges between the two men, some of which show Olmsted's painstaking replies to Vaux's critique. He labored over the report, revising and rephrasing right up to the time of presentation, which caused Vaux some concern that significant changes would occur after his last reading. As late as a week before they presented the report, Vaux was sending comments and corrections to Olmsted.[151] The scheduled date for the presentation was Tuesday, February 22, 1887, but on Saturday the 19th came news that the meeting of the commissioners had been postponed for a week. John C. Olmsted described Olmsted's harried last days of preparation:

> He worried a good deal over the opening of the report and was rather "cut up" about the postponement of the meeting. Being all primed and cocked he naturally wanted to fire. Then, too, he had been working every night and getting but little sleep saying to himself that it would all be over on Tuesday and thinking that he could stand it till then. He can't take writing easily. He must worry over it till the moment when it is delivered and he can alter no more.[152]

Olmsted and Vaux submitted their report and plan on March 1, 1887, and the commissioners formally submitted the report and plan to the state legislature on March 19. The commission approved the report and sought an appropriation to begin construction, but that was denied during the year 1887. The text presented here is taken from a version of the report that was published in March in New York City in an edition of 300, for circulation to influential citizens and the press.[153]

Construction was slow to begin thereafter, in part because of the small size of appropriations provided by the legislature. In fact, Olmsted was convinced that a whole new campaign would be required, similar to the one for creating the reservation, in order to secure adequate funding to carry out his and Vaux's plan.[154] By 1889, however, the unsightly structures had been removed from Bath Island and the mainland shore. By the time of Vaux's death in 1895 and Olmsted's retirement the same year, a circuit carriage drive had been constructed on Goat Island. Olmsted and his firm had little to do with the construction, while Vaux was involved in road building and architectural work. He designed the two principal stone bridges on Goat Island, one to Luna Island and the other to the first Sister Island. He also designed the simple iron railing that was installed at places overlooking the falls. His son Downing Vaux designed at least two shelters on Goat Island.[155]

Although the report of 1887 published below was Olmsted's last statement concerning the Niagara Reservation in New York, he later consulted with commissioner C. S. Gzouski about the plan for the Canadian reservation that was acquired in the summer of 1887 and opened in May 1888. Olmsted was concerned that the Canadian reservation would have a "garden park character rather than a forest scenic character" and that the intention to have the reservation pay for itself "by restaurants and playthings and to draw business by attractions to picknickers" would result in proliferation of the kinds of artificial entertainments that it had been his purpose to abolish on the American side. Gzouski approached Olmsted concerning his fee for helping plan the reservation, and Olmsted replied that he would engage to do so if Vaux were to join with him. No such project developed, but Olmsted did visit the Canadian reservation with Gzouski in August 1887. Seeking to have the Canadian reservation supplement that on the New York side, he urged that the carriage drive be moved close to the edge of the gorge instead of running it 300 yards inland, as was being planned. This would provide the best access to the direct view of the falls that Olmsted and Vaux had emphasized in their 1887 report as the special advantage of the Canadian side. The area back of the road to the steep wooded slope on the border of the reservation should, Olmsted recommended, appear as "a broad quiet, simple unbroken park-like body of land." Since the Canadian reservation was so large, requiring a five-mile walk to make a circuit of it, he proposed two large picnic grounds with shelters. In connection with these he wished to provide limited restaurant service, something he had excluded from the smaller New York reservation.[156] Olmsted's concept for the Canadian reservation, therefore, called for treatment quite different from that on the American side of the Niagara gorge: one would complement the other. But no such coherent and unified plan for both reservations has ever been fully articulated.

"Plan for a Public Park on the Flats South of Buffalo," 1888

At the time that Olmsted rejoined Calvert Vaux to plan the Niagara Reservation he also returned, without Vaux, to planning the Buffalo park system. This opportunity came in 1887, after a hiatus of a dozen years. The growth of industry and population in the southern part of the city had led to growing demands for parks and parkways in that section. A petition from citizens led the Common Council in February 1887 to request the park commissioners to create a park and parkways. The commissioners turned to Olmsted, who visited the city in March. At the public meeting held during his visit, most of the advocates who spoke were more interested in the route of parkways to the new lakeside park site than they were in the park itself. Part of their interest stemmed from the fact that abutting owners would be assessed for only half the cost of streets that were defined as parkways. The remaining cost would be funded by general taxation, since parkways were considered to benefit the entire city.[157]

In a report of April 1887 Olmsted urged the importance of addressing the barrier to travel posed by the one-half-mile-wide swath of railroad tracks that separated the south side of Buffalo from the older city north of Buffalo Creek. Such a situation was dangerous as well as inconvenient. He cited the testimony of one park commissioner who said that in order to visit a nearby suburb it was necessary to make twenty-four crossings of railroad tracks at grade. Fatal accidents at the crossings were all too frequent, and the time lost while conveyances waited at track crossings was becoming increasingly costly. As a solution, Olmsted urged that the city and the railroad companies work out an agreement to combine and relocate some of the lines on the south side. Then a single "grand trunk" viaduct should be constructed spanning the belt of railroads. The viaduct should have separate ways for different conveyances — one for carts and wagons, others for carriages and street railways. Several parkways could then be constructed running through the southside ward: one would lead to the new park, while Olmsted held out the prospect that numerous broad avenues would lead in other directions "so that, eventually, without excessive indirectness, branches from them would really come to every man's door, and all the country beyond be made conveniently accessible."[158]

In his final report on the subject in 1888, Olmsted proposed such a crossing at Abbot's Corners Road, a mile east of the lake and two miles south of Niagara Square. The crossing would provide a route by which a carriage could be driven to the new south park "from a point on an average nearest to the homes" of the whole city. A parkway 90 to 120 feet wide would run to the new park along the route of existing streets.[159]

However, Olmsted believed that the ready access to the park offered by railroad lines running through the eastern section of the site would provide more significant access. Another route, more pleasant than either the parkway or the railroads would be along the edge of the lake. Like the proposed parkway, its development was closely tied to larger issues of city planning on Buffalo's south side. Much of that section was low and poorly drained, a situation aggravated by the many railroad embankments being constructed in the area. Olmsted was convinced that a comprehensive plan must be adopted that would control further building in the area. Otherwise the problem would grow increasingly expensive to solve. Accordingly, he requested the city engineer to examine the two most likely solutions. One was to raise the level of land by filling to the point where storm drainage and sewer systems could operate by gravity flow; the other was to construct a series of levees against flooding and secure adequate drainage by pumping, as practiced in Holland. The engineer concluded that filling to a minimal height would cost one million dollars, while a pump-driven drainage system would cost a third of that sum.[160] Olmsted accordingly recommended the latter solution. It had the added benefit of creating a particularly attractive route of access to the new park. The levee to be constructed along the lake would create a grand five-mile promenade, providing a fine view of the lake and permitting access by carriage, horseback, and street railway. The dredging required to build the levee would produce a canal on its inland side by which private boats and commercial launches could carry visitors to the park.

The park itself would have a large area of waterways and islands for pleasure boating, created by the same procedure of dredging and filling. This area of lagoons would also be tied to another element of the city planning of the south side — the diversion of Cazenovia Creek. Flooding by the creek was growing increasingly dangerous, and the city engineer had already proposed diverting it directly to the lake.[161] The new route could bring a source of water to the new park for the boating facilities that Olmsted had in mind.

Olmsted's plan for the park itself, as set forth in the report published below, reflected his desire to make this second park for Buffalo distinctly different from the first, Delaware Park. The fact that he and Vaux had planned the Front and the Parade at the same time that they designed Delaware Park had enabled them to dedicate that park exclusively to quiet recreation and the enjoyment of the scenery of meadow, grove, and lake. Still, the original northside system had contained only one park. Now, for the first time since he and Vaux had planned the Chicago South Park in 1871, Olmsted had the prospect of designing two parks of several hundred acres for a single city. The new park had the added advantage of being at the opposite end of the city from Delaware Park. The question, as Olmsted phrased it in his report of 1888, was: *"Twenty years hence shall Buffalo have one park, of a poor, confused character, or two, each of a good, distinct character?"* Without the new park, there was danger that the desire for a place where "gayety, liveliness, and a slight spirit of adventure" was stimulated would lead to demands to supply such facilities "by a succession of small, feeble, imperfect and desultory interpolations" upon the design of Delaware Park.[162]

In general, the plan for the new park resembled the one that Olmsted and Vaux had drawn up for Jackson Park in Chicago in 1871, as Delaware Park resembled the open greens, picnic areas and Mere of Washington Park. But Olmsted offered a new concept in the Buffalo South Park. Previously, his concern had been the exhaustion caused by the stress of application to business and economic activity. Now he observed that something more than "tranquilizing natural scenes" was desired by workers in industrial enterprises — those, as he phrased it, "who pass most of their time in monotonous occupations and amid sombre surroundings." The previous year he had addressed this problem in his first plan for Charlesbank in Boston, a recreation ground near the tenement district of the West End. There he planned extensive open-air exercise facilities. These included a gymnastic ground for men and a playground and running track for women. The final design of 1892 included a gymnastic ground for women. These were the first "scientifically designed and administered open-air gymnasiums to be operated free of charge in a public park."[163] In keeping with this new concern, Olmsted's plan for the Buffalo South Park design included an oval "athletic ground" or "out-of-door Gymnasium" with a bicycle and running track around the perimeter. There were also facilities for bathing, both in Lake Erie and in a sheltered interior pool. For the eighty-five-acre section of the park east of the railroad embankment that bisected it, Olmsted proposed more active, even exciting, recreation. He suggested that the area be used as a firing range by local militia during the summer. In winter it would be flooded and adapted for skating, sledding, and tobogganing.

Finally, the South Park gave Olmsted the opportunity at last to create a large park in Buffalo that took advantage of the city's situation on the shores of Lake Erie. His first, and last, desire for the city was to make this happen, and the thirty-two-acre Front that he and Vaux had included in their original park system plan was too small to permit many of the activities that Olmsted wished to foster. His concept for Jackson Park in Chicago had not been realized, and there was no prospect that it would be, at least under his guidance. This must have made him all the more anxious to seize the occasion in Buffalo to create a park with lakeshore bathing activities and extensive interior lagoons for boating. For those not wishing to row and paddle amongst the numerous islands in the lagoons, Olmsted proposed a system of public launches that would make a four-mile circuit in three-quarters of an hour.

However, it was in Chicago's Jackson Park, rather than Buffalo, that Olmsted finally realized his dream of a great water park. The Buffalo park commissioners were reluctant to act on his proposal. They felt that the cost of construction would be too great and the risk of frequent damage from storms on the lake too high. They also felt that the site was too far from the residential areas on the south side and were concerned by the absence of good building sites for residences in the low-lying area adjoining the park. Instead, they selected two inland sites that Olmsted described as "too large for local grounds, too narrow and cut up for parks — dilemmas."[164]

His successors in the Olmsted firm drew up the plans for these in the late 1890s, creating a small area for boating in 76-acre Cazenovia Park by damming the creek running through it, and making an arboretum of 150-acre South Park.[165] Thus, the park system developed by the firm for Buffalo's south side differed greatly from Olmsted's vision of a great boating park and lakeside promenade embankment and canal.

Advice to the People of Cincinnati, 1894

Olmsted's last major report that combined an explication of the nature of the urban park with a description of a particular plan was *Notes on the Plan of Franklin Park and Related Matters* of 1886. Thereafter, his reports on parks, like that for the South Park in Buffalo, concentrated on the design issues of the particular project in hand. In other situations, however, he continued to explain the nature of parks, the responsibilities of park commissions, the role of professional landscape architects, and the psychological effect of scenery. In 1886, for instance, he visited Minneapolis, where H. W. S. Cleveland had just begun to design a park system. The report Olmsted wrote to the park commission dealt primarily with the purpose of a park, the responsibilities of park commissions, and the importance of securing prime park sites while the land was still inexpensive.[166] Among Olmsted's papers relating to the Rochester park system are many pages of fragmentary and apparently never-completed statements concerning the nature of parks and the duties of park commissions that he wrote c. 1890. The laborious rewording and reworking that he imposed on himself is evident in these fragmentary and repetitious remains. Likewise, when the park commissioners of his city of birth — Hartford, Connecticut — finally approached him during his last year of professional practice to guide them in planning a park system, he undertook first to explain to them the nature and purpose of landscape architecture. He never completed this discourse, and the many pages of fragmentary beginnings and revisions reveal both how seriously he viewed the task and how difficult it still was for him to write on theoretical topics. But the urgency, the sense of importance of once again clarifying the nature of his art and the role to be played by park commissioners and their professional advisors, was strong.

The most complete of the numerous attempts that Olmsted made in his last years of practice to explain his art once again to new groups of park commissioners is the report he wrote for Cincinnati in 1894. In early January of that year he visited the city at the invitation of the park commissioners. They originally had asked him to inspect their parks, offer suggestions on the treatment of Eden and Burnet Woods parks, and comment on the suitability of some new land the commissioners were thinking of acquiring. Subsequent opposition by local businessmen led them instead to ask him only for advice on improving existing parks. During his visit, the commissioners were distressed that he refused to provide them instantly with instructions concerning certain details of the parks he visited. It became clear to him that even if funds were available for improvement of the parks and acquisition of new sites, no coherent landscape treatment over time would be possible under the existing park administration. The problem was of long standing and had led Cincinnati's preeminent landscape gardener, Adolph Strauch, to resign in 1876 as superintendent of the parks after a difficult three years in that position.

This was reason enough to move Olmsted to attempt to educate the people of Cincinnati in proper park management. By the time he completed his report at the end of January, moreover, the state legislature had abolished the park commission and put Cincinnati's parks under the control of a board that was responsible for numerous other public works in the city. These developments gave added importance to Olmsted's report, and he asked his partners John C. Olmsted and Charles Eliot to read his draft of it carefully. "The circumstances give us possibly a rare opportunity to say something for our faith, & we should use it," he wrote John. Since he wished to convince the city's businessmen of the rationality and true economy of his approach, he sought to make his statement "moderate and sensible, cool and quiet."[167]

On the day Olmsted completed his report, the commission to which he wrote it ceased to exist. But he hoped to rally public support by having the report printed in the city's newspapers. He instructed his partners to have it translated into German and sent several copies to the superintendent of parks, R. H. Warder, for distribution. "What we want is to do the best thing we can under the circumstances for the public interests, for the spread of sound ideas, and for the good standing of our art and profession . . . ," he explained to Warder. Accompanying the report, Olmsted included a note addressed to "the Citizens of Cincinnati" saying that since the park commission had been abolished he felt "that it should be placed directly before you."[168]

The report addressed once again the vexing issues of the nature of a park, the evils in cities that parks are designed to counteract, the need for continuity of administration and employment of professional landscape architects by park boards. In the process Olmsted included a stern indictment of the city's failure to follow the plans of Adolph Strauch. The problems of the park system stemmed from a failure to use common sense in recognizing the purpose of a park commission and then applying "ordinary business principles" to that purpose. It was this, rather than advice on design by outsiders, that the parks needed. Rely on the professionals that you already employ, he counseled, and clearly define their responsibilities so that they have no excuse for not meeting them, "especially no excuse of that class of excuses commonly referred to in political affairs as 'influences,' of which the effect always is a practical dissipation of official responsibility." Such had been Olmsted's theme for over a decade, since well before his dismissal from the New York parks department and the publication of *The Spoils of the Park* that followed.

There is no evidence that any Cincinnati newspaper published the report, although copies may have been circulated privately. The following year the park department included an innocuous and extensively excerpted portion of Olmsted's statement in its annual report. His attempt to rally the people of Cincinnati to the cause of good government and responsible park administration had not succeeded.[169] Still, this was but one battle of many, each charged with real significance for the future of Olmsted's vision of public parks in the American democracy.

As the documents in this volume illustrate, Olmsted had many such battles during his career. Over a period of nearly half a century, from the publication of his article on Birkenhead Park in the *Horticulturist* in 1851 to his retirement in 1895, he found many occasions to explain the principles of park design, use, and administration to the public. During those years he and his partners created more than a dozen major parks and nearly one hundred other recreation grounds and parkways. With a carefully defined set of basic principles, he sought to create landscapes with powerful and beneficial psychological effect, while at the same time providing adequately for the need of people to come together in large numbers. In addition, he strove to place responsibility for managing the parks in the hands of park boards that were independent of political pressures and thus able to pursue long-term policies that would permit the realization of his design concepts. He placed this work within the broader setting of his historical concept of the evolution of the city and his firm belief that the park movement of the nineteenth century represented a "self-preserving instinct of civilization." While he considered such universal elements, he also sought in his individual designs to develop a unique solution based on the nature of the site and the social need it served, giving clear individuality to each design.

1. See Frederick Law Olmsted, *Report Upon a Projected Improvement of the Estate of the College of California, at Berkeley, near Oakland,* June 29, 1866 (*Papers of FLO,* 5: 546–73); and Frederick Law Olmsted, *A Few Things to be Thought of before Proceeding to Plan Buildings for the National Agricultural Colleges,* [Dec. 1866] (*Papers of FLO,* 6: 130–50).
2. Frederick Law Olmsted, *The Park For Detroit* (Brookline, Mass., 1882).
3. F. L. Olmsted and J. B. Harrison, *Observations on the Treatment of Public Plantations, More Especially Relating to The Use of the Axe* (Boston, 1889).
4. See page 250 below.
5. George F. Chadwick, *The Park and the Town* (New York, 1966), p. 68.

6. See page 71 below.
7. See Charles E. Beveridge, "In Search of Olmsted's England," *The Planner: Journal of the Royal Town Planning Institute* 70 (July 1984): 15–16; [A. J. Downing], "Mr. Downing's Letters from England," *Horticulturist* 6 (June 1851): 281–86; [A. J. Downing], "The New-York Park," ibid. (Aug. 1851): pp. 345–49.
8. See FLO to Board of Commissioners of the Central Park, Sept. 9, 1858 (*Papers of FLO*, 3: 202–4); "Map of Central Park Showing Construction Completed as of January 1, 1862, in BCCP, *Fifth Annual Report* [1862].
9. Frederick Law Olmsted, *Preliminary Report in Regard to a Plan of Public Pleasure Grounds for the City of San Francisco*, March 31, 1866 (*Papers of FLO*, 5: 536–42).
10. See *Papers of FLO*, 5: 564–65, 572.
11. F. L. Olmsted, *Plan of Public Pleasure Grounds for San Francisco* (*Papers of FLO*, 5: 522).
12. Frederick Law Olmsted, "Preliminary Report upon the Yosemite and Big Tree Grove," [August 1865] (*Papers of FLO*, 5: 503, 504).
13. See pages 83 and 129 below.
14. See page 155 below.
15. *Papers of FLO*, 5: 659.
16. "Æsop at Play," in Æsopus, *The Fables of Æsop, and Others, with Designs on Wood, by Thomas Bewick* (1818; rpt. ed., New York, 1975), pp. 333–34.
17. See page 89 below.
18. See page 87 below.
19. Ibid.
20. For the enlarged promenade on Prospect Lake, see *Papers of FLO*, 6: 414–15.
21. Frederick Law Olmsted, "The Future of New-York," *New York-Daily Tribune*, Dec. 28, 1879, p. 5.
22. "Document No. 3," in BCCP, *Minutes*, Jan. 11, 1866, pp. 9–10, 13–14, 39–45.
23. Ibid., pp. 64–65.
24. See page 129 below.
25. See pages 148, 151, and 152 below.
26. Jay Appleton, *The Experience of Landscape* (London, 1975), pp. 68–80.
27. "Communications from Fred. Law Olmsted, Esq.," in City of Buffalo. Park Commission, *Fifth Annual Report of the Buffalo Park Commissioners. January 1875* (Buffalo, N.Y., 1875), pp. 11–12; "The Act of the Legislature," in City of Buffalo. Park Commission, *Preliminary Report Respecting a Public Park in Buffalo . . .* (Buffalo, N.Y., 1869), pp. 29–48; *Buffalo Express*, Feb. 11, 1869, p. 20; City of Buffalo. Common Council, *Proceedings*, Nov. 1, 1869, p. 715; ibid., Nov. 25, 1869, pp. 766–69.
28. See page 167 below.
29. FLO to George E. Waring, Jr., April 13, 1876.
30. FLO to JCO, June 13, 1893.
31. Cynthia Zaitzevsky, *Frederick Law Olmsted and the Boston Park System* (Cambridge, Mass., 1982), pp. 34–37; Henry Villard to FLO, Dec. 8, 1869; James Haughton to FLO, [c. Dec. 1869]; James T. Fields to FLO, Nov. 15, 1869; Edward Everett Hale to FLO, Nov. 24, 1869; Robert M. Copeland to FLO, Dec. 3, 1869; James T. Fields to FLO, Dec. 8, 1869. Fields's remark that the material beginning on page 34 of Olmsted's manuscript was the sort of thing he wanted for the article indicates the similarity between both the length and progression of topics of that manuscript and the article published here, which is based on Olmsted's lecture of February 1870.
32. Henry Villard to FLO, Dec. 8, 1869.
33. See Olmsted, Vaux & Co., *Preliminary Report upon the Proposed Suburban Village at Riverside, Near Chicago*, Sept. 1, 1868 (*Papers of FLO*, 6: 273–89).
34. See page 180 below.
35. See pages 183–84 below; see *Papers of FLO*, 6: 361–68, 374–78, 442–52.

36. "The Central Park and other City Improvements," *New York Herald*, Sept. 6, 1857, p. 4: see *Papers of FLO*, 3: 272–73.
37. Papers of FLO, 6: 442–52; see page 197 below.
38. See *Papers of FLO*, 5: 593–94, 605–6.
39. Daniel Bluestone, *Constructing Chicago* (New Haven, 1991), p. 26; *Chicago Times*, Feb. 20, 1867, p. 5.
40. D. Bluestone, *Constructing Chicago*, pp. 46–52; Theodore Turak, "William Le Baron Jenney: Pioneer of Chicago's West Parks," *Inland Architect* 25 (March 1981): 39–45.
41. FLO to Joseph Donnersberger, April 20, 1894, A33: 889, OAR/LC.
42. The Ramble in Washington Park was drawn directly from Paxton's Birkenhead Park: it had excavated mounds on a flat terrain that were densely planted with shrubs, and it contained an area with large rocks and a fernery, as did Birkenhead Park.
43. *Papers of FLO*, 3: 354.
44. The Central Park competition rules called for inclusion of a parade ground, three playgrounds, a hall for exhibitions and concerts, a "principal fountain," a prospect tower, a flower garden of two to three acres and a site for ice skating: see *Papers of FLO*, 3: 178.
45. FLO to Rudolph Ulrich, March 24, 1891, A13: 186, OAR/LC.
46. The Long Meadow in Prospect Park, for instance, is 90 acres in area, and the meadow in Buffalo's Delaware Park is 150 acres.
47. The only time that Olmsted called a section of one of his parks a "prairie" was in 1881 at Belle Isle in Detroit. In this case the apparent reason was not because he felt that he was in a "prairie" region, but rather that he wished to indicate a roughness of character and low level of maintenance that he did not apparently desire for the meadows of Washington Park. (F. L. Olmsted, *Park for Detroit*, pp. 50–52).
48. See page 213 below.
49. FLO to Ignaz Anton Pilat, Sept. 26, 1863 (*Papers of FLO*, 5: 85).
50. See page 213 below.
51. FLO to Rudoph Ulrich, March 24, 1891, A13: 185–87, OAR/LC.
52. Frederick Law Olmsted, "The Landscape Architecture of the World's Columbian Exposition," *Inland Architect and News Record* 22 (Sept. 1893): 18–20.
53. Horace W. S. Cleveland to FLO, July 25, 1888.
54. See page 251 below.
55. See page 248 below.
56. FLO to Parke Godwin, Aug. 1, 1858 (*Papers of FLO*, 3: 201).
57. Frederick Law Olmsted, "Report of the Landscape Architect on the Recent Changes in the Keepers' Service," July 17, 1873 (*Papers of FLO*, 6: 613).
58. Ibid., p. 612.
59. "The Central Park and other City Improvements," *New York Herald*, Sept. 6, 1857, p. 4. See *Papers of FLO*, 3: 272–73, and page XXX below.
60. See *Papers of FLO*, 6: 627, n. 7.
61. F. L. Olmsted, "Report on Recent Changes in the Keepers Service" (*Papers of FLO*, 6: 617–18, 619).
62. FLO to Board of Commissioners of Central Park [1860], in *Forty Years*, 2: 439–40.
63. F. L. Olmsted, "Report on Recent Changes in the Keepers Service" (*Papers of FLO*, 6: 620).
64. Ibid., pp. 624–25.
65. See page 291 below.
66. Jan Vier, "Central Park in Danger," *New-York Daily Tribune*, May 28, 1873, pp. 4–5; Jan Vier, "The Central Park Investigation," ibid., May 29, 1873, p. 5; Frederick Law Olmsted, "Central Park Changes," June 3, 1873 (*Papers of FLO*, 6: 607).

67. FLO, manuscript fragment, summer 1873; see *Papers of FLO*, 6: 44–45; DPP, *Minutes*, Sept. 25, 1873, p. 296.
68. See *Papers of FLO*, 4: 40–42, 463, 466–70; Charles E. Beveridge, "Frederick Law Olmsted: The Formative Years 1822–1865" (Ph.D. diss., University of Wisconsin, 1966), pp. 423–33.
69. See page 304 below.
70. See page 299 below.
71. For Tompkins Park, see report of Olmsted, Vaux & Co., in BPC, *Eleventh Annual Report* [1871], pp. 33–35; *Papers of FLO*, 6: 24–25, 395–98.
72. See page 309 below.
73. See page 313 below.
74. Whereas he had said of Birkenhead Park near Liverpool that "though small, it is by its admirable plan the most complete, and for its age the most agreeable park in Europe;" he now wrote that the 120-acre space "though too small in scale and too garden-like for the general popular use of a large community, is very pleasing, and is one of the most instructive to study in Europe." He excised his earlier statement regarding Phoenix Park in Dublin that "in its natural character it is the best public park in the world" (having said something of the sort in the new article concerning the equally extensive Fairmount Park in Philadelphia); and he changed his view of the English Garden in Munich from "its scenery, in the English style, is more agreeable than that of any other large public park on the continent," to "It has serious defects, but its scenery in the English style has been considered more agreeable than that of any other public park on the continent" (see *Papers of FLO*, 3: 347, 352).
75. See page 346 below.
76. FLO to Commissioners of Mount Royal Park, Nov. 21, 1874.
77. FLO to H. A. Nelson, Dec. 28, 1875, June 6, 1876, and March 26, 1877.
78. See page 405 below.
79. FLO to H. A. Nelson, March 26, 1877.
80. FLO to H. A. Nelson, July 26, 1876, Archives Municipales de Montréal, Montreal, Quebec, Canada.
81. FLO to W. J. Picton, Sept. 30, 1876.
82. FLO to H. A. Nelson, April 4, 1876, Archives Municipales de Montréal, Montreal, Quebec, Canada.
83. FLO to Mount Royal Park Commission, April 28, 1877.
84. FLO to H. A. Nelson, Oct. 16, 1876, Archives Municipales de Montréal, Montreal, Quebec, Canada.
85. FLO to H. A. Nelson, Nov. 3, 1876, Archives Municipales de Montréal, Montreal, Quebec, Canada.
86. FLO to JCO, Oct. 7, 1877, John C. Olmsted Papers, Frances Loeb Library, Graduate School of Design, Harvard University, Cambridge, Mass.
87. FLO to H. A. Nelson, Dec. 26, 1879.
88. Olmsted described his symptoms in 1863, saying "to write a single sheet entirely interrupts my digestion, sets my brain throbbing, my ears singing and half suffocates me — also my eyes twitch . . ." (FLO to E. L. Godkin, Dec. 25, 1863 [*Papers of FLO*, 5: 160]).
89. FLO to Charles Loring Brace, March 7, 1882.
90. "Our Parks. Lecture by Mr. Olmsted," *Montreal Daily Star*, Sept. 29, 1877, p. 2; FLO to Commissioners of Mount Royal Park, Aug. 1, 1881.
91. William Woodruff Niles to FLO, July 11, 1881.
92. See page 366 below.
93. See page 374 below.
94. See pages 393–94 below.

95. FLO to Samuel C. Dawson, Aug. 2, 1881, Archives Municipales de Montréal, Montreal, Quebec, Canada.
96. FLO to James McMillan, Nov. 12, 1881; FLO to John Sterling, Dec. 30, 1881.
97. James McMillan to Detroit Common Council, in City of Detroit, *Journal of the Board of Councilmen*, Oct. 3, 1882, p. 535.
98. Ibid., April 11, 1882, p. 145.
99. FLO to Belle Isle Park Commissioners, Dec. 1, 1882.
100. F. L. Olmsted, *Park for Detroit*, p. 32.
101. Frederick Law Olmsted, "Map to illustrate proposed drainage arrangmnts," March 17, 1883; Vincent Scully, Jr., *The Shingle Style: Architectural Theory and Design from Richardson to the Origins of Wright* (New Haven, 1955), pp. 91–154.
102. FLO to JCO, March 22, 1883.
103. FLO to JCO, Oct. 12, 1883; FLO to John Sterling, Feb. 13, 1884.
104. Charles Eliot Diary, Sept. 9 and Oct. 7, 1883, Charles Eliot Papers, Frances Loeb Library, Graduate School of Design, Harvard University, Cambridge, Mass.
105. Ibid., March 30, 1884.
106. FLO to JCO, Decoration Day, 1884.
107. FLO to Mr. Smith, Nov. 24, 1884.
108. FLO to Elliott T. Slocum, Feb. 8, 1887, A1: 627, OAR/LC.
109. FLO to Charles H. Dalton, April 8, 1876.
110. F. L. Olmsted, *Park for Detroit*, pp. 21, 27.
111. "City Document No. 15," in City of Boston, *Fifth Annual Report of the Board of Commissioners of the Department of Parks* (Boston, 1881), p. 12.
112. FLO to Boston Park Commissioners, in City of Boston. Department of Parks, *Twelfth Annual Report of the Board of Commissioners for the Year 1886* (Boston, 1887), p. 16.
113. See FLO, *Notes on the Plan of Franklin Park and Related Matters*, (1886), page 483 below.
114. FLO to Charles H. Dalton, Dec. 9, 1879.
115. FLO to A. E. Verrill, Feb. 8, 1879.
116. FLO to Charles H. Dalton, Jan. 24, 1880.
117. Ibid.
118. For a discussion of the Boylston Street bridge, see C. Zaitzevsky, *Frederick Law Olmsted and the Boston Park System*, pp. 164–68.
119. See sketches for bridges in ibid., pp. 168, 169.
120. See Frederick Law Olmsted, *Report Upon a Projected Improvement of the Estate of the College of California, at Berkeley, Near Oakland*, June 29, 1866 (*Papers of FLO*, 5: 564–65).
121. See map showing state of construction in the Fens at the end of 1885 in C. Zaitzevsky, *Frederick Law Olmsted and the Boston Park System*, p. 157.
122. *American Architect and Building News*, March 20, 1880, p. 117; ibid., April 17, 1880, p. 169; ibid., April 3, 1880, p. 145.
123. Frederick Law Olmsted, "Remarks About a Difficulty Peculiar to the Park Department of City Governments, Addressed, upon Invitation, to the New England Club, 26th January 1889," in City of Boston. Department of Parks, *Fourteenth Annual Report of the Board of Commissioners for the Year 1888* (Boston, 1889), pp. 31–34.
124. Ibid.; Charles Eliot Norton to FLO, March 5, 1885, Charles Eliot Norton Papers, Houghton Library, Harvard University, Cambridge, Mass.; JCO to Joshua Crane, Jan. 27, 1889.
125. FLO to Charles W. Eliot, July 20, 1886; FLO to Sylvester Baxter, March 20, 1886.
126. FLO to Charles Eliot Norton, Feb. 25, 1886.
127. FLO to Charles W. Eliot, Feb. 25, 1886.

128. FLO to William McMillan, March 16, 1885.

129. FLO to JCO, Sept. 8, 1891.

130. FLO to JCO, May 15, 1892. In the end, the Schoolmaster Hill shelter had a tile roof instead: see C. Zaitzevsky, *Frederick Law Olmsted and the Boston Park System*, p. 180.

131. Sylvester Baxter, *Boston Park Guide Including the Municipal and Metropolitan Systems of Greater Boston* (Boston, 1896), p. 21.

132. See the discussion of the Refectory in C. Zaitzevsky, *Frederick Law Olmsted and the Boston Park System*, pp. 180–81.

133. Ibid., pp. 66, 77–78.

134. FLO to C. K. Remington, May 28, 1888, A2: 531–33, OAR/LC.

135. See *Papers of FLO*, 5: 472, n. 57.

136. FLO, manuscript fragment, Olmsted Papers; see *Papers of FLO*, 5: 465.

137. "Notes by Mr. Olmsted," in New York (State), *Special Report of New York State Survey on the Preservation of the Scenery at Niagara Falls . . . for the Year 1879* (Albany, N.Y., 1880), pp. 28, 29.

138. Ibid., p. 29.

139. Ibid., p. 30.

140. Ibid., pp. 27–30.

141. James T. Gardner, "Report of the Director on the Plan for a Proposed State Reservation at Niagara," in ibid., pp. 19–30.

142. FLO to James T. Gardner, Oct. 3, 1879, James Terry Gardner Manuscripts, New York State Library, Albany, N.Y.

143. See *Papers of FLO*, 4: 284, 618–20; ibid., 5: 63–65.

144. FLO to Charles Eliot Norton, May 11, 1883, Charles Eliot Norton Papers, Houghton Library, Harvard University, Cambridge, Mass.; FLO to J. Hampden Robb, June 4, 1883.

145. CV to FLO, May 30, 1865; FLO to CV, March 25, 1864 (*Papers of FLO*, 5: 210); see *Papers of FLO*, 3: 55–59, 317–19.

146. FLO to Charles Eliot Norton, June 21, 1883, Charles Eliot Norton Papers, Houghton Library, Harvard University, Cambridge, Mass.

147. Howard Potter to FLO, May 19, 1883; Charles Eliot Norton to FLO, May 11, 1883, Charles Eliot Norton Papers, Houghton Library, Harvard University, Cambridge, Mass.

148. FLO to Charles Eliot Norton, June 21, 1883, Charles Eliot Norton Papers, Houghton Library, Harvard University, Cambridge, Mass.

149. William Dorsheimer to FLO, May 15, 1885; FLO to Charles Eliot Norton, Aug. 4, 1885.

150. CV to FLO, May 21, [1886]; FLO to CV, May 24, 1886; George Radford to FLO, May 26, 1886; Andrew H. Green to William Dorsheimer, July 21, 1886; Minutes of Commissioners of the Niagara Reservation, June 9, Oct. 6, and Nov. 3, 1886.

151. FLO to Mariana Griswold Van Rensselaer, May 16, 1887; CV to FLO, Feb. 21, [1887]; CV to FLO, Feb. 22, [1887].

152. JCO to CV, [Feb.] 22, 1887 [transcription in Olmsted Papers microfilm, reel 36, frame 220, misdated "22nd September, 1887"].

153. New York (State), *Fourth Annual Report of the Commissioners of the State Reservation at Niagara, for the Year 1887* (Troy, N.Y., 1888), p. 5; CV to FLO, [March] 21, [1887].

154. FLO to Mariana Griswold Van Rensselaer, May 18, 1887.

155. George Radford to JCO, Jan. 14, 1892; CV to FLO, [April 5, 1887] (Olmsted Papers microfilm, reel 36, frame 199); New York (State), *Ninth Annual Report of the Commissioners of the State Reservation at Niagara, for the Year 1892* (Albany, N.Y., 1893), p. 50; idem, *Tenth Annual Report of the Commissioners of the State Reservation at*

Niagara, for the Year 1893 (Albany, N.Y., 1894), p. 49; idem, *Eleventh Annual Report of the Commissioners of the State Reservation at Niagara, for the Year 1894* (Albany, N.Y., 1895), pp. 50, 53; idem, *Sixteenth Annual Report of the Commissioners of the State Reservation at Niagara, for the Year 1899* (Albany, N.Y., 1900), pp. 32, 33.

156. FLO to C. S. Gzouski, Aug. 15, 1887, A1: 944, OAR/LC.

157. F. L. and J. C. Olmsted, "Report on the South Parkway Question," in City of Buffalo. Park Commission, *The Projected Park and Parkways on the South Side of Buffalo. Two Reports by the Landscape Architects* (Buffalo, N.Y., 1888), p. 28.

158. Frederick Law Olmsted, "Proposed Extension of the Park System," in City of Buffalo. Park Commission, *Eighteenth Annual Report of the Buffalo Park Commissioners. January 1888* (Buffalo, N.Y., 1888), p. 38.

159. F. L. and J. C. Olmsted, "Report on the South Parkway Question," pp. 35–37.

160. Ibid., p. 41.

161. F. L. Olmsted, "Proposed Extension of the Park System," in City of Buffalo, *Eighteenth Annual Report*, p. 34.

162. See page XXX below.

163. C. Zaitzevsky, *Frederick Law Olmsted and the Boston Park System*, p. 97; FLO to Boston Park Commissioners, in City of Boston, *Twelfth Annual Report*, pp. 15–17. Previously, Olmsted had provided exercise equipment only for children, as with the well-equipped playgrounds he and Vaux had designed for Prospect Park in 1868 and Buffalo's Parade in 1870. They had also included gymnastic grounds for adults, as in their plan for Walnut Hill Park in New Britain, Connecticut, in 1870, but these plans indicated no facility beyond a stretch of lawn. The plan for the men's gymnastic area at Charlesbank of 1891 had trapezes and swinging rings, horizontal and parallel bars, and pulleys with weights, as well as a running track and places for the broad jump, pole vault, shot put, weight throwing, and quoits. The women's gymnastic ground had swings, ladders, and giant strides (See pp. XXX and XXX below; *Papers of FLO*, 6: 363; City of Boston. Department of Parks, *Seventeenth Annual Report of the Board of Commissioners for the Year 1891* (Boston, 1892), pp. 47–59).

164. City of Buffalo. Park Commission, *Nineteenth Annual Report of the Buffalo Park Commissioners. January, 1889* (Buffalo, N.Y., 1889), pp. 10–11; FLO to JCO, Dec. 5, 1891.

165. Arleyn A. Levee, "The Olmsted Firm in Buffalo: The Next Generation," in *The Best Planned City: The Olmsted Legacy in Buffalo*, ed. Francis R. Kowsky (Buffalo, N.Y., 1992), pp. 29–32.

166. FLO to the Park Commission of Minneapolis [1886]; William H. Tishler, "H. W. S. Cleveland," in *American Landscape Architecture: Designers and Places*, ed. William H. Tishler (Washington, D.C., 1989), p. 27.

167. Report of Visits, Jan. 1, 2 and 3, 1894, E4: 126–30, OAR/LC; FLO to JCO, Jan. 25, 1894.

168. FLO to Reuben H. Warder, Jan. 30, 1894; FLO to the citizens of Cincinnati, Feb. 3, 1894.

169. Jessie P. Boswell to JCO, Feb. 24, 1915; City of Cincinnati, Board of Administration, *Annual Report of the Park Department of the City of Cincinnati. 1894* (Cincinnati, Ohio, 1895), pp. 14–16.

WRITINGS ON PUBLIC PARKS, PARKWAYS, AND PARK SYSTEMS

The People's Park at Birkenhead, near Liverpool.
by W., Staten Island, New-York.

[May 1851]

BIRKENHEAD is the most important suburb of Liverpool, having the same relation to it that Brooklyn has to New-York, or Charlestown to Boston.[1] When the first line of Liverpool packets was established, there were not half a dozen houses here; it now has a population of many thousands, and is increasing with a rapidity hardly paralleled in the New World.[2] This is much owing to the very liberal and enterprizing management of the land-owners, which affords an example worthy of consideration in the vicinity of many of our own large towns. There are several public squares, and the streets and places are broad, and well paved and lighted. A considerable part of the town has been built with uniformity, and a reference to general effect, from the plans, and under the direction of a talented architect, Gillespie Graham, Esq., of Edinburgh.[3]

We received this information while crossing the Mersey in a ferry-boat,[4] from a fellow passenger, who, though a stranger, entered into conversation, and answered our inquiries, with frankness and courtesy. Near the landing we found, by his direction, a square of eight or ten acres, enclosed by an iron fence, and laid out with tasteful masses of shrubbery, (not trees,) and gravel walks. The houses about were detached, and though of the same general style, were sufficiently varied in details not to appear monotonous. These were all of stone.[5]

We had left this, and were walking up a long, broad street, when the gentleman who had crossed the ferry with us, joined us again, and said that as we were strangers, we might like to look at the ruins of an abbey which were in the vicinity, and he had come after us; that if we pleased he might conduct us to it. What an odd way these Englishmen have of being "gruff and reserved to strangers," thought I.[6]

*   *   *   *   *

Did you ever hear of Birkenhead Abbey?[7] I never had before. It has no celebrity, but coming upon it so fresh from the land of Youth as we did, so unexpecting of anything of the kind — though I have since seen far older ruins, and more renowned, I have never found anything so impressively aged.[8]

*   *   *   *   *

At the Market place[9] we went into a baker's shop, and while eating some buns, learned that the poorest flour in the market was American, and

69

GRAND ENTRANCE TO BIRKENHEAD PARK

the best, French. French and English flour is sold in sacks, American in barrels. The baker asked us if American flour was *kiln dried*, and thought it must be greatly injured, if it was not, on that account. When we left, he obligingly directed us to several objects of interest in the vicinity, and showed us through the market. The building is very large, convenient, and fine. The roof, which is mostly of glass, is high and airy, and is supported by two rows of slender iron columns, giving to the interior the appearance of three light and elegant arcades. The contrivances to effect ventilation and cleanliness, are very complete. It was built by the town, upon land given to it for the purpose, and cost $175,000.

The baker had begged of us not to leave Birkenhead without seeing their new Park, and at his suggestion we left our knapsacks with him, and proceeded to it. As we approached the entrance, we were met by women and girls, who, holding out a cup of milk, asked us — "Will you take a cup of milk, sirs! Good, cool, sweet, cow's milk, gentlemen, or right warm from the ass." And at the gate were a herd of donkies, some with cans of milk strapped to them, others saddled and bridled, to be let for ladies and children to ride.

The gateway, which is about a mile and a half from the ferry, and quite back of the town, is a great massive block of handsome Ionic architecture, standing alone, and unsupported by anything else in the vicinity, and looking, as I think, heavy and awkward. There is a sort of grandeur about it that the English are fond of, but which, when it is entirely separate from all other architectural constructions, always strikes me unpleasantly. It seems intended as an impressive preface to a great display of art within. But here, as well as at Eaton Park,[10] and other places I have since seen, it is not followed up with great things — the grounds immediately within the grand entrance being very simple, and apparently rather overlooked by the gardener. There is a large archway for carriages, and two smaller ones for those on foot; on either side, and over these, are rooms, which probably serve as inconvenient lodges for the laborers. No porter appears, and the gates are freely open to the public.

Walking a short distance up an avenue, we passed through another light iron gate into a thick, luxuriant, and diversified garden. Five minutes of admiration, and a few more spent in studying the manner in which art had been employed to obtain from nature so much beauty, and I was ready to admit that in democratic America, there was nothing to be thought of as comparable with this People's Garden. Indeed, I was satisfied that gardening had here reached a perfection that I had never before dreamed of. I cannot attempt to describe the effect of so much taste and skill as had evidently been employed; I will only tell you, that we passed through winding paths, over acres and acres, with a constant varying surface, where on all sides were growing every variety of shrubs and flowers, with more than natural grace, all set in borders of greenest, closest turf, and all kept with most consummate neatness. At a distance of a quarter of a mile from the gate, we came to an open field of clean, bright, green-sward, closely mown, on which a large tent was pitched, and a party of boys in one part, and a party of gentlemen in another, were playing cricket. Beyond this was a large meadow with rich groups of trees, under which a flock of sheep were reposing, and girls and women with children, were playing. While watching the cricketers, we were threatened with a shower, and hastened back to look for shelter, which we found in a pagoda, on an island approached by a Chinese bridge. It was soon filled, as were the other ornamental buildings, by a crowd of those who, like ourselves, had been overtaken in the grounds by the rain; and I was glad to observe that the privileges of the garden were enjoyed about equally by all classes. There were some who even were attended by servants, and sent at once for their carriages, but a large proportion were of the common ranks, and a few women with children, or suffering from ill health, were evidently the wives of very humble laborers. There were a number of strangers, and some we observed with note-books, that seemed to have come from a distance to study from the garden. The summer-houses, lodges, bridges, &c., were all well constructed, and of undecaying materials. One of the bridges which we crossed was of our countryman, Remington's patent, an extremely light and graceful erection.[11]

I obtained most of the following information from the head working gardener.

The site of the Park and Garden was ten years ago, a flat, sterile, clay farm. It was placed in the hands of Mr. Paxton in June, 1844, by whom it was

71

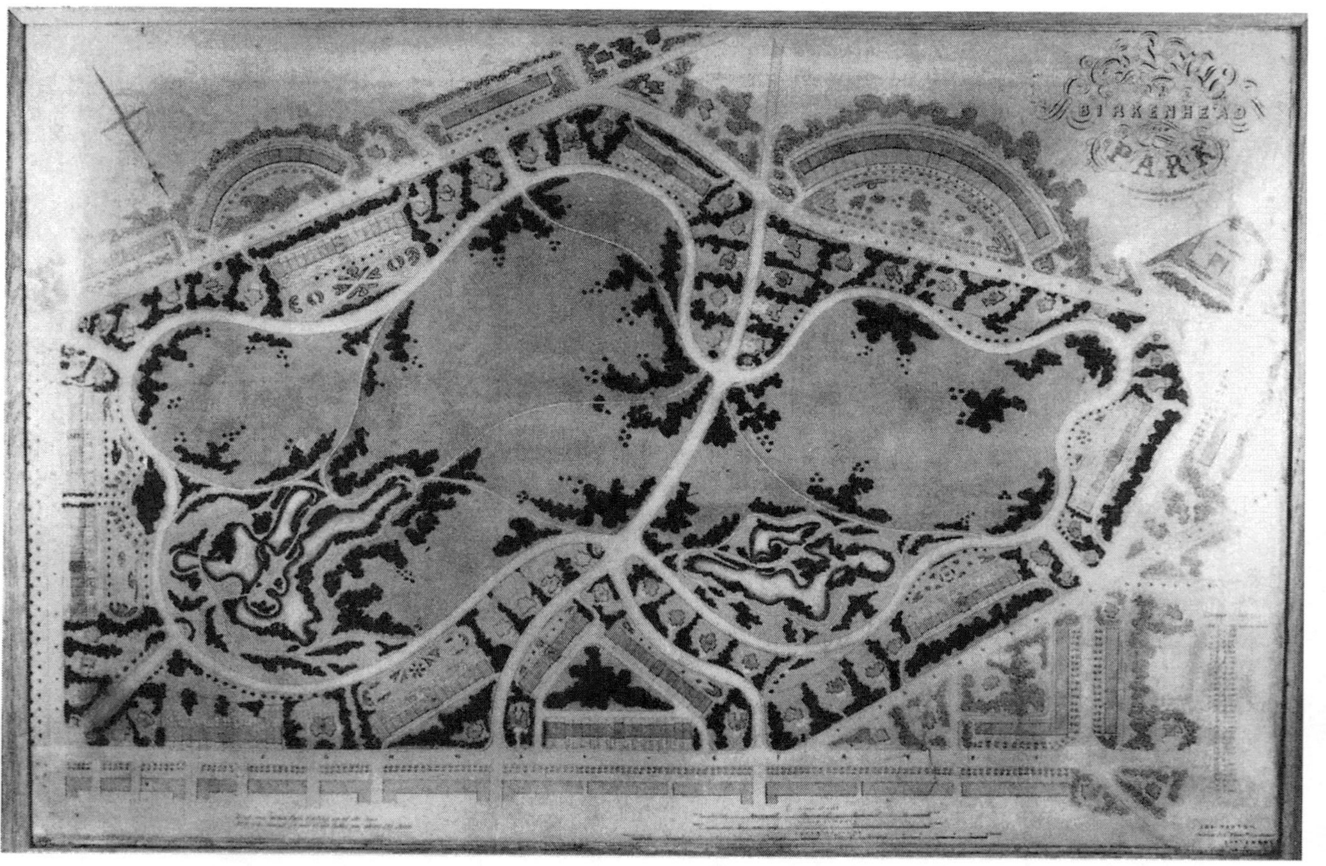

Plan of Birkenhead New Park, 1844

laid out in its present form by June of the following year.[12] Carriage roads, thirty-four feet wide, with borders of ten feet, and walks varying in width, were first drawn and made. The excavation for a pond was also made, and the earth obtained from these sources used for making mounds and to vary the surface, which has been done with much *naturalness* and taste. The whole ground was thoroughly under-drained, the minor drains of stone, the main, of tile. By these sufficient water is obtained to fully supply the pond, or lake, as they call it, which is from twenty to forty feet wide, and about three feet deep, and meanders for a long distance through the garden. It is stocked with aquatic plants, gold fish and swans.

The roads are McAdamised.[13] On each side of the carriage way, and of all the walks, pipes for drainage are laid, which communicate with deep main drains that run under the edge of all the mounds or flower beds. The walks are laid first with six inches of fine broken stone, then three inches cinders, and the surface with six inches of fine rolled gravel. All the stones on the ground which were not used for these purposes, were laid in masses of rock-work, and mosses and rock-plants attached to them. The mounds were then planted with shrubs, and Heaths, and Ferns, and the beds with flowering plants. Between these, and the walks and drives, is everywhere a belt of turf, which, by the way, is kept close cut with short, broad scythes and shears, and swept with house-brooms, as we saw. Then the rural lodges, temple, pavilion, bridges, orchestra for a band of instrumental music, &c., were built. And so, in one year, the skeleton of this delightful garden was complete.

But this is but a small part. Besides the cricket and an archery ground, large valleys were made verdant, extensive drives arranged — plantations, clumps, and avenues of trees formed, and a large park laid out. And all this magnificent pleasure-ground is entirely, unreservedly, and forever the People's own. The poorest British peasant is as free to enjoy it in all its parts, as the British Queen. More than that, the Baker of Birkenhead had the pride of an Owner in it.

Is it not a grand good thing? But you are inquiring who *paid* for it. The honest owners — the most wise and worthy town's people of Birkenhead — in the same way that the New-Yorkers pay for the Tombs,[14] and the Hospital, and the *cleaning*, (as they amusingly say,) of their streets.

Of the farm which was purchased, one hundred and twenty acres have been disposed of in the way I have described. The remaining sixty acres, encircling the Park and Garden, were reserved to be sold or rented, after being well graded, streeted and planted, for private building lots. Several fine mansions are already built on these, (having private entrances to the park,) and the rest now sell at $1.25 a square yard. The whole concern cost the town between five and six hundred thousand dollars. It gives employment at present, to ten gardeners and laborers in summer, and to five in winter.*

* "When the important advantages to the poorer classes, of such an extensive

The generous spirit and fearless enterprise, that has accomplished this, has not been otherwise forgetful of the health and comfort of the poor.† Among other things, I remember, a public wash and bathing house for the town is provided. I should have mentioned also, in connection with the market, that in the outskirts of the town there is a range of stone slaughter-houses, with stables, yards, pens, supplies of hot and cold water, and other arrangements and conveniences, that enlightened regard for health and decency would suggest.

The consequence of all these sorts of things is, that all about, the town lands, which a few years ago were almost worthless wastes, have become of priceless value; where no sound was heard but the bleating of goats and braying of asses, complaining of their pasturage, there is now the hasty click and clatter of many hundred busy trowels and hammers. You may drive through wide and thronged streets of stately edifices, where were only a few scattered huts, surrounded by quagmires. Docks of unequalled size and grandeur are building,[15] and a forest of masts grows along the shore; and there is no doubt that this young town is to be not only remarkable as a most agreeable and healthy place of residence, but that it will soon be distinguished for extensive and profitable commerce. It seems to me to be the only town I ever saw that has been really built at all in accordance with the advanced science, taste, and enterprising spirit that are supposed to distinguish the nineteenth century. I do not doubt it might be found to have plenty of exceptions to its general character, but I did not inquire for these, nor did I happen to observe them. Certainly, in what I have noticed, it is a model town, and may be held up as an example, not only to philanthropists and men of taste, but to speculators and men of business.

After leaving the Park, we ascended a hill, from the top of which we had a fine view of Liverpool and Birkenhead. Its sides were covered with villas, with little gardens about them. The architecture was generally less fantastic, and the style and materials of building more substantial than is usually employed in the same class of residences with us. Yet there was a good deal of the same *stuck up*, and uneasy pretentious air about them, that the suburban houses of our own city people so commonly have. Possibly this is the effect of association in my mind, of steady, reliable worth and friendship with

---

and delightful pleasure ground, are taken into consideration, no one will be inclined to say that such an expenditure does not merit the most unbounded success, and the deepest public gratitude. Here nature may be viewed in her loveliest garb, the most obdurate heart may be softened, and the mind gently led to pursuits which refine, purify, and alleviate the humblest of the toil-worn."[16]

† "Few towns, in modern times, have been built with such regard to sanitary regulations, as Birkenhead, and in no instance has so much been done for the health, comfort and enjoyment, of a people, as by those energetic individuals with whose names the rise and progress of Birkenhead are so intimately connected." *Dr. J. H. Robertson.*[17]

plain or old fashioned dwellings, for I often find it difficult to discover in the buildings themselves, the elements of such expression. I am inclined to think it is more generally owing to some disunity in the design — often perhaps to a want of keeping between the mansion and its grounds or its situation. The architect and the gardener do not understand each other, and commonly the owner or resident is totally at variance in his tastes and intentions from both; or the man whose ideas the plan is made to serve, or who pays for it, has no true independent taste, but had fancies to be accommodated, which only follow confusedly after custom or fashion. It is a pity that every man's house cannot be really his own, and that he cannot make all that is true, beautiful, and good, in his own character, tastes, pursuits and history, manifest in it.

But however fanciful and uncomfortable many of the villa houses about Liverpool and Birkenhead appear at first sight, the substantial and thorough manner in which most of them are built, will atone for many faults. The friendship of nature has been secured to them. Dampness, heat, cold, will be welcome to do their best. Every day they will improve. In fifty or a hundred years, fashions may change, and they will appear, perhaps, quaint, possibly grotesque — at any rate, picturesque — but still strong, homelike, and hospitable. They have no shingles to rot, no glued, and puttied, and painted gim-crackery, to warp and crack, and moulder, and can never look so shabby, and desolate, and dreary, as will nine-tenths of the buildings of the same denomination now erecting about New-York, almost as soon as they lose the raw, cheerless, impostor-like airs which seem almost inseparable from their newness.

WAYFARER[18]

The text presented here is taken from the *Horticulturist* of May 1851, volume 6, pages 224–28. Olmsted included a slightly longer version of this article as chapter eight of his book *Walks and Talks of an American Farmer in England,* which would be published in 1852.

In the late 1840s the *Horticulturist*'s editor, Andrew Jackson Downing (1815–1852), advocated the creation of public parks in U.S. cities. By May 1851, the same time that Downing published Olmsted's article presented here, New York City Mayor Ambrose C. Kingsland recommended to the Common Council that land be set aside for a public park. Olmsted and Downing corresponded after Olmsted's return from England in 1850, and it is possible that Downing asked Olmsted for this article as a way of introducing the importance of a public park for New York City to an American audience (*Walks and Talks,* 1: 74–84; *Papers of FLO,* 3: 90–91).

1. Birkenhead in Cheshire, lying on the west bank of the River Mersey opposite Liverpool (*Guide to Liverpool, Birkenhead, Wallasey* . . . [London, n.d.], p. 92).
2. Coastal steamship service to and from Liverpool was established in the 1810s and 1820s. Birkenhead's population in 1818 was about fifty inhabitants but had grown to 24,285 by 1851 (George Chandler, *Liverpool Shipping: A Short History* [London, 1960], p. 50; *The County Borough of Birkenhead: The Official Guide* [London, 1970?],

75

p. 8; *EB*; J. Thomas and T. Baldwin, eds., A *Complete Pronouncing Gazetteer, or Geographical Dictionary, of the World* . . . [Philadelphia, 1855], s.v. "Birkenhead").

3. James Gillespie Graham (1776–1855), an architect born in Dunblane, Perthshire, Scotland. Gillespie Graham (he adopted the second surname after the death of his father-in-law in 1825) received several commissions in Scotland and England during his career including the town of Birkenhead, which he laid out between 1825 and 1828 (Adolf K. Placzek, ed., *Macmillan Encyclopedia of Architects*, 4 vols. [New York, 1982], 2: 235).

4. The Woodside ferry providing service from Birkenhead to Liverpool was established as early as the thirteenth century. In 1822 a steam ferry was introduced. Twenty years later the Birkenhead commissioners purchased the ferry from private owners, which the town continued to operate (see n. 7 below; *County Borough of Birkenhead*, pp. 8, 15; *The Strangers' Guide through Birkenhead* [Birkenhead, 1847], pp. 9–11).

5. Hamilton Square, the only square built to Gillespie Graham's design. The square, near the center of town and three minutes' walk from the ferry landing, was laid out soon after 1833. Hamilton Square contained six-and-one-half acres of gardens and walks enclosed by a parapet and iron railings. The square itself was surrounded on all sides by elegant stone-fronted houses, home to the founding families of Birkenhead (*Strangers' Guide through Birkenhead*, pp. 12–13; *Guide to Liverpool*, p. 93).

6. Here the text omits three paragraphs describing Birkenhead Abbey that Olmsted included in *Walks and Talks* (*Walks and Talks*, 1: 76–77).

7. Birkenhead Abbey or Priory was founded in 1250 by Hamon de Masci, Baron of Dunham Massey, for the Benedictine Order. Among its many grants and privileges, the most important was the exclusive right of ferrying passengers between Liverpool and Birkenhead. After the dissolution of the English monasteries by Henry VIII in 1535, the priory and its grounds fell into the hands of the crown, and in 1545 it was passed on to Ralph Worsley of Worsley, in Lancashire. Thereafter the priory was left to deteriorate (Charles Grey Mott, *Reminiscences of Birkenhead* [Liverpool, 1900], pp. 39–40; *EB*).

8. Here the text omits one paragraph describing Birkenhead Abbey that Olmsted included in *Walks and Talks* (*Walks and Talks*, 1: 77).

9. The wholesale market, located on Hamilton Street south of Hamilton Square, was established in 1833 (*Guide to Liverpool*, p. 93).

10. Eaton Hall and Park, located in Chester, England, belonged to the Duke of Westminster. Olmsted probably entered Eaton Park by way of Grosvenor Lodge, also known as Chester gate, an imposing structure built similarly to St. Augustine's Abbey Gate at Canterbury. Olmsted described it as "a great, fresh pile of bombastic towers and battlements." In describing the park within the gate he noted that he was

> surprised to find within only a long, straight road, with but tolerable mowing lots alternating by the side of it, with thick plantations of trees, no way differing from the twenty-year old natural wood of my own farm, except that hollies, laurels, and our common dog-wood were planted regularly along the edge. After a while we pushed into this wood, to see if we could not scare up some of the deer. We soon saw daylight on the outside, and about twelve rods from the road, came to an open field, separated from the wood only by a common Yankee three-rail fence, which I had not expected to see in England; very poor it was too, at that.

(John Leyland, ed., *Gardens Old and New: The Country House & Its Garden Environment*, 3 vols. [London, 1900–8], 2: 203–4; J. Hemingway, *Panorama of the Beauties, Curiosities, and Antiquities of North Wales* . . . [London, 1845], p. 133; *Walks and Talks*, 1: 116, 134).

11. John R. Remington from Lowndes County, Alabama, patented a design to increase

the strength of truss bridges without the use of truss frames by bracing or tying down the ends of the sleepers and thereby preventing them from breaking in the middle (U.S. Patent Office. Patent no. 3,095, May 19, 1843).

12. Sir Joseph Paxton (1803–1865), English landscape designer, botanist, and architect. Paxton is probably best known for designing the Crystal Palace for the International Exhibition in Hyde Park in 1851. He also served as head gardener for Chatsworth Estate in Derbyshire, England, from 1826 to 1858. Paxton obtained the commission to lay out Birkenhead Park in 1844, and it was opened to the public in April 1847 (A. K. Placzek, ed., *Macmillan Encyclopedia of Architects*, 3: 378–79; George F. Chadwick, *The Park and the Town* [New York, 1966], pp. 68–71).

13. A system of paving using hard, broken stones to create roadbeds and named for its inventor, John Loudon McAdam (1756–1836) (*DNB*).

14. In 1833 New York City passed a law providing for the building of a new prison in the downtown area. When members of the selection committee saw a picture of an Egyptian tomb in a recently published travel book, they were so impressed with the structure that they recommended the prison have a similar appearance and be named "The Tombs" (Charles Sutton, *The New York Tombs: Its Secrets and its Mysteries* [1874; rpt. ed., Montclair, N.J., 1973], p. 48).

15. In 1843 the shipbuilder John Laird formed a company that undertook the construction of shipping docks along the River Mersey at Birkenhead. By 1847 the first of these docks was completed. Thus began a heated rivalry between Liverpool and Birkenhead until the Mersey Docks and Harbour Board was established in 1858 and took control of the harbourage on both sides of the river (*Guide to Liverpool*, p. 95).

16. This quotation is from *The Strangers' Guide through Birkenhead*, page 35.

17. This statement first appeared in Dr. James Hunter Robertson's *The Present Sanatory Condition of Birkenhead*, published in 1847. Olmsted took the quotation he used here, however, from *The Strangers' Guide through Birkenhead*. The editors of *The Strangers' Guide* altered the text and punctuation of Robertson's statement, and Olmsted's version matches those changes (James Hunter Robertson, *The Present Sanatory Condition of Birkenhead* [London, 1847], p. 6; *Strangers' Guide through Birkenhead*, p. 64).

18. At the end of the article Downing included an editorial note that read:

> We are very much indebted to our correspondent for his clear and pleasing account of one of the most interesting public places of enjoyment in all Europe—and all the more interesting, because it has been formed by the people themselves, and not made and presented to them by the sovereign. We only regret that the people of our large cities, generally, cannot see, with their own eyes, the beauty, and realize the advantages of such parks in the midst of towns. New-York, for instance, now one of the largest cities in the world, has no public park, whatever—no breathing place, no grounds for the exercise and refreshment of her jaded citizens—for to call the little *yards* of land, covered with turf, and planted with trees, in various parts of the town, *parks*, is as much a misnomer as it would be to spread one's handkerchief down on the floor of the rotunda of a capitol, and call it a carpet.
>
> The fact is, Americans generally, have no conception of the value, extent, or importance to the people of large cities, of public parks—and among the good results that will grow out of the World's Fair in London, will be that of showing thousands of them, Hyde Park, where the Crystal Palace stands—a building that covers twenty acres, and appears to take up as little room there, as if it were in an oak opening in Illinois.

We are glad to be able to say, *en passant,* that the government at Washington are manifesting a lively interest in this subject. The large tract of unimproved public lands lying south of the city of Washington — consisting of between one and two hundred acres, has just been taken in hand, at the desire of the President, with the view of making a NATIONAL PARK — something really worthy of the name. If his views can be fully carried out, that Park may exert an influence on the public taste of the whole country, as well as embellish and improve, in the highest degree, its seat of government. ED.

Preliminary Report to the Commissioners for
Laying Out a Park in Brooklyn, New York:
Being a Consideration of Circumstances of Site and
Other Conditions Affecting the Design of
Public Pleasure Grounds

Index of Subjects.

REPORT.

JANUARY 24th, 1866.

To the Board of Commissioners:[1]
GENTLEMEN:

We have been instructed to lay before you at this time such plans, accompanied by information and advice, as would aid you in a final review of the boundaries of the park proposed to be formed under your government. The study herewith submitted has been prepared for this purpose, and though not designed to be full or accurate in all details, is intended to be complete in those respects which are essential to an understanding of the advantages to be gained by such changes of the boundaries as we would recommend to be secured, before a plan of construction is definitively settled upon.

We proceed to show what these changes are, and why they are considered desirable.

In selecting a site for a park, it is evidently important that such natural advantages should be secured as are found in well grown woods, an agreeable variety of surface and fair prospects both of distant and local scope. It is true, that a site may be deficient in any of these characteristics, and yet, with time enough and money enough, be convertible by well directed labor, into a park of varied and attractive scenery. If, however, such conditions as are most desirable to be added, should have been already provided by nature in the immediate vicinity of a site, it would be felt, on the one hand, to be an extravagance to repeat them by artificial means upon it; while, on the other, the disadvantage of its being without them would be greater, because more obvious. Moreover, there are two possible misfortunes of a site, which in no period of time, and by no expenditure of labor, can ever be remedied. These are, inadequate dimensions, and an inconvenient shape.

Our first duty has been to examine the site to which you have asked our attention, with reference to the several conditions we have thus indicated; that is to say, with reference to —

1. Convenience of its shape.
2. Amplitude of its dimensions.
3. Its topographical conditions, and the surrounding circumstances, in relation to which the value of its topographical conditions must in part be estimated.

The fact which first claims attention is the complete bisection of the site by a broad and conspicuous thoroughfare, (Flatbush avenue,) much used for ordinary and indispensable public travel, between Brooklyn and an important suburb that connects it with a large district of agricultural country.[2] It is obvious that this division must seriously interfere with the impressions of amplitude and continuous extent, that the general dimensions of the ground assigned for a park would otherwise convey. To establish convenient communication between the two parts would involve a considerable outlay in bridge construction, which would not be called for if the public highway skirted the ground instead of traversing it. A thoroughfare crossing the park might be a useful and even necessary adjunct, if it were so situated that it served to connect two districts of the city that were likely in future to be closely built up, and that would otherwise be widely separated. Such, however, is not the case in the present instance, and a glance at the map of Brooklyn is sufficient to show that the line of travel, accommodated by the park section of Flatbush avenue, could be diverted, without much inconvenience, to Warren street and Washington avenue. If cross roads for business purposes are required at all, it is in a direction nearly at right angles to Flatbush avenue. The city, however, is so laid out, that no real necessity is apparent for any merely traffic-roads across the property.

Proceeding to consider the two main divisions of the site separately, the Reservoir is found to encroach so seriously on the smaller section east of Flatbush avenue, that it is in effect subdivided again into two portions of very insignificant dimensions for park purposes. The formation of the ground is, moreover, of a character that would make its improvement very expensive, and when the best possible had been done, it would always present a cramped, contracted and unsatisfactory appearance. For these reasons, we think it our duty to advise, that so much of the site as lies east of Flatbush avenue should be abandoned for park purposes.

The great reduction which we have thus suggested in the dimensions of the park site, as originally provided,[3] would oblige you either to be content with a much smaller park than has hitherto been contemplated, or to determine on an extension of its original boundaries in some other direction.

As the number and value of the health and pleasure giving circumstances possible in any park must of course be limited by its size, the question of size may be thought to depend on the restrictions fixed in regard to the number of these circumstances; and it may perhaps be thought that a large park has advantages over a small one only in the greater number and the greater variety, of the pleasures which it offers. But it would be a serious mistake to entertain any such idea, as will be evident to anyone who will ask himself: Is there any pleasure which all persons find at all times in every park, and if so, what does that pleasure depend upon?

The answer unquestionably must be, that there is such a pleasure,

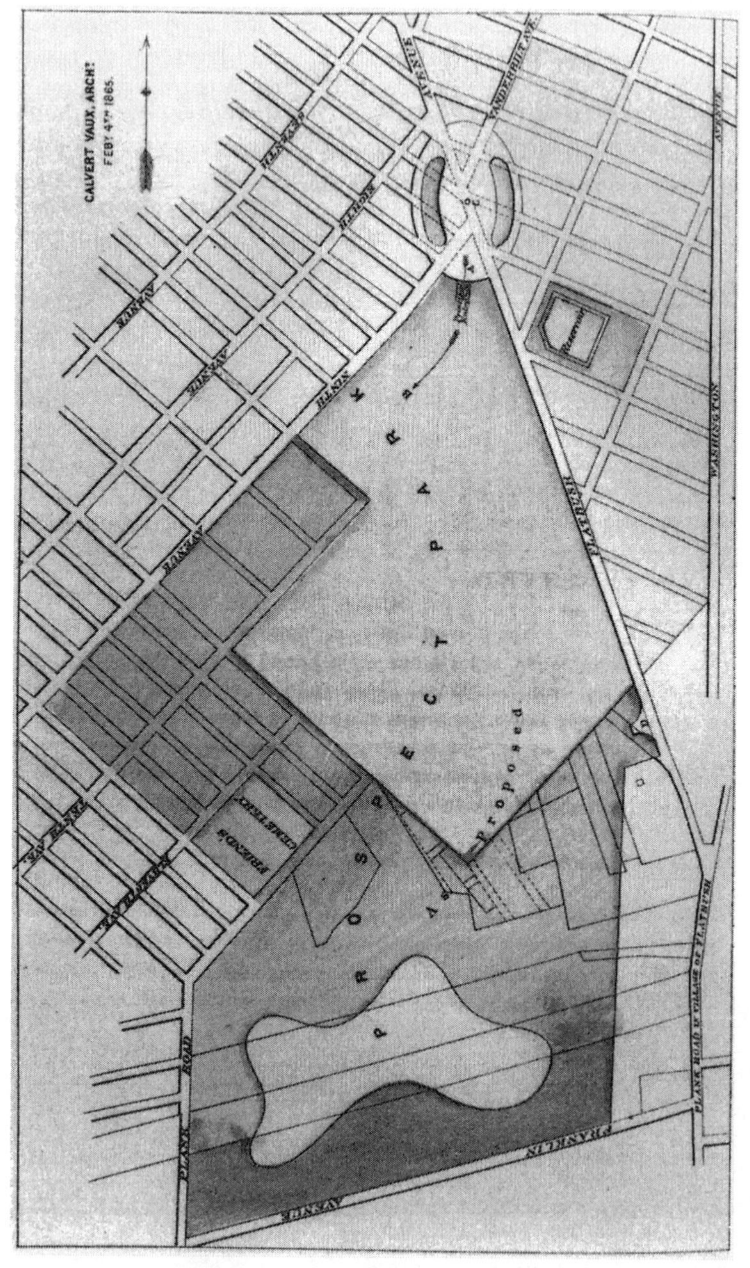

Calvert Vaux, "Plan Showing Present & Proposed Boundaries of Prospect Park Brooklyn," February 4, 1865 Light-toned area west of Flatbush Avenue is land already selected for Prospect Park that Vaux proposed to retain. Darker-toned area is land he proposed to add to the park.

common, constant and universal to all town parks, and that it results from the feeling of relief experienced by those entering them, on escaping from the cramped, confined and controlling circumstances of the streets of the town; in other words, *a sense of enlarged freedom* is to all, at all times, the most certain and the most valuable gratification afforded by a park. The scenery which favors this gratification is, therefore, more desirable to be secured than any other, and the various topographical conditions and circumstances of a site thus, in reality, become important very much in the proportion by which they give the means of increasing the general impression of undefined limit. The degree of this impression, which will be found in any particular park, must unquestionably depend very much upon the manner in which it is laid out; that is to say, on the manner in which the original topographical conditions are turned to account by the designers; but as no degree of art can make the back yard of a town house seem unlimited, and as no art at all is required to make a prairie of some hundred square miles seem unlimited to a man set down in the midst of it, it is obvious that a certain distance between the points of resort within the park, and its exterior limits, is necessary in order to allow the fence or wall that would otherwise definitely establish the position of the boundary to be obscured by planting, if nothing more; and that therefore, until all other necessary requirements are provided for, it will not be entirely practicable to determine where the boundary lines of the park may be established, with a true economy of space.

We have first then to determine what accommodations are desirable to be secured within the park, and next how these shall be situated with reference to one another, and to exterior topographical circumstances. Our conclusions will depend first upon our understanding of the purposes which any town park should be designed to fulfill, that is to say, of the general principles to be observed, and secondly upon our estimate of the number and the special character of the people who are to use the particular park in question.

With regard to the latter point, we need only remark that we regard Brooklyn as an integral part of what to-day is the metropolis of the nation, and in the future will be the centre of exchanges for the world, and the park in Brooklyn, as part of a system of grounds, of which the Central Park is a single feature, designed for the recreation of the whole people of the metropolis and their customers and guests from all parts of the world for centuries to come. With regard, however, to the purposes which town parks in general should be intended and prepared to fulfil, this being a matter upon which little has ever been said or written, and upon which very different ideas prevail, and inasmuch as a clear understanding upon it must be had before a fair judgment can be formed of any plan for a town park, we propose to indicate the views which we have adopted, and out of which our plan has grown.

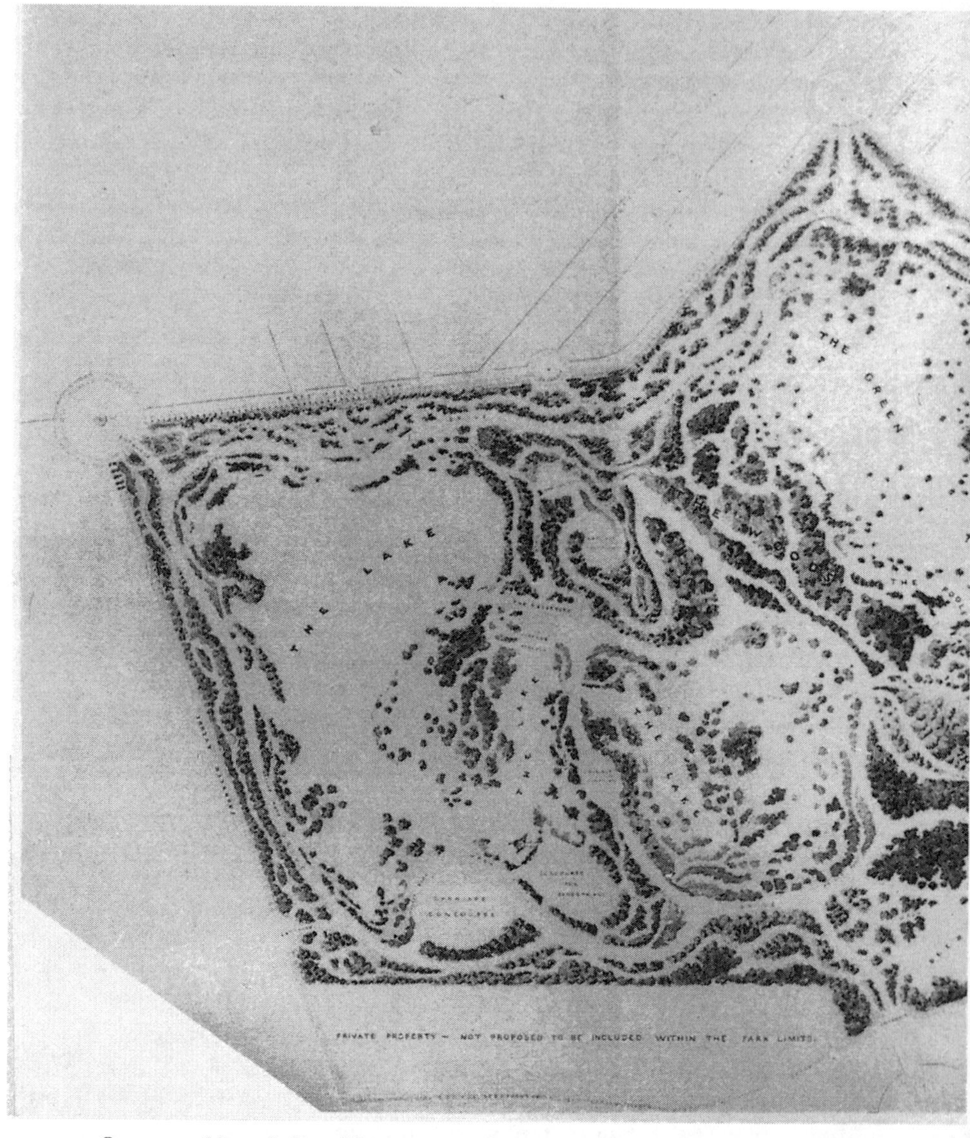

Olmsted, Vaux & Co., "Preliminary Study of a Design for Prospect Park

PURPOSES OF A PARK.

The word park has different significations, but that in which we are now interested has grown out of its application centuries ago, simply to hunting grounds; the choicest lands for hunting grounds being those in which the

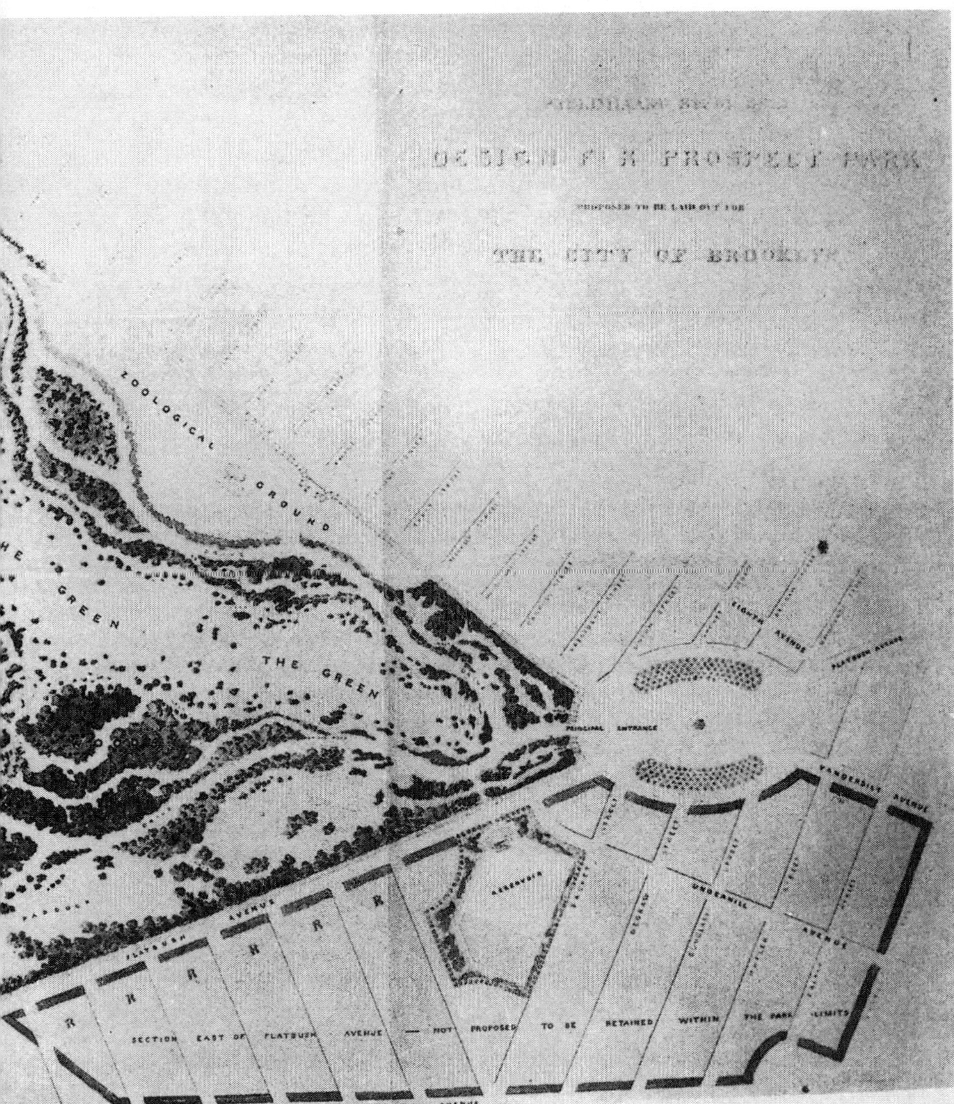

Proposed to be Laid Out for the City of Brooklyn," 1866

beasts of the chase were most happy, and consequently most abundant, sites were chosen for them, in which it was easy for animals to turn from rich herbage to clear water, from warm sunlight to cool shade; that is to say, by preference, ranges of well-watered dale-land, broken by open groves and dotted with spreading trees, undulating in surface, but not rugged. Gay parties of pleasure occasionally met in these parks, and when these meetings occurred the enjoyment otherwise obtained in them was found to be increased. Hence, instead of mere hunting lodges and hovels for game keepers, extensive buildings and other accommodations, having frequently a festive character, were after a time provided within their enclosures. Then it was found that people took pleasure in them without regard to the attractions of the chase, or of conversation, and this pleasure was perceived to be, in some degree, related to their scenery, and in some degree to the peculiar manner of association which occurred in them; and this was also found to be independent of intellectual gifts, tranquilizing and restorative to the powers most tasked in ordinary social duties, and stimulating only in a healthy and recreative way to the imagination. Hence, after a time, parks began to be regarded and to be maintained with reference, more than anything else, to the convenient accommodation of numbers of people, desirous of moving for recreation among scenes that should be gratifying to their taste or imagination.[4]

In the present century, not only have the old parks been thus maintained, but many new parks have been formed with these purposes exclusively in view, especially within and adjoining considerable towns, and it is upon our knowledge of these latter that our simplest conception of a town park is founded. It is from experience in these that all our ideas of parks must spring.

This experience shows that the great advantage which a town finds in a park, lies in the addition to the health, strength and morality which comes from it to its people, an advantage which is not only in itself very great and positive but which as certainly results in an increase of material wealth as good harvests or active commerce. And the reason is obvious: all wealth is the result of labor,[5] and every man's individual wealth is, on the whole, increased by the labor of every other in the community, supposing it to be wisely and honestly applied; but as there cannot be the slightest use of the will, of choice between two actions or two words, nor the slightest exercise of skill of any kind, without the expenditure of force, it follows that, without recuperation and recreation of force, the power of each individual to labor wisely and honestly is soon lost, and that, without the recuperation of force, the power of each individual to add to the wealth of the community is, as a necessary consequence, also soon lost.

But to this process of recuperation a condition is necessary, known since the days of Æsop, as the unbending of the faculties which have been tasked,[6] and this *unbending* of the faculties we find is impossible, except by the occupation of the imagination with objects and reflections of a quite different character from those which are associated with their bent condition. To secure such a diversion of the imagination, the best possible stimulus is found to be the presentation of a class of objects to the perceptive organs, which shall be as agreeable as possible to the taste, and at the same time entirely different from the objects connected with those occupations by which the faculties have been tasked. And this is what is found by towns-people in a park.

If now we ask further, what the qualities of a park are which fit it to meet this requirement? we find two circumstances, common to all parks in distinction from other places in towns, namely, scenery offering the most agreeable contrast to that of the rest of the town; and opportunity for people to come together for the single purpose of enjoyment, unembarrassed by the limitations with which they are surrounded at home, or in the pursuit of their daily avocations, or of such amusements as are elsewhere offered.

It may be observed, that these two purposes are not quite compatible one with the other; for that scenery which would afford the most marked contrast with the streets of a town, would be of a kind characterized in nature by the absence, or, at least, the marked subordination of human influences. Yet, in a park, the largest provision is required for the human presence. Men must come together, and must be seen coming together, in carriages, on horseback and on foot, and the concourse of animated life which will thus be formed, must in itself be made, if possible, an attractive and diverting spectacle.

How can these opposing requirements be harmonized?

Perfectly harmonized they cannot be, and, because they cannot be, success in realizing either must be limited. Yet, by a careful adjustment of parts, and by accommodating the means necessary to the effecting of one purpose to those necessary to the effecting of the other, both may be accomplished in a degree which experience shows is satisfactory.

In the endeavor to accommodate the requirements of the one purpose to those of the other, a perfect compromise at all points is not essential. On the contrary, it is desirable that each should be carried out at certain points in high degree and if the natural topography of the site chosen is varied, it will not be difficult to select points suitable for doing this.

It is, however, necessary, to a satisfactory result, that what is wholly incompatible with one purpose and at the same time not absolutely necessary to the other should be everywhere rigidly avoided and excluded. For instance, a railroad station, a manufactory with chimnies and steam engines, advertising displays, wagons for commercial traffic, fast driving, gambling booths, a market place, though all of these may be seen in some town parks, are clearly there by mistake and want of proper consideration.* We may add that what-

---

*There will always be a temptation to make use of the ground of a park for other public purposes than those to which it is primarily devoted, and, if this is not guarded against at the outset, there is great danger that after a time the purposes for which a park is especially designed will be subordinated, and all that has been done to meet them sacrificed to purposes which, with proper forethought and economy, would be equally well met on other sites. A park is a center about which public buildings are most appropriately placed, but if there is to be an obvious relation between the buildings and

ever the numbers to be accommodated, it is incompatible with the rural character required in a park, that anything like the embarrassing turmoil, confusion and discordant din, common to the crowded streets of the town should be necessarily encountered within it, while it is equally evident that no regard for scenery should be allowed to prevent the assemblage and movement of great crowds within the park — of crowds much greater than will occur anywhere else in the town.

To admit of this, and at the same time maintain anything of a rural, natural, tranquilizing and poetic character in the scenery, the driving room, riding room, walking room, sitting room, skating, sailing and playing room, must be not only liberally designed, but must be studied and adapted to all the natural circumstances of the site with the greatest care.

HOW THE OBJECTS OF A PARK ARE TO BE PURSUED.

To illustrate the practical application of these views, we will take one of the many classes of arrangements for the accommodation of the movements of the public through a park: The drive, or carriage way, and consider what is required in it.

A drive must be so prepared that those using it shall be called upon for the least possible exercise of judgment as to the course to be pursued, the least possible anxiety or exercise of skill in regard to collisions or interruptions with reference to objects animate or inanimate, and that they shall, as far as possible, be free from the disturbance of noise and jar.[7]

To secure these negative qualities, the course of the road must be simple; abrupt turns must be avoided, steep grades that would task the horses or suggest that idea must not be encountered. The possibility of the road becoming miry must be securely guarded against; its surface must also be smooth and be composed of compact material.

These being the first and essential engineering considerations, it is necessary, secondly, that they should be secured in a manner which shall be compatible with the presentation of that which is agreeable to the eye in the surrounding circumstances; that is to say, the drive must either run through beautiful scenery already existing or to be formed, and for this purpose it may be desirable at any point to deviate from the line which an engineer would be bound to choose as that which would best meet the first class of requirements. It must also be remembered that although the drive can hardly be expected in itself to add to the beauty of the scenery, it must always be more or less in view as part of it, and it should therefore be artistically designed so

---

the scenery of the park, both should be parts of the same design. If no such relation is required, the buildings should not be seen from within the park. This subject is further discussed under the head of "Museums and other Edifices."

as to interfere as little as possible with the views, and to present at all points
agreeable and harmonious lines to the eye. Moreover, as it is desirable that
at some point in the course of a drive through every park, there should be an
opportunity for those in carriages to see others and be seen by others, some
portion of the ground, which by development of natural suggestions cannot
be readily made very attractive to the eye, should be chosen for that purpose.
And here it will be proper that the application of art to inanimate nature, as
in architectural objects, and by festive decorations of the outlines of the drive
itself, should distinctly invite attention, and aid to produce a general suggestion of sympathy with human gaiety and playfulness.

It is unnecessary to show here how the same general principles need
to be regarded in planning the rides, the walks, the seats, the playing grounds,
the skating fields, the places of refreshment, and in whatever other accommodations are proposed to be occupied by those who use the park. We would
only remind you that no park has yet been made for the people of a large
civilized town which has not been much more used than its designers had
anticipated; and that all danger of damage, misuse and wasteful destruction
of public property practically amounts to nothing, except as it results from
insufficient extent of the means of communication and of rest within the
park, or from an appearance of slovenliness, or want of completeness and
finish in its arrangements for gratifying the eye, which adjoin these accommodations.

THE ARTISTIC ELEMENT IN THE DESIGN OF A PARK.

The general principles in regard to scenery, which have governed us
in our study, remain to be indicated; and inasmuch as some misapprehension, in our judgment, generally prevails concerning the province of art in
the formation of scenery, and especially of scenery in the natural style, we
propose to briefly express our views upon that subject.

A mere imitation of nature, however successful, is not art, and the
purpose to imitate nature, or to produce an effect which shall seem to be
natural and interesting, is not sufficient for the duty before us.

A scene in nature is made up of various parts; each part has its individual character and its possible ideal. It is unlikely that accident should bring
together the best possible ideals of each separate part, merely considering
them as isolated facts, and it is still more unlikely that accident should group
a number of these possible ideals in such a way that not only one or two but
that all should be harmoniously related one to the other. It is evident, however, that an attempt to accomplish this artificially is not impossible, and that
a proper study of the circumstances relating to the perfect development of
each particular detail will at least enable the designer to reckon surely on a
certain success of a high character in that detail, and a comprehensive bring-

ing together of the results of his study in regard to the harmonious relations of one, two or more details may enable him to discover the law of harmonious relation between multitudinous details; and if he can discover it, there is nothing to prevent him from putting it into practice. The result would be a work of art, and the combination of the art thus defined, with the art of architecture in the production of landscape compositions, is what we denominate landscape architecture.

The first process in the application of this art upon any given site, is the formation of a judgment upon the capabilities and the limitations of that site, with reference to the artistic purpose. It is obviously impossible, for instance, to produce in the vicinity of Brooklyn such scenery as will affect the mind as it is affected by the Alps or the Sierras, on the one hand, or by the luxuriant vegetation of a tropical swamp on the other.

Moreover, there are certain kinds of scenery which experience shows to be most satisfactory within a town park, which require an extensive aggregation of their elements. It will be readily seen, for instance, that if all the wood, water and turf, within a certain area of ground, were distributed in patches, strips and pools, however extensive as a whole, and however varied in detail it might seem to those who should thoroughly explore all its parts, there would be no part which would not seem confined, there could be no large open single scene, and no such impression or effect on the mind would be produced as there would be, if all the water were collected in one lake, all the trees in one grove, all the strips of grass in one broad meadow. Such aggregations, and consequently the degree of the impression intended to be produced by them, must be limited by consideration for two other purposes: the purpose of variety of interest, and the purpose to make all the scenery available to the satisfaction of the public by ways of communication. Other limitations upon the artistic purpose, again, are imposed by conditions of soil and exposure, by rock and springs. How far each of these can be overcome, as by blasting, draining, grading, screening, manuring and other processes, must be in every case a special study, and the artistic purposes of the plan must be affected in every part and particular by the conclusions arrived at.

In the case before us, it is obvious that we should attempt nothing which is incompatible with, or inappropriate to, comparatively slight variations of surface, and a climate of considerable rigor. On the other hand, there are no protruding ledges of rock, no swamps difficult of drainage, and there is no especial bleakness, or danger to trees from violent winds, to be apprehended. It is under similar conditions to these that we find in nature that class of scenery, already referred to, as the original and typical scenery of parks or hunting grounds, and which is termed pastoral. It consists of combinations of trees, standing singly or in groups, and casting their shadows over broad stretches of turf, or repeating their beauty by reflection upon the calm surface of pools, and the predominant associations are in the highest degree tranquilizing and grateful, as expressed by the Hebrew poet: "He maketh me to lie

VIEW OF LONG MEADOW, PROSPECT PARK

down in green pastures; He leadeth me beside the still waters."[8] We know of no other landscape effects that can be commanded, within the limitations fixed by the conditions of this site, which experience shows to be more desirable in a town park than these. This being the case, no other should be sought for or retained, if, by discarding them, we can the better secure these. Only so far then as we can, without sacrificing anything that will contribute to the highest practicable ideal of pastoral scenery, should we endeavor to secure any degree of those other ideals, of which the best types are found under widely dissimilar circumstances.

Although we cannot have wild mountain gorges, for instance, on the park, we may have rugged ravines shaded with trees, and made picturesque with shrubs, the forms and arrangement of which remind us of mountain scenery. We may perhaps even secure some slight approach to the mystery, variety and luxuriance of tropical scenery, by an assemblage of certain forms of vegetation, gay with flowers, and intricate and mazy with vines and creepers, ferns, rushes and broad-leaved plants. But all we can do in these directions must be confessedly imperfect, and suggestive rather than satisfying to the imagination. It must, therefore, be made incidental and strictly subordinate to our first purpose.[9]

Having formed these general plans, we find, in further studying the site, its most important circumstance to be the fact, that a large body of trees already exist upon it, not too old to be improved, yet already old enough to be of considerable importance in a landscape. These trees are in two principal divisions, between which a space of two or three hundred feet in width is found, of undulating ground, not wholly ungraceful, and now mainly covered with a ragged turf. A few trees stand out singly upon this space. It is more nearly level, and less occupied by trees, than any other portion of the site. There is no rock in place upon it, nor would it be at all impracticable to reduce its few abrupt and graceless hillocks, and fill up its gravel pits and muck holes. If we imagine this to be done, and then look at it in connection with the surrounding groves, it is obvious that all that is required to form here a fair example of pastoral scenery is, first, an improvement of the turf, and, secondly, greater space, so that the observer may not see all the boundaries of free sunlight before him at a glance. The former requirement is certainly within our power, all that is needed to secure it being the drainage, deep tillage and enrichment of the soil, and the substitution of finer grasses for the present coarse grasses and weeds. Something may be done also with regard to the second, by cutting in upon the borders of the woods, where the ground lies in gentle slopes, leaving only the finer trees to stand out singly, or in small groups, upon the turf to be formed upon the new ground thus obtained. Were this done, however, the open space would still be comparatively an unimportant one in relation to the whole park. The observer would take it all in at a glance, and if this were all he felt that he could look for, the result would be tantalizing rather than satisfactory.

As a very important suggestion springs from this observation, we shall be pardoned for referring to a portion of the Central Park, New York, where somewhat similar conditions formerly existed, and where our views have been adopted and realized. Entering by the turn to the right, at the Merchant's Gate,[10] in a few moments the visitor's eye falls upon the open space called the Cricket Ground,[11] where originally was a small swamp, enlarged at great expense in the construction of the park, in order to meet a similar artistic purpose to that above explained, by the removal of several large ledges of rock, and now occupied by an unbroken meadow, which extends before the observer to a distance of nearly a thousand feet. Here is a suggestion of freedom and repose, which must in itself be refreshing and tranquilizing to the visitor coming from the confinement and bustle of crowded streets. But this is not all. The observer, resting for a moment to enjoy the scene, which he is induced to do by the arrangement of the planting, cannot but hope for still greater space than is obvious before him, and this hope is encouraged, first, by the fact that, though bodies of rock and foliage to the right and left obstruct his direct vision, no limit is seen to the extension of the meadow in a lateral direction; while beyond the low shrubs, which form an undefined border to it in front, there are no trees or other impediments to vision for a distance of half a mile or more, and the only distinct object is the wooded knoll of Vista Rock,[12] nearly a mile away, upon the summit of which it is an important point in the design, not yet realized, to erect a slight artificial structure, for the purpose of catching the eye, and the better holding it in this direction. The imagination of the visitor is thus led instinctively to form the idea that a broad expanse is opening before him, and the more surely to accomplish this, a glimpse of a slope of turf beyond the border of shrubs in the middle distance has been secured. As the visitor proceeds, this idea is strengthened, and the hope which springs from it in a considerable degree satisfied, if not actually realized, first by a view of those parts of the Cricket Ground which lie to the right and left of his previous field of vision, afterwards by the broad expanse of turf on either side and before him, which comes into view as he emerges from the plantations at or near the marble archway.[13]

The carrying out of this most important purpose in the scenery of the Central Park, owing to the rocky and heterogeneous character of the original surface, involved much more labor and a larger expenditure than any other landscape feature of that undertaking.

For the same reason that induced us to recommend that expenditure to the Commissioners of the Central Park, we feel dissatisfied with the limits of the space we are now regarding. It is evident at a glance, however, that if we do not restrict ourselves to the artificial boundary formerly fixed upon for the park, this space may readily be more than doubled in extent without encroaching upon any considerable natural elevation, and at a very moderate expense.[14] Thus our second requirement would be met.

In addition to the special artistic advantage which the acquisition of this ground would secure, there are two other very important considerations in favor of obtaining it: First, such an addition is almost indispensable to a proper provision of playing grounds, there being no space of moderately level ground, not occupied by groves of trees of much value, sufficient for this purpose, upon the territory now controlled by your Commission; second, its acquisition will enable us to make a very great improvement upon any general plan of drives, rides and walks, which would otherwise be practicable, and in these and other ways, to which we shall hereafter allude, it will greatly lessen the danger of overcrowding the park.

Next to groves and greensward, a sheet of water is the most important element in the character of the scenery which we desire to realize. We find no place suited to the formation of such a feature of sufficient extent within the limits of the site now held by your Commission. At a short distance beyond them, there is, however, a broad plain, overlooked on the park side by the highest ground in the vicinity,[15] from the top of which there is a prospect to the southward, which includes a large sweep of the ocean, the Highlands of Navesink, Sandy Hook, and all the outer harbor of New York. The formation of a lake on the low ground referred to, in such a manner that this elevation would be reflected upon its surface, would add such an unquestionable advantage to the landscape attractions of the park, that we should feel obliged to take the same course with reference to it as we have done in regard to the previously proposed extension of the limits of the site, even if no other considerations favored it. The great value of a park lake in this climate, however, for skating, and the attractiveness of the spectacle which crowds of skaters afford to others, added to its value for the recreation of rowing, afford additional inducements of no small consequence in favor of this course. With the further addition, which we therefore advise, it will be practicable to form a sheet of water having more than twice the accommodation for skaters of that in the Central Park. The Central Park lake, though many objected to it originally as larger than necessary for any artistic purpose, while it occupied space which might be otherwise used to advantage, is already found much too small for the comfortable accommodation of those who are prepared to use it, and many turn from it, in consequence, to those small ponds where the payment of an admission fee secures greater space to individual skaters.[16] If this is now the case, the need of very much larger skating space will be a very pressing one in the future, as population increases. We cannot doubt that a sheet of ice in Brooklyn, equally near to the present centre of population of the metropolis, and more than twice as large as that in the Central Park, would soon attract a larger number of persons than have ever yet resorted to the latter. This number has on several occasions been above one hundred thousand in a day and five hundred thousand in a week. If we consider that the opportunity afforded for this recreation would be worth in the acquisition of health and vigor to the whole body of citizens an amount equal to a dime for each visitor, it will be evident that the whole cost of purchasing the land in view, and of constructing the lake, might be defrayed by the use which would be made of it in a single season.

Supposing the more hilly land to be covered by plantations, and a green-sward to be formed upon the open ground which we have described, and the low plain to be mainly occupied by a lake, we have the three grand elements of pastural landscape for which we were seeking. What remains consists of limited strips of surface, generally stony and somewhat rough, and may be left to be treated incidentally, as before explained. To the important features of the greensward, the wood, the lake and the hill, the roads and walks must be accommodated in such a way as to give the visitor the best advantage, consistent with ease and comfort, for enjoying whatever charm they may be made to possess. Before referring particularly to the system of communications, however, it will be best to speak of certain other detached arrangements.

PLACES OF CONGREGATION AND REST.

Besides the green, our study provides three places, each adapted to the assemblage of large numbers of people, and for their remaining together for some time at rest.

The first of these we designate the Look-out.[17] The circumstances which make a special arrangement for the accommodation of an assemblage at this point desirable are, 1st, the view which is obtained here, and nowhere else in the park, of the outer harbor, the distant mountain ranges of New

Jersey and the ocean offing; 2d, the peculiar advantages which the elevation offers for the enjoyment in hot weather of the sea breeze; 3d, the interest of the local scenery, which it is our intention should be quite different from that of any other part of the park; and 4th, The bird's eye view which will be presented of military evolutions, if the projected parade-ground should be formed south of the park.

We propose to form here a terraced platform, one hundred feet in length, with seats and awnings, connected by a broad terrace walk and staircase with an oval court for carriages, three hundred feet long and one hundred and fifty wide. On the west side of the platform, provision is made for a small low building, designed for the special accommodation of women and children, and at which they may obtain some simple refreshment. This building is also intended to serve the purpose of shutting off the view westwardly from the lookout platform, as this would otherwise detract from the effect obtained in other directions.[18]

All the principal walks of the park tend to lead the visitor from whatever entrance he starts, to finally reach the lookout, though he may visit every other part of the park, and yet avoid this if he prefers. From the lookout, broad walks lead across the park to the east end of the lake, where, at a point commanding the largest water view, together with a rich open meadow landscape, backed by the highest elevation of the park, pinnacled with evergreens, arrangements for open-air concerts are proposed. The orchestra will be situated upon an island in a bay of the lake, so that it can be seen from three sides. On the main land, within a distance of two hundred and twenty-five yards of this island — at which distance the music of a well appointed band can be perfectly appreciated — standing room is provided for horses and carriages in a circular space about five hundred feet in diameter and, in an oval space at a higher elevation, three hundred feet long and one hundred and seventy-five feet wide,[19] while directly in front, at a distance varying from one hundred to five hundred feet, a space is provided, to be occupied by shaded seats, sufficient for over ten thousand people.[20] Provision is made for the rapid dispersion of the audience, however large it may be, on foot, in carriages, and on horseback; also for checking the movement of carriages within the circular space, during the performance of music.

Midway between the lookout concourse and the music concourse, and with approaches for footmen and carriages from both, a series of terraces and arcades is provided, within which there will be room for a large restaurant. These look out upon the lake, and the floor of the lower arcade will be nearly on a level with the surface of the lake, so that it can be readily entered from the ice in winter or from boats in summer. The upper terrace is five hundred feet in length by sixty feet in width, and the remaining floor space of the structure one hundred and seventy-five by two hundred feet. The arcades are intended to be the principal architectural feature of the park.[21]

SYLVAN FEATURES.

There are four sylvan features of considerable importance in the plan. First, upon the green, the meadow, and the slopes of the upper lake, a display of the finest American forest trees, standing singly and in open groups, so as to admit of the amplest development of individuals, which will be further encouraged by the best attainable conditions of soil and situation.

Second, in the central portions of the park, an open grove of forest trees, in which visitors may ramble in the shade without impediment of underwood, and without danger of doing harm to anything through carelessness or any ordinary selfish impulse.

Third, a collection, arranged in the natural way, of the more delicate shrubs and trees, especially evergreens, both coniferous and of the class denominated in England American plants, such as Rhododendrons, Kalmias, Azaleas and Andromedas: these would be situated on the interior slopes of the Lookout and the Friend's Hill, and in the valley between them, where, from the peculiar circumstances of exposure and protection they will be likely to thrive.[22]

Fourth, picturesque groups of evergreens and deciduous trees and shrubs on the shore of the lake.

PLAY GROUNDS AND GREENSWARD.

A portion of the green, nearest the Flatbush railroad and the refectory, and where the surrounding road and walks are at the greatest distance from the centre, is proposed to be fitted to be used for a ball playing ground, by the children of the public schools and others.[23]

We should advise that the whole of the green, upon special occasions at least, if not at all times, should be open to all persons on foot, as a common. If the ground is properly prepared, there is no danger that the beauty of the turf would be seriously impaired, except perhaps immediately after heavy rains, at which time it would seldom occur that the park would be greatly crowded with visitors. If this is done, and the interior groves also thrown open to pedestrians, through their whole extent between the bridle road and the green, we consider that the danger that the walks and resting places would be overcrowded so as to force or sorely tempt visitors to go upon ground where they would really injure the elements of the scenery, or create disturbance, embarrassment and waste, would be very small.[24]

ZOOLOGICAL GROUND.

The tract of broken ground, near the Ninth avenue, now partly occupied by gardens and residences, the features of which are quite varied, but rather diminutive for desirable park effects, we propose should be held in reserve for zoological collections, and, as it may properly be placed under the control of a special corporation for this purpose, we refrain at this time from suggesting in what manner it should be laid out. This subject will be recurred to.[25]

GRAZING GROUND FOR DEER.

The narrow sheltered strip of meadow, on the opposite side of the park, we propose to enclose with a sufficient iron paling and make use of as a pasture ground for deer, antelopes, gazelles, and such other grazing animals as can be satisfactorily herded together in summer upon it.[26]

WATER WORKS AND DRAINAGE.

In regard to the water needed for the lake, we are informed that sufficient may be spared from the general supply already brought to the city by the Nassau Water Works. We recommend, however, that arrangements be had in view, not only for securing an independent supply, but also for keeping up a constant circulation, by pumping the water from the lake to the spring on the west side of the Friend's Hill, so that it may always be flowing from that point in a natural stream. The pump for this purpose would be worked by steam, in connection with the kitchen of the refectory. The stream furnished by the spring is intended to take first the character of a series of pools, overhung on the one side by the trees upon the north side of the Friend's Hill, and margined on the other by banks of turf. It would then assume more of the usual character of a small mountain stream, taking a very irregular course, with numerous small rapids, shoots and eddies, among rocks and ferns, until it emerged from the shadow of the wood upon a grassy slope; thence it would flow more quietly until, after falling over a body of rock, in connection with a foot bridge on the side of the park opposite that on which it started, it would assume the appearance of a small river with high and shaded banks and at length, passing the refectory and music concourse in two reaches, empty into the eastern bay of the lake. Here, on the north shore would be a low flat meadow with a few large trees and small thickets of bushes overhanging the water.[27] In the coves would be beds of pond lilies and other aquatic plants, and, on the shores near them, flags, cat-tails, bulrushes and the like. This arrangement would give opportunity for every variety of water scenery which is practicable within the space of the park, with any moderate supply of water.

The natural outlet for the surplus water of the park would be in a southerly direction, and a plan of drainage may be adopted that will be more simple and less expensive than would usually be practicable upon a site of this extent, having such a considerable variety of surface.

DRIVES, RIDES AND WALKS.

The more important features of scenery and of local accommodations for various purposes, having been thus pointed out, we now turn to the several ways of communication by which they are connected and related one to another.

The drive, commencing with a width of sixty (60) feet, at the centre of the north or principal entrance to the park, is carried in a southerly direction for some little distance, but diverges slightly to the east, so as to accommodate itself to some high ground in the neighborhood. It there branches to the southeast and southwest, and becomes a part of the circuit drive, which is proposed to be of an average width of forty (40) feet. The arrangement of the lines and curves, at the junction, is such that carriages coming into the park will continue to proceed for a few hundred feet in a southeasterly direction, after reaching the circuit drive, and will thus be fairly started on the road that it is intended they should follow, for, although the formation of the ground naturally suggests this treatment of the lines, we should, under any circumstances, have made an effort to arrange the plan in some such way as is indicated in the design, because the southeasterly branch leads more directly into the heart of the park. It commands, moreover, from a point very near the entrance, a view in the direction of the length of what is now an unplanted stretch of ground, but which is treated in the design as open lawn or meadow, dotted with trees, it being the intention to reduce the height of a low, narrow ridge that crosses this piece of ground, so that its real extent may be fairly seen from the drive.

Continuing on the course already indicated, the road soon curves to the right, and ascends to a point from which it is proposed to obtain an extensive view, in a westerly direction, over the great green of the park. From this point, the road descends into the wooded defile where an old wayside inn now stands, marking the ground held by the Continental forces in an engagement during the battle of Long Island, at which point it will be practicable in perfecting the plan of the park to provide for some architectural memento of that important struggle.[28]

Passing through the defile, a view is obtained over a pretty glade of turf to the left, intended to be used as a grazing ground for deer, and bounded on the opposite side by the thick coppice-wood which already effectually conceals the Flatbush avenue. Keeping to the right of the deer paddock, the drive continues to pass through the woods, but presently divides into two somewhat narrower branches, by which means full advantage is taken of the already existing opportunities for shade, and the standing trees are less interfered with than would otherwise be necessary, and then, reuniting, continues to run in a southerly direction, till it approaches the proposed Franklin avenue boundary line. At this point it divides again, and one branch enlarges almost directly into the open space previously described as the music concourse. The other branch or main line of drive, after passing the two entrances to the concourse, is carried round the head of the lake, and along the shore in a westerly direction, till it approaches the proposed Coney Island road boundary. It then curves to the northward, still following the shore of the lake, until it reaches the west side of the lookout hill. Although there is nothing interesting in the natural scenery of this stretch, the bank of the lake will be made so artificially, and there will be very agreeable views across the water, the north shore being the most picturesque part of the park. This is intended to be used more particularly as the promenade or common course of the park. The drive is consequently laid out of unusual width, and the bridle road, together with a broad walk, is carried in close connection with it.

The western foot of the look-out hill is one of the most important points on the whole line of drive. It is very desirable that the road should retain its circuit character, and continue on in a northerly direction when the hill is reached, as the whole lake has by this time been seen, the social or gregarious disposition is supposed to have been satisfied, and a considerable change is therefore needed in the landscape effect. The way in which we propose that this shall be managed will be readily understood by an examination of the plan; and, although the contour lines of the strip of ground proposed to be added in this immediate neighborhood will need to be somewhat modified, the object in view is really so essential to the development of the whole design, that its successful accomplishment will justify any reasonable expenditure that it may be necessary to incur for the sake of securing it. The main drive continues, therefore, in a westerly direction, leaving the Friends' Hill to the northward, and afterwards opening directly upon and keeping in view the most purely rural, and at the same time the most expanded and extended, view within the park. On approaching the Ninth avenue boundary, it curves to the east round the green, enters the western woods, divides again into two branches, and, after reuniting, passes on for some distance, still in the midst of groves, until, after passing along the side of the meadow stretch that was viewed in the direction of its length, at the commencement of the drive, it reaches the starting point near the main entrance.

In addition to the circuit drive thus described, a cross-road is introduced about the middle of the park, from which will be obtained a fine open out-look towards the country beyond the southern boundary. A loop from this interior road leads to the refectory and across a bridge, over an arm of the lake, to a carriage concourse of smaller size than the one already described, which it is proposed to construct on somewhat elevated ground, overlooking the lake and the music stand. A branch from this cross-road is proposed to lead up the slopes on the side of the look-out hill, to the open area on the upper level, which will command a view of the ocean. The connections with the various entrances are proposed to be made as shown on the plan, and the whole length of drive thus provided for is about five miles and a half.

The bridle road is so laid out on the plan, that by increasing the size of some archways needed for other purposes, it may, if desired, be kept distinct from the carriage road and the footpaths through the whole length of its circuit. It follows generally the line of the main road, sometimes in immediate connection with it, and sometimes passing along at a considerable distance from it. The whole length of the bridle road laid out on the plan is about four miles.

The drive and the bridle road being thus arranged for, the system of walks proposed by the plan next requires attention. It is very important to the comfort of pedestrians, that they should be able to proceed into the park from the entrances that will be chiefly used, without having to cross over the circuit drive or bridle road, and that, when once fairly in among the trees and grass stretches, they should be able to ramble over the whole extent of the property with as much apparent freedom as if the whole park had been intended solely for their enjoyment.

There are two points in the design which may be said to be central points, so far as the walk system is concerned: the summit level of the lookout hill overlooking the ocean, and the large open air hall of reception shown on the plan, near the principal carriage concourse already described. All the leading lines will be found to tend in these directions, and the intermediate walks are designed to give variety and intricacy, without interfering with this general intention of the design. From the main entrance two walks are proposed to start. One passes near the north-eastern boundary, and leads to the reservoir bridge over Flatbush avenue; it then continues in a southerly direction, skirting the deer paddock, and terminates at the music concourse. A branch of this walk passes under the carriage road, near the main entrance, and opens directly onto the meadow stretch which forms the northern division of the great green. The walk passes around this meadow, and crossing the green commands a full view of its whole extent; then through the woods into a ravine by the side of the brook and by an arched passage under the carriage road to the lawn-like open ground north of the lookout hill; then again through the woods till it meets the line, already described, which leads to the music concourse.

The second walk that starts from the main entrance passes in a rather more westerly direction. It has the same general tendency as the walks above mentioned, and leads both to the look-out and to the music concourse.

A walk extends all around the lake and around the green, and a system of walks is introduced to connect the music concourse and the look-out with the refectory; but it is not necessary to describe all these walks in detail.

From the principal entrance at the junction of Flatbush and Ninth avenues, from the entrance at the corner of Fifteenth street and Ninth avenue, from the foot entrance at the junction of Sixteenth street and the Coney Island road, and from the entrance from Flatbush avenue, near the Willink property,[29] it is proposed to have walks, leading to the principal points of interest, that will not be interfered with by the carriage road. From the other two entrances, surface cross-walks are proposed, as it would be difficult, on account of the embankment that will be necessary to retain the waters of the lake, to adopt the plan used elsewhere.[30]

BOUNDARY ARRANGEMENTS.

Outside the exterior drives and walks, such extent of ground only is wanted as is necessary to enable us, by planting and otherwise, to shut out of view that which would be inharmonious with and counteractive to our design. This extent we find in all cases, without carrying the boundary beyond the nearest street line, as laid down on the city map, and except at the two points where the ground, which might otherwise seem to be more than is required to enable us to plant out the boundary, is occupied by the zoological grounds and the deer paddock before described, it will be found that the amount of ground taken into the park, beyond what is absolutely necessary for this purpose, is nowhere equal to the depth of an ordinary lot. Practically there will not be a foot of ground within the boundary the use of which will not add to the interest of the park and its value to the citizens. At one point, the boundary is kept a long distance within the nearest street line. This is where the orchards and villa gardens, on the east of the drive, near the music concourse, admit of a narrower margin than would otherwise answer.[31] The fronts of these valuable grounds near the park are not likely to be built upon before its border trees will have become well grown, nor until a street has been opened along the boundary line. Any buildings then likely to be erected here will consequently be placed at such a distance as not to be conspicuous from the park, while the arrangement enables the city to avoid the purchase of any land having special value from its association with highly improved residences.

By adopting the line of Franklin Avenue for the boundary on the south, about half the space between an observer standing on Look-out Hill and the horizon, will seem to be occupied by the lake and the park. This effect will of course be merely an optical one, but a visit to the site will show at once that it will be all-sufficient to divert the attention of the visitor from the land occupied for agricultural purposes, and will serve to render the sea view more attractive. This advantage will be considerably increased, if the ground immediately beyond Franklin avenue should be appropriated for a parade ground, or any other public purpose which will prevent it from being occupied by tall buildings.[32] A nearer boundary than Franklin avenue would probably fail to realize the effect desired in this particular.

It is proposed to widen Vanderbilt avenue to one hundred feet, as far as the limits of the property at present owned by the Commissioners; also to widen Ninth avenue to one hundred feet, as far as the limits of the park are proposed to extend; also to widen Fifteenth street, the Coney Island road and Franklin avenue, as shown on the plan, wherever they connect with the proposed boundary lines. In all these cases, the additional width is proposed to be added on the side of the road next to the park, leaving the lines on the opposite {side} of the road as already laid down on the city map.

On the additional ground thus obtained, it is proposed to construct a thirty-feet sidewalk, shaded by a double row of trees, so that an ample gas-lighted and umbrageous promenade will be offered to the public in the immediate vicinity of the park, after the gates are closed at night. The comparatively close planting of these avenue trees will moreover help to shut out the houses that will be built on the opposite side of the street from the view of the visitors who may be in the interior of the park.

ARRANGEMENT OF EXTERIOR STREETS.

In conclusion, we wish to offer a few suggestions with regard to the management of some parts of the ground outside of the park boundaries.

Although, for the reasons given, at the beginning of this report, we think it desirable that the section of the site as originally established, lying east of Flatbush avenue, should be abandoned as a part of the park, it does not follow that the lines laid down on the city map, before the project of a park in this vicinity had been suggested, should be re-adopted, and considerable advantages may be obtained, in our judgment, by adjusting them with reference to the park.

We have indicated on our study the manner in which this may be done. It will be seen that while the streets north of the reservoir follow the old lines, those south of it are set out at right angles to Flatbush avenue, instead of diagonally as formerly; and as Grand and Classon avenues cannot cross the park, they are stopped at Washington avenue.

This district, if re-arranged in the manner suggested, will most probably be occupied to a considerable extent by residences of a first-class character, and as the blocks will be sixty feet more than the usual width, it will be easy in execution, if thought desirable, to subdivide the property in such a way that, while on one street the lots will be of ordinary length, on the other they will be so much longer that ample room will be provided for stables that will have a convenient lane access between the two.

An open place or square is suggested at the junction of Grand and Washington avenues, and Washington avenue is proposed to be widened ten feet along the whole length of the property now owned by the Commissioners. A design is also shown for a possible future improvement opposite the park gate, in the vicinity of the present Willink property, so that Franklin avenue may be included in our general scheme for the arrangement of the approaches to this important entrance. As there is a fine distant view from the top of the reservoir, and as this structure belongs inalienably to the city, we also propose to reserve some of the ground about it so as to be able to flank it with agreeable groups of trees, and to connect it by means of a light foot-bridge over Flatbush avenue with the walks of the park, as indicated on our study. The formation of the ground is suitable for the purpose and the fine view to be obtained from the upper level of the reservoir can thus be associated with the attractions of the park.

In addition to the principal entrance, provision is made for gates to the park on Flatbush avenue, near the Willink property; on Franklin avenue, near the southeast corner of the proposed boundaries; at the junction of Franklin avenue, with the Coney Island road; at the junction of Sixteenth street and the Coney Island road, and from the junction of Ninth avenue and Fifteenth street. Another entrance is indicated on the Ninth avenue, opposite Third street, which can either lead into the park or connect simply with the zoological garden, as may be ultimately determined.

Improvements are suggested, in connection with three of these entrances, which seem to be necessary for the purpose of securing easy and agreeable approaches; and the advantage proposed to be gained in each case will be so readily understood, by reference to the plan, that we deem further explanations in regard to this part of the design unnecessary.

MUSEUMS AND OTHER EDUCATIONAL EDIFICES.

Although the ground now held by your Commission, east of Flatbush avenue, does not appear to us desirable to be retained for the purpose for which it has been assigned, it will nevertheless be an advantage to the park, if a small section of it, abutting on Flatbush avenue and facing the park, remains in the possession of the city. We therefore desire to offer a suggestion as to the use to which it may be appropriated.

It is undesirable that any duties or responsibilities should be assumed by legislative bodies that can be equally well undertaken by citizens, either individually or associated in their private capacity. The exact limit of judicious legislation in this way cannot however be defined, and while there are many public responsibilities that clearly cannot be assumed by individual citizens, and many more that can, there are some few that are of an intermediate character, and that require special consideration. It is generally conceded that a system of popular education is an essential part of a republican government, for instance, but it is by no means determined what means of education should be secured to all, and to what extent the public can be taxed, with reasonable assurance of a saving to the tax payers, through a reduction of taxes for courts, police, prisons and poorhouses, and the general cheapening of the necessaries of life by the increased capacity for productive labor of the whole community which may be obtained through the improvement of the education system.

It is very desirable therefore that plans should, if possible, be adopted by our municipal bodies, which will admit of strict construction, and at the same time be no bar to the progressive improvement of our methods of education. At present, book learning and education are generally considered correlative terms, but the conviction is evidently fast gaining ground in the public mind, which has long been established with those who have given the most thorough consideration to the subject, that, although the ordinary chances of observation may be sufficient to make many branches of knowledge which are inculcated in books sufficiently intelligible, there are others, progress in which is of special value with reference to the enlargement of the mind and the development of healthy inclinations and habits, which cannot be pursued with much advantage in this second-hand way.

Hence, it may be anticipated that the common-school system of a large city will, sooner or later, be generally considered incomplete, unless ample opportunity is found within it for the direct exercise by every student of his perceptive faculties in regard to a large class of objects not likely to come under his ordinary observation. The idea of education, it must be confessed by all, unquestionably culminates in the development of the reflective faculties, but the reflective faculties — which are secondary — can never, it is obvious, be healthily exercised if the perceptive faculties — which are primary — are neglected and starved.[33]

The question therefore is pertinent, even at present, whether the city, without absolutely assuming the whole expense and the whole control of undertakings for this end, may not wisely offer some encouragement to associations voluntarily formed by citizens for the purpose.

Having some such views in mind as these, when we were preparing the design of Central Park, we advocated the retention of the building near the boundary, north of the Scholars' Gate,[34] formerly used as an arsenal, simply because it would probably, if retained, be found to be of sufficient value to be converted into a suitable building for a museum, and although it was very inconveniently located for any such purpose, we felt that the opportunity was one that ought not to be lost. Our suggestion was adopted by the Commissioners, and the Historical Society has since asked for and obtained possession from them of this site and this building with the understanding that it is to be improved and converted into a public museum at the expense of the society.[35]

We have before shown the impropriety, as a general rule, of placing edifices, which are not strictly auxiliary to the primary purpose of a park, within its boundaries, and this illustration is, of course, presented with no purpose of favoring their introduction but rather to show that they ought in some other way to be provided for in season. The suggestion we have to make in this case is that the stretch of ground abutting on Flatbush avenue, fronting towards the park (marked R.R. on the plan), and now in the possession of the Commissioners, should be distinctly set apart for such purposes as we have indicated. If this suggestion is accepted, the lots on this part of Flatbush avenue, will probably, in course of time, be occupied by handsome buildings, the objects of which will in some way be connected with the educational system of the city, but which will not be erected or owned by it, the terms on which the different sites would be given being such as to secure a share of control in the management of each institution, sufficient to ensure to the city an adequate return for the value of the land it parts with.

SUBURBAN CONNECTIONS.

It will be observed that we have indicated the commencement of a road leading out of the west side of the circle, in connection with the southern entrance to the park. We have done so from a conviction, that a shaded pleasure drive in extension of that of the park, and free from the embarrassments which will inevitably be associated with a road partially occupied by a line of railway, and which is also used as a trotting course for fast horses, will soon be demanded by the frequenters of the park. Such a road, whatever may be the character of the country through which it passes, should be in itself of a picturesque character. It should, therefore, be neither very straight nor very level, and should be bordered by a small belt of trees and shrubbery.

We have made no special survey with reference to the course which should be followed by such a road, but the first objective point in view would unquestionably be the ocean beach, and this might very properly be its terminus.[36] It has occurred to us, however, that either from some point a little further east on the beach, thus made accessible by carriages from the park, or from a point more directly in connection with the park drives, a similar road may be demanded in the future which shall be carried through the rich country lying back of Brooklyn, until it can be turned, without striking through any densely occupied ground, so as to approach the East River, and finally reach the shore at or near Ravenswood.[37] From this point, either by ferry or high bridges, it may be thrown over the two narrow straits into which the East River is divided in this neighborhood, and connection may thus be had with one of the broad streets leading directly into the Central Park, and thus with the system of somewhat similar sylvan roads leading northward, now being planned by the Commissioners of the Central Park.[38] Such an arrangement would enable a carriage to be driven on the half of a summer's day, through the most interesting parts both of the cities of Brooklyn and New York, through their most attractive and characteristic suburbs, and through both their great parks; having a long stretch of the noble Hudson with the

Palisades in the middle distance, and the Shawangunk range of mountains in the back-ground, in view at one end, and the broad Atlantic with its foaming breakers rolling on the beach, at the other.

The whole might be taken in a circuit without twice crossing the same ground, and would form a grand municipal promenade, hardly surpassed in the world either for extent or continuity of interest.

This suggestion forms no part of our plan and may seem premature, but there can be but little danger of too extended a prevision with reference to future improvements which may grow out of so important a work as that upon which your Commission is engaged, and we have, therefore, in the preparation of the design herewith submitted endeavored, as far as possible, to arrange for a proper connection with any undertakings of the character indicated which may hereafter be found to be required.

Respectfully,

OLMSTED, VAUX & CO.,
Landscape Architects.

The text presented here was published by the Board of Commissioners of Prospect Park for public circulation in 1866. It was also published, without headings for the different sections, as "Report of the Landscape Architects" in Board of Commissioners of Prospect Park, *Sixth Annual Report* (Brooklyn, 1866), pages 11–38.

1. The twelve-member Board of Commissioners of Prospect Park, with James S. T. Stranahan as president. The original board of seven was appointed by the state legislature in the law of 1860 creating the commission. An enlarged board of thirteen commissioners was appointed for a five-year term by Chapter 340, Laws of 1861. Vacancies occurring at the end of terms were filled by the mayor of Brooklyn with the approval of two-thirds of the Common Council (BPC, *Annual Reports, 1861–1873*, pp. 17, 67).
2. Flatbush Avenue, which connected Brooklyn with the suburb of Flatbush (M. Dripps, *Map of Brooklyn and Vicinity* [New York, 1866]).
3. The original boundaries of "Mount Prospect Park" were proposed in a report of February 1860 by a commission created by the state legislature in April 1859 to select grounds for public parks in Brooklyn. Creation of a park in that location was then authorized by the legislature in April 1860. The boundaries are shown on the map on page 324 of volume 6 of the Olmsted Papers. President of the board James S. T. Stranahan wished to expand the park to the south and west and in late 1865 solicited Calvert Vaux's advice in the matter. Vaux urged him, in particular, to extend the park to a flat area to the south in order to create what became Prospect Lake. In February 1865 Vaux submitted a report recommending the change in boundaries discussed in this report, eliminating the area east of Flatbush Avenue, creating the entrance area between two crescent-shaped berms that became Grand Army Plaza, and greatly expanding the park to the south and west. He also proposed to expand the park westward to include an area one block deep along the south side of Ninth Avenue between 3rd and 9th streets and three blocks deep between 9th and 14th streets (but excluding the Quaker cemetery that lay east of Eleventh Avenue between 11th and 14th streets).

This land included a considerable portion of what became the Long Meadow. In this report, Olmsted and Vaux proposed in addition to extend the park to 15th Street and to include the area of the Quaker cemetery within the park.

    In early 1866 the Prospect Park commissioners published and circulated numerous copies of the report presented here. Satisfied that sufficient public support existed, they then sought authorization from the legislature to acquire the necessary additional land. On April 30, 1866, the legislature approved most of the proposed expansion of the park and the property was acquired on March 27, 1867. However, the legislature declined, ostensibly on the grounds of expense, to approve acquisition of twelve blocks of land between Ninth and Tenth avenues from 3rd Street to 15th Street. One of the residences in that area was the mansion of Edwin Clark Litchfield, designed by Alexander Jackson Davis; the other belonged to the Democratic "boss" of Brooklyn, Hugh McLaughlin. The commissioners applied again to the legislature for authority to acquire the land, which finally gave its approval in April 1868. Purchase of this property, at a cost of over $1,705,000 (in contrast to the $2,269,000 paid previously for the rest of the park) took place in April 1869 (BPC, *Annual Reports, 1861–1873*, pp. 6–7, 11, 80–85, 123–25, 130–31, 162–63, 240, 325; CV to FLO, Jan. 9, 1865 [*Papers of FLO*, 5: 296]; *Papers of FLO*, 6: 338, n. 22).

4. In the epistemology, based particularly on the writings of John Locke, that underlay the concepts of human thought and experience from which Olmsted drew in this passage, the imagination was a faculty that was directly acted upon by visual stimuli. It made possible a direct response, both pleasurable and spiritual, to such scenes as park landscapes (see Ernest Lee Tuveson, *The Imagination as a Means of Grace: Locke and the Aesthetics of Romanticism* [Berkeley, Calif., 1960], pp. 92–102).

5. This passage expresses Olmsted's belief that the function of individuals in society was to serve the other members of society, to meet their needs in an efficient and effective way. In so far as such labor was "wisely and honestly applied" this meant that the labor of individuals in a community was mutually beneficial. This passage also repeats a belief that Olmsted had stated in his writings on the economy of the antebellum South that "Labor is the creator of wealth" ("The South," number 7, *New-York Daily Times*, March 17, 1853 [*Papers of FLO*, 2: 109]).

6. This passage identifies the source for Olmsted's use of the phrase "*unbending* of the faculties" to describe the beneficial effect on the human organism of the experience of park scenery. The concept of the importance of the unbending of faculties to the process of recuperation is not to be found in the fables of Aesop, but rather in a tale told about the life of Aesop himself. Most editions of the fables do not include these anecdotes, but the incident to which Olmsted refers appears in an illustrated British edition of 1818. The fable is as follows:

Æsop at Play

An Athenian one day found Æsop entertaining himself with a company of little Boys at their childish diversions, and began to jeer and laugh at him for it. Æsop, who was too much a wag himself to suffer others to ridicule him, took a bow unstrung, and laid it upon the ground. Then calling the censorious Athenian, Now philosopher, says he, expound the riddle if you can, and tell us what the unstrained bow implies. The Man, after racking his brains a considerable time to no purpose, at last gave it up, and declared he knew not what to make of it. Why, says Æsop, smiling, if you keep a bow always bent, it will lose its elasticity presently; but if you let it go slack, it will be fitter for use when you want it.

Application.

The mind of man is not formed for unremitted attention, nor his body for uninterrupted labour; and both are in this respect like a bow. We cannot go through any business requiring intense thought, without unbending the mind, any more than we can perform a long journey without refreshing ourselves by due rest at the several stages of it. Continual labour, as in the case of the bended bow, destroys the elasticity and energy of both body and mind. It is, therefore, absolutely necessary for the studious man to unbend, and the laborious one to take his rest, or both lose their tone and vigour, and become dull and languid. It is to remedy these extremes, that pastimes and diversions ought to be kept up, provided they are innocent. The heart that never tastes of pleasure, shuts up, grows stiff, and is at last incapable of enjoyment.

(Æsopus, *The Fables of Æsop, and Others, With Designs on Wood, by Thomas Bewick* [1818; rpt. ed., New York, 1975], pp. 333–34).

7. These elements of a park drive were all necessary if those viewing a park from a carriage were to benefit to any extent from the "unconscious influence" of the scenery through which they passed. These elements would reduce to a minimum the distractions caused by fear of accidents and collision, and those caused by any need to make decisions concerning the route to take through the park. This section of the report is Olmsted's classic exposition of the qualities necessary in a park drive.

8. The quotation is from the twenty-third Psalm, attributed to David, the King of Judah and Israel in the tenth century B.C.

9. The descriptive terms that Olmsted uses here, especially his reference to the "mystery, variety and richness of tropical scenery" and to vegetation that is "intricate and mazy" indicates that he is describing the "picturesque" style of scenery, whose effects he had experienced most fully while crossing the Isthmus of Panama in 1863. While "pastoral" landscape was the most desirable in a park, Olmsted usually included some passages of the "picturesque" as well, partly for variety and partly because it was much better adapted to steep and rough terrain. (For explication of why picturesque should be the secondary and subordinate style in a park, see discussion of the role of picturesque in a park in Olmsted's article "Park" for the *New American Cyclopaedia* of 1875, below.) (Charles E. Beveridge, "Frederick Law Olmsted's Theory of Landscape Design," *Nineteenth Century* 3 [Summer 1977]: 38–43; *Papers of FLO*, 5: 83, 85–91).

10. The Merchant's Gate is at Columbus Circle at the southwest corner of Central Park, the intersection of 59th Street, Central Park West, and Broadway.

11. The Cricket Ground, in the southwestern corner of Central Park, is indicated by the letter E on the map of Central Park in the article "Park," page 325, below.

12. Vista Rock, marked B on the Central Park map on page 325 below, at the top of the Ramble, just above the 79th Street transverse road. The Belvedere, designed by Calvert Vaux, was later constructed at that point.

13. A reference to the area that became known as the Sheep Meadow (D on the Central Park map on page 325). The Marble Arch was at the southwest corner of the Mall and provided a passageway for pedestrians under the carriage drive.

14. For the original boundary of Prospect Park east of Flatbush Avenue, see Calvert Vaux's sketch of the original and proposed new boundaries of February 4, 1865, on page 82. As the plan accompanying this report indicates (pages 84–85), Olmsted and Vaux by January 1866 were proposing to extend the park three blocks farther east than contemplated in Vaux's report of a year previous.

15. A reference to Lookout Hill, where Olmsted and Vaux planned the Overlook terrace and carriage concourses (indicated by D on map of Prospect Park on page 327 below).

16. The twenty-acre Lake in Central Park is just north of the Bethesda Terrace, which is indicated by C on the map of Central Park on page 325. The opportunity for skating that Central Park provided, beginning in the winter of 1859–60, soon led to the creation of privately operated skating ponds, many of which were formed in sunken lots

near the park. A considerable number were lit at night and provided music for the skaters. Numerous other such ponds were created in other parts of the New York City area—particularly in Hoboken, Brooklyn, and along the lines of the Harlem and New Haven railroads (Clarence C. Cook, A *Description of the New York Central Park* [1869; rpt. ed., New York, 1972], pp. 66–68).

17. The Look-out is indicated by D on the map of Prospect Park on page 327 below.

18. That is, the proposed building would block the view of Greenwood Cemetery, which lay nine blocks west of Prospect Park. Olmsted was anxious to eliminate the view of a cemetery, and the associations suggested by it, from a pleasure ground like Prospect Park, in part because he felt the inappropriateness of the custom that had grown up in New York and other cities prior to the creation of parks of using rural cemeteries for picnics and walks. He regarded such a practice as barbarous. One of the great benefits of parks was that their creation meant that people no longer need be subjected to the sight of graves and funeral corteges when they sought relaxation and recreation in the open air.

19. The carriage concourse on Breeze Hill, indicated by E on the map of Prospect Park on page 327 below.

20. The Concert Grove, indicated by F on the map of Prospect Park on page 327 below.

21. This proposed arcade-terrace-restaurant complex was never constructed.

22. That is, along the carriage drive between Lookout Hill and the hill north of it, where the Quaker (or Friends') Cemetery was located. Olmsted and Vaux's plan of 1865 indicates that they assumed the cemetery would be removed and its space devoted to park purposes.

23. That is, the southern end of the Green (or Long Meadow, as it came to be called) nearest 15th Street, along which the Coney Island Rail Road ran. Consistent with his views expressed at various times during his career, Olmsted here proposes that only children should be allowed to play team sports in the park. He preferred that such facilities be provided as part of a public school education, although he was also willing to permit working boys to play team sports in some parks (FLO to Henry G. Stebbins, [c. July 10, 1873] [*Papers of FLO*, 6: 630–31]; see also FLO, "Public Parks and the Enlargement of Towns," Feb. 25, 1870, n. 24, below).

24. Olmsted here proposes much freer access to greensward than he had felt was advisable in Central Park, with its more limited area of open turf. There he had devised an elaborate system of regulating free access to lawn and meadow areas, in order to protect them from overuse during particularly dry or wet weather (*Papers of FLO*, 3: 279).

25. The state legislature did not give the Prospect Park commission authority to purchase the area here proposed for a zoological garden until the spring of 1868, and the property was acquired by condemnation in April of the next year. No zoo was established in the area proposed, however. Instead, administrative offices for the park staff were installed in the Litchfield Mansion, which is in that section of the park.

   Olmsted and Vaux drew up no further proposals that have survived concerning a zoo in that area. In 1934, during the Robert Moses era of the New York Parks Department, a zoo was constructed in Prospect Park in the area that Olmsted and Vaux had planned as a deer paddock (BPC, *Annual Reports, 1861–73*, pp. 123–25, 156–57, 240–43, 252–53, 311–12; Joy M. Kestenbaum, "Chronology of Prospect Park Perimeter," [1983]; David Schuyler, "First Historic Landscape and Structures Report: The Perimeter Lands, Prospect Park, Brooklyn, New York," [1983], p. 60).

26. The Deer Park is indicated by C on the map of Prospect Park on page 327 below.

27. The Nethermead, indicated by B on the map of Prospect Park on page 327 below.

28. A reference to the Valley Grove Tavern, constructed in a pass that was in the center of the defensive line of Continental troops during August 27, 1776, the first day of the

"Battle of Brooklyn" that marked the beginning of the British invasion of New York (Henry R. Stiles, A *History of the City of Brooklyn* . . ., 3 vols. [Brooklyn, 1867–70], 1: 280–81).

29. That is, the entrance opposite the large traffic circle shown on the accompanying plan into which Washington and Franklin avenues both run. The entrance was just north of the property of the Willink family on the west side of Flatbush Avenue, and the adoption of Olmsted and Vaux's proposal led to acquisition of a portion of the estate for the entrance. However, the boundaries of the park proposed by Olmsted and Vaux, as shown in the accompanying plan, jogged away from Flatbush Avenue just before reaching the Willink mansion, avoiding that building and the houses beyond it on Flatbush Avenue (Henry W. B. Howard, ed., *The Eagle and Brooklyn: The Record of the Progress of the Brooklyn Daily Eagle* [Brooklyn, 1893], p. 82; "Preliminary Map Showing Lineal and Topographical Surveys of Prospect Park Brooklyn, Over Areas Included by Present and Proposed Boundaries . . . 1865," in BPC, *Annual Reports, 1861–1873*, between pp. 90 and 91).

30. Only two of the four entrances discussed here were provided with arches enabling pedestrians to reach the internal park without crossing the carriage drive at grade. One was the principal entrance at Flatbush and Ninth avenues (later Grand Army Plaza), for which Calvert Vaux designed two arches, Meadowport Arch and Endale Arch, for the footpaths that entered the park on each side of the "Principal Entrance"; the other, East Wood Arch, was near the entrance on Flatbush Avenue near the Willink property. All three arches were constructed between 1867 and 1869. Such arches for separation of ways were not constructed for the west-side entrances — neither the arch shown on the plan under the circuit drive near Ninth Avenue opposite 12th Street, nor the two arches shown on the plan that would have permitted paths leading from the circle at the intersection of 15th Street and Coney Island Road to pass under the circuit drive (J. M. Kestenbaum, "Chronology of Prospect Park").

31. That is, the orchards and gardens of the Willink estate and other residences on Flatbush Avenue.

32. This area was acquired by the city of Brooklyn for a Parade Ground in May 1867 (J. M. Kestenbaum, "Chronology of Prospect Park").

33. The primacy of the perceptive faculties was due to the nature of experience as defined by Lockean psychology: the primary source of ideas was the experience of phenomena through the senses. The reflective faculty, or understanding, then further developed "another set of ideas, which could not be had from things without." (E. L. Tuveson, *Imagination as a Means of Grace*, pp. 15–18).

34. The Scholars' Gate is the principal entrance to Central Park at Fifth Avenue and 59th Street. The text of the published report at this point reads "Artist's Gate," and the correction was written in the margin of the copy used for the text published here, which is in Olmsted's collection of park reports at the Frederick Law Olmsted National Historic Site, Brookline, Massachusetts. The Artists' Gate was at 59th Street and Sixth Avenue.

35. In May 1865 the Central Park commissioners set aside a four-acre tract in Central Park surrounding and including the New York State Arsenal at Fifth Avenue and 64th Street, for museum buildings for the New-York Historical Society. The society received permission to remodel or replace the arsenal (BCCP, *Minutes*, May 11, 1865, pp. 15–18).

36. Ocean Parkway, the second parkway in Brooklyn constructed in accordance with the proposals in this report, runs to Coney Island from the circle described here. Constructed in the early 1870s at a width of 210 feet, it followed the line of the Coney Island Plank Road and so runs in a straight line rather than along the curving course proposed in this report.

37. Ravenswood was on the East River opposite Blackwell's Island and the lower section of Central Park.
38. At this time the commissioners of Central Park were responsible for constructing 150-foot-wide extensions of Sixth and Seventh avenues from Central Park at 110th Street northward to the Harlem River at 150th and 155th streets, respectively. The combined length of the two new drives was four and one-half miles (*Papers of FLO*, 5: 544, n. 4).

Report of the Landscape Architects and Superintendents.

BROOKLYN, January 1st, 1868.

To the President of the Board of Commissioners of Prospect Park, Brooklyn:[1]
SIR: —

In our Annual Report of last year, we described the organization which had been made under instructions from your Board for carrying out the design of the Park upon the ground. This organization remains to the present time essentially unchanged.

In June last, Mr. J. P. Davis having resigned the position, Mr. C. C. Martin was appointed to the office of Engineer in Charge.[2]

DEVELOPMENT OF THE DESIGN.

During the year it has been found practicable to carry forward the design for the Park without intermission, although at many points the works, which it would have been most desirable to press to completion, have been suspended in consequence of the uncertainties in regard to boundary lines that still continue to embarrass operations.[3]

So much of the land required for the Park as lies to the south of that upon which work was last year commenced, came into the actual possession of the Commissioners during the month of June last, and active operations were at once extended over a large part of the new territory.[4]

A portion of the road system in this section of the ground has been developed, the carriage concourse proposed in our original design to be constructed on Briar Hill has been subgraded and the ground in the vicinity of this concourse has been partially shaped. It was found practicable in execution to enlarge the area of this feature of the design, and the dimensions have been somewhat increased, it being evident that the position was one that would offer special attractions to visitors in carriages.[5]

On the east side of the Park, north of the deer-paddock, the design as it stood last year has been so far modified in execution as to admit of the introduction of a series of arrangements adapted especially to meet the wants of children. The plan as approved, and now well advanced in execution, contemplates suitable accommodations for running sports and for playing various games, it also includes croquet grounds, a pond for the sailing of toy boats, and a maze.[6]

112

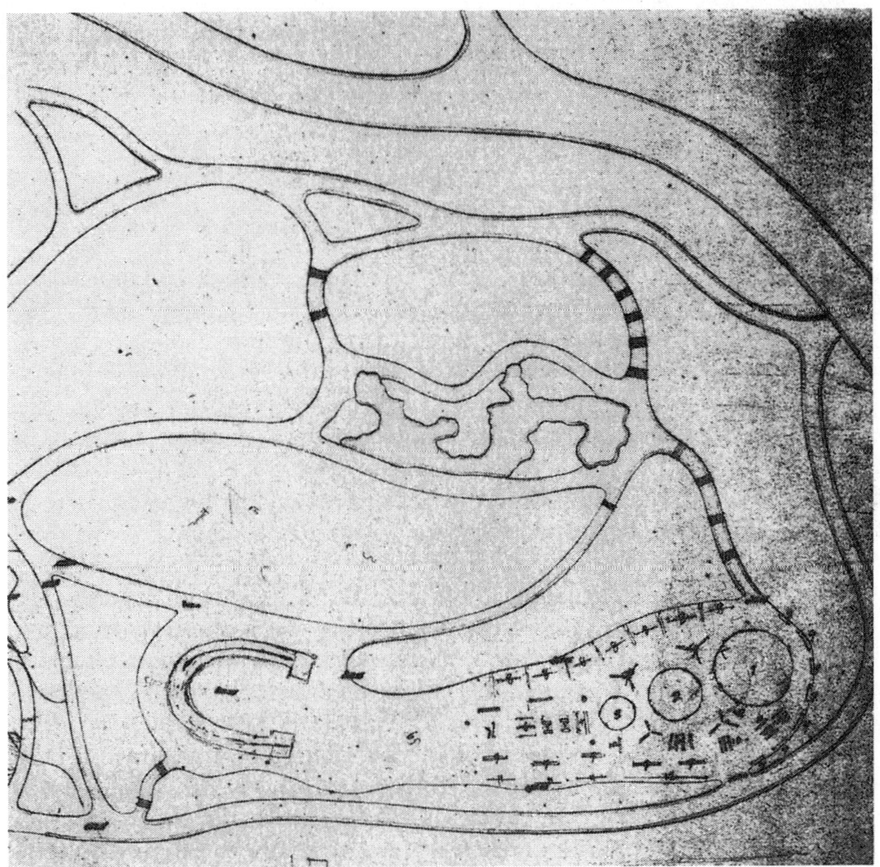

OLMSTED, VAUX & CO., PLAN FOR PLAYGROUND IN PROSPECT PARK NEAR FLATBUSH
AVENUE, DECEMBER 10, 1868
1. [illegible]; 2. Giant Stride Pole; 3. Giant Stride Pole; 4. Parallel Bars; 5. Horses;
6. Horizontal Bar; 7. Trapeze; 8. Swings (5 to each with double faced seat between);
9. Seats (double & single); 10. See Saws; 11. Bouncing Boards; 12. Balancing Walk.

In other respects but little variation has been made in the outline of
the design from our first study.

CONSTRUCTION.

You will find appended a full account of the progress of the methods
used, and of the means and materials employed, which has been prepared by
Mr. Martin and his principal aids, Mr. Bogart and Mr. Culyer.[7]

Two arch-ways have been partially constructed during the year, and
work has been commenced upon several other architectural features, our

studies for which have been approved by the Board.[8] The development in detail of this department of the work is under the more immediate charge of Mr. E. C. Miller,[9] who has fulfilled the duties of Assistant Architect since the beginning of July last.

PUBLIC USE OF THE PARK.

It was found necessary in the spring to close the country roads by which the public had previously crossed the Park territory, but on the 20th of October, a portion of the drive at the east side was so far completed that, by making temporary connections with old roads, a thoroughfare for carriages across the Park was again opened. At the same time regulations for the conduct of visitors and for the management of the work with reference to the convenience of the public were promulgated, and a beginning was made in the organization of a permanent body of Park-keepers, conjointly with a body of gardeners, according to a plan which had some time before been adopted by the Board.[10] Although the short piece of good road opened at this time was accessible with difficulty, and the grounds through which it passed were in a quite unfinished condition, it was immediately resorted to by visitors in large numbers. Besides those in carriages, many came on horse-back, and although no walks had been opened, many more on foot. A tabular statement of the number of each class prepared from the returns of the gate-keepers is given by Mr. Culyer.[11] The fact is noted that a considerable portion of the visitors evidently did not come merely from motives of curiosity, but after their first visit, repeatedly returned. During all the remainder of the season, indeed, not a few resorted to the Park as a daily habit, of whom some came from the more distant parts of the town. Considering the extreme inconvenience with which the Park is at present reached and the very limited attractions which as yet it offers, this circumstance is a gratifying indication of the value which it will hereafter possess.

THE PARK WAY—APPROACHES AND CONNECTIONS.

The unsatisfactory character of the approaches to the Park has been recognized by your Board, from the outset of its undertaking, as calculated to seriously detract from the value of the service which it would otherwise be able to render the city, and it has accordingly been an incidental part of our duty to devise means of improvement. To do so it has been necessary that we should extend our field of study beyond the territory under your jurisdiction. Our first suggestion led, through the subsequent action of your Board, to the special appropriation of the ground necessary for the formation of the Plaza, and to the establishment of the several circular spaces by which amplitude, symmetry, and dignity of character was sought to be secured on the street side of each of the Park gates.[12] Through the promptness of the necessary legisla-

114

tive action, and of the subsequent proceedings in regard to the Plaza, a very great advantage was gained at a comparatively small cost for the necessary land, much of the adjoining ground having since been sold in the open market at rates indicating an advance of several hundred per cent. upon the prices paid by the city.

In our Preliminary Report, accompanying the first study of the plan of the Park, without making any definite recommendations, we suggested the leading features of a general scheme of routes of approach to and extension from the Park, through the suburbs, in which the sanitary, recreative and domestic requirements of that portion of the people of the city living at the greatest distance from the Park should be especially provided for.[13] In our Annual Report of last year portions of this project were somewhat more distinctly outlined, and the economical advantages were pointed out of preparing and adopting plans for the purpose well in advance of the public demand, which it was intended to anticipate, and while land properly situated might yet be selected in the suburbs of such moderate value that no private interests of much importance would be found to stand in antagonism in this respect to those of the public.[14]

RELATIONS OF THE PARK TO THE STREET ARRANGEMENTS OF THE CITY.

Your Board having brought these suggestions before the public,[15] they have during the last year attracted considerable attention. One of the minor recommendations has been already taken up by a body of citizens and an organized effort to carry it out is understood to be in progress. Under your instructions a topographical survey has also been made of a section of the ground to which the larger scheme applies, being that lying immediately east of the Park and extending from it to the city line;[16] and a study has been prepared, also under your instructions and which is herewith presented, for a revision of a part of the present city map of this ground with a view to the introduction of the suggested improvement.

The period seems to have arrived, therefore, for a full and comprehensive inquiry as to the manner in which the scheme would, if carried out, affect the substantial and permanent interests of the citizens of Brooklyn and of the metropolis at large.

The project in its full conception is a large one, and it is at once conceded that it does not follow but anticipates the demand of the public; that it assumes an extension of the city of Brooklyn and a degree of wealth, taste, and refinement, to be likely to exist among its citizens which has not hitherto been definitely had in view, and that it is even based upon the presumption that the present street system, not only of Brooklyn but of other large towns, has serious defects for which, sooner or later, if these towns should continue to advance in wealth, remedies must be devised, the cost of

which will be extravagantly increased by a long delay in the determination of
their outlines.

ELEMENTS OF ORDINARY STREET ARRANGEMENTS.

What is here referred to under the designation of our present street
system, is essentially comprised in the two series of thoroughfares extending
in straight lines to as great a distance within a town as is found practicable,
one series crossing the other at right angles, or as nearly so as can be conveniently arranged. Each of the thoroughfares of this system consists of a way
in the center, which is paved with reference solely to sustaining the transportation upon wheels of the heaviest merchandise, of a gutter on each side of
this wheel-way, having occasional communication with underground channels for carrying off water, and a curb which restricts the passage of wheels
from a raised way for the travel of persons on foot, the surface of which, to
avoid their sinking in the mud, is commonly covered with flags or brick.

This is the system which is almost universally kept in view, not only
in the enlargement of our older towns, but in the setting out of new; such, for
instance, as are just being projected along the line of the Pacific Railroad.[17] If
modifications are admitted, it is because they are enforced by some special
local conditions which are deemed, by those responsible for the arrangement,
to be unfortunate. The reason for this is probably found chiefly in the fact,
that it is a plan which is readily put on paper, easily comprehended, and
easily staked out; it makes the office of an Engineer or Surveyor at the outset
almost a sinecure, as far as the exercise of professional ability is concerned,
and facilitates the operations of land speculators.

Its apparent simplicity on paper is often fallacious, and leads either
to unnecessary taxation or to great permanent inconvenience. It is obviously
incomplete, and wholly unsuited to the loading and unloading of goods
which require storage, but, where it can be well carried out, offers very great
advantages for the transportation of merchandise between distant points. It is
also well adapted to equalize the advantages of different parts of a town, and
thus avoid obstructions to improvement which mercenary jealousies might
otherwise interpose.

In our judgment, advantages such as these have hitherto been pursued far too exclusively, but, as the presumption is always strong against any
considerable innovation upon arrangements which have been long associated with the general conditions of prosperity and progress of all civilized
communities, we desire, before giving reasons for this conviction, first, to remove any reasonable prejudice against the introduction of the entirely new
elements into the street plan of Brooklyn, which we shall have to propose, by
showing under what conditions of society and with reference to what very
crude public requirements, compared with those which now exist, our present street arrangements have been devised.

WHY ORDINARY ARRANGEMENTS ARE INADEQUATE TO PUBLIC REQUIREMENTS.

At present, large towns grow up because of the facilities they offer mankind for a voluntary exchange of service, in the form of merchandise; but nearly all the older European towns of importance, from which we have received the fashion of our present street arrangements, were formed either to strengthen or to resist a purpose involving the destruction of life and the plunder of merchandise. They were thus planned originally for objects wholly different from those now reckoned important by the towns which occupy the same sites, and an examination of the slow, struggling process by which they have been adapted to the present requirements of their people, may help us to account for some of the evils under which even here, in our large American towns, we are now suffering.

HISTORICAL DEVELOPMENT OF EXISTING STREET ARRANGEMENTS, FIRST STAGE.

They were at the outset, in most cases, entrenched camps, in which a few huts were first built, with no thought of permanence, and still less with thought for the common convenience of their future citizens. The wealth of their founders consisted chiefly in cattle, and in the servants who were employed in herding and guarding these cattle, and the trails carelessly formed among the scattered huts within the entrenchments often became permanent foot-ways which, in some cases, were subsequently improved in essentially the same manner as the sidewalks of our streets now are, by the laying upon them of a series of flat stones, so that walkers need not sink in the mud. If the ground was hilly, and the grades of the paths steep, stairs were sometimes made by laying thicker slabs of stone across them. Convenience of communication on foot was, of course, the sole object of such improvements.

If, in these early times, any highways were more regularly laid out, it was simply with reference to defence. For example, although two nearly straight and comparatively broad-ways were early formed in Paris, so that reinforcements could be rapidly transferred from one gate to another when either should be suddenly attacked,[18] no other passages were left among the houses which would admit of the introduction of wheeled traffic; nor in all the improvements which afterwards occurred, as the city advanced in population and wealth, were any of the original pathways widened and graded sufficiently for this purpose until long after America had been discovered, and the invention of printing and of fire-arms had introduced a new era of social progress.

The labor required for the construction of permanent town walls, and the advantage of being able to keep every part of them closely manned during an attack, made it desirable that they should not be unnecessarily extended. To admit of a separate domiciliation of families within them, therefore, the greatest practicable compactness in the arrangement of dwelling-houses soon became imperative. As families increased, the demand for additional house-room was first met by encroachments upon the passages which had been left between the original structures, and by adding upper stories, and extending these outward so as to overhang the street. Before this process had reached an extreme point, however, the town would begin to outgrow its walls, and habitations in the suburbs would occur, of two classes: first, those formed by poor herdsmen and others, who, when no enemy was known to be near at hand, could safely sleep in a temporary shelter, calculating to take their chance in the town when danger came; and, second, those formed by princes, and other men of wealth and power, who could afford to build strongholds for the protection of their families and personal retainers, but who, in times of war, yet needed to be in close vicinity to the larger fighting forces of the town. Neither the castle nor the hovel being placed with any reference to the enlargement of the town, or to public convenience in any way, streets were formed through the suburbs, as they became denser, in much the same way as they had been in the original settlement; then, as the walls were extended, the military consideration again operated to enforce the idea of compactness in every possible way.

The government of these towns also, however its forms varied, was always essentially a military despotism of the most direct and stringent character, under which the life, property, health and comfort of the great body of their people were matters, at best, of very subordinate consideration.

Thus the policy, the custom and the fashion was established in the roots of our present form of society of regarding the wants of a town, and planning to meet them, as if its population were a garrison, to be housed in a barrack, with only such halls and passages in it, from door to door, as would be necessary to turn it in, to sleep and feed, and turn it out, to get its rations.

It naturally fell out that when at length the general advance of society, in other respects, made it no longer necessary that a man should build a castle, and control, as personal property, the services of a numerous body of fighting men, in order to live with some degree of safety in a house of his own, apart from others, all the principal towns declined for a time in wealth and population, because of the number of opulent citizens who abandoned their old residences, and moved, with servants and tenants, to make new settlements in the country.

The excessive suppression of personal independence and individual inclinations which had before been required in town-life caused a strong reactionary ambition to possess each prosperous citizen to relieve himself as much as possible from dependence upon and duties to society in general, and it became his aim to separate himself from all the human race except such part as would treat him with deference. To secure greater seclusion and at the same time opportunity for the only forms of out-door recreation, which the rich, after the days of jousts and tournaments, were accustomed to engage in, all those who could command favor at Court, sought grants of land abounding in the larger game, and planted their houses in the midst of enclosures called parks, which not only kept neighbors at a distance, but served as nurseries for objects of the chase.

The habits of the wealthy, under these circumstances, though often gross and arrogant, and sometimes recklessly extravagant, were far from luxurious, according to modern notions, and as, in order to realize as fully as possible the dream of independence, every country gentleman had his private chaplain, surgeon, farrier, tailor, weaver and spinner, raised his own wool, malt, barley and breadstuffs, killed his own beef, mutton and venison, and brewed his own ale, he was able to despise commerce and to avoid towns. The little finery his household coveted was accordingly brought to his door on pack-mules by traveling merchants. The vocation of a merchant, in its large, modern sense, was hardly known, and the trade of even the most considerable towns was, in all respects, very restricted. Thus the old foot-way streets still served all necessary requirements tolerably well.

As the advance of civilization continued, however, this disinclination to the exchange of service, of course, gave way; demands became more varied, and men of all classes were forced to take their place in the general organization of society in communities. In process of time the enlargement of popular freedom, the spread of knowledge by books, the abatement of religious persecutions, the voyages of circumnavigators, and finally the opening of America, India and the gold coast of Africa to European commerce, so fed the mercantile inclinations, that an entirely new class of towns, centres of manufacturing and of trade, grew upon the sites of the old ones. To these the wealthy and powerful were drawn, no longer for protection, but for the enjoyment of the luxuries which they found in them, while the more enterprising of the lower classes crowded into them to "seek their fortune."

Second Stage of Street Arrangements.

Wagons gradually took the place of pack-trains in the distribution of goods through the country, and, as one man could manage a heavy load, when it was once stowed, as well as a light one, the wagons were made very large and strong, and required the employment of many horses.

In comparatively few town-streets could two of these wheeled merchantmen, with the enormous hamper they carried on each side, pass each other. The seats and hucksteries of slight wood-work with which the streets had been lined were swept away; but, as the population rapidly increased, while the house accommodation was so limited that its density, in the city of London, for instance, was probably three times as great as at present, any attempt to further widen the streets for the convenience of the wagoners had to encounter the strongest resistance from the house-holders.

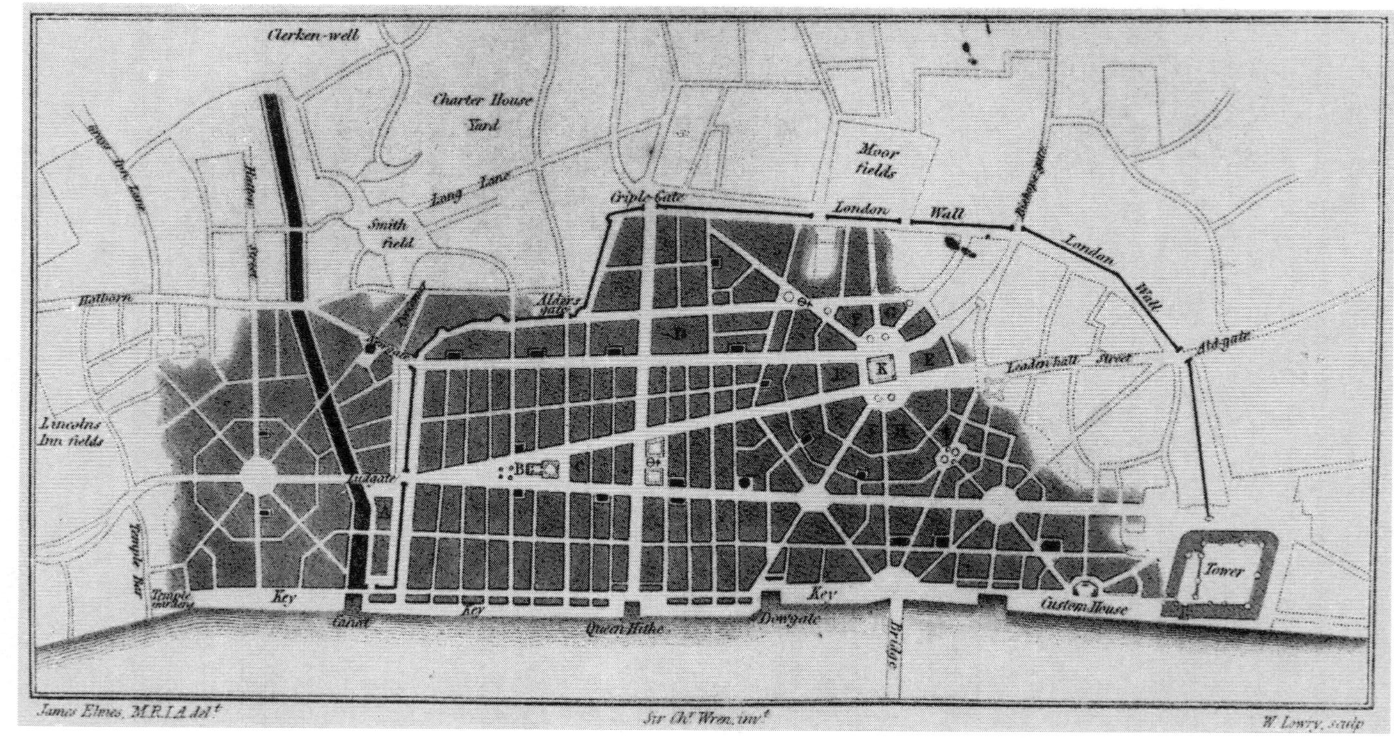

CHRISTOPHER WREN'S PLAN FOR LONDON, 1666

Thus, without any material enlargement, the character of the streets was much changed. They frequently became quite unfit to walk in, the more so because they were used as the common place of deposit for all manner of rubbish and filth thrown out of the houses which was not systematically removed from them.

Although London then occupied not a fiftieth part of the ground which it does now, and green fields remained which had been carefully preserved for the practice of archery within acomparatively short distance of its central parts, to which the inhabitants much resorted for fresh air on summer evenings; although the river still ran clear, and there was much pleasure-boating upon it, the greater part of the inhabitants were so much confined in dark, ill-ventilated and noisome quarters, that they were literally decimated by disease as often as once in every two years, while at intervals fearful epidemics raged, at which times the mortality was much greater. During one of these, four thousand deaths occurred in a single night, and many streets were completely depopulated.[19] All who could by any means do so, fled from the town, so that in a short time its population was reduced more than fifty per cent. It had not yet filled up after this calamity, when a fire occurred which raged unchecked during four days, and destroyed the houses and places of business of two hundred thousand of the citizens. Its progress was at length stayed by the widening of the streets across which it would have advanced if the buildings which lined them had not been removed by the military.[20]

Five-sixths of the area occupied by the old city was still covered with smoking embers when the most distinguished architect of the age seized the opportunity to urge a project for laying out the street system of a new town upon the same site.[21] The most novel feature of this plan was the introduction of certain main channel streets, ninety feet wide, in which several wagons could be driven abreast upon straight courses from one end of the city to the other. It was also proposed that there should be a series of parallel and intersecting streets sixty feet wide, with intermediate lanes of thirty feet. The enormous advantages of such a system of streets over any others then in use in the large towns of Europe were readily demonstrated; it obtained the approval of the king himself, and would have been adopted but for the incredible short-sightedness of the merchants and real estate owners. These obstinately refused to give themselves any concern about the sacrifice of general inconvenience or the future advantages to their city, which it was shown that a disregard of Wren's suggestions would involve, but proceeded at once, as fast as possible, without any concert of action, to build anew, each man for himself, upon the ruins of his old warehouse. There can be little question, that had the property-owners, at this time, been wise enough to act as a body in reference to their common interests, and to have allowed Wren to devise and carry out a complete street system, intelligently adapted to the requirements which he would have been certain to anticipate; as well as those which were already pressing, it would have relieved the city of London of an incalculable expenditure which has since been required to mend its street arrangements; would have greatly lessened the weight of taxation, which soon afterwards rose to be higher than in any other town of the kingdom, and would have saved millions of people from the misery of poverty and disease.

Although in a very few years after the rebuilding of the city, its commerce advanced so much as to greatly aggravate the inconveniences under which street communication had been previously carried on, the difficulties were allowed to grow greater and greater for fully a century more before anything was done calculated to essentially alleviate them. They seem to have been fully realized and to have been constantly deplored, nor were efforts of a certain kind wanting to remedy them; the direction of these efforts, however, shows how strongly a traditional standard of street convenience yet confused the judgment even of the most advanced. A town being still thought of as a collection of buildings all placed as closely as possible to one centre was also regarded as a place of necessarily inconvenient confinement, and therefore, of crowding, hustling and turbulence. An enlargement of the population of a town could only aggravate all the special troubles and dangers to which those living in it were subject, add to the number of its idle, thriftless, criminal and dangerous classes, and invite disease, disorder and treasonable tumults. As, therefore, to amplify the street arrangements or otherwise enlarge the public accommodations for trade or residence, would be to increase its attractions, the true policy was generally assumed to be in the other direction. In London, not only its own Corporation followed this policy, but Parliament and Sovereign systematically did the same.

Once, for instance, a proclamation was issued, to forbid under heavy penalties the erection of any houses, except such as should be suitable for the residence of the gentry, within three miles of the town; another followed which interdicted householders from enlarging the accommodations for strangers within the town; another enjoined all persons who had houses in the country to quit the town within three weeks, while constant efforts were made to ship off those who had none to Ireland, Virginia, or Jamaica.[22]

In spite of all, new houses were built on the sides of the old country roads, the suburban villages grew larger and larger till at length they were all one town with London, and the population became twice as great and the commerce much more than twice as great as at the time of the great fire. Even when at last plans of real improvement began to be entertained, it was no thought of resisting the increase of disease, pauperism and crime, by other means than fencing it out, that produced the change, but mainly the intolerable hindrance to commerce of the old fashioned arrangements. Though some refused to see it and still protested against the plans of improvement as wholly unnecessary, hazardous, reckless, and extravagant, and denounced those who urged them, as unprincipled speculators or visionary enthusiasts, the merchants generally could no longer avoid the conviction that their prosperity was seriously checked by the inadequacy of the thoroughfares of the town for the duty required of them. Parliament was therefore induced in the latter part of the last century, to authorize a series of measures which gradually brought about in the course of fifty years, larger and more important changes than had occurred before during many centuries.

As the definite aim of these changes was to get rid of certain inconveniences which had previously been classed among the necessary evils of large towns, and as the measure with reference to which the purpose of their design was limited is thus clearly established, it is evident that before we can realize the degree in which they were likely to approach the ultimatum of civilized requirement, we need to know more exactly what the inconveniences in question amounted to.

It appears then that the imperfect pavements, never having been adequately revised since the days of hand-barrow and pack-horse transportation, were constantly being misplaced and the ground worn into deep ruts by the crushing weight of the wheels; the slops and offal matters thrown out of the houses were combined with the dung of the horses and the mud to make a tenacious puddle, through which the people on foot had to drag their way in constant apprehension of being run down or crushed against the wall. In the principal streets strong posts were planted at intervals behind which active men were accustomed to dodge for safety as the wagons came upon them. Coaches had been introduced in the time of Elizabeth, but though simple, strong and rudely hung vehicles, they were considered to be very dangerous in the streets and their use within the town was for some time forbidden. Sedan chairs for all ordinary purposes superseded them and for a long time had been in common use by all except the poorer classes upon every occasion of going into the streets. When George the Third went in the state coach to open Parliament, the streets through which he passed were previously prepared by laying faggots in the ruts to make the motion easier. There was little or no sewerage or covered drainage, and heavy storms formed gullies of the ruts and often flooded the cellars destroying a great deal of merchandise.

This was the condition in which after several hundred years, the town had been left by the transformation of the passages, first occurring between the huts of the entrenched camp of a tribe of barbarians, from the serviceable foot ways of the early middle ages to the unserviceable wagon ways of the generation but one before the last.

THIRD STAGE OF STREET ARRANGEMENTS.

To remedy its evils, in the construction of new streets, and the reconstruction of old, the original passage for people on foot was restored, but it was now split through the middle and set back with the house fronts on each side so as to admit of the introduction of a special road-way for horses and wheels, at a lower level. A curb was placed to guard the foot way from the wheels; gutters were used to collect the liquid and floating filth, and sewers were constructed which enabled the streams thus formed to be taken out of the streets before they became so large as to flood the sidewalks. At the same time an effort was made to so straighten and connect some of the streets that goods could be taken from one quarter of the town to another by direct courses, and without the necessity of doubling the horse-power at certain points in order to overcome the natural elevations of the ground.[23]

Thus, just one hundred years after Wren's suggestions were rejected by the merchants, their grandsons began to make lame efforts to secure some small measure of the convenience which his plan had offered them.

A few of the latter improvements had been adopted in other towns at a somewhat earlier period than in London. In the plans of St. Petersburg and of Philadelphia, for instance, directness and unusual amplitude of roadway had been studied, and some of the free cities of Germany had, at an earlier date, possessed moderately broad and well-paved streets, but the exceptions do not affect the conclusion which we desire to enforce.

To fully understand the reason of this long neglect to make any wise preparation for the enlargement of population which it would seem must surely have been anticipated, we need to consider that while a rapid advance was all the time occurring from the state of things when a town was intended to be governed with little direct regard for the interests of any but a very few of its occupants, at the same time direct responsibility for the care of its interests was being diffused and held for shorter intervals, and was, consequently, less and less felt, as a motive to ingenuity and energy, by any one of the several individuals who partook in it. The theory and form of town government changed more slowly than the character and modes of life of those who were called upon to administer it, but an adherence to the antiquated forms was only calculated to make a personal duty, with reference to the actual new conditions of the people, less easily realized and less effectively operative. What is everybody's business is nobody's, and although, of late years, experts, with professional training in special branches, are not infrequently engaged by municipal bodies to study particular requirements of the people, and invent means to satisfy them, still, as a general rule, improvements have come in most cities, when they have come at all, chiefly through the influence of individual energy, interested in behalf of special mercantile or speculative enterprises, by which the supineness of the elected and paid representatives of the common interests of the citizens has been overborne.

ERRONEOUS VIEW OF THE NECESSARY DISADVANTAGES
OF TOWN LIFE.

What is of more consequence, however, not merely that we may avoid injustice to our ancestors, but that we may realize the changes which have occurred in the standard of requirement, with reference to which the merits of a street system are now to be judged, is the fact that when these improvements were devised, it was still pardonable to take for granted that the larger the population of a town should be allowed to become, the greater would be the inconvenience and danger to which all who ventured to live in it would necessarily be subject, the more they would be exposed to epidemic diseases, the feebler, more sickly, and shorter their lives would be; the greater would be the danger of sweeping conflagrations; the larger the proportion of mendicants and criminals, and the more formidable, desperate and dangerous the mobs.

Evils of Town-Life Have Diminished as Towns Have Grown Larger.

We now know that these assumptions were entirely fallacious, for, as a matter of fact, towns have gone on increasing, until there are many in Europe which are several times larger than the largest of the Middle Ages, and in the largest the amount of disease is not more than half as great as it formerly was; the chance of living to old age is much more than twice as great; epidemics are less frequent, less malignant and more controllable; sweeping fires are less common, less devastating and are more sooner got under; ruffians are much better held in check; mobs are less frequently formed, are less dangerous, and, when they arise, are suppressed more quickly and with less bloodshed; there is a smaller proportion of the population given over to vice and crime and a vastly larger proportion of well-educated, orderly, industrious and well-to-do citizens. These things are true, in the main, not of one town alone, but of every considerable town, from Turkey on the one side to China on the other, and the larger each town has grown, the greater, on an average, has been the gain. Even in Mahomedan Cairo, chiefly through the action of French engineers, the length of life of each inhabitant has, on an average, been doubled.[24] The question, then, very naturally occurs: What are the causes and conditions of this amelioration? and Can it be expected to continue?

Reason for Anticipating an Accelerated Enlargement of Metropolitan Towns.

If the enormous advance in the population of great towns which has been characteristic of our period of civilization, is due mainly to the increase of facilities for communication, transportation and exchange throughout the world, as there is every reason to believe that it is, we can but anticipate, in the immediate future, a still more rapid movement in the same direction.

We are now extending railroads over this continent at the rate of more that fifteen hundred miles a year, and before our next President takes

his seat, we shall have applied an amount of labor which is represented by
the enormous sum of two thousand millions of dollars, to this work, most of
it preparatory, and more than half of it directed to the opening up of new
lands to profitable cultivation. The productive capacity of the country thus
laid open, and the demand upon commerce of its people, has scarcely yet
begun to be manifested. We have but half made our first road to the Pacific,
and we have only within a year begun to extend our steam navigation to Japan
and China, where the demands upon civilized commerce of a frugal and
industrious population, much larger than that of all Christendom, yet remain
to be developed. We are ourselves but just awake to the value of the electric
telegraph in lessening the risks of trade on a large scale, and giving it order
and system.[25] Thus, we seem to be just preparing to enter upon a new chapter
of commercial and social progress, in which a comprehension of the advantages that arise from combination and co-operation will be the rule among
merchants, and not, as heretofore, the exception.

Conditions Under Which the Evils of Large Towns Have Diminished.

The rapid enlargement of great towns which has hitherto occurred,
must then be regarded as merely a premonition of the vastly greater enlargement that is to come. We see, therefore, how imperative, with reference to
the interests of our race, is this question, whether as the enlargement of towns
goes on the law of improvement is such that we may reasonably hope that
life in them will continue to grow better, more orderly, more healthy? One
thing seems to be certain, that the gain hitherto can be justly ascribed in
very small part to direct action on the part of those responsible for the good
management of the common interests of their several populations. Neither
humanity nor the progress of invention and discovery, nor the advancement
of science has had much to do with it. It cannot even, in any great degree, be
ascribed to the direct action of the law of supply and demand.

Shall we say, then, that it has depended on causes wholly beyond the
exercise of human judgment, and that we may leave the future to take care
of itself, as our fathers did? We are by no means justified in adopting such a
conclusion, for, if we cannot yet trace wholly to their causes, all the advantages we possess over our predecessors, we are able to reach the conviction,
beyond all reasonable doubt, that at least, the larger share of the immunity
from the visits of the plague and other forms of pestilence, and from sweeping
fires, and the larger part of the improved general health and increased length
of life which civilized towns have lately enjoyed is due to the abandonment
of the old-fashioned compact way of building towns, and the gradual adoption of a custom of laying them out with much larger spaces open to the sunlight and fresh air; a custom the introduction of which was due to no intelligent anticipation of such results.

Evidence of this is found in the fact that the differing proportions between the dying and the living, the sick and the well, which are found to exist between towns where most of the people still live on narrow streets, and those in which the later fashions have been generally adopted; and between parts of the same town which are most crowded and those which are more open, are to this day nearly as great as between modern and ancient towns. For instance, in Liverpool, the constant influx of new-comers of a very poor and ignorant class from the other side of the Irish Channel, and the consequent demand for house-room, and the resulting value of the poor, old buildings which line the narrow streets, has, till recently, caused the progress of improvement to be much slower than in the much larger town of London, so that, while the average population of Liverpool is about 140,000 to the square mile, that of London is but 50,000; the average age at death in Liverpool is seventeen, and that in London, twenty-six. In the city of Brooklyn the number of deaths for each thousand of population that occurred this last year in the closer built parts, was twice as large as in those where the streets are wider and there are many gardens.

Comparisons of this kind have been made in such number, and the data for them have been drawn from such a large variety of localities in which the conditions of health in all other respects have been different, that no man charged, however temporarily and under whatever limitations, with municipal responsibilities, can be pardoned for ignoring the fact that the most serious drawback to the prosperity of town communities has always been dependent on conditions (quite unnecessary to exist in the present day) which have led to stagnation of air and excessive deprivation of sun-light.

Again, the fact that with every respiration of every living being a quantity is formed of a certain gas, which, if not dissipated, renders the air of any locality at first debilitating, after a time sickening, and at last deadly; and the fact that this gas is rapidly absorbed, and the atmosphere relieved of it by the action of leaves of trees, grass and herbs, was quite unknown to those who established the models which have been more or less distinctly followed in the present street arrangements of our great towns.[26] It is most of all important, however, that we should remember that they were not as yet awake to the fact that large towns are a necessary result of an extensive intercourse between people possessing one class of the resources of wealth and prosperity and those possessing other classes, and that with each increase of the field of commerce certain large towns must grow larger, and consequently, that it is the duty of each generation living in these towns to give some consideration, in its plans, to the requirements of a larger body of people than it has itself to deal with directly.

Change in the Habits of Citizens Affecting the Structural Requirements of Towns.

If, again, we consider the changes in the structure of towns which have occurred through the private action of individual citizens we shall find that they indicate the rise of a strong tide of requirements, the drift of which will either have to be fairly recognized in the public work of the present generation or it will, at no distant day, surely compel a revision of what is now done that will involve a large sacrifice of property.

Separation of Business and Domestic Life.

In the last century comparatively few towns-people occupied dwellings distinctly separate from their place of business. A large majority of the citizens of Paris, London and of New York do so to-day, and the tendency to divisions of the town corresponding to this change of habits must rapidly increase with their further enlargement, because of the greater distance which will exist between their different parts. The reason is obvious: a business man, during his working-hours, has no occasion for domestic luxuries, but needs to have access to certain of his co-workers in the shortest practicable time, and with the smallest practicable expenditure of effort. He wants to be near a bank, for instance, or near the Corn Exchange, or near the Stock Exchange, or to shipping, or to a certain class of shops or manufactories. On the other hand, when not engaged in business, he has no occasion to be near his working place, but demands arrangements of a wholly different character. Families require to settle in certain localities in sufficient numbers to support those establishments which minister to their social and other wants, and yet are not willing to accept the conditions of town-life which were formerly deemed imperative, and which, in the business quarters, are yet, perhaps, in some degree, imperative, but demand as much of the luxuries of free air, space and abundant vegetation as, without loss of town-privileges, they can be enabled to secure.

Those parts of a town which are to any considerable extent occupied by the great agencies of commerce, or which, for any reason, are especially fitted for their occupation, are therefore sure to be more and more exclusively given up to them, and, although we cannot anticipate all the subdivisions of a rapidly increasing town with confidence, we may safely assume that the general division of all the parts of every considerable town under the two great classifications of commercial and domestic, which began in the great European towns in the last century, will not only continue, but will become more and more distinct.

It can hardly be thought probable that street arrangements perfectly well adapted in all respects to the purposes to be served in one of these divisions are the very best in every particular that it would be possible to devise for those of the other.

RECREATIVE REQUIREMENTS AND DISTANCE OF SUBURBS.

Another change in the habits of towns-people which also grows out of the greatly enlarged area already occupied by large towns, results from the fact that, owing to the great distances of the suburbs from the central parts, the great body of the inhabitants cannot so easily as formerly stroll out into the country in search of fresh air, quietness, and recreation. At the same time there is no doubt that the more intense intellectual activity, which prevails equally in the library, the work shop, and the counting-room, makes tranquilizing recreation more essential to continued health and strength than until lately it generally has been. Civilized men, while they are gaining ground against certain acute forms of disease, are growing more and more subject to other and more insiduous enemies to their health and happiness, and against these the remedy and preventive cannot be found in medicine or in athletic recreations but only in sunlight and such forms of gentle exercise as are calculated to equalize the circulation and relieve the brain.

CHANGE IN THE CHARACTER OF VEHICLES.

Still another important change or class of changes in the habits of the people of towns may be referred to the much greater elaboration which has recently occurred in the division of labor and the consequent more perfect adaptation to the various purposes of life of many instruments in general use. A more striking illustration of this will not readily be found than is afforded by the light, elegant, easy carriages which have lately been seen in such numbers in your Park. When our present fashions of streets was introduced sedan chairs were yet, as we have shown, in general use for taking the air or making visits to neighbors. The few wheeled vehicles employed by the wealthy were exceedingly heavy and clumsy and adapted only to slow travel on rough roads, a speed of five miles an hour by what was called the "flying coach," being a matter for boasting. Now we have multifarious styles of vehicles in each of which a large number of different hands has been ingeniously directed to provide in all their several parts for the comfort, pleasure, and health with which they may be used. For the sake of elegance, as well as comfort and ease of draft, they are made extremely light and are supplied with pliant springs. They are consequently quite unfit to be used in streets adapted to the heavy wagons employed in commercial traffic, and can only be fully enjoyed in roads expressly prepared for them. In parks such roads are provided in connection with other arrangements for the health of the people.[27]

129

Inadequate Domestic Access to Suburbs and Parks.

The parks are no more accessible than the suburbs, however, from those quarters of the town occupied domestically, except by means of streets formed in precisely the same manner as those which pass through the quarters devoted to the heaviest commercial traffic. During the periods of transit, therefore, from house to house and between the houses and the Park there is little pleasure to be had in driving. Riding also, through the ordinary streets, is often not only far from pleasant, but, unless it is very slowly and carefully done, is hazardous to life and limb. Consequently much less enjoyment of the Park is possible to those who live at a distance than to those who live near it and its value to the population at large is correspondingly restricted. The difficulties of reaching the Park on foot for those who might enjoy and be benefited by the walk, are at the season of the year when it would otherwise be most attractive, even greater, for they must follow the heated flags[28] and bear the reflected as well as the direct rays of the sun.

But we cannot expect, even if this objection were overcome, that all the inhabitants of a large town would go so far as the Park every day, or so often as it is desirable that they should take an agreeable stroll in the fresh air. On the other hand we cannot say that the transportation of merchandise should be altogether interdicted in the domestic quarters of a town, as it is in a park, and as it now is through certain streets of London and Paris during most hours of the day. On the contrary it is evidently desirable that every dwelling house should be accessible by means of suitable paved streets to heavy wheeled vehicles.

New Arrangements Demanded by Existing Requirements.

It will be observed that each of the changes which we have examined points clearly towards the conclusion that the present street arrangements of every large town will at no very distant day require, not to be set aside, but to be supplemented, by a series of ways designed with express reference to the pleasure with which they may be used for walking, riding, and the driving of carriages; for rest, recreation, refreshment, and social intercourse, and that these ways must be so arranged that they will be conveniently accessible from every dwelling house and allow its occupants to pass from it to distant parts of the town, as, for instance, when they want to go to a park, without the necessity of travelling for any considerable distance through streets no more convenient for the purpose than our streets of the better class now are.

We may refuse to make timely provisions for such purposes in our suburbs, and we may by our refusal add prodigiously to the difficulty and the cost of their final introduction; but it is no more probable, if great towns continue to grow greater, that such requirements as we have pointed out will not eventually be provided for than it was two hundred years ago that the obvious defects of the then existing street arrangements would continue to be permanently endured rather than that property should be destroyed which existed in the buildings by their sides.

THE POSITION OF BROOKLYN.

If we now take the case of Brooklyn we shall find that all the reasons for an advance upon the standards of the street arrangements of the last century which apply to great towns in general, are applicable to her special situation with particular emphasis.

With reference to general commerce, Brooklyn must be considered as a division merely of the port of New York. The city of New York is, in regard to building space, in the condition of a walled town. Brooklyn is New York outside the walls.

The length of suitable shore for shipping purposes which the city of New York possesses is limited. Many operations of commerce cannot be carried on in the northern parts of the island. It may be reckoned upon as certain that the centre of the commercial arrangements of the port will be in the lower part of New York island.

It may be also reckoned upon as certain that everywhere, within a limited distance back from its shores, all the ground will be required for commercial purposes. The amount of land enclosed by this commercial border remaining to be devoted to purposes of habitation will then be comparatively small and will be at a considerable distance north of the commercial centre, probably not nearer on an average than the upper part of the Central Park, which is more than seven miles from the present Custom House. On each side of it, north, south, east, and west, will be warehouses and manufacturing and trading establishments, and, at a little greater distance, wharves and shipping.

The habitable part of New York island will then necessarily be built up with great compactness and will in every part be intersected with streets offering direct communication for the transportation of merchandise between one part of its commercial quarter and another.

If now, again, we look on the Long Island side of the port we find a line of shore ten miles in length which is also adapted to the requirements of shipping. It may be assumed that the land along this shore will be wanted, as well as that along the shore of New York island and for an equal distance back from the water, for mercantile and manufacturing purposes. Supposing that the district thus occupied shall, after a time, reach as far back as the corresponding district on New York island; in the rear of it, (and still at a distance from the commercial centre of the port, not half as great on an average as the Central Park), we find a stretch of ground generally elevated, the higher parts being at an average distance of more than a mile from any point to which merchandise can be brought by water.[29] East of this elevation the ground slopes to the shore, not of a harbor or navigable river, but of the ocean itself. A shore in the highest degree attractive to those seeking recreation or health but offering no advantages for shipping, manufacturing or mercantile purposes. At present this slope is occupied chiefly by country seats, and the habitations of gardeners and farmers, and only through the most perverse neglect of the landowners of their own interests is it likely to be built upon for other purposes.

The Opportunity of Brooklyn.

Here, then, there is ample room for an extension of the habitation part of the metropolis upon a plan fully adapted to the most intelligent requirements of modern town life. A large part of the elevated land which has been referred to lies not more than half as far from the commercial centre as the habitation district of New York island, the ground is better formed with reference to sanitary considerations; it is open to the sea breezes and lies in full view of the ocean; it can never be enclosed on all sides by commerce as the habitable part of New York island soon will be; and, its immediate back country being bounded by the sea, the commercial traffic through it is always likely to be light and will be easily provided for in a few special channels. Thus it seems set apart and guarded by nature as a place for the tranquil habitation of those whom the business of the world requires should reside within convenient access of the waters of New York harbor.

It does not follow, however, that it will be so occupied. In the drift of the population of towns it is generally found that natural advantages alone go for but little, and except in the part controlled by your Commission no other arrangements as yet exist with reference to the convenience, health, and pleasure of residents upon this land than such as would have been formed if it were desired to invite to it nothing but factories, ship yards, or the warehouses and offices of merchants. One or two streets were laid out through it some years ago with an avowed intention of being especially adapted to residences;[30] they were so designed however, as to offer every advantage to commercial transportation and consequently for shops and factories but, except in mere width, without intelligent regard to the alleged purpose in view. They are nevertheless adapted to serve an important purpose in concentrating such commercial traffic as must pass through their neighborhoods and in furnishing sites for shops and public buildings which will in any case be needed to meet local requirements.

Upon the manner in which there are good grounds for confidence that the elevated district which has been indicated will be occupied in the future, depends the valuation which can justly and sagaciously be now placed upon it, and upon this valuation mainly depends the financial prosperity of the city of Brooklyn.

How the Opportunity May be Misused and how Availed of.

It would be a perfectly simple problem to cause this land to be given up in a few years almost exclusively to shanties, stables, breweries, distilleries, and swine-yards, and eventually to make the greater part of it a district corresponding, in the larger metropolis which is hereafter to exist on the shores of New York harbor, to that which the Five Points has been in the comparatively small town we have known.[31]

The means by which it may be made a more suitable and attractive place of domestic residence than it is possible that any other point of the metropolis ever will be, are equally within command.

Influence of the Park on the Value of Property.

The effect of what has already been done, under the direction of your Commission, has been to more than quadruple the value of a certain portion of this land,[32] and we have thus an expression of the most simple character, in regard to the commercial estimate which, at this period in the history of towns, is placed upon the circumstance of convenient access from a residence to a public pleasure-ground, and upon the sanitary and social advantages of a habitation thus situated. The advance in value, in this case, is quite marked at a distance of a mile, and this local advantage has certainly not been attended by any falling back in the value of other land in Brooklyn.

If we analyze the conditions of this change in value, we shall find that it is not altogether, or even in any large degree, dependent upon mere vicinity to the sylvan and rural attractions of the Park, but in very large part, in the first place, upon the degree in which these attractions can be approached with security from the common annoyances of the streets, and with pleasure in the approach itself. If, for instance, the greater part of the Park were long and narrow in form, other things being equal, the demand for building sites, fronting on this portion of it, would not, probably, be appreciably less than for those fronting on the broader part. Secondly, the advance in value will be found to be largely dependent on the advantages of having near a residence, a place where, without reference to the sylvan attractions found in a large park, driving, riding, and walking can be conveniently pursued in association with pleasant people, and without the liability of encountering the unpleasant sights and sounds which must generally accompany those who seek rest, recreation or pleasure in the common streets.

There are other things to be valued in a Park besides these, but these are the main positive advantages which would make the value of a residence, if upon the Park, much greater than if at a distance from it.

How the Advantages of Vicinity to a Park May be Extended.

So far, then, as it is practicable, without an enlargement of the Park in its full breadth and compass, to extend its attractions in these especial respects, so far is it also practicable to enlarge the district within which land will have a correspondingly increased attraction for domestic residences. The further the process can be carried, the more will Brooklyn, as a whole, become desirable as a place of residence, the higher will be the valuation of land, on an average, within the city, and the lighter will be the financial burden of the Corporation.

Example of a Fourth Stage of Street Arrangements.

We come, then, to the question of the means by which such an extension can be accomplished. Although no perfect example can be referred to, there have been in Europe a few works by which a similar end, to a certain extent, has been reached. Of these, the most notable is the Avenue of the Empress, in Paris, which connects a palace and a pleasure-ground within the town, with a large park situated far out in the suburbs. This avenue, with its planted border, occupies so much ground (it is 429 feet in width) that it may be considered to constitute rather an intermediate pleasure-ground than a part of the general street system. It is lined with a series of detached villa residences, and building-lots facing upon it are much more valuable than those facing upon the Park.[33]

The celebrated Linden Avenue, at Berlin,[34] leads likewise from a palace and palace grounds, to a great rural park on the opposite side of the town, through the very midst of which it passes. The finest private residences and hotels of the town, as well as many public buildings, such as Art Galleries and Museums, front upon it, and it is equally convenient for all the ordinary purposes of a street with any other. It nevertheless differs essentially from an ordinary business street, in that the process which we have described, by which wagon-ways were introduced into the old streets, has been carried one step further, the wagon-way having itself been divided as the foot-way formerly was, and a space of ground having been introduced, within which there is a shaded walk or mall, and a bridle-road, with strips of turf and trees.

The Parkway. — A Fifth Stage.

The "Parkway" plan which we now propose advances still another step, the mall being again divided into two parts to make room for a central road-way, prepared with express reference to pleasure-riding and driving, the ordinary paved, traffic road-ways, with their flagged sidewalks remaining still on the outside of the public mall for pedestrians, as in the Berlin example. The plan in this way provides for each of the several requirements which we

Avenue de l'Impératrice, Paris

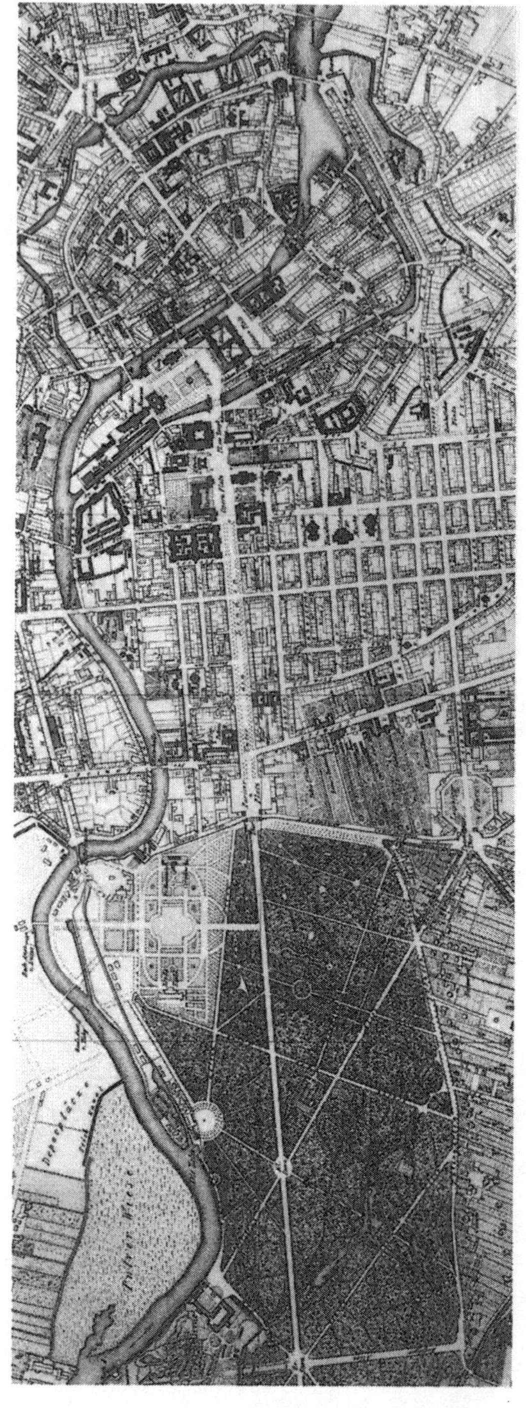

Plan of Unter den Linden and Thiergarten, Berlin

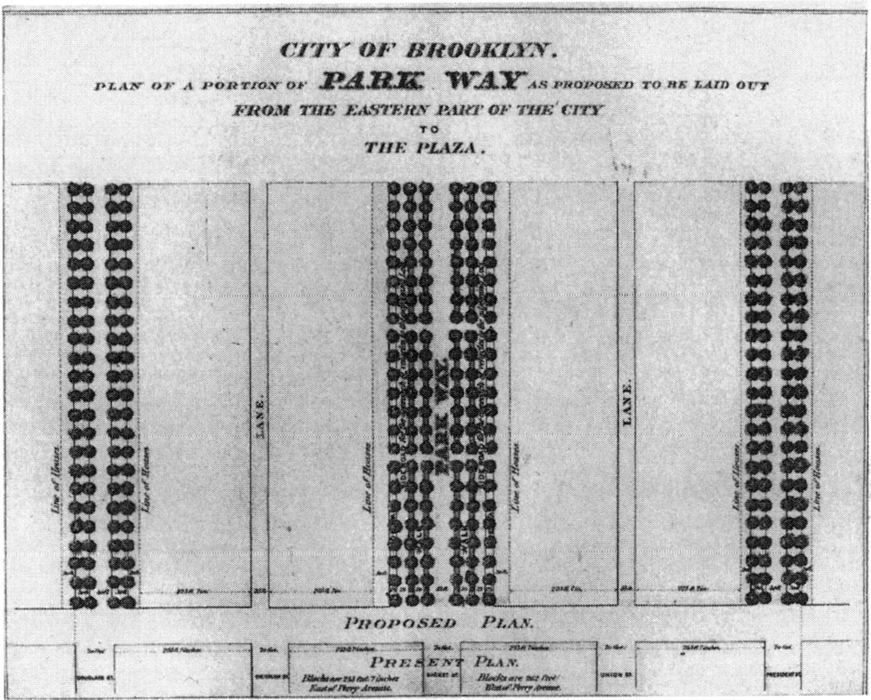

OLMSTED, VAUX & CO., PLAN FOR PARKWAY IN BROOKLYN, 1868

have thus far examined, giving access for the purposes of ordinary traffic to all the houses that front upon it, offering a special road for driving and riding without turning commercial vehicles from the right of way, and furnishing ample public walks, with room for seats, and with borders of turf in which trees may grow of the most stately character. It would contain six rows of trees, and the space from house to house being two hundred and sixty feet, would constitute a perfect barrier to the progress of fire.

PRACTICABLE FUTURE EXTENSIONS OF THE PARKWAY.

With modifications to adapt it to variations of the topography and the connecting street arrangements, the plan should eventually be extended from the Park, in one direction, to Fort Hamilton, where ground for a small Marine Promenade should be secured, overlooking the Narrows and the Bay; and in the other to Ravenswood, where it should be connected by a bridge with one of the broad streets leading on the New York side to the Central Park. A branch should extend from it to the ocean beach at Coney Island, and other branches might lead out from it to any points at which it should appear that large dwelling quarters were likely to be formed, at such a distance from the main stem that access to it from them would otherwise be inconvenient.

There are scarcely any houses at present standing on the general line indicated and it would pass nearly parallel to, and be everywhere within from fifteen to thirty minutes walk of the wharves of the East River. The distance between its extreme points would be about ten miles and the average distance of residences upon it from Wall Street would be about half the distance to the Central Park. Spacious and healthful accommodations for a population of 500,000 could be made within ten minutes walk of this Parkway.

PLAN OF THE PARKWAY NEIGHBORHOOD.

Our plan, it will be observed, covers more ground than is necessarily required to be taken for the purposes which have been indicated. The object of this is that in addition to providing for an enlargement of the Park advantages, throughout its whole extent, the Parkway may also constitute the centre of a continuous neighborhood of residences of a more than usually open, elegant, and healthy character. It is believed that such a neighborhood would not merely be more attractive, to the prosperous class generally, of the metropolis, than any which can be elsewhere formed within a much greater distance from the commercial centre, but that it will especially meet the requirements of an element in the community that is constantly growing larger and that is influenced by associations and natural tastes that unquestionably deserve to be fostered and encouraged. A typical case, for the sake of illustrating the class in view may be thus presented. A country boy receives a common school education, exhibits ability and at a comparatively early age finds himself engaged in business in a provincial town; as his experience and capacity increase, he seeks enlarged opportunities for the exercise of his powers and being of superior calibre, ultimately finds himself drawn by an irresistible magnetic force to the commercial cities; here he succeeds in becoming wealthy by close attention to his specialty and the sharp country boy becomes the keen city man. Trees and grass are, however, wrought into the very texture and fibre of his constitution and without being aware of it, he feels day by day that his life needs a suggestion of the old country flavor to make it palatable as well as profitable. This is one aspect of the natural phenomena with which we are now attempting to deal; no broad question of country life in comparison with city life is involved; it is confessedly a question of delicate adjustment, but we feel confident that whenever and wherever, in the vicinity of New York, this delicate adjustment is best attended to, and the real needs of these city-bred country boys are most judiciously considered, there they will certainly throng. We do not of course mean to argue that the tastes to which we have referred are limited solely to citizens whose early life has been passed in the country, but only that the existence of the special social element thus typified gives one of the many assurances that such a scheme as the proposed Parkway neighborhood would be successful, if judiciously carried out within the lines suggested, before the demand is more or less perfectly met in some other locality.

It is clear that the house lots facing on the proposed Parkway would be desirable, and we assume that the most profitable arrangement would be to make them, say 100 feet wide, and of the full depth between two streets, convenient sites for stables being thus provided. The usual effect of such a plan of operations would be an occupation of the rear street by houses of inferior class, and it is with a view of avoiding any such unsatisfactory result that the design is extended over four blocks of ground. If the two outermost streets are widened to 100 feet and sidewalks shaded by double rows of trees introduced in connection with them, the house lots on these streets will be but little inferior to those immediately facing the Parkway, for they also will be of unusual depth and will be supplied with stable lots that can be entered from the street already mentioned, which should be made suitable for its special purpose, and with the idea that it is only to be occupied by such buildings as may be required in connection with the large lots which are intended to be arranged throughout back to back, with the stable street between them.

Thus, so far as this arrangement should be extended, there would be a series of lots adapted to be occupied by detached villas each in the midst of a small private garden. This arrangement would offer the largest advantages possible to be secured in a town residence, and there is no good reason why they should not be of a permanent character. With the modern advantages for locomotion which would be available, the departure from the old-fashioned compactness of towns might be carried to this extent, in that part of them devoted to residences, without any serious inconvenience. The unwholesome fashion of packing dwelling-houses closely in blocks grew, as we have shown, out of the defensive requirements of old towns; it may possibly be necessary to continue it under certain circumstances, as, for the reasons already indicated, on the island of New York, but where there is no necessary boundary, either natural or artificial, to the space which is to be occupied by buildings, as is the case with Brooklyn, it is, to say the least, unwise to persist in arrangements which will permanently prevent any indulgence of this kind.

Those who availed themselves of the opportunity here proposed to be offered would not benefit themselves alone, but the whole community. The Romans seem to have been wiser than we have been in this particular. Rich people were offered every facility for surrounding their houses with open garden spaces, and the larger part of the Eternal City was composed of what we should now term detached villas, while in no part was it permitted that a new house, even though intended for the residence of slaves, should be built within five feet of walls previously erected.[35]

How far it might be desirable for property-owners to extend the plan in the peculiar form suggested, is, of course, an open question, depending on the anticipated demand for lots of the size indicated, but it will be readily seen that as the proposed subdivisions are not of the ordinary contracted character, a comparatively small number of residents will suffice to fill up a considerable stretch of ground laid out in this way, and it is also evident that if, within a reasonable time, it should become certain that a specific number of blocks would be carried out on this plan, the lots included within the boundaries determined on would not require to be improved in regular succession, but would be selected with reference to slight, fancied advantages anywhere along the line, every purchaser feeling satisfied that the main question of good neighborhood had been settled on a satisfactory basis at the outset.

Advantages of the Parkway Likely to be Secured to Brooklyn Exclusively.

Having so fully described, in its principal aspects, the question of the desirability of developing, in Brooklyn, a plan of public improvement of the general character indicated, it may be proper for us to enquire whether the broad streets which are proposed to be opened on New York island under the name of Boulevards during the next few years, are calculated to interfere with the probable success of such a scheme.

While the Central Park was in its earlier stages of progress, a Commission was appointed to prepare a plan for laying out the upper end of New York island, and some years later this responsibility was transferred to the Central Park Commission, whose plan is published in their last annual report.[36]

The same document contains an elaborate discussion of the subject by Mr. A. H. Green, on the part of the Board, and as our professional relations with the Commissioners have not been extended over this department of their work, and we are not aware of their intention in regard to this improvement, except so far as it is set forth in the plan and public statement above mentioned, we make, for the purposes of this Report, the subjoined quotation, which sets forth clearly the limitations that are to be recognized in New York as controlling the designs of the Commissioners:

"We occasionally, in some country city, see a wide street ornamented with umbrageous trees, having spaces of green interposed in its area, the portion used for travel being very limited. This arrangement is only possible where thronging population and crowding commerce are not at liberty to overlay and smother the laws that are made to secure the legitimate use of the public streets. It would seem inexpedient, at any rate, until some better permanent administration of our streets is secured, to attempt these fanciful arrangements to any great extent in a commercial city, under our form of government."[37]

It is clear, therefore, that the Central Park Commissioners have no intention of carrying out, in New York, any such scheme as the "Parkway," and consequently, if, as we believe, the requirements that such a plan is designed to meet are already felt to exist in this community, Brooklyn can soon be made to offer some special advantages as a place of residence to that portion of our more wealthy and influential citizens, whose temperament, taste or education leads them to seek for a certain amount of rural satisfaction in connection with their city homes.

Although the plots of ground appropriated to the Brooklyn and Central Parks are entirely different in shape, while their landscape opportunities and general possibilities of design are equally dissimilar, a generic family resemblance will yet be found between the two pleasure-grounds, simple because they are both called into existence to meet the same class of wants, in the same class of people, at the same Metropolitan centre.

The Brooklyn Parkway, on the other hand, will, if executed, be a practical development of the ideas set forth in this Report, which seem to be particularly applicable to the city of Brooklyn, and which, as we have shown, are considered by those in authority to be unsuitable for development in the city of New York; it will consequently have no such family resemblance to the New York Boulevards as exists between the two parks, and its attractions will, for a time, at any rate, be of a special and somewhat individual character.

In pursuing the general question of approaches to the Park, in accordance with your instructions, we have thus been led to the examination of some other scarcely less important topics, and although the consideration of such problems as those we have adverted to can only come before your Commission in an indirect and incidental way, we have thought it best to lay the results of our study thus fully before you, because during the investigations and consultations of the past year it has become more and more evident that the early adoption of some such scheme as the "Parkway" would have the effect of adding very greatly to the advantages which your Commission is endeavoring to secure to the citizens of Brooklyn in the construction of the Park.

Respectfully,

OLMSTED, VAUX & CO.,
Landscape Architects and Superintendents.

The text published here is taken from the Board of Commissioners of Prospect Park, *Eighth Annual Report* (Brooklyn, 1868), pages 29–56. A separate edition, without the first few pages dealing with the process of construction of Prospect Park, was published in 1868, apparently by the park commissioners, with the title *Observations on the Progress of Improvements in Street Plans. With Special Reference to The Park-Way Proposed to be Laid Out in Brooklyn.* It contained a prefatory note by Olmsted, Vaux & Company indicating the subject matter of the publication.

During 1868 the Prospect Park commissioners were attempting to secure authority from the legislature to direct the laying out of streets in Kings County outside the city of Brooklyn. This authority was needed in order to carry out the full system of parkways envisioned by Olmsted and Vaux in this report. The separate publication of this report was presumably part of the commissioners' campaign. They failed to secure the desired legislation during 1868, and the next year the legislature instead authorized the supervisors of the towns in Kings County to lay out the streets and roads there. However, on May 6, 1868, the legislature did authorize the Prospect Park commissioners to widen Sackett Street to 210 feet, thus providing for construction of Eastern Parkway following the plan by Olmsted, Vaux & Company included in this report. The parkway ran two miles east to the city boundary. On May 15 the legislature also authorized the Prospect Park commissioners to widen the Coney Island Plank Road in Kings County by 40 feet, which made possible the construction of Ocean Parkway. Both parkways were constructed in a straight line, instead of following the curvilinear course that Olmsted and Vaux had anticipated in previous descriptions of parkways for Brooklyn. In their report of 1866, published above, they had described a "shaded pleasure drive" that would have a "picturesque character" and would be "neither very straight nor very level." In their report to the Prospect Park commissioners of 1867, they proposed an avenue running from the eastern entrance of Prospect Park along the city line to the Ridgewood reservoir. "The route suggested," they observed, "would make frequent curves and considerable inequalities of surface desirable . . ." (BPC, *Annual Reports, 1861–1873*, pp. 157–58, 251–52; New York [State], *Laws of the State of New York, Passed at the Ninety-Second Session of the Legislature . . .* [Albany, N.Y., 1869], chap. 670; see page 105 above; Olmsted, Vaux & Co., "Report of the Landscape Architects & Superintendents," Jan. 1, 1867 [*Papers of FLO*, 6: 157]).

1. The president of the Board of Commissioners of Prospect Park was James S. T. Stranahan (BPC, *Annual Reports, 1861–1873*, p. 154).
2. Joseph Phineas Davis (1837–1917) a civil engineer, graduated from Rensselaer Polytechnic Institute in 1856. He immediately went to work for the city of Brooklyn and assisted in the construction of the Brooklyn waterworks. After serving in the U.S. Army during the Civil War, Davis returned to Brooklyn and from 1866 to 1867 he worked with Olmsted and Calvert Vaux on the construction of Prospect Park as chief engineer. His successor at Prospect Park was Charles Cyril Martin (1831–1903), who held the position until 1870 (*NCAB*; *Papers of FLO*, 6: 162, n. 26; ibid., 6: 271, n. 10; see also, FLO, "Paper on the Back Bay Problem and its Solution," April 2, 1886, n. 14, below).
3. The commissioners of the park were still attempting to acquire a twelve-block area along Ninth Avenue between 3rd and 15th streets, an area essential for creation of the Long Meadow (BPC, *Annual Reports, 1861–1873*, pp. 155–56; see OVC, *Preliminary Report to the Commissioners for Laying Out a Park in Brooklyn, New York,* Jan. 24, 1866, n. 5, above).
4. The largest section of the land acquired by the commission in June 1867 was the flat area that became the site of Prospect Lake.
5. The carriage concourse on what is now called Breeze Hill, overlooking the Concert Grove between the Cleft Ridge Span and Terrace Bridge. At this time the shape of the concourse was elongated and its size slightly enlarged. The 1874 plan reproduced

on page 666 of volume 6 of the Olmsted Papers shows the shape of the concourse as it was revised in 1868.

6. Olmsted and Vaux planned this playground as part of the "children's ground" that included a small pool in the dell that later came to be called the Vale of Cashmere. Both the pool and the playground appear for the first time on the 1868 plan of the park. The playground was on high ground between the pool and Flatbush Avenue, opposite the residential blocks just south of the reservoir indicated by "R" on the 1866 Prospect Park plan (page 327 above). Within two years Olmsted and Vaux designed a similar playground for the Parade in Buffalo, containing a trapeze, horizontal bars, horses, parallel bars, giant strides, ships, see-saws and swings, an aviary, a carrousel and a "Bear Pit." In 1895–96 the playground in Prospect Park was redesigned as a rose garden by Rudolph Ulrich, superintendent of the park (*Papers of FLO*, 6: 327, 430; Joy M. Kestenbaum, "Chronology of Prospect Park Perimeter" [1983]).

7. The Assistant Engineers in Charge of Prospect Park, John Bogart (1836–1920) and John Y. Culyer (1839–1924), both of whom had previously worked with Olmsted on Central Park (BPC, *Annual Reports, 1861–1873*, p. 154; *Papers of FLO*, 6: 162, nn. 24 and 25).

8. The two archways under construction were Endale Arch at the north end of the Long Meadow and East Wood Arch near the Willink Entrance on Flatbush Avenue. The other architectural features must have included the Thatched Shelter near the principal entrance and the vine-covered trellis overlooking the children's ground, which were completed during the next year (J. M. Kestenbaum, "Chronology of Prospect Park Perimeter"; BPC, *Annual Reports, 1861–1873*, pp. 258–59).

9. Edward C. Miller (1811–1872), who worked for Olmsted on Central Park before the Civil War, assisted him as a surveyor on several commissions in California in 1864–65, and then worked for the firm of Olmsted, Vaux & Company until taking the position of Assistant Architect on Prospect Park in 1867 (*Papers of FLO*, 5: 299, 398–401; ibid., 6: 272).

10. The keepers force consisted of fourteen keepers, who were assisted during periods of heavy park use by forty-eight gardeners (BPC, *Annual Reports, 1861–1873*, pp. 160–61, 170–72, 221).

11. John Culyer reported that from October 20 to December 31, 1867, the park was visited by 42,089 carriages, 9,766 equestrians, and 54,242 pedestrians, making a total visitation that he calculated at 180,868 persons (ibid., p. 222).

12. In his "Preliminary Report on Boundaries" of February 1865, Calvert Vaux had proposed creation of an entrance area enclosed by two crescent-shaped mounds at the intersection of Ninth Avenue and Flatbush Avenue. The first published plan for the park by Olmsted, Vaux & Company, which accompanied its report of January 24, 1866, showed this arrangement and proposed circles at four other entrances. The City of Brooklyn acquired the additional land needed for the plaza on February 4, 1866, and the area for the entrance circles was included in the expansion of the park authorized by the legislature on April 30, 1866 (J. M. Kestenbaum, "Chronology of Prospect Park Perimeter"; BPC, *Annual Reports, 1861–1873*, pp. 130–31).

13. See pages 105–6 above.

14. The text of this report is published in *Papers of FLO*, 6: 157–59.

15. Presumably a reference to the commissioners' publication of the report by Olmsted, Vaux & Company of January 1, 1867, in their *Seventh Annual Report*.

16. A topographical survey of the land east of Flatbush Avenue was being carried out under the direction of John Bogart (BPC, *Annual Reports, 1861–1873*, pp. 146, 210).

17. The Union Pacific Railroad, which received large grants of land from the National Domain along its route, engaged in extensive townsite planning and promotion, as did numerous transcontinental and western railroads thereafter. The streets of these

towns were almost universally laid out in a simple grid pattern (John W. Reps, *The Forgotten Frontier: Urban Planning in the American West Before 1890* [Columbia, Mo., 1981], pp. 76–81).

18. A reference to la Croisée de Paris, two streets crossing in the center of Paris that were paved with flagstones at the command of King Philip Augustus circa 1184 (*The History of Paris from the Earliest Period to the Present Day . . .*, 3 vols. [London, 1827], 3: 183).

19. A reference to the plague epidemic in London of 1665 (Nathaniel Hodges, *Loimologia: or, An Historical Account of the Plague in London in 1665 . . .* [London, 1720], pp. 19–20).

20. A description of the Great Fire of London of 1666 (Samuel Pepys, *Diary and Correspondence of Samuel Pepys . . .*, 5 vols. [London, 1848–49], 3: 276–77).

21. Olmsted is referring to the plan of London drawn up after the Great Fire by Christopher Wren (see FLO, "Public Parks and the Enlargement of Towns," Feb. 25, 1870, n. 20, below).

22. The period during which royal proclamations such as those described by Olmsted were most commonly issued not after the Great Fire of 1666, but rather during the reigns of James I and Charles I: see especially proclamations by James I of September 16, 1603, October 24, 1614, December 9, 1615, July 17, 1620, and November 20, 1622, and by Charles I of May 2, 1625, and July 16, 1630 (James Ludovic Lindsay Crawford, *A Bibliography of Royal Proclamations of the Tudor and Stuart Sovereigns and of Others Published under Authority, 1485–1714. With an Historical Essay on Their Origin and Use, by Robert Steele,* 2 vols. [Oxford, 1910], 1: 111, 136, 139, 152, 159, 167, 190–91).

23. Numerous laws passed in the reigns of George II and George III provided for rerouting and paving streets in greater London. Of special note is the act of 1760 for opening and widening streets in the City of London and its suburbs. The act provided for the demolition of many houses in order to create new passages ranging from twenty to fifty feet wide in a dozen wards (Great Britain, Laws, statues, etc., 1727–1760 [George II], *Anno Regni Georgii II . . . Tricesimo Tertio . . .* [London, 1760], pp. 487–516).

24. The editors have not been able to identify the sanitary improvements carried out by French engineers in Cairo prior to 1868 to which Olmsted makes reference here.

25. Olmsted had experienced the role of the telegraph in conducting business over long distances when he was manager of the Mariposa Estate in California in 1863–65. During that period the telegraph could convey information between New York and San Francisco in one or two days rather than the month needed either by land or water routes. As soon as he arrived on the estate, Olmsted made arrangements to extend the telegraph the more than one hundred miles from San Francisco to his offices at Bear Valley, but the line was not constructed during the time he spent there (*Papers of FLO*, 5: 10).

26. According to leading public health authorities of the time, the breathing of each person exhausted the oxygen in 14 cubic feet of air each hour, and in the process each person exhaled sufficient carbonic acid to vitiate dangerously some 100 cubic feet of air (Citizens' Association of New York. Council of Hygiene and Public Health, *Report of the Council of Hygiene and Public Health of the Citizens' Association of New York upon the Sanitary Condition of the City* [New York, 1865], pp. xc, 257–58).

27. Since the 1850s there had been a proliferation of light, spring-suspension carriages, which was encouraged by the construction of public carriage drives such as those in Central and Prospect parks (Ezra M. Stratton, *The World on Wheels; or, Carriages, with Their Historical Associations from the Earliest to the Present Time . . .* [New York, 1878], pp. 449–67).

28. That is, flagstones.

29. A reference to Harbor Hill Moraine, which ran from east to west along the southern boundary of the City of Brooklyn.
30. Presumably a reference to Flatbush and Fulton avenues.
31. The Five Points area on Manhattan's lower East Side was legendary for the squalor of its tenements and noted as a center for the criminal element of the city (Charles Lockwood, *Manhattan Moves Uptown: An Illustrated History* [Boston, 1976], pp. 108–10).
32. It is unclear what particular area Olmsted had in mind in making this assertion. At this time the park commission was proudly pointing to the fact that the assessed value of real estate in the entire Eighth Ward, which adjoined the park, had increased from $4,913,274 in 1864 to $7,983,200 in 1867, an increase of 60 percent (BPC, *Annual Reports, 1861–1873*, p. 164).
33. The Avenue de l'Imperatrice in Paris ran between the Arc de Triomphe and the Bois de Boulogne, a distance of nearly a mile. It served as an extension of the Avenue des Champs Elysées, which connected the Place de l'Etoile with the royal palace of the Louvre and its attendant Tuileries gardens. The Avenue de l'Imperatrice was laid out under the direction of Baron Haussmann as one of the civic improvements initiated by Napoleon III between 1850 and 1870. In the center of the avenue was a drive for carriages sixteen meters wide with a path for pedestrians on one side and a bridle path on the other, each twelve meters wide. The only separation between these three ways for different modes of travel was the gutters of the carriage drive: it thus lacked the separation of ways by means of planted medians with trees and grass that characterized the parkways designed by Olmsted and Vaux. On either side of the three ways was a strip thirty-one meters wide planted with grass and trees. Outside of each of these ran a service drive six meters wide flanked by two sidewalks one and one-half meters in width. Outside of these was a strip ten meters wide densely planted with shrubs and ornamental plantings. The total width of the avenue was one-hundred-forty meters, or 460 feet (Jean-Charles-Adolphe Alphand, *Les Promenades de Paris* [1867–73, rpt. ed., Princeton, N.J., 1984]).
34. Unter den Linden in Berlin, which ran between the Emperor's palace and the Brandenburg Gate, beyond which was the extensive Thiergarten. Unter den Linden had a central carriage drive flanked by two double rows of trees (Henry Vizetelly, *Berlin under the New Empire . . .*, 2 vols. [1879; rpt. ed., New York, 1968], 1: 177–94).
35. Olmsted's source is probably the *Annals* of Tacitus, 42–43, which describes the rebuilding of Rome under Nero following the disastrous fire of A.D. 64. Tacitus reports that Nero offered rewards for rapid construction of new houses, and that each building was to be free-standing and not attached to the walls of its neighbors. Historians have determined, however, that only a small proportion of the buildings of Rome were single-family villas. Most were multi-family apartment structures or *insulae* (Jérôme Carcopino, *Daily Life in Ancient Rome: The People and the City at the Height of the Empire*, ed. Henry T. Rowell and trans. E. O. Lorimer [New Haven, Conn., 1940], pp. 23–24).
36. In April 1860 the New York state legislature created a seven-member commission to lay out the streets of Manhattan above 155th Street, an area that had been beyond the jurisdiction of the Commission of 1811 that created the gridiron street pattern between 14th and 155th streets. Olmsted and Calvert Vaux were appointed "Landscape Architects & designers" to this commission, which presented no official plan before going out of existence in 1865. In 1865 the legislature authorized the board of commissioners of Central Park to lay out the area above 155th Street. As Olmsted testifies here, the commissioners did not seek the assistance of Olmsted and Vaux in this task, although they had been appointed in July 1865 as landscape architects to the board. Instead, Andrew H. Green, the controller of the board and one of its most

powerful members, took the lead in planning the new street system. On January 11, 1866, he submitted a long report to the commissioners proposing an approach to planning the streets as ordered by the legislature ([FLO] to Henry H. Elliott, [Aug. 27, 1860] [*Papers of FLO*, 3: 259–67]; BCCP, *Ninth Annual Report* [1866], p. 52; "Document No. 3," in BCCP, *Minutes*, Jan. 11, 1866, pp. 1–75).

37. Olmsted is quoting from Andrew H. Green's report to the Central Park board (ibid., p. 64).

Address to {the} Prospect Park Scientific Association

[May 1868]

You have asked me to talk to you upon the subject of the treatment of natural woods with reference to park purposes. There is a difficulty which always stands in the way of useful debate of any of the elements by which our work here is distinguished from the great body of works in which the principles of engineering science and architectural art are more especially applied. A difficulty which arises from the insufficiency and chiefly from the looseness & vagueness of the nomenclature of the class of works in question we are prevented from comparing ideas, prevented from elaborating ideas by mutual efforts, prevented from giving & recvg instruction, by the want of words which are certain to call up in the minds of all of us or of any two of us, the same images or ideas. This arises from the fact that hitherto, there has been little occasion for exact discussion; that so far as works of this kind have been carried on at all they have been carried on without much careful thought, or at least without the benefit of exact thought in many minds. There has been but little criticism; little debate consequently little explanation or occasion for explanation of the principles of science & art upon which they are designed. In fact, public works of this class are new in the world. There have been public parks before now certainly, but till quite lately the construction of those parks has not been pursued fully & fairly as a public work, open to general, thorough & searching criticism, to anything like professional scientific criticism. Responsibility for these works has not been felt to be a responsibility to the public. Accountability has been felt only to some individual or to some few individuals and provided their intentions were realized, provided they were gratified, criticism of them has been regarded as nobody else's business. There has been no interest therefore demanding & leading to anything like precise, exact & searching debate & consequently precision of thought & clear means of expressing precise & thorough thought has not been developed.

Thus a necessity exists in the discussion of such a topic for instance as this we have in hand, to use a great deal of circumlocution or to dwell a great deal upon elementary ideas & to define elementary terms. I must do so or I shall be liable to convey impressions to you very different from those I wish you to recve. To reach good results our process must be studious, elaborate, slow, perhaps tedious.

Take this term, park purposes. What are we to understand by it. It is your business to plan and superintend constructions in which the materials of the earth's surface, clay, sand & stone, are to be largely & scientifically dealt with. You are called upon in your professional capacity to provide a certain town with a park as you might be to provide it with water-works, bridges, docks or canals. What is the idea your clients have when they demand of you a park? To begin let us say, they want a place of recreation? But that is a very insufficient definition. A theatre is a place of recreation, so is a flower garden, so is a conservatory. The vacant lots between X & XI av. & 3ᵈ & 9ᵗʰ St have been a place of recreation; of out of door recreation, for a long time, both the wooded parts & the open. But now we are asked to take this land & more & make a park of it. How shall we get at what it is they want? Where did they get the word? It is an English word and we must go to England if we would know to what it has been formerly applied. There are several thousand pieces of ground which for many centuries have been called parks — some of which were called parks at the period when more especially the English language was consolidated. The term park was not used to distinguish them as places set apart or fitted especially for recreation, certainly not for any kind of recreation that your modern townspeople want ground to be set apart & prepared for. What then is their common characteristic? In what did the park differ from other divisions of ground?

What was the *common quality* they possessed which made it necessary that they should have a *common designation*? They were not public properties but when the state of society was yet essentially barbarous were selected and taken possession of, prized, fought for & held solely by the rich and powerful — and when society became better organized and less rude, these same pieces of ground still remained a peculiar possession of the more fortunate and arrogant, who had residencies in the midst of them. It continued the same through all the changes of manners and customs, the increase of luxury and the progress of refinement to the present day when at length we find people who cannot have a park for a private possession uniting with others to obtain one which can be used in common. Why should the particular pieces of land to which the term park was first applied have been regarded as choice & peculiarly desireable possessions for so long a time & by men of such very different wants & habits? Pretty certainly, it appears to me, because of some topographical conditions in which they originally differed from other pieces of land, which topographical conditions have all the time been found peculiarly convenient for the indulgence of certain propensities which are a part of human nature and which the progress of civilization does not affect, as it does mere manners & customs.

To illustrate and more fully fix in your minds this hypothesis, I shall narrate to you a personal experience. When I was a young man I made a long journey through England on foot, in company with my brother, in the course of which we became very familiar with the finest & most characteristic park scenery. A few years afterwards my brother & I started to go overland by the Southern or Gila route to the Pacific. On account of the outbreak of an Indian war and the refusal of parties which we had expected to join to take the risk without military escort which could not be spared us, we were compelled to wait on the frontier during a period of several months. We undertook therefore, for our amusement and information an exploration of so much of the country beyond settlements as it was at all safe for us to cruise in, as well as some of the border land a little beyond the line of safety and of the other border a little within the line of outermost settlement.[1]

Travelling with a pack-mule and for the most part living on the country, being in no haste, we usually broke camp about 9 $^{o'ck}$, and soon after noon began to look out for a new camping ground. That is to say if at any time after noon we saw a promise anywhere to the right or left or right ahead of certain topographical conditions, we moved in that direction, and whenever we came upon a site which was particularly satisfactory to us as a place for camping, though it was but just after noon, there we would end our day's march. If we found nothing satisfactory we would keep on till dusk, and then do the best we could. If we were fortunate in this respect on Saturday we generally rested on Sunday, and sometimes at a camp that particularly pleased us laid up for several days, it being our object to keep our stock in good condition. Thus I may say that it was our chief business for some months to study the topography of the country more especially with reference to the selection of satisfactory camping places. Now with fresh recollections of the old country parks[2] we found that the topographical conditions which we were accustomed to look for were such that we sometimes questioned whether if an Englishman had been brought blindfolded to our tent, and the scene disclosed to him he would be readily persuaded that he was not in some one of those old parks.[3] Yet I need not say the conditions were perfectly natural, that no Engineer or gardener had had a hand in fashioning them — nay I suppose that sometimes no white man ever had before been on the ground.

What then were the governing circumstances of our selection?

First, we wanted good, clear water close at hand, both for bathing and for drinking.

2^d good pasturage in which with little labor or care to us we could keep our cattle in good condition.

3^d wood at convenient distance, both small wood to readily kindle up, and logs to keep the fire through the night.

4th We preferred seclusion, partly because in seclusion there was greater safety for though we did not fear the Indians or Border ruffians by day light, the chance of an attempt to steal our horses at night was just enough to make us feel a little more comfortable if our situation was a somewhat cosy one. When at the greatest distance from settlements the danger was sufficient to induce us to shift camp after cooking our supper lest the fire should have advertised us too closely. Partly for this reason we preferred seclusion, and partly because we were frequently visited after nightfall by the sudden blast of a norther, in which case an elevated or exposed position was far from com-

fortable either for us or our horses, which whatever the range we gave them during daylight were always staked within close pistol shot of our bed at nightfall.

5th We liked to have game near at hand, and

6th We made it a point to secure if possible as much beauty as possible in the view from our tent door.

This last brings us to the question: What is the beautiful? but it is a question which we {will} not here discuss. I only wish you to observe that the beauty which we enjoyed in this case depended on elements of topography of a very simple character. I assume that such beauty of scenery gives pleasure even to savages.

Now, if you think of it, you will see that all these conditions of a pleasant camp would also be the conditions of a pleasant family residence of a more permanent character, provided that the wants of the family were very simple or rude, provided, i.e. it was not greatly dependent for its comfort on the labor of others; provided it was prepared to live mainly within itself as the phrase is.

In fact we found that wherever the pioneers were settling in this country, they were selecting just such places[4] & plainly because the less artificial wants of men were in such situations more conveniently provided for, provided for with less exertion, effort and anxiety of mind, than in any other. For example, in such a situation it would be easy to get water when wanted, easy to get wood when wanted, easy to find shelter from wind, easy to find shelter from sun, easy to make shelter from rain, easy to spy game at a distance, easy to enclose stock, easy to keep watch of stock, when turned out, easy to follow stock when strayed, easy for stock when turned out to find good grazing, water & shelter, easy, if desired, to enclose land, to cultivate it, &, to house the crops from it.[5]

In one word the topography of such a situation is of a character which suggests to an observer an easy gratification of a great variety of the elementary human impulses and thus, leaving out of consideration entirely the impulse to associate or marry with that quality of natural objects whatever it is which we describe as the beautiful.[6]

And this topography as I have shown is also the characteristic topography of the old parks; this is what a park was, this & nothing more when certain pieces of land were first enclosed & called parks. This gives us, therefore, the original, radical & constant definition of the topography which is wanted to be selected or constructed when a park is called for. I do not mean that this is all of a park, but that an idea of a park centres & grows upon this. If it is an insufficient definition, it is because the condition of ease is merely a negative condition. The absence of obstruction is the condition of ease of movement, and a park as a work of design should be more than this; it should be a ground which invites, encourages & facilitates movement, its topographical conditions such as make movement a pleasure; such as offer inducements in variety, on one side and the other, for easy movement, first by one promise of pleasure then by another, yet all of a simple character & such as appeal to the common & elementary impulses of all classes of mankind.[7] But this quality of ease, must underlie the whole. You must first secure this, and if this is not all, it is at least the framework of all. But is a park, you may ask, a mere study of topography, the work merely of an engineer? I answer that that depends on what limit the engineer chooses to put upon the field of his professional study. My own opinion is that the science of the engineer is never more worthily employed than when it is made to administer to man's want of beauty. When it is carried into works not merely of art but of fine art.

Now Herbert Spencer in an Essay on Gracefulness[8] says:

> grace as applied to motion, describes motion that is effected with an economy of muscular power, grace as applied to animal forms describes forms capable of this economy. Grace as applied to postures, describes postures which may be maintained with this economy, & grace as applied to inanimate objects, describes such as exhibit certain analogies to these attitudes & forms.
>
> That this generalization, if not the whole truth, contains at least a large part of it, will I think become obvious on considering how habitually we couple the words easy & graceful.

Whether the philosophy here is perfect & the analysis final & complete or not, we must admit that the association of ideas pointed out is inevitable; and you will see that by simply substituting the word grace for the word ease in the statement of the conclusions to which we have arrived in our study of the engineering question which we have hitherto had before us, we raise our aim at once into the region of esthetic art.[9] Let us call grace the idealization of ease, and then let us take the final step, and add a positive quality to the negative one of ease or grace, and we shall find ourselves prepared to form what I consider to be the true conception or ideal of a park, in distinction from any other ground, or any other place of recreation.

That is to say we must study to secure a combination of elements which shall invite and stimulate the simplest, purest and most primeval action of the poetic element of human nature, and thus tend to remove those who are affected by it to the greatest possible distance from the highly elaborate, sophistical and artificial conditions of their ordinary civilized life.

Thus it must be that parks are beyond anything else recreative, recreative of that which is most apt to be lost or to become diseased and debilitated among the dwellers in towns.

With reference to construction, or the artificial formation of topography then, we may say that park-purposes means a purpose to make gracefully beautiful in combination with a purpose to make interesting and inviting, or hospitable by the offer of a succession of simple, natural pleasures as a result of easy movements.

These, I mean, are *park*-purposes, primarily, in distinction from all

other pleasure-ground purposes. So far as we are to do anything at the {. . .}
Ground for instance, it is with these purposes we are to do it. If we cannot
make it more graceful, more interesting, more inviting, more convenient,
then we are to do nothing.[10]

It does not follow that all parts of our enclosure should be of this
simple easy flowing topography which I have indicated. Grace like any other
quality which acts upon us through our sense of vision is enhanced by contrast, and if we can employ accessories which will have this effect & at the
same time serve a direct purpose of any value they will be proper and desirable within our enclosure, but they will not be the characteristic features of
the park. It is chiefly important that they do not become of so much relative
importance as to lose their character as accessories.

Rocks for instance may be such accessories so may thick wood, so
may shrubbery. So may buildings, monuments &c but these are not what
make a park; they are not characteristic of it.

The word park as a common noun, as a descriptive word, should
indicate such graceful topography, such open pastoral, inviting hospitable
scenery as I have indicated.

When I speak of the treatment of wood with reference to park purposes, I mean first of all with reference to the production or improvement of
such scenery, & secondly with reference to the production of improvement
of such accessories.

There may be another class of park purposes, of a quite different
character, & to discriminate between the two, you must recollect that the
word park is used as a proper as well as a common noun.

Phoenix Park, for instance is *the* park of Dublin and includes, a vice-
regal palace, with orchards & kitchen gardens; Barracks, a magazine, an arsenal; parks of artillery, & other features which are far from being graceful and
equally far from presenting inducements for an indulgence in simple natural
enjoyments. Yet all of which are a part of what is called the Park when the
word is used as a proper noun, as much as that which, using the word again
as a common noun, is the park itself, which consists of few other elements
than turf and trees.

When we know that such things as barracks, arsenals and buildings
intended solely for domestic or public business purposes, which are wholly
incongruous with the purposes of a park, are referred to under the same general head with turf & trees, we are in no danger of confusing the common &
the proper noun. But there may be accessories of a park, which contribute to
its main purpose by predisposing the mind or removing impediments of the
mind to the kind of recreation which it is adapted to stimulate, as by means
of relief from thirst or hunger or excessive fatigue or shelter from rain and
these may be included under the term park-purposes, even with reference to
topographical construction and artistic design, though in themselves they are
the reverse of graceful or suggestive of easy movement.

And it is possible to add these & many other auxiliaries to the means of accomplishing our primary purposes not only without lessening, but in such a manner as to positively increase the special value of the latter. For the influence of grace of topography like any other quality which influences our minds through the senses is enhanced by contrast.

Elements designed to *increase* park effects by contrast must however be used with caution, lest instead of heightening the impression sought to be primarily produced by certain elements of topography we obscure or confuse them. To this end it is chiefly important that the contrasting circumstances should be unmistakeably auxiliary, subordinate, and accessory in every respect to the general design. This principle & this caution in the application of the principle, applies to the use of woods or trees as well as to more purely constructional objects.

What then is the part; what are the duties, of trees?

Christopher North asks:[11]

But the more important qualities of trees in landscape are those of termination and obscuration of the view of an observer, though the two may be considered as one, for the termination of landscape by trees is effected by a high degree of obscuration.

You will recollect that I used the term hospitable as descriptive of the essential characteristic of park topography, and that while I hinted at a more recondite significance, in the possible appeal of a hospitable landscape to the simplest instincts of our race, I also described this quality of hospitality to consist in conditions which make the ground appear pleasant to wander over. Among such conditions, one will be the absence of anything which should cause severe exertion to the wanderer and another the presence of opportunities for agreeable rest at convenient intervals. Together these conditions imply general openness & simplicity with occasional shelter and shade, which latter will result both from trees and from graceful undulations of the surface.

Bearing in mind this deduced significance of the term hospitable as descriptive of the general character of a park topography, you will see that the more unlimited the degree of hospitality of landscape, the more unmeasured the welcome which the broad face of your park can be made to express, the better will your purpose be fulfilled,[12] and that it follows that all absolute limits should be so screened from view by trees that the imagination will be likely to assume no limit, but only acknowledge obscurity in whatever direction the eye may rove. As, however, to comply with the conditions previously established, the range of clear vision must be constantly limited in most directions, it is desireable that there should be an occasional opportunity of looking upon a view over turf and between trees so extended that even obscurity, that is to say uncertainty of extent, to the hospitable elements of the topography, shall be impossible.

I trust you recognize the paramount importance of these purposes of trees, because ignorance of them or forgetfulness of them or the subordination of them to other purposes of trees is a besetting sin of most planters.

In subordination to them, strictly, strenuously, always & every where within a park, in subordination to them, trees are to be regarded as individuals, and as component parts of groups, which groups are again to be regarded both individually, and in relation one to another as components of landscapes as seen from special points of view.

I hope that you will see that I am not studying a mere word all this time. I want you to see that when people ask for a park, it may be perfectly possible to please them very much with something which is not a park or which is a very poor and much adulterated kind of park and that it would nevertheless be dishonest, quackish, to do so. A park is a work of art, designed to produce certain effects upon the mind of men. There should be nothing in it absolutely nothing — not a foot of surface nor a spear of grass — which does not represent study, design, a sagacious consideration & application of known laws of cause & effect with reference to that end.

The original, a draft in pencil in Olmsted's hand, was discovered by members of the Olmsted Papers staff at the Frederick Law Olmsted National Historic Site, rolled up with plans of the late 1870s for the Twenty-third and Twenty-fourth wards of New York City. On the wrapper is the notation "Ad. to P. Park/Scientific Assoc./May 1868." Olmsted apparently delivered the lecture in response to a request from the "Board of Control of the Park Association" that he deliver an address to them on May 6, 1868, "upon the subject of treatment of natural woodlands for Park purposes or such other subjects as he may select" (Charles C. Martin to FLO, April 8, 1868).

1. In *Walks and Talks of an American Farmer in England*, Olmsted described the first part of his walking tour of 1850 with his brother, John Hull Olmsted, and their friend Charles Loring Brace. In 1853–54 Olmsted and his brother made a five-month horseback journey through Texas, including a two-week trip from San Antonio to San Fernando in Mexico, just beyond the Rio Grande. While returning to San Antonio the brothers encountered a group of armed Lipan Indians near Castroville who committed no violence but put them in the position of "prisoners under escort." A few days later these Indians began a two-year campaign of marauding against white settlers. As they neared San Antonio, the brothers intended to visit an outlying sheep ranch. They changed their plans and learned soon after that on the night they would have spent at the ranch it was attacked by Indians who killed two shepherds (*Papers of FLO*, 2: 294–95, 473–79; Frederick Law Olmsted, *A Journey Through Texas* [New York, 1857], pp. 290–95).

2. The old country parks that Olmsted had in mind were those that he and his brother, John Hull Olmsted, had visited during their walking tour of the British Isles in the summer of 1850 — as is indicated by a crossed-out section in this part of the manuscript:

    A few years before we had spent a summer in England travelling on foot and visiting and luxuriating in the various old parks that came in our way.

    In *Walks and Talks*, which chronicles the first month of that trip, Olmsted briefly described his visit to the parks of three estates in Cheshire and Wales: Eaton Park near Chester, Wynstay Park near Ruabon, and Chirk Castle near Chirk (*Walks and Talks*, 1: 133, 135–36, 202, 212).

3. In describing a camping site near San Marcos, Texas, Olmsted wrote:

> We pitched our tent at night in a live-oak grove, by the side of a deep pure spring, at the mouth of a wooded ravine closed by rugged hills toward the north. Behind us were the continuous wooded heights, with a thick screen of cedars; before us, very beautiful prairies, rolling off far to the southward, with the smooth grassed surface, varied here and there by herds of cattle, and little belts, mottes and groups of live-oak (F. L. Olmsted, *Journey Through Texas*, p. 137).

4. In the original version, Olmsted began a new sentence after "places":

> These conditions involve, first a stream of water-courses the banks of which are not generally abrupt but gently slopeing and grassed to the water's edge, otherwise they would be constantly under-mining . . .

5. Here Olmsted originally wrote, and then crossed out, a passage, the surviving portion of which is as follows:

> Can it be supposed that a man of cultivation & wealth want the same topographical conditions about his residence with a careless wanderer or a poor pioneer. Yes no man wants to be compelled to use great exertion whenever he goes out of his house whatever his purpose: however different his purpose from the purposes of a rude pioneer. Take the citizen of a town jaded with any exertion, & needing recreation. It is not severe but quiet exercise he needs.

6. Olmsted wrote and then crossed out the following passage at this point:

> But as no movement is easy if indefinitely prolonged, the topography must also offer suggestions of opportunity of rest & refreshment such as are furnished by shade & shelter and water.

7. Here Olmsted originally continued:

> Therefore a dead flat, upon which movement would be easiest will not answer. The topographical conditions must not be monotonous or repetative, but varied.

> Two other passages that Olmsted crossed out are also relevant to the discussion at this point. In one passage, Olmsted wrote:

> Ground that is pleasant to wander over, must have two qualities, first that which makes wandering easy, that is to say, graceful contours, and second that degree of obscurity in some directions which presents a motive to wandering. A third may be added in an alternation of sun-light and shade which promises an agreeable option in regard to temperature to the wanderer. An excessive degree of planting would be incompatible with the first.

> In another passage, Olmsted observed: "Positive hospitality on the other hand is chiefly to be obtained by the alternation of light and shadow."

8. Herbert Spencer (1820–1903), English philosopher. Olmsted is quoting a series of examples in Spencer's essay "Gracefulness" that illustrate his contention that "given a certain change of attitude to be gone through — a certain action to be achieved, then it is most gracefully achieved when achieved with the least expenditure of force" (*EB*; Herbert Spencer, *Essays: Moral, Political and Æsthetic* [New York, 1878], p. 313).

9. On the back of a page, Olmsted wrote the following passage that relates to this section of the address:

But I would not limit the field of art in park–making to this, the {imitation} of natural graceful scenery. Art means more than this. Nature never throws all possible treasure upon one piece of ground. Man is but one of nature's instruments and is so in the exercise of his free will. We may then exercise our free will in such a way as to obtain a higher impression of grace than nature minus the agency of man would have produced. What I mean is that we should not restrict our efforts to mere reproduction of certain natural effects.

10. Here Olmsted wrote and later crossed out the following passage:

In a secondary sense the term means more than this, but I want you to carefully discriminate between this primary sense & the secondary sense because the first alone is that in which strictly speaking the term can be used with advantage with reference to topographical construction. A secondary sense of the word park has arisen from the fact that it is used as a proper as well as a common noun — that is to say as designative of a particular locality parts or the whole of which may be far from park like in topography or scenery.

11. A reference to John Wilson (1785–1854), who, under the pseudonym of Christopher North, wrote a series of articles for *Blackwood's Magazine* entitled *Noctes Ambrosianae*. One passage that Olmsted especially noted was what he called "old Kit North's rhapsody on trees" and which he quoted as: "Light, shade, shelter, coolness, freshness, music, dew, and dreams dropping through their umbrageous twilight — dropping direct, soft, sweet, soothing, and restorative from heaven." The second "rhapsody" in North's "Soliloquy on the Seasons" contains rhapsodic descriptions of several species of trees in different seasons but does not address the question of the "duties" of trees (*EB*, s.v. "Wilson, John"; Frederick Law Olmsted, *A Journey in the Seaboard Slave States* [New York, 1856], pp. 417–18; *Papers of FLO*, 1: 325; ibid., 2: 160; John Wilson, "Soliloquy on the Seasons" in *The Recreations of Christopher North* [Boston, 1854], pp. 253–54).

12. In a discarded version of this section, Olmsted continued at this point as follows:

Two rules follow of universal application
First, the greater the distance to which your purely park views can be extended the better.
Second, Any necessary limit to views in any direction within your park which are not calculated to suggest to the imagination a still continuing hospitality in that direction, should be rendered indefinite by the interposition of trees so arranged that the imagination may not only penetrate but look beyond their obscurity, and that thus they may serve to enlarge instead of limiting the prospect of ground pleasant to wander over, so that even at such points there shall be a negative if not a positive hospitality.

110 Broadway,
October 1st 1868.

William Dorsheimer Esq:
Sir;

On the 12th of August last you asked our advice for a body of gentlemen[2] who wished to present the main outlines of a scheme for establishing a public park in Buffalo to the consideration of their fellow citizens. We shortly afterwards visited your city, studied its plan with you and made a cursory examination under your guidance of its immediate suburbs, giving special attention to three localities the merits of which for the purpose in view we understood from you had been already under discussion.[3]

We have since gone more carefully over the ground, tested soils, examined maps and obtained all the information we could, without making a topographical survey, of the conditions of the general problem you have to solve and have subjected our first impressions to a close and deliberate review, the result of which we now propose to give to you. In doing so we shall restrict our advice to such general suggestions as it is practicable for us to offer with entire confidence, upon points which need to be well considered before any legislative action could be properly asked for; assuming that all questions, except those bearing directly upon the general and approximate outlines of the proposed scheme, should be left to a body officially accountable to the whole body of citizens interested.

We think it right to distinctly state the fact that if you, or any of the gentlemen whom you represent, have had any special interests, predilections, purposes or opinions in this matter, which it is hardly possible should not have been the case, they have been perfectly concealed from us and that our judgment of what would be for the best interests of the citizens at large, without regard to classes or localities, has been consulted in the simplest and fairest manner possible.

We think it necessary, first of all, to urge that your scheme should be comprehensively conceived, and especially that features, the desirableness of which are most apparent, should not at the outset be made so important as to cause others, the possible value of which may seem more distant, to be neglected.

For this purpose it should be well thought of that a park exercises a very different and much greater influence upon the progress of a city in its general structure than any other ordinary public work, and that after the design for a park has been fully digested a long series of years must elapse before the ends of the design will begin to be fully realized. Even in the initiatory discussions of a plan for such a work therefore it would be unwise to have in view merely the satisfaction of the probable demands of those who will be expected to use it in the immediate future. If a park should prove not adapted to the requirements of those who are to come after us and even of those who are to come after our immediate successors, the outlay which will be needed for it would be an extravagant one.

This caution applies especially to questions of situation, extent, general outlines, approaches and relations with other public ways and places. Minor interior arrangements may be adapted merely to suit immediate and clearly obvious requirements, as the cost of adding to these when found advisable will not necessarily be very formidable, provided the ground first secured shall have been of good shape, wisely located and the general plan of improving it shall have been a well balanced one. It is universally found, however, when this has not been the case and when a growing town has once begun to accommodate itself to a large park that any essential modification of its outlines becomes an undertaking of greater difficulty than the original enterprise itself.

To establish the advantages of a careful prevision, in this respect, we may mention that after land for the Central Park of New York had been acquired, but before work had been commenced upon it, we called attention to the value of certain improvements which might be made in the park and its approaches by the addition of a small amount of land to that already secured. The necessary land for most of these improvements has since been acquired and they have been carried out but their cost has been increased by the neglect to provide for them at the outset from 800 to 2500 per cent., while one of the most desirable, which might have been adopted originally at small expense, will probably never be realized on account of the occupation of the land by important constructions, the undertaking of which was induced by the opening of the park.[4] Prompt action on similar advice to the city of Brooklyn, in one case, secured land for the enlargement of an approach at a cost of only one fifth what it would have cost two years afterwards, while a delay of three years in securing a tract of sixty acres foolishly omitted in the original purchase for a park has cost that city over a million of dollars.[5]

Similar facts are found in the recent experience of London, Liverpool and Paris. Nor are they peculiar to very large towns. To slightly straighten the boundaries, enlarge the ball grounds, widen the adjoining streets and amplify the approaches of the little park laid out nine years ago in the town of Hartford, Conn[t], improvements very obviously desirable and the requirement of which should have been anticipated, would now probably involve an expense larger than was necessary for the purchase of all the land included in the park and several times larger than would have been originally necessary had the project been formed with a sufficiently comprehensive exercise of forethought.[6]

The still smaller town of Bridgeport acquired a tract of land for a park of seventy acres which, less than two years ago, we were called upon to examine. We enquired as to the practicability of making some change of the boundaries and were told that the land had already advanced so much since the purchase for the park had been made that the idea could not be entertained.[7] It happened, however, that upon an explanation which we made to the owner of a large adjoining field used for agricultural purposes, of the improvement which could be made in the plan of the park if a slight addition were made to it from his property, he wisely but generously offered to make a free gift to the city of what was required; the offer was accepted and the gentleman informs us that he has recently sold a part of the remainder of the field in question for building lots at more than twice the valuation he had placed upon it at that time, and that he considers that the acquisition of any land required for a modification of the boundaries of the park or for an enlargement of the approaches to it would now be assessed at sixteen times as much as it would have been originally.

It must be observed, also, that a really fine, large and convenient park exercises an immediate and very striking educational influence which soon manifests itself in certain changes of taste and of habits and consequently in the requirements of the people.

To understand the character of these changes and their bearing upon the task we have in hand it will be necessary to understand what a park is, or rather what it may be if properly designed and administered.

The main object we set before us in planning a park is to establish conditions which will exert the most healthful, recreative action upon the people who are expected to resort to it. With the great mass such conditions will be of a character diverse from the ordinary conditions of their lives in the most radical degree which is consistent with ease of access, with large assemblages of citizens with convenience, cheerfulness and good order, and with the necessities of a sound policy of municipal economy.

Much must necessarily be seen in any town park which sustains the mental impressions of the town itself, as in the faces, the dresses and the carriages of the people and in the throngs in which they will at times here and there gather and move together. Inasmuch as there are these necessary limitations to the degree in which a decided and at the same time a pleasing contrast to the ordinary conditions of town life are possible to be realized in a park, and inasmuch as the town is constituted by the bringing together of artificial objects, the chief study in establishing a park is to present nature in the most attractive manner which may be practicable. This is to be done by first choosing a site in which natural conditions, as opposed to town conditions, shall have every possible advantage, and then by adding to and improving these original natural conditions. If this is skillfully done, if the place possessing the greatest capabilities is taken and nature is not overlaid but really aided discreetly by art, it follows as a matter of course that in a few years the citizens resorting to the locality experience sensations to which they have before been unaccustomed, disused perceptive powers are more and more exercised, dormant tastes come to life, corresponding habits are developed and a new class of luxuries begins to be sought for, superseding to some extent certain others, less favorable to health, to morality and to happiness, if not wholly wasteful and degrading. The demand thus established will of course sooner or later make itself felt in several other ways besides those which pertain to the park.

Before laying out a park, therefore, it is best to consider what the character of the demand which must thus be expected to grow up with it will be and see if it cannot be anticipated with advantage.

It is easy to determine that its character will be that of a liking for things which are in no way essential to the requirements which had led to the building up of the town as it was before the park was called for. For example, the demand for convenience in getting quickly from places where business is done to places where such rest and sustenance can be had as are necessary to maintain the ability to do business, and for convenience of transferring goods from shops and shipping to stores obliges the obliteration of all natural objects, gives occasion for compact building, causes the removal of whatever would obstruct wheeling and walking between buildings, and leads to the construction of solid and rigid pavements, and the general prevalence of noise, jarring and confusion.

All these things are compatible with a great deal of luxury, especially with the luxury of architectural grandeur and elegance, but the tastes which will be fostered by a park will demand luxuries not only of another kind but such as cannot be associated intimately with these things, luxuries more natural, more healthful and more desirable to be brought within easy reach of the citizens.

The park, as we have described it, must necessarily be large and costly; to place it in the midst of the town would be to make it excessively costly in the first place and permanently a great obstruction to business. It should then be placed at such a distance from the great body of citizens that time will necessarily be spent in going to and coming from it, time which will either be spent unpleasantly or at best with reference to the gratification in any degree of the tastes under consideration, will be wasted. The demand then will be that means of escaping from streets bearing the character which inevitably attaches to the greater part of the compact business parts of a city shall be put everywhere more nearly within reach of all the people than they would be merely by the formation of a park, however large, at some one point in the suburbs.

For these reasons we would recommend that in your scheme a large park should not be the sole object in view but should be regarded simply as the more important member of a general, largely provident, forehanded, comprehensive arrangement for securing refreshment, recreation and health to the people. All of such an arrangement need not be undertaken at once but the future requirements of all should be so far foreseen and provided for that when the need for any minor part is felt to be pressing it may not be impossible to obtain the most desirable land for it.

A comprehensive and well prepared scheme seems to us for several reasons to be peculiarly desirable for Buffalo; first, because Buffalo is a place of singular mobility and progressiveness, rapidly increasing in population and wealth, with every reason for expecting a prolonged career of prosperity, and a more than usually rapid development of advance in the common requirements of civilization; second, because the immediate environs of the town in the conditions they are now and have been for a number of years are not generally at all attractive, and young people in search of recreation especially, have very little inducement to a pure, healthy, natural exercise of their faculties and tastes, and, in consequence, there are special inducements to offer them facilities and stimulants to unwholesome substitutes for recreation; third, the relation of the town to its canals and railroads and the lake and rivers is such as to make an escape from it in several directions, to anything like rural quiet, difficult and disagreeable if not impossible;[8] fourth, during a considerable part of the year that portion of the environs which is otherwise least repellant to rural exercise is swept by harsh, damp winds, very trying to those who are in most need of quiet open air recreation.[9]

Each of the three sites to which our attention has been called possesses some special advantages to which we shall now refer.

The first is the most elevated ground in the city on High street near the old Potters field.[10] From this a finer lookout may be had over the city than from any other point and the distant wooded plains, backed by blue hills, make a beautiful background to the view on the South. It is nearer to the more densely populated parts of the city than any other site having distinctive natural advantages. In a few years unless soon reserved for a public ground it will probably be occupied and surrounded by buildings when the view from it can no longer be had.

The second site referred to is one adjoining Fort Porter.[11] It is also comparatively elevated and has attracted attention because of the view which is commanded from it over the lake. This, especially at sunset in certain states of the atmosphere, is a very fine one and it is within the province of art to enhance the sense of beauty in the distance by forming a substitute for a part and a screen for the remainder of a foreground which is at present rude, discordant and essentially disagreeable. The outer scene thus framed and emphasized would be peculiar to Buffalo and would have a character of magnificence admirably adapted to be associated with stately ceremonies, the entertainment of public guests and other occasions of civic display.

The third site to which our attention was directed is to be found on the banks of the creek west of the Forest-lawn Cemetery.[12] By the construction of an embankment about half a mile below the road which is a prolongation of Delaware Street[13] a body of living water might here be formed about twenty acres in extent with a very agreeable natural line of shore, the greater part of which would be shaded by beautiful groves of trees, already on the ground, and most of which are now in their prime and of very desirable species. This water would be well adapted to the requirements of ornamental water fowl, to skating and boating; the groves adjoining it would furnish a cool place to be resorted to for rambling and rest on a hot day, the views over the water might easily be made charming and appropriate and the general situation is one to which your citizens could go, and in which they could remain, for several hours during many days of the spring and autumn, when most other places in the suburbs, and especially the two elevations which have been considered, would be made disagreeable by the harshness of the winds which sweep them.

On the east side of the road and north of the Cemetery there is a series of large open fields which are graced by a number of remarkably fine, umbrageous trees such as are never found except under unusually favorable conditions of soil and climate. The general aspect of this ground is not only beautiful but its beauty is of that kind which is appropriately termed park-like. Taking these circumstances in connection with the groves and the creek we cannot hesitate to conclude that whatever advantages for pleasure grounds of a certain kind the other sites we have examined may offer they are not to be compared for a moment with that which is here offered you, when the question is of what we call, by distinction, a park.

The objections to the situation which may be anticipated are those which would be felt by some portion of the people of the city to any situation, namely distance, and difficulty of access from certain quarters.

We have seen no other situation nearer the centre of population in which it would be possible to form a spacious park, even at an expense several times larger than would be required for one at this point, where it would not very certainly prove a great inconvenience to business and involve large changes in the general plan upon which the building up of the city is otherwise likely to advance. The site which we have in view is now either waste land, or is occupied, with the exception of a single unimportant manufacturing establishment, exclusively for agricultural purposes, and, for farming land near a large town, can be bought at an extraordinary low rate.[14] A park would neither interfere with nor be interfered with by any existing or probable line of business communication, the character of the topography of the neighborhood not having encouraged the formation of roads from either side through it. It would be feasible by a slight divergence from the present route to carry the only existing public thoroughfare across it, whenever it shall be found desirable, where by means of a natural depression of the surface it would be out of view from the pleasure routes of the park.

Due weight being given to these facts we doubt not that it will be clear to you that no other situation would on the whole be equally convenient for the main purposes which a park should be designed to serve, and that a park in no other situation would occasion so little inconvenience to those living or doing business, even in the parts of the city to which the objection of distance and difficulty of access may be considered to be of the most consequence.

If you are thus prepared to adopt the conclusions that the principal feature of your scheme should be a park, intended for the general enjoyment of all citizens of Buffalo, as Buffalo may be expected to be a generation or two hence, and that this park shall be situated as we have advised, then you will find it necessary to consider how the people of the more distant parts of the city can be secured access to this park without a journey long, fatiguing and discordant with the sentiment and purposes of recreation in view, and what compensation can be offered them for the distance at which they will be placed by the location of the park as proposed.

To reach sound conclusions on these points you will need to reflect that public pleasure grounds are chiefly used in three ways, as follows: First, for recreation of a decided character, involving an absence of some hours from ordinary pursuits, and that such recreation is either taken after the main business of the day is over by those who are able to leave their business somewhat early in the afternoon, or that it involves a holiday or half holiday. Second, for the airing, exercise and recreation of children, invalids, women, and others who are not methodically occupied by any regular business yet are necessarily much confined within walls. Third, for a slight diversion of those whose business usually holds them so late that they are able to leave it only for short periods during the day but to whom an attractive recreation ground would be worth perhaps more than to any other, if it could be put within their easy reach.

For both the latter purposes a large park outside a city is resorted to by those living or working within a limited distance of it, but it cannot serve these purposes, so far as the larger body of citizens is concerned. Grounds need to be provided, therefore, less complete in their opportunities for a variety of forms of recreation and adapted to accommodate a smaller number of persons at a time, but to which many can resort for a short stroll, airing and diversion, and where they can at once enjoy a decided change of scene from that which is associated with their regular occupations.

The sites near Fort Porter and on High Street are both suitable for this class of grounds; each would be conveniently accessible from a different quarter of the town, and each of these quarters would have less direct access to the main parks than to any other quarter where vacant land can be found offering any advantages for the formation of pleasure grounds.

If you accept the conclusion thus suggested the question only remains of making the main park more readily and more agreeably and more appropriately accessible from a distance.

Fortunately the plan of Buffalo is such that the proposed site of the main park is already accessible by the most direct way possible from the very centre of population, and from the only quarter not proposed to be otherwise

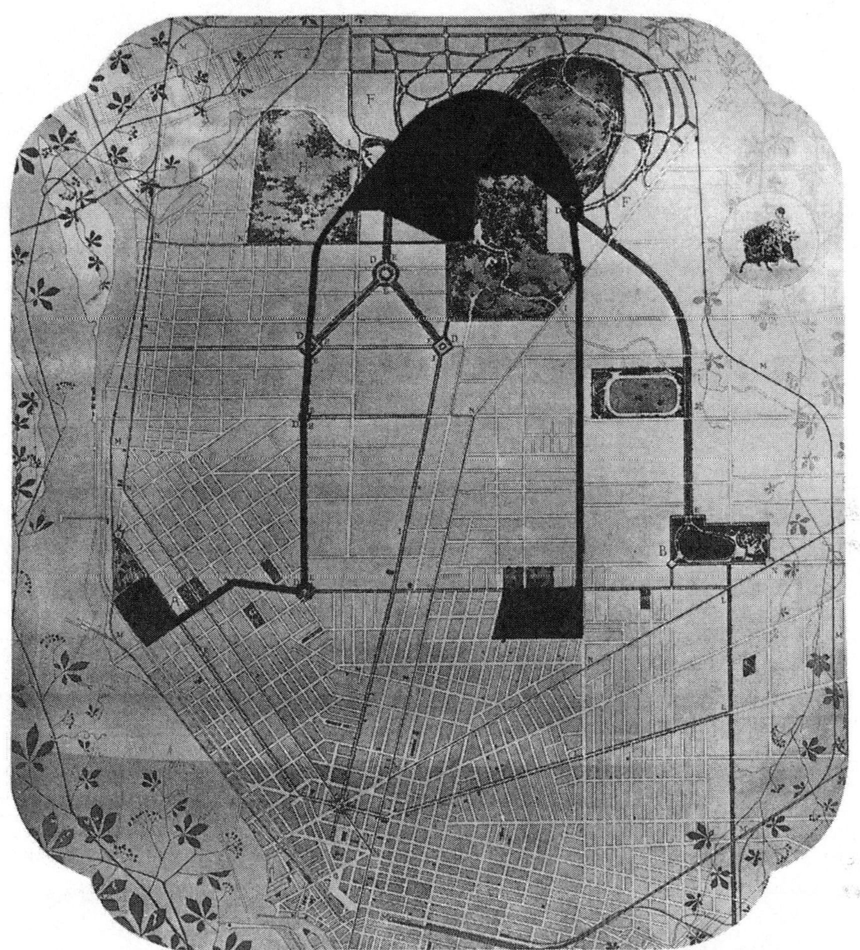

OUTLINE OF BUFFALO PARK SYSTEM PROPOSED IN OLMSTED'S REPORT OF OCTOBER 1, 1868, SUPERIMPOSED ON THE PLAN OF THE SYSTEM AS CONSTRUCTED, C. 1876

provided with a local pleasure ground, by Delaware avenue, an approach of stately proportions.[15] So far as this quarter of the city is concerned a better solution of the difficulty is thus at once offered than can often be obtained at large expense in other cities. The avenue is susceptible also of great improvement at a very moderate outlay.

For the rest, we would suggest that the two ends of the main park on the Southeast and West be gradually narrowed and curved toward the town, so that the greater part of the ground taken would be included within a crescent-shaped figure, and that strips of ground, at least two hundred feet wide, be acquired, extending from them toward the North and West parts of the city on one side, and the South and East parts on the other. Through these strips a series of roads and walks adapted exclusively for pleasure travel should eventually be formed and outside of them roadways to answer the purpose of streets, for ordinary traffic, which could thus be disassociated from the movement to and from the park. So much of these strips as would not be wanted for passage-ways should be occupied by turf, trees, shrubs and flowers; they should follow existing lines of streets as far as practicable, so as not to interfere unnecessarily with the present divisions of property, and they should be so laid out as to connect the two subordinate grounds which have been indicated with the main park.

Thus, at no great distance from any point of the town, a pleasure ground will have been provided for, suitable for a short stroll, for a playground for children, and an airing ground for invalids, and a route of access to the large common park of the whole city of such a character that most of the steps on the way to it would be taken in the midst of a scene of sylvan beauty and with the sounds and sites of the ordinary town business, if not wholly shut out, removed to some distance and placed in obscurity. The way itself would thus be more park-like than town-like.

Such a park-way on the East might follow the line of Jefferson Street from Genesee or Batavia Street to near Main Street, and soon after crossing the latter begin to expand into the crescent ends of the park itself.[16] On the West, starting from an architectural construction and esplanade on the bluff at or near the present base-ball grounds, it might divide and enclose the Niagara and York Street Public Gardens[17] and continue in a straight course to Rogers Street, then follow Rogers Street to Clinton Grove, near which it might slightly expand and take a more picturesque character than would be desirable nearer the town, and finally open fully into the park itself near the foot of the proposed ornamental water, half a mile west of the Cemetery.[18]

At a point near the entrance of the Race Course, and at the crossing of important streets, the Parkways might, for greater convenience in crossing and turning, be expanded in a circular or elliptical form, and such points would, in the future, offer suitable positions for fountains, statues, trophies and public monuments.[19]

It is impracticable to form even an approximate estimate of the cost of such arrangements as we have suggested without a plan based upon a careful topographical survey, but it will be readily seen that the opportunity may be secured for them and held by the city at a very moderate expense.

The most costly items in the acquisition of a park by a city usually are; first, the land; second, grading; third, the foundation or stone work of roads; fourth, constructions of masonry. The land which you would require for the park is mere farming land, with no costly buildings upon it, instead of being as is usually the case town building-lots more or less occupied by expensive structures and for important business purposes. Its surface is almost everywhere gently sloping, so that the necessary grading to adapt it to park purposes

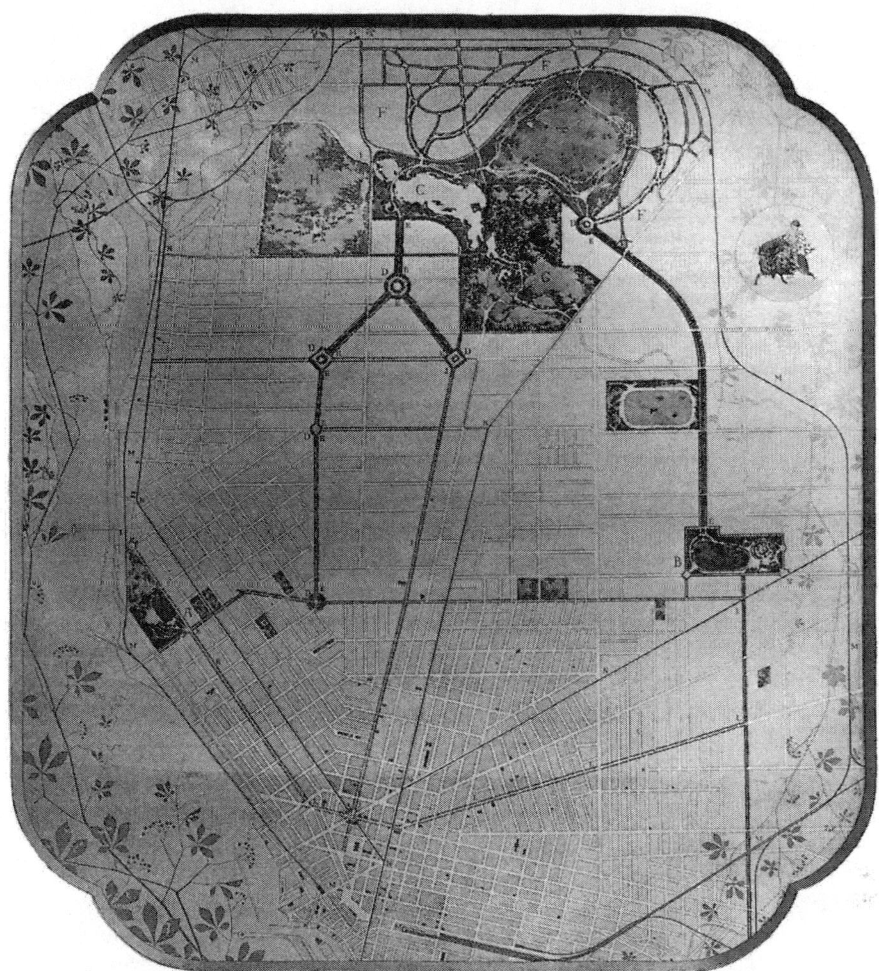

PLAN OF BUFFALO PARK SYSTEM, AS DISPLAYED AT THE CENTENNIAL EXHIBITION IN
PHILADELPHIA, 1876

would be extraordinarily light. The chief topographical change suggested
would be effected by the construction of a simple embankment, about one
hundred feet in length and the natural action of the water which would accumulate above it. An abundance of stone suitable for road foundation is found
on the ground, in quarries already opened and the facility with which these
can be worked and the stone prepared is such that we are informed that contracts for road-metal may be made at less than half the prices we have usually
found it necessary to pay elsewhere. There is no necessity for any large work
of masonry and what little may be required will, for the reasons first indicated,
be inexpensive.

167

On reviewing all the circumstances it cannot be doubted that they present an opportunity of acquiring a property at comparatively moderate cost, which when gradually improved, as from year to year may be deemed expedient, will ultimately be of inestimable value to your city.

We are, with great respect for the generous and impartial public spirit with which our counsel has been sought and received by your associates and yourself,

Your obedient servants,

Olmsted Vaux & C°
Landscape Architects.

The original of this report, in a clerk's hand with revisions by Olmsted and signed for the firm by Olmsted, was included in the manuscript minutes of the Buffalo Common Council, November 23, 1868. An edited version of the report was later published in City of Buffalo. Park Commission, *Preliminary Report Respecting a Public Park in Buffalo . . .* (Buffalo, N.Y., 1869), pages 11–28.

1. William Edward Dorsheimer (1832–1888), lawyer and politician in Buffalo, New York. Long active in civic affairs, Dorsheimer was in the forefront of the movement to establish a public park in Buffalo. Dorsheimer and Olmsted became friends and worked together in the effort to establish the Niagara Reservation in the 1880s. As lieutenant governor of New York in the mid-1870s, he transferred the designing of the new state capitol from the original designer to Olmsted and the architects Henry Hobson Richardson and Leopold Eidlitz (*DAB*; *Papers of FLO*, 6: 547; Francis R. Kowsky, "Delaware Avenue, Buffalo, New York," in *The Grand American Avenue: 1850–1920*, eds. Jan Cigliano and Sarah Bradford Landau [San Francisco, 1994], pp. 47–48; FLO and CV, *General Plan for the Improvement of the Niagara Reservation*, [1887], below).

2. On August 12, 1868, William Dorsheimer, writing on behalf of several Buffalo citizens, requested that Olmsted visit and discuss the feasibility of laying out a park in the city. Olmsted visited Buffalo August 16 and 17, and returned on August 25. As he got off the train he was startled to discover that a public meeting concerning the preparation of a park in Buffalo at which he would be the principal speaker had been arranged for that evening (William Dorsheimer to FLO, Aug. 12, 1868; FLO to MPO, Aug. 23 and 25, 1868 [*Papers of FLO*, 6: 266–69]; ibid., 6: 271).

3. The three localities already under consideration for a park were the site of the "old Potters field" near High Street, a site adjacent to Fort Porter, located at the confluence of the Niagara River and Lake Erie, and a site adjacent to Forest Lawn Cemetery in the northern part of the city. The localities became the Parade, the Front, and the Park (later renamed Delaware Park) (see nn. 10, 11, and 12, below).

4. A reference primarily to the extension of Central Park in New York from 106th Street to 110th Street (see FLO, *Notes on the Plan of Franklin Park and Related Matters* [1886], n. 43, below).

5. Probably a reference to the change in boundaries and the additional purchase of land for Prospect Park in Brooklyn, New York (see ibid., n. 59, below).

6. A reference to "The Park" in Hartford (later named Bushnell Park) laid out in 1859 by Jacob Weidenmann. In a letter published in 1869 in *Hearth and Home*, Horace

Bushnell, the driving force behind the creation of the park and for whom it was named, noted that

> the Council . . . have enlarged the original ground, by taking possession of buildings and lots on the north and east sides of the river, to clear away the nuisance of so many filthy rears, and form a street and green-slope bank facing Park-ward on that side; an addition that was contemplated from the first, but which, to reduce expense, was not included in the original purchase.

(*Papers of FLO*, 6: 451; Horace Bushnell, "Hartford Park," *Hearth and Home*, Feb. 6, 1869, p. 102).

7. In 1867 Olmsted and Vaux designed Seaside Park in Bridgeport, Connecticut. At the time Olmsted and Vaux prepared their plan for Seaside Park, the park comprised about forty acres, but by 1871 it had expanded to seventy acres. Much of the land for the park was donated by public-spirited citizens like P. T. Barnum, the famous showman, and Nathaniel Wheeler, manufacturer and inventor. The rest of the land was purchased for $13,478 (George C. Waldo, Jr., *History of Bridgeport and Vicinity*, 2 vols. [New York, 1917], 1: 277–79; Department of Parks, *Bridgeport Municipal Register for 1873* [Bridgeport, Conn., 1873], pp. 117–18; *DAB*).

8. Buffalo, the western terminus of the Erie Canal, is situated at the eastern end of Lake Erie at the point where it narrows to become the Niagara River, flowing rapidly northward toward Niagara Falls. In addition, Buffalo is bounded on the south by Big Buffalo Creek and, at the time Olmsted was writing this report, by numerous smaller ship-canals and slips. First a port city, Buffalo became an important railroad center as well, and several railways crossed the southern part of Buffalo from east to west (*Walling's Route and City Guides: Erie Railway* [New York, 1867], pp. 47–48).

9. A reference to the effect of winds blowing off Lake Erie.

10. The "old Potters field" between North and Best streets, one block north of High Street, had been created in 1832 to serve as a common burial ground during a cholera epidemic. Given Olmsted's desire for the park on this site to include the highest ground in the vicinity, the most likely boundary streets would have been Best Street on the north, Jefferson Street on the east, High Street on the south, and Michigan Street on the west. Although Olmsted was very enthusiastic about this site, it was not purchased, and the Parade was laid out about a mile to the east of it. This was probably because the language of the enabling legislation authorizing the purchase of park property specified that one-fifth of the land taken had to lie east of Jefferson Street (H. Perry Smith, ed., *History of the City of Buffalo and Erie County* . . ., 2 vols. [Syracuse, N.Y., 1884], 2: 504; New York [State], *Laws of the State of New York, Passed at the Ninety-Second Session of the Legislature* . . . [Albany, N.Y., 1869], chap. 165; see also, FLO and CV, "Plan for a Public Park on the Flats South of Buffalo," Oct. 1, 1888, n. 3, below).

11. Fort Porter, a U.S. Army post, was built in 1843 on a bluff on the shore of Lake Erie at the point where the Erie Canal reached the Niagara River. The park site proposed by Olmsted adjoined Fort Porter on the south. From the bluff at that point there were impressive views over the lake. Elsewhere, Olmsted wrote that from this spot there was "a river effect such as can be seen, I believe, nowhere else — a certain quivering of the surface and a rare tone of color, the result of the crowding upward of the lake waters as they enter the deep portal of the Niagara" (Robert W. Bingham, ed., *Niagara Frontier Miscellany* [Buffalo, N.Y., 1947], pp. 148–49; Frederick Law Olmsted, "A Healthy Change in the Tone of the Human Heart," *Century Illustrated Monthly Magazine* 23 [October 1886]: 963).

12. Forest Lawn Cemetery, located on Scajaquada Creek and laid out in 1853. Olmsted and Vaux proposed to lay out the Park, the largest of the three parks discussed in this report, in a crescent that would envelope the cemetery on the north and west (Francis

R. Kowsky, "Municipal Parks and City Planning: Frederick Law Olmsted's Buffalo Park and Parkway System," *Journal of the Society of Architectural Historians* 46 [March 1987]: 53, 55).

13. Delaware Street bisected the proposed site of the Park and ran in a southerly direction to the center of the city of Buffalo about four miles away. Here, Olmsted and Vaux are proposing the damming of Scajaquada Creek for the creation of the Lake (ibid., p. 55).

14. The land for the Park was purchased for $600 an acre in 1869 (City of Buffalo. Park Commission, *Sixth Annual Report of the Buffalo Park Commissioners. January 1876* [Buffalo, N.Y., 1876], p. 8).

15. Delaware Street was one of four wide streets that extended radially from Niagara Square, the central focus of Joseph Ellicott's plan for the city of 1804. In the years following the Civil War it was the city's "premier residential street," with numerous residences designed by architects of distinction (F. R. Kowsky, "Delaware Avenue, Buffalo, New York," pp. 35–55).

16. Olmsted proposed to have this parkway connect the Parade with the Park; however, since the site of the Parade was moved about a mile to the east, the parkway could not be laid out as originally planned and fulfill its purpose of linking the two public spaces. In Olmsted and Vaux's plan of 1870 this function was performed by Humboldt Parkway (see n. 10 above).

17. That is, Prospect Place, a public pleasure area bounded by Connecticut Street on the north, Prospect Street on the east, York Street (later renamed Porter Street) on the south, and Niagara Street on the west (*Reese & Kaye's New Map of the City of Buffalo* [Buffalo, N.Y., 1871]).

18. Olmsted proposed that this series of parkways would link the Front with the Park. Starting from the Front, York and North streets were widened as far as the latter's intersection with Rodgers Street. Rodgers Street (renamed The Avenue) was widened and as proposed here would have been the principal approach to the Park. Olmsted was unable to complete this parkway as originally planned, because the northwestern end of the parkway would have traveled through property set aside in 1870 for the Buffalo State Hospital for the Insane. Instead, in the final design the Avenue ended at Bidwell Place, which was connected by Bidwell Parkway to Soldiers Place, which in turn connected to the Park by Lincoln Parkway (*Papers of FLO*, 6: 454).

19. The law for the creation of the Buffalo driving park was passed in 1868. It provided for the laying out of "walks, roads, riding and driving tracks, and fair or show grounds." The driving park first appeared on Buffalo maps in 1871 and was located between Delaware Park and the Parade and bounded on the east by Humboldt Parkway (New York [State], *Laws of the State of New York, Passed at the Ninety-First Session of the Legislature* . . . [Albany, N.Y., 1868], chap. 91; *Reese & Kaye's New Map of the City of Buffalo*).

Public Parks and
the Enlargement of Towns.[*]

THE last "Overland Monthly" tells us that in California "only an inferior class of people can be induced to live out of towns. There is something in the country which repels men. In the city alone can they nourish the juices of life."[1]

This of newly built and but half-equipped cities, where the people are never quite free from dread of earthquakes, and of a country in which the productions of agriculture and horticulture are more varied, and the rewards of rural enterprise larger, than in any other under civilized government! With a hundred million acres of arable and grazing land, with thousands of outcropping gold veins, with the finest forests in the world, fully half the white people live in towns, a quarter of all in one town, and this quarter pays more than half the taxes of all. "Over the mountains the miners," says Mr. Bowles, "talk of going to San Francisco as to Paradise, and the rural members of the Legislature declare that 'San Francisco sucks the life out of the country.'"[2]

Nearer home the newspapers again tell us that twenty-five thousand men, to say nothing of women, are asking for work in Chicago;[3] each of the great cities of the Mississippi region is reported to be increasing in population at a wonderful rate; gold and wheat are fast falling in their markets, but rents keep up, and it is complained that builders do not supply the demand for dwellings suited to the requirements of new-comers, who are chiefly men of small capital and young families, anxious to make a lodgment in the city on almost any conditions which will leave them a chance of earning a right to remain.

To this I can add, from personal observation, that if we stand, any day before noon, at the railway stations of these cities, we may notice women and girls arriving by the score, who, it will be apparent, have just run in to do a little shopping, intending to return by supper time to farms perhaps a hundred miles away. We shall observe trains advertised with special reference to the attendance of country people upon the evening entertainments of the town. Leaving the cars at some remote and lonely station, we may find a poster in its waiting-room, announcing matinée performances at a city theatre. If we push across the prairie, and call on a farmer who has been settled

---

[*] A paper read before the American Social Science Association at the Lowell Institute, Boston, February 25, 1870.[4]

171

and doing well upon his land for twenty years, an intelligent and forehanded man, we shall hardly fail to see that very little remains to him or his family of what we formerly, and not very long ago, regarded as the most essential characteristics of rural life.

Formerly it was a matter of pride with the better sort of our country people that they could raise on their own land, and manufacture in their own household, almost everything needed for domestic consumption. Now their tables are furnished with all kinds of city delicacies. The housewife complains of her servants. There is no difficulty in getting them from the intelligence offices in town, such as they are; but only the poorest, who cannot find employment in the city, will come to the country, and these, as soon as they have got a few dollars ahead, are crazy to get back to town. It is much the same with the men, the farmer will add; he has to go up in the morning and find someone to take "Wolf's" place. You will find, too, that one of his sons is in a lawyer's office, another at a commercial college, and his oldest daughter at an "institute," all in town. I know several girls who travel eighty miles a day to attend school in Chicago. If under these circumstances the occupation of the country school-master, shoe-maker, and doctor, the country store-keeper, dress-maker and lawyer, is not actually gone, it must be that the business they have to do is much less relatively to the population about them than it used to be; not less in amount only, but less in importance. An inferior class of men will meet the requirements.

And how are things going here in Massachusetts? A correspondent of the "Springfield Republican" gave the other day an account of a visit lately made to two or three old agricultural neighborhoods, such as fifty years ago were the glory of New England.[5] When he last knew them, their society was spoken of with pride, and the influence of not a few of their citizens was felt throughout the State, and indeed far beyond it. But as he found them now, they might almost be sung by Goldsmith.[6] The meeting-house closed, the church dilapidated; the famous old taverns, stores, shops, mills, and offices dropping to pieces and vacant, or perhaps with a mere corner occupied by day laborers; but a third as many children as formerly to be seen in the school-houses, and of these less than half of American-born parents.

Walking through such a district last summer, my eyes were gladdened by a single house with exceptional signs of thrift in fresh paint, roofs, and fences, and newly planted door-yard trees; but happening as I passed to speak to the owner, in the second sentence of our conversation he told me that he had been slicking his place up in hopes that some city gentleman would take a fancy to it for a country seat. He was getting old, had worked hard, and felt as if the time had fully come when he was entitled to take some enjoyment of what remained to him of life by retiring to the town. Nearly all his old neighbors were gone; his children had left years ago. His town-bred granddaughters were playing croquet in the front yard.

You know how it is here in Boston. Let us go on to the Old World.

We read in our youth that among no other people were rural tastes so strong, and rural habits so fixed, as with those of Old England, and there is surely no other country where the rural life of the more fortunate classes compares so attractively with their town life. Yet in the "Transactions of the British Social Science Association," we find one debater asserting that there are now very few more persons living in the rural districts of England and Wales than there were fifty years ago; another referring to "the still increasing growth of our overgrown towns and the stationary or rather retrograding numbers of our rural population;" * while a third remarks that the social and educational advantages of the towns are drawing to them a large proportion of "the wealthy and independent," as well as all of the working classes not required for field labor. †

When I was last in England,[7] the change that had occurred even in ten years could be perceived by a rapid traveler. Not only had the country gentleman and especially the country gentlewoman of Irving[8] departed wholly with all their following, but the very embers had been swept away of that manner of life upon which, so little while ago, everything in England seemed to be dependent. In all the country I found a smack of the suburbs — hampers and packages from metropolitan tradesmen, and purveyors arriving by every train, and a constant communication kept up with town by penny-post and telegraph.

In the early part of the century, the continued growth of London was talked of as something marvelous and fearful; but where ten houses were then required to accommodate new residents, there are now a hundred. The average rate at which population increases in the six principal towns is twice as great as in the country at large, including the hundreds of other flourishing towns. So also Glasgow has been growing six times faster than all Scotland; and Dublin has held its own, while Ireland as a whole has been losing ground.

Crossing to the Continent, we find Paris absorbing half of all the increase of France in population; Berlin growing twice as fast as all Prussia; Hamburg, Stettin, Stuttgart, Brussels, and a score or two of other towns, all building out into the country at a rate never before known, while many agricultural districts are actually losing population. In Russia special provision is made in the laws to regulate the gradual compensation of the nobles for their losses by the emancipation of the serfs, to prevent the depopulation of certain parts of the country, which was in danger of occurring from the eagerness of the peasantry to move into the large towns. ‡

Going still further to the eastward, we may find a people to whom the movement has not thus far been communicated; but it is only where

* *Transactions*, 1864.[9]
† *Transactions*, 1861.[10]
‡ *Nation*, vol. x. p. 161.[11]

obscurity affords the best hope of safety from oppression, where men number their women with their horses, and where labor-saving inventions are as inventions of the enemy.

Of the fact of the general townward movement of the civilized world, and its comprehensiveness, there can be no doubt. There is a difference of opinion apparently as to its causes and as to the probability of its continuance, for we hear anticipations of a reaction expressed. I see no grounds for them. It appears to me to look much more as if what we had thus far witnessed was but the beginning. I do not propose to go to the root of the matter; it is sufficient for our purpose to point out that the strength of the movement at any point seems to correspond closely with the degree in which the habits of the people have been recently changed by the abolition of feudalism, slavery, and government by divine right; by the multiplication and cheapening of schools, newspapers, and books; and by the introduction of labor-saving arrangements, especially of that class which are only available at all where they can be used to the direct benefit of many, such as railroads and telegraphs.

Consider that the standard of education is still advancing. There is yet no halt in the onward march of liberty of thought; telegraph stations are multiplying, new railroads are building, and the working capacity of old ones is increasing. Consider what we have been doing in our own country. Our public lands have been divided in square plats, so as to discourage the closer agricultural settlement which long and narrow divisions favor. We have given away the pick of them under a plan well adapted to induce a scattering settlement for a time, but also calculated to encourage waste of resources. We have no longer the best to offer.

Again, we have said to the world, "Here are countless deposits of the precious metals, scattered about over many millions of acres of wild land. We will give them away as fast as they can be found. First come, first served. Disperse then, and look for them." In spite of this policy, we find that the rate of increase of our principal towns is even now greater than that of the country.

But the same cause has also had the effect of giving us, for a time, great command of ready money and easy credit, and we have thus been induced to spend an immense sum — say two thousand millions — in providing ourselves with the fixtures and machinery of our railroad system. This system, while encouraging the greater dispersion of our food-producers, has tended most of all to render them, as we have seen, independent of all the old neighborhood agencies of demand and supply, manufacture and exchange, and to educate them and their children in familiarity with and dependence on the conveniences and habits of towns-people.

We all recognize that the tastes and dispositions of women are more and more potent in shaping the course of civilized progress, and again we must acknowledge that women are even more susceptible to this townward drift than men. Ofttimes the husband and father gives up his country occupations, taking others less attractive to him in town, out of consideration for his wife and daughters. Not long since I conveyed to a very sensible and provident man what I thought to be an offer of great preferment. I was surprised that he hesitated to accept it, until the question was referred to his wife, a bright, tidy American-born woman, who promptly said: "If I were offered a deed of the best farm that I ever saw, on condition of going back to the country to live, I would not take it. I would rather face starvation in town." She had been brought up and lived the greater part of her life in one of the most convenient and agreeable farming countries in the United States. Few have lived long in the city without having experiences of a similar feeling. Is it astonishing? Compare advantages in respect simply to schools, libraries, music and the fine arts. People of the greatest wealth can hardly command as much of these in the country as the poorest work-girl is offered here in Boston at the mere cost of a walk for a short distance over a good, firm, clean pathway, lighted at night and made interesting to her by shop fronts and the variety of people passing.

It is true the poorer work-girls make little use of these special advantages, but this simply because they are not yet educated up to them. When, however, they come from the country to town, are they not moving in the way of this education? In all probability, as is indicated by the report (in the "New York Tribune") of a recent skillful examination of the condition and habits of the poor sewing women of that city, a frantic desire to escape from the dull lives which they have seen before them in the country, a craving for recreation, especially for more companionship in yielding to playful girlish impulses, innocent in themselves, drives more young women to the town than anything else.[12] Dr. Holmes may exaggerate the clumsiness and dreariness of New England village social parties; but go further back into the country among the outlying farms, and if you have ever had part in the working up of some of the rare occasions in which what stands for festivity is attempted, you will hardly think that the ardent desire of a young woman to escape to the town is wholly unreasonable.[13]

The civilized woman is above all things a tidy woman. She enjoys being surrounded by bright and gay things perhaps not less than the savage, but she shrinks from draggling, smirching, fouling things and "things out of keeping" more. By the keenness with which she avoids subjecting herself to annoyances of this class, indeed, we may judge the degree in which a woman has advanced in civilization. Think what a country road and roadside, and what the back yard of a farm-house, commonly is, in winter and spring-time; and what far-away farmers' gardens are in haying time, or most of them at any time. Think, again, how hard it is when you city people go into the country for a few weeks in summer, to keep your things in order, to get a thousand little things done which you regard as trifles when at home, how far you have to go, and with how much uncertainty, how much unaccustomed management you have to exercise. For the perfection and delicacy — the cleanness — with which any human want is provided for depends on the concentration of human ingenuity and skill upon that particular want. The greater the division of labor at any point, the greater the perfection with which all wants may be satisfied. Everywhere in the country the number and variety of workmen, not agricultural laborers, proportionately to the population, is lessening as the facility for reaching workmen in town is increasing. In one year we find fifty-four new divisions of trade added to the "London Directory."[14]

Think of all these things, and you will possibly find yourself growing a little impatient of the common cant which assumes that the strong tendency of women to town life, even though it involves great privations and dangers, is a purely senseless, giddy, vain, frivolous, and degrading one.

The consideration which most influences this tendency of women in families, however, seems to be the amount of time and labor, and wear and tear of nerves and mind, which is saved to them by the organization of labor in those forms, more especially, by which the menial service of households is simplified and reduced. Consider, for instance, what is done (that in the country is not done at all or is done by each household for itself, and, if efficiently, with a wearing, constant effort of superintendence) by the butcher, baker, fishmonger, grocer, by the provision venders of all sorts, by the ice-man, dust-man, scavenger, by the postman, carrier, expressmen, and messengers, all serving you at your house when required; by the sewers, gutters, pavements, crossings, sidewalks, public conveyances, and gas and water works.

But here again there is every reason to suppose that what we see is but a foretaste of what is yet to come. Take the difference of demand upon invention in respect to cheap conveyance for example. We began experimentally with street railways twenty years ago. At present, in New York, one pair of horses serves to convey one hundred people, on an average, every day at a rate of fare about one fiftieth of the old hackney-coach rates, and the total number of fares collected annually is equal to that of the population of the United States. And yet thousands walk a number of miles every day because they cannot be seated in the cars. It is impossible to fix a limit to the amount of travel which really ample, convenient, and still cheap means of transportation for short distances would develop. Certain improvements have caused the whole number of people seeking conveyances in London to be doubled in the last five years, and yet the supply keeps nowhere near the demand.

See how rapidly we are really gaining and what we have to expect. Two recent inventions give us the means of reducing by a third, under favorable circumstances, the cost of good McAdam roads. There have been sixteen patents issued from one office for other new forms of perfectly smooth and nearly noiseless street pavement, some of which, after two or three years' trial, promise so well as to render it certain that some improvement will soon come by which more than one of the present special annoyances of town life will be abated.[15] An improvement in our sewer system seems near at hand also, which will add considerably to the comparative advantages of a residence in towns, and especially the more open town suburbs.

Experiments indicate that it is feasible to send heated air through a town in pipes like water, and that it may be drawn upon, and the heat which is taken measured and paid for according to quantity required.[16] Thus may come a great saving of fuel and trouble in a very difficult department of domestic economy. No one will think of applying such a system to farm-houses.

Again, it is plain that we have scarcely begun to turn to account the advantages offered to towns-people in the electric telegraph; we really have not made a beginning with those offered in the pneumatic tube, though their substantial character has been demonstrated. By the use of these two instruments, a tradesman ten miles away on the other side of a town may be communicated with, and goods obtained from him by a housekeeper, as quickly and with as little personal inconvenience as now if he were in the next block. A single tube station for five hundred families, acoustic pipes for the transmission of orders to it from each house, with a carriers' service for local distribution of packages, is all that is needed for this purpose.[17]

As to the economy which comes by systematizing and concentrating, by the application of a large apparatus, of processes which are otherwise conducted in a desultory way, wasteful of human strength, as by public laundries, bakeries, and kitchens, we are yet, in America, even in our larger cities, far behind many of the smaller towns of the Old World.

While in all these directions enterprise and the progress of invention are quite sure to add rapidly to the economy and convenience of town life, and thus increase its comparative attractions, in other directions every step tends to reduce the man-power required on the farms for the production of a given amount of the raw material of food. Such is the effect, for instance, of every improvement of apparatus or process in ploughing, mowing, reaping, curing, thrashing, and marketing.

Another tendency arising from the improvement of agricultural apparatus, and which will be much accelerated when steam shall have been as successfully applied to tillage as it is already to harvesting and marketing operations, is that to the enlargement of fields and of farms. From this will follow the reduction in number and the greater separation and greater isolation of rural homesteads; for with our long-fronted farms, it will be centuries before we can hope to have tolerable roads on which rapid steam travelling from farm to farm will be practicable, though we may be close upon it wherever hard, firm, and always smooth roads can be afforded.

It should be observed that possession of the various advantages of the town to which we have referred, and, indeed, of all the advantages which are peculiar to large towns, while it very certainly cannot be acquired by people living in houses a quarter or a half mile apart, does not, on the other hand, by any means involve an unhealthy density of population. Probably the advantages of civilization can be found illustrated and demonstrated under no other circumstances so completely as in some suburban neighborhoods where each family abode stands fifty or a hundred feet or more apart from all others, and at some distance from the public road. And it must be remembered, also, that man's enjoyment of rural beauty has clearly increased rather than diminished with his advance in civilization. There is no reason, except in the loss of time, the inconvenience, discomfort, and expense of our present arrangements for short travel, why suburban advantages should not be almost indefinitely extended. Let us have a cheap and enjoyable method of conveyance, and a building law like that of old Rome,[18] and they surely will be.

As railroads are improved, all the important stations will become centres or sub-centres of towns, and all the minor stations suburbs. For most ordinary every-day purposes, especially house-keepers' purposes, these will need no very large population before they can obtain urban advantages. I have seen a settlement, the resident population of which was under three hundred, in which there was a public laundry, bath-house, barber's shop, billiard-room, beer-garden, and bakery. Fresh rolls and fresh milk were supplied to families before breakfast time every morning; fair fruit and succulent vegetables were delivered at house doors not half an hour after picking; and newspapers and magazines were distributed by a carrier. I have seen a town of not more than twelve hundred inhabitants, the streets and the yards, alleys, and places of which were swept every day as regularly as the house floors, and all dust removed by a public dust-man.

The construction of good roads and walks, the laying of sewer, water, and gas pipes, and the supplying of sufficiently cheap, rapid, and comfortable conveyances to town centres, is all that is necessary to give any farming land in a healthy and attractive situation the value of town lots. And whoever has observed in the French agricultural colonies how much more readily and cheaply railroads, telegraph, gas, water, sewer, and nearly all other advantages of towns may be made available to the whole population than under our present helter-skelter methods of settlement, will not believe that even the occupation of a farm laborer must necessarily and finally exclude his family from a very large share of urban conveniences.

But this opens a subject of speculation, which I am not now free to pursue. It is hardly a matter of speculation, I am disposed to think, but almost of demonstration, that the larger a town becomes because simply of its advantages for commercial purposes, the greater will be the convenience available to those who live in and near it for coöperation, as well with reference to the accumulation of wealth in the higher forms, — as in seats of learning, of science, and of art — as with reference to merely domestic economy and the emancipation of both men and women from petty, confining, and narrowing cares.

It also appears to be nearly certain that the recent rapid enlargement of towns and withdrawal of people from rural conditions of living is the result mainly of circumstances of a permanent character.

We have reason to believe, then, that towns which of late have been increasing rapidly on account of their commercial advantages, are likely to be still more attractive to population in the future; that there will in consequence soon be larger towns than any the world has yet known, and that the further progress of civilization is to depend mainly upon the influences by which men's minds and characters will be affected while living in large towns.

Now, knowing that the average length of the life of mankind in towns has been much less than in the country, and that the average amount of disease and misery and of vice and crime has been much greater in towns, this would be a very dark prospect for civilization, if it were not that modern Science has beyond all question determined many of the causes of the special evils by which men are afflicted in towns, and placed means in our hands for guarding against them. It has shown, for example, that under ordinary circumstances, in the interior parts of large and closely built towns, a given quantity of air contains considerably less of the elements which we require to receive through the lungs than the air of the country or even of the outer and more open parts of a town, and that instead of them it carries in to the lungs highly corrupt and irritating matters, the action of which tends strongly to vitiate all our sources of vigor — how strongly may perhaps be indicated in the shortest way by the statement that even metallic plates and statues corrode and wear away under the atmospheric influences which prevail in the midst of large towns, more rapidly than in the country.

The irritation and waste of the physical powers which result from the same cause, doubtless indirectly affect and very seriously affect the mind and the moral strength; but there is a general impression that a class of men are bred in towns whose peculiarities are not perhaps adequately accounted for in this way. We may understand these better if we consider that whenever we walk through the denser part of a town, to merely avoid collision with those we meet and pass upon the sidewalks, we have constantly to watch, to foresee, and to guard against their movements. This involves a consideration of their intentions, a calculation of their strength and weakness, which is not so much for their benefit as our own. Our minds are thus brought into close dealings with other minds without any friendly flowing toward them, but rather a drawing from them. Much of the intercourse between men when engaged in the pursuits of commerce has the same tendency — a tendency to regard others in a hard if not always hardening way. Each detail of observation and of the process of thought required in this kind of intercourse or contact of minds is so slight and so common in the experience of towns-people that they are seldom conscious of it. It certainly involves some expenditure nevertheless. People from the country are ever conscious of the effect on their nerves and minds of the street contact — often complaining that they feel confused by it; and if we had no relief from it at all during our waking hours, we should all be conscious of suffering from it. It is upon our opportunities of relief from it, therefore, that not only our comfort in town life, but our ability to maintain a temperate, good-natured, and healthy state of mind, depends. This is one of many ways in which it happens that men who have been brought up, as the saying is, in the streets, who have been the most directly and completely affected by town influences, so generally show, along with a remarkable quickness of apprehension, a peculiarly hard sort of selfishness. Every day of their lives they have seen thousands of their fellow-men, have met them face to face, have brushed against them, and yet have had no experience of anything in common with them.

It has happened several times within the last century, when old artificial obstructions to the spreading out of a city have been removed, and especially where there has been a demolition of and rebuilding on a new ground plan of some part which had previously been noted for the frequency of certain crimes, the prevalence of certain diseases, and the shortness of life among its inhabitants, that a marked improvement in all these respects has immediately followed, and has been maintained not alone in the dark parts, but in the city as a whole.

But although it has been demonstrated by such experiments that we have it in our power to greatly lessen and counteract the two classes of evils we have had under consideration, it must be remembered that these means are made use of only with great difficulty — how great, one or two illustrations from experience will enable us perhaps better to understand.

When the business quarter of New York was burnt over, thirty years ago, there was a rare opportunity for laying out a district expressly with a view to facilitate commerce.[19] The old plan had been arrived at in a desultory way; and so far as it had been the result of design, it had been with reference more especially to the residence of a semi-rural population. This had long since passed away; its inconvenience for commercial purposes had been experienced for many years; no one supposed from the relation of the ground to the adjacent navigable waters that it would ever be required for other than commercial purposes. Yet the difficulties of equalizing benefits and damages among the various owners of the land prevented any considerable change of the old street lines. Every working day thousands of dollars are subtracted from the profits of business, by the disadvantages thus reëstablished. The annual loss amounts to millions.

Men of barbarous habits laid out a part of London in a way which a thousand years later was found to be a cause of immeasurable waste of life, strength, and property. There had been much talk, but no effective action, looking toward improvement, when the great fire came, and left every building a heap of ashes. Immediately upon this, while the fire was still burning, a great man, Sir Christopher Wren, prepared a plan for avoiding the old evils.[20] This plan, a simple, excellent, and economical one, he took to the king, who at once approved it, took a strong interest in it, and used all his royal power to have it carried out. It was hailed with satisfaction by all wise and good men, and yet so difficult was it to overcome the difficulties entailed by the original rural laying out of the ground, that the attempt was finally abandoned, and the new city was built with immaterial modifications under the old barbarous plan; and so it remains with only slight improvement, and that purchased at enormous cost, to this day.

Remedy for a bad plan, once built upon, being thus impracticable, now that we understand the matter we are surely bound, wherever it is by any means in our power, to prevent mistakes in the construction of towns. Strange to say, however, here in the New World, where great towns by the hundred are springing into existence, no care at all is taken to avoid bad plans. The most brutal Pagans to whom we have sent our missionaries have never shown greater indifference to the sufferings of others than is exhibited in the plans of some of our most promising cities, for which men now living in them are responsible.

Not long since I was asked by the mayor of one of these to go before its common council and explain the advantages of certain suggested changes, including especially the widening of two roads leading out of town and as yet but partially opened and not at all built upon. After I had done so, two of the aldermen in succession came to me, and each privately said in effect: "It is quite plain that the proposition is a good one, and it ought to be adopted; the city would undoubtedly gain by it; but the people of the ward I represent have less interest in it than some others: they do not look far ahead, and they are jealous of those who would be more directly benefited than themselves; consequently I don't think that they would like it if I voted for it, and I shall not, but I hope it will be carried."[21]

They were unwilling that even a stranger should have so poor an opinion of their own intelligence as to suppose that they did not see the advantage of the change proposed; but it was not even suggested to their minds that there might be something shameful in repudiating their obligations to serve, according to the best of their judgment, the general and permanent interests committed to them as legislators of the city.

It is evident that if we go on in this way, the progress of civilized mankind in health, virtue, and happiness will be seriously endangered.

It is practically certain that the Boston of to-day is the mere nucleus of the Boston that is to be. It is practically certain that it is to extend over many miles of country now thoroughly rural in character, in parts of which farmers are now laying out roads with a view to shortening the teaming distance between their wood lots and a railway station, being governed in their courses by old property lines, which were first run simply with reference to the equitable division of heritages, and in other parts of which, perhaps, some wild speculators are having streets staked off from plans which they have formed with a rule and pencil in a broker's office, with a view chiefly to the impressions they would make when seen by other speculators on a lithographed map. And by this manner of planning, unless views of duty or of interest prevail that are not yet common, if Boston continues to grow at its present rate even for but a few generations longer, and then simply holds its own until it shall be as old as the Boston in Lincolnshire now is, more men, women, and children are to be seriously affected in health and morals than are now living on this Continent.

Is this a small matter — a mere matter of taste; a sentimental speculation?

It must be within the observation of most of us that where, in the city, wheel-ways originally twenty feet wide were with great difficulty and cost enlarged to thirty, the present width is already less nearly adequate to the present business than the former was to the former business; obstructions are more frequent, movements are slower and oftener arrested, and the liability to collision is greater. The same is true of sidewalks. Trees thus have been cut down, porches, bow-windows, and other encroachments removed but every year the walk is less sufficient for the comfortable passing of those who wish to use it.

It is certain that as the distance from the interior to the circumference of towns shall increase with the enlargement of their population, the less sufficient relatively to the service to be performed will be any given space between buildings.

In like manner every evil to which men are specially liable when living in towns, is likely to be aggravated in the future, unless means are devised and adapted in advance to prevent it.

Let us proceed, then, to the question of means, and with a seriousness in some degree befitting a question, upon our dealing with which we know the misery or happiness of many millions of our fellow-beings will depend.

We will for the present set before our minds the two sources of wear and corruption which we have seen to be remediable and therefore preventible. We may admit that commerce requires that in some parts of a town there shall be an arrangement of buildings, and a character of streets and of traffic in them which will establish conditions of corruption and of irritation, physical and mental. But commerce does not require the same conditions to be maintained in all parts of a town.

Air is disinfected by sunlight and foliage. Foliage also acts mechanically to purify the air by screening it. Opportunity and inducement to escape at frequent intervals from the confined and vitiated air of the commercial quarter, and to supply the lungs with air screened and purified by trees, and recently acted upon by sunlight, together with the opportunity and inducement to escape from conditions requiring vigilance, wariness, and activity toward other men — if these could be supplied economically, our problem would be solved.

In the old days of walled towns all tradesmen lived under the roof of their shops, and their children and apprentices and servants sat together with them in the evening about the kitchen fire. But now that the dwelling is built by itself and there is greater room, the inmates have a parlor to spend their evenings in; they spread carpets on the floor to gain in quiet, and hang drapery in their windows and papers on their walls to gain in seclusion and beauty. Now that our towns are built without walls, and we can have all the room that we like, is there any good reason why we should not make some similar difference between parts which are likely to be dwelt in, and those which will be required exclusively for commerce?

Would trees, for seclusion and shade and beauty, be out of place, for instance, by the side of certain of our streets? It will, perhaps, appear to you that it is hardly necessary to ask such a question, as throughout the United States trees are commonly planted at the sides of streets. Unfortunately, they are seldom so planted as to have fairly settled the question of the desirableness of systematically maintaining trees under these circumstances. In the first place, the streets are planned, wherever they are, essentially alike. Trees are planted in the space assigned for sidewalks, where at first, while they are saplings, and the vicinity is rural or suburban, they are not much in the way, but where, as they grow larger, and the vicinity becomes urban, they take up more and more space, while space is more and more required for passage. That is not all. Thousands and tens of thousands are planted every year in a manner and under conditions as nearly certain as possible either to kill them outright, or to so lessen their vitality as to prevent their natural and beautiful development, and to cause premature decrepitude. Often, too, as their lower limbs are found inconvenient, no space having been provided for trees in laying out the street, they are deformed by butcherly amputations. If by rare good fortune they are suffered to become beautiful, they still stand subject to be condemned to death at any time, as obstructions in the highway.*

What I would ask is, whether we might not with economy make special provision in some of our streets — in a twentieth or a fiftieth part, if you please, of all — for trees to remain as a permanent furniture of the city? I mean, to make a place for them in which they would have room to grow

---

* On the border of the first street laid out in the oldest town in New England, there yet stands what has long been known as "the Town Tree," its trunk having served for generations as a publication post for official notices. "The selectmen," having last year removed the lower branches of all the younger roadside trees of the town, and thereby its chief beauty, have this year deliberately resolved that they would have this tree cut down, for no other reason, so far as appears in their official record, than that if two persons came carelessly together on the roadway side of it, one of them might chance to put his foot in the adjoining shallow street-gutter. It might cost ten dollars to deepen and bridge this gutter

naturally and gracefully. Even if the distance between the houses should have to be made half as much again as it is required to be in our commercial streets, could not the space be afforded? Out of town space is not costly when measures to secure it are taken early. The assessments for benefit where such streets were provided for, would, in nearly all cases, defray the cost of the land required. The strips of ground reserved for the trees, six, twelve, twenty feet wide, would cost nothing for paving or flagging.

The change both of scene and of air which would be obtained by people engaged for the most part in the necessarily confined interior commercial parts of the town, on passing into a street of this character after the trees had become stately and graceful, would be worth a good deal. If such streets were made still broader in some parts, with spacious malls, the advantage would be increased. If each of them were given the proper capacity, and laid out with laterals and connections in suitable directions to serve as a convenient trunk-line of communication between two large districts of the town or the business centre and the suburbs, a very great number of people might thus be placed every day under influences counteracting those with which we desire to contend.

These, however, would be merely very simple improvements upon arrangements which are in common use in every considerable town. Their advantages would be incidental to the general uses of streets as they are. But people are willing very often to seek recreation as well as take it by the way. Provisions may indeed be made expressly for recreation, with certainty that if convenient, they will be used.

The various kinds of recreation may be divided primarily under two heads. Under one will be included all of which the predominating influence is to stimulate exertion of any part or parts needing it; under the other, all which cause us to receive pleasure or benefit without conscious exertion. Games chiefly of mental skill, as chess, or athletic sports, as base-ball, are examples of means of recreation of the first division, which may be termed that of *exertive* recreation; music and the fine arts generally, of the second or *receptive* division.

Considering the first by itself, it will be found not a very simple matter to determine for what forms of exertive recreations opportunities can be provided in a large town, consistently with good order, safety, and economy of management. Mr. Anthony Trollope[22] might recommend fox-hunting; hurdle-racing has been seriously urged by gentlemen who have given special attention to the advantages of that form of exercise. In New York, on the other hand, after several years' deliberation, and some experiments in a small way,

---

substantially. The call to arms for the Old French War, for the War of the Revolution, the war for the freedom of the seas, the Mexican War, and the War of the Rebellion, was first made in this town under the shade of this tree, which is an American elm, and, notwithstanding its great age, is perfectly healthy and almost as beautiful as it is venerable.[23]

it has been decided that the city cannot expediently undertake to provide grounds even for base-ball, cricket, and foot-ball clubs, to the great disappointment of a very large and influential element of the population.[24]

I do not propose now to discuss the various details of this question, but to leave out of consideration all that class of pastimes which, except in the open country, cannot easily be pursued without danger to persons not taking part in them, and to adopt the conclusion that only school-boys should be provided at public expense with every-day grounds for ball-playing, and this as a part of the educational rather than the recreative system of the town. I will only remark that you will find no purposes of athletic recreation which cannot be accommodated either by such trunk roads as I have suggested we should here and there introduce, or by a sufficient number of comparatively small spaces of open ground, and that, although there are certain advantages more particularly to be gained by pursuing the forms of exertive recreation named on grounds of large rather than small area, it would be better on the whole to have a number of small grounds than to establish any very large ground with special reference to them.

Let us now proceed to the consideration of receptive recreations. As we shall consider such forms of recreation as are pursued socially or by a number of persons together, it will be convenient to again divide our subjects into sub-heads, according to the degree in which the average enjoyment of them is greatest when a large congregation of persons is assembled, or when the number coming together is small, and the circumstances favorable to the exercise of personal friendliness. Our pleasure in recreations of the first of these classes appears to me to be dependent upon the existence of an instinct in us of which I think not enough account is commonly made, and I shall therefore term it the *gregarious* class of social receptive recreations. The other will be sufficiently distinguished from it by the term *neighborly*.

Purely gregarious recreation seems to be generally looked upon in New England society as childish and savage, because, I suppose, there is so little of what we call intellectual gratification in it. We are inclined to engage in it indirectly, furtively, and with complication. Yet there are certain forms of recreation, a large share of the attraction of which must, I think, lie in the gratification of the gregarious inclination, and which, with those who can afford to indulge in them, are so popular as to establish their importance of the requirement.

If I ask myself where I have experienced the most complete gratification of this instinct in public and out of doors, among trees, I find that it has been in the promenade of the Champs Elysées. As closely following it I should name other promenades of Europe, and our own upon the New York parks. I have studiously watched the latter for several years. I have several times seen fifty thousand people participating in them; and the more I have seen of them, the more highly have I been led to estimate their value as means of counteracting the evils of town life.

Consider that the New York Park and the Brooklyn Park[25] are the only places in those associated cities where, in this eighteen hundred and seventieth year after Christ, you will find a body of Christians coming together, and with an evident glee in the prospect of coming together, all classes largely represented, with a common purpose, not at all intellectual, competitive with none, disposing to jealousy and spiritual or intellectual pride toward none, each individual adding by his mere presence to the pleasure of all others, all helping to the greater happiness of each. You may thus often see vast numbers of persons brought closely together, poor and rich, young and old, Jew and Gentile. I have seen a hundred thousand thus congregated, and I assure you that though there have been not a few that seemed a little dazed, as if they did not quite understand it, and were, perhaps, a little ashamed of it, I have looked studiously but vainly among them for a single face completely unsympathetic with the prevailing expression of good nature and light-heartedness.

Is it doubtful that it does men good to come together in this way in pure air and under the light of heaven, or that it must have an influence directly counteractive to that of the ordinary hard, hustling working hours of town life?

You will agree with me, I am sure, that it is not, and that opportunity, convenient, attractive opportunity, for such congregation, is a very good thing to provide for, in planning the extension of a town.

I referred especially to the Champs Elysées, because the promenade there is a very old custom, not a fashion of the day, and because I must needs admit that this most striking example is one in which no large area of ground — nothing like a park — has been appropriated for the purpose.[26] I must acknowledge, also, that the alamedas of Spain and Portugal supply another and very interesting instance of the same fact.[27] You will observe, however, that small local grounds, such as we have said might be the best for most exertive recreations, are not at all adapted to receptive recreations of the type described.

One thing more under this head. I have but little personal familiarity with Boston customs; but I have lived or sojourned in several other towns of New England, as well as of other parts of the country. I have never been long in any one locality, south or north, east or west, without observing a *custom* of gregarious out-of-door recreation in some miserably imperfect form, usually covered by a wretched pretext of a wholly different purpose, as perhaps, for instance, visiting a grave-yard. I am sure that it would be much better, less expensive, less harmful in all ways, more health-giving to body, mind, and soul, if it were admitted to be a distinct requirement of all human beings, and appropriately provided for.

I have next to see what opportunities are wanted to induce people to engage in what I have termed neighborly receptive recreations, under conditions which shall be highly counteractive to the prevailing bias to degeneration and demoralization in large towns. To make clearer what I mean, I need an illustration which I find in a familiar domestic gathering, where the prattle of the children mingles with the easy conversation of the more sedate, the bodily requirements satisfied with good cheer, fresh air, agreeable light, moderate temperature, snug shelter, and furniture and decorations adapted to please the eye, without calling for profound admiration on the one hand, or tending to fatigue or disgust on the other. The circumstances are all favorable to a pleasurable wakefulness of the mind without stimulating exertion; and the close relation of family life, the association of children, of mothers, of lovers, or those who may be lovers, stimulate and keep alive the more tender sympathies, and give play to faculties such as may be dormant in business or on the promenade; while at the same time the cares of providing in detail for all the wants of the family, guidance, instruction, and reproof, and the dutiful reception of guidance, instruction, and reproof, are, as matters of conscious exertion, as far as possible laid aside.

There is an instinctive inclination to this social, neighborly, unexertive form of recreation among all of us. In one way or another it is sure to be constantly operating upon those millions on millions of men and women who are to pass their lives within a few miles of where we now stand. To what extent it shall operate so as to develop health and virtue, will, on many occasions, be simply a question of opportunity and inducement. And this question is one for the determination of which for a thousand years we here to-day are largely responsible.

Think what the ordinary state of things to many is at this beginning of the town. The public is reading just now a little book in which some of your streets of which you are not proud are described.* Go into one of those red cross streets[28] any fine evening next summer, and ask how it is with their residents? Oftentimes you will see half a dozen sitting together on the door-steps, or, all in a row, on the curb-stones, with their feet in the gutter, driven out of doors by the closeness within; mothers among them anxiously regarding their children who are dodging about at their play, among the noisy wheels on the pavement.

Again, consider how often you see young men in knots of perhaps half a dozen in lounging attitudes rudely obstructing the sidewalks, chiefly led in their little conversation by the suggestions given to their minds by what or whom they may see passing in the street, men, women, or children, whom they do not know, and for whom they have no respect or sympathy. There is nothing among them or about them which is adapted to bring into play a spark of admiration, of delicacy, manliness, or tenderness. You see them presently descend in search of physical comfort to a brilliantly lighted basement, where they find others of their sort, see, hear, smell, drink, and eat all manner of vile things.

* *Sybaris*, by the Rev. E. E. Hale.[29]

Whether on the curb-stones or in the dram-shops, these young men are all under the influence of the same impulse which some satisfy about the tea-table with neighbors and wives and mothers and children, and all things clean and wholesome, softening and refining.

If the great city to arise here is to be laid out little by little, and chiefly to suit the views of land-owners, acting only individually, and thinking only of how what they do is to affect the value in the next week or the next year of the few lots that each may hold at the time, the opportunities of so obeying this inclination as at the same time to give the lungs a bath of pure sunny air, to give the mind a suggestion of rest from the devouring eagerness and intellectual strife of town life, will always be few to any, to many will amount to nothing.

But is it possible to make public provision for recreation of this class, essentially domestic and secluded as it is?

It is a question which can, of course, be conclusively answered only from experience. And from experience in some slight degree I shall answer it. There is one large American town, in which it may happen that a man of any class shall say to his wife, when he is going out in the morning: "My dear, when the children come home from school, put some bread and butter and salad in a basket, and go to the spring under the chestnut-tree where we found the Johnsons last week. I will join you there as soon as I can get away from the office. We will walk to the dairy-man's cottage and get some tea, and some fresh milk for the children, and take our supper by the brook-side;" and this shall be no joke, but the most refreshing earnest.

There will be room enough in the Brooklyn Park, when it is finished, for several thousand little family and neighborly parties to bivouac at frequent intervals through the summer, without discommoding one another, or interfering with any other purpose, to say nothing of those who can be drawn out to make a day of it, as many thousand were last year. And although the arrangements for the purpose were yet very incomplete, and but little ground was at all prepared for such use, besides these small parties, consisting of one or two families, there came also, in companies of from thirty to a hundred and fifty, somewhere near twenty thousand children with their parents, Sunday-school teachers, or other guides and friends, who spent the best part of a day under the trees and on the turf, in recreations of which the predominating element was of this neighborly receptive class. Often they would bring a fiddle, flute, and harp, or other music. Tables, seats, shade, turf, swings, cool spring-water, and a pleasing rural prospect, stretching off half a mile or more each way, unbroken by a carriage road or the slightest evidence of the vicinity of the town, were supplied them without charge, and bread and milk and ice-cream at moderate fixed charges. In all my life I have never seen such joyous collections of people. I have, in fact, more than once observed tears of gratitude in the eyes of poor women, as they watched their children thus enjoying themselves.

The whole cost of such neighborly festivals, even when they include excursions by rail from the distant parts of the town, does not exceed for each person, on an average, a quarter of a dollar; and when the arrangements are complete, I see no reason why thousands should not come every day where hundreds come now to use them; and if so, who can measure the value, generation after generation, of such provisions for recreation to the overwrought, much-confined people of the great town that is to be?

For this purpose neither of the forms of ground we have heretofore considered are at all suitable. We want a ground to which people may easily go after their day's work is done, and where they may stroll for an hour, seeing, hearing, and feeling nothing of the bustle and jar of the streets, where they shall, in effect, find the city put far away from them. We want the greatest possible contrast with the streets and the shops and the rooms of the town which will be consistent with convenience and the preservation of good order and neatness. We want, especially, the greatest possible contrast with the restraining and confining conditions of the town, those conditions which compel us to walk circumspectly, watchfully, jealously, which compel us to look closely upon others without sympathy. Practically, what we most want is a simply, broad, open space of clean greensward, with sufficient play of surface and a sufficient number of trees about it to supply a variety of light and shade. This we want as a central feature. We want depth of wood enough about it not only for comfort in hot weather, but to completely shut out the city from our landscapes. These are the distinguishing elements of what is properly called a park.

There is no provision for recreation so valuable as this would be; there is none which will be so important to place judiciously in the plan of the city merely as a space, and as an interruption of direct communication between its different parts. There is nothing, therefore, for which we should be more anxious to find and early secure and hold in reserve a suitable site.

A Promenade may, with great advantage, be carried along the outer part of the surrounding groves of a park; and it will do no harm if here and there a broad opening among the trees discloses its open landscapes to those upon the promenade. But recollect that the object of the latter for the time being should be to see *congregated human life* under glorious and necessarily artificial conditions, and the natural landscape is not essential to them; though there is no more beautiful picture, and none can be more pleasing incidentally to the gregarious purpose, than that of beautiful meadows, over which clusters of level-armed sheltering trees cast broad shadows, and upon which are scattered dainty cows and flocks of black-faced sheep, while men, women, and children are seen sitting here and there forming groups in the shade, or moving in and out among the woody points and bays.

It may be inferred from what I have said, that very rugged ground, abrupt eminences, and what is technically called picturesque in distinction from merely beautiful or simply pleasing scenery, is not the most desirable for a town park. Decidedly not in my opinion. The park should, as far as possible, compliment the town. Openness is the one thing you cannot get in buildings. Picturesqueness you can get. Let your buildings be as picturesque as your artists can make them. This is the beauty of a town. Consequently, the beauty of the park should be the other. It should be the beauty of the fields, the meadow, the prairie, of the green pastures, and the still waters. What we want to gain is tranquillity and rest to the mind. Mountains suggest effort. But besides this objection there are others of what I may indicate as the house-keeping class. It is impossible to give the public range over a large extent of ground of a highly picturesque character, unless under very exceptional circumstances, and sufficiently guard against the occurrence of opportunities and temptations to shabbiness, disorder, indecorum, and indecency, that will be subversive of every good purpose the park should be designed to fulfill.

Nor can I think that *in the park proper*, what is called gardenesque beauty is to be courted; still less that highly artificial and exotic form of it, which, under the name of subtropical planting, the French have lately introduced,[30] and in suitable positions with interesting and charming results, but in following which indiscreetly, the English are sacrificing the peculiar beauty of their simple and useful parks of the old time. Both these may have places, and very important places, but they do not belong within a park, unless as side scenes and incidents. Twenty years ago Hyde Park[31] had a most pleasing, open, free, and inviting expression, though certainly it was too rude, too much wanting in art; but now art is vexed with long harsh lines of repellant iron-work, and here and there behind it bouquets of hot house plants, between which the public pass like hospital convalescents, who have been turned into the yard to walk about while their beds are making. We should undertake nothing in a park which involves the treating of the public as prisoners or wild beasts. A great object of all that is done in a park, of *all* the art of a park, is to influence the mind of men through their imagination, and the influence of iron hurdles can never be good.

We have, perhaps, sufficiently defined the ideal of a park for a large town. It will seldom happen that this ideal can be realized fully. The next thing is to select the situation in which it can be most nearly approached without great cost; and by cost I do not mean simply cost of land or of construction, but cost of inconvenience and cost of keeping in order, which is a very much more serious matter, and should have a great deal more study.

A park fairly well managed near a large town, will surely become a new centre of that town. With the determination of location, size, and boundaries should therefore be associated the duty of arranging new trunk routes of communication between it and the distant parts of the town existing and forecasted.

These may be either narrow informal elongations of the park, varying say from two to five hundred feet in width, and radiating irregularly from it, or if, unfortunately, the town is already laid out in the unhappy way that New York and Brooklyn, San Francisco and Chicago, are, and, I am glad to say, Boston is not, on a plan made long years ago by a man who never saw a spring-carriage, and who had a conscientious dread of the Graces,[32] then we must probably adopt formal Park-ways. They should be so planned and constructed as never to be noisy and seldom crowded, and so also that the straightforward movement of pleasure-carriages need never be obstructed, unless at absolutely necessary crossings, by slow-going heavy vehicles used for commercial purposes. If possible, also, they should be branched or reticulated with other ways of a similar class, so that no part of the town should finally be many minutes' walk from some one of them; and they should be made interesting by a process of planting and decoration, so that in necessarily passing through them, whether in going to or from the park, or to and from business, some substantial recreative advantage may be incidentally gained. It is a common error to regard a park as something to be produced complete in itself, as a picture to be painted on canvas. It should rather be planned as one to be done in fresco, with constant consideration of exterior objects, some of them quite at a distance and even existing as yet only in the imagination of the painter.

I have thus barely indicated a few of the points from which we may perceive our duty to apply the means in our hands to ends far distant, with reference to this problem of public recreations. Large operations of construction may not soon be desirable, but I hope you will agree with me that there is little room for question, that reserves of ground for the purposes I have referred to should be fixed upon as soon as possible, before the difficulty of arranging them, which arises from private building, shall be greatly more formidable than now.

To these reserves, — though not a dollar should be spent in construction during the present generation, — the plans of private construction would necessarily, from the moment they were established, be conformed.

I by no means wish to suggest that nothing should be done for the present generation; but only, that whatever happens to the present generation, it should not be allowed to go on heaping up difficulties and expenses for its successors, for want of a little comprehensive and business-like foresight and study. In all probability it will be found that much can be done even for the present generation without greatly if at all increasing taxation, as has been found in New York.

But the question now perhaps comes up: How can a community best take this work in hand?

It is a work in which private and local and special interests will be found so antagonistic one to another, in which heated prejudices are so liable to be unconsciously established, and in which those who would be disappointed in their personal greeds by whatever good scheme may be studied out, are so likely to combine and concentrate force to kill it (manufacture public opinion, as the phrase is), that the ordinary organizations for municipal business are unsuitable agencies for the purpose. It would, perhaps, be a bold thing to say that the public in its own interest, and in the interest of all of whom the present public are the trustees, should see to it that the problem is as soon as possible put clean out of its own hands, in order that it may be taken up efficiently by a small body of select men. But I will venture to say that until this in effect is done, the danger that public opinion may be led, by the application of industry, ingenuity, and business ability on the part of men whose real objects are perhaps unconsciously very close to their own pockets, to overrule the results of more comprehensive and impartial study, is much greater than in most questions of public interest.

You will not understand me as opposing or undervaluing the advantages of public discussion. What I would urge is, that park questions, and even the most elementary park questions, questions of site and outlines and approaches, are not questions to which the rule applies, that every man should look after his own interests, judge for himself what will favor his own interests, and exert his influence so as to favor them; but questions rather of that class, which in his private affairs every man of common sense is anxious, as soon as possible, to put into the hands of somebody who is able to take hold of them comprehensively as a matter of direct, grave, business responsibility.

It is upon this last point far more than upon any other that the experience of New York is instructive to other communities. I propose, therefore, to occupy your time a little while longer by a narration of those parts of this experience which bear most directly upon this point, and which will also supply certain other information which has been desired of me.

The New York legislature of 1851 passed a bill providing for a park on the east side of the island. Afterwards, the same legislature, precipitately and quite as an after-thought, passed the act under which the city took title to the site of the greater part of the present Central Park.[33]

This final action is said to have been the result of a counter movement, started after the passage of the first bill merely to gratify a private grudge of one of the city aldermen.

When in the formation of the counter project, the question was reached, what land shall be named in the second bill, the originator turned to a map and asked: *"Now where shall I go?"* His comrade, looking over his shoulder, without a moment's reflection, put his finger down and said, "Go there;" the point indicated appearing to be about the middle of the island, and therefore, as it occurred to him, one which would least excite local prejudices.[34]

The primary selection of the site was thus made in an off-hand way, by a man who had no special responsibility in the premises, and whose previous studies had not at all led him to be well informed or interested in the purposes of a park.

It would have been difficult to find another body of land of six hundred acres upon the island (unless by taking a long narrow strip upon the precipitous side of a ridge), which possessed less of what we have seen to be the most desirable characteristics of a park, or upon which more time, labor, and expense would be required to establish them.

But besides the topographical objections, when the work of providing suitable facilities for the recreation of the people upon this ground came to be practically and definitely considered, defects of outline were discerned, the incomplete remedy for which has since cost the city more than a million of dollars. The amount which intelligent study would have saved in this way if applied at the outset, might have provided for an amplification of some one of the approaches to the Park, such as, if it were now possible to be gained at a cost of two or three million dollars, I am confident would, if fairly set forth, be ordered by an almost unanimous vote of the tax-payers of the city. Public discussion at the time utterly failed to set this blundering right. Nor was public opinion then clearly dissatisfied with what was done or with those who did it.

During the following six years there was much public and private discussion of park questions; but the progress of public opinion, judged simply by the standard which it has since formed for itself, seems to have been chiefly backward.

This may be, to a considerable degree, accounted for by the fact that many men of wealth and influence — who, through ignorance and lack of mature reflection on this subject, were unable to anticipate any personal advantage from the construction of a park — feared that it would only add to their taxes, and thus were led to form a habit of crying down any hopeful anticipations.

The argument that certain towns of the old country did obtain some advantage from their parks, could not be refuted, but it was easy to say, and it was said, that "our circumstances are very different: surrounded by broad waters on all sides, open to the sea breezes, we need no artificial breathing-places; even if we did, nothing like the parks of the old cities under aristocratic government would be at all practicable here."

This assertion made such an impression as to lead many to believe that little more had better be done than to give the name of park to the ground which it was now too late to avoid taking. A leading citizen suggested that nothing more was necessary than to plough up a strip just within the boundary of the ground and plant it with young trees, and chiefly with cuttings of the poplar, which afterwards, as they came to good size, could be transplanted to the interior, and thus the Park would be furnished economically and quite well enough for the purposes it would be required to serve.

Another of distinguished professional reputation seriously urged through the public press, that the ground should be rented as a sheep-walk. In going to and from their folds the flocks would be sure to form trails which would serve the public perfectly well for foot-paths; nature would in time supply whatever else was essential to form a quite picturesque and perfectly suitable strolling ground for such as would wish to resort to it.

It was frequently alleged, and with truth, that the use made of the existing public grounds was such as to develop riotous and licentious habits. A large park, it was argued, would inevitably present larger opportunities, and would be likely to exhibit an aggravated form of the same tendencies, consequently anything like refinement of treatment would be entirely wasted.

A few passages from a leading article of the "Herald" newspaper, in the seventh year of the enterprise, will indicate what estimate its astute editor had then formed of the prevailing convictions of the public on the subject: —

> "It is all folly to expect in this country to have parks like those in old aristocratic countries. When we open a public park Sam will air himself in it. He will take his friends whether from church, street, or elsewhere. He will knock down any better dressed man who remonstrates with him. He will talk and sing, and fill his share of the bench, and flirt with the nursery-maids in his own coarse way. Now we ask what chance have William B. Astor and Edward Everett[35] against this fellow-citizen of theirs? Can they and he enjoy the same place? Is it not obvious that he will turn them out, and that the great Central Park will be nothing but a great bear-garden for the lowest denizens of the city, of which we shall yet pray litanies to be delivered?"

In the same article it was argued that the effect of the construction of the Park would be unfavorable to the value of property in its neighborhood, except as, to a limited extent, it might be taken up by Irish and German liquor dealers as sites for dram-shops and lager-bier gardens.[36]

There were many eminent citizens, who to my personal knowledge, in the sixth, seventh, and eighth year after the passage of the act, entertained similar views to those I have quoted.

I have been asked if I supposed that "gentlemen" would ever resort to the Park, or would allow their wives and daughters to visit it? I heard a renowned lawyer argue that it was preposterous to suppose that a police force would do anything toward preserving order and decency in any broad piece of ground open to the general public of New York. And after the work began, I often heard the conviction expressed that if what was called the reckless, extravagant, inconsiderate policy of those who had the making of the Park in charge, could not be arrested, the weight of taxation and the general disgust which would be aroused among the wealthy classes would drive them from the city, and thus prove a serious injury to its prosperity.

"Why," said one, a man whom you all know by reputation, and many personally, "I should not ask for anything finer in my private grounds for the use of my own family." To whom it was replied that possibly grounds might not unwisely be prepared even more carefully when designed for the use of two hundred thousand families and their guests, than when designed for the use of one.

The constantly growing conviction that it was a rash and ill-considered undertaking, and the apprehension that a great deal would be spent upon it for no good purpose, doubtless had something to do with the choice of men, who in the sixth year were appointed by the Governor of the State, commissioners to manage the work and the very extraordinary powers given them. At all events, it so happened that a majority of them were much better known from their places in the directory of banks, railroads, mining, and manufacturing enterprises, than from their previous services in politics; and their freedom to follow their own judgment and will, in respect to all the interior matters of the Park, was larger than had for a long time been given to any body of men charged with a public duty of similar importance.[37]

I suppose that few of them knew or cared more about the subject of their duties at the time of their appointment, than most other active business-men. They probably embodied very fairly the average opinion of the public, as to the way in which it was desirable that the work should be managed. If, then, it is asked, how did they come to adopt and resolutely pursue a course so very different from that which the public opinion seemed to expect of them, I think that the answer must be found in the fact that they had not wanted or asked the appointment; that it was made absolutely free from any condition or obligation to serve a party, a faction, or a person; that owing to the extraordinary powers given them, their sense of responsibility in the matter was of an uncommonly simple and direct character, and led them with the trained skill of business men to go straight to the question: —

"Here is a piece of property put into our hands. By what policy can we turn it to the best account for our stockholders?"

It has happened that instead of being turned out about the time they had got to know something about their special business, these commissioners have been allowed to remain in office to this time — a period of twelve years.

As to their method of work, it was as like as possible to that of a board of directors of a commercial corporation. They quite set at defiance the ordinary ideas of propriety applied to public servants, by holding their sessions with closed doors, their clerk being directed merely to supply the newspapers with reports of their acts. They spent the whole of the first year on questions simply of policy, organization, and plan, doing no practical work, as it was said, at all.

When the business of construction was taken hold of, they refused to occupy themselves personally with questions of the class which in New York usually take up nine tenths of the time and mind of all public servants, who have it in their power to arrange contracts and determine appointments, promotions, and discharges. All of these they turned over to the heads of the executive operations.

Now, when these deviations from usage were conjoined with the adoption of a policy of construction for which the public was entirely unprepared, and to which the largest tax-payers of the city were strongly opposed, when also those who had a variety of private axes to grind, found themselves and their influence, and their friends' influence, made nothing of by the commissioners, you may be sure that public opinion was manufactured against them at a great rate. The Mayor denounced them in his messages; the Common Council and other departments of the city government refused to coöperate with them, and were frequently induced to put obstructions in their way; they were threatened with impeachment and indictment; some of the city newspapers attacked them for a time in every issue; they were caricatured and lampooned; their session was once broken up by a mob, their business was five times examined (once or twice at great expense, lawyers, accountants, engineers, and other experts being employed for the purpose) by legislative investigating committees.[38] Thus for a time public opinion, through nearly all the channels open to it, apparently set against them like a torrent.

No men less strong, and no men less confident in their strength than these men — by virtue in part of personal character, in part of the extraordinary powers vested in them by the legislature, and in part by the accident of certain anomalous political circumstances — happened to be, could have carried through a policy and a method which commanded so little immediate public favor. As it was, nothing but personal character, the common impression that after all they were honest, saved them. By barely a saber's length they kept ahead of their pursuers, and of this you may still see evidence here and there in the park, chiefly where something left to stop a gap for the time being has been suffered to remain as if a permanence. At one time nearly four thousand laborers were employed; and for a year at one point, work went on night and day in order to put it as quickly as possible beyond the reach of those who were bent on stopping it.[39] Necessarily, under such circumstances, the rule obtains: "Look out for the main chance; we may save the horses, we must save the guns;" and if now you do not find everything in perfect parade order, the guns, at all events, were saved.

To fully understand the significance of the result so far, it must be considered that the Park is to this day, at some points, incomplete; that from the centre of population to the midst of the Park the distance is still four miles; that there is no steam transit; that other means of communication are indirect and excessively uncomfortable, or too expensive. For practical everyday purposes to the great mass of the people, the Park might as well be a hundred miles away. There are hundreds of thousands who have never seen it, more hundreds of thousands who have seen it only on a Sunday or holiday. The children of the city to whom it should be of the greatest use, can only get to it on holidays or in vacations, and then must pay car-fare both ways.

It must be remembered, also, that the Park is not planned for such use as is now made of it, but with regard to the future use, when it will be in the centre of a population of two millions hemmed in by water at a short distance on all sides; and that much of the work done upon it is, for this reason, as yet quite barren of results.

The question of the relative value of what is called off-hand common sense, and of special, deliberate, business-like study, must be settled in the case of the Central Park, by a comparison of benefit with cost. During the last four years over thirty million visits have been made to the Park by actual count, and many have passed uncounted. From fifty to eighty thousand persons on foot, thirty thousand in carriages, and four to five thousand on horseback, have frequently entered it in a day.

Among the frequent visitors, I have found all those who, a few years ago, believed it impossible that there should ever be a park in this republican country, — and especially in New York of all places in this country, — which would be a suitable place of resort for "gentlemen." They, their wives and daughters, frequent the Park more than they do the opera or the church.

There are many men of wealth who resort to the Park habitually and regularly, as much so as business men to their places of business. Of course, there is a reason for it, and a reason based upon their experience.

As to the effect on public health, there is no question that it is already great. The testimony of the older physicians of the city will be found unanimous on this point. Says one: "Where I formerly ordered patients of a certain class to give up their business altogether and go out of town, I now often advise simply moderation, and prescribe a ride in the Park before going to their offices, and again a drive with their families before dinner. By simply adopting this course as a habit, men who have been breaking down frequently recover tone rapidly, and are able to retain an active and controlling influence in an important business, from which they would have otherwise been forced to retire. I direct school-girls, under certain circumstances, to be taken wholly, or in part, from their studies, and sent to spend several hours a day rambling on foot in the Park."

The lives of women and children too poor to be sent to the country, can now be saved in thousands of instances, by making them go to the Park. During a hot day in July last, I counted at one time in the Park eighteen separate groups, consisting of mothers with their children, most of whom were under school-age, taking picnic dinners which they had brought from home with them. The practice is increasing under medical advice, especially when summer complaint is rife.

The much greater rapidity with which patients convalesce, and may be returned with safety to their ordinary occupations after severe illness, when they can be sent to the Park for a few hours a day, is beginning to be understood. The addition thus made to the productive labor of the city is not unimportant.

The Park, moreover, has had a very marked effect in making the city attractive to visitors, and in thus increasing its trade, and causing many who have made fortunes elsewhere to take up their residence and become taxpayers in it, — a much greater effect in this way, beyond all question, than all the colleges, schools, libraries, museums, and art-galleries which the city possesses. It has also induced many foreigners who have grown rich in the country, and who would otherwise have gone to Europe to enjoy their wealth, to settle permanently in the city.

And what has become of the great Bugaboo? This is what the "Herald" of later date answers: —

> "When one is inclined to despair of the country, let him go to the Central Park on a Saturday, and spend a few hours there in looking at the people, not at those who come in gorgeous carriages, but at those who arrive on foot, or in those exceedingly democratic conveyances, the street-cars; and if, when the sun begins to sink behind the trees, he does not arise and go homeward with a happy swelling heart," and so on, the effusion winding up thus: "We regret to say that the more brilliant becomes the display of vehicles and toilettes, the more shameful is the display of bad manners on the part of the —— extremely fine-looking people who ride in carriages and wear the fine dresses. We must add that the pedestrians always behave well."[40]

Here we touch a fact of more value to social science than any other in the history of the Park; but to fully set it before you would take an evening by itself. The difficulty of preventing ruffianism and disorder in a park to be frequented indiscriminately by such a population as that of New York, was from the first regarded as the greatest of all those which the commission had to meet, and the means of overcoming it cost more study than all other things.

It is, perhaps, too soon to judge of the value of the expedients resorted to, but there are as yet a great many parents who are willing to trust their school-girl daughters to ramble without special protection in the Park, as they would almost nowhere else in New York. One is no more likely to see ruffianism or indecencies in the Park than in the churches, and the arrests for offenses of all classes, including the most venial, which arise simply from the ignorance of country people, have amounted to but twenty in the million of the number of visitors, and of these, an exceedingly small proportion have been of that class which was so confidently expected to take possession of the Park and make it a place unsafe and unfit for decent people.

There is a good deal of delicate work on the Park, some of it placed there by private liberality — much that a girl with a parasol, or a boy throwing a pebble, could render valueless in a minute. Except in one or two cases where the ruling policy of the management has been departed from, — cases which prove the rule, — not the slightest injury from wantonness, carelessness, or ruffianism has occurred.

Jeremy Bentham, in treating of "The Means of Preventing Crimes," remarks that any innocent amusement that the human heart can invent is useful under a double point of view: first, for the pleasure itself which results from it; second, from its tendency to weaken the dangerous inclinations which man derives from his nature.[41]

No one who has closely observed the conduct of the people who visit the Park, can doubt that it exercises a distinctly harmonizing and refining influence upon the most unfortunate and most lawless classes of the city, — an influence favorable to courtesy, self-control, and temperance.

At three or four points in the midst of the Park, beer, wine, and cider are sold with other refreshments to visitors, not at bars, but served at tables where men sit in company with women. Whatever harm may have resulted, it has apparently had the good effect of preventing the establishment of drinking-places on the borders of the Park, these not having increased in number since it was opened, as it was originally supposed they would.

I have never seen or heard of a man or woman the worse for liquor taken at the Park, except in a few instances where visitors had brought it with them, and in which it had been drank secretly and unsocially. The present arrangements for refreshments I should say are temporary and imperfect.

Every Sunday in summer from thirty to forty thousand persons, on an average, enter the Park on foot, the number on a very fine day being sometimes nearly a hundred thousand. While most of the grog-shops of the city were effectually closed by the police under the Excise Law on Sunday, the number of visitors to the Park was considerably larger than before. There was no similar increase at the churches.

Shortly after the Park first became attractive, and before any serious attempt was made to interfere with the Sunday liquor trade, the head-keeper told me that he saw among the visitors the proprietor of one of the largest saloons in the city. He accosted him and expressed some surprise; the man replied, "I came to see what the devil you'd got here that took off so many of my Sunday customers."

I believe it may be justly inferred that the Park stands in competition with grog-shops and worse places, and not with the churches and Sunday-schools.

Land immediately about the Park, the frontage on it being seven miles in length, instead of taking the course anticipated by those opposed to the policy of the Commission, has advanced in value at the rate of two hundred per cent. per annum.

The cost of forming the Park, owing to the necessity of overcoming the special difficulties of the locality by extraordinary expedients, has been very great ($5,000,000); but the interest on it would even now be fully met by a toll of three cents on visitors coming on foot, and six cents on all others; and it should be remembered that nearly every visitor in coming from a distance voluntarily pays much more than this for the privilege.

It is universally admitted, however, that the cost, including that of the original off-hand common-sense blunders, has been long since much more than compensated by the additional capital drawn to the city through the influence of the Park.

Finally, to come back to the question of worldly wisdom. As soon as the Park came fairly into use, public opinion began to turn, and in a few months faced square about. The commissioners have long since, by simple persistence in minding their own proper business, come to be by far the most popular men who have had to do with any civic affairs in the time of the present generation. They have been, indeed, almost uncomfortably popular, having had need occasionally to "lobby" off some of the responsibilities which there was an effort to put upon them.

A few facts will show you what the change in public opinion has been. When the commissioners began their work, six hundred acres of ground was thought by many of the friends of the enterprise to be too much, by none too little for all park purposes. Since the Park has come into use, the amount of land laid out and reserved for parks in the two principal cities on the bay of New York has been increased to more than three times that amount, the total reserve for parks alone now being about two thousand acres, and the public demand is now for more, not less. Twelve years ago there was almost no pleasure-driving in New York. There are now, at least, ten thousand horses kept for pleasure-driving. Twelve years ago there were no road-ways adapted to light carriages. There are now fourteen miles of rural drive within the parks complete and in use, and often crowded, and ground has been reserved in the two cities and their suburbs for fifty miles of park-ways, averaging, with their planted borders and inter-spaces, at least one hundred and fifty feet wide.

The land-owners had been trying for years to agree upon a new plan of roads for the upper part of Manhattan Island. A special commission of their own number had been appointed at their solicitation, but had utterly failed to harmonize conflicting interests. A year or two after the Park was opened, they went again to the Legislature and asked that the work might be put upon the Park Commissioners, which was done, giving them absolute control of the matter, and under them it has been arranged in a manner, which appears to be generally satisfactory, and has caused an enormous advance of the property of all those interested.[42]

At the petition of the people of the adjoining counties, the field of the commissioners' operations has been extended over their territory, and their scheme of trunk-ways for pleasure-driving, riding, and walking has thus already been carried far out into what are still perfectly rural districts.

On the west side of the harbor there are other commissioners forming plans for extending a similar system thirty or forty miles back in to the country, and the Legislature of New Jersey has a bill before it for laying out another park of seven hundred acres.[43]

In speaking of parks I have not had in mind the private enterprises, of which there are several. One of the very men who, twelve years ago, thought that anyone who pretended that the people of New York wanted a park must be more knave than fool, has himself lately devoted one hundred and fifty acres of his private property to a park designed for public use, and simply as a commercial operation, to improve the adjoining property.[44]

I could enforce the chief lesson of this history from other examples at home and abroad. I could show you that where parks have been laid out and managed in a temporary, off-hand, common-sense way, it has proved a penny-wise pound-foolish way, injurious to the property in their neighborhood. I could show you more particularly how the experience of New York, on the other hand, has been repeated over the river in Brooklyn.

But I have already held you too long. I hope that I have fully satisfied you that this problem of public recreation grounds is one which, from its necessary relation to the larger problem of the future growth of your honored city, should at once be made a subject of responsibility of a very definite, very exacting, and, consequently, very generous character. In no other way can it be adequately dealt with.

The text presented here is taken from a version of the paper printed in 1870 by the American Social Science Association and includes written corrections made by Olmsted. It was later published as "Public Parks and the Enlargement of Towns," in the *Journal of Social Science* in 1871, volume 3, pages 1–36.

1. The *Overland Monthly* was started in 1868 by Anton Roman, a San Francisco publisher and book seller. The purpose of the magazine was to promote California "boosterism" and provide a forum for a group of San Francisco writers to publish their work. The monthly's first chief editor was the American short-story writer Bret Harte.

    Olmsted is quoting from Socrates Hyacinth's article "A Flock of Wool" about the state of sheep-ranching in California. The exact quotation reads, "California resembles ancient Greece in the inferiority of its rural population, both served and serving, compared with city dwellers. There is something dry, something dusty, something windy about the country which repels men; in the city alone can they nourish up the juices of life" (Frank Luther Mott, *A History of American Magazines, 1865–1885* [Cambridge, Mass., 1957], pp. 402–3; Socrates Hyacinth, "A Flock of Wool," *Overland Monthly* 4 [February 1870]: 143).

2. Samuel Bowles (1826–1878), editor of the *Springfield [Massachusetts] Republican* and friend of Olmsted. It is unclear where Olmsted obtained the entire quotation for which he credits Bowles here; however, the excerpt "San Francisco brokers and bankers may have sucked the life out of the interior" appears in Bowles's book *Across the Continent* (*Papers of FLO*, 6: 60–62; Samuel Bowles, *Across the Continent . . .* [Springfield, Mass., 1868], p. 163).

3. A reference to an article in the *New-York Times* that related the previous year's business activities in Chicago. The article noted that 20,000 people were unemployed in the city (*New-York Times*, Jan. 8, 1870, p. 1).

4. The American Social Science Association was founded in 1865 in Boston. Its goals were the collection of facts, distribution of knowledge, and the stimulation of inquiry regarding the advancement of social welfare in the United States. Many of Olmsted's friends and acquaintances were members, and Olmsted joined the association in 1866. The Lowell Institute in Boston, established and endowed in 1839 by James Lowell, served as a forum for free public lectures (*Papers of FLO*, 6: 9, 677; *EB*).

5. A reference to an article in the *Springfield Republican* about the village of Blandford, Massachusetts, located in western Hampden County, fifteen miles west of Spring-

field. Blandford had been a thriving dairy community, but according to the article, farms had been abandoned and mills and churches were closed (*Springfield Republican*, Feb. 5, 1870, p. 4).

6. Oliver Goldsmith (1728–1774), English poet. Olmsted is alluding to Goldsmith's poem "Deserted Village" published in 1870. In it Goldsmith praises the pastoral charm of the fictional farming village of Auburn but laments the passing of such villages with the beginnings of industrialization (*DNB*; Margaret Drabble, ed., *Oxford Companion to English Literature* [Oxford, 1985], p. 269).

7. Olmsted had last visited England in 1859 when he traveled there on business for the Central Park commission.

8. Olmsted is alluding to Washington Irving's characters in his collection of short stories published as *Bracebridge Hall* under the pseudonym Geoffrey Crayon. In this book Irving presents a highly romanticized view of the English gentry and their daily lives (*DAB*; Washington Irving, *Bracebridge Hall, or the Humourists* [1822; rpt. ed., New York, 1896], passim).

9. Olmsted took the first statement from John Yeats's article "On Human Growth in Towns." The second statement is a quotation from Sir Robert Christison's "Address on Public Health." Both articles were published in the *Transactions* for the 1863 meeting of the National Association for the Promotion of Social Science. The organization's purpose was to ferret out existing social problems, investigate and report on them, and finally recommend reform legislation that might ameliorate the conditions (John Yeats, "On Human Growth in Towns," in *Transactions of the National Association for the Promotion of Social Science. 1863*, ed. George W. Hastings [London, 1864], p. 536; Professor Christison, "Address on Publich Health," in ibid., p. 113; *DNB*; Philip Abrams, *The Origins of British Sociology: 1834–1914* [Chicago, Ill., 1968], pp. 44–47).

10. Olmsted is quoting from John Beddoe's, "On the Physical Degeneration of Town Population," in *Transactions of the National Association for the Promotion of Social Science. 1861*, ed. George W. Hastings (London, 1862), page 501.

11. A reference to a review in the *Nation* of the book *Modern Russia* by Julius Eckardt published in 1870. In his book Eckardt included a discussion of the effect of emancipation on the serfs and the government's enactments of laws to provide the peasants with land as incentive not to leave the agricultural areas of northern Russia for the cities (*Nation*, March 10, 1870, p. 161).

12. On February 26, 1870, the *New-York Daily Tribune* published an article detailing the lives of sewing women in the city (Shirley Dare, "One End of the Thread," *New-York Daily Tribune*, Feb. 26, 1870, pp. 1–2).

13. Oliver Wendell Holmes (1809–1894), physician, essayist, and poet born in Cambridge, Massachusetts. Olmsted may well have been thinking of Holmes's novel *Elsie Venner: A Romance of Destiny* when he wrote these words. In the novel Holmes noted

> — A great party given by the smaller gentry of the interior is a kind of solemnity, so to speak. It involves so much labor and anxiety, — its spasmodic splendors are so violently contrasted with the homeliness of every-day family-life, — it is such a formidable matter to break in the raw subordinates to the *manége* of the cloak-room and the table, — there is such a terrible uncertainty in the results of unfamiliar culinary operations, — so many feuds are involved in drawing that fatal line which divides the invited from the uninvited fraction of the local universe, — that, if the notes requested the pleasure of the guests' company on "this solemn occasion," they would pretty nearly express the true state of things.

(*DAB*; Oliver Wendell Holmes, *Elsie Venner: A Romance of Destiny* [Boston, 1861], p. 87.)

14. *Kelly's Post Office London Directory* for the year 1869 noted that "about fifty new

trades" were added that year. The directory added an additional fifty-three trades in 1870 (*Kelly's Post Office London Directory* [London, 1869], p. iv; ibid., [London, 1870], p. v).

15. Probably a reference to the U.S. Patent Office's granting of several patents in the late 1860s and early 1870s for asphalt pavement. Asphalt was used for the first time in the United States when a section of street in front of the city hall in Newark, New Jersey, was paved with it in 1870 (U.S. Patent Office, *Annual Report of the Commissioner of Patents for the Year 1868*, 4 vols. [Washington, D.C., 1870], 2: 13, 391, 631; idem, *Annual Report of the Commissioner of Patents for the Year 1869*, 4 vols. [Washington, D.C., 1871], 2: 101; idem, *Annual Report of the Commissioner of Patents for the Year 1870*, 3 vols. [Washington, D.C., 1872], 2: 1, 503, 769, 832, 917; *The Encyclopedia Americana*, 30 vols. [Danbury, Conn., 1995], s.v. "asphalt").

16. Olmsted is drawing on the research of Lewis Leeds, an engineer specializing in the ventilation, heating, and lighting of hospitals and other large buildings. Leeds noted that steam heat was healthy, less costly that other heating methods, and "under the pressure of an ordinary boiler it will travel seven miles in one minute." Olmsted probably knew Leeds, since he had been employed by the U.S. Sanitary Commission early in the Civil War. In addition, in 1867 Olmsted wrote Leeds commending him on a series of lectures on ventilation that he was delivering at the time to the Franklin Institute in Philadelphia (Lewis W. Leeds, *Lectures on Ventilation* . . . [New York, 1868], p. 48; idem, *A Treatise on Ventilation* . . . [New York, 1871], p. 217).

17. The use of pneumatic tubes for transmittal of written dispatches was introduced in London in 1853, and in the 1860s the British introduced an underground pneumatic railway for the transportation of mail in London. At the time Olmsted was writing this paper, the New York City newspapers were publishing articles concerning the building of pneumatic railways that would transport passengers and merchandise. In 1869–70 Alfred E. Beach, an inventor, constructed a 200-foot tunnel, 8 feet in diameter under Broadway at the corner of Warren Street, as an experiment. His railway could carry cars of up to ten passengers. On February 19, 1870, the major newspapers in New York City published an article concerning the possibility of building an above-ground pneumatic railroad that could carry mail, freight, and fresh produce from one part of the country to another faster and more economically than by conventional railroad (B. C. Batcheller, *The Pneumatic Despatch Tube System of the Batcheller Pneumatic Tube Co.* . . . [Philadelphia, 1897], pp. 10–11, 19, 25–26; *New-York Daily Tribune*, Jan. 11, 1870, p. 8; ibid., Feb. 19, 1870, p. 4; *New-York Times*, Feb. 19, 1870, p. 2).

18. For a reference to the building laws of Rome, see Olmsted, Vaux & Co., "Report of the Landscape Architects and Superintendents," Jan. 1, 1868, note 35, above.

19. A fire destroyed the financial district of New York City on December 16 and 17, 1835. The rapid spread of the fire was attributed to the old and narrow streets of the city that enabled the fire to jump from building to building and street to street (Isaac Newton Phelps Stokes, *The Iconography of Manhattan Island, 1498–1909*, 6 vols. [New York, 1915–28], 5: 1735).

20. Christopher Wren (1632–1723), English architect. The Great Fire of London started on September 2, 1666, and raged until September 5, destroying most of the city. On September 12, Wren presented Charles II with a preliminary plan for rebuilding London. Wren's plan provided for wide streets radiating out from a central space. While the plan was well received, it was considered too expensive and was never implemented (*DNB*; *EB*; Robert Gray, *A History of London* [New York, 1979], pp. 173–84).

21. Possibly a reference to Walnut Hill Park in New Britain, Connecticut, for which Olmsted and Calvert Vaux prepared a report and plan in 1870. In the report Olmsted and Vaux suggested that Hart Avenue, bordering the park on the south, and Vine Street, bordering the park on the west, be widened to 100 feet and that eventually

"broad streets be laid out at right angles to them." While Olmsted and Vaux's plan for the park was largely carried out, their suggestions for the widening of Hart Avenue and Vine Street were not (OVC to the Board of Park Commissioners of the Borough of New Britain, Conn., March 23, 1870 [*Papers of FLO*, 6: 361–68]).

22. Anthony Trollope (1815–1882), English novelist (*DNB*).

23. Olmsted may be referring to an American elm planted along Leyden Street in Plymouth, Massachusetts (James Thacher, *History of the Town of Plymouth* . . . [Boston, 1835], p. 310).

24. In 1866 the Central Park commission in response to a request from the city's Board of Education did allow public school boys and girls to play ball and croquet on the "Green" (later the "Sheep Meadow") three days each week. The children had to present certificates of "good standing and regular attendence" for permission to participate in these activities. The board refused, however, to grant adults these same privileges. It did not want the intrusion of baseball and cricket clubs, citing potential damage to the park plantings as well as the "objectionable features that have become the frequent attendant of these games" (BCCP, *Tenth Annual Report* [1867], pp. 36–37; idem, *Twelfth Annual Report* [1869], pp. 24–26; idem, *Thirteenth Annual Report* [1870], pp. 46–47; Roy Rosenzweig and Elizabeth Blackmar, *The Park and the People: A History of Central Park* [Ithaca, N.Y., 1992], pp. 248–49).

25. That is, Central Park in New York City and Prospect Park in Brooklyn.

26. The Champs Elysées in Paris extends from the Place de la Concorde to the Place de l'Etoile at the site of Napoleon's Arc de Triomphe. In his first version of "Park" published in 1861, Olmsted noted that "the Champs Élysées forms the most magnificent urban or interior town promenade in the world" (Frederick Law Olmsted, "Park," [1861] [*Papers of FLO*, 3: 352]).

27. See FLO, *Notes on the Plan of Franklin Park and Related Matters* (1886), and note 35, below.

28. During the seventeenth century a red cross was painted on the doors of infected houses during the London plagues. In the nineteenth century red crosses or dots were used in mapping tenement districts of U.S. cities to mark the streets and homes where infectious diseases were found (*OED*; New York [City], *Annual Report of the Board of Public Health of the Department of Health, 1870/71* [New York, 1870–71], pp. 26–35, 53–60; David Vecchioli, "Epidemiologic Maps of Washington DC, 1878–1909," *Public Health Reports* 111 [July–Aug. 1996], pp. 315–19).

29. Edward Everett Hale (1822–1909), Unitarian minister and author. Hale had been an acquaintance of Olmsted's ever since they had worked together in the mid-1850s for free-labor colonization in the west. Hale's book *Sybaris and Other Homes*, published in 1869, discussed the need for decent suburban communities for the laboring classes (*DAB*; Edward Everett Hale, *Sybaris and Other Homes* [Boston, 1869], passim; FLO to Edward Everett Hale, Oct. 21, 1869 [*Papers of FLO*, 6: 346–49]).

30. Subtropical gardening or the use of subtropical plants was introduced in Parc de Monçeau in Paris in the early 1860s by Jean-Pierre Barillet-Deschamps. This practice consisted of using plants with large, brightly colored or ornamental leaves planted in informal groups. The use of subtropical gardening spread to England where John Gibson adopted its use in London's Battersea Park in the late 1860s (Geoffrey Jellicoe et al., eds., *The Oxford Companion to Gardens* [Oxford, 1991], pp. 38, 540; George F. Chadwick, *The Park and the Town* [New York, 1966], pp. 160–61).

31. Hyde Park, one of the royal parks in London, was opened to the public in 1635 by Charles II.

32. In mythology the Graces were daughters of Zeus. These three sisters were the goddesses of charm and beauty and were concerned with those things that added gentleness and refinement to the lives of the gods and men (George Howe and G. A. Harrer, *A Handbook of Classical Mythology* [Detroit, Mich., 1970], p. 61).

33. In 1851 the New York state legislature enacted a law providing for a New York City park on a site known as Jones Wood. After considerable opposition to the creation of a park at Jones Wood, a new site, that of present-day Central Park, was selected in 1853 (Frederick Law Olmsted, "Passages in the Life of an Unpractical Man," [undated] [*Papers of FLO*, 3: 84–85, 91–92]).
34. See note 33 above.
35. William Backhouse Astor (1792–1875), New York capitalist and real estate investor, and Edward Everett (1794–1865), Unitarian minister and orator (*DAB*).
36. A reference to the *New York Herald* article "The Central Park and Other City Improvements" published on September 6, 1857 (*New York Herald*, Sept. 6, 1857, p. 4).
37. In April 1857 the New York state legislature passed a law establishing the Board of Commissioners of Central Park. In compliance with the law the governor of New York, John King, appointed eleven men to the park board. As Olmsted mentions here, many were businessmen and most were wealthy; however, the objective of the legislative act was to remove the park from the control of city politicians and place its development in the hands of a nonpartisan park board (*Forty Years*, 2: 32–33; Robert Sobel and John Raimo, eds., *Biographical Directory of the Governors of the United States, 1789–1978*, 4 vols. [Westport, Conn., 1978], 3: 1083; R. Rosenzweig and E. Blackmar, *The Park and the People*, pp. 98–99).
38. The mayor was Daniel Fawcett Tiemann (1805–1890), elected in 1857. Shortly after taking office Tiemann announced that all city projects, including the Central Park, should be controlled by the mayor and city aldermen rather than an independent park board. In 1860 opponents of the board called for an examination of the board's management of the park, and the state senate passed a resolution empaneling a special commission to investigate the matter. The commission exonerated the Central Park board of all charges against it (*Papers of FLO*, 3: 114, 247–48).
39. In the summer of 1859, 3,800 laborers were employed on Central Park. Work continued twenty-four hours a day for months to excavate the tunnel for a transverse road under Vista Rock (*Forty Years*, 2: 534).
40. The editors have been unable to locate this quotation in the *New York Herald*.
41. Jeremy Bentham (1748–1832), English jurist and writer. Olmsted is paraphrasing from Bentham's *Principles of Penal Law* part three, chapter four (*DNB*; *The Works of Jeremy Bentham* . . ., 11 vols. [Edinburgh, 1843], 1: 540).
42. A reference to the New York state legislature's enactment of a law for the formation of a commission to lay out the streets and roads in Manhattan north of 155th Street (see OVC, "Report to the Brooklyn Park Commission," Jan. 1, 1868, n. 36, above).
43. Olmsted may be referring to a communication presented to the New Jersey state senate on February 8, 1870, that included resolutions regarding a public park for Newark. The communication was tabled and no action was taken on it (New Jersey Senate, *Journal of the Twenty-sixth Senate of the State of New Jersey* . . . [Newton, N.J., 1870], p. 184).
44. Possibly, Howard Potter (1826–1877), New York City banker and friend of Olmsted. In 1866 Potter and his partner Louis B. Brown owned a 150-acre tract of beach-front property in Long Branch, New Jersey, that they wished to develop for seaside cottages. Potter asked Olmsted to visit the site to make suggestions for its development. Olmsted, in turn, recommended that they donate part of the land fronting the ocean for public access and use. Potter noted that, "the idea . . . of dedicating a part of a seafront to the common use & enjoyment I think a very valuable one & not to be lost sight of" (FLO to Howard Potter, [Aug. 13, 1866] [*Papers of FLO*, 6: 104–10]).

Report.

<hr>

March, 1871.

To the Chicago South Park Commission:[1]
Gentlemen:

We present for consideration at this time a design, prepared under your instructions,[2] for laying out the three tracts of land which are comprised under the title of the South Park,[3] and before proceeding to describe the special features of our plan, we wish to draw your attention to the leading considerations which have determined its general character.

There are two broad types of public parks, by reference to which the discussion of a plan may be most readily opened. Richmond Park is, for instance, a very useful adjunct of the park system of London,[4] and Fontainebleau of that of Paris,[5] but both are useful in a quite different way from St. James's[6] or the Parc de Monceau;[7] the first being great roaming grounds, to which people go out by railway, generally spending a day in the excursion; the other, garden-like enclosures, into which people are constantly strolling in great numbers for a short diversion from the ordinary occupations of the day.

Your territory lies at the distance of six miles from the center of business of Chicago, and quite beyond its corporate limits. Its neighborhood is mainly an uncultivated country, much of it unenclosed and sparsely inhabited — the thousand acres of the park site having included not more than a dozen small dwellings.

Under these circumstances, it may be thought that the park to be formed upon it will not be much used by the citizens of Chicago, except as a distant suburban excursion ground. The population of the city might indeed be doubled several times, and if it should be built as compactly as most great towns hitherto have been, and the advance of building should spread equally to the North, South and West, the South Park would, undoubtedly, still be in the midst of a rural district.

Against any such presumption, however, stands the fact that in all large and flourishing cities throughout the world, there has been manifest of late, a strong and steadily increasing tendency to abandon the old, cramped manner of building, and to adopt a style of dwellings with individual and villa-like characteristics that involve a greater ground space, and a corresponding tendency at the same time to widen streets and public places, and separate

206

domestic more and more distinctly from commercial quarters. This tendency is especially strong where it has free play in American communities, and except where it goes so far as to lead people to dispense with appliances of health, which, on account of their costliness, require a certain degree of density of building, there is abundant evidence that it is, in the long run, economical, beneficent and favorable to the prosperity of the whole community.[8] This being the case, it may be observed incidentally, that in designing a park in the environs of a rapidly growing town, it is proper to have in view, as a secondary purpose, the general improvement of the neighborhood with reference to its healthfulness as a residence, as, for instance, by facilitating its drainage.

In Chicago the banks of the navigable streams are unattractive for domestic purposes and cannot fail to be required for commerce. Special business quarters may hereafter grow up in some directions at a considerable distance from them, but if so a more or less complete connection of business streets will soon follow between the two, and, under the operation of the tendency to separate domestic from commercial life, the intermediate districts will become less and less valuable for dwellings. The most desirable domestic quarters therefore in the early future are likely to be those in which building has never been compact and which are in no danger of being invaded for commercial purposes.

In regard to the district about your site there are, in the first place, nowhere near it any special inducements to the rise or extension of a commercial quarter; in the second place, the interpolation of the large closed spaces of the Park, turning transportation out of direct channels, will be obstructive to business, and finally, the advantage which will come with the Park for securing domestic comfort can hardly fail to soon establish a special reputation for the neighborhood and give assurance of permanence to its character as a superior residence quarter.

There are other circumstances which it is unnecessary to specify here which add weight to these considerations, and it thus becomes highly probable that before any proper plan of a park designed at the present time shall be fully realized, not only will a large number of the citizens of Chicago be living much nearer to your site than now, but it will be in the center of a really populous and wealthy district. In addition then, to its holiday use by the whole body of citizens, a large number must be expected to resort to it for their daily exercise and recreation. To be well adapted to such habitual use, it will need to have a much greater variety of features and much larger and more varied accommodations than if it were so remote to the population of the city on an average, that few would see it except occasionally and it were only rarely to be used by great numbers, and then as a pic-nic and roving ground.

If it were now to be improved with a view to the latter use only, it would be impossible at a later period to change its character, by the introduction of much enlarged accommodations and new landscape features of interest, without destroying and wasting much of what had first been prepared, and this consideration would probably prevent any but feeble and insufficient changes being made.

Regarding it on the other hand as an urban park, that is to say, as a ground to which large numbers of people will resort every day, rather than as a remote or holiday park, it has to be considered that it will be but one of a series of such grounds and will be further from the present town centre than any of the others. It is then a question how far it should be treated purely as a local park.

It is clearly most undesirable that the existing territorial divisions of interest and policy by which all comprehensive improvement of your city are embarrassed should be unnecessarily perpetuated, and with whatever motives the choice has been made of the park sites now fixed in its general plan, present duty is first of all to the whole city. We are bound, that is to say, to look upon the park to be formed on your site simply as one member of a general system of provisions upon which as a whole the health of the city, its attractiveness as a residence and its prosperity will in all future time be largely dependent. In the process of design, therefore, one of the first duties is to study the comparative value of one or another possible function, or class of features or source of interest of each site.

The marked circumstances of the South Park site when compared with the others are, first, the groves of comparatively large trees which it contains; second, the greater spaciousness of two of its divisions; and, third, the longer frontage and greater depth of that division of it which looks upon the Lake.

The first, though it makes the Park more available for certain purposes at an early day, is of little importance with reference to a plan except as it may be an indication that the natural conditions are more favorable than elsewhere for the growth of large trees, and we are of opinion that with skillful management very much better trees than any on the South Park may be grown upon each of the other park sites of the city.

It is an advantage of great space that one part of those who resort to a park for recreation can be engaged in a class of exercises which, in order to be pursued by different parties without clashing, require much breadth of open ground, that another part can look upon the first from a suitable distance with convenience and safety, while a third, interested neither as participants nor spectators, can seclude themselves completely from both and straying into other parts of the Park pursue entirely different methods of recreation. Another advantage is that, without any sacrifice of convenience for the class of exercises first referred to, elements of interest may be multiplied and yet, if the natural features oppose no obstacle, a larger, simpler and more tranquil landscape character be given to the Park as a whole.

Of the other park sites reserved for the future benefit of Chicago but one offers this class of advantages in any degree to compare with that of the South Park, and that, as it should be, is the one which is at the greatest distance from it. The two outer divisions of the South Park being connected more directly, however, and by a division considerably wider than any connecting any other two park divisions of the whole series, it is possible to associate them much more intimately in design than any other two, so that each may in many particulars complement the other and the whole be classed together as one park. If we add to this possibility those which grow out of its situation with reference to the Lake, there can be little room for doubt that you have the opportunity, and consequently the duty, of adopting a scale of scenery and at certain points a scale of public accommodations larger than can elsewhere be attempted, without a restriction upon design with reference to depth and variety of sylvan elements of interest, which would be unfortunate.

By a course of reasoning thus barely indicated, but which will be more evident as we proceed with the consideration of details, we are led to think that, while the local urban use of the South Park will not be unimportant, its availability for general purposes in which the city as a whole will be interested is considerably greater than that of any other of the sites which have been reserved for parks.

It follows that the South Park should belong to a third class, of which the type in London is found in Hyde Park with Kensington Gardens, and in Paris in the Bois de Boulogne; a class which should not be a compromise between the two extremes first named, but in which the advantages of each should be completely reconciled and united.[9]

That some one park will be required to assume this position and will be more or less satisfactorily adapted to it, may, from the experience of other cities, be assumed and that neither of the others is as well suited to the purpose, must, we believe upon a comparison of situations, outlines and topographical conditions, be admitted.

Before discussing what should be demanded in such a park and the availability for various required provisions of different parts of your ground, it is necessary that the fact should be recognized that none of the sites and no part of any one of the sites which have been reserved for parks at Chicago, would generally elsewhere be recognized as well adapted to the purpose. The undertaking involved in the series is, indeed, a bold one and can be justified only by the conviction that a city of great importance to the world at large — a city which should have a metropolitan character and influence, and to which great numbers of men should be drawn, not only on account of its commercial, but of its scientific, artistic, scholarly, domestic and social advantages — is here to be built upon ground plans now forming and foundations now laying. It is undeniable that it would be a most serious drawback to such a city not to be provided with parks. It is equally undeniable that when the best has been done that is possible, it will be a long time before parks can be formed for it which will compare satisfactorily with such as already have been secured by most important cities of the civilized world. It is a courageous forecast which reasons from these premises that the sooner all that is done that is possible to be done for overcoming this disadvantage of the city is set about, the better.

If this is the justification of the enterprise which in its most important feature it has been given you to inaugurate, it follows that while the immediate reward of those who now plan, prepare and tax themselves for the general good in this matter, should be reasonably consulted, their benefit should not be held of paramount importance, nor should any plan be adopted or anything be done with a view to their gratification, by which a permanent obstacle would be placed in the way of arrangements which would be appropriate and sufficient for a city of several times the present population and wealth of Chicago.

The general class, scope and character of the proposed park having been thus approximately determined, we may proceed to consider the limitations fixed by the conditions of the site upon the design.

The first obvious defect of the site is that of its flatness. That this is to be regretted is undeniable, yet it is a mistake to suppose that a considerable extent of nearly flat ground is inadmissable or undesirable in a great park, or that it must be overcome, at any cost, by vast artificial elevations and depressions, or by covering the surface with trivial objects of interest.

The Central Park of New York, having been laid out for the most prodigal city in the world, is one of the most costly constructions ever made for public, open air recreation. The view just expressed may then be thought to be strengthened by the fact that one of the largest items in its cost, and unquestionably, one of the most profitable, was that for reducing considerable portions of its surface to a prairie-like simplicity. In our judgment, it still comes far short in this particular of what is chiefly desirable in the principal recreation ground of a large city, in a temperate climate.

It should especially be considered that where there is a broad meadow with ever so little obvious play of surface, an irregular border formed by massive bodies of foliage will in a great degree supply the place in landscape of moderate hills and particularly will this be the case if it contains water in some slight depression, so situated as to double these masses.

Chicago in the future would no doubt be glad if there should have been provided for it, somewhere within the thousand acres of its principal park, a considerable district of a highly picturesque character, a mountain glen with a dashing stream and cascades, for example, but, agreeable as this might be if it were to be obtained by the simple appropriation and development of conditions already existing; as in the valley of Wissahickon at Philadelphia,[10] it would, after all, in a thoroughly well ordered park, be an episode, not essential, and far less useful than a district of low rolling prairie.

There is but one object of scenery near Chicago of special grandeur or sublimity, and that, the Lake,[11] can be made by artificial means no more grand or sublime. By no practical elevation of artificial hills, that is to say, would the impression of the observer in overlooking it be made greatly more profound. The Lake may, indeed, be accepted as fully compensating for the absence of sublime or picturesque elevations of land.

There are three elements of scenery, however, which must be regarded as indispensable to a fine park to be formed on your site, the first being turf, the second foliage, the third still water. For each of these you are bound, at the outset, to make the best of your opportunities, because if you do not, posterity will be likely to lay waste what you have done, in order to prepare something better.

Water wells up abundantly a few feet below the surface in nearly all parts of your ground, and may therefore be easily introduced when required in your plan. Turf may also be secured in a few years, by the common agricultural process. But the adequate development of foliage is not so sure and simple a matter.

Great, spreading trees, are the distinctive glory of all park scenery in which broad spaces of level greensward are the central features. But park-like great trees are hardly more natural to your conditions than hills, crags, or dashing streams. There is no difficulty in making young trees live and flourish in Chicago, but sooner or later, always before they reach what should be their finest estate, they seem to lose vigor, and a large number come to untimely death. The trees at present on your ground are, many of them, of considerable size, but not one of these has a character which would be of high value in a park. Most of them are evidently struggling for mere existence, and the largest are nearly all decrepid. The unfortunate influences affecting them are of two classes, those which act upon the foliage, and those which act upon the root.

In regard to the first we have seen an effect produced upon tender foliage and twigs by a high wind suddenly coming off the Lake after a warm day in Spring, so remarkable that if often repeated it could not fail to result in permanent constitutional injury. This and other atmospheric difficulties you cannot expect to lessen, on the contrary, as the fumes, smoke and dust of the town increase, they are likely to be aggravated. The obvious root evils are a cold, wet, sometimes permanently water-soaked soil or sub-soil, and inadequate or unsuitable root food. By reducing the general level of the ground water as far as practicable, the temperature of the soil in your Upper Division may probably be elevated from ten to fifteen degrees of Fahrenheit, and the average length of the season in which wood will grow and ripen may be extended about a month. With an improved ground temperature and deep soil, moderately rich but not at all stimulating, trees may be expected to grow which will possess much greater vigor and powers of resistance and recuperation with reference to harmful atmospheric influences than any hitherto grown under the conditions which naturally prevail near Chicago, and there are many of the most desirable species and varieties which could probably be brought to exhibit their peculiar beauties in the highest degree.

The light mould at present found in some parts of your ground is of that character, the fertility of which is quickly exhausted, and while it should be carefully husbanded is of little permanent value. It will be necessary therefore to bring upon the ground a large amount of surface material to form a moderately rich, wholesome loam, and this operation however tedious and costly, should go before every other but drainage and grading. The turning in of a series of green crops, forced to rankness by stimulating manures, after a dressing of clay, will probably be the most economical way of improving the character of the soil on a large scale.

We have spoken of the advantage which is to be gained by reducing the level of the ground water in the Upper Division. In the Lower Division one-third of all the surface is below the high-water level of the Lake, the greater part of the remainder is much too low, too wet and cold for upland trees to flourish upon it, and adequate drainage is out of the question.

If it should be undertaken to form a large market garden in such a district as this, the first thing to be done would be, if possible, to secure a free outlet through the beach, so that water flowing in from the west would, under no circumstances, be so checked in its outflow as to rise appreciably higher than the lake. This would be accomplished, if at all, by building out a crib upon the beach, and then opening a channel, the mouth of which would be on its south side. A series of cross channels would then be laid out mainly parallel with and equidistant from one another, the breadth, depth, and distances between them being so adjusted that the material excavated, when thrown out, should be sufficient to raise the surface of all the intermediate ground just so far above the level of the lake as should be thought necessary for the thrifty growth of the crops proposed to be cultivated.

The same process may be adopted for your purpose, with such modifications as the difference between a park and a vegetable garden requires, the difference being, that in the park the divisions of land and water should have a natural appearance and be interesting in landscape effect, and that they should be adapted to the convenient movement of a large number of persons pursuing recreation in a variety of ways.

Searching for a natural type of what is thus desirable, we look first for local suggestions. The present formation is the result of an encroachment of the shore upon the lake, and this appears to have occurred first by the formation of a large outer bar, and of minor bars within it, the outer bar rising gradually more and more above the surface, and finally completely separating the water behind it, except perhaps at one or two inlets, from the main lake. In subsequent storms the outer bar has been more or less broken down, and sand, driven by wave and wind, mixed with some wash from the land side, has gradually filled up the inner basins.

Had the situation been less bleak, had the outer bar been firmer and composed of different material, had the streams flowing in been more rapid and the country swept by them richer in vegetation, and had the climate been hot and moist certain plants would have taken root upon the shallows, silt would have been caught by them and drift stuff lodged upon them; fish, birds, insects would have made contributions and soil would accumulate, other plants would in time overgrow the first, and, the process continuing, scenery would finally result of a most interesting and fascinating character, that, namely, of the wooded lagoons of the tropics.

You certainly cannot set the madrepore or the mangrove at work on the banks of Lake Michigan, you cannot naturalize bamboo or papyrus, aspiring palm or waving parasites, but you *can* set firm barriers to the violence of winds and waves, and make shores as intricate, as arborescent and as densely overhung with foliage as any. You can have placid and limpid water within these shores that will mirror and double all above it as truly as any, and thus, if you cannot reproduce the tropical forest in all its mysterious depths of shade and visionary reflections of light, you can secure a combination of the fresh and healthy nature of the North with the restful, dreamy nature of the South that would in our judgment be admirably fitted to the general purposes of any park, and which certainly could nowhere be more grateful than in the borders of your city, not only on account of the present intensely wide-awake character of its people, but because of the special quality of the scenery about Chicago in which flat and treeless prairie and limitless expanse of lake are such prominent characteristics.

Taste and convenience would require that some portions of the lagoon waters should be broader than the economy of a mere market garden would prescribe, but to avoid great length of haul in filling over the marshy ground, the water spaces would need to be distributed from end to end and from the beach to the rear of the Lower Division.

This course of thought leads towards two important conclusions, viz.: 1st. By any feasible and moderately economical plan of making a public pleasure resort on your Lower Division, water must be so distributed through it that the land will be broken up into comparatively small areas and no great breadth of green landscape will be available. 2d. Command of the Lake upon a shore line of more than a mile and a half in length; accessibility from the heart of the city by water-passage, and the great extent and necessary ramifications of its interior waters would give such marked distinctions to this part of the Park, that, so long as they were in view, a comparison of it with parks elsewhere, more fortunate in other respects, would be out of the question. For beauty of hill and dale your ground certainly will never be distinguished; it may never be for the grandeur of its trees, but it may have a beauty and an interest of its own such as we have partly indicated, in which the citizens of Chicago for generations to come, shall take a just pride, and all the more so that it has been the result of their fathers' work upon a sand-bar.

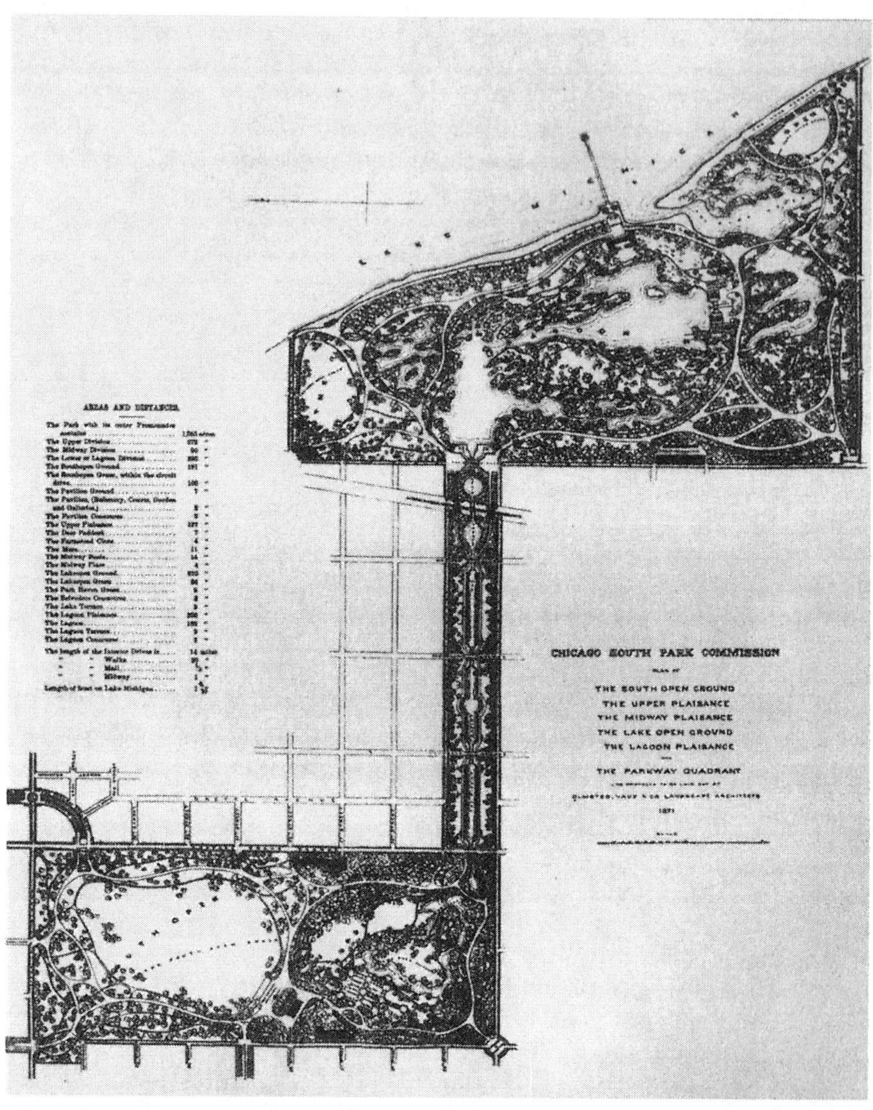

"Chicago South Park Commission, Plan of The South Open Ground, The Upper Plaisance, The Midway Plaisance, The Lake Open Ground, The Lagoon Plaisance, and The Parkway Quadrant, As Proposed to be Laid Out by Olmsted, Vaux & Co. Landscape Architects, 1871"

In every distinct field of design, however multitudinous the intentions to be served in its details, some one source of interest should dominate, and either by contrast or harmony, all details should be auxiliary to this central interest. In a work of the kind before us there may be — almost necessarily

214

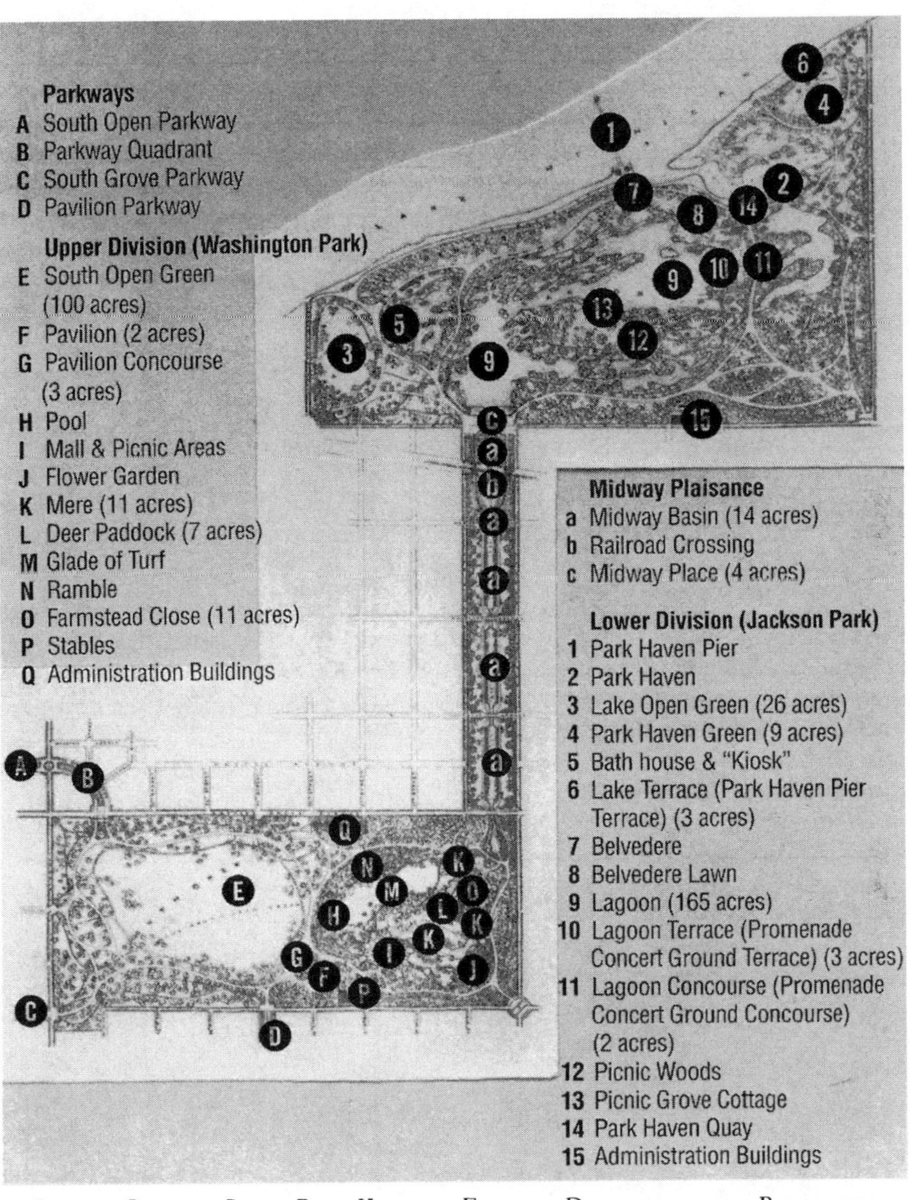

PLAN OF CHICAGO SOUTH PARK, KEYED TO FEATURES DESCRIBED IN THE REPORT BY OLMSTED, VAUX & CO. OF 1871

215

must be — several more or less distinct fields of design, but it is desirable that there should be a studied artistic relation of support by harmony, and of emphasis by contrast of character between the different fields. The element of interest which undoubtedly should be placed first, if possible, in the park of any great city, is that of an antithesis to its bustling, paved, rectangular, walled-in streets; this requirement would best be met by a large meadowy ground, of an open, free, tranquil character. The necessity of sub-dividing the ground by the ramifications of the water system, and of generally planting the shores, if you would gain the beauty of reflections, half-lights, and shaded coves of foliage over water, as we have proposed, will prevent your realizing any considerable breadth of open landscape within your Lower Division. It will be equally impossible within your Middle Division, on account of its narrowness. Fortunately, there is no similar objection to the realization of this desideratum in the Upper Division, the proper general landscape character of which, as well as that of the Lower Division, may thus be considered as determined.

We proceed to consider what is required more specifically in the Lower Division. It naturally divides into two fields of landscape, the exterior Lake expanse with its necessarily simple, raw, storm-lashed foreground, and the interior Lagoon scenery, intricate, sequestered, sylvan and rich in variety of color and play of light and shade, both having the common and continuous element of water. Still, considering this park as the principal recreation ground of the city and one in which more than any other a general attendance from all parts of the city should be expected, invited, and prepared for, the fact remains that the distance to it from the centre and more northern quarters is so long that the access to it by land will be often uninteresting and tedious. Were it to be very much more so, were approach by land to the Park wholly impracticable, as from Venice to the Lido,[12] the means of access by water and the connection of the Park by water with the heart of the commercial part of the city would be so admirable that under ordinarily favorable conditions of weather, there would be thousands of the very class of citizens whose convenience most needs to be considered, to whom the Park would practically begin at the mouth of the Chicago river. Where great numbers are to be carried short distances, there is no transportation so cheap or so agreeable as that by water, and the time should be expected when the toiling population of Chicago, relieved from work at an early hour on the last of the week, will be carried to the South Park by many tens of thousands at the cost of a few cents. Its advantages in this respect will correspond to those of the Haga Park of Stockholm, one of the most popular and delightful public grounds in the world.[13]

Aside from the actual advantages of access which it thus offers, it is most desirable that whatever sources of interest there may be in the Lake should be as closely as possible associated with those of the Park and be made to appear, as much as possible, part and parcel of the Park. The introduction of artificial water with natural outlines and no perceptible current, so near the great Lake, is, as a matter of Art, not a little hazardous, and to fully insure it against a paltry and childish aspect it is indispensable that the character of the Lagoon as an arm of the Lake should be distinctly manifest. For this reason the channel between the water of the Lake and the water within the Park should be given importance in the design, so that at all times, even when few or no boats are passing, this privilege of the Park will be felt by land visitors as an important distinction.

The channel must be cut through the beach, the break in it being guarded against the drift of sand from the northward by a pier, which should be fully two hundred feet in length, in order to create a strong eddy at the mouth of the inlet. It must be presumed that in any case the channel will need occasional dredging.

Such a pier would be the most prominent object connecting the Park with the Lake, and experience shows that where an offset into the water from a tame coast has been thus formed people are strongly drawn to gather upon and near it. So well established is this attraction that at many of the places of resort on the English and French coasts, long piers have been built simply for the gratification of visitors.[14]

For these reasons the pier and inlet must be treated as most important members of the design; they should not be thrust into a corner, but located as near to the heart of the Park as possible, and as visitors will inevitably be drawn to the pier, special provision should be planned for the comfortable coming together of a large number in connection with it. From the view of the Lake which these would command, the transition should be made easy and natural to some other point, also adapted to the coming together of large numbers, which will have a like central position with reference to the Lagoon.

We wish to present one other class of preliminary considerations before referring to our plans. Among the purposes for which public grounds are used is that of an arena for athletic sports, such as baseball, football, cricket, and running games, such as prisoner's base,[15] and others which are liable to come again much more in fashion than they have been of late. Another is that of a ground for parades, reviews, drills, processions and public meetings and ceremonies in which large spaces are required. Experience shows that neither upon fields used for these purposes nor on ground where large numbers of people are liable to come together strongly interested in them, is it practicable to guard shrubs and low branching trees from injury. For all these purposes turf is much more favorable to the skill and comfort of those engaged in the exercises and more agreeable to the eye of spectators than gravel; it is also generally much less costly. If at any particular point, however, it is much used it wears out and leaves unsightly and slippery ground in its stead. Consequently it is impossible to keep grounds used for these purposes in decent order unless the open fields of turf are very large and the plantations about them are of an open character, and composed almost wholly of strong, clean trunked trees.

It is also impossible to keep grounds in good order in which the breadths of turf are smaller and decorated with shrubbery and low foliage, if the same freedom of movement and action is permitted in them which it is desirable to allow upon the larger open grounds. Consequently an entirely different scheme of regulations needs to be applied to them. To enable these to be enforced the line between one class of grounds and the other must be sharply defined so that it cannot be passed unconsciously even under excitement.

The distinction between grounds to be used by day only, and grounds to be open night and day, needs also to be considered. It is impossible to make grounds in the midst of large towns which offer numerous places of complete obscurity, safe places of general resort after nightfall. Wherever it has been attempted in Europe or America, decent people have soon been driven from them, and they have become nurseries of crime and immorality.

The tarry vapor which escapes from gas-pipes is poisonous to trees, and grounds which are closely planted, or which abound in shrubs and underwood, cannot be so lighted artificially that their landscape beauty may be enjoyed, or so that those wishing concealment in them can be clearly recognized, and their movements surely followed. For this reason, when such grounds are not closed at dusk, they require a much larger police force by night than by day, and it is always questionable whether, at best, their advantages for evil purposes do not outweigh those for good.

Disregarding here very small places we thus show a necessity for two classes of grounds, one characterized by broad, nearly level spaces of turf suitable for reviews and athletic exercises, and open plantations offering no coverts, and which may be artificially lighted and safely resorted to after nightfall; the other, not designed to be artificially lighted nor to be used at night, adapted only to quiet and moderate exercises; in which shrubbery, underwood and brooding trees may be common elements of scenery, and if circumstances admit of it, what is technically styled the picturesque in distinction from the simply beautiful in nature may be cultivated.

The scenery of the first class of grounds is distinctively "park scenery," because the private parks of Europe are generally pastured by deer or cattle, and consequently, up to a distinct browsing line, are clear of foliage. The scenery of the second class is that of what is usually distinguished from the park as the "pleasure ground" or "kept ground," being managed in a more garden-like way. We shall term the first "open," and shall apply the old word "plaisance" to such as is intended to be enclosed with a high fence and used only by day.

Your territory is so extensive and so large a population may be expected eventually to resort exclusively to it for out-door recreation that it is clear that provision of both classes should be found in it, and its extreme points being three miles apart (exclusive of the Parkways), it should not even be necessary for a boy who has reached one end to go half around it to find himself free to run upon the turf, or that a man living near it and going out after dusk with his wife and daughters, should find no better place in which to stroll than an ordinary street side-walk. For these reasons there should be enough "open" ground at least for local use, night and day, near each of the extreme parts of your plan.

It is impracticable to close any ground at night through which important thoroughfares are carried unless by the expedient of carrying one line of transit under another as in the New York Park.[16] This is a costly arrangement and can rarely be used so that landscape opportunities shall not be marred by it; it should only be adopted therefore under considerations of special necessity.

We are instructed that your Upper Division must be crossed by a thoroughfare near its middle from east to west. It is not to be hoped and there is no reason to believe that there ever will be a business quarter on the east side of this ground, nor at least very near it on the west. As the space in the east is quite limited and is likely to be occupied almost exclusively with dwellings of people of wealth, and therefore not densely, there is not likely to be much need for driving through the Park except with pleasure carriages. Coal, building materials, hay, and most market supplies will be brought in from the north, and the principal occasion for crossing with business wagons will be early in the morning, as of milkmen and bakers. Under these circumstances the movement of pleasure carriages is not likely to be so unpleasantly interfered with as at all to justify the construction of a sunken traffic road across the Park. The only important question involved is as to the night use, with which we shall deal presently.

We shall now refer to our plans, which are upon three sheets: No. 1 representing the Upper Division; No. 2, the space six hundred feet wide connecting it with the Lower Division, which is shown on No. 3.

The Upper and Lower Divisions are each subdivided into an open and an enclosed ground, and the whole of the Middle Division is enclosed. The open ground of the Upper Division is designated the Southopen Ground; the other, looking upon the Lake, the Lakeopen Ground; different parts of the enclosed ground are designated respectively the Upper Plaisance, the Midway Plaisance, and the Lagoon Plaisance.

The various subdivisions are connected by a common system of drives and walks, as well as by the arrangement of water. The drives are generally forty feet wide. In the Midway Division, where there are two parallel stretches so near together as almost to form one, the width of each part is thirty-five feet, and on the Lake shore, where carriages are likely to be driven

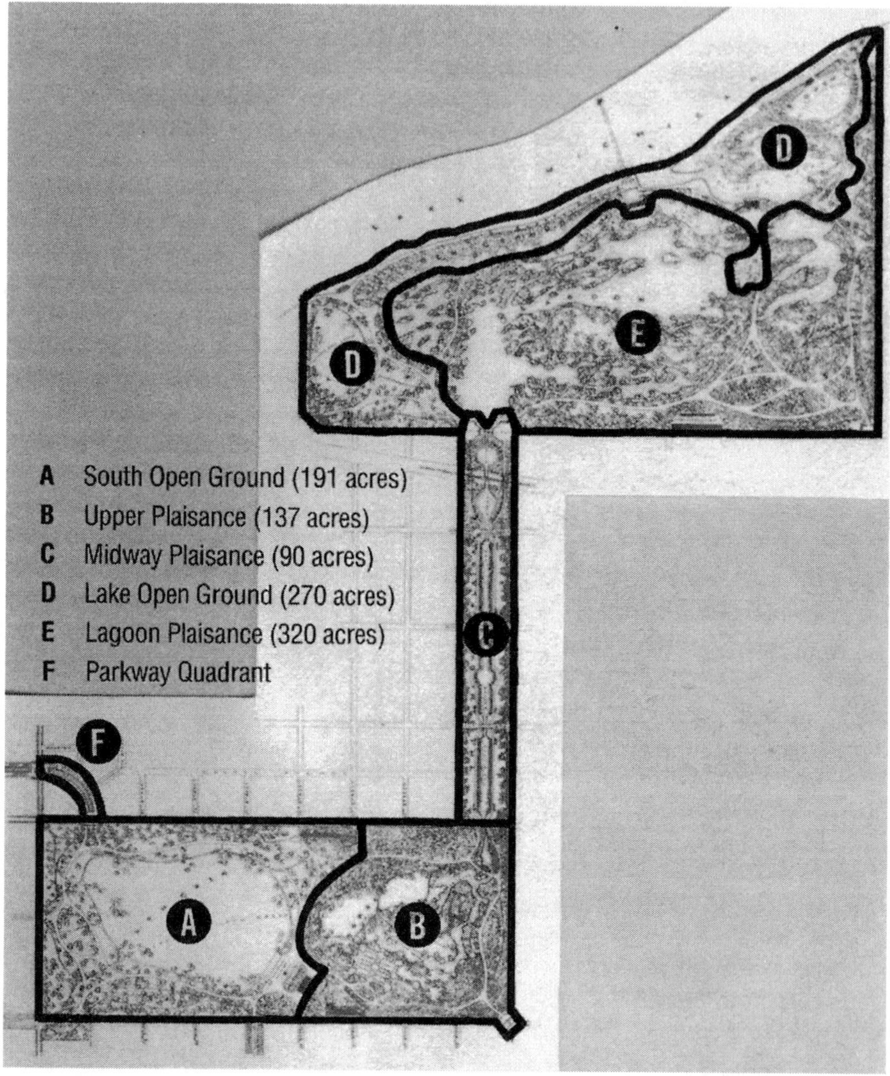

PLAN OF CHICAGO SOUTH PARK, SHOWING "OPEN" AND "PLAISANCE" AREAS AS
DESCRIBED IN REPORT BY OLMSTED, VAUX & CO. OF 1871

back and forth repeatedly, and the number wishing to occupy the road is likely to be larger than elsewhere, the width is increased to fifty feet.

Five open places are also introduced in the system, each two or more acres in extent, in order to allow carriages to stand together, so that their occupants may engage in conversation, listen to music or look upon some prospect of special interest, without interrupting the circulation upon the drives.

We have presumed that the same principle of construction which has applied in the Lincoln Park[17] drives would be adopted in yours, the conditions of the ground and the materials at your command being similar, while it is probable that with the use of a heavy steam roller, more efficient arrangements for drainage and more care in details, a road may thus be formed more agreeable than the best stone or concrete roads, and at much less cost. Two stretches of bridle road are introduced on a part of the ground where there will be no occasion for anyone to be walking. Equestrians may thus have an opportunity to gallop at speed, but, as, with the unusual extent of ordinary roads provided for, their length being about fourteen miles, they are seldom likely to be much crowded with carriages, and as, with the construction suggested, they will be satisfactory under the saddle as well as in carriages, we have not thought it necessary to indicate any great extent of roads designed especially for riding. Should it be desired, a pad may be introduced by the side of the ordinary road anywhere in the Upper or Lower Division, or a bridle road thrown off on the west and south sides of the Lower Division in the same manner as in the upper. Thirty miles of walks are indicated with similar arrangements for occasional congregation, the more important of which will be referred to in the description of the several subdivisions of the plan which follows.

The Southopen ground, which will be found on the left of plan No. 1, consists simply of a nearly level meadow with a grove of large trees surrounding it on all sides but one, where the character of the plantation, as it is extended into the adjoining closed district, changes to that of a denser and more picturesque wood, with glades of turf reaching far into it from the meadow. Entering the park from either of the two principal approaches from the city, the visitor, as he passes through the outer grove, will thus find a view opening before him over a greensward without a perceptible break, considerably beyond the limits of the Open Ground itself, and ending in one direction in a glimmer of water reflecting tall trees nearly a mile away. Advancing further, if late in the day, the shadows of the trees falling across the meadow, will be a quarter of a mile in length, sheep and cows will be grazing upon it and boys and men playing here and there, as on a village green. A carriage road passes around it, on each side of which, at a short distance, there are walks with numerous branches and connections, one series under the shade of the grove and the other upon the open green. The space of turf inclosed by the circuit drive contains a hundred acres, and the space available for reviews is about the same as that of the Champ de Mars at Paris,[18] and much larger than any parade or playground thus far provided for anywhere in this country.

Of the two approaches which have been referred to, one is planned more especially with reference to the rapid movement of a great number of persons driving, riding or walking, being planted openly with straight rows of clean trunked trees. This, having in mind its terminus as well its plan, we have designated the Southopen Parkway. The other is designed with a view

221

to more quiet and leisurely movement, and its principal feature is a walk or series of walks passing somewhat indirectly through a grove with frequent interludes of shrubbery, fountains and arbors to invite rest and contemplation. This we have accordingly designated the Southgrove Parkway. In a town where local nomenclature can so rarely be based on topographical circumstances, any tolerable names of this class should be welcomed. Even if they seem outlandish at first, if at all euphonious, a very little usage makes them familiar and much more agreeable than arbitrary names.[19]

The third grand approach to the Park will enter the Southopen Ground from the west near its southern end, and from this point, which in the afternoon would be chosen as the best for looking across the Green, we have planned arrangements for the principal place of assemblage of the upper park. At the junction of roads from four directions there is a Concourse for carriages; in its rear a stand for music; back of this again an extensive area covered by trellises and surrounded by galleries, one of which, overlooking the Concourse and the Green, is intended to serve the purpose of a grand stand on occasion of parades, match games and exhibitions. To this series of structures is added a large Refectory building, and the whole, on account of its opensided character, is termed the Pavilion. Promenade concerts are designed to be held here, the audience, not in carriages, walking on or under the galleries or in alleys under the vine-covered trellises, at the sides of which will be seats and tables for ices and coffee.

Being on the Open Ground the Refectory need not be closed at night.

The Pavilion may be brilliantly illuminated and fireworks may be safely exhibited on the Green opposite, where they will be seen to great advantage from the front gallery. The public road here crossing the park, being also entirely within the Open Ground, may be open at night.

The grand approach from the west entering the park in front of the Pavilion, we have designated the Pavilion Parkway.[20]

It has been shown that in the view from the north end of the Green no line of demarcation is designed to be seen at its south boundary. To accomplish this a broad artificial depression in the southern part of the Green will be required, the needed depth at the middle not being more than two feet. South of the transverse road a deeper excavation is to be made for a small pool, at each end of which will be an island which will receive the fence, the pool serving as a fence across the intermediate space. The water of this pool will not be seen in the view from the north end of the Green but the eye will range over it and through a continuation of the depression, southerly, to the more distant water.

The Southopen Ground will need no enclosure except a low guard rail; (of course, in saying this we presume that cattle will not be allowed to range through the adjoining streets). The grass should be kept short by a sufficient number of sheep and a few cows, the milk of which may be sold by the glass to visitors as is done in St. James' Park in London.[21]

We have before indicated the advantages of an open ground thus detached for certain purposes, though artistically united to the enclosed portion of the park. As the practical application of our views will now, however, be better understood, we recapitulate them:

1st, The arrangement avoids the temptation which has elsewhere been found irresistible to trespass upon the enclosed park for purposes which within it are illegal, destructive and demoralizing, such as military and semi-military parades and political demonstrations.

2d, It reduces and strictly defines the area within which it is necessary to require visitors to conform themselves to regulations of a special character, and desirable that they should be under special police observation.

3rd, It enables the park authority to exclude visitors from the enclosed grounds without forcing them to leave the park altogether, the outer ground offering all necessary advantage for air, exercise and recreation from a short time after sunset till after sunrise. It thus brings much of the necessary attendance upon visitors within the limits of a day's service, so that within the enclosed ground one set of men will answer for it instead of two.

4th, It makes a much greater freedom from restraint practicable on greensward playgrounds than could be permitted with safety if they were surrounded by closely planted or finely decorated grounds.

5th, It simplifies and reduces the expense of keeping the ground in order.

Against the advantages there is to be placed the necessity of keeping the Open Ground very well lighted and patrolled at night, and the artistic disadvantage of dispensing with underwood within its borders. The latter objection is of less weight in this case than it would be if the distance from the Green to any exterior and incongruous objects were not so great.

South of this Open Ground lies the enclosed district, which we have designated the Upper Plaisance.

Adjoining the entrance to it on the side of the Pavilion, a mall will be observed having the form of a hall nearly a quarter of a mile in length, out of which, near its centre, four square apartments open. The outlines are marked by rows of trees and the floor is of gravel. The object is to provide a convenient open air rendezvous and assembly ground for large pic-nic parties and for societies, fraternities, Sunday school and other organizations, and also to supply a suitable ground for such plays as would be destructive to turf. The four square apartments are also designed with reference to entertainments and exhibitions in which the use of stagings or platforms may be desirable, as in the festivals of the Turners.[22]

Formal lines are here introduced in the plan because the same clear space of shaded ground thus bounded will be more commodious and will admit of a greater degree of freedom of movement when occupied by a large number of persons than any other. Outside of the lines of trees other trees are disposed irregularly, so that the formality of the arrangement, although so conspicuous on the paper plan, will not destroy the general naturalness of the landscape design of this division of the park.

At the east central entrance of the Mall there is a descent to a landing on the Mere, which is the head of the boating water of the Park.

On the opposite side of the Mere there is a Paddock, seven acres in extent, for deer. These will appear from the Mall to be free, but are to be confined by an under-water fence, as it is not safe for deer to range where there are children.

The walks opening southward from the Mall lead into a flower garden attached to which are shrubbery walks, sheltered seats, and balconies over the water.

The northern part of the Mall looks eastwardly upon a lawn, the edges planted with shrubbery and divided by a knoll, closely planted with trees and underwood, from the Deer Paddock.

Still further to the east the lawn merges into a large glade of turf terminating at the lower part on the Mere near the south-east corner of the Division.

The walks leading eastward from the glade pass into a region of broken ground, designated as the Ramble on the plan, to be formed by excavating deeply for the walks and mounding the material thus obtained between them. It is to be planted thickly; mostly with large shrubs, and to be made as shady, sequestered and picturesque in the character of its details as practicable. It will be desirable that a few small ledges of rock should be transferred to it, and ferns, mosses and alpine plants used in connection with them but only in a very simple and delicately natural manner. It is also to be finished with substantial seats and arbors.

The outer parts of the Upper Plaisance on each side, through which the drives are carried, are to have the character of rather dense natural woods, affording an agreeable change from the Open Ground.

A stable and sheds for the deer, and the sheep and cows to be kept in the Open, for the birds that will require winter protection and for such horses, carts, etc., as may be required, and a house for the stock keeper, are provided in the enclosure, (named the Farmstead Close on the plan), east of the Deer Paddock.

The plan of the Midway Plaisance is shown on drawing No. 2. The earth excavated in making the Basin and the drives and walks, which are to be at an elevation of four feet only above the water, is to be mounded as naturally as possible on each side, the more elevated parts being generally planted centrally with trees and in front with shrubbery; the recesses, which will be glades of turf with a few detached groups of shrubs, will reach with slightly undulating slope nearly or quite to the side walks of the adjoining streets.

These streets are proposed to be widened to eighty-six feet, ten feet of which would be taken off the park ground; the side-walk being planted with a double row of trees, the opposite houses would not be unpleasantly conspicuous from the water and land ways of the Park.

Three streets are proposed to be carried across the Midway besides those at its end; the water-way, carriage-way and walks of the park system passing under viaducts. As the track of the Illinois Central Railway is too low to pass under with carriages, and as we are informed by the Engineer of the Company that it cannot be sufficiently raised, it is designed to be arched over, the trains upon it being kept out of view by a parapet of earth and shrubbery.

An open area, designated Midway Place, in two symmetrical parts, connected by a bridge over the Basin, terminates the Midway Plaisance on the east. As will be seen on drawing No. 3, to which we now turn, it opens to the right upon that division of the closed ground which we have designated the Lagoon Plaisance; on the left, upon the Lake Open Ground, and looking east, commands a view over the head of the Lagoon through a gradually narrowing perspective of points and islands, with the Lake seen through a depression of the dunes which are here to be clothed with prostrate shrubs.

In studying the general arrangement of parts in the Lower Division we have already shown that the feature of most controlling importance is the Pier, and have stated the considerations which approximately fix its position. A natural ridge, partly wooded, the longitudinal axis of which is nearly at right angles with the coast line, indicates the most desirable course for the outlet and entrance channel and consequently establishes more precisely the proper place for the Pier.

We suppose that a public road will be formed along the beach beyond the park limits, each way, and have considered that when the regions south of the east half of the Lagoon Division of the Park shall have become populous, a route or routes of communication between it and the north side of the Park more direct than is afforded by Hyde Park Avenue, will be of considerable importance, and also that access from it to the boats running between the Park and Chicago river, will be very desirable. At the same time it is of even more importance that small steamers and sail boats should be able at all times to make a harbor at the Park, and a drawbridge at the harbor's mouth is not only to be deprecated on account of its inconvenience, but because by establishing a harsh and conspicuous line across the channel, it would be most unfavorable to an impression of unity between the Park and the Lake.

These conflicting objects of a continuous shore road and of a harbor opening by an unbridged channel upon the Lake, are as far as possible harmonized by a detour of the shore road, which following closely the bank of the channel and the Park Haven, is returned upon an island with two bridges towards the Lake shore, and passes out of the Park at its south east corner. A branch road leads westerly out of the Park from the point of the detour furthest from the Lake, offering a short-cut to the middle parts of the region south of the Park. The Park gates and fence are then placed west of this branch and of the shore road from end to end, so that they may always be left open, together with the harbour, for use at night. A large Green is also thrown out at the north end, indicated as the Lakeopen Green, and a smaller Green outside of the harbour at the south end, the latter designated the Park Haven Green. These are intended more especially for ball playing and other athletic exercises, and each is provided with a lodge for dressing rooms and the shelter of lookers-on at the games. The whole is adapted like the Southopen Ground, to be lighted and left open at night.

The Lakeopen Green is at the nearest point of this division of the park to the town and is entered directly from a station of the Illinois Central and Michigan Central railways. Visitors taking this way out may be engaged in ball playing or floating on the Lagoon within half an hour after they have left a school house, an office or a shop in the midst of the city. In London excursion trains frequently take over fifty thousand people an hour to or from the Crystal Palace Park at Sydenham, at a charge of a penny a mile.[23]

As the water of the Lagoon will probably be much warmer than that of the Lake, it is suggested that arrangements for bathing and swimming in the north bay should be made at the house indicated in the plan opposite the Lakeopen Green.

Within the Lakeopen Ground there are two places especially adapted to large assemblies, one at the Pier, the other on the lake shore in front of the Park Haven Green. The latter is in the form of a terrace and gives the outer position to carriages. On the Pier a broad walking space is arranged outside of the carriage Concourse, and from the solid pier which extends 250 feet outward from the present shore line, a narrower open work pier is proposed, to eventually extend to a block about a thousand feet further out.

Immediately behind the Concourse on the Pier a large building will be observed, designated the Belvedere, which would be the principal refectory of this Division of the Park. It fronts on one side upon the Lake, on the other upon a lawn which slopes to a bay opening upon the middle of the Lagoon, opposite which is a cluster of islands in a wooded cove. An elevated outlook is intended to be here provided for, and this suggests the name of the building.

The Belvedere lawn, which is within the Lagoon Plaisance, and would be entered from the Belvedere by doors closed at night, extends on the south to the central feature of this division of the plan, a Promenade Concert Ground upon a Terrace formally planted. The Park gate being open at the head of the harbour, carriages pass readily south of the lawn to the Concourse south of the Terrace platform, the trees upon which are arranged with reference to the view northward, which extends through a long vista formed by narrows of the Lagoon; the vista point being a Kiosk, seen beyond a bridge, at the head of the South Bay. The Orchestra is to be stationed upon a small island, and the music, floating over the water, will reach the Pic-nic woods on the west and the walks upon the Belvedere lawn on the east, as well as the terrace, where the principal part of the audience, both on foot and in carriages, is expected to assemble. The correspondence of the principal features of the plan from the Pier to the Lagoon Terrace with the requirements developed in the earlier part of the Report, will be evident.

The Pic-nic district above referred to includes the best of the woods now growing upon the grounds. It is to be further planted in groups and open groves and near the water with underwood, and fitted with swings and other means of amusement. A cottage with separate accommodations and attendance for men and women and several shelters or summer houses looking upon the Lagoon will also be observed. There are open glades for croquet parties and children's dances. Further to the southward there are shaded drives and walks through deeper woods.

There is a Quay on the Park Haven for steamboats and masted boats that cannot pass the bridges, and at different points on the Lagoon nine boat landings, to each of which a sheltered seat is attached. A number of other sites are indicated for shelters and bowers, and balconies over the water.

It will be observed that there are numerous islands without boat landings; some of these are intended to be specially protected against the approach of boats by flat, rushy shores, the object being to provide entirely isolated and sequestered coverts as breeding places for birds. The Lagoon is intended to be abundantly stocked with all water fowl that will endure the climate, and your Commission is recommended to take early measures to procure and domesticate the American swan and other fine birds of the upper lakes and of the far West.[24]

The increase of such birds will be in request for the Zoological Gardens and private parks of Europe, and black swans or other rare and beautiful birds of Asia, Australia, and the Antarctic regions would be gladly exchanged for them. The bleak and humid situation of Chicago is most unfavorable for general Zoological or Botanical gardens, but in Ornithology a better living collection could very soon be established in your ground than now exists in the world. The complete success of the recent attempt to naturalize the English sparrow, of which thousands are now propagated every year in the New York and Brooklyn parks, and which has completely relieved those cities and their suburbs of a serious nuisance, indicates that a little enterprise in this direction might be expected to accomplish results of great interest.[25] The naturalization of some of the common song birds of the north of Europe, which would be a delightful acquisition, is probably quite feasible and the process would not be expensive if undertaken in connection with a general aviary establishment.

If a voluntary organization should be formed for this purpose of sufficient strength, the exclusive use might be given it of all desirable ground for breeding purposes, together with the privilege of establishing a museum and convenient offices in the park, proper guarantees of public benefit being agreed upon. The Ornithological Society of London is thus accommodated in St. James's Park.[26] If desired, inconspicuous arrangements may also be studied out on the Lower Division of the Park for special classes of animals to which the circumstances would be congenial, as Bisons, Elks, Bears; or amphibians, as Seals and Sea Lions; the general rule being observed, to admit nothing in the management of which a distinguished success, without sacrifice of matters of more primary interest, cannot be confidently expected. No bird or animal should be allowed in the Park which will not surely be healthy and happy in it.

The manner in which the water is disposed in all of the Lower Division is such that except at a few narrow points of connection, it occupies only a part of the ground which is now flooded or liable to be so when the Lake is highest. The water surface of the Lagoon will be 165 acres in extent at ordinary summer level. An excavation sufficient to give a general depth of 6 feet, with slope of 6 to 1, will yield about 1,300,000 yards of material. This will be sufficient to add about 2 feet to the general elevation of the rest of the Division. We suppose that 2 to 4 inches of clay, brought from without will be mixed with this to give trees a better support. The surface of most of the land will then lie from 4 to 4½ feet above the highest ordinary, and 2 to 2½ above the occasional extraordinary summer level of the Lake. A less general elevation than this could not, in our judgment, be made agreeable to the eye, nor would it be wholesome for any but a few aquatic trees.

The outlines of the shores of the Lagoon may at first sight seem to be unduly complicated, but the introduction of numerous points and narrow islands is here demanded by considerations of cost as much as by fidelity to the type of natural scenery which is had in view.

The same water level is designed to be carried through the Midway Basins to the Mere, and economy will probably require that the excavation of the Lagoon shall precede that of the Midway Basin, the Basin that of the Mere, and the Mere the shaping of the surface generally of the Upper Plaisance. The depth of water in the Midway, should also be at least 6 feet, in summer, or there will be trouble with water plants. It will then fall everywhere to 4 during the skating season.

If it were not for the experience of other cities where the cost of forming parks has been more than met by the increased taxable valuation of real estate benefited by them, and for the rise in the value of certain property which has already accrued on account of the South Park undertaking, the excavation for water required by the plan would probably be thought too costly to be soon entered upon. Even as it is, it may be questioned whether the delay which will be involved by it in meeting the expectations upon which the present value of property depends, will not, after a time, be so disappointing as to render advisable some different plan of dealing with the Middle and Upper Divisions, dispensing with the water connection, and giving the public the use of the ground sooner in a finished condition.

We shall give some reasons for thinking that nothing would really be gained by such a course.

The expectations upon which the rise in the value of real estate has depended and will depend, are partly of a definite and partly of a very indefinite character. A few years ago the district more especially affected by the undertaking of the South Park was commonly regarded as waste land and as hardly susceptible of much improvement. Whatever change has occurred in the public judgment in this respect is due, in the first place, to the results of private enterprise by which it has been proved that it can generally be relieved of surface water, be clothed with fine greensward, and that trees can, up to a certain point at least, be made to flourish upon it.[27] These experiments give definite and tangible ground of expectation as to its future. But beyond this, secondly, there is a blind faith that your Commission, having larger proportionate means at command, and being able to direct a business-like study to the question of the possibilities of improvement, will find a way to do more on a large scale than private enterprise has yet done even on a small scale. Suppose, then, that after several years work, a finish shall have been given to the whole of the Upper and Middle Divisions, but that the character of this finish does not vary materially from that of the adjoining door yards as they are now seen, the improvements by drainage, manuring, greensward and tree planting having been essentially the same. The result would be that nothing more would be found in the Park than the realization of the defined and experimentally grounded expectations of the present, and it may be doubted whether this would not really be somewhat disappointing.

But suppose, on the other hand that, with less extent of superficial finish, it should be evident that the operations in progress were to result in much more substantial far-reaching improvements than had been definitely imagined — improvements of a really organic character, directly affecting the whole region — it is clear that it would not only satisfy, but induce a strong advance upon, present expectations.

The great increase in the value of real estate produced by the construction of the New York park did not begin until sometime after it was commenced, nor until the public began to see that the ground had much greater capabilities than had at first been imagined. The President of the Brooklyn Park Commission, in a public address two years ago,[28] quoting a statement that the opening of a small part of the park the previous year had caused an advance of real estate in that city to the amount of ten millions of dollars, observed that it was not because the public then first realized that the city was to have a park, but because the character of the first improvements which had been made for the purpose really advanced the rank of the city in the public estimation and suddenly caused a new class of expectations to be formed of its future.

Looking again at the Baltimore and Philadelphia parks, the natural advantages of the sites of which are much greater than those possessed in New York and Brooklyn, and where the improvements thus far made, though quite extensive, have been of a more superficial and commonplace class, we find that they have produced no very extraordinary increase of value in neighboring real estate.

Among the advantages of the plan we propose, which would be permanently barred by the substitution for it of any plan which could be executed very much more cheaply and quickly, are the following:

First.   It secures a deep thorough drainage[29] of the Upper and Middle Divisions, and thus adds greatly to the chances of making trees flourish upon them.

Second.   It locks the three divisions of the Park into one obvious system, so that their really disjointed character will be much less impressed upon the minds of observers passing through them than would be the case if the connecting element of a common body of water were lacking.

Third.   It practically places the Upper or Inland Division of the Park upon a navigable arm of Lake Michigan and thus makes it accessible by boats from the heart of the commercial part of the city. The aquatic character of the Park will thus be more remarkable. It will also be an advantage that the water fowl and fish may swim freely between the Upper Plaisance and the Lake. The skating advantage is also obvious.

Fourth.   It offers to those coming by rail, in public carriages, or on foot, a means of traveling through nearly all parts of the Park quietly, agreeably and without fatigue, and by a method much less expensive than that of wheeled carriages. This will be of great value to invalids, convalescents, and mothers with children in arms. There is a very limited extent of water in the New York Park, yet it is found that from four to six thousand persons use the small boats daily, in fine weather, and at a charge of ten cents they yield a satisfactory profit.

Fifth.   The material excavated from the Basins and Mere will, if skillfully used upon the banks, overcome, to a certain extent, the chief landscape defect of all the Chicago pleasure grounds, namely, their nearly level surface. Presuming that the work will be done by steam dredges, in no other way can so considerable an improvement in this respect be made as cheaply. Here, therefore, if anywhere, the city can afford a little luxury in undulation.

Sixth.   By offering upon the Midway and the Upper Plaisances to the view of those who come to the Park in boats a shore with, generally, much higher banks than it will be practicable to form upon the Lagoon, the value of the boating privileges of the Park, and consequently of its Lake approach, will be greatly increased.

Seventh.   The incidental effect of this operation upon all the country surrounding the Park as well as that within it will be most valuable. It will gradually bring about a change in its character equivalent to that which would be gained by lifting its surface several feet above its present level. It will make gardens practicable where otherwise nothing but swamp plants will grow. It will at once make a considerable district suitable for residences which will otherwise remain not only unwholesome for that purpose within itself, but a source of ill health to others until a costly system of sewers has been constructed. In connection with the better growth of trees which will result, the climate of the whole south part of the city will be essentially improved by it, so much so, for instance, that there will be appreciably less liability to rheumatic and pulmonary complaints and the epidemics of children.

In view of the advantages thus promised, it would, in our judgment, be prudent and politic to enter at once upon the necessary works, even though, to carry them on, all other improvements had to be postponed until they were completed. We judge, however, that this would not be at all necessary. The process of excavation and embankment should be mainly by steam apparatus, and when once begun should go steadily on at a nearly regular per diem rate, otherwise idle capital would be charged upon the Park. The total amount of the outlay which would thus be required per annum, would not, we suppose, exhaust your resources. The construction of the Southopen Ground being an undertaking by itself, need wait for nothing. It nowhere involves very heavy work, and the chief need for discretion will be in regard to the means and methods to be used for improving the soil. We should recommend that the outer parts be dressed heavily with soil, clay, and well-rotted manure, and trees planted of much larger size than we should advise to be used under other circumstances, but that for the sake of economy the Green should be improved more slowly by the process already suggested. Before it was ready to be seeded for turf the Pavilion might be built, and the grove to the north of it being fitted up as a temporary pic-nic ground, it would probably be found at once a source of income equivalent to the interest on its cost.

At the same time the Park Haven pier should be built and there would be nothing in the way of the construction of the shore road, the Concourse on the Pier, and the Belvedere. By the times these had been completed, the dredging would be so far advanced that boats could run from the city into the harbor and finishing operations could be begun on the Belvedere lawn and other parts of the interior Park.

We make these suggestions as to the course of operations simply to show that if the construction of the Lagoon and Midway Basin should be immediately undertaken, it would not necessarily involve a delay in making the Park fully available in certain important particulars for public use.

In speaking of the depth of the Lagoon, and generally in referring to the depth of excavations, we have had in view the minimum requirements of the plan. It is to be expected that roads and walks throughout the Park will generally be graded as low as shall be consistent with efficient drainage and

231

a graceful continuity of parts, and by this means material will be obtained for a slight modulation of adjoining surfaces. By the occasional introduction in the shores of a surface but a few inches above high water level, and in which only rushes and water plants will grow, the average elevation of the filled ground may be made higher at other points, and a variety attained altogether desirable. Adjoining the basin and the Mere, occasional elevations of at least twenty feet can be easily managed with long flowing contours and without any appearance of being artificially mounded. The excavation of two feet, which we have before said is required in the Southopen Ground, and which should be extended from the central point in long shallow depressions to the north-east and north-west, and to the south-west beyond the Pool, together with the deeper excavation required for the Pool itself, will yield sufficient material to give a perceptible play of surface upon the lower part of the South-open Green, and in grading the drives and walks something may be cheaply added.

By slight and inexpensive changes of the surface, such as we have thus advised, provided always that trees of a satisfactory character can be insured, the scenery of this part of the Park may be rendered appropriate and pleasing. We do not say that it would under no circumstances be desirable to vary the surface much more, but only that it is not indispensable to do so, and as any considerably increased modulation beyond what we have indicated, would be expensive, the question of undertaking it may be regarded as one of detail, to be determined when necessary with fair consideration of resources which shall then be available.

If it could be afforded, for instance, it would be desirable to form an irregular depression extending from the vicinity of the Pool through the Glade to the Mere on the east side of the Upper Plaisance, its depth being sufficient to disclose the Mere at this point to view from the north-western part of the Green. The material obtained would be used chiefly to elevate the Ramble district. The drive east of this may have considerable depression and the material thus obtained should be chiefly used to elevate the surface still further to the eastward.

The shores of the Mere, the swells of the Midway slopes and the points and islands of the Lagoon could generally be increased several feet in height beyond what will be convenient with the material provided for, by increasing the proposed depth of the excavation for water. There will be a decided advantage in all such increase and no disadvantage, except that of cost, which within desirable limits will not at all advance with the depth the dredging machine is required to work.

The consideration hereafter of what can be afforded in this way will perhaps be affected favorably to larger operations than we have spoken of as absolutely necessary by the adoption of a temporizing policy wherever it can be applied without entailing permanent defects upon the Park. You have for instance a great extent of woods and walks upon your plan. It is very important that all of these should be laid out, and in the management of the plantations should be constantly regarded as if in existence, but it is entirely unnecessary for this purpose that finely constructed wheel and foot ways, of full width and adapted to use in all weathers, should be formed within their outlines. The way being left open, this part of the work can be postponed until required by the immediate convenience of the public. The character of your ground is very favorable to such a course. Again, you have a cheap lumber market, and if such buildings, bridges and fences as are at once required by the public accommodation should be built of wood, no opportunity would have been lost and little expenditure would have been wasted, if, when they were found decaying or inadequate, it should be decided to supplant them with structures of greater dignity and permanence.

On the other hand, if, before making your plantations, you should neglect to take every practicable precaution to secure the constant, vigorous growth and health of the trees, the defect which you will have fastened upon the Park, is one which, by no subsequent liberality, can be made good. A temporizing policy in this direction, therefore, would be most disloyal to the Future, which you are bound first of all to be faithful to.

As grading operations must be essentially complete before the preparation of surfaces for planting can be begun, we would again, therefore, most earnestly press the consideration upon you that a comparatively small body of vigorous, well developed trees, will in a few years, produce more elevated sky lines, more apparent variety of surface, and give greater satisfaction than can be obtained by the expenditure of millions in heaping up earth. Consequently, however desirable a little more play of surface may be, it is of much less consequence than that all available means should be used for developing the highest horticultural capabilities of your ground.

It only remains for us to refer to some suggestions which we have offered in the plan, in regard to approaches and exterior streets.

The important line of communication which we call the Southopen Parkway, does not, at present, connect properly with the Southopen Ground, but it may be made to do so by the acquisition on the part of your Commission, of a comparatively small piece of land, and we have therefore thought it desirable to show on our design how a satisfactory adjustment may thus be arrived at.

The difficulty in regard to the Southgrove Parkway, as at present laid down on the maps, is of a more serious character. It turns abruptly at right angles, a few hundred feet away from the Park, and the actual provision for entrance when it reaches its extreme corner, is so wholly inadequate that some considerable improvement will inevitably be required.

A close study of all the circumstance of this case, has led us to avoid any attempt to solve the difficulty by direct addition to the Park territory, and we have been led to think on the other hand that the necessary improvement should be made in the form of an extension of the Parkway on a scale commensurate with the importance of its position and having a marked artistic character of its own.

About fifty years ago the Quadrant leading from Pall Mall to Regent Street was made one of the finest thoroughfares in London. No such connection had been originally contemplated, but the demand for some adequate means of communication in this direction having become imperative, the new street was at length cut through a quarter of the city that had been solidly built up with expensive structures.[30] We suggest the adoption of a somewhat similar expedient in your case, before any houses are erected in the neighborhood, and if the Parkway Quadrant can be carried out as shown on our Plan, the curved line of approach will, we think, have a sufficiently bold sweep to be easy and agreeable in connection with the long, straight line of the Southgrove Parkway, and the main Park entrance to which it leads will be relieved of any appearance of awkwardness.

An unusual volume of traffic will naturally be accumulated on the boundary streets of the Park, and we propose, for this reason, and also to improve their promenade character, that they should be somewhat widened on each side of the present centre line. The suggestion to increase the width of two of these streets to eighty-six feet, has been already referred to, and the others should, we think, be at least a hundred feet wide, and their walks on the Park side continuously shaded. Improvements of this character are almost invariably called for sooner or later in the vicinity of urban parks, and their costliness increases with every year they are postponed. We have seen many hundred thousand dollars saved in a few years by prompt action on similar advices in other cases, and many more lost by inattention to it.

In the progress of a public improvement like that of the Chicago South Park, undertaken with so much reference to the distant future as its justification necessarily predicates, and the completion of which, in all its parts, must be so far off, the introduction of subsidiary elements of design of greater or less importance will undoubtedly from time to time be proposed. It is not to be expected that a plan will be made at the outset so complete, that no additions to it or modifications of it in detail will be admissable, but it is of the utmost consequence that the essential ends should be clearly seen before the work is organized, and that from the moment it begins to the end, be that five or fifty years hence, and under whatever changes of administration and changes of fashion, these great ruling ends should be pursued with absolute consistency. Work of the character designed constantly requires ability of high order in its supervision, and it is undesirable that the exercise of this ability should be hampered by unnecessarily specific instructions.

Under the influence of these considerations our object has been simply to develop a series of the most desirable features practicable of realization under the very peculiar conditions of your site and circumstances, and we have endeavored to carry the design of these only so far as to establish the characteristic end of each, whether it be an artistic effect on the imagination or simply an accommodation for convenience and comfort.

The plan having, after due deliberation, been adopted as the constitutional law of the park construction, no proposition involving change or addition in any locality, should be entertained, however attractive in itself, which is not harmonious with the purpose intended to rule in that locality. All propositions on the other hand, intelligently designed to strengthen and emphasize its main purposes, may be heartily welcomed, and their adoption be simply a question of practical business expediency.

Trusting that the plan which wc have now presented may meet with your approval and that time will justify the confidence with which you have honored us.

> We remain, gentlemen,
> Yours respectfully,

OLMSTED, VAUX & CO.
Landscape Architects.

The original was published as Olmsted, Vaux & Company, *Report Accompanying Plan for Laying Out the South Park* (Chicago, 1871), pages 3–40.

1. The Chicago South Park Commission established by the February 24, 1869, law provided for the creation of the South Park; its members were appointed by the governor of Illinois (Illinois, *Private Laws of the State of Illinois, Passed by the Twenty-sixth General Assembly, Convened January 4, 1869*, 4 vols. [Springfield, Ill., 1869], 1: 358–66; Alfred Theodore Andreas, *History of Chicago*, 3 vols. [1884–86; rpt. ed., New York, 1975], 3: 167).

2. Olmsted and Vaux were not given any formal, written instructions except to "prepare plans of the Parks." They proceeded to prepare the report presented here and plans for the parks and their connecting boulevards (James P. Root to OVC, April 5, 1870).

3. The South Park was composed of three tracts of land, which Olmsted and Vaux designated as the Lower Division (later named Jackson Park), located on the shore of Lake Michigan between 56th and 67th streets; the Upper Division (later named Washington Park), bounded by Cottage Grove Avenue on the east and Kankakee Avenue on the west between 51st and 60th streets; and the 600-foot-wide Midway Plaisance, bounded by 59th Street on the west and 60th Street on the east, which connected the larger two divisions of the park (Illinois, *Private Laws of the State of Illinois*, 1: 360).

4. Richmond Park, located south of the River Thames and about six miles southwest of the center of London, was created by King Charles I in 1636 as a 2,500-acre deer park and rural retreat. Although Charles fenced in the park with a ten-mile-long wall, the public was allowed entry almost from the beginning (Guy R. Williams, *The Royal Parks of London* [London, 1978], p. 154; Susan Lasdun, *The English Park: Royal, Private & Public* [1991; rpt. ed., New York, 1992], p. 40; see also, FLO, "Park," [1875], below).

5. The 41,000-acre forest of Fontainebleau, located thirty-six miles from Paris, was a popular recreation ground and favorite subject of French landscape painters (A. Vin-

cent, *Fontainebleau: The Palace, the Town, the Forest* [Paris, c. 1920], pp. 88, 90–98; see also, FLO, "Park," [1875], below).

6. St. James's Park, consisting of fifty-nine acres and one of London's royal parks, is located in the heart of London and surrounded by Buckingham Palace, St. James's Palace, Whitehall, and the Wellington Barracks. St. James's Park was a fashionable place for promenading by London society in the eighteenth century. In 1826 John Nash redesigned the park, giving it a more picturesque appearance (G. R. Williams, *Royal Parks of London*, pp. 21, 36; S. Lasdun, *English Park*, pp. 124–25; see also, FLO, "Park," [1875], below).

7. The Parc de Monçeau, located in the northwestern part of Paris, was redesigned by Jean-Charles-Adolphe Alphand in 1861 as one of three smaller parks to be used by local patrons (George F. Chadwick, *The Park and the Town* [New York, 1966], pp. 157–58; see also, FLO, "Park," [1875], below).

8. In their 1868 report to the Riverside Improvement Company concerning the laying out of a suburban village near Chicago, Olmsted and Vaux emphasized the importance of this change in designing cities and towns. They noted that there were

> symptoms of a change . . . found in the constant modification which has occurred in the manner of laying out all growing towns, and which is invariably in the direction of a separation of business and dwelling streets, and toward rural spaciousness in the latter. The broader the streets are made, provided they are well prepared in respect to what are significantly designated "the modern conveniences," and especially if some slight rural element is connected with them, as by rows of trees or little enclosures of turf and foliage, the greater is the demand for dwelling-places upon them.

They also discussed in their report the scientific findings of Henry W. Rumsey, an English physician, who cited overcrowded conditions in cities as a direct threat to public health (Olmsted, Vaux & Co., *Preliminary Report upon the Proposed Suburban Village at Riverside, Near Chicago*, Sept. 1, 1868 [*Papers of FLO*, 6: 273–89, and n. 4]).

9. London's 380-acre Hyde Park, originally a royal hunting park, and the more formal 290-acre Kensington Gardens, which adjoins Hyde Park. The Bois de Boulogne in Paris, a 2,500-acre royal forest, was designed as a public park in the 1850s (see FLO, "Park," [1875], below).

10. The Wissahickon Creek and Valley in Philadelphia, extending northeasterly from the Schuylkill River, has been described as "a miniature Alpine gorge." The valley, consisting of a lush, green waterway and wooded slopes, was appropriated by the Fairmount Park Commission in 1868 to protect the city's water source and "preserve the beauty of its scenery" (Thomas Augustine Daly, comp., *The Wissahickon* [Philadelphia, 1922], pp. 9–10, 38–39; Francis Burke Brandt, *The Wissahickon Valley, within the City of Philadelphia* [Philadelphia, 1927], p. 6).

11. That is, Lake Michigan.

12. The Lido, a narrow island, is located between Venice and the open sea. Fashionable as a bathing resort, it was accessible only by water (Bruno Alfieri, *Venice: A Guide to the City of the Lagoon*, trans. Elena Ciriello, 4th ed. [Venice, 1953], pp. 97–98; Augustus J. C. Hare, *Venice* [London, 1884], p. 181).

13. In 1780 King Gustaf III commissioned the laying out of his royal chateau at Haga as a public park in the English landscape style. Haga Park, lying north of Stockholm on the Brunnsviken, is accessible by both land and water (Sacha Segal Scarlat, *Key to Stockholm* [Stockholm, 1960], p. 89).

14. These seaside resort piers, first constructed in the 1810s and 1820s, were designed as landing piers to which visitors to the coastal towns could disembark from steamboats. Owners of the piers, however, noticed that people were coming simply to stroll along

the piers. By the 1840s and 1850s the piers' functions were changing, and by the 1860s piers were being built for the pleasure of visitors. Admission fees were charged, and the piers included shelters, refreshment stalls, bandstands, and promenades, usually erected at the seaward end of the pier. These piers became so popular that scores were built along the English coast. France followed England's lead and constructed its own piers in the last half of the nineteenth century (Simon H. Adamson, *Seaside Piers* [London, 1977], pp. 13, 14, 19, 21, 43).

15. A children's game in which players of one team attempt to tag and imprison players of the other team if they venture from their home territory or "base" (*EB*).

16. Olmsted is referring to the use of sunken transverse roads on Central Park, a unique aspect of the Greensward Plan, which carried crosstown traffic safely under the park at all hours, thus eliminating the need to keep the park open at night (*Papers of FLO*, 3: 180, n. 14).

17. During the same month that the South Park and West Parks commissions were created, the Illinois state legislature also passed legislation for the creation of a North Park commission and the laying out of a public space later named Lincoln Park. The 250 acre Lincoln Park was located in the northern part of the city on the shore of Lake Michigan (A. T. Andreas, *History of Chicago*, 3: 182–83).

18. The Champ-de-Mars in Paris, created in 1790 and extending over 3,000 feet from the École Militaire northwesterly to the present-day Eiffel Tower, was used for military reviews and parades (Karl Baedeker, *Paris and Northern France* [London, 1867], p. 159).

19. The Southopen Parkway, extending north from the northwest corner of Washington Park became known variously as Kankakee Boulevard, Grand Boulevard, South Open Parkway, and today as Martin Luther King Drive. The Southgrove Parkway, extending north from the northeast corner of Washington Park was renamed Drexel Boulevard (Daniel Bluestone, *Constructing Chicago* [New Haven, Conn., 1991], p. 55).

20. Pavilion Parkway, renamed Garfield Boulevard, extended westward from Washington Park along the preexisting 55th Street for about four miles. The boulevard was widened to 200 feet and contained a 90-foot-wide planting strip at its center with two 40-foot-wide drives and two 15-foot-wide walks on either side (ibid.).

21. During the eighteenth and nineteenth centuries milkwomen were allowed to pasture their cows in London's St. James's Park for a fee. Twice a day the women would herd their cows to the far end of the park, near Whitehall, and sell milk to the public for a penny a mugfull (Evelyn Cecil, *London Parks and Gardens* [London, 1907], p. 64; Hazel Thurston, *Royal Parks for the People* [London, 1974], p. 41).

22. Turners were members of *Turnvereine*, or gymnastic societies, first established in Germany by F. L. Jahn in the 1840s for the promotion of physical education. German immigrants brought their *Turnvereine* with them in the mid-1800s when they came to the United States and participated in annual *Turnfeste*, or festivals. The festivals included exercises in free and apparatus gymnastics as well as lectures on physical education (*OED*; Henry Metzner, *A Brief History of the American Turnerbund* [Pittsburgh, Pa., 1924], pp. 7–8, 11).

23. About 5,500 people per day visited the Crystal Palace at Sydenham. During special events, however, as many as 30,000 people would attempt to travel to the Crystal Palace at the same time, and railway companies were forced to add extra lines to accommodate the crowds. Olmsted is accurate in that it cost about seven pence to travel third class the seven-and-one-half miles to the Crystal Palace; a first-class, one-way ticket cost £1.3 (Patrick Beaver, *The Crystal Palace* [London, 1970], pp. 105, 111; C. T. Goode, *To the Crystal Palace* [Berkshire, 1984], p. 54).

24. See F. L. & J. C. Olmsted, "Plan for a Public Park on the Flats South of Buffalo," Oct. 1, 1888, note 17, below.

25. Attempts to propagate English (or house) sparrows in New York began in 1850. They

were introduced in Central Park in 1864. Americans in their zeal to advance the sparrow population in the United States were under the mistaken assumption that the birds were insect eaters and would keep down the insect population. Studies found, however, that the birds were not insect eaters but rather preferred grain, seeds, and fruit. The birds did not relieve the cities of nuisances but were in fact pests themselves (Walter B. Barrows, *The English Sparrow [Passer domesticus] in North America, Especially in its Relations to Agriculture*, in *Bulletin no. 1*, U.S. Dept. of Agriculture [Washington, D.C., 1889], pp. 17–18, 22, 98).

26. The Ornithological Society was founded in 1837 for the purpose of collecting and propagating species of water fowl in the London parks. In 1840 the society was granted the privilege of building a cottage and aviary on Duck Island in St. James's Park ("Report of the Council," in *Sixth Annual Report of the Acclimatisation Society of Great Britain, and Ornithological Society of London* [London, 1866], p. 10; Donald Edgar, *The Royal Parks* [London, 1986], p. 88).

27. Olmsted may be alluding to the fact that practical drainage techniques such as thorough drainage could be used with success on the South Park site (see n. 29 below).

28. James Samuel Thomas Stranahan (1808–1898) was president of the Prospect Park commission from 1860 until 1882. Stranahan's address, to which Olmsted here refers, was before a public meeting on March 30, 1869, regarding the Prospect Park boundaries. At the time of Stranahan's speech about 200 acres of the park had been improved, but he stated that "it has been said by those who should know, that the day we opened the park saw a rise in value of the real estate of our city of ten millions of dollars" (*DAB*; BPC, *Annual Reports, 1861–1873*, p. 349).

29. Thorough drainage is a comprehensive system of draining land using underground tile or wooden drainpipes. Olmsted made considerable use of thorough drainage on Central Park (*Papers of FLO*, 3: 101, n. 2).

30. In 1811 the Prince Regent of England commissioned John Nash to lay out Regent's Park in London. As part of his design Nash proposed to link Regent's Park with St. James's Park, Pall Mall, and Charing Cross to the south. He planned to lay out a street roughly following the lines of existing streets as far as Piccadily. The difficulty was that the southern end of what would become Regent Street would be considerably off line with the northern part above Piccadily because of existing fashionable homes, squares, and roadways. To link the two parts of Regent Street, Nash created Piccadily Circus and then the Quadrant, which he called in his plan a "bending street." In actuality, it was a crescent that swept around to the east to Piccadily Circus which fed into the southern part of Regent Street, thus eliminating awkward or right-angle turns. In addition to laying out this roadway, Nash also designed the buildings along the Quadrant, creating a highly fashionable area of London (John Summerson, *The Life and Work of John Nash, Architect* [Cambridge, Mass., 1980], pp. 76–77; Terence Davis, *John Nash: the Prince Regent's Architect* [Cranbury, N.J., 1967], pp. 63–64, 65, 74–75).

A Review of Recent Changes,
and Changes which have been Projected, in the Plans
of the Central Park:

LETTER I.

A Consideration of Motives, Requirements and Restrictions
Applicable to the General Scheme of the Park.

New York, January, 1872.

To the Honorable H. G. Stebbins,[1]
President of the Department of Public Parks:
Sir: —

In 1870, the preparation of the Central Park had been fourteen years in progress under the Commission of which you were then President.

A few objects had been accepted as practicable to be associated with the main scheme, suitable provisions for which remained to be established, but the primary construction of the Park in its essential elements, except at the outskirts where joint action with other departments of the city had been required, was complete, and the public enjoyed such use of it as can be had of any park the plantations of which are but just planted, their finer details incomplete, and all parts yet raw and blotchy.

Nearly six million dollars had been expended to bring the undertaking to this point, when the Commission was superseded by the Department under the charter of 1870.[2]

Eighteen months later, another change having occurred restoring you to the head of the administration, it is found that while, in the meantime, little or nothing has been done on the unimproved outskirt ground, numerous alleged defects have been discerned in the plans formerly pursued, remedies for these devised, and to some slight extent carried out, and that the Park stands charged with an additional expenditure of two and a quarter millions of dollars.[3]

At the time the old plans were reviewed and their revision resolved upon, we retained the position which we had held from the beginning of the work, as the professional advisers of the Board in respect to matters of design.

Referring to these facts, you have been kind enough to suggest that an explanation is due from us of the changes which have been thought necessary, more especially as the Annual Report of the Department, while presenting sub-reports from eight junior officers, contains nothing, as you observe, from us and refers in no way to our service.[4]

Thanking you for the opportunity, we shall, as briefly as possible, relieve ourselves from responsibility in respect to the change of plans, and afterwards discuss the occasion and character of this change.

Soon after our re-appointment, in May, 1870,[5] we made a concise written report on the purposes and design of the various structures in progress on the Park, and took several occasions to show our wish to explain these more fully to the new Commissioners.[6] When subsequently we were casually informed of newly conceived projects,[7] we sought opportunity to point out the relations which they would have, and which were liable to be overlooked, to parts of the design already executed, but no reply was made to our requests for appointments for this purpose. As late as November we had not been officially advised of any dissatisfaction with the plans, nor had we been asked to explain those elements of our design which appear from the Report to have been regarded as inscrutable.[8]

On the 25th of November, having then learned, though not officially, that radical changes had been determined on, we addressed a letter to the President of the Department, of which a copy is appended.[9]

The receipt of this was formally acknowledged, but no action taken on the request conveyed, and on the 1st of December, the Department having openly disregarded the terms of its engagement with us, our duties to it were concluded.[10]

The Annual Report of the Department (of the sub-reports attached to which we had no knowledge until you recently placed the printed copy in our hands) embodies a studied inculpation of previous administrations of the Park, the more emphatic charge being that of gross inconsiderateness of the reasonable requirements of the public in the designs of different parts of the work; the specifications of this charge being incorporated in the explanation of various local changes undertaken by the late administration.

The imputations thus made upon the plan of the Park are of a class with criticisms which have been constant since the inception of the work; criticisms heretofore more commonly expressed, however, in the form of suggestions and inquiries, and thus with an acknowledgment of incomplete study. As the ground, officially stated, of changes by which not only much previous work is sentenced to be undone, but in which a further expenditure of some millions of dollars is involved, they now demand examination.

By a similar method of criticism, changes equally costly may be demanded and apologized for under every successive administration of the Park.

Its characteristic defect being that it takes no account of the larger number of motives which have influenced the design of the features assumed to be under review, a reply in detail, in which all such overlooked considerations should be set forth, would require a volume much larger than the Report itself. Before attempting a comprehensive reduction of this duty by the development of a general theory of design applicable to the Park, it may be desired, however, that we should fully exhibit this alleged defect

An example, which will enable us to do so within moderate limits, is offered in a small group of associated objects, in which the motives of design, requiring consideration, are unusually local and limited. First presenting these, we shall then quote the criticism of the Report, and lastly refer to the changes, in this case slight, which have been made with a view of improvement.

Children will come to the Park in large numbers while yet too young to have the tastes and habits with regard to which its arrangements are generally designed, and localities in which they can be more particularly cared for are thus desirable. Ball-grounds have been prepared, in and about which boys have special privileges and special guardianship. Girls and boys, too small to use these, like to flock together also, and it is both better for them and more convenient for their elders that they should be encouraged and facilitated in doing so.

This was one of the considerations to which we have referred; another was suggested by the frightful increase of mortality among very young children which annually occurs in this city about midsummer; the number of deaths of infants, notwithstanding so many are taken out of town, often being double as many in a day about the middle of July as in any day of several previous months. The causes act in part directly upon the children, but largely, also indirectly, by inducing nervous irritation with nursing mothers.

A visit to the country offers the surest means of escaping the danger, and, in incipient stages, the best means of cure of the special disorders in which the danger lies. To most mothers, however, this is impracticable, and

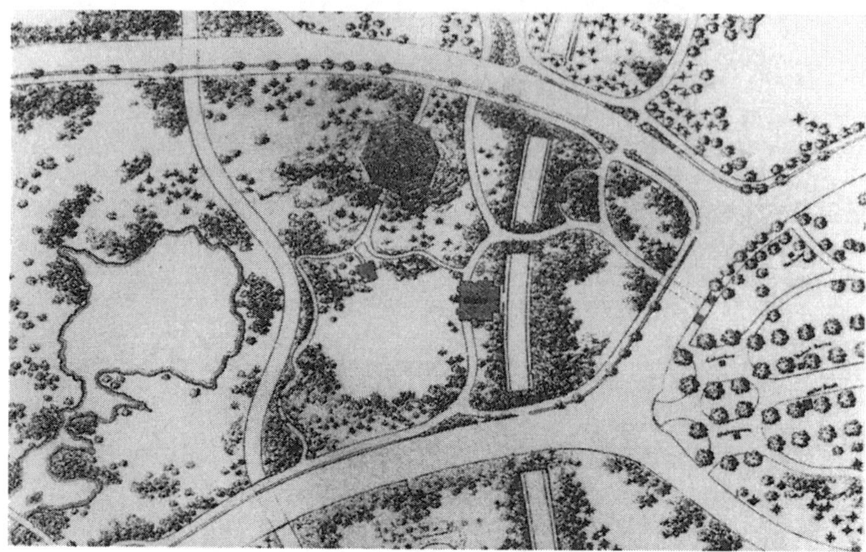

PLAN SHOWING "CHILDREN'S DISTRICT" OF CENTRAL PARK, c. 1873

the best that can be done is to spend an occasional day or part of a day on the Park. It has been for some years a growing practice with physicians to advise this course.

The whole Park is, of course, open as much to mothers with children as to any other class; but on a hot day a mother carrying a sick child, and perhaps leading other children, if she follows the throng, is liable to become more heated and feverish through fatigue, anxiety and various slight embarrassments, than if she remained quietly within a close, dark chamber. If she comes with a party of friends, she will be glad to find some quiet nook in which, while others wander, she can be left with her baby. The class of considerations thus suggested had influenced the treatment of several localities, but had been controlling in a larger way than elsewhere at the point in question.

There were here two masses of rock around both of which the main drive passed as a loop. On the borders and in the clefts of these rocks, the ground being impracticable for cultivation, loose thickets of sassafras, dogwoods, sumachs, bitter-sweet, and their common rock-edge associates, had sprung up, so that just here, in the midst of the general bleakness, barrenness and filth of this quarter of the Park site, there was a pretty bit of natural scenery, having a somewhat wild and secluded character. It was designed to follow up the natural suggestions of this class, and by thickening and extending the original sylvan defences, secure a more decided effect of rural retirement.[11]

The advantages for this purpose supplied one ground for the selection of the spot, the proximity of the play-grounds for larger children, another; and that of one of the sunken roads of the Park another; but the main reason for it was the fact that *it was the precise point in the Park which could be reached with the fewest steps* on an average, by visitors coming from the denser parts of the city by seven different lines of railway, and after the Park should be entered, wholly along walks by which the crossing of any carriage road would be avoided. From the Eighth Avenue and the "Belt" lines, access to it could be had by the Park carriages in five minutes; it was ten minutes' walk from the Sixth and Seventh Avenue and Broadway lines, and was approached by six walks, each fourteen feet wide, laid out from as many entrances to the Park, with no more indirectness than was necessary to avoid with easy curves considerable rocky elevations.

The most noticeable feature of the special local arrangements consisted of a series of seats and tables shaded by trellised vines, so placed as to

THE CHILDREN'S SHELTER IN CENTRAL PARK

cover with verdure the larger part of a broad, flat, uninteresting mass of rock, which otherwise would have been a bleak and sterile blot in the view at a point almost of introduction to the more luxuriant landscape in the design of the lower park. A few arrangements for amusing and taking care of children were placed within easy reach, and also a building which had been designated the Dairy,[12] because it was intended to make sure that with a few other simple refreshments for children, perfectly fresh pure milk should be sold in it at a moderate charge. Its lower story, containing a store-room, ice-room and other offices, not interesting to the public, and accordingly completely concealed from its view, opened upon the sunken road by which its supplies could be received and its waste removed in carts without annoyance to visitors. The upper part, consisting of a sales-room, with a counter for refreshments and the loan or sale of playthings, and a broad gallery, was constructed for coolness and was open to the South breeze which it was found, even when calm elsewhere, would be drawn towards it from the South Pond.[13] A bay of this water, with a bold dark shore opposite, rising to an eminence crowned with firs, was looked down upon, over a narrow glade of turf which, between the rocks and coppices, formed the foreground of a little local landscape promising some day to be quite interesting. Upon the bit of green-sward in front, it had been intended that a cow or two, an ewe with lambs, and a few broods of chickens, should be kept for the amusement of children, and a small stable had been built for them hard by, which also served to mask a dressing-room and water-closet.[14]

It was considered that the same conditions which promised advantages for mothers, especially at midsummer, would be also grateful to convalescents, invalids, and aged persons who should desire to be as much as possible with comfort out of doors, especially in the early spring and late autumn; the Dairy being sheltered on the north, northwest and northeast, by elevations planted with evergreens, and giving upon a warm, dry southern slope, and a walk connecting with it, a quarter of a mile in length, having similar advantages of shelter and geniality.

Although more particularly designed for the benefit of the classes indicated, no attempt to exclude other visitors would have been practicable, nor was any intended. It was simply not desired, by making any of the group of structures unnecessarily prominent, to seem to recommend passersby, who would be likely to enjoy other points of the Park more, to turn off their course and tarry here. A special invitation for people to leave their carriages to obtain meals at the Dairy, was, perhaps, more especially designed *to be avoided*, as the parts of the roadway nearest it were among the most unsuitable on the Park for the stoppage and collection of carriages; and two minutes' drive beyond, a place had been specially prepared where a number might stand together without interrupting the regular movement upon the drive, and visitors in them could be served, if they chose, without alighting.[15] It was thought, however, that people coming to the Park in carriages would fre-

The Dairy in Central Park

Lawn Below the Dairy in Central Park, with the Children's Cottage

quently find it convenient to leave nurses and children for a short time, as they passed near the Dairy, and there were three convenient routes of access to it from the drive — the distance by the most direct, being less than a hundred paces, by none a hundred and twenty. It had been intended that all the local arrangements should be ready for use before midsummer, and when the new administration took charge in May, the Dairy was well advanced.

Although no inquiry was made of us in regard to this structure, and we did not suspect that any other view of it was taken than that which has been above explained, we twice referred, in written communications to the Department, to the fact that it had been designed as an attachment to the "Children's District," (the various other constructed features of which were once fully enumerated and their relations to it indicated), at the same time urging its immediate completion.[16] The result is shown in the following paragraph of the Annual Report, no other reference to any of the whole group of arrangements being found in the volume:

> "The remaining structure in progress was the Dairy House adjacent to the transverse road at Sixty-fifth street, in a very inappropriate location. It is hidden from direct view; is difficult of access; and no direct path leads to it from the main drive; so that the criticism is often popularly made that a Dairy building, intended for general use of persons frequenting the Park, has been placed, as much as possible, out of sight and reach. Of course, it was necessary to complete it according to the original plans, because it had progressed too far for alteration. It has been finished in accordance with the plans of those who conceived it. It may not, however, be uninteresting to know that this inconsiderable building has cost about fifty thousand dollars — nearly all of it expended before this department took office."[17]

In accordance with the theory of design thus indicated, the Dairy has been used as a common eating-house, no stipulations having been made with the tenant[18] other than apply to the general restaurant at Mount St. Vincent;[19] the stable has been turned into a paint-shop; the coppices thinned and trimmed up, and, with the rocks, put partially out of sight, and wholly out of countenance by rows of prim garden-shrubs. By making gaps in the established plantations, straightening two slight curves of the walks, and planting a granite stepping-stone, twenty feet long, on the edge of the drive, it has been opened to view, and the distance to it therefrom shortened six paces.

These changes, as we have said, are comparatively slight. Looking at the building as the authors of the Report had chosen to do, simply as a roadside inn, standing detached from the road, but in their eyes more detached from all else on the Park, if changes were to be made, it is only to be wished that they could have been more efficacious. But slight, or rather feeble, as they are, interpreted by the significant brevity of their explanation, if the building had been leveled, and all the ground around had been plowed and salted, a willing ignorance of the real elements of value in all the work of the neighborhood, and a blind disdain of the study which had been given to the harmonious and equitable adjustment of its several motives could not have been more distinctly manifested.

It will appear probable that those who had taken the responsibility of administering the public trust of this property regarded the building as an item by itself; that they neither knew nor cared for its relations with any other elements of the Park; that they chose, however feebly, to force it into a relation with the drive, for which, by their own declaration, it was not adapted; that the tendency of their policy was to lessen, if not wholly cancel, its value with reference to its characteristic original purposes; and that, when their Report was prepared, they saw no reason to suppose that the public did not, with one voice, consent to and applaud such a method of dealing with their trust.

The construction of the Park has been watched by a large number of intelligent citizens, and more closely than any other public work of the city; it has unquestionably excited more general interest, and been more popular, than any other, and yet it is true that but little weight is commonly given to many important motives of its design, either in commendations which are heard of it, or in propositions for its amendment.

It is not difficult to partly see how, with the necessarily superficial consideration given to it by most intelligent observers, this happens.

The various works which, since 1857, have been in progress on the site of the Park, may be considered under two classes: one comprehending changes in the surface of the ground and the production of landscape effects, the other limited to the formation of various structures in stone, brick, concrete and metal. Value receivable for the first will only be due in important amount after years of careful culture, and, for the present, few city-bred men can be expected to fully understand wherein the value is to consist. Structures in masonry, on the other hand, often reveal their full design the moment the builders' scaffolds are removed, and the quality of those on the Park has been at all times directly comparable with that of much other work with which the citizens of New York are familiar. The roads on the Park, as fast as opened section after section, were found to be superior to any other roads generally known, and being the only public pleasure roads of the city, they have been greatly frequented and obtained much favorable consideration. It has thus been brought about that encomium and criticism of the Park has alike been mainly directed to works of the second class, and most commonly from points of view in which each of them has been seen in a detached form.

The brick, stone, and iron parts of the Park have thus assumed an importance in comparison with its landscape elements somewhat analogous to that of the solid walls of a public building in comparison with its plaster, paint, frescoes, hangings, and furniture. To most persons they yet, including roads and walks, appear the essential elements of the Park. Take them out, and the Park would seem to be without plan. But leaving them in, from the practice of considering the several structures each by itself, the analogy of a public building would commonly be felt to be defective chiefly in that the plan of the Park is presumed to be much less coherent than that of any building.

It thus occurs that propositions respecting the Park have been constantly made, the like of which are never heard in regard to any public building.

The new Court House[20] has been a great deal discussed during the last few years, but, in all that has been written, a demand has probably not been made that certain of its rooms should be fitted up with billiard tables or suitably for religious services or public demonstrations in anatomy; the lack of a convenient carriage way to the roof or to the lunch-counter has not been complained of, nor has it been proposed to remedy the present cramped, inconvenient and unattractive arrangements for refreshments by devoting the more spacious of the court rooms to this purpose.

The fact that such changes of the plan would, in some limited view, be improvements, does not hide the larger fact that the acceptance of but a few propositions of the same character would soon completely ruin the building for the purposes which it has been built expressly to serve, and in reference to which, whatever value it may have is presumed to lie.

But propositions quite as fantastic are not infrequently made with earnestness in regard to the Park. It has, for example, been seriously proposed that it should be used as a place of burial for the more distinguished dead of the city; that all religious sects should be invited to build places of worship upon it, and often that some central feature should be introduced corresponding in obvious importance to the dwelling in private grounds; that this should be a grand people's cathedral in which all sects might unite in a common litany; that it should be an exhibition and advertisement of the goods for sale in the city; that it should be many other things as diverse in character as the worship of God and of Mammon.

It has been urged that the plan of the Park should be so contrived that an illustration would be presented on a large though miniature scale of the geography of the continent; an illustration of the geological structure of the earth; a living cabinet of botany; a living museum of zoology.

Provided the principal constructions in roads, bridges, arches and buildings are not required to be destroyed, no structure which in itself promises to be in any way valuable to the public, would seem to be thought, by many intelligent citizens, out of place anywhere on the site of the Park. Thus the location of great buildings in positions where they would utterly destroy the scale of the growing landscape, where they would, indeed, obliterate the most important park features, is frequently urged.

The right has been often claimed to use any part of the Park for any purpose which is lawful to be pursued in the streets of the city; to go anywhere upon it, either on foot or in any vehicle.

A street railway through the midst of the Park has been called for;

New County Court House, New York, 1871

steamboats, and even a full rigged ship have been proposed to be placed in its waters.

New roads have been called for, crossing and practically destroying, for their original purpose, the most important features of the design. It has been proposed to widen every principal walk not laid directly along side of a drive, and throw it open to carriages.

A demand has more than once been made for a change in important features of the plan, for no other reason than that particular business speculations would be thereby rendered more promising.

The use of various parts of the ground, assumed to be at present unoccupied, has been asked for horse-races, for steeple-chases, for experiments with sundry new machines, for various kinds of advertising, for the sale of various wares, for popular meetings, for itinerant preaching, for distributing controversial tracts.

Room on which to erect tents, and make enclosures within the Park for circuses, concerts, trials of strength and skill, and all manner of popular exhibitions, has been frequently applied for with confidence.

As the city grows larger, projects for the public benefit multiply, land becomes more valuable, and the Park more and more really central, applications for the use of ground upon it for various more or less plausible purposes, are likely to become increasingly frequent and increasingly urgent, and there will thus be a strong tendency to its conversion into a great, perpetual metropolitan Fair Ground, in the plan and administration of which no general purpose need be recognized, other than to offer, for the recreation of those who may visit it, a desultory collocation of miscellaneous entertainments, tangled together by a series of crooked roads and walks, and richly decorated with flowers and trees, fountains and statuary.

The only solid ground of resistance to dangers of this class will be found to rest in the conviction that the Park throughout is a single work of art, and as such, subject to the primary law of every work of art, namely, that it shall be framed upon a single, noble motive, to which the design of all its parts, in some more or less subtle way, shall be confluent and helpful.

To find such a general motive of design for the Central Park, it will be necessary to go back to the beginning and ask, for what worthy purpose could the city be required to take out and keep excluded from the field of ordinary urban improvements, a body of land in what was looked forward to as its very centre, so large as that assigned for the Park? For what such object of great prospective importance would a smaller body of land not have been adequate?

To these questions a sufficient answer can, we believe, be found in the expectation that the whole of the island of New York would, but for such a reservation, before many years be occupied by buildings and paved streets; that millions upon millions of men were to live their lives upon this island, millions more to go out from it, or its immediate densely populated suburbs, only occasionally and at long intervals, and that all its inhabitants would assuredly suffer, in greater or lesser degree, according to their occupations and the degree of their confinement to it, from influences engendered by these conditions.

The narrow reservations previously made offered no relief from them, because they would soon be dominated by surrounding buildings, and because the noise, bustle, confinement and noxious qualities of the air of the streets would extend over them without important mitigation.

Provisions for the improvement of the ground, however, pointed to something more than mere exemption from urban conditions, namely, to the formation of an opposite class of conditions; conditions remedial of the influences of urban conditions.

Two classes of improvements were to be planned for this purpose: one directed to secure pure and wholesome air, to act through the lungs; the other to secure an antithesis of objects of vision to those of the streets and houses which should act remedially, by impressions on the mind and suggestions to the imagination.

The latter only require our present attention, and the first question with reference to them is: What class of objects are best adapted to the purpose?

Experience would lead most men to answer that they are chiefly such as give the characteristic charm to gardens, pleasure grounds, and rural landscapes. But some consideration may be required to determine by what mode of selection from among these, and by what general principle of arrangement, the highest practicable degree of the desired effect is to be attained.

It sometimes occurs that a certain species of trees grow naturally, under conditions favoring such a result, in forms of extraordinary symmetry, their heads each having the outline of a haycock set upon a straight, perpendicular post. Occasionally several such trees may be found in nature growing together. Any number of objects of that character would have but limited value, if any, for the purpose of the Park, because it is a character more nearly compatible in a tree than any other with the convenience of men when living compactly in streets and houses. Trees of that form might be, and, in fact, sometimes are, grown along the streets of the city between rows of houses.

A series of rose bushes, grown in pots, trained to single stems, sustained by stakes, would have even less value. Trim beds of flowers, such as might be set on a drawing-room table, or in the fore-court of a city dwelling, still less.

A cluster of hornbeams and hemlocks, the trunks of some twisting over a crannied rock, the face of the rock brightened by lichens, and half veiled by tresses of vines growing over it from the rear, and its base lost in a tangle of ground pine, mosses and ferns, would be of considerable value, partly because of the greater difficulty of reconciling the presence of such an assemblage of natural objects with the requirements of convenience in the streets, but mainly because the intricate disposition of lights and shadows seen in the back parts of it would create a degree of obscurity not absolutely impenetrable, but sufficient to affect the imagination with a sense of mystery.

A broad stretch of slightly undulating meadow without defined edge, its turf lost in a haze of the shadows of scattered trees under the branches of which the eye would range, would be of even higher value, and if beyond this meadow occurred a depression of the surface, and the heads of other trees were seen again at an uncertain distance, the conditions would be most of all valuable for the purpose in view, first, because there would be positive assurance of a certain considerable extent of space free of all ordinary urban conditions, and, in the soft, smooth, tranquil surface of turf, of immunity from the bustling, violent and wearing influences which act upon the surface of the streets, and secondly, because the imagination, looking into the soft commingling lights and shadows and fading tints of color of the background would have encouragement to extend these purely rural conditions indefinitely.

Considering that large classes of rural objects and many types of natural scenery are not practicable to be introduced on the site of the Park — mountain, ocean, desert and prairie scenery for example — it will be found that the most valuable form that could have been prescribed is that which we have last indicated, and which may be distinguished from all others as pastoral. But the site of the Park having had a very heterogeneous surface, which was largely formed of solid rock, it was not desirable that the attempt should be made to reduce it all to the simplicity of pastoral scenery. What would the central motive of design require of the rest? Clearly that it should be given such a character as, while affording contrast and variety of scene, would, as much as possible, be confluent to the same end, namely, the constant suggestion to the imagination of an unlimited range of rural conditions.

The pleasing uncertainty and delicate, mysterious tone which *chiaro-oscuro*[21] lends to the distance of an open pastoral landscape certainly cannot be paralleled in rugged ground, where the scope of vision is limited; but a similar influence on the mind, less only in degree, is experienced as we pass near the edge of a long stretch of natural woods, the outer trees disposed in irregular clusters, the lower branches sweeping the turf or bending over rocks, and underwood mingling at intervals with their foliage. Under such circumstances, although the eye nowhere penetrates far, an agreeable suggestion is conveyed to the imagination of freedom, and of interest beyond the objects which at any moment meet the eye. While, therefore, elements of scenery of this class (which may, for the present purpose, be distinguished as picturesque sylvan scenery) would both acquire and impart value from their contrast with the simpler elements of open pastoral landscapes, their effect, by tending to withdraw the mind to an indefinite distance from all objects associated with the streets and walls of the city, would be of the same character.

The question of localizing or adjusting these two classes of landscape elements to the various elements of the natural topography of the Park next occurs, the study of which must begin with the consideration that the Park is to be surrounded by an artificial wall, twice as high as the Great Wall of China, composed of urban buildings. Wherever this should appear across a meadow-view, the imagination would be checked abruptly at short range. Natural objects were thus required to be interposed, which, while excluding the buildings as much as possible from view, would leave an uncertainty as to the occupation of the space beyond, and establish a horizon line, composed, as much as possible, of verdure.

No one, looking into a closely-grown wood, can be certain that at a short distance back there are not glades or streams, or that a more open disposition of trees does not prevail.

A range of high woods, then, or of trees so disposed as to produce an effect, when seen from a short distance looking outwardly from the central parts of the Park, of a natural wood-side, must be regarded as more nearly indispensable to the purpose in view — that of relieving the visitor from the city — than any other available feature.

The site of the Park being naturally very broken and largely composed of masses of rock, the extent to which the meadow-like surfaces of pastoral scenery could be introduced in the plan was limited.

It was, then, first of all, required that such parts of the site as were available and necessary to the purpose should be assigned to the occupation of elements which would compose a wood-side, screening incongruous objects without the Park as much as possible from the view of observers within it.

Secondly, of the remaining ground, it was required to assign as much as was available to the occupation of elements which would compose tranquil, open, pastoral scenes.

Thirdly, it was required to assign all of the yet remaining ground to elements which would tend to form passages of scenery contrasting in depth of obscurity and picturesque character of detail with the softness and simplicity of the open landscapes.

There are other elements yet to be considered; but those thus classified and assigned to various quarters of the site alone contribute directly to the general characteristic purpose of the Park, and are, therefore, to be distinguished as its essential elements.

This should be clearly recognized. As neither glass, nor china, nor knives and forks, nor even table and chairs are the essential elements of a dinner, so neither bridges, towers, shelters, seats, refectories, statues, cages for birds and animals, nor even drives and walks are the essential elements of the Park. But as what is well designed to nourish the body and enliven the spirits through the stomach makes a dinner a dinner, so what is well designed to recreate the mind from urban oppressions through the eye, makes the Park the Park. All other elements of it are simply accessories of these essentials.

Accessory elements, by which walking, driving, riding, resting, eating and drinking are facilitated, were also to be required in the design of the Park, in so far as they would be instruments necessary to be used to obtain the benefit of its essential elements.

But if people were to be allowed to straggle at will anywhere upon the ground, and if provision were to be made for their doing so comfortably and with cleanliness, all the ground would need to be specially prepared for the purpose; there would be no turf and no trees upon it, and it would afford no relief from the city. It will thus be seen that these accessory elements of the Park are admissible only where and so far as the advantages they offer in making its essential elements available compensate for any curtailment their introduction may involve in these essential elements. They are desirable to be seen, so far as they aid the essential elements in inviting the observer to rest or move forward in one way or another, as shall most conduce to his recreation. They are undesirable to be seen, so far as they tend to weaken, divide, blot or make patch-work of the essential or natural landscape elements.

The first consideration, then, in a truly critical study of the size, form, and place in the Park of any required construction for the accommodation of visitors was, originally, and always should be, that the degree of display which may be allowed in it should correspond, as nearly as other considerations will permit, with the importance of the need it is designed to meet; this being measured, not only by its average value to each user, but with regard also to the number of those who will have occasion to use it.

The second consideration is, that whatever serves to display an artificial construction required for the convenience of visitors is *undesirable*:

1st.   In the degree in which the border-screen is required to be broken.

2d.   In the degree in which the scope of meadow-surface is required to be broken.

3d.   In the degree in which picturesque passages are required to be disconcerted.

And the location of such constructions as are necessary to convenience should, as far as possible, be regulated by this scale.

But a class of possible accessories requires consideration which are not strictly necessary to make the essential elements of the Park available, yet which may be adapted to indirectly increase the public value of those elements. For example, a great space of ground is not necessary to the performance or the enjoyment of music, but the effect of good music on the Park is to aid the mind in freeing itself from the irritating effect of urban conditions, and by increasing the pleasure of a visit to the Park, it will tend to enlarge the number of visitors to it, and prolong the average period in which the special means of recreation afforded by its essential elements are active. The simple question, then, in regard to the admissibility of musical entertainments on the Park is: will the necessary means of providing such entertainments, as the fixed orchestra, the seats or standing places of the audience, lessen the value of the essential elements of the Park?

Similar considerations will apply to various entertainments which are partially scientific and educational and partially amusing—a cage of monkeys or parrots, for example. But it being understood that to accommodate adequately the numbers of visitors to be expected on the Park, the necessary accessory elements alone must occupy the eye more than is desirable, it may appear that no considerable structures for such purposes can be justifiable.

There are, however, certain localities which may be regarded as exceptional in this respect. They occur from the fact that the Legislature found it convenient to define the legal bounds of this body of the city property by the pre-existing street lines, which do not precisely coincide with the desirable limits of the Park as a work of art, which must nevertheless be all included within them; there are, therefore, along the boundary, several small spaces of ground, buildings within which, if properly designed, will not affect the park landscapes, and which, regarding the Park as a work of art, and with reference to the purpose of affording recreation by scenery from urban conditions, may be considered as extraneous.[22] Questions of height, size and style of building being involved, these exceptional outer districts cannot be here more accurately defined. The extent of such debatable ground is, however, quite limited, and the question of the legitimate occupation and disposition of all parts of the Park site proper need not be complicated in the present discussion by the slight opening thus admitted for exceptions.

We submit that such requirements and restrictions as have been thus developed, commend themselves to common sense as well adapted to secure the desired end of the undertaking of the Central Park.

That the original plans were formed in accordance with them, and that they were respected by the original Commission, has been, as we know, sincerely and intelligently doubted.

We propose, in another letter, to consider the more common grounds of such intelligent doubt before examining the course of alleged improvement which has been more recently adopted.

We are, Mr. President,
Very respectfully yours,

OLMSTED & VAUX,
Landscape Architects.

LETTER II.

Examination of the Design of the Park and
of Recent Changes Therein.

New York, February, 1872.

To the Honorable H. G. Stebbins,
President of the Department of Public Parks:
Sir:

In the present letter we shall hope to establish the conviction that the restrictions and requirements set forth in our last had been faithfully regarded in all classes of work under the original Commission, and shall afterwards indicate the course with respect to them which has since been taken.

255

A complete review of all the work being neither practicable nor necessary, we shall address ourselves to points in regard to which intelligent doubt has appeared, and, with reference to the recent works, to such as are most significant of the spirit and intention of alleged improvements.

The preliminary study of the original plan, it will be remembered, was first presented in competition with thirty-three others. One of its distinctions was, that it presented larger unbroken surfaces of turf and of water than any other; it was designated the "Greensward" plan.[23] In actual construction the extent of open pastoral surface had been made even larger than was suggested in the preliminary study. It will not be denied that, wherever it had been practicable to complete the work up to the boundary before the Commission was superseded, the required screening woods had been planted, while one of the criticisms upon the Park has been that, in much of the remaining ground, a wild negligence and seclusion has been suffered to prevail which was not in good taste.

Assuming, then, that, with more or less skill the prescribed requirements had been regarded in the design, as far at least as the primary blocking out of natural features is concerned, the question remains, and is one upon which a substantial difference of judgment undoubtedly exists, as to how far, in the subsequent introduction of accessories, or convenient furniture for use, the advantages so gained have been unnecessarily sacrificed?

The architectural features of the Park are numerous and costly, more numerous and costly, it is sometimes said, than those of any other modern pleasure-ground. From this fact, with the influences, explained in our first letter, fixing public attention very strongly upon the architectural works during the period of construction, it has happened that an impression has been very generally adopted, even with qualified judges, that the interest of the Park has been designed to be found largely, if not chiefly, in this class of its works.

The existence of such an impression is placed in very strong light by a not uncommon criticism that these works are so situated as nowhere to be seen to advantage; that they are not individually imposing structures, and that they are never so associated as to produce grand combined effects, such as might have been obtained had a series of boldly projected and well-designed objects of no greater costliness been arranged symmetrically in one noble composition, supported by corresponding plantations, as in the works of the old architectural school of gardening.[24]

Perhaps the existence of the same impression is shown, however, even more strongly, when the Park is spoken of in terms of approval, which could not be applied to natural scenery, as "a magnificent garden," for instance. It has naturally followed, also, from the same impression, and as a retort to misapplied compliments, that regret has been often expressed that the Commissioners had not had the good taste to prefer a plan purely in the natural style.[25]

To persons who have not given special study to this subject, the frequent reference thus made to schools is liable to withdraw attention from the only point of any real importance that these comments prove to be in question, by making it appear necessary to understand the whole art of gardening before it can be intelligently answered. That this is not the case, we shall attempt to make clear by considering upon what purity of style, in a work of the class in question, depends. This may be seen by examining the conditions, and consequent human wants, in which each of the two schools referred to originated.

The architectural style of gardening was in vogue long before the period of Christian civilization; its finest examples probably had been formed in regions of grand landscape features, but of arid climate and with a general aspect of stern, wild and savage nature. The primary motive of design under this school, is, accordingly, to produce a splendid urbanity.

The natural school originated in the last century, and was based on the experience that in northern countries of perennial turf and of gentle topography, modern civilized men, however they may admire the magnificence of the ancient pleasure-grounds, find more refreshing and more lasting pleasure in certain not at all extraordinary types of natural landscape. An extreme statement of such an experience is found by Mr. Robinson, in an account by Sidney Smith of a visit to "a very grand place," with which at first he had been enchanted. He says: — "It seemed something so much better than nature that I really began to wish the earth had been laid out according to the latest principles of improvement. . . . In three days' time I was tired to death; a thistle, a nettle, a heap of dead bushes — anything that wore the appearance of accident and want of intention — was quite a relief. I used to escape from the made grounds, and walk upon an adjacent goose-common, where the cart-ruts, gravel-pits, bumps, irregularities, coarse, ungentleman-like grass, and all the varieties produced by neglect, were a thousand times more gratifying than the monotony of beauties the result of design, and crowded into narrow confines."[26]

The landscape or natural school proceeds upon an analysis of such experiences to design the means of similar gratification, as far as may be practicable in any given situation, artificially, and to reconcile the means of doing so with the cleanliness, convenience and comfort of those for whom the ground is prepared.

The two schools do not stand in opposition to each other, any more than the shoe-maker and the hatter. The question, if there must be a question of schools, is not, which do you like best? which is most to your taste? or which is the latest fashion? but which, in this or that particular case, promises to provide most toward the fullness of life? and this is wholly a question of special circumstances and conditions.

But as there is no doubt that an attempt to combine motives of such opposite character is sure to produce a feeble result, it is a perfectly reasonable demand that, in a work like that of the Central Park, it shall not be uncertain which has been adopted. Whether the number of architectural and avowedly artificial constructions on the Central Park established such an uncertainty, depends on the special motive of each of these constructions, as will be evident from the following considerations:

In all much frequented pleasure-grounds, constructions of various kinds are necessary to the convenience and comfort of those to be benefited; their number and extent being proportioned to the manner in which they are to be used, and to the number of expected users. If well adapted to their purpose, strongly and truly built, the artificial character of many of these must be more or less displayed. It is not, then, by the absence nor by the concealment of construction that the natural school is tested.

On the other hand, the principal elements of scenery in architectural gardens, even of such extreme types as that of Versailles,[27] is found in verdure. It is not, then, by the absence nor the concealment of productions of nature that the architectural school is known. What remains as the essential distinction between the two would seem to be, simply, that in architectural gardening, natural features are employed adjunctively to designs, the essential pleasure-giving elements of which are artificial, while in natural gardening artificial elements are employed adjunctively to designs, the essential pleasure-giving character of which is natural.

It being admitted that the main purpose of the Central Park, as defined in our previous letter, exacts the predominance of natural elements; if this simple requirement in respect to its necessary artificial constructions is kept in view, no further consideration of what, under other circumstances, has been the practice of one school or the other, need enter into a critical review of its design. Neither need the special science of the gardener be brought in question. As Mr. Palgrave, in the preface to his Essays on Art, says of judgment upon what are more commonly and conventionally spoken of as works of art: it "is a matter which simply resembles other branches of human knowledge: a certain natural faculty or bias must always be presupposed; with this, as in case of mathematics or of language, taste is obtained by study and observation; and, as in those sciences, leads to a practical power of decision. Some few strictly technical qualities remain, on which the artist alone is a judge. But this exception does not invalidate the criticism of spectators, * * * * * the technical qualities are only means to a public end, and the question which remains always is, how far do they tend to the object of all the fine arts — high and enduring pleasure."[28]

To a fair understanding of the architectural elements of the design of the Central Park, it is first of all necessary that some effort should be made to realize what extent of accommodation will be required in this particular ground when it shall be in the centre of a city of perhaps two millions of people, surrounded by water and by densely populated suburbs for some distance beyond the water.

Obviously, not only in extent, but in solidity of construction, the means of accommodation which must at times be actually occupied in various ways by visitors will need to be somewhat different from those commonly associated with natural rural scenery. Somewhat different, also, from those required in most foreign public pleasure-grounds — the people of London, Paris, Vienna and Berlin, for example, having each nearly as many thousands of acres to scatter over in pursuit of their recreation as those of New York have hundreds.

By far the most extensive and important of the constructed accommodations of the Central Park are those for convenience of locomotion. How to obtain simply the required amount of room for this purpose, without making this class of its constructions everywhere disagreeably conspicuous, harshly disruptive of all relations of composition between natural landscape elements on their opposite borders, and without the absolute destruction of many valuable topographical features, was the most difficult problem of the design. If anyone has doubts of this, it will only be necessary to drive through the Park, pausing at frequent intervals to consider what would be the difference of effect were the groups of foliage, even in their present partial development, thrown back twenty feet on each side, and were the rocks blasted out or the slopes of the surface broken, which will be seen within that distance.

In dealing with this problem, the following considerations had weight. In any roadway much frequented by pleasure-vehicles, and little used otherwise, half a dozen heavily laden carts often cause more divergence from direct movement, and thus more impede such use of it as is chiefly desired, than as many hundred carriages driven at nearly equal moderate speed. A woman attempting to lead a child across the road when it is all crowded with rapidly moving vehicles, will often cause three or four horses to be pulled up to avoid her, and this will oblige others in the rear of them to be turned out of their course; or, if they are near the curb, also to be pulled up to avoid a collision. Consequently, under these conditions, the distance between the curbs will be frequently found, no matter how great it is, inconveniently narrow for those who wish to drive at a steady trot, and a given number of pleasure-carriages will move with greater regularity and be better accommodated in a wheel-way forty feet wide, from which ordinary slow traffic and people on foot are excluded, than in one eighty feet wide to which these sources of obstruction and disturbance are admitted. Again, in crowded thoroughfares, continuous straight-forward movement on the walks is chiefly impeded by people — especially women, children and infirm — who stand fearful and hesitating at the crossings, and whom, under these circumstances, others sometimes find it difficult not to press upon.

These and other observations of similar import, both in our streets and in European parks, led to the planning of a system of independent ways: 1st, for carriages: 2d, for horsemen wishing to gallop; 3d, for footmen; and 4th, for common street traffic requiring to cross the Park. By this means it was made possible, even for the most timid and nervous, to go on foot to any district of the Park designed to be visited, without crossing a line of wheels on the same level, and consequently, without occasion for anxiety or hesitation.[29]

Incidentally, the system provided, in its arched ways, substantial shelters scattered through the Park, which would be rarely seen above the general plane of the landscape, and which would be made as inconspicuous as possible, but to be readily found when required in sudden showers.

Without taking the present occasion to argue the point, we may simply refer to another incidental advantage of the system which, so far as we have observed, has not been publicly recognized, but which, we are confident, may be justly claimed to exist, in the fact that to the visitor, carried by occasional defiles from one field of landscape to another, in which a wholly different series of details is presented, the extent of the Park is practically much greater than it would otherwise be.

The system was elaborated with great care in detail to accomplish the necessary introduction of its numerous arches and variations of surface, in such a manner as that the ravines and ridges should not appear to have been constructed to order; natural depressions of surface were generally made available for approaches to the subways,[30] but sometimes the construction of picturesque defiles through rock, and even tunneling was resorted to in order to avoid disturbance of important landscape features. In most cases rocky banks were worked up boldly against the masonry of the arches, so that as little as possible of it should be exposed; these banks were planted in such a manner as to obscure it still more. The arches were often so made that a thicket of bushes could be substituted for an obviously artificial parapet. The necessary railing of others was used as a trellis, so that it disappeared under a drapery of twining foliage.

In the majority of cases where, two years ago, the design had not yet been at all realized, we believe that visitors, in passing over the arches, often did so without being aware of it, and in passing under them did so with an experience of gratification. In the single instance where a choice is offered between crossing the drive by the same number of steps upon the surface, or by an arched way,[31] the latter is generally chosen by habitués of the Park.

More than nine-tenths of the so-called architectural objects of the Park have been built as necessary elements of this special system, which had been designed to supply the maximum of accommodation with the minimum of disturbance of its natural scenery, and especially of the more important features of its natural scenery. (In looking across the two principal meadows, in no direction is an archway to be seen. There is one on the edge of a third and smaller meadow, but it is so retired and shaded as in summer to be undiscernible.)[32]

GREYWACKE ARCH IN CENTRAL PARK WITH NEW PLANTINGS DESIGNED
TO OBSCURE IT FROM VIEW, C. 1863

It may here be mentioned that there had been, under the old Commission, but two permanent buildings erected upon or in the edge of the
open grounds, and both of these were flanked by groves of trees; one, was a
cottage containing dressing-rooms for ball-players; the other, a small, tent-
like structure, the mineral spring pavilion.[33] As yet, the appearance of even
such small structures, seen often against the sky and in sunlight, is glaring
compared with what it will be when the planted trees shall curtain round and
overhang them.

Taking all the architectural features of the Park together, we believe
that when the natural elements of the design have been fairly developed,
those which had been established under the original Commission will be
found to very moderately affect its landscape character, and that rarely will
more than one of them be distinguishable from any particular point of view.

It is not to be assumed that in such cases it will always be seen undesirably. It is, to say the least, doubtful if the most effective anti-climax to

the lofty buildings and paved levels of the city is to be found in a scene absolutely devoid of evident human handiwork. No authority on landscape design has contended for this. Mr. Ruskin has shown the value of a bridge or chálet introduced in a representation of even the grandest scenes of nature.[34] Uvedale Price, who, in his zeal for the picturesque, argues that even rudeness resulting from storms, decay and the depredations of beasts should be reproduced by the gardener, cuts trees away to bring a mill, a village spire, or a cottage into his park compositions.[35] Shenstone says, "a rural scene is never complete without the addition of some kind of building."[36]

To determine whether any structure on the Park is undesirable, it should be considered, first, what part of the necessary accommodation of the public on the Park is met by it, how this much of accommodation could be otherwise or elsewhere provided, and in what degree and whence the structure will be conspicuous after it shall have been toned by weather, and the plantations about and beyond it shall have taken a mature character.

Under the peculiar plan adopted in laying out the roads and walks of the Central Park, no one, we believe, who will candidly study it, can doubt that there is a much smaller parting and displacement of the essential natural elements of the Park and a much smaller display of artificial elements than there would needs be, had it been undertaken to provide an equal amount of public accommodation without the architectural constructions of the archways.

Even, however, if a doubt can be maintained on this point, it can be no more than a doubt. Fifteen years ago, the grounds of doubt were very clearly before the administration of the Park, and they were cautiously and deliberately weighed; every argument against the expedient which has since been raised being fully presented and considered before it was adopted. Having been adopted, there is no part of the drive, no part of the ride, and but little of the walk system which is not studiously adjusted to the arches, and planned, in respect to course, breadth, curves and grades, with a constant purpose to avoid leading people on foot to wish to occupy ground on which others have a right to drive horses. That a certain advantage was promised by the arrangement, there has never been a doubt; that a certain advantage is experienced from it, there can be no present doubt. To justify setting aside this advantage, be it considered large or small, after all that has been expended to secure it, there should be clear evidence that some greater advantage is to be gained which cannot be secured without its sacrifice.

The serious and intelligent questionings of the plan of the Park to which we have thus replied, are nowhere recognized in the Annual Report of the Department, but in its undertakings of improvement a disposition to give up the advantages of the archway system has, as we shall show, been quite unnecessarily manifested, while the appliances originally used to avoid undue prominence in its necessary architectural elements have been neglected and in some cases dismantled. In the structures originating with the late administration, indeed, the reverse purpose is evinced; each, no matter how humble its purpose, being made as conspicuous, both by location and design of elevation, as its purpose will allow, and no consideration being paid to the manner in which the natural features will be affected by it, either in scale, color or composition.

The Annual Report, however, contains a series of strictures upon some points of the Commission's policy, of minor consequence, but for a fair understanding of which some explanation seems desirable. It should be remembered that a good deal of forecast had been necessary in regard to the housekeeping work of a place in which the wants of some hundred thousand people would require purveyance, often for several days in succession, and, in which, especially the wear, tear, and litter of that number of visitors would need to be cared for by means and methods which would not be unseemly, would not obstruct their movements and would not interfere with their pleasure. To this end a considerable amount of handy fixtures of the class of dust-bins, tool, store, and other closet-rooms would need to be provided. As an illustration, turf must be kept close or it will run out; the cheapest and best way of keeping it close on the pastoral surface of the Park is to graze it with sheep, and for the sheep thus required, shelter is sometimes necessary. Until the Commission was superseded, old buildings, temporarily left upon the Park for the purpose, and slight temporary structures had been used for these offices. One of permanent character only had been begun, the general barn and stable, which had been so designed and placed that, although its roof, as now completed, is much larger than any other built upon the Park, not one visitor of a thousand has probably ever seen it. It is, at the same time, centrally located, and has direct communication with the streets, clear of the Park drives and walks.[37] The same will be true of the range of workshops which has been begun under the late administration, in a situation and upon a plan previously prepared. Other buildings of this class had been designed to be similarly dealt with. We shall show later that a different policy has been initiated since, in respect to them.

In the original design of the Park, there had been no provision for zoological buildings or yards. Gifts of living animals having been afterwards made to the city, temporary quarters were provided for them in one of the old buildings, formerly occupied as a State Arsenal, and which was used likewise for various administrative purposes.[38] Temporary enclosures were also made for pasturage in two places on the borders of the Park. As the collection gradually increased, mainly from gifts to the city, it became evident that better provision for it would be necessary.

By taking advantage of the circumstances referred to at the close of the preceding letter, and carefully adjusting the required buildings, yards, paddocks, roads and walks to the plan of the Park, a considerable collection of the hardier birds, beasts and reptiles might be provided for without serious encroachment upon its important features; but if a general exposition of the zoology of the world were to be undertaken, including moderately liberal provision for giraffes, elephants, camels and other large tropical graminivorous animals, which, besides airy shelters and strongly enclosed open grounds for a satisfactory exhibition of their characteristic movements and habits in summer, with ample approaches and accommodations for crowds of lookers-on, need also roomy and artificially warmed winter apartments, it was seen that, with all possible skill in the arrangement of these appliances, the Park must be grievously injured with respect to its essential purposes. It was also seen that it would be a measure of economy to bring all required buildings for tropical animals near together for convenience of heating.

The suggestion was, therefore, made and adopted that a piece of un-improved land belonging to the city, lying near the Park, should be placed in the hands of the Commission — such parts of it as were needed, to be occupied by the tropical section of a popular zoological exhibition.[39]

The impression is very emphatically conveyed in the Annual Report, that the ground given to the Commission in accordance with this suggestion, is wet, cold, and impossible to be drained, and that this consideration, which makes it utterly unsuitable for the purpose, had wholly escaped our attention. As the late administration itself proposed to erect buildings for men and women upon the same site, it is hardly necessary to refer to this argument further than to state that surveys had been made and two distinct plans of drainage, with estimates, prepared, either of which was perfectly feasible. There was no formidable difficulty in making it dryer, more sheltered and warmer than any ground upon the Park.[40]

Besides living animals, the Park had been made a receptacle for a variety of gifts to the city: some of them illustrations of art, others of history, others of science.

The policy of your Commission had been to cautiously foster the formation of collections mainly by the voluntary associated action of citizens, in which, through its negotiations, the public should be secured certain rights, rather than establish museums to be solely managed by the civic authorities.[41]

A question had arisen as to whether any suitable buildings or building sites could be offered for this purpose; and this leading to the inquiry where on the Park *a large range of buildings could be placed at the least disadvantage to its essential elements*, a plat of ground east of the old reservoir had been indicated.[42] The reason for this selection was that a large range of buildings at this point would be seen from no other point of the Park, the locality being bounded on two sides by the reservoir walls, on a third by a rocky ridge, and on the fourth by exterior buildings, while the whole of the territory thus enclosed was too small for the formation of spacious pastoral grounds, and was less well adapted and less required than any other equal space for contrasting picturesque effects.

Public interest had been rapidly increasing, and public agitations rapidly growing and tending to comprehensive and liberal combination in respect to these associated and incidental purposes of the Commission's work; and although the time was not thought to have arrived for a definite and final study of plans, it was seen that some extensive public or semi-public buildings, in connection with the Park and on city property, would soon be called for, in the basements and courts of which it was not unlikely that some of the necessary accessories of the Park would be incidentally provided. Under these circumstances, the policy of the Commission being a waiting one, temporary accommodations continued to be patched up and used for many purposes, more and longer than was consistent with its own convenience or perfect efficiency of management for the time being.

The old arsenal, for example, was found a useful make-shift during the period of construction, but was regarded as a conspicuously ugly and ill-placed building. A part of the permanent buildings to which its contents would be transferred, had already begun; projects for others were forming. Pending the question of its evacuation and demolition, expense had been as much as possible avoided in fitting it for its temporary duties, and, so far as its exterior was concerned, outlay had been chiefly directed to subduing its color, making it less conspicuous by reducing its height, and training over it the vines which the late administration has torn down and uprooted. The same temporizing policy led to the maintenance of various humble arrangements which are dealt with in the Annual Report, as if they were permanent, prominent and characteristic elements of the Park.[43]

Most of the structures really permanent in character, which were built by your Commission, are unquestionably well built, and, like all firm and well-built permanent works, they were honestly costly. A doubt is admitted whether, in respect to arrangements of temporary convenience, a somewhat more liberal policy would not have been more economical. On the other hand, while there can be no question of the great improvements made in this respect under the late administration, there may be a question whether their costliness is fully justified. But this is a matter of minor consequence, and we now turn to the main question of the alleged improvements of the permanent elements of the Park.

During fourteen years the whole work of the Central Park centered, as has been shown, upon three branches of a single purpose: first, the putting out of view of exterior buildings by a suitable disposition of tall growing trees; second, the formation of a series of broad, simple meadow surfaces, with, when practicable, such a disposition of umbrageous trees, without underwood, as would render their limits defined; third, the development of a series of landscape passages *strongly contrasting* with those of the pastoral and high wood districts in complexity of grouping, and the frequent density, obscurity, and wild intricacy of low growing foliage, especially on broken and rock-strewn surfaces. The permanent accessory elements of roads, walks, arches, and other structures had been located and designed in strict sequence and subordination to these purposes; as little as possible to conflict with them, as much as possible to support them.

The question now before us is, how have these purposes been served during the last year and a half; how far has the value which had been gained previously been increased, and in what degree, with reference to these purposes, has the design of the Park been improved by the changes made?

First: as to the screening woods?

The Department has done nothing to advance, and but little practically to thwart this branch of the design, but it has published the declaration (page 20 of the Annual Report) that it is an illegal undertaking; that an unobstructed view across the Park from any house that may be built around it is one of the rights of the owners of the adjoining land that cannot be interfered with for the public benefit.[44] In that case, unquestionably, much of the work which has been done upon the Park, under the late administration itself, as well as previously, has been worse than wasted, for much earth and rock has been heaped up, as well as trees planted, which must have this illegal effect, and it would seem to be necessary for compliance with the requirement, to reduce its surface everywhere to the level of the adjoining streets.

Second; as to open landscapes?

The Department has begun the erection of a large series of buildings, which is intended to be followed by the construction of a series of small yards, of walks between them, and of lines of trees following these walks, upon the largest meadow of the park.[45] The first of the houses may be seen, exteriorly nearly complete, about 400 yards south of Mount St. Vincent.[46] The meadow is intended to entirely disappear, and in defending its course (pages 23 and 280, Annual Report) the late administration has not considered the landscape value of this opening worth mentioning.[47] The argument of the defence is based, as we have shown, upon a fallacy.

In the site of the lower Park there were originally two spaces besides those excavated for water, where, by the reduction and covering with soil of a few comparatively small ledges of rock, it was possible to obtain some expanse of landscape.[48] One was at a lower elevation than the other, and they were separated by a rocky ridge and rapid slope. Along this slope it was thought necessary, for reasons of exterior convenience, that one of the roads for common business purposes crossing the park should be carried.[49] This was graded eight feet below the natural surface, and a ledge to the north of it having been blasted out for the purpose, an opening about 200 feet in width was thus secured, by which the range of the eye from both sides was greatly extended, looking from the south, considerably more than half a mile. Walks leading from the main walks were laid out near the edge of the sunken road, from which however the masonry of its walls was concealed. A row of English elms "breaking joints," with a row of silver maples, pruned as street trees, to long naked trunks, has been planted by the late administration, following the lines of these walks. The effect, if they should be allowed to grow as intended, will be to completely close this opening, previously secured at so much expense.

Third: as to the more picturesque elements?

It must be admitted that the plantations of the Park, and particularly the more picturesque plantations, at the period of the change of administration, did stand, as claimed in the Annual Report, in need of extensive revision.[50] The construction of the Park had proceeded by districts, one after another being taken up in succession. From the time in which drainage and grading work began, until the roads and walks of any district were finished, was generally a period of from two to three years. It was necessary to finish roads and walks before the ground adjoining them could be surfaced and planted. As soon, however, as roads and walks were finished, the public eagerly thronged upon them. The desire was strong with the Commission that when this occurred the impression produced by the appearance of the adjoining ground should not be so disagreeable as it was likely to be if left in the extremely rough and cumbered condition which the border of a road under construction must have. It often happened that the first opportunity of clearing them occurred very late in the planting season; in the spring, so late that only coniferous trees could be planted safely.

The Commission had declined to adopt the policy urged upon it at an early day to establish a large and varied nursery of its own.[51] It began with the trial of some not very successful experiments to obtain its trees, like brick, stone and cement, by contracts to the lowest bidder. It had been found impossible, through ordinary channels to obtain many desired trees and plants, and especially to obtain anything like the number of many that was required. Of some that were then costly, there was a certain doubt, since wholly removed, that they would endure the climate of the Park, at least until its surface should become less bleak.

These and many other considerations (some of which are indicated in the printed document of the Commission, No. 4, of 1859, pages 5 and 6),[52] led to a habit of occasionally giving a temporary finish to the ground, and often to the planting of unsuitable trees, especially strong conifers, which would serve to give it a fresh, green appearance, and at once cover its nakedness, with the intention of subsequently removing them to the outer parts of the Park.

Owing to successive changes of policy of other departments of the city, the finishing of the outer parts of the Park was delayed, and for this and other reasons the necessary measures for securing an adequate supply of many desired plants had not yet been taken when the Commission was removed.[53] It sometimes happened, therefore, that only the central or interior members of the principal masses and groups of planting had yet been planted, while cheap lots of the commonest nursery stock had been dropped in along the borders of the drives and walks in front of them.

With similar motives, indigenous trees and shrubs had been suffered to remain untouched in some localities, where, when full grown, they would destroy important landscape compositions, and these had already partly overgrown and obscured some points of interest.

The intended revision, by the removal of temporary material and the introduction of finer detail, the cutting away of low growth in some cases, the establishment of low growth in others, had, it cannot be denied, been in many parts postponed longer than was desirable.

A vigorous remedy for this neglect has, during the last year been in progress. The result is frequently, that in parts of the Park in which the intricacy of low growth and picturesque obscurity had been required in the design, the natural underwood has been grubbed up, the original admirably rugged surface made as smooth and meadow-like as ledge-rock would allow, and the trees, to a height of from ten to fifteen feet, trimmed to bare poles.[54]

The object of these operations is stated in the Annual Report to have been that of securing "a circulation of air," "opening beautiful views of lawn and scenery," and clearing the Park of "cat-briars and tangled weeds."[55] The undergrowth removed was, in fact, largely of indigenous azaleas, clethra, cephalanthus, and the commonly associated interesting wood shrubs, with plenty of asters, gentians, golden rod and the like. No shrubbery or low growth seems to have been valued unless it could be seen within a clean-edged dug border.

The extent to which this kind of improvement has been carried, is partly indicated by the fact that the quail, both Eastern and California, with which the Park was well stocked, and which were breeding in it freely before the destruction of the covers, have now almost wholly disappeared.

The bolder rocky parts of the Park had been in some cases, especially in the more recent work, left with a smooth surface of turf or of clean, bare ground between and about the base of the rocks, and with smooth, turf-covered flanking slopes, conditions scarcely ever seen in nature, incongruous and uninteresting. The intention had been to give a temporary finish to these parts that would save a destructive wash of the surface; and afterwards, at a convenient time, to add peat and wood earth, and bring to them a large number of low plants from the mountains, ferns, mosses, and creepers. Nothing like this has been done, but the late administration has, in some of these cases, undertaken an improvement by the introduction of a variety of beds in arabesque patterns, planted with flower-garden annuals.[56]

On the borders of the open ground, where the indigenous trees required thinning, an additional number have in some cases been planted, and

THE SHEEPFOLD, CENTRAL PARK

in others an improvement has been attempted by lopping off lower limbs in the manner before described, so as to lessen their umbrageousness and produce the character of street trees.

A large number of structures have been projected, some planned, and the plans of others, half built, recast, but to show how little respect has been paid to the requirements originally recognized in this class of the accessories of the Park, it will be sufficient to refer to two buildings for the humblest purposes, which have been projected, planned and completely constructed since the removal of the original Commission.

No one can visit the Park without having his attention called to a structure placed on a slight elevation, where, in the original design, the principal meadow view from the north part of the Mall was designed to become dim under large trees, which were also to hide the buildings on the Eighth avenue, which lies sixty paces beyond. It consists of a central building, two stories in height, with low wings, extending diagonally on each side toward the Green, and terminating in two handsome pavilions of greater elevation. It has throughout a high pitched, slate roof, decorated with turrets and gilded iron work; the walls are of pressed brick, with trimmings of cut blue stone and polished granite, and its general aspect suggests a large English parochial school. Its cost has been $70,000. It is officially designated a "sheepfold," and its ostensible purpose is to provide a shelter, at night and in severe winter

269

weather for the sheep used to keep down the grass on the adjoining Green. The pavilions at its ends, however, are designed for the use of visitors, and it has been intended that portraits of sheep and specimens of wools should be hung upon their walls. It is expected, as stated in the Annual Report, to be "a great attraction to all classes." It can, nevertheless, only be reached by foot-men, after crossing the Bridle Road on the surface at a point where, owing to its grades and curves, a rider would not see persons crossing before him until too close upon them to pull up a galloping horse. So little was this objection to the site and arrangement valued, that when the attention of the Department was called to it officially, it obtained no attention. A flower-garden was designed to be formed in front of the sheep-shed, between which and the door to its public rooms the Bridle Road passed.[57]

A "cottage" may be seen a little to the north of this edifice. It is situated between two branches of the Bridle Road, which must be crossed on the surface by everyone visiting it.

Situations for both these buildings, free from this objection, in which they would have been more convenient for their purposes, and much less obtrusive, might have been found within a stone's throw of their present positions.

On the drive east of the old reservoir, one of the archways of the walk system has been lengthened: in rebuilding its end, the original arrangement, by which a screen of shrubbery was carried across the arch, entirely concealing the artificial work, has been changed, a broad platform of blue stone, with a substantial iron railing, substituted, and the face of cut stone work over the arch has been doubled in depth.[58]

The Central Park, on account of the narrowness of its site and the way in which it is broken by the reservoirs and numerous rocky ledges, and because of the constructions indispensable to the convenient and harmonious use of it, in diverse methods and under various circumstances, of the vast body of people of all classes, which will need to be accommodated when the centre of population, now four miles away, shall be in the midst of it, could not be given a landscape character of as much simplicity, tranquility and unsophisticated naturalness as, for its primary purpose, was desirable. If the work done upon it during the first fourteen years was designed, without undignified tricks of disguise, or mere affectations of rusticity, to get as far as practicable the better of these difficulties, and secure as much as possible of this desirable character as we have given reasons for claiming, all that has been done and projected since has been directed by the reverse motive and necessarily to the waste of what had before been gained.

In judging what should now be done with the Park, there are a variety of minor considerations which seem to require more attention than, in public discussions, they always receive.

The Central Park is not by any means to be the only place of resort in the city for pleasure-driving and walking. To say nothing of the smaller grounds now in use, at least twenty miles of shaded "boulevards" are already laid out upon the island, besides four notable pleasure grounds, which remain to be prepared.[59] From two of these grounds, and from a number of points in the boulevard system, views much more grand than any on the Central Park will be permanently commanded, and each of the pleasure grounds will be likely in some respects to excel the Central Park in beauty.[60]

The boulevards, five miles of one of which, 150 feet wide, is nearly complete in its constructive features, will offer much better opportunities for a display of equipage and for general public promenade than can be presented in the Central Park.[61]

No part of any of the lands now owned by the city on the island is suitable to be formed into a parade ground, which the present Governor has declared to be a necessity of the city, the demand and agitation for which has already been heated and is sure to occur again and with increasing force.[62]

Four broad avenues of communication, running parallel with the principal drives of the Park, are now under construction, and will in a few years be open to public use. These will withdraw an important element of the travel that now passes through the Park.[63]

As population increases and lodges nearer the Park, those who will resort to it for a short stroll on foot or for lounging and resting — who will require walks, seats and shelter — will increase in number much more rapidly than those who come to it in carriages and on horseback. It may in time even be superseded as the fashionable promenade, but, unless greatly mutilated and mismanaged, in no other grounds can there be offered any comparable degree of simple rural effects or of advantages, in that respect, of relief from the city. This special quality of value, then, in the Central Park, should be carefully guarded against a disposition to extend the wheel-ways, or crowd the limited open spaces with artificial objects of interest which would soon have greater value elsewhere.

The value of the Park to the city will be greatly affected by the degree in which good nature and a liking for good order and decorum prevail among those who resort to it. Nothing is so unfavorable to an increase of its value in this respect as temporary, make-shift, incomplete or imperfectly finished arrangements by which the convenience and comfort of visitors is affected and their esthetic impressions are confused. The best means of education in good order is good order.

The walks, especially the concrete walks and gutters, borders of the walks, wooden foot bridges and wood work generally, are now in bad order, and partly from neglect of timely repair, much of their original material will require to be replaced, The present condition of the various works of all classes, executed from eight to fifteen years ago, demonstrates the superior economy of the more substantial and, in the first cost, more expensive structures, and also of a judiciously liberal policy in maintenance.

The existing arrangements for supplying refreshments in the Park are temporary and incomplete: the buildings in which they are served are none of them adapted to be used precisely as they are at present.

The Central Park was designed in all its parts to be closed at nightfall, and to be environed by a walk thirty feet wide and six miles long, to be brilliantly lighted for a night promenade. The time must soon come when, if the Park proper is left open at night, it will be impossible by any practicable force of police to prevent the occurrence of frequent crimes and gross outrages upon it. The advantages for clandestine purposes offered in its numerous coverts of rock and foliage, will tend not only to bring the Park itself into disrepute, but to form a bad neighborhood about it. The attempt, recently projected, to light it with gas, while the cost in original outlay and continuous expense would be very great, could not possibly make it a safe or decent place of resort at night.[64] The difficulty of closing and clearing it will increase the longer it is left open after dark. It can hardly be closed, however, at least to carriages, until the adjoining avenues are made ready for use.

The due return for what has already been expended in the Park undertaking, remains not only in abeyance, but, as recent experience has shown, in special peril, so long as the completion of its deferred works is delayed.

Of these there are three classes: First, those dependent on works outside the Park proper. Until, for example, the grading of Eighth avenue is complete, a body of trees within the Park, of the first importance in its landscape design, must remain unplanted, although they will need thirty years' growth to fully realize their purpose, and the trees with which they are to combine, and with which great inequality is undesirable, have already been planted ten years.

Second, those which are yet but vaguely projected, and the location and extent of which, so far as they are to come on the Park at all, is undetermined, as the proposed museums of science, of art, and of living animals.

Third, the refinement and filling out with delicate detail of the present but roughly sketched-in landscape design, especially by suitable horticultural treatment. This, which would not be very costly work, may and should be at once diligently prosecuted.

The increased value of life in this city which has been thought to be promised in the Park, and the expectations of trade, population and wealth to be held and attracted to it, returns more to the city treasury, through its effect on the value of real estate, than the cost of acquiring the Park, as it now stands, has taken from it.

It is quite possible that a large additional outlay may be made on the

Park with the eventual result of abating and disappointing the expectations which have been formed of it.

On the other hand, not only may the highest estimates hitherto entertained of its value be realized, but by well directed outlay, they may, profitably, be very much enlarged.

We are, Mr. President,
Very respectfully yours,

OLMSTED & VAUX,
Landscape Architects.

The text presented here is taken from "Appendix B," in New York (City), Department of Public Parks, *Second Annual Report* (New York, 1872), pages 67–113.

1. Henry George Stebbins (1811–1881), New York City financier. Stebbins was appointed to the Board of Commissioners of Central Park in 1859 and elected president of that board later in the same year. He served on the commission without interruption until May 1870 when the Tweed Ring board took over. Stebbins was reappointed to the park board in November 1871 and remained until 1877 except for a five-month leave of absence in 1872 (*BDAC*; *Papers of FLO*, 6: 66–67; *New-York Times*, Dec. 11, 1881, p. 2; New York [City], *The City Record. Official Journal*, Feb. 5, 1878, p. 1).
2. On April 5, 1870, the New York state legislature passed an act calling for a new charter for the city of New York (which became known as the Tweed Charter). Among the changes included in the new charter was the creation of a Department of Public Parks to supercede the old Central Park Board of Commissioners and its jurisdiction. The new department was headed by five commissioners under the presidency of Peter B. Sweeny, and its jurisdiction was "all public parks and public places above Canal Street." Only one member of the old Central Park board remained a commissioner in the new department: Andrew H. Green (Isaac Newton Phelps Stokes, *Iconography of Manhattan Island, 1498–1909*, 6 vols. [New York, 1915–28], 5: 1938; DPP, *Minutes*, May 3, 1870, p. 3).
3. The financial statements in Appendix A of the Department of Public Park's *Second Annual Report* show that $2,174,000 was spent for the maintenance, construction, and permanent improvements of Central Park between April 20, 1870, and November 22, 1871 (DPP, *Second Annual Report* [1872], pp. 60–61).
4. A reference to the *First Annual Report of the Board of Commissioners of the Department of Public Parks for the Year ending May 1, 1871*.
5. On May 19, 1870, the new park board passed a resolution recognizing "Messrs. Olmsted & Vaux as Chief Landscape Architects, as such, advisers to the Board, and continue their employment under the resolution of the late Board, adopted in January, 1865" (DPP, *Minutes*, May 19, 1870, p. 36).
6. On May 30, 1870, Olmsted and Vaux presented the board with a document specifying the works in progress on Central Park. At the request of the board, they prepared a second report on June 6, 1870, delineating the probable cost of completing those projects. While the board ordered both documents printed, there is no indication that it took the slightest interest in what Olmsted and Vaux had to say (DPP, *Minutes*, May 31, 1870, p. 60; ibid., June 7, 1870, p. 90; "Document No. 10," in ibid., May 30, 1870, pp. 3–4; "Document No. 13," in ibid., June 6, 1870, pp. 3–6).

273

7. The "newly conceived projects" that most upset Olmsted were the plans to construct a sheepfold on the western side of the park just north of the 65th Street transverse road and a zoological garden on the Northern Meadows (DPP, *First Annual Report* [1871], pp. 20, 22–23; see nn. 40 and 57, below).

8. Among those parts of Olmsted and Vaux's design that were the least understood by the new park commissioners seemed to be the placement and function of the Dairy, the location and design of the Belvedere, and many of the plantings. In its *First Annual Report*, the park board considered the Dairy to be in a poor location making it inaccessible to park visitors.

    Olmsted and Vaux considered the Belvedere, located just north of the 79th Street transverse road at the southwest corner of the old reservoir, to occupy "a critical position in reference to the general design." They also noted that

> every available opportunity should be taken advantage of to give facilities for the gathering and shelter of a number of visitors in an informal picturesque way at this attractive point; the present plan was therefore prepared, adopted, and the foundation work executed. As it would be out of character to prepare for any rich architectural work at this point, which is the antithesis to the *Terrace*, and as it was a site of too great prominence to justify apparent cheapness of design, the work, though rough in actual surface, has been executed with special care and accuracy, so as to attract some attention as a piece of stone-work.

The park board, however, viewed the Belvedere as too costly and resolved "to eliminate from the plan every item of extravagance that could be avoided" including one of the towers.

    Finally, the board completely failed to comprehend much of the planting in the Central Park design. Olmsted and Vaux had intended that parts of the park, particularly the lower park, be planted with lush and varied plantings to provide a picturesque effect in sharp contrast to the pastoral character of the upper park. The park board ordered the clearing out of many of the plantations in order to open up extended views (DPP, *First Annual Report*, [1871], pp. 16–17, 18, 26; "Document No. 13," in DPP, *Minutes*, June 6, 1870, p. 5; for the Dairy, see nn. 12 and 18 below; for plantings in Central Park, see nn. 54 and 55 below).

9. The following is the appended letter to Olmsted and Vaux's report:

No 110 Broadway,
New York, November 25th, 1870.

To the Honorable PETER B. SWEENY,
President, Department of Public Parks:
SIR: —

    We first learn by the public prints to-day that the Department has had under discussion, and has resolved upon a proposition to transform the open ground of the north division of the Central Park into a Zoological Garden.

    When we accepted the office of Chief Landscape Architects Advisory to your Department, the terms of the resolution secured to us an opportunity to report on the effect on the general design of the Park of all propositions involving the introduction of new structures upon it.

    As the location now proposed for the Zoological Garden buildings would seem to involve a neutralization of features which have hitherto been deemed important elements of the executed design of the Park, we should be glad of an opportunity to carefully examine the scheme and to submit a report thereon before the termination of our present relations with the Department.

    Respectfully,

OLMSTED, VAUX & CO.,
Landscape Architects.

274

10. On November 22, 1870, Commissioner Henry Hilton offered the following resolution: "That the existing arrangement for the services of Messrs. Olmsted & Vaux shall terminate on the first of December next, and that it be referred to the Executive Committee to make such new and other engagement with them as may seem desirable." No new arrangements were forthcoming, however (DPP, *Minutes*, Nov. 22, 1870, p. 274).

11. A reference to the lawn area between the South Pond and the Dairy.

12. Olmsted and Vaux intended the Dairy to be an important part of the Children's District in the southern end of the park. The Dairy, designed by Calvert Vaux, was nearly completed when the Sweeny board took control of the park. In their report to the board on June 6, 1870, Olmsted and Vaux noted it would only need $3,000 for completion ("Document No. 13," in DPP, *Minutes*, June 6, 1870, pp. 3–4; see n. 18 below).

13. The South Pond was just below the Dairy in the southeast corner of the park.

14. A reference to the Children's Cottage just south of the Dairy.

15. A reference to the carriage concourse and Casino, or Refreshment House, a short distance north of the Dairy and just east of the Mall.

16. A reference to the two reports that Olmsted and Vaux sent to the board in May and June of 1870 (see n. 6 above).

17. This is a quotation from the Department of Public Park's *First Annual Report*, page 18.

18. In his report to the park board, the superintendent, B. F. Crane, noted that after construction of the Dairy was completed it was prepared as a restaurant. The tenant may well have been Stetson and Radford who at that time had all of the restaurant concessions on the park (ibid., p. 309; Thomas Addison Richards, *Guide to the Central Park* [New York, 1870], p. 83).

19. Mount St. Vincent, located on the eastern side of the park at 105th Street, was the site of a convent used by the Vincentian Sisters. Before the Civil War it was used by Olmsted as an office and residence. During the war it was the site of a military hospital, from which the last patient was discharged in August 1865. In 1866 the park board proceeded to refurbish the buildings of Mount St. Vincent for a restaurant (Sister Marie de Lourdes Walsh, *The Sisters of Charity of New York, 1809–1959*, 3 vols. [New York, 1960], 1: 155, 3: 174; *Papers of FLO*, 3: 323; BCCP, *Ninth Annual Report* [1866], p. 38; *The Hotel Guests' Guide for the City of New York, 1871–72* [New York, 1871], p. 85).

20. A reference to the New York County Courthouse designed by John Kellum. Construction of this "Tweed Ring" courthouse, located to the north of City Hall, began in 1861 and was completed in 1874. When finished the courthouse had cost the city over thirteen million dollars and had "nothing to boast of but size." The extravagance and corruption associated with the courthouse helped lead to the downfall of the Tweed Ring (*Papers of FLO*, 6: 308, n. 4; *Hotel Guests' Guide for the City of New York*, p. 138; I. N. P. Stokes, *Iconography*, 5: 1951).

21. That is, the effect of light and shade in nature (*OED*).

22. That is, the park was laid out as a rectangle two-and-one-half miles long by one-half mile wide. Its boundaries were defined by the existing Fifth and Eighth avenues on the east and west and 59th and 106th (later extended to 110th) streets on the south and north.

23. In the fall of 1857 the Central Park commission announced a public competition for a design for the park. Calvert Vaux invited Olmsted to join him in preparing a plan, and their winning collaborative effort was known as the Greensward plan ("Description of a Plan for the Improvement of the Central Park: 'Greensward,'" [1858] [*Papers of FLO*, 3: 119–87]).

24. This architectural or formal style of gardening had been in use in public and private gardens for centuries. It combined straight walkways with geometrical flower beds and designs. These gardens usually contained statues, vases, urns, and other forms of sculpture (Edward Kemp, *Landscape Gardening: How to Lay out a Garden*, rev. by F. A. Waugh, 4th ed. [New York, 1912], pp. 107–8, 111).

25. The natural style of landscape gardening was characterized by irregular shapes and serpentine lines with extensive use of native rather than exotic plants (ibid., pp. 123–24).

26. William Robinson (1838–1935), English landscape gardener and Sydney Smith (1771–1845), English clergyman and essayist. The quotation that Olmsted includes here is an epigraph at the beginning of Robinson's *The Wild Garden*, published in 1870 (*DNB*).

27. The gardens at Versailles have often been viewed as the quintessential example of the architectural school of design. Commissioned by Louis XIV in 1661, André Le Nôtre's plan included terraces, an amphitheater, a mile-long canal, statuary, and other elaborate ornamental groves and small gardens laid out in geometric patterns (Geoffrey Jellicoe et al., eds., *The Oxford Companion to Gardens* [Oxford, 1991], pp. 584–86).

28. Francis Turner Palgrave (1824–1897), English poet and critic. Palgrave's book *Essays on Art*, from which this quotation is taken, was published in 1866 (*DNB*; Francis Turner Palgrave, *Essays on Art* [London, 1866], p. vi).

29. That is, Olmsted and Vaux proposed a "separation of ways" of the interior walkways, bridle paths, carriage drives, and transverse roads on Central Park, reducing the possibility of injury and heightening the enjoyment of those using the park (*Papers of FLO*, 3: 25–26; see also, FLO to the Board of Commissioners of the Central Park, May 31 and Sept. 9, 1858 [ibid., 3: 193–96, 202–4]).

30. That is, an underground tunnel by which pedestrians may pass from one point to another below a roadway (*OED*).

31. Presumably a reference to the area where the carriage drive crosses the northern end of the Mall. Visitors have the choice of passing under the drive by a wide staircase that descends to the Bethesda Terrace, or of crossing the drive at grade and then reaching the Terrace by two exterior stone staircases.

32. The two principle meadows were the Northern Meadows and the Green (now the Sheep Meadow). The third, smaller, meadow was the Playground: the arch to which Olmsted refers is Dalehead Arch, on its western edge.

33. The ballplayers' cottage was located between the Playground and the Green (or Sheep Meadow) just south of the 65th Street transverse road. The Mineral Spring Pavilion was located on the northern edge of the Green.

34. John Ruskin (1819–1900), English art critic and social reformer (*DNB*).

35. Sir Uvedale Price (1747–1829), English author of *An Essay on the Picturesque* (1810) (*DNB*).

36. William Shenstone (1714–1763), English poet and essayist. This quotation is from Shenstone's "Unconnected Thoughts on Gardening," in *Essays on Men and Manners*. The exact quotation reads, "a rural scene to me is never perfect without the addition of some kind of building . . ." (*DNB*; William Shenstone, *Essays on Men and Manners* [London, 1868], p. 150).

37. This stable was located in the center of the park between the old Croton reservoir and the 85th Street transverse road.

38. The New York State Arsenal, located just inside the lower park at Fifth Avenue and 64th Street, was completed in 1851. The Central Park commissioners acquired it in 1858. Apparently the zoo animals were kept in cages in the basement and first floor of the arsenal, sharing their space with clerks on the first floor and the Central Park

police in the basement (*Papers of FLO*, 3: 184; DPP, *First Annual Report* [1871], pp. 13–14).

39. As early as 1865, the Central Park board discussed the idea of placing a zoological garden on Manhattan Square, located on the western side of the park between 77th and 81st streets. In 1867 Olmsted and Vaux presented the park board with a plan for doing so, but it was never implemented and in 1871 Manhattan Square became the site for the American Museum of Natural History (BCCP, *Ninth Annual Report* [1866], pp. 13–14; Olmsted & Vaux to the President of the Board of Commissioners of the Central Park, [1867] [*Papers of FLO*, 6: 184–89]).

40. In the report to which Olmsted here refers, the park commissioners stated that

> How this square could ever be used for the purpose of a zoological garden, is not easy to understand. The first necessity for such a garden is ample drainage for the refuse of animals, and a spot incapable of being properly drained, must necessarily be an improper place for a zoological garden.

The two plans for providing for the drainage of Manhattan Square may have been in 1865 and in 1867. In 1865 the Central Park board reported that the Croton Aqueduct Department was preparing a plan to drain the square by way of a sewer through 75th Street to the North River. Apparently that plan was never implemented, and after Olmsted and Vaux presented their report proposing the creation of a zoo at Manhattan Square in 1867, construction of a sewer was commenced that would have carried drainage away from the square to the Hudson River, but it had not been completed before the Central Park board was superseded by the Department of Public Parks (DPP, *First Annual Report* [1871], pp. 22–24, 273–79; BCCP, *Ninth Annual Report* [1866], pp. 13–14; *Papers of FLO*, 6: 189; see n. 39 above).

41. In 1859 the New York state legislature enacted a law allowing individual bequests or donations to be made to New York City for the "improvement and ornamentation" of Central Park as well as the establishment of museums within the park. The park commissioners, however, believed that it was inappropriate to expend park funds for the erection of such structures (New York [State], *Laws of the State of New York, Passed at the Eighty-Second Session of the Legislature* . . . [Albany, N.Y., 1859], chap. 349; BCCP, *Third Annual Report* [1860], p. 11).

42. A reference to the section of the park between 80th and 84th streets that became the site of the Metropolitan Museum of Art in 1872 (I. N. P. Stokes, *Iconography*, 5: 1950).

43. In the *First Annual Report*, the commissioners noted that they had approved the construction of several buildings surrounding the Arsenal to house the zoo animals. In addition, they approved extensive renovations to the Arsenal itself. All the floors in the building had been remodeled: the basement was refitted for a parkkeeper's station; the first floor was refitted with offices at either end and a gallery for statues and flowers in the center; the second and third floors were remodelled with glass exhibition cases for the American Museum of Natural History; and the fourth floor was redesigned for the Meteorological Department. In his report to the board, Superintendent B. F. Crane noted that "Outside, what was an old building of discolored brickwork, with vines and iron fastenings here and there, now is a fine structure, tastefully painted, surrounded by a series of neat structures for birds and animals, forming a group both useful and ornamental" (DPP, *First Annual Report* [1871], pp. 21–22, 309–10).

44. A reference to the park board's abandonment of a plan to construct the Paleontology Museum in the southwest corner of the park at 63rd Street. The board cited the costliness of the museum as well as the fact that if the building was erected it would "interfere with the right of a property owner upon the avenue to enjoy the full and free view

of the Park. The right to an unobstructed view from his residence opposite the Park is one of the benefits and advantages for which the avenue owner has been assessed" (ibid., pp. 18–20).

45. A reference to the building of a zoological garden on the Northern Meadows of the park.

46. Probably a reference to the "Deer House" situated on the East Meadow in the upper part of the park. The Deer House was the first structure designed by the architect-in-chief of the park, Jacob Wrey Mould, under the aegis of the Sweeny board for the newly intended zoological garden. At the time Mould submitted his report in April 1871, the Deer House was still in the planning stage; however, by the time the Sweeny board was removed, the building was probably well under construction (ibid., pp. 388, 417).

47. In both instances to which Olmsted is here referring, the park board and the engineer-in-chief, M. A. Kellogg, ignored the purpose of the meadow and stressed the fact that the ground was ideal for the zoo because it was easily drained (ibid., pp. 23, 279–80; see nn. 39 and 40 above).

48. That is, the Playground and the Green (Sheep Meadow).

49. That is, the 65th Street transverse road.

50. Presumably, a reference to landscape gardener Frank Pollard's report to the park commissioners included in the *First Annual Report*, in which he stated that many of the trees that had been planted early in the park's construction had become too crowded and needed to be thinned. He noted that "the trees were crowding and interfering with each other to such an extent that many would soon be killed or reduced to mere masts" (DPP, *First Annual Report* [1871], pp. 295–96).

51. It is unclear when the park board determined to establish a nursery on the park grounds; however, by 1865 one had been created just east of Mount St. Vincent (BCCP, *Eighth Annual Report* [1865], p. 62; T. A. Richards, *Guide to the Central Park*, p. 86).

52. In the pages cited here, Olmsted had expressed his annoyance at constantly having to hire laborers for park work who were patronage appointments with few skills. For this reason he was unable to hire more qualified individuals to perform the necessary work on the park (*Papers of FLO*, 3: 236–38; *Forty Years*, 2: 307–8).

53. The Board of Commissioners of the Central Park was at the mercy of the Department of Public Works, the Department of Streets, and the Croton Aqueduct Department for the completion of sewers, streets, and drainage outside of the park proper. All of the work was contracted out and much of it took years to finish. In 1865 the board complained that "the unfinished condition of the avenues and streets surrounding the Park, not under the jurisdiction of the Board, has, to a considerable extent, embarrassed the progress of the work" (BCCP, *Ninth Annual Report* [1866], pp. 13, 14, 38–39).

54. Having received instructions from the park commissioners to "reform the present planting," Frank Pollard noted that "the work of clearing out was actively conducted." He stated that a "large portion of this land has already been grubbed up, cleared of stone and rubbish, and thrown into grass." In addition, the lower branches of American elms growing along both sides of the Mall as well as along the Fifth Avenue sidewalk had been removed to eliminate any obstruction of view (DPP, *First Annual Report* [1871], pp. 296–97; see n. 55 below).

55. A quotation from the Department of Public Park's *First Annual Report*. In December 1870 the park board requested that the landscape gardener

> reform the present planting of the Park upon the principle that distance, expanse, and extent of vision should be constantly aimed at; that in all cases where the soil will permit an undergrowth of grass the trees should be thinned out for their better

development; and that shrubbery which obstructs the view and impedes the circulation of the air, and is not necessary to conceal imperfections, should be especially avoided.

(DPP, *First Annual Report* [1871], pp. 26, 296; idem, *Minutes*, Dec. 6, 1870, p. 314.)

56. Probably a reference to the Sweeny board's planting of ornamental flowerbeds north of the Esplanade and "beds of bulbs . . . extensively laid out in various conspicuous portions of the Park" (DPP, *First Annual Report* [1871], pp. 298, 300).

57. The quotation is from the park commission's *First Annual Report*, page 20. After its completion the park board touted the sheepfold as "a beautiful structure, and generally admired." After the dismissal of the Sweeny board in 1872, however, superintendent of the park Columbus Ryan noted that the sheepfold, "an extensive and costly structure, was designed and erected without proper regard to light and ventilation — two indispensable requisites — the absence of which totally unfits it, in my judgement, for its ostensible purpose. It is also extremely damp." (DPP, *Minutes*, Oct. 24, 1871, p. 278; DPP, *Second Annual Report* [1872], p. 118.)

58. Perhaps a reference to the archway one block north of the 79th Street transverse road (arch no. 23). The Sweeny board proposed and arranged for the widening of the East and West drives from thirty-three feet to forty-five feet between 79th and 104th streets. This archway would have been lengthened to accommodate the widening of the East Drive at that point (DPP, *First Annual Report* [1871], p. 202).

59. The smaller grounds already in use in New York City included the Battery, City Hall Park, Madison Square, Tompkins Square, Washington Square, and Mount Morris Square.

The approximately twenty miles of boulevards may well have been: Sixth Avenue from the north end of Central Park to the Harlem River (2 miles); Seventh Avenue from the north end of Central Park to the Harlem River (2 miles); a public drive north of 155th Street (6 miles); the Avenue St. Nicholas from Central Park to 155th Street (2 miles); Manhattan Street from the Avenue St. Nicholas to the Hudson River (1 mile); and the "Boulevard" (or Broadway) from 34th Street to 155th Street (6 miles).

At least three of the four pleasure grounds remaining to be prepared may have been Union Square for which Olmsted and Vaux prepared a plan in 1872 and Morningside and Riverside parks for which Olmsted prepared reports and plans in 1873 (BCCP, *Minutes*, May 3, 1870, p. 8; New York [State], *Laws of the State of New York, Passed at the Eighty-Eighth Session of the Legislature* . . . [Albany, N.Y., 1865], chaps. 564 and 565; idem, *Laws of the State of New York, Passed at the Eighty-Seventh Session of the Legislature* . . . [Albany, N.Y., 1864], chap. 275; idem, *Laws of the State of New York, Passed at the Eighty-Ninth Session of the Legislature* . . . [Albany, N.Y., 1866], chap. 367; idem, *Laws of the State of New York, Passed at the Ninety-Second Session of the Legislature* . . . [Albany, N.Y., 1869], chap. 890; Olmsted & Vaux to Henry G. Stebbins, March 13, 1872 [*Papers of FLO*, 6: 531–37]; "Report of the Landscape Architect on Riverside Park and Avenue," March 29, 1873 [ibid., 6: 596–600]; FLO and CV to Salem H. Wales, Oct. 11, 1873 [ibid., 6: 651–60]).

60. Possibly, a reference to Morningside and Riverside parks. Parts of Morningside Park contained steep hillsides providing views of the Harlem River. Similarly, Riverside Park included steep high ground with fine views of the Hudson River (see n. 59 above).

61. A reference to the "Boulevard," as Broadway above 59th Street was called.

62. This controversy over a parade ground began in the fall of 1869 when Governor John T. Hoffman (1828–1888) wrote to the park board asking if it would be possible to make room for a parade ground in Central Park. The military had been using Tompkins Square since 1866, but the facilities there proved inadequate and the space too

small. Andrew H. Green wrote a lengthy but polite letter to the governor stressing the impracticality of his request. Yet, in his annual message to the state legislature on January 5, 1870, Governor Hoffman declared that the First Division of the National Guard needed a proper parade ground and that Central Park would be a suitable site. The following year, however, the state legislature provided that a public square be laid out north of 59th Street for a parade ground, and in 1872, Olmsted recommended an eighty-one-acre site located near Inwood Depot and landing and adjacent to Fort George on the Hudson River in the northernmost part of Manhattan Island. Apparently, nothing came of Olmsted's proposal, and the military continued to use Tompkins Square. In 1875 Olmsted prepared a plan to improve the square and make it adequate for the use by the military as well as the public (BCCP, *Thirteenth Annual Report* [1869], pp. 153–71; *New-York Times*, Jan. 5, 1870, p. 1; "Document No. 40," in DPP, *Minutes*, Oct. 16, 1872, pp. 1–4; *Papers of FLO*, 6: 632).

63. Probably a reference to Fifth, Eighth, and Eleventh avenues and the "Boulevard" above 59th Street.

64. In July of 1872 Olmsted formally addressed the issue of lighting the park and leaving it open at night. He argued that the installation of gas lights within the park would be harmful to the trees in the park, and the safety of those using the park might not be guaranteed. Nevertheless, in 1873 the park was opened until nine o'clock at night in the winter and eleven o'clock in the summer (*Forty Years*, 2: 416–17).

Department of Public Parks.

---

*General Order for the Organization and Routine of Duty
of the Keepers' Service of the Central Park.*[1]

[March 31, 1873]

Branches of the Service.

The organization for attendance on visitors in the Central Park will consist of three branches, with the superintending officers.

First. — *Patrol-keepers*, whose duties will require much activity of movement, and who, besides attending directly on visitors, will act as sub-officers for the other two branches of the service.

Second. — *Post-keepers*, who will be chiefly stationed at gates and other posts.

Third. — *Extra-keepers*, who will be uniformed workingmen, for the most part charged with keeping in order each a certain division of the walks with the connected structures, and who will incidentally to this duty assist in preventing the misuse of the Park under their view. The number of extra keepers to be placed on duty will vary according to circumstances.

There will be a special body of watchmen for the care of the Park after visitors leave at night.

Patrol-Keepers.

Organization of Patrol-keepers. — The Patrol-keepers will be organized in three sections; one for morning duty, which will take the care of the Park from the night watchmen; one for evening duty, which will take the care of the Park from the morning section, and one for reserve duty, which will ordinarily be used to strengthen the evening section.

Each man will be specially assigned for each period of duty, some to a designated beat ("beat duty"); others to a designated route ("round duty").

BEAT DUTY.

"All-day Beats." — There will be four regular all-day beats, as follows:

First. — The Harlem beat will be the drive from the Farmer's Gate to Mt. St. Vincent, with all the ground to the eastward and so much to the westward as is under observation from the drive.

Second. — The Hill beat will be the drive from the Warrior's Gate to the Glen Span, with all of the ground on both sides of it west of the Harlem beat.

Third. — The Ramble beat will be the whole of the Ramble.

Fourth. — The Terrace beat will be all of the ground from the East to the West Drive, between the Lake, on the north, and the walks north of the Green and south of the Music-stand, on the south.[2]

Keepers assigned to the Harlem and Hill beats will make a close inspection of the gates upon them once every hour.

Other beats and posts of duty will be established at the discretion of the commanding officers.

Evening beats. — There will be a series of beats to be covered (by the reserve section) after 7 P.M., which will be designated on a map.

ROUND DUTY.

Routes. — Routes for round duty will be respectively designated the West and East routes according as the keeper is required to pass northwards on the east or west side of the Park. Each will be more particularly defined hereafter.[3] In each, the circuit drive is to be followed, with certain regular diversions (directed below) and such others, as it may appear to the keeper will enable him better to accomplish the purposes in view. Each route may be easily passed in two hours and a half, but not less than two hours and forty minutes is to be used. If regular time is made, ten minutes can ordinarily be occupied in rest at the stations. Between the beginning of one round and the beginning of the next there will thus be a period of two hours and fifty minutes.

Routine Inspections. — In the course of each round inspections will be made of two classes: close and passing inspections.

Each patrol-keeper on round duty will make a close inspection of one-half of the gates he passes, and a passing inspection of the other half. In the close inspection he will observe, in approaching the gate, if the post-keeper is attentive to his duties; he will see that the walk and border is clean within fifty feet of the gate each way, and, if not, direct it to be made so. He will see that the post-keeper is tidy in his appearance and wears his uniform properly, and require the correction of any faults. He will examine the post-keeper's book and judge if he has been keeping correct accounts. He will write his number and the time of his inspection in the book. In the passing

CENTRAL PARK KEEPER AT GATE

inspection the patrol-keeper will come near enough to distinctly see the post-keeper. If he appears to require no instruction or assistance, the patrol-keeper may then pass on without approaching nearer.

Passing inspections will be made of all post and extra keepers on or near the route, as will be more particularly directed later.

The East Route. — Keepers assigned to the east route will proceed as follows: from the station southward along the walk to 64th Street gate (passing inspection), along walk to Scholars' Gate (close inspection); thence by drive to the Children's Gate[4] (passing inspection); thence by drive and walk through Trefoil Arch and the Glade to the Miner's Gate (close inspection); thence by walk through Greywacke Arch and the drive to the Engineer's Gate (passing inspection); thence to the Woodman's Gate (close inspection); thence to the Girl's Gate (passing inspection); thence to Mt. St. Vincent Station, (report to Sergeant); thence to the Boy's Gate (close inspection); thence to All Saints' Gate (passing inspection); thence to the Mariner's Gate (close inspection); thence to the Woman's Gate, (passing inspection); thence to the Merchant's Gate (close inspection); thence along walk to Artisan's Gate (close inspection); thence under the Dipway Arch to Spur Rock and return; thence by walk to the Artist's Gate (passing inspection); thence by drive to the south end of the Mall; thence by drive and Museum walk to 64th Street Gate (close inspection); and thence to the Station.

The West Route. — The keeper assigned to the west route will make close inspections where passing inspections are above ordered, and will reverse the order of proceeding, with the following variations: After close inspection of the Artist's Gate, return to Drive, by the Copcot Shelter, thence follow the Drive westward, making passing inspection of the Artisan's Gate from the Dipway Arch, thence take the shortest way of the Drive to the Woman's Gate, after close inspection of which, pass by the west branch of the Drive to the Lake shore, and so north. Also, in returning on the east side, from the Engineer's Gate to the Miner's Gate, and thence to the Children's Gate, follow the Drive.

ASSIGNMENTS FOR ROUND DUTY.

There will be six regular series of rounds for the patrol keepers, the first series beginning at 5:30 A.M., the last series at 7:40 P.M.

The morning section will supply keepers for three series of rounds, the first beginning at 5:30 A.M. The evening section will supply keepers for the three series of rounds beginning at 2 P.M. The reserve section will be used to increase the number of keepers on round duty from 2 P.M. to 7 P.M., or for other duty, as occasion may require.

The keepers assigned to round duty will proceed in succession, one following another at an interval, the length of which will vary with the number of men available for duty, an adjustment for this purpose being made by the station sergeant as the different squads report for duty, according to the number of men reporting, as will be hereafter directed.

DAILY ROUTINE OF MOVEMENTS.

Morning: All-day beats. — Four keepers are to be sent from the station at 5.30 A.M. to occupy the all-day beats. In going north they are to proceed by different routes; one by the West Drive and one by the East to Mt. St. Vincent; one by the Dene Walk and the Mall to the Terrace beat, and the fourth by the Dairy, the Middle Drive, the Lake Concourse and Bow Bridge to the Ramble beat. Those assigned to the upper beats will report to the sergeant at the sub-station before going on them. (At 1.55 P.M. eight keepers are to report for duty at the station, and to be sent out to relieve the first on the all-day beats. These will hold them until the hour for closing the park.)

Morning: Round duty. — At 5.25 A.M. one-half the keepers assigned to morning round duty are to report at the station. At 5.30 A.M. one is to be sent out, the rest following in a regular sequence, alternately on the east and west routes. The length of the intervals will depend on the number of keepers ready for duty, as many intervals of equal length being made between 5.30 A.M. and 6.55 A.M. (85 minutes) as there are keepers — thus, if there are five keepers, the intervals will be seventeen minutes; if four keepers, twenty-one minutes; if three keepers, twenty-eight minutes.

At 6.50 A.M. the second half of the keepers of the morning section are to report for duty at the station; at 6.55 the first is to be sent out, and the others in succession at regular intervals, dividing the time till 8.20 A.M. (85 minutes) by the number of keepers ready for duty.

At 8.10 A.M. the first keeper sent out will be due on his return; at 8.20 he is to be sent out on his second round; the time from 8.20 to 11.10 A.M. (170 minutes) is to be divided by the full number of keepers on round duty, and those returning from the first round are to be sent out on the second as nearly as practicable at the successive intervals thus indicated. The first round of the second series is to be completed at 11 A.M., and the third to begin at 11.10.

If, on account of making an arrest, or other necessity, any keeper on round duty is prevented from keeping his place in the sequence, his place is to be taken with as little delay as practicable by the next following.

In all cases of disarrangement of the sequence, the officer in charge of the station will shorten rests and hasten movements, so as to secure the nearest approach to the regular order in the disposition of the whole body of keepers on round duty as is practicable.

The keeper making the first round will, in regular order, complete his third round at 1:50 P.M., and unless there is an extraordinary necessity for further service, will then be dismissed for the day; others of the section on morning duty will be dismissed as they return, in regular succession.

Evening: All-day Beats. — Three men will be taken from the evening section and three from the reserve section for the all-day beats, the Ramble and Terrace beats each being divided for evening duty into two. These will report for duty at 1:55 P.M., and between 2 and 2:05 P.M., will be sent out; care being taken that no two proceed in company after leaving the station.

Evening: Round duty. — At 1:55 P.M., one-half the remainder of the evening and reserve sections will report for duty. The keepers for round duty of the evening section will be sent out at intervals determined by the same method as before directed to be used for the morning section, the first at 2 P.M., the west and east routes being taken alternately, as before. If the reserve section is not required for special duty (as will be the case on concert days, etc.), it will be sent out in the same way on round duty — a keeper of the reserve section leaving the station one minute after each keeper of the evening section, but taking the east route when the keeper of the evening section takes the west, and *vice versa*. Thus, one-half the keepers of each section will be sent on each route.

At 3:20 P.M. the remainder of the evening and (ordinarily) of the reserve sections will report for duty, and the process will continue as above, the first keeper for round duty of the evening section going out at 3:25 P.M. The second series of evening rounds will begin at 4:50; the third (for the evening section only) at 7:40 P.M.; the keeper assigned to the first evening round will end his last round at 10:20 P.M., and be dismissed, and the others as they come in, in regular succession.

ASSIGNMENTS FOR EVENING BEATS.

At 7 P.M. the keepers of the reserve section on round duty, wherever they may be, will discontinue that duty and proceed each man to the evening beat previously assigned him, where, until the hour for closing the Park, he will patrol the walks, from which, at 7 P.M., the extra keepers are to be withdrawn.

GENERAL SUPERVISORY DUTIES.

Extra keepers, not in charge of houses, will each have a district of walks to cover. Outside the all-day beats, some part of each extra keeper's district, and generally the larger part, will be open to view from the route of the patrol-keepers on round duty, and it will be the duty of the patrol-keepers, whether on round or beat duty, to watch for occasions to instruct or assist each extra and post-keeper whom he passes. The patrol keeper on round-duty, will try to make a passing inspection on every round of each extra keeper on the Park who is not within the all-day beats; but is not required to accomplish this purpose when it will involve a break of sequence. Short diversions from the drive, at the discretion of the patrol-keeper, for better observation of the walks, the meadows and the water, are allowed and desirable. Shelters and urinals on the beats are to be inspected by the beat-keepers every half-hour, and each of those within fifty paces of the routes is to be inspected by each patrol-keeper on round-duty at least as often as every second time he passes it.

Patrol-keepers are directed, for the most part, to follow the drive, because by doing so, and judiciously crossing from side to side, according to circumstances, they may observe, and may bring themselves to the notice of, a larger number of walking visitors than in any other way, as well as because they will thus best superintend the post and extra keepers. Care must be taken not to let attention be drawn too much from their more important duties in these respects by the carriages on the drive. All necessary directions and cautions to drivers may, generally, be given by gestures and without stopping. So long as visitors are in carriages they are little liable to misuse the Park to its serious injury. They are, therefore, of secondary interest in park-keeping.

Shifting Sections.

A shift of sections will be made monthly, the morning section becoming the evening section, the evening section the reserve, and so on.

Shortening Field Force.

In stormy or extremely inclement weather, when there are no visitors for recreation on the Park, the Captain, and, in his absence, the Lieutenant, may put two beats in one, divide periods of beat duty, and lengthen the intervals of sequence in round duty at his discretion; all held at the station may then be placed under drill or instruction, and the usual time of dismissal for the day anticipated.

Leave of Absence.

Leave of absence, except for less time than one period of duty, is to be granted only to keepers on the reserve section, but exchanges may be made between keepers of the morning and evening sections and the reserve, as a preliminary to leave of absence.

Temporary Vacancies.

When absences occur in the morning and evening sections without leave, as may happen from illness, the vacancies will be made good as soon as practicable by transfers from the reserve.

Vacancies occurring in the evening section will in all cases be immediately filled. Vacancies in the morning section may be temporarily made good by transfers from the post-keepers; vacancies in the post-keepers being filled by draft on the extra keepers.

Post Keepers.

The post-keepers will be organized in three sections; one to cover the gates during the first half of the day; another to cover the gates during the second half of the day, and the third to cover such other posts, at and during such periods of time as may be designated from day to day by the officer in command, it being intended that the keepers composing it shall be generally posted during the afternoon at points within the Park where visitors are most apt to crowd, and to need assistance, advice and caution.

Revised and Additional Rules for the Conduct of Patrol and Post Keepers.

The rules and customs of the keepers' force heretofore established, not inconsistent with the present orders, will continue to apply to patrol and post keepers. The following are in part old rules, which have fallen to some extent into neglect, or which are now given a more defined form than they have hitherto had. They are hereafter to be exactly followed and rigidly enforced.

Note. — Keepers in uniform, waiting orders at the stations and elsewhere, and not called for, will be on "waiting duty." After being dispatched from the stations, whether in proceeding to posts, on posts, on beats, on rounds, or carrying orders or messages, they will be on "active duty."

I.

Wearing the uniform will signify that a keeper is on duty, and subject to the rules and discipline of duty in all respects.

II.

No outer clothing is to be worn on duty except the prescribed uniform.

III.

No part of the uniform is to be worn out of the stations without all parts.

IV.

No keeper is to wear the uniform or any part of it out of the stations, unless he is prepared in all respects for active duty.

V.

No keeper is to wear any other clothing which is likely to be mistaken for a part of the uniform, even though his own property, and when off duty.

VI.

Post keepers, on whose posts watch-boxes are placed, may enter the boxes and remain standing in them, in a position suitable for observation, in stormy or very inclement weather, when few visitors are passing. They may shift and deposit over-clothing in the watch-boxes, as required by changes of weather. They may also enter and stand in them for a space of not more than ten minutes, while eating a lunch, once during each period of duty. They are forbidden to enter the watch-boxes for rest or shelter except as above authorized. They are forbidden when in the watch-boxes to sit or lounge. Patrol keepers, on route duty, will carry no food with them from the station, will receive none, and will eat none. Patrol keepers while on beat duty will receive no food, and if they find it necessary to take sustenance will temporarily exchange duties with post keepers on gate duty, and follow the rule applicable to that duty.

VII.

From the time that a keeper comes on active duty, until he reports and is dismissed, or returned by his officer to waiting duty, including all of the time in which he shall be in uniform, out of a station or office of the Department, he is to carry and deport himself in a vigilant, decorous and soldier-like way. When proceeding to a post or beat, or when on route duty, he is to move at a quick march, or if there is special need to move slowly for observation, he is to carefully avoid any appearance of sauntering or listlessness. He is to seek no shelter, and to occupy no position or locality unfavorable to his duty of preventing the misuse of the Park, and aiding and giving confidence to visitors in its proper use. Nor is he, without special necessity, to enter any building or take any position or action in which he may appear to others to be seeking his own ease or comfort, or disengagement from activity and vigilance.

When illness, a call of nature, or any irresistible necessity would otherwise prevent a compliance with these requirements, he is to call on and temporarily resign his duty to some other member of the force; to an extra keeper if no other is available. This is to be done formally, and with a statement of the reason; he is at the same time to remove his shield and put it out of sight. He may afterwards return, if able, replace his shield, and resume his duty. The time of the resignation and resumption of duty is to be noted and reported, with other particulars, by both keepers.

VIII.

He is not to try to surprise visitors; is not to play the detective; is not to move furtively or use slyness, in any way, for any purpose.

IX.

He is not to suffer himself to be drawn into private conversation.

X.

He is not to engage in disputes or discussions on questions of his duty or that of visitors, or other matters.

XI.

To lessen the liability of falling into conversation, not required by his duty, and of an appearance of neglect of duty, he will, while in necessary communication with others, stand in the position of "attention," or if in movement, will take special care to maintain a brisk and vigilant carriage.

XII.

He is not to address visitors in a loud voice, when occasion for doing so can be avoided by his own activity.

XIII.

He is not to exhibit ill-temper, vexation, impatience or vindictiveness in manner, tone of voice, words or acts.

XIV.

The authority to make arrests is to be used with extreme caution; only when to refrain from using it will bring the law, as represented by the keeper, into disrespect, or be followed by other results harmful to general public interests.

XV.

Persons to be arrested, and while under arrest, must be saved from all unnecessary indignity.

XVI.

When the keeper is obliged, for the vindication of the law, to use force, he must be cautious to avoid unnecessary violence or harshness.

XVII.

The worst criminal having a right to a hearing by a magistrate before condemnation to punishment, the punishment of offenders can be no business of the keeper. No conduct or language toward a visitor, which conveys *an intention of punishment*, is therefore, under any circumstances, to be justified.

XVIII.

The Captain or Lieutenant will, as soon as practicable after every arrest, inquire into the cause and motive of it, the manner in which it was made, the language used, and the treatment of the prisoner from first to last.

XIX.

Keepers are not to carry clubs, unless by special order, and are not, under any circumstances to carry pistols, or other weapons, concealed or exposed.

XX.

Two members of the force will never move side by side in company, unless under orders of an officer, or to meet a special necessity. If, by chance, two come side by side, both proceeding the same way, the one who has the highest number on his shield will quicken, and the other moderate speed, until there is a space of at least one hundred paces between them.

XXI.

Patrol keepers meeting on the drive, and having no occasion of duty for verbal communication, will pass on opposite sides, each taking the left (because by so doing, each will face the nearest approaching carriages).

XXII.

When a section or squad is to move in a body, and no officer with it, the keeper having the lowest number on his shield will be in command, military order will be preserved, and no talking allowed.

XXIII.

A keeper finding visitors sick, swooning, sun-stricken, deranged, paralyzed, in stupor, or apparently drugged or intoxicated, may suspend all other duty in order to help them either to find relief or to leave the Park. If they can in any way be disposed of with more kindness to themselves and less annoyance to others or injury to the Park without bringing them to the station, that way is to be preferred. In urgent cases they may be taken to the nearest cottage, or other suitable shaded or sheltered place, and an extra keeper or other trusty messenger sent for a surgeon or to obtain a conveyance.

XXIV.

When persons are found not in their sober senses and inclined to disorder or violence, keepers are not to consider whether they came so by intemperance or otherwise, but to regard their condition as an infirmity, the evils of which it is their duty for the time being to skilfully restrict as far as they can.

XXV.

The action of the Commissioners in establishing different grades of responsibility and authority in the keepers' force must be rigidly respected by all its members. That habits of subordination and respect may be cultivated and guarded, a proper reserve and formality of manner must be preserved in the intercourse between those of different ranks.

XXVI.

Conduct, language and manners tending unnecessarily to provoke or foster jealousies, prejudices or ill-will between different members of the force, whether of the same or of different ranks, by which a spirit of mutual support and co-operation would be discouraged, are to be studiously avoided. The intrusion of personal interests, and especially of personal differences between keepers into proceedings of official duty is strongly reprobated.

XXVII.

Officers and keepers of each rank may suspend those of a lower rank, and may discontinue suspensions made by those of a lower rank, in every case reporting their action as soon as practicable to their own superiors. A keeper suspended while on active duty will remove his shield, and report at the station as soon as practicable thereafter. Suspensions are to be made only where there is an appearance of grave fault or incompetency for duty, and those making them are to be held to strict account for the grounds of their action.

XXVIII.

It is the duty of officers to watch for, consider and report errors or neglect of duty in the conduct of their subordinates. It is not the duty of keepers to watch for faults in their officers or in one another, and it is inconsistent with their duty to countenance useless grumbling, or idle reports, gossip or scandal tending to insubordination or the injury of their officers or comrades.

XXIX.

When a keeper, against whom no charges are pending, has knowledge of grave misconduct on the part of an officer, or reasonable grounds of complaint against an officer, it will be proper for him to make the same known to that officer's superior without unnecessary delay: But after charges have been made against any keeper, and while they are pending, it will not be proper for him to bring accusations against those making them or the witnesses to be examined, unless this is necessary to his own vindication, in which case the accusations must be made in writing, formally and specifically, so that due notice may be given those accused.

XXX.

The resignation of no member of the force will be accepted while a charge is pending against him.

Conditions of Holding Appointments.

By resolution of the Commissioners of the Department of Public Parks the following are established as conditions of holding an appointment as patrol or park keeper. Any keeper failing to comply with them will forfeit his position:

I.

A keeper shall be engaged in no other business, trade or calling, but shall hold himself ready for keeper's duty, when required by his officers, at all times.

II.

Each keeper shall carry out all lawful instructions from persons placed in authority over him, in good faith, according to their true intent and meaning to the best of his understanding and ability.

III.

He shall not, upon any occasion, or for any reason, take money or any gratuity from any person without the express permission of the Commissioners.

IV.

He shall not seek to obtain promotion or favor from his officers or the Commissioners by the aid or interposition of others, or on other grounds than that of his just credit for intelligent and faithful service.

V.

He shall enter into no agreement, intrigue or understanding with others to bring about the discredit or the advance of any member of the force.

VI.

6th. He shall not seek to evade or prevent a fair trial of himself or other keepers when charged with delinquencies.

General Observations on the Conduct Required of the Keepers of the Central Park.

Among the circumstances which have obliged considerable changes to be ordered in the regulations for the keeping of the Park, are the following:

After the dismissal of more than a third of the force, represented by its officers to be its least promising members, and after much effort to secure improvement under existing rules, a satisfactory appearance of vigilance, discipline and activity in a keeper on duty has remained exceptional.

Moreover, although a keeper, while on his beat or post, rarely comes under the observation of an officer unexpectedly to himself, instances have continued to be disgracefully common of keepers seen by their officers under conditions raising a strong presumption of intentional neglect of duty.

It has been but too evident, from these and other circumstances, that a habit of disregarding the just claims upon them of the Commissioners and of the public, had been strongly established with many members of the force, and, that under existing arrangements, the Commissioners have been unable to enforce a faithful compliance with the contract which is, in effect, made between themselves and each keeper at his appointment, and which is renewed and ratified whenever the keeper puts on his uniform.

This being a duty resting on the Commissioners second in importance to no other, as will be later shown, the subject has, for sometime, been one of constant and close study, with a view to new arrangements on a sounder basis.

Most of the cases of apparent neglect of duty reported, have been found, after investigation, to divide more or less distinctly, into three classes:

First. — Those in which the keeper has frankly confirmed the statement of the officer, acknowledged himself at fault, and in which it has been probable that the error was a casual one, quite out of his usual habits.

Second. — Those in which the statement of the officer has been essentially confirmed by the keeper, and some reason given for the apparent neglect, which has been assumed by the keeper to be a justification of it.

Third. — Those in which the keeper has either admitted the facts, as represented by the officer, or has denied only some quite unimportant particulars of them, but has seemingly not recognized that they established any neglect of duty.

There has really been but a single instance of the first class; that of one of the oldest of the keepers, whose character has always been, and is, of the highest. Of the second class of cases there have been many. The following are examples of the grounds on which justification for an admitted relaxation from, or temporary putting aside of, duty, has been commonly claimed:

1st. — Compulsion of heat, cold, or storm; sickness, fatigue, or exhaustion from exposure or excessive tours of duty.

2d. — Calls of nature.

3d. — Hiding from visitors while eating, or when making some change or adjustment of clothing.

4th. — Receiving necessary food from home, and standing apart to converse with the person bringing it.

5th. — Communication with other keepers.

6th. — Civilities to a friend.

7th. — Trying to detect a visitor in wrong-doing.

It has been evident that if, in the comparatively few cases of neglect of duty which would come under official notice, it should continue the case that the keepers, called to account, had only need to assert that they were acting under some one of these classes of alleged necessities in order to clear themselves, men wholly unfit for the business, with no pride in it, and no sense of honor in relation to it, might remain in the force for years, and the requirements upon them be easier than they would be upon the true men.

One object of the changes now to be made is to debar such excuses for neglect of duty.

It will be readily seen that most of them are precluded under the new rules, and that they are so in a manner which involves no excessive requirement of self-control or endurance. The keeper who offers them, hereafter, will show either that he does not know his business or that he is incompetent for it.

As for the first, it is intended that every man appointed or retained as a keeper, shall have such strength of constitution, vigor, stamina and muscles, as he must have to bear his share in meeting all the obvious requirements upon the force as a whole, without excessive strain or discomfort.

The surgeon certifies that all who have been retained on the force are so at this time.

This being the case, in determining what the Commissioners may reasonably require of each man, it is to be remembered that they provide him with outer clothing more or less fitting to the season but that he supplies his own under-clothing, and can wear thick or thin; single, double or triple layers as in his judgment may most conduce to his comfort. No man is required to report for duty when he is unwell. Consequently, when a man reports for duty, he is supposed to be clothed as nearly as possible suitably for his period of duty, and to be in sufficiently vigorous condition to bear any exposure or discomfort to which a change of weather occurring within it would subject him. If, then, he is found to be inactive; to be taking rest or shelter; to be throwing off or adding to his dress, except as regularly provided for, he makes one of two things evident; either that he is physically disqualified for his duty, or that he prefers to disobey orders rather than endure the measure of fatigue and discomfort which is involved in the obligations he has assumed with his uniform.

In either case he shows that he cannot rightly be retained in the employment of the Commissioners as a keeper.

Under the new arrangements, most of the patrol keepers will regularly call at a station, where, when necessity exists, they can be excused from duty by an officer, as often as once in every hour and a half. Special provisions are made in the rules for those who will not do so. Post keepers will be in communication with patrol keepers at least every half-hour, and will be constantly within signalling distance of an extra keeper. In case of real necessity, therefore, any member of the force can soon get another to take his place under the rules.

Failing to do so, suspension, abandonment or neglect of duty cannot be attributed to illness, unless it shall be of so sudden and prostrating a character as to require the immediate aid of a physician. Of this, the only evidence which can be considered conclusive will be that of the surgeon.

In the third class of cases it has been evident that, if the keeper's statements were sincere, it had been possible for men to hold appointments for some time in the force with scarcely the least idea for what purposes it is maintained by the Commissioners, and whose conduct had, on the whole, probably tended to promote that which they had been paid for aiding to prevent.

Hereafter no man will be retained on the force who cannot be made to realize that it is the smallest part of his duty to avoid being absent from his place, and while in it to perform those few acts, for which he may find occasion as a common officer of the law. No man can be retained who fails to understand the special purposes of the system of park keeping, or how he may steadily contribute to those purposes without a moment's intermission during all of such time as he is on active duty.

That there may be the less excuse for failure, the purposes of the system and the method by which they are chiefly to be promoted will here be explained in the most elemental way, at the same time the error of certain habits into which there has been much tendency to fall will be exposed.

The Park Commissioners are trustees and managers for the whole body of owners of a large amount of public property. Their business with it is of two kinds, first, that of forming parks; second, that of keeping them.

The first of these duties employs many the more men, costs much the more money, and makes greatly the larger show to the eye, but the second is the graver responsibility, and the Commissioners are to be holden to a stricter account if the arrangements they make for it are ill-judged, or if they delegate it to faithless or inefficient agents.

What is here meant by the keeping of the Parks in distinction from the forming of them, and why it has so much more importance than the comparative extent of business would indicate may be suggested by an illustration:

A man may buy and fit up a costly house, but if, after he has done so, he finds coal and ashes scattered over his carpets, if decorated ceilings are stained and marred, if pictures are defaced, if books and dishes are piled on his chairs, windows and doors kept open during storms, beds used as tables and tables as beds, and so on, all that he has obtained for his expenditure will be of little value to him for the time being, and the possibility of its ever again being made of much value will lessen with every day that such misuse is suffered, through *inefficiency of housekeeping*, to prevail.

In the same way a park, as in the case of the Central Park, having been formed and furnished with a great variety of appliances, each, like chairs, and tables, and beds, and dishes, and carpets, and pictures in a house, designed to be used in a different way and for different ends, though all for the one general end of the comfort of the occupants, whatever value the owners are to enjoy for the twelve million dollars or more they have laid out upon the park will depend on the prevention of misuse, which again is a question of the efficiency of the park-keeping.

For example, rock has been removed, drains laid, deep soil formed and fine, short greensward gradually established upon the soil in certain places in order to secure that particular form of gratification which may be produced by a rich color and texture of turf, and by the contrast of this color and texture with that of other associated objects. To a limited extent and under certain conditions, the turf may be trodden upon without injury, but if walking upon it were generally allowed, the particular object for which much labor during many years has been thus expended would be wholly lost. Hence it is an imperative part of the business of the Commissioners to prevent this misuse of it.

Again, the Park is furnished with a bridle-road, the object being to have a place where horses can be ridden with a free hand and at a rapid rate of speed. This is forbidden by law anywhere else in the city, because nowhere else have arrangements been made by which it could be done with safety. In the Park they have been, at great cost. This bridle-road might be used by people in carriages or on foot but it is not necessary to the comfort of anyone that it should be, as there are on the Park above nine miles of road much better adapted to driving, and nearly thirty miles better adapted to walking; and, as to drive or walk upon it would greatly injure its value for its special purposes, it is the business of the Commissioners to prevent such misuse of it.

Similar illustrations might be multiplied by the hundred, and keepers must realize that every foot of the Park's surface, every tree and bush, as well as, every arch, roadway and walk has been fixed where it is *with a purpose*, and upon its being so used that it may continue to serve that purpose to the best advantage, and upon its *not being otherwise used*, depends its value.

There are ways, however, in which the Park may be misused, not so distinctly definable as those above illustrated, the general nature of which may be indicated as follows:

The Park is not simply a pleasure-ground, that is, a ground to which people may resort to obtain some sort of recreation, but a ground to which people may resort for recreation in certain ways and under certain circumstances *which will be conducive to their better health*.

Physicians order certain classes of their patients to visit the Park instead of prescribing medicine for them, because, they need first of all the tranquilizing influence upon the nerves which they may find in it, and the insensible advantage which is gained in this way by thousands who visit it without this purpose definitely in view, but whose strength and powers of usefulness are thus increased, and whose lives thus prolonged, constitutes its chief value.

Any conduct which tends on the whole to restrict this value is a misuse of the Park, and in considering what conduct would have this effect it must be remembered that a large majority of all the inhabitants of the city are women and children, sickly and aged or weakly, nervous and delicate persons, and that the Park is adapted to benefit none so much as those who have barely the courage, strength and nerve required for a visit to it.

Incidentally to the prevention of misuse in the two forms which have been indicated, it is required in the keeping of the Park, that such assistance should be given to visitors as is necessary to their profitable use of it.

Those most needing assistance (in the way chiefly of directions, information and advice) will be people of home-keeping habits, retiring disposition, helpless, sensitive, modest. The difficulty here is not in supplying all necessary advice that shall be asked, but *in giving those most needing to obtain advice confidence to ask and accept what they need*.

From all that has been said it will be seen that the administration of this most important part of the Departments' business does not turn simply upon the question, by what means can the misuse of the park be prevented? but that it must also be considered how the agencies employed for this purpose may best aid the proper use of the park, and especially how trustfulness in the means of prevention and confidence in the use of the aid to be provided may best be inspired.

There are apt to be certain preconceived ideas in the minds of those who have not studied the subject which stand in the way of sound convictions as to the methods by which the park can best be kept and, that they may be removed, it is desirable that the following considerations should be well weighed.

There are frequent occasions when the number of visitors on the Park is many times larger than is usual. The walks and seats being then crowded, the temptation to each visitor to pursue his pleasure out of the beaten tracks, and so to misuse the Park in various ways, is correspondingly greater than usual. To employ a sufficient number of keepers on such occasions to guard every point where these temptations will occur, and to give a caution or check directly and personally to everyone who might need it, would be wholly impracticable.

But even if it were practicable, it will be evident that the pleasure and value of a ramble in the Park would be destroyed, and, instead of a tranquilizing, an irritating effect would be produced if at every turn a visitor were to be made to feel himself superintended in all his conduct like a lunatic by his keeper, or a child by its nurse.

It is not, then, by the frequent overhauling of visitors that the park is to be successfully kept.

There have been many occasions when each keeper employed within the gates of the Park has had to cover a space on an average of fifty acres, most of these spaces abounding with bushes, hollows and rocks favorable to those wishing to escape notice while misusing it, and when there will have been on each such space three or four thousand visitors. If it could be supposed that any considerable part of these visitors were influenced by positive hostility to the purposes of the keeper, it will be apparent that the evidences of misuse which they would leave behind them would be much greater than they ever have been. To see this more clearly, however, let a common example of misuse be studied.

Certain spots have been prepared in a peculiar manner, with a view to secure a luxuriant growth of ferns and wild flowers in association with rocks and other adjoining objects. There are some of the owners of the Park to whom the intended effect would give great delight, aiding them to forget their troubles, momentarily at least, and producing something of the good result which a visit to the mountains brings to a fagged-out man or a jaded woman. The places have been carefully selected and prepared so that it need be little, if any, inconvenience for visitors to avoid walking on them, and so that the plants, once well established, will in a great degree take care of themselves. The danger in this case that the intended result will not be attained, is chiefly this, that a few persons, perhaps one in ten thousand of all who pass near any such place, will tramp across it, and in so doing, stamp out the life of the plants, or will, one by one, pick and misappropriate the flowers to private use. They have no more right to do either than to pick their neighbor's pockets, throw stones at his windows or vitriol at his coat. Yet, of the comparatively small number of visitors who will crush out the life of the ferns, or steal the flowers, it will certainly be a still very much smaller number who are capable of being led intentionally to do any such wrong to their neighbor.

The truth is, then, that even of the comparatively small number of those who would make such a misuse of the Park, much the larger part are capable of being tempted to it only because having had no occasion, under ordinary circumstances, in walking along the streets, or when in the country, through the woods and fields, to consider the rights of others in the way that is necessary in the Park, it fails to be clear to their minds that they will be wronging others when they feel the impulse to such misconduct.

There is the same explanation often to be made even for people who carry themselves rudely in the Park, disputing loudly with one another, using threatening, profane or obscene language, crowding others off the walks, excluding others unnecessarily from seats, and so on. It is not with intention of troubling others that they do these things, but in most cases from sheer unmindfulness that others are being unpleasantly affected by them.

But a little further thought will satisfy the keeper that not only is it to be fairly presumed that visitors, as a rule, are indisposed to misuse the Park, but that they have an active desire and intention to avoid its misuse. Consider, for example, how much pleasanter it is in a hot summer's day to step on turf than on gravel or concrete walks, yet how few, comparatively, make a practice of stepping off the walks upon the turf whenever they have reason to think they might do so without danger of reproof from a keeper.

Even of the more lawless class a larger number commonly keep within the bounds of decent use of the Park than, when it is an easy matter to keep out of the sight of a keeper for hours together, can be accounted for by the mere danger of reproof or arrest. In what other way can it be explained that bad men, abandoned women and mischievous boys make no more misuse of the Park than they do?

Let the keeper who is at all doubtful of the answer ask himself if he were going with a friend to a theatre, or a church or a funeral, and while walking in the streets should be smoking or engaged in a warm debate and talking loudly with his friend, whether he would be at all likely to continue smoking or talking aloud after entering the house? or, supposing that by any mischance he did so for a moment, whether he would continue long to do so? If not, let him ask himself again, why he would not wait until admonished or threatened with arrest by an officer of the law?

Reflection will satisfy him that he would be led by the silent and unconscious influence of others present to regard the custom and proprieties of the occasion and the place. A little more reflection will further satisfy him that no man however hardened, no woman however brazened, is wholly proof against such an influence. Remembering then, that, on the other hand, this class has not often much to gain by any marked defiance of custom or propriety in the Park, it will be seen that its protection rests almost wholly on the loyal disposition of the great body of visitors to side with the keepers in discountenancing its misuse.

Keeping this last consideration in mind, let the keeper imagine a man entering the Park, fully aware that he does so as one of its rightful owners, under obligations to no one; that, presently, through heedlessness or ignorance, he disobeys some rule for its proper use; that immediately a man whose livery shows that he is one of his servants, employed for his pleasure and paid with his money, accosts him, not, as it appears, with a purpose to respectfully aid him toward a better understanding of what is due to others, as one gentleman might manage to aid another who was a stranger to him, but as a watchdog might accost a sneak-thief, growling, and with a look of seizing hold of him. Suppose that the visitor has not only been so treated himself, but has observed similar conduct on the part of other keepers toward other visitors, and that both experiences have been often repeated. Let the keeper consider whether a desire will not grow with this visitor to take care of himself when he is in his Park, and no thanks to anybody; whether a disposition to try conclusions with the whole force of keepers, to see whether they shall prevent him from going where he likes and behaving as he pleases, will not be established in his mind?

To fully realize the danger of thus enlisting the self-respect of visitors against the purposes of the force, it must be remembered that there are many Jacks-in-office who, commanding but little of the respect of others in their own proper persons, enjoy to presume on the respect of others for any slight authority of law with which they may be briefly clothed, and that, consequently, there has grown up a common and not unreasonable predisposition in the public mind to find all public servants, more or less officious and meddlesome.

Now, if the keeper sees that it is not by activity in reproof of misuse, or by exciting fear of his authority to arrest, that he is chiefly to contribute to the efficiency of the force for its purposes, it must also be plain to him, without argument, that the occasional sight of a man who is simply distinguished from men in general by a badge and some peculiarities of clothing, is going to check misuse of the park very little. It will also be plain to him that a visitor, knowing that men so distinguished are the only representatives of those who are charged with the duty of keeping the park, and who sees one of them lounging listlessly, talking with friends, making himself comfortable, and who reflects that he is maintained in this way of living at public expense, is likely to have his respect for the ordinances established by the Commissioners to prevent the misuse of the park in no way increased.

But, now, let the keeper who cannot see what way is left to him for contributing to the object of the force, suppose that a visitor has, through some previous observation, come to be aware that there is an organized system for aiding visitors to avoid its misuse and for giving them all needed directions for its use; that in whatever part of the park he has been he has, at intervals, found agents of this system, and has observed a striking uniformity not only in their attire but in their carriage and manner, making it evident they were acting under common authority, common instructions, and with a common responsibility strictly enforced.

Suppose that they had invariably appeared to him watchful, vigilant, active and with their minds so fully occupied with their business of keeping the Park that they could think of nothing else. That whenever any one of them had been seen addressing a visitor, it had been obviously because it was his duty to do so, and that whomsoever he found occasion to address, a swaggering, impudent man, or a poor shrinking girl, and for whatever purpose, to check a misuse of the Park or to show the way to a seat, it had been with a manner of studied official respect.

Suppose that having himself had need occasionally for some information or advice, and having applied to keepers for it, it had been given with no more words than necessary, but with all desirable fullness, accuracy and clearness, and with perfect courtesy: not with an air as if it were a matter of grace with the keeper, nor with a hurried, irritated manner, as if he were impatient of it, but simply as if it were a constant duty for which he had carefully prepared himself, and in which he had no right to do otherwise than as well as possible.

It will be readily seen that one result of such an experience would be that, to this visitor, every Park-keeper would distinctly represent the general, permanent and legal interests which he possessed, in common with all other citizens, in the Park, in distinction from the momentary, selfish, illegal, individual interests which alone can be served through its misuse.

If then, at any time, such a visitor were carelessly misusing the Park, the mere sight of a keeper would be sufficient to recall those larger, deeper, nobler interests to his mind, and self-respect, instead of prompting him to persist in a spirit of defiance, would lead him to cease from the misuse, and to proceed in the proper use and enjoyment of the Park with more consideration.

If, on the other hand, he were misusing the Park through ignorance, and the keeper should ask him to desist, the request, so far from being felt as a personal affront, would be received with all respect and cheerfully complied with.

But if this would be the result of such an experience of the keepers with one man, it would equally be the result with thousands — with the great body of fairly well disposed visitors — and thus the force of custom would act, out of the keeper's sight, in resistance to the misuse of the Park, with a strong, constant pressure, upon even the more recklessly selfish class.

It cannot, then, be too strongly borne in mind, that any conduct which tends to wound the self-respect of visitors tends also to promote a disposition to misuse the Park, and that, in so far as there is anything in the appearance of a keeper at any moment while he is on active duty, which seconds those general influences of the Park, by which the self-respect or civic pride of the citizen is gratified, he will at that moment be actively contributing to the general purpose of the organization.

Moreover, it may be fairly estimated that however slight such influence may be at any particular moment, on any particular visitor, the sum of all the influence which each keeper may so exert will be a larger contribution to the general end which he has undertaken, as the business of his life, to serve, than he will be able to make in all other ways.

It is very desirable that the officers of the force, especially, should realize that the great difficulty with which they have to contend is just here, in the proneness, that is to say, of keepers, in common with mankind in general, to have too little respect for or faith in influences which operate quietly and graciously, and to magnify the importance of acts of which the results are direct and obvious; in the proneness, also, of keepers to imagine that their usefulness lies in what each man accomplishes from day to day, by himself, rather than in the ultimate results of a system to which any contributions that any one of them can make will be chiefly valuable in proportion as he sustains a general influence proceeding from all with whom he is placed in co-operation.

The points more important to be fixed in the keeper's mind of what has been said may be recapitulated as follows:

First. — The most pressing responsibility upon the Commissioners, with reference to the Central Park, is that of the prevention of its misuse.

Second. — The degree in which the Park will be wilfully and gravely misused corresponds to the degree in which any misuse of it will be given the apparent sanction of custom, through thoughtless and slight misuse of it.

Third. — The keeper can do little towards preventing misuse of the park, by arrests or by threats or admonitions addressed personally to visitors.

Fourth. — What is chiefly to be relied upon for keeping within necessary limits the thoughtless and slight misuse of the park, and through this all misuse, is the impression which may from time to time be produced on the minds of well-intentioned visitors by the mere presence and manner of the Park-keepers.

Fifth. — This impression will be valuable for the purpose in proportion as it is uniform, and as it manifests systematic vigilance, order, discipline, considerateness and courtesy.

Sixth. — The Commissioners cannot afford, in justice to their own responsibility, to retain men in the position of keepers who fail to contribute constantly, when on active duty, to such an impression.

Ordinances Applicable to the Ordinary Use of the Central Park.[5]

The Board of Commissioners of the Department of Public Parks, this thirty first day of March, A.D. 1873, adopt and ordain the following ordinances for the use of the Central Park, to be observed by all persons not in the service of the Department.

I. No one shall enter or leave the Park except at the established entrance ways, nor shall anyone enter or remain in it after eleven o'clock at night, during the six months beginning May first; nor after nine o'clock at night during the six months beginning November first, except as, on special occasions, its general use may be authorized beyond the regular hours.

II. No one shall climb upon or in any way cut, break, injure or deface any wall, fence, shelter, seat, statue or other erection, nor any turf, tree, shrub, or other plant, nor throw stones or other missiles, nor discharge, fire or carry any firearm, fire-cracker, torpedo or fire-works, nor make a fire, nor play any musical instrument, nor offer or expose things for sale, nor post or display any sign, placard, flag, banner, target, transparency, advertisement or device of business, nor solicit business or fares, nor beg or publicly solicit subscriptions or contributions, nor tell fortunes, nor play games of chance or with any table or instruments of gaming, nor make any oration or harangue, nor utter loud threatening, abusive or indecent language, nor do any indecent or obscene act.

III. No quadrupeds except those placed in the Park by the Commissioners, and except dogs when controlled by a line of suitable strength not more than six feet in length, and horses and others used for pleasure travel, shall be driven or conducted into the Park or allowed to remain in it.

IV. The drive shall be used only by persons in pleasure carriages or on horseback; the ride only by persons on horseback; animals to be used on either shall be well broken and constantly held in such control, that they may be easily and quickly turned or stopped; they shall not be allowed to move at a rate of speed which shall be alarming or cause danger, nor under any circumstances at a rate of speed on the drive of more than seven miles, nor on the ride of over twelve miles an hour; and when any park-keeper shall deem it necessary to safety, good order, or the general convenience, that the speed of an animal shall be checked, or that it should be stopped, or its course altered, and shall so direct, by gesture or otherwise, it shall be the duty of the rider or driver of such animal to follow such direction; and no horse or other beast of burden or draft shall be driven or suffered to stand anywhere, except on the drive or ride.

V. No hackney-coach or other vehicle for hire shall stand within the Park, for the purpose of taking up passengers, other than those whom it has brought in. No omnibus or express-wagon, and no wagon, cart or other vehicle, carrying, or ordinarily used to carry merchandise, goods, tools or rubbish, and no fire-engine or other apparatus on wheels for extinguishing fires shall enter or be allowed upon any part of the Park.

VI. No military or target company, and no civic, funeral or other procession, or a detachment of a procession, and no hearse or other vehicle, or persons, carrying the body of a dead person shall enter, or be allowed on any part of the Park.

VII. No person shall bathe or angle, or take fish, or send or throw or place any animal or thing in or on the waters, or disturb or annoy the birds or animals in the Park.

VIII. No person shall go on the turf except when and where the word "common" is posted as an indication that at that time and place all persons are allowed to go on it.

IX. No person shall bring into or carry within the Park any tree, shrub, plant or flower, nor any newly plucked branch or portion thereof.

X. When necessary to the protection of life or property, the officers and keepers of the Park may require all persons to remove from, and keep off any designated part thereof.

XI. On the arrest of a person in the Park, he shall be forthwith conducted to one of the keepers' stations, the officer in charge of which shall determine whether he shall thence be conveyed before a magistrate or be discharged.

By order of the Board of Commissioners of the Department of Public Parks.

HENRY G. STEBBINS,
President.

F. W. Whittemore,
Secretary.[6]

The text presented here is taken from "Document No. 43," in New York (City), Department of Public Parks, *Minutes*, March 31, 1873, pages 3–37.

1. The Central Park keepers' service had been created in February 1858 and placed under Olmsted's supervision. The purpose of the keepers' force was to maintain order on the park and to educate visitors in its proper use. After May 1870, when the Sweeny board replaced the old Central Park commission, the keepers' force was filled with patronage appointments. Crime and vandalism rose in the park while morale and discipline among the keepers declined. After the collapse of the Tweed Ring and the Sweeny board, conditions in the keepers' service did not improve, and in November 1872 the Central Park board ordered Olmsted to reorganize the keepers' force. In February 1873 Olmsted presented his reorganization plan to the board, and it was adopted the following month. The principal change in the keepers' service as outlined in Olmsted's report was the introduction of the "round system," which forced the keepers to walk at a continuously fast pace until they completed their circuit (*Papers of FLO*, 6: 41–43; see also, FLO and CV, "Report of the Landscape Architect on the Recent Changes in the Keepers' Service," July 8, 1873 [ibid., 6: 610–30]).
2. That is, the Harlem beat was the area of the East Drive between the Farmer's Gate, at 110th Street and Sixth Avenue, and the refectory at Mount St. Vincent, which was just east of the drive opposite 105th Street. The Hill beat was the area of the West Drive between the Warrior's Gate, at 110th Street and Seventh Avenue, and the Glen Span arch, which crossed the stream valley between the Pool and the Loch opposite 102nd Street. The Ramble beat covered the hillside between the Lake and the old Croton receiving reservoir at 79th Street. The walks marking the southern boundary of the Terrace beat were approximately on the line of 70th Street: the Music-stand was in the Concert Ground, in the northern section of the Mall.
3. The keepers on round duty made a full circuit of the park, primarily following the drive, between 59th Street and Mount St. Vincent, which was on the East Drive opposite 105th Street. Between them, the East Route and West Route achieved "close inspection" of the gate-keepers at all of the gates.
4. In this description, references to the Children's Gate must instead be to the Inventor's Gate, a carriage and pedestrian entrance at Fifth Avenue and 72nd Street. By the time the keepers reached this point they had already inspected the Children's Gate, which was a pedestrian entrance at the Old Arsenal at Fifth Avenue and 64th Street, and which in this document is called the 64th Street gate.
5. Although these ordinances appear to be a separate document attached to the report, Olmsted wrote them as well (FLO to H. A. Nelson, March 24, 1876).
6. Frederick W. Whittemore served as secretary to the Board of Commissioners of the Department of Public Parks from July 1872 through May 1873 (DPP, *Minutes*, June 4, 1873, p. 23).

"Park"

from the

American Cyclopedia

[1875]

Park, a space of ground used for public or private recreation, differing from a garden in its spaciousness and the broad, simple, and natural character of its scenery, and from a "wood" in the more scattered arrangement of its trees and greater expanse of its glades and consequently of its landscapes. For the sake of completeness, recreation grounds not properly called parks will be considered under the same title. The grounds of an old English manorial seat are usually divided into two parts, one enclosed within the other and separated from it by some form of fence. The interior part, immediately around the dwelling, is distinguished as the pleasure ground or kept ground, the outer as the park. The park is commonly left open to the public, and frequently the public have certain legal rights in it, especially rights of way. A parish church is sometimes situated within the park. The use of the park as part of a private property is to put the possibilities of disagreeable neighborhood at a distance from the house and the more domestic grounds, to supply a pleasant place of escape from the confinement and orderliness of the more artificial parts of the establishment, and for prolonged and vigorous out-of-door exercise. The kept grounds, being used incidentally to in-door occupations, are designed in close adaptation to the plan of the house, richly decorated, and nicely, often exquisitely, ordered by the constant labor of gardeners. Anciently the kept grounds were designed as a part of the same general architectural plan with the house, and were enclosed and decorated with masses of foliage clipped in imitation of cut and sculptured stone. Their lofty hedges often completely intercepted the view from the house toward the park. A recognition of the fact that the parks were much more beautiful than the kept grounds when thus fashioned, led early in the 16th century to the art of landscape gardening, or, as it is more generally called out of England, landscape architecture. The aim of the new art was, while still keeping the park fenced off, to manage the pleasure grounds in such a way that they would provide a harmonious and appropriate foreground to landscapes extending over the park, and to make such changes in the park itself as would improve the composition of these landscapes. The scenery of the old parks often has great beauty of a special character, which is the result of the circumstances under which the more ancient and famous of them have been

308

"WINDSOR PARK"

formed. These were originally enclosed many centuries since for keeping deer. In choosing ground for this purpose, rich land having broad stretches of greensward pasturage, with trees more sparingly distributed than usually in the forest, was to be preferred, and this character would be increased intentionally by felling a portion of the trees, and unintentionally by the browsing of the deer; water, either flowing or still, was a necessity. In process of time the proprietors of parks established residences in them, and at length the size of their trees and the beauty of their grouping came to be matters of family pride. As the old decayed, new trees were planted, with the purpose of maintaining the original character, or perhaps of carrying it nearer its ideal. Properties of this class, being associated with that which was oldest and most respectable in the land, came to be eagerly sought for, and to be formed to order as nearly as possible after the older type; and they are to be seen now in England by thousands. As a general rule, each element in their scenery is simple, natural to the soil and climate, and unobtrusive; and yet the passing observer is very strongly impressed with the manner in which views are successively opened before him through the innumerable combinations into which the individually modest elements constantly rearrange themselves; views which often possess every quality of complete and impressive landscape compositions. It is chiefly in this character that the park has the advantage for public purposes over any other type of recreation ground, whether wilder or more artificial. Other forms of natural scenery stir the observer to warmer admiration, but it is doubtful if any, and certain that none which under ordinary circumstances man can of set purpose induce nature to supply him, are equally soothing and refreshing; equally adapted to stimulate simple, natural, and wholesome tastes and fancies, and thus to draw the mind from absorption in the interests of an intensely artificial habit of life.

Private and public parks differ only in the extent of their accommodations for certain purposes, and most of the public parks in Europe are old private parks adapted to public use. When this is not the case, and a park for public use has to be formed essentially from the bare ground, its value will chiefly depend on provisions that cannot be fully matured or have their best operation for many years after their groundwork is established. For this reason the selection of a site, the design for laying out, and the system of continuous management of a public park should be determined with great caution. The aim should be to produce the park rather than the more elaborate pleasure ground or garden style of scenery, not only for the reasons above indicated but because a ground of this character can be consistently and suitably maintained at much less cost; because, also, it will allow the necessary conveniences for the enjoyment of it by large numbers of persons to be introduced in such a way as not to be unpleasantly conspicuous or disastrously incongruous; and because it favors such a distribution of those who visit it that few shall be seen at a time, and that the ground shall not seem overcrowded. It is a common impression that the loftier and more rugged and mountain-like the site of a public ground may be, and the more wild, picturesque, and grand scenery can be imitated in its improvement, the better it will answer its purpose. A principle of art however interposes, which M. Taine, in a discussion of the unimpressiveness of certain forms of mountain scenery, explains as follows: "A landscape in order to be beautiful must have all its parts stamped with a common idea and contributing to a single sensation. If it gives the lie here to what is said yonder, it destroys itself, and the spectator is in the presence of nothing but a mass of senseless objects."[1] It is extremely difficult to provide suitably extensive and varied conveniences for the public use of a piece of ground, the elements of which are strongly picturesque with an approach to grandeur, without destroying much of its original character; and the result of such attempts, unless under unusually fortunate circumstances and the guidance of unusual taste and skill, with the use of large means, is sure to be confusing and ineffective. Sites of much natural grandeur or even of bold picturesqueness are, therefore, to be selected for a park only where all necessary improvements for the convenience of a great number of visitors can be so managed that they will in some way strengthen rather than weaken the prevailing character. No instance of a public park exists in which this has been accomplished, but the principle is illustrated in various landscapes of the great painters. Examples may be found, for instance, in almost any book of engravings after Turner,[2] in which the original effect of a crag of rock is shown to be augmented by buildings designed for the purpose, the bases of which are skilfully merged in its face, or where a single great building of very simple outline is given a firm and tranquil standing in a wild and broken landscape of steep declivities and rugged heights. Under good direction, sites with features of much natural grandeur, on a scale so large and of such a character that the necessary constructions for the intended visitors can be insignificant, are to be preferred to any other; but such sites have not yet been appropriated to the purpose with the advantage of a sufficiently long continued adequate direction of their improvement, and there can be but few cases where they will be. After them, and more commonly attainable, are sites the natural character of which would usually and significantly be termed "park-like." If the ideal of the old English park scenery is kept in view, rather than either that of a more picturesque or more artificially refined, finical, and elaborately embellished kind, it will be readily seen that in the site for a public recreation ground it is desirable that views of considerable extent should be controllable within its borders, and that in order to command them it should not be necessary that views beyond its borders be opened, the elements of which cannot be controlled, and are liable, even in the distant future, to be made inharmonious with those of the park; especially so, where such elements will have urban rather than rural associations. It is generally better, therefore, that the outer parts should be the higher, the central parts the more depressed; that the surface should be tame rather than rugged, gently undulating rather than hilly. Water is desirable, and it will be best situated where it can be seen from the greatest number of widely distributed points of view. Relatively to the residences of those who are expected to benefit by it, the park will be best situated where there can be but little occasion to make thoroughfares through it. Otherwise, the less the distance and the more convenient and agreeable the intermediate roads, the better. As roads which radiate from a town are usually more important to be kept open than those which cross them, and as land near a town is relatively more needed for other uses than that more distant, it is commonly better that the breadth of the site should increase with its distance from the nearest point to the town, as in Prospect park, Brooklyn, N.Y. In the improvement of the site, attractive and suitable scenery has to be formed, and unsuitable elements of existing scenery changed or obscured; and at the same time and on the same ground accommodations of various kinds are to be prepared for great numbers of people, many in carriages and on horseback, many ignorant, selfish, and wilful, of perverted tastes and lawless dispositions, each one of whom must be led as far as possible to enjoy and benefit by the scenery without preventing or seriously detracting from the enjoyment of it by all others. The most essential element of park scenery is turf in broad, unbroken fields, because in this the antithesis of the confined spaces of the town is most marked. In the climate of Great Britain turf will endure on favorable soils twice as much foot wear as it will in that of Paris or northern France or the United States; yet in the more frequented London parks it is found necessary to surround with strong iron hurdles the glades on which their landscape attraction is dependent. For this and other obvious reasons, a great extent of ground must be prepared expressly for the wear of feet and wheels. In the two principal recreation grounds of Paris, the woods of Boulogne and Vincennes, though both are suburban parks and not readily used by the mass of the people, the extent of such flooring, prepared by macadamizing, paving, and otherwise, is 480 acres, or ten times the whole recreation ground of Boston, "the Common." In the Central park of New York it is 100 acres, and there is a constant public demand for its enlargement, which can only be met by reducing the verdant elements of landscape, and consequently the benefit to be obtained by the use of the park. In a public park for a city, therefore, the purpose of establishing such natural beauty as soil, climate, and topography would otherwise allow to be aimed at, must be greatly sacrificed under the necessity of providing accommodations for the travel and repose of many thousands of men and horses; and on the other hand, the extent of such accommodations must be made less than would otherwise be thought desirable, in order that the special objects of the park may be secured in a suitable degree. A plan for a park is good, indifferent, or bad, mainly according to the ingenuity, tact, and taste with which these conflicting requirements are reconciled, and to the degree in which local circumstances are skilfully turned to account if they can be made favorable, or skilfully overcome if unfavorable for this purpose. The problem is sufficiently difficult under the simplest conditions, and it is undesirable that it should be unnecessarily complicated by a requirement to provide for various purposes which have nothing in common with that of tranquillizing rest and exercise, and to which the element of landscape beauty is not essential. Soldiers, for example, drill and manœuvre, horses race, gymnasts and ball players exercise, on a piece of flat ground surrounded by buildings as well as in the glades of a wood. It is true that, when a suburban park is very spacious relatively to the number of people resorting to it for park recreation, a limited use of the larger turf areas for athletic exercises will injure it but little; but their frequent use for such purposes, especially if large assemblages of spectators are likely to be attracted, will be destructive of the value of the ground as a park, in the specific sense of the term. It is also to be considered that the proper rules and police arrangements for a park are different from those for a parade, ball, or gymnasium ground, or for a race course. Hence, when the most suitable ground near a town for these purposes adjoins that which is most suitable for a park, it is yet much better that there should be a marked division between them. Public buildings can be reconciled with the purposes of a park only in a limited degree. Ground about any building designed for an important public service should be laid out with a view, first, to convenience of communication with it; secondly, to its best exhibition as a work of architectural art. The neighboring grounds should be shaped and planted in strict subordination to these purposes, which will involve an entirely different arrangement from that which the purpose of forming a quiet rural retreat would prescribe. A similar consideration will prevent monuments and statues from being placed profusely in a park, or at all in situations where they will be obtrusive. The same cautions apply to the introduction of botanic, zoölogical, and other gardens. Their main object is as different from that of a park as that of a billiard room from a library. Both one and the other may serve for recreation, and there is an advantage in being able to pass from one to the other; but the kind of recreation to be gained by one is not that of the other, the appropriate furniture of the one is not that of the other; and their perfect combination being impracticable, the two can be much better used apart, one at a time.

In the larger part of the civilized world, circumstances are as unfavorable to park-like scenery as to grand scenery in the vicinity of large towns. The climate of France is nowhere as favorable to it as that of Great Britain, and even in the north it cannot be found in perfection unless on unusually suitable soil. In the south of France, in Italy, and on all the borders of the Mediterranean, in Mexico and California, and in short wherever a rich close perennial turf cannot be established, parks properly so called ought not to be attempted. In these cases, the two natural elements of scenery to be developed in a suburban public ground of great extent are forests (or "woods") and water. While trees in woods are by no means as beautiful as trees in parks, and a forest is apt to be gloomy and to produce an oppressive sense of confinement, the mystery of this confinement, so different from that of the walls of a town, makes it interesting and recreative. In the midst of well grown woods, public accommodations, no matter how obviously artificial, nor within reasonable limits how large they may be, detract but little from the main impression, and if fairly well designed supply a grateful relief to what might otherwise be too prolonged a mass and too nearly a monotone of color. The introduction of long strips of clear ground, even if covered with gravel or poor herbage (as at Versailles and most of the great old gardens), giving vistas through which the light may stream in visible beams, touching the walls of foliage at the side with an infinite number of lustrous flecks, produces a most agreeable impression. Bodies of water, whether formal or naturalistic in outline, in the midst of deep dark tall "woods," are still more effective. For the same reason statues, monuments, and gardens of highly colored flowers may be introduced in the midst of woods to much better advantage than in parks.

The use in America of the word park as a general designation for gardens, green courts, and all sorts of public places, is an exaggeration of a French application of the word to the more private or kept grounds of a château connected with a forest. To avoid confusion, open spaces for public use in a city may be termed "places;" grounds in turf and trees within places, "place parks;" and broad thoroughfares planted with trees and designed with special reference to recreation as well as for common street traffic, "parkways." The value of public gardens, places, place parks, and parkways, in distinction from parks and "woods," is dependent less on the extent of their sylvan elements than on the degree of convenience with which they may be used; those being the most valuable, other things being equal, through which the greatest number of people may be induced to pass while following their ordinary occupations and without serious hindrance or inconvenience.

Hence the most important improvement made of late in the general plan of cities has been the introduction or increase in number and breadth of parkways which, if judiciously laid out, become principal channels or trunk lines of common traffic, to which the ordinary streets serve as feeders, so that a man wishing to go to a considerable distance shall find it a saving of time and trouble to take one of them on his way. In this respect Paris has taken the lead, having formed since 1855 over 80 m. of such trunk lines of communication from 100 to 300 ft. in width, provided with borders of trees or shrubbery, walks and drives of a special character, seats, special lighting arrangements, and other conditions more interesting and agreeable than those of common streets. The total length of boulevards and avenues lined with trees under the direction of the municipality within the enceinte of Paris is 120 m. Most of the large towns of Europe are making similar improvements, and at Washington, Chicago, Cleveland, Buffalo, Syracuse, and Brooklyn excellent examples of them exist or are in process of formation. New York, with an area of about 42 sq. m., has 7 m. of planted parkways, all of which are suburban and as yet but partly finished.[3] Simple places, piazzas, or plazas (the two latter being equivalent terms derived from the Italian and Spanish) have the sanitary value of making a city more airy than it would be without them. If furnished with parks (place parks), they have the additional advantage of providing refreshment to the eye through the mind. If a piece of ground of one or two acres in the midst of a busy town is laid out and managed with a view to providing upon it the greatest practicable degree of plant beauty in trees, shrubs, flowers, and turf, and on the same general principles that a private garden for the same purpose would be, it will be of comparatively little use; for the walks will probably be indirect, the low planting of the outer parts will obscure the general view for passers by, and there will be frequent crowding and jostling and disturbance of quiet. Neatness and the maintenance of orderly conduct among visitors in such a ground becomes also exceedingly difficult. Hence, as a rule, at least in the United States, public grounds designed with this motive soon become more forlorn than open places would be. It is much better to decorate them in such a manner as will not destroy their openness or cause inconvenience to those who have occasion to cross them. For this purpose their plans should be simple and generally formal in style, their passages should be broad and direct, and they should be provided with seats in recesses or on the borders of the broader paved or gravelled spaces, leaving ample room for free movement. Their trees should be high-stemmed and umbrageous; conifers, except in rare instances, as permanent dwarfs, should be excluded, and flowers and delicate plants little if at all used except in vases and baskets (*corbeilles*) or as fringes of architectural objects. Interest will desirably centre in a fountain.

Every considerable town in Europe now possesses grounds which are resorted to for public recreation, and most have several different types specially prepared and kept at public expense. In France the state has long held

"Fontainebleau — View from the Chateau"

and managed extensive "woods and forests," remnants of the original forests which covered the country in the time of Cæsar. More than 20 such are found within a distance from Paris which makes them available for a day's pleasuring by means of railway excursion trains. They vary in extent from about 1,000 acres, as at St. Cloud, to 41,000, as at Fountainebleau. Each of these contains a château which at some time has been a royal residence, in connection with which there is a "park" or garden of several acres, generally containing a lake, fountains, statuary, monuments, parterres (as in the above engraving), and sometimes conservatories, aviaries, or other interesting objects. More or less historical interest also attaches to each, and in some quaint old customs are maintained, by which visitors are attracted. The forest proper is wilder, and in its depths many animals are found in a state of nature. It is however divided, by a network of broad avenues crossed by first, second, and third class roads and walks, into spaces of five to ten acres, so that in passing through it vistas open at frequent intervals on both sides and in all directions. Some of these forests are distinguished for great rocks, trees, and picturesque scenery; some contain in their depths broad meadows and savannas, others lakes or streams with cascades; all are guarded from depredations and policed by an organized body of men thoroughly trained in their duties under a military discipline. Among the more noted of these suburban resorts around Paris are those of Boulogne, Vincennes, St. Cloud, Marly, St. Germain, Rambouillet, Chantilly, and Compiègne, which together contain more than 170,000 acres. The first five are within 10 m. of the city, and may be reached by rail in less than half an hour. Versailles is another resort yet more famous, and in which the woods are of less importance than the palace and gardens. The

"Fontainebleau — View in the Forest"

woods of Boulogne and Vincennes, being nearest the city, one at its west and the other at its east side, have since 1854 been placed under the jurisdiction of the municipality, and fitted by extensive and important improvements, the better to serve as recreation grounds for the daily use of the citizens. The wood of Boulogne contains about 2,500 acres, and the fortified line of the city forms its eastern boundary. The soil is naturally gravelly and poor, the trees are generally thickly sown, spindled, and weak, and the scenery flat and uninteresting. Several departmental roads (broad, straight, paved wagon ways) pass through it. Except in the refreshing wildness of a forest, it offered as late as 1855 but little to attract a visitor. Yet because of its close vicinity to the city it was already much frequented by the Parisians, and Napoleon III. saw in the neglect to which it had been abandoned the opportunity of making one of those sensations, to the frequent succession of which he owed so much of his popularity. The coarse, silicious soil was less costly to handle than better earth; good roads could be cheaply graded in it, and the materials of a sufficiently firm superstructure for so porous a base were to be had on the spot by simply screening its pebbles; for the same reason scarcely any artificial drainage was necessary. There were open meadows which could be extended to the banks of the Seine. The plan of improvement was adroitly adapted to turn all these advantages to account, so that in a short time, to those who kept to certain routes, the character of the wood seemed to have been completely changed. On the immediate borders of the new roads, and on the lines of certain vistas opening from them, the surface of the ground and the foliage appear varied and picturesque, and there are certain features of scenic interest, as a cascade and grotto, the rock of which was brought from the distant forest of Fontainebleau and skilfully wrought into masses with patches of concrete imitation of stone. The greater part of the old wood remained, as far as

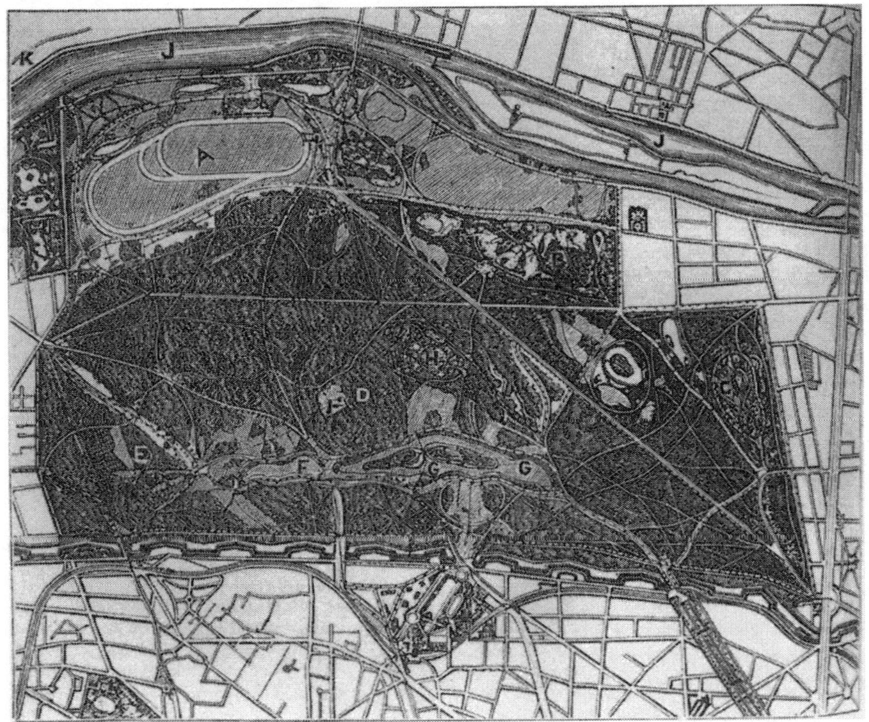

"MAP OF THE BOIS DE BOULOGNE"
A, Hippodrome; B, Bagatelle; C, Zoological Garden; D, Military Magazine; E. Nursery;
F, Upper Lake; G, Lower Lake; H, Pré Catalan; II, Avenue Bois de Boulogne; JJ, the
Seine; K, Palace and Park of St. Cloud.

the operations of improvement are concerned, little changed and as uninteresting as a wood might be. The approach to the improved ground from the
central parts of the town is first through the Champs Élysées, afterward for a
distance of 1⅛ m. by the new avenue Bois de Boulogne (formerly de l'Impératrice).[4] This consists of a driveway 60 ft. wide, a bridle road on one side of it
40 ft. wide, and a walk opposite of the same width, with borders of lawn-like
ground on each side, the whole space being 300 ft. in width. In the original
design this avenue was expected to become the fashionable promenade of
Paris; but, probably because it was not in the outset sufficiently well shaded,
fashion pushed further out to the road on the south bank of a new lake in the
wood 1⅔ m. in length, where no tolerable provision had been made for it.
To meet the demand, the original drive on the lake was widened to 45 ft.,
and a pad or bridle path introduced by its side, 40 ft. wide. Under ordinary
circumstances the greater part of the visitors to the wood concentrate on these

317

roads and the adjoining walk. There were in the whole wood of Boulogne before 1870, when a considerable space both of the old and new planting was cleared in preparation for the defence of Paris against the Germans, 1,009 acres of wooded land, 674 of unshaded turf, 75 of water surface, and 286 of drives, rides, and walks (not including the race track). The race ground of Longchamps, which is a part of the property, contains 195 acres, the ground leased to the acclimation society for a zoölogical garden, 50 acres, and the leased amusement garden, the Pré Catalan, in the midst of the wood, to which a charge for admission is made, 21 acres. There are 36 m. of public drive (including the old straight forest and departmental highways), 7 m. of ride, and 15 m. of walk. The larger part of the pleasure drives are 25 to 36 ft. broad, the widest 48 ft.; the rides 12 to 17 ft.; the walks 8 to 12 ft. The wood of Vincennes, similar in other respects to that of Boulogne, contained an ancient castle which was the centre of a great military establishment, and a large plain in the midst of the wood, used as a training ground. This has been maintained, but in other respects the design for improvement has been similar to that for the wood of Boulogne, the principal difference being that the accommodations and attractions for foot visitors at Vincennes are relatively more important. The extent of the ground is 2,225 acres, of which about half is wooded. There is a race course on the plain, and a lake of 60 acres. The public ways, not including the race track, take up 183 acres. There are no large parks within the fortified lines of Paris, but several beautiful place parks and gardens. (See Paris.) A detailed account of them and of their admirable method of administration may be found in Robinson's "Parks, Promenades, and Gardens of Paris" (London, 1869),[5] and one still more complete in *Les promenades de Paris*, by M. Alphonse, the chief designer of the recent improvements.[6] The extent of the public recreation grounds within the fortified lines of the city is about 250 acres. The area of suburban grounds commonly resorted to for recreation and maintained at public expense, not including those too far away for an afternoon excursion, may be estimated at 20,000 acres. The extent of pleasure drive maintained by the municipal government is 87 m., being about 3 m. of roadway to each square mile of the city, or, counting the parkways (boulevards) shaded and with asphalt driveways, over 7 m. to the square mile. New York has less than a quarter of a mile to the square mile.

The parks and open spaces of London are very numerous, and their total extent is larger perhaps than that of those belonging to any other metropolis of the first magnitude. They are very various in area, ranging from one to several hundred acres. It has been long recognized that London owes a great deal of its physical and political health to its parks and open spaces. All the year round they act as great lungs to the mighty city, while in summer and even to a considerable extent in winter they are the Sunday resort of the weary workers. The open spaces of London are not confined to any quarter. The East End has Victoria park (300 acres); Finsbury park (115 acres), too new to

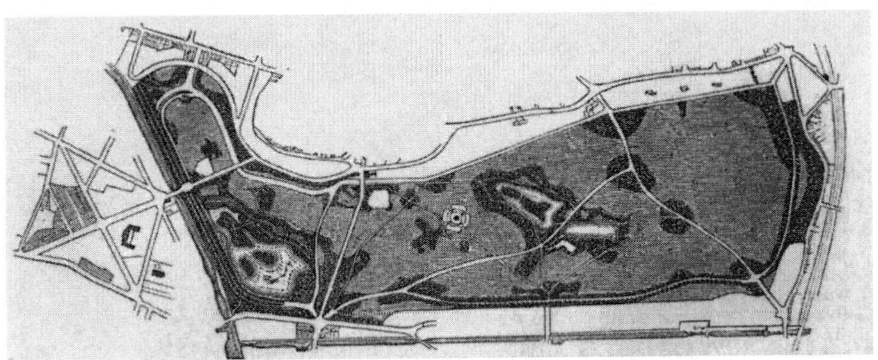

"Map of Victoria Park"

be so pleasant to the eye, but still rapidly becoming what it is intended to be; and the half dozen "downs," "fields," and "commons" that go under the general name of Hackney Downs (50 acres). It has also, lying just outside its boundaries, the two forests of Epping and Hainault, and several green breadths that may be called everybody's and yet no man's land. South London has some of the finest of the parks and open spaces. To the southeast lie Woolwich common, Greenwich park (174 acres), and Greenwich common, and nearer at hand Lewisham common, Peckham Rye, and Southwark park (63 acres). Directly south lie Camberwell (55 acres) and various little remnants of ancient greens and commons, while the grounds of the Crystal palace may almost be said to answer as a park for the wide districts of Sydenham, Norwood, and Penge. Southwest lie Clapham common (10 acres), Wandsworth common (302), and Wimbledon common (628). Tooting Beck and Tooting Graveney commons and Battersea park (230 acres) also belong to this district. In the north lie Hampstead heath (240 acres), the Greenlanes, the grounds of Alexandra park (192), and Primrose hill. In the west are found Hyde park (about 400 acres), the Green park, St. James's park, Regent's park (450), Kensington gardens (290), and several small "greens," such as Shepherd's Bush. All these parks, commons, and open spaces are within the actual metropolitan district. Taking in a little wider radius, the heaths, downs, parks, and greens within easy reach of London become almost innumerable. First, beginning at the southeast and sweeping round by the south, west, north, and east, we find Chiselhurst common; a little southwest of this Hayes common, a great resort of cockneys in summer, where any day a score of pleasure vans may be seen; a little further to the west Addington common, also much frequented; still further west Mitcham common and Banstead downs, not to speak of those of Epsom, famous for horse races, or of the score of small spaces kept "open" by the strong hand of the law and the general consent of the people. Approaching the Thames by a northwest course, we next meet with Richmond park (2,253 acres) the largest park near London except that

319

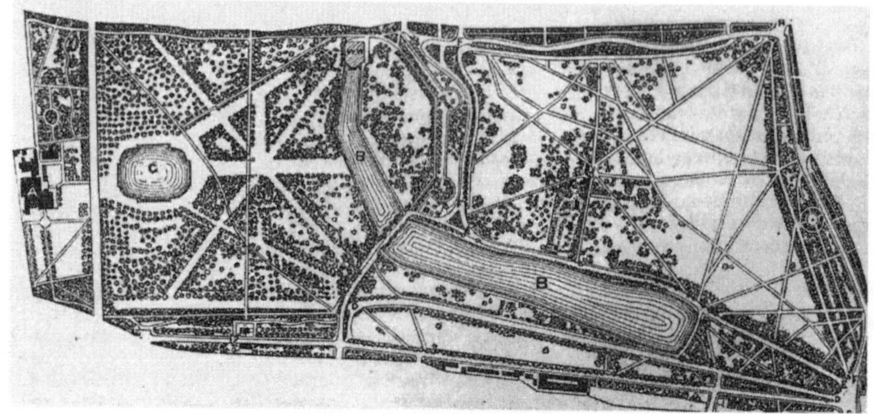

"MAP OF HYDE PARK AND KENSINGTON GARDENS"
A, Kensington Palace; BB, the Serpentine; C, Round Pond; DD, Rotten Row; EE, the Ladies' Mile; FFF, the Ring; G, Hyde Park Corner; H, Marble Arch; I, Prince Consort's Memorial.

at Windsor (3,800), Hampton Court park and Bushy parks (1,842), and Kew park and gardens (684), the finest botanic garden in England. Crossing the river, we come next upon Ealing and Acton greens (leaving Hounslow heath on the left as out of our radius), Wormwood Scrubs, and numerous little greens and commons. North of Hampstead and Alexandra park the open spaces are fewer and smaller, and owing to a more scattered population less required. Northeast lie Epping and Hainault forests, mentioned before, each of them very large and full of natural beauty. Hyde park, the most noted of the public grounds of London, takes its name from the ancient manor of Hyde, which at one time belonged to the abbey of Westminster, became public property in 1535, was sold by order of parliament in 1652, and again recovered to the crown on the restoration in 1660. It was originally of the usual character of English private parks, a broad piece of quiet pasture ground, with numerous fine great trees scattered over it singly and in groups and masses. In 1730–'33 a body of water was introduced (the Serpentine), but with no care to give it a natural or even a graceful outline. Roads have also been formed in the park from time to time, less with a view to public pleasure driving than for convenient passages. What is called the Rotten Row (a corruption of the French *route du roi*) was originally the passage for the king and his cavalcade between Westminster and his palace of Kensington; it is a mile long and 90 ft. wide, has a surface of loose fine gravel, and is used by the public only on horseback; it is separated from the Serpentine and "ladies' mile" (45 ft. wide), the fashionable drive of London, by a walk and strip of turf of variable width. It divides and overpowers what might otherwise be a pleasing landscape expanse, and no attempt has been made to mitigate the harshness of the invasion. Parts of Hyde park have lately been made into gardens, and in these during parts of the summer there is a very brilliant display of flowers, "specimens," and subtropical plants; but the old trees are disappearing more rapidly than the young ones are brought forward; the turf is not well kept, and to avoid its destruction in many parts iron hurdles are placed along the walks. It is thus gradually losing its beauty as a park, for which its streaks of fine gardening here and there offer no compensation. The crystal palace was erected in Hyde park in 1851, and on the site now stands the Albert memorial, completed in 1872. (See LONDON.) Regent's park, formerly part of old Marylebone park, was laid out in 1812. There is a drive of nearly two miles around it, and within are the botanic and zoological gardens, and a lake. Victoria park in E. London was opened to the public in 1845. A fine drinking fountain, 60 ft. high and costing £5,000, given by Lady Burdette-Coutts, was erected in it in 1862. St. James's park was formed and walled in by Henry VIII., was much improved under Charles II., and was arranged as it now appears chiefly under George IV. The public property in many of the larger commons of London is so complicated by ancient manorial and local rights that its extent cannot be accurately stated. The aggregate area of the several public and crown parks that have been named, together with so much of the commons lying within the metropolitan district as is under the board of works, is about 13,000 acres. There is also in the squares and gardens (place parks), most of which have been established by landlords and are private property but of great public advantage, about 1,200 acres.

Liverpool and its suburb Birkenhead have six parks, five of which are recent acquisitions and yet incompletely prepared for public use. The largest, Sefton park, contains 387 acres. Birkenhead park contains 120 acres, besides the leased villa grounds (60 acres) by which it is surrounded. It was undertaken as a land speculation, and though too small in scale and too garden-like for the general popular use of a large community, is very pleasing, and is one of the most instructive to study in Europe, having been laid out and the trees planted under the direction of the late Sir Joseph Paxton, over 30 years ago.[7] The corporation of Leeds has lately purchased a noble park of 800 acres, containing a fine stream of water and a lake, formed by the previous owner, of 33 acres. Its scenery is diversified, and it commands fine distant rural views. These advantages and its exemption from injury by factory smoke compensate for the necessity the citizens will be under of reaching it by rail, its distance from the town being 4 m. Birmingham, Manchester, Bradford, and other manufacturing towns of England have acquired parks by subscriptions of citizens or by joint-stock companies. At Halifax a park has been formed and given to the town by a benevolent citizen. Derby is provided in the same way with an arboretum. The city of Lincoln is forming an arboretum on land purchased for this purpose. Most of the small towns of England have some place of recreation, as for instance the old city walls and the river banks above the town at Chester, the common and the old castle grounds at Hereford,

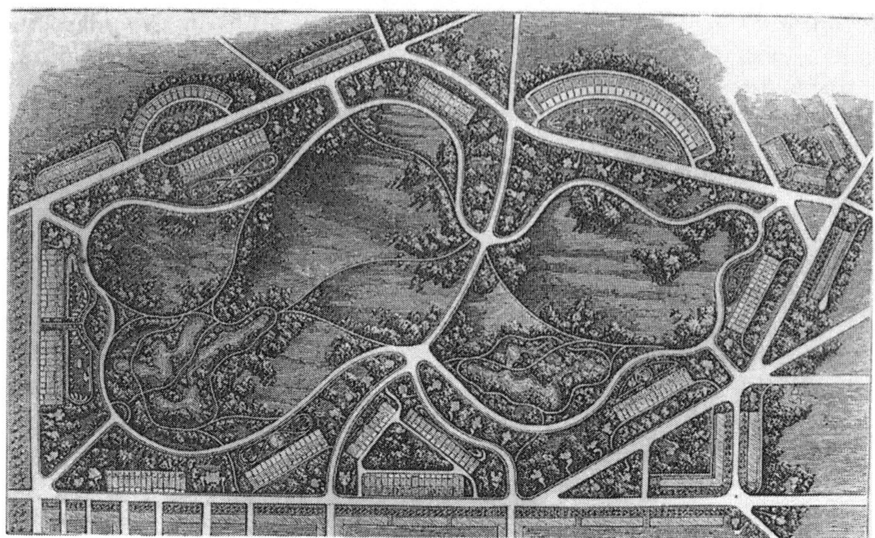

"Map of Birkenhead Park and adjoining Villa Sites"

and the cathedral greens at Salisbury and Winchester.[8] These consist in each case either of a long broad walk pleasantly bordered and leading to fine views, or a few acres of smooth turf with shaded borders. Most villages in England have a private park near them, which people are allowed to use. When this is not the case, even a hamlet almost invariably has at least a bit of cricket ground or common, where, on benches under a patriarchal oak or elm, the old people meet to gossip and watch the sports of the vigorous youth. Phœnix park at Dublin (1,752 acres) is a fine upland meadow fringed and dotted with trees, but badly laid out and badly kept, being much larger than the town requires or can afford to take suitable care of.

The old towns of the continent have generally provided themselves with recreation grounds by outgrowing their ancient borders of wall and moat and glacis, razing the wall, filling part of the moat, and so, with more or less skilful management of the materials, making the groundwork of a garden in the natural style. This is done admirably at Frankfort, Leipsic, and Vienna. Elsewhere simple broad walks bordered with trees have been laid out upon the levelled ramparts. The principal promenade of Vienna is the Prater, the chief feature of which is a straight carriage road over a mile long, with a walk on one side and a riding pad on the other. It contains near the town a great number of coffee houses and playhouses; but as it is 5 m. long, considerable portions are thoroughly secluded and rural. Before the recent improvements of the Bois de Boulogne, it was the most frequented large recreation ground in the world. There are numerous other public grounds at Vienna, both urban and suburban. The English garden at Munich was laid out under the direction of Count Rumford by the baron von Skell. It has serious defects, but its scenery in the English style has been considered more agreeable than that of any other public park on the continent; it is about 4 m. long and half a mile wide. The Thiergarten at Berlin contains over 200 acres of perfectly flat land, chiefly a close wood, laid out in straight roads, walks, and riding pads; its scenery is uninteresting. The Prussian royal gardens of Sans Souci, Charlottenburg, and Heiligensee are all extensive grounds, the two former in mixed, the latter in natural style. Public gardens worthy of a traveller's attention exist at Cologne, Dresden, Düsseldorf, Stuttgart, Hanover, Brunswick, Baden, Cassel, Darmstadt, Gotha, Weimar, Wörlitz, Schwetzingen, Teplitz,[9] Prague, and Hamburg. Coffee or beer houses are important adjuncts of German public gardens. The refreshments furnished are plain and wholesome, and the prices moderate. Many families habitually resort to these for their evening meal, especially when, as is usually the case, there is the additional attraction of excellent music furnished by the government. The gardens of Antwerp, the Hague, and Warsaw, and the "city grove" of Pesth, are also remarkable. The famous summer gardens of St. Petersburg are not extensive, being but half a mile long by a quarter of a mile wide, and formal in style. They contain fine trees, are rich in statuary (boxed up in winter), and are the most carefully kept public gardens in the world, as shown in the exceeding freshness and vigor of the plants and flowers and in the deep vivid green of the turf. The more fashionable promenade of St. Petersburg is in the gardens of Katharinenhof, where on the first of May an annual procession of private carriages of almost endless length is headed by that of the emperor. A remarkable ground is that of Tzarskoye Selo, in which is the residence of the imperial family, about two hours from St. Petersburg. Besides the palace, it contains temples, banqueting houses, and theatres, a complete village in the Chinese style, a Turkish mosque, a hermitage, and numerous monuments of military and other achievements. But beyond this museum of incongruous objects there is a part in which there is natural and very beautiful scenery both open and wooded, and much of it is simple. The keeping of the ground employs 600 men. Stockholm has a great variety of delightful waterside rural walks; but the chief object of pride with its people is the Djurgard or deer park, which is a large tract of undulating ground about 3 m. in circumference, containing grand masses of rock and some fine old trees. The Haga park, also at Stockholm, is picturesque, and has the peculiarity of natural water communications between its different parts and the city, so that it is much visited in boats. The environs of Copenhagen contain many grounds of public resort, but the notable promenade of the city is the royal deer park (*Dyrhave*). In all the Italian cities, the chief public rural resorts are gardens attached to the villas of ancient noble families. The Cascine of Florence is an old pasture of the dairy of the former grand dukes on the banks of the Arno, passing through which are broad straight carriage drives. It contains little that is attractive, but commands delicious views. At a space whence several roads radiate, a band of music usually performs at intervals during the promenade hours. The municipality is now preparing promenades and recreation grounds which promise to be of remarkable interest. The fashionable promenade of Rome has been on the Pincian hill, which has few attractions except in its magnificent distant views. Since Rome was made the capital of the new kingdom of Italy, large public grounds in other quarters have been projected and in great part formed by the municipality. At Naples the fashionable promenade is the Riviera di Chiaja, a public street. It is divided into a ride, a drive, and a walk, and is nearly a mile in length, with a breadth of 200 ft. A part of it is separated from the shore of the bay of Naples by the villa Reale, planted in the garden style. Most towns of Spanish or Portuguese origin are provided with a promenade of formal avenues, to which, generally at dusk, custom brings the ladies in open carriages and the gentlemen on foot or on horseback.

Until some years after the middle of the present century no city in North America had begun to make provision for a park. To a certain extent cemeteries were made to serve the purpose. In 1849 Mr. A. J. Downing began in the "Horticulturist" a series of papers which were widely copied and did much to create a demand on this subject. At length a large tract of land was provided in New York, upon which in 1858 the preparation of the present Central park was begun. The topography of the ground was in all important respects the reverse of that which would have been chosen with an intelligent understanding of the desiderata of a park. The difficulties presented could only have been tolerably overcome by an enormous outlay. The popularity of the parts of the park first prepared, however, was so great that the necessary means for improvements on a large scale were readily granted. The magnitude of the operations (nearly 4,000 men being at one time employed on the works), the rapidity of the changes wrought, and the novelty of the scenes presented, soon gave the enterprise great celebrity; and the rapid rise in the taxable value of the land near it more than met the interest on its cost. An efficient management of its public use was maintained, and though frequented by great crowds of people it was found, contrary to general expectation, that a degree of good order and of social amenity prevailed, nowhere surpassed and rarely equalled in the public places of Europe. Philadelphia, Brooklyn, Albany, Providence, Baltimore, Buffalo, Chicago, St. Louis, Cincinnati, Montreal, and San Francisco have since each acquired land for one or more parks of considerable extent, the average being over 500 acres. As in the case of New York, the selection of ground has often been made more with reference to other considerations than to that of fitness for the intended use. Some are as yet only held for future use, while in others provisions essentially temporary, and which will be in the way of substantial improvement, are made; none are so far complete and well fitted as fairly to illustrate the ends which a park should be designed to serve.

The Central park of New York is 2½ miles long and half a mile wide,

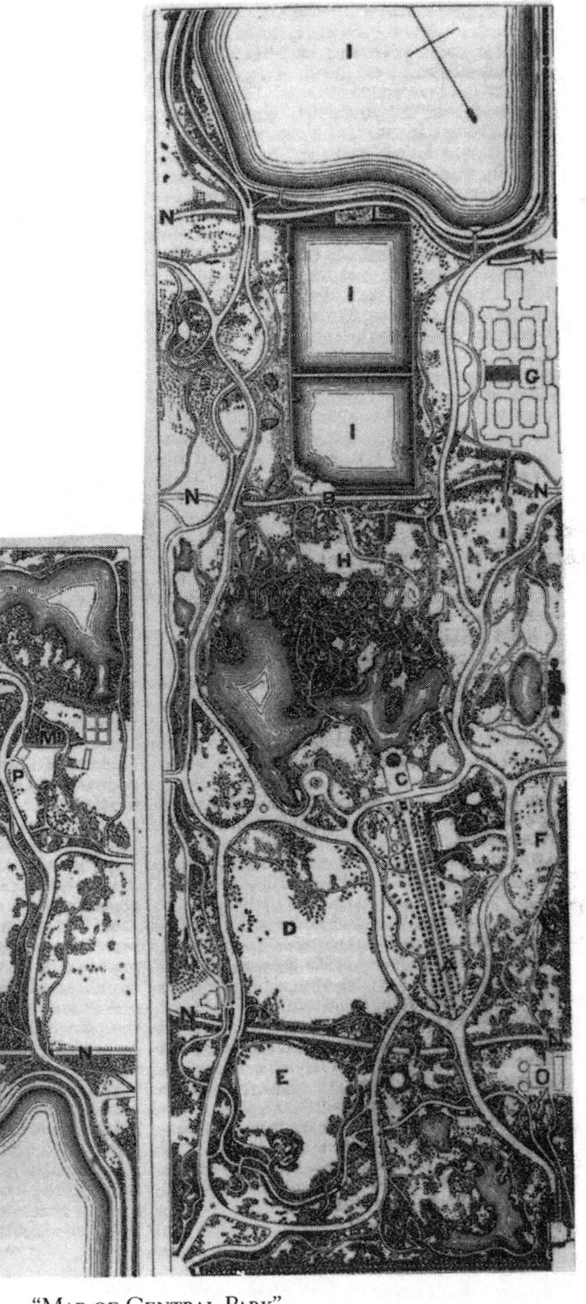

"Map of Central Park"

A, the Mall; B, Belvedere; C, Terrace; D, Green; E, Ball Ground; F, East Green; G, site
for Art Museum; H, Ramble; III, Reservoirs of City Water Works; KK, the Meadows;
L, Harlem Heights; M, Mount St. Vincent; NN, Subways for street traffic; O, temporary
Museum and Offices; P, temporary Museum, Refectory, and Offices.

325

but this space is practically divided by the reservoirs of the city water works, which are elevated above its general level and occupy 142 acres. Deducting besides this certain other spaces occupied for special public purposes, the area of the park proper is 683 acres. Of this, 55 acres is meadow-like ground, 54 in smaller glades of turf, 400 of rocky and wooded surface, 43 in six pieces of water, the largest being of 20 acres, 15 in riding ways, 52 in carriage ways, and 39 in walks. There are 5½ m. of rides, 9½ m. of drives, and 28 m. of walks. Omitting a few by-roads, the average breadth of the drives is 50 ft., and of the walks 13 ft. There are 8 bridges (over water) and 38 tunnels and subway arches, 15 of which are concealed from view by plantations carried over them, and all of which are expedients for reconciling within narrow limits the large amount of foot, horse, and wheel room required with sylvan and pastoral landscapes. On the east side, near the middle of the parallelogram containing the park and reservoirs, ground is reserved for a great museum of art; and beyond its boundary on the west side another plot is held for a museum of natural history. The first block of each is now building. There are carriage and foot entrances at the two southern corners, and between them on the south end, at the termini of street railroads, there are two foot entrances; and 14 other entrances are in use or provided for. From the S.E. or Fifth avenue approach, which is most used, the visitor is led by a nearly direct course to a slightly elevated point in the interior of the park, northwardly from which, at great cost in reducing the original rocky knolls, broad green surfaces have been prepared (D, E on the map), and views of a tranquil landscape character obtained of considerable extent. At the most distant visible point a small tower of gray stone (B) has been built to draw the eye, and the perspective effect is aided by the character and disposition of the foliage, and especially by an avenue of elms (A) leading toward it. At the end of this avenue, termed the mall, the ground falls rapidly to the arm of a lake, and here a structure called the terrace (C) has been introduced, which, though mainly below the general plane of the landscape and unobtrusive, supplies a considerable shelter and place of reunion. It is designed to be richly decorated with sculptured works. On one side of it is the concert ground of the park, on the other a fountain surmounted by a bronze typifying the angel of Bethesda. The concert ground is overlooked by a shaded gallery called the Pergola, back of which is a small house of refreshment in cottage style. On the opposite side of the water is a rocky and wooded slope, threaded by numerous paths, called the Ramble (F). These with the green (D), play ground reserved for the scholars of the public schools, two irregular bodies of water, and several rocky knolls (on one of which is the Kinderberg, a place for little children), form the chief features of the south park. Those of the north are a central meadow (K) divided by a rocky spur, the high wooded ground beyond it (L), with a steep rocky face on the north, and an intermediate glen with a chain of waters. The number of visits to the park sometimes exceeds 100,000 in a day, and is about 10,000,000 a year.

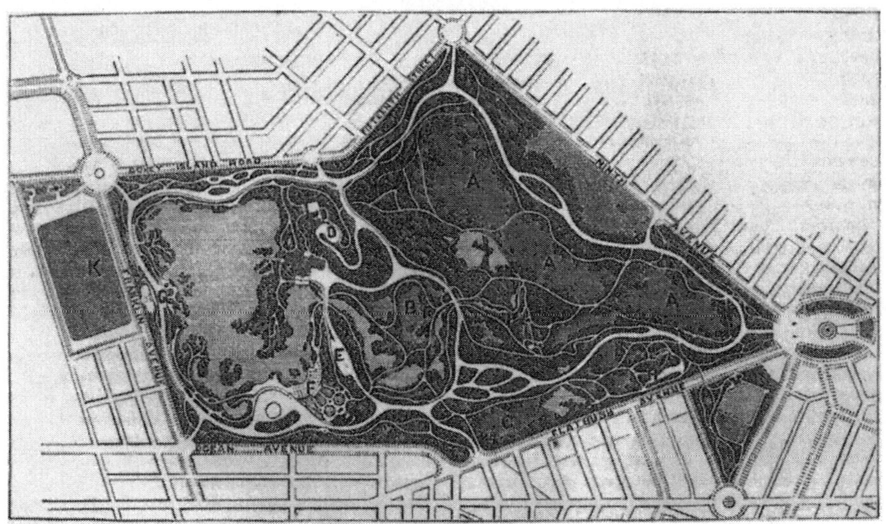

"MAP OF PROSPECT PARK"
AAA, the Long Meadow; B, the Neter Mead; C, Deer Park; D, Lookout Hill; E, Breeze
Hill; F, Concert Grove; G, Promenade; H, Children's Play Ground; I, Picnic Ground;
K, Parade Ground.

Prospect park of Brooklyn, N.Y., contains, with the adjoining parade
ground, 550 acres. There is included in it a considerable amount of old wood,
and for this reason, and because of the better soil, climate, and early horticultural management, it has a finer rural and more mature character than the
New York park, though its construction was begun eight years later. It has
about 6 m. of drives, 4 m. of ride, and 20 m. of walks. Its artificial water covers
a space of 50 acres, and is supplied from a well by a steam pump. It commands a fine view over the ocean. (See BROOKLYN.) There are 33 smaller
public grounds in New York and Brooklyn, all but three of which are improved and in use, the total pleasure ground space of the two cities being
1,600 acres.

Fairmount park of Philadelphia is a body of land 2,740 acres in extent, having a great variety of surface, all of it of considerable natural beauty.
The heights command fine distant prospects; it bears many noble trees, and
at the part most remote from the city there is a glen through which dashes a
charmingly picturesque stream. It is divided by the Schuylkill river and
crossed by a common highway and in two directions by railroads, the cuttings
and embankments of which unfortunately completely break the naturally
most quiet scenes. These with other structures, some of which have been
recently erected and are designed to be permanent, greatly disturb its natural
beauty.[10] The object of the city in acquiring the ground was to control it
against such occupations as would peril its water supply, and its permanent

327

disposition is not fully determined. Appropriations have been already made for two large reservoirs, for pumping works, and for a zoölogical garden. No measure has yet been taken looking to the permanent preservation or special preparation of any considerable part distinctly as a park; but drives, rides, and walks have been formed, mainly temporary, by which all parts are traversed or laid open to view. Several houses which were originally private villas are used as refectories; the river is well adapted to pleasure boating; the spaces are so large that few restrictions on the movements of visitors are necessary; and in spite of the defects to which allusion has been made, the ground offers better and larger opportunities for popular rural recreation than are possessed in a single property by any other city in the world. Druid Hill park in Baltimore, of 600 acres, is a very beautiful old wood, acquired by the city in 1860, the original private improvements of which have been enlarged and extended for public use. Buffalo is forming the most complete system of recreation grounds of any city in the United States. It will consist of an inland suburban park of 300 acres, of very quiet rural character, with an ample approach from the centre of the city, and parkways 200 ft. wide extending from it in opposite directions, one to a promenade overlooking Lake Erie, the other to a parade ground and a garden on the opposite side of the town. There is a fine natural growth of trees in the main park, a lake of 46 acres has been formed, and several miles of fair macadamized roads and walks constructed, together with various suitable buildings. The work was begun in 1871, and has been advanced very steadily and economically. The aggregate area of ground occupied, including the parkways, is 530 acres. Chicago is situated in a region most unfavorable to parks, and should she ever have any that are deserving the name, it will be because of a persistent wisdom of administration and a scientific skill as well as art in the constant management of those which she is setting about, such as has been nowhere else applied to a similar purpose. The grounds appropriated are flat, poor in soil, and devoid of desirable natural growth, or, except two which look upon Lake Michigan, of any natural features of interest. In one it is proposed to transform a series of marshes partly overflowed by high water of the lake into lagoons, the quiet water surface of which is designed to take the place ordinarily given to lawns in sylvan landscapes; this, if the idea is consistently carried out, will be unique and interesting.[11] The Chicago park system contains nearly 1,900 acres of land in six parks of an average extent of 250 acres each, three in one chain, and all with one exception connected by parkways. About 20 m. of parkway, from 200 to 250 ft. wide, has been laid out (in the city and suburbs), nearly half of which is already provided with good macadamized or concrete roads and well planted. St. Louis now controls 2,100 acres of lands held for recreation grounds, of which about 100 are in place parks, the greater part improved and in use, and the remainder suitable for parks proper, the smallest field being of 180 acres and the largest of 1,350. Of the latter, one only, Tower Grove park, containing 277 acres, is yet at all adapted to use. A parkway 120 ft. wide and 12 m. long is under construction. Cincinnati has a little over 400 acres of public recreation ground, 207 being in Eden park, which lies on undulating ground commanding fine distant views, and 168 in Burnett wood, which has a similar surface with a fine growth of indigenous trees. There will be about 3 m. of pleasure road in each. Cincinnati possesses in Spring Grove cemetery the best example in the world, probably, of landscape gardening applied to a burial place;[12] and her parks are likely to be improved with the same taste and skill. San Francisco holds 1,100 acres of land for recreation grounds, of which over 1,000 acres is in one body, called the Golden Gate park. This borders on the ocean, and is very bleak and partly covered with drift sand; no trees grow upon it except in an extremely dwarfed and distorted form, and turf can only be maintained by profuse artificial watering; but wherever shelter, fertility, and sufficient root moisture can be secured, a low, southern, almost subtropical vegetation may be maintained throughout the year, of striking luxuriance and beauty. Experiments in arresting the sand and forming a screen of foliage on the shore have been made with promising success. If steadily, boldly, and generously pursued, with a cautious humoring of the design to the unique natural conditions, and skilful adaptation of available means, a pleasure ground not at all park-like, but strikingly original and highly attractive, may be expected. Nearly 7 m. of carriage road has already been formed on the ground, and it is much used. A parkway stretching 3 m. along the shore is provided for, the reservation for it ranging from 200 to 400 ft. in breadth.

For other information concerning the parks mentioned above, see the articles on the cities where they are situated; and for accounts of the so-called national parks see WYOMING (territory), and YOSEMITE.

The original was published in George Ripley and Charles A. Dana, editors, *The American Cyclopaedia: A Popular Dictionary of General Knowledge*, 16 volumes (New York, 1873–76), volume 12 (1875), pages 95–108. This article is an illustrated and much revised version of "Park" that was published in the *American Cyclopaedia* in 1861 and included in the *Papers of Frederick Law Olmsted*, volume 3, pages 346–60.

1. Hippolyte Adolphe Taine (1828–1893), French philosopher, literary historian, and art critic. This quotation comes from book 2, chapter 4 of *A Tour Through the Pyrenees* (*EB*, Hippolyte Adolphe Taine, *A Tour Through the Pyrenees*, trans. J. Safford Fiske [New York, 1874], pp. 162–64).
2. Joseph Mallord William Turner (1775–1851), English landscape artist (*DNB*).
3. Possibly a reference to the public drive laid out above 155th Street in Upper Manhattan. The drive extended northerly along the Harlem River side of Manhattan until Inwood Street where it turned to the northwest, crossed Manhattan to the Hudson River and then proceeded south, intersecting with Eleventh Avenue (New York [State], *Laws of the State of New York, Passed at the Eighty-Eighth Session of the Legislature . . .* [Albany, N.Y., 1865], chap. 565).
4. The Avenue Bois de Boulogne, renamed Avenue Foch.

5. William Robinson wrote several books including the volume Olmsted cites here, *The Wild Garden* (1870), *Alpine Flowers for English Gardens* (1870), and *The English Flower Garden* (1883) (DNB).
6. Jean-Charles-Adolphe Alphand (1817–1891), French civil engineer, who was responsible for the improvements of the Parisian public parks, including the Bois de Boulogne, in the 1850s. Alphand published *Les Promenades de Paris* in installments between 1867 and 1873 (*Papers of FLO*, 3: 241; ibid., 6: 470).
7. Sir Joseph Paxton designed Birkenhead Park in the 1840s (see FLO, "The People's Park at Birkenhead, near Liverpool," [May 1851], and n. 12, above).
8. Olmsted visited and described these four sites in detail in *Walks and Talks of an American Farmer in England* (*Walks and Talks*, 1: 111–18, and 2: 67, 136–38, 150).
9. In Olmsted's day Teplitz was in Bohemia and part of the Austrian Empire. Now called Teplice, it is in the present-day Czech Republic (*EB*).
10. In December 1867 Olmsted and Calvert Vaux had prepared a report outlining desirable boundaries for Fairmount Park. The two men were appointed "advising and consulting Landscape Gardeners and Architects" to the Fairmount Park commissioners in 1868, and in 1871 they prepared a plan for the old park on the east side of the Schuylkill River below Girard Avenue. They had expectations of being engaged to design the larger section on the west side of the river, but the commissioners took no action on their proposals. Instead, the commissioners turned in 1873 to the park's engineer, John C. Cresson, and the architect/engineer Herman J. Schwarzmann to plan 450 acres of the west park for the Centennial Exhibition of 1876. The "glen through which dashes a charmingly picturesque stream" was Wissahickon Valley and Wissahickon Creek. The "recently erected" structures were buildings designed to house the Centennial Exhibition (OVC to the Chairman of the Committee on Plans of the Park Commission of Philadelphia, Dec. 4, 1867 [*Papers of FLO*, 6: 231–45]; FLO to George E. Waring, March 1871; John W. Field to George E. Waring, March 17, 1871; Theo Cuyler to Olmsted, Vaux & Co., Feb. 4, 1870, B15: #121, OAR/LC; FLO to Theo Cuyler, Oct. 28, 1872; J. S. Ingram, *The Centennial Exposition* . . . [Philadelphia, 1876], pp. 109–14).
11. A reference to Lincoln and Jackson parks in Chicago. Jackson Park was part of the South Park plan developed by Olmsted and Vaux in 1871. They proposed to create the lagoon effect described here in Jackson Park (see OVC, "Report Accompanying Plan for Laying Out the South Park," March 1871, above).
12. Olmsted greatly admired Spring Grove Cemetery and Adolph Strauch, the man responsible for improving the cemetery grounds beginning in the 1850s (see Olmsted, Olmsted, and Eliot to Joseph Thomas Carew, Jan. 30, 1894, nn. 16, 17, 19, and 20, below).

A Consideration of the Justifying Value
of a Public Park.

January 28, 1881,

Our large town parks are public trusts, so loosely defined as to fix no clear limits to the use which may be legitimately or honorably made of the lands, materials, funds, or official "influence," which belong to them. The most essential duty under them may be neglected without wreck of character or sense of shame. To say as to any point in question of their management "it is a matter of taste," generally means that every trustee is as to that point a law unto himself. This paper, which touches the question of a possible basis of stricter accountability, has been printed in the Journal of the American Social Science Association,[1] but with such errors, owing to a miscarriage of proofs, that I wish to offer corrected copies to those having a special interest in the topic discussed. The feeling which has lately been evinced against plans urged by able and worthy men for subverting the most important features of the Central Park of New York by buildings, roads, walks, and decorative garden-work suitable to a world's fair ground,[2] and a growing dislike shown elsewhere to the introduction of objects and methods of decoration in public grounds thought to be incongruous with their character, may be hoped to indicate a ripening of public opinion favorable to the ends of the paper.

A bill has just been introduced in the Legislature of New York by Senator Astor, entitled "An Act to Define and Limit the Uses of Public Parks," which declares that all properties so classed under the laws of the State, when exceeding 100 acres in extent, "are intended and shall be appropriated for the recreation of the people by means of their rural, sylvan, and natural scenery and character," that they must be used and managed in accordance with this definition and that "no ground in them shall be appropriated or used in such a manner as to lessen their value and advantages for such recreation."[3]

A striking illustration of the equivocal use which prevails of the word park and of the harm liable to result from it, has recently occurred. Lord Dufferin, deploring the destruction of the appropriate scenery of Niagara Falls, and seeking means to arrest it and restore a natural aspect to the shores, suggested a scheme for what he, unfortunately, though with strict propriety, termed an international park.[4] It is a serious obstacle to the purpose which he had in view, that under this term few seem to suppose that anything can be intended which does not involve costly gardening "decoration" which would be simply savage.

F.L.O.

The Justifying Value of a Public Park.

After the Paper now to be read had been mainly prepared I was advised of a wish that it might lead on to a discussion of the subject of parks at low cost for small towns. The topic which I had adopted being a more comprehensive one, I will introduce it by a few observations, showing how the question of cost for parks of any class, for towns large or small, cannot well be discussed independently of it.

The cost of a park depends on two considerations back of economy of management; back, also, of a plan as commonly understood: the first is the use intended to be made of it, or the general aims of the undertaking; the second, the degree in which the site to be improved is adapted to these aims. As to the first, it is liable to be overlooked that the aims of a park may be so low that the result will be of less value than no park at all. This has been proved over and over again. As to adaptation of site, it is also liable to be forgotten that a hundred acres of land in one situation may be turned, at a given cost, into a more useful park than two hundred in another; and that two hundred acres of land, of one sort, may be prepared for a given use, of a given population, at less cost than one hundred of another sort.

These considerations being recognized, the special perplexity of park business will be understood to lie in the fact that, whatever determinations as to use you set out with, whatever aims control your choice of site and your plan of improvements; whatever rules for economy you fix upon, you have no assurance in law, custom or public common sense, that they will not soon be thrown overboard. This, again, being understood, it will not be difficult to realize that the great danger to be guarded against in setting about a park, is one which is commonly disguised under the phrase, "practical business tact," or "practical common-sense," meaning a habit of mind, cultivated in commercial life, of judging values by the market estimate. What answers to the market estimate, in park values, is commonly a guess as to what the public will think of the results of a proposed operation at a time when these results, although the operation shall be apparently complete, are yet immature, provisional and tentative; and, as in this condition, they will be regarded from the point of view, not of mental relaxation, but of commercial competition. Under these circumstances, most important elements of value are liable to be wholly disregarded.

For example, in any well-designed park-work, the character of each of several parts is largely determined with a motive (over and above any that appears in the work as seen by itself) of enhancing the value of all other parts, and of gaining enhancement of value by the character to be given all other parts. Again, much the larger share of the value to be ultimately earned by the park, depends on the gradual merging together of elements of value originally detached, and which, as seen in this detached condition (as they must be for years after work has apparently ceased with reference to them), show nothing, and to most minds, suggest nothing of the value which they potentially possess.

These, I think, are two plain reasons, but as it happens to apply more directly to my main purpose, I should like to refer also to another embarrassment of the ordinary pleasure-seeker's judgment, which is not so plain. I may, indeed, be excused for doubting if, in this scientific audience, there are many who suspect the degree in which considerations of stability and endurance enter into any sound estimate of the value of park-work, or who realize in what manner these elements of value may be represented in objects which, to the mind seeking relaxation, exhibit qualities of an entirely different character; objects of little more apparent stability than the maize in the farmer's field, which next month is to be cleared of it, and ploughed over for a spring sowing of oats. So few are prepared to accept what is sound in this respect and it has so much to do with the question, what it is worthwhile for a small but promising town to undertake in a park, and of what is low cost with reference to it, that I beg to offer a little evidence bearing on the point.

It is more than two hundred years since Mr. Pepys wrote of going in his new coach to the King's Park, and of the "innumerable appearance of gallants," which he there found, sauntering among the trees.[5] Of those trees it is possible that some have not yet succumbed to the acrid atmosphere of London. It is certain that many held their own long enough, and were enough valued, to preserve the general outlines and surface of the park against all suggestions of change, and thus indirectly to influence the leading lines of miles of streets, and establish the position of later park plantings, of which we now have the result. What had then been done, determines where today shade shall be found, where prospects screened or opened, where millions of men and women are yet to direct their steps. Mr. Pepys's road is still in use, and not many years ago it was plainly to be seen where its grade was affected, its breadth contracted, and its course deflected, out of respect to a single tree which he probably saw as a sapling, the trunk and roots of which had grown into it. Of most of the bridges, conduits, markets, and landing-places of London of that period, only curious fragments remain. The King's Park was never as much, or as well used as it is at present, and for the purposes of its most important use, has few substantial advantages or disadvantages not to be traced to determinations formed long, long ago; when London, in comparison with its present state, was a very small town.

In Paris, the series of groves and greens which lie between the ruins of the Tuileries and the long-since leveled gate toward the Woods of Boulogne had its beginning as far back, at least, as the sixteenth century, when, as we now reckon, Paris, also, was a small town; and no motive has had more weight in determining the plan of the great town growing from it, than that of sparing and providing for the extension and uninterrupted use of these grounds.[6]

The present town park of Dijon was laid out by Le Nôtre before these waters of Saratoga had been tasted by a white man, and its plan is as different from any modern park as the personal costume of that day differs from that we are wearing. But, visiting it not long since, I found the town forester following orders which Le Nôtre had given, and the ground better realizing the pictures which must have been in his mind, than it could possibly have done while he lived.[7] The roads, walks, seats; the verdant carpets, the leafy vistas, — in none of these had the original work lost value. Never before were they as well adapted to their designed use, or worth as much for it. Where is the public building of the same date, of which, as a town property, the same can be said?

Most old, large towns would supply some like evidence. there are woody resorts in Rome which have been woody resorts from the time of the Cæsars.[8] The Mount of Olives still serves as a place of retreat from the confinement and bustle of the streets of Jerusalem, and its present groves are believed to have sprung from the roots of trees planted centuries before the summer days when the humble friends of a certain unpractical Jew were apt to look for him among the afternoon strollers under their shade.[9]

There is no people in the world who would take more honest and respectable pride and satisfaction in having their work done with a view to considerations of intrinsic and lasting value than our own; but it is at present impossible that the impression we casually form of our inceptive park-work shall take fairly into account its substantial merits or short-comings. Parks, of all things, should not be taken hold of as frontier expedients. Makeshift, temporizing, catch-penny work upon them is always extravagant work. The men hitherto more directly in trust of our parks have not been specially prone to the trading view of them. Though raw in respect to park service, they have usually been high-minded servants of the public. But they have been constrained by public opinion to waste much of what their free judgment would secure, and there is but one way in which the difficulty can be got over. It is by bringing public opinion itself to take a larger interest in the lasting conditions of accruing value in a park; and experience suggests that this is of even more importance, and of greater difficulty, in small towns, and in regard to parks for moderate use, than with respect to undertakings the magnitude and costliness of which is better fitted to affect the imagination in this respect.

One of the chemists engaged in the discussion of this Association on the subject of the Adulterations of Food, the other night, said that all were agreed that everything should be known in the market by its own name: that if we wanted glucose we should not have to take it with the name of sugar; if oleomargarine, not as butter. There is a difficulty in discussing questions of cost and value in parks, lying in the fact that the public is so far from a common understanding of what the unadulterated substance of a park may be. If I now proceed upon my own notion in this respect, I may be met, as a dealer once told me that he had been by a young housekeeper who complained that if she left the stuff which he sold her for milk to stand a little while "a nasty yellow scum rose on it." "So it always does, madam, on good milk." "Never, sir," she rejoined, "never, on what I call milk."

I have lately known the word "park" applied to the protecting belt of a reservoir, to a fish-pond, a sea beach, and a jail yard; to scores of things which have the least possible public interest in common. I have seen a low rocky shore having what I regard as park-value beyond estimate, in tints, lights and shadows and reflections of translucent and opaque foliage over rippling water, and full of poetic mystery, — of beauty such as no painter can render. I have seen such a shore so changed that the water lay dead upon a wall of raw stone, capped by an inclined plane of turf; all possible architectural beauty lost through meaningless meanderings; all value which might have been in a simple breadth of turf, destroyed by pinning it down with prim pegs of living spruce and arbor vitæ. And this result I have heard praised as park-like.

Therefore, I had begun my paper (which I now reach) with some observations on this point, recalling the fact that while the few public properties which had the name of park with us, twenty-five years ago, did not differ from others known as greens, commons, or yards; yet the word had a meaning by no other so well given. Scores of times I have heard plain country people, Northern and Southern, Eastern and Western, describe something they had seen as "park-like," or "pretty as a park," or as "a perfect natural park." It might be Blue Ridge table-lands, oak openings further west, mesquite-grass prairies beyond the Trinity, or passages of the Genesee Flats or Connecticut Bottoms. What did the word mean? Nothing in the least practical. It reported nothing of the soil, of the water-power, of quarries or quartz lodes. It told of a certain influence of *conditions solely of scenery*, — soothing and reposeful influences. If we trace back this use of the word, it will carry us to the immigrations of the early part of the seventeenth century, before the replanting of English parks under the urgings of Evelyn, the Royal Society and the Admiralty, when there were generally broader spaces of greensward within them, and yet more of spacious seclusion from all without than even at present.[10]

I beg that this significance of the word may be kept in mind a little while.

Twenty-five years ago we had no parks, park-like or otherwise, which might not better have been called something else. Since then a class of works so called has been undertaken which, to begin with, are at least spacious, and which hold possibilities of all park-like qualities. Upon twenty of these works in progress, there has been thus far expended upwards of forty millions of dollars, — well nigh if not fully fifty millions, — and this figure does not tell the whole story of cost, as I will later show. Considering that in none of the towns making this outlay the necessity of a park was a little while ago at all felt, a remarkable progress of public demand is thus manifested. It will be found the more remarkable when it is considered that, in all Europe, but one notable public park had been laid out in the first half of this century; that this was formed on ground previously a royal hunting park, not by the government of the town, not by taxing the town, and not with an eye single to the town's advantage.[11] But to see the full significance of the fact it is further necessary to consider that within the same period, since 1850, as many parks have been laid out for the people of large towns in Europe as with us, and that the area which has been for the first time legally and definitely appropriated to that end is larger there than here. What has been secured for London alone is of greater extent than all the town parks of America together.[*] At the same time there has been a radical change in the management of many of the old parks.

Allow me to use the term *park movement*, with reference to what has thus recently occurred on both continents. With us, it dates from Mr. Downing's writings on the subject in 1849.[12] But these could not have obtained the public attention they did, nor have proved the seed of so large a harvest, but for their timeliness, and a condition of expectancy in the soil upon which they fell.

Our first act of park legislation was in 1851. In 1853, the first Commissioners for the Central Park entered upon their duties.[13] It was only in the latter year that some ill-considered steps were taken toward supplying Paris with its first public park.[14] It was not till 1855 that Mr. Alphand came from Bordeaux, and gave the work its final form and impetus.[15] A little earlier, three small park undertakings had been entered upon in England, the leading one under the direction of Paxton, afterwards Sir Joseph.[16] I know of none in Germany, Italy or Belgium; but a few years afterward, I saw in each of these countries evidence that, about the same time, planting and gardening for the public benefit had taken new life.[17]

Parks have plainly not come as the direct result of any of the great inventions or discoveries of the century. They are not, with us, simply an improvement on what we had before, growing out of a general advance of the arts applicable to them. It is not evident that the movement was taken up in any country from any other, however it may have been influenced or accelerated. It did not run like a fashion. It would seem rather to have been a common, spontaneous movement of that sort which we conveniently refer to the "Genius of Civilization."

I do not take this way of disposing of the question of its origin, impulse and aim, which I will discuss later. I wish here only that the reflection

---

[*] Chiefly in recent action in respect to Epping Forest.[18]

may be made that a wide-spread popular movement is not, naturally, all at once perfectly clear-headed, coherent and perspicuous in its demands. In other words, it is hardly to be supposed that the popular demand represented in parks has yet taken the fully mature, self-conscious form of thoroughly-reasoned purposes and principles, and has insisted on an accurate embodiment of them in the works ordered. It is more reasonable to assume that it has not.

I wish to present this assumption in a practical form. Let me suppose that a man has become possessed, near a town, of adjoining properties comprising one or two farms, with marsh land, wood-land, pastures, mill-pond, quarry and brickyard. It is crossed by roads, upon which there is some pleasure-driving; the pond is used for skating, the hill-sides for coasting, the pastures for kite-flying, base ball and target-firing; snipe are shot in the marshes, rabbits trapped in the woods. There are neglected private properties so used for recreation by the public near most of our towns. Now, suppose that the man dies, leaving an infant heir; twenty years afterwards the heir dies, and the entire property is to come by will to the town on condition that the town spends half a million dollars to make it a park. Suppose the old roads are improved and furnished with sidewalks and shade trees; the brickyard fitted for a parade ground, the marsh for a rifle range; and that the quarry, with masonry and gates added, becomes a town reservoir. Part of the ground is taken for a cemetery; a statue of the former owner is set on the highest hill; a museum and public library take the place of the homestead; an armory is provided, a hospital, poor-house, high school, conservatory, camera-obscura, prospect tower, botanic and zoological garden, archery, lawn-tennis and croquet-grounds, billiard-house, skating-rink, racket court, ten-pin alley, riding-school, Turkish bath, mineral springs, restaurants, pagodas, pavilions, and a mall, terrace and concert garden. Suppose that the town has spent its half million, several times over, in these things, and that the courts can have found reason (I know not how) to decide that the condition of the bequest has been complied with. Suppose that a due part of all the town outlay in the premises has been set down in the town books to old accounts, so far as applicable, as to account of waterworks, street improvements, schools, hospitals, and so on; and that, after all, there is found something which must be charged under the new head of "parks."

Now, suppose that a question is raised whether this expenditure has been made in good faith, with reference to the proper objects and distinctive value of a park, and has been judiciously and economically directed, and that a popular judgment (not a technical court judgment) is asked upon this issue, what would be the result? Few men would have a sufficiently clear idea of the objects and the conditions of value of a park to form a judgment; those who had would differ widely in their ideas, and most of the more judicial and properly leading minds would hold such ideas as they had with enough of doubt to make them slow either to fully support or decisively condemn those responsible. This, unquestionably, would be the case much more than it would be in regard to any other large matter of town expenditure.

Let this unreadiness of popular judgment be considered for a moment in connection with certain faults in our methods of public business. This Association needs no explanation of them. It is sufficient to say that changes in the fundamental laws of our parks, in the boards governing them, or in the bodies governing these boards, occur annually. A certain weakness of human nature, usually exhibited in some degree after such changes, is expressed in the proverb, "New brooms sweep clean." There is generally a disposition with each new man in office to find an *ex post facto* reason for his being there. In the absence of any restraint, such as lies with reference to other public works, in a definite and well established public understanding of what is to be accomplished, there is nothing to prevent a novice in a park board, or in the office of mayor, comptroller or member of city council, from aiming to make changes of organization, and to force a course of operations adapted to discountenance some of the aims of work previously done, and with this motive to lay waste what funds under the same trust had before been used to obtain. There have already been such cases. In one a large outlay has been made, and the money is claimed to have been honestly used, with the unquestionable intent of nullifying what at least half a million dollars had been previously spent to gain. It has happened more than once that plans have been adopted, work advanced under them, then thrown aside by new men, new plans adopted, and, after some years, these in their turn abandoned, and the original plans resumed. The change of purpose in such cases will have been deliberate and intentional. But changes as great and as wasteful are more likely to occur through the passing of park works under the control, direct or indirect, of men who, through simple ignorance, forgetfulness, or indifference to such aims as have before-time been had in view, let a large share of the value that has been once secured slip through their fingers.*

But now, if I have suggested the special hazard under our special political customs, of the lack of a well-understood central and distinctive purpose in the management of these large town properties, I wish to add that, back of this, but closely united with it, there is a more positive and a deeper seated difficulty. Briefly, it is the difficulty of dispossessing the mind of ideas which are associated with an object when, through lapse of time and change of circumstances, the nature of that object and its conditions of value have

---

*In the short history of one of our parks, a change in the immediate direction of the plantations has occurred not less than six times, and in each case the new appointee has shown a disposition to upset the methods of his predecessor, and twice, at least, such changes have been thus accomplished, amounting to serious changes of general design. Upon another park, for which I am supposed to have some responsibility, the resident professional superintendent was changed five times in three years.[19]

been radically changed. This difficulty, in individual experience, is not an uncommon one, but, with regard to this matter of parks, it is largely a transmitted experience, and I can think of no quite parallel case by which to explain it.

Its full elucidation would carry me into a history of a class of property unknown with us, but which, throughout the Old World, has for many centuries been of importance. Its value has been in two kinds; forest materials and game. It has been managed with reference to each, systematically, by classes of men specially trained to their duties, and since no other equally extensive property has had so much of what is called sentimental value, as to none has service been so much handed down from father to son, and as to none have traditional ideas been more persistent. There are many thousands of such properties, of which the character and methods of management and use have changed little since the period of the Crusades. In England they are mostly called parks, and there the changes have been greater, as a rule, than on the continent. Still, in some essential particulars, the sentiment of conservatism with regard to them, not only with their owners for the time being, but with the people at large, is very strong.

Some few of these old forest and hunting properties, once belonging to kings, and situated near growing towns, came after a time to be used by the townspeople for their own amusement, much as neglected private lands near our towns often are now. Gradually such use of them established something like a vested right, and so, by very slow degrees, from kings' parks, they came to be regarded as at least pseudo-public parks.

I say by slow degrees. A single fact will indicate how slowly, and suggest, with reference to their management, how imperfectly. That great park which we know so well for its Merry Wives' recreations; with its antlered stags in waiting for royal hunting parties; its phantom huntsman; its foresters' saw-pits with children hiding in them; is now surrounded with towns and villages, and is an important feature of suburban London.[20] It is nearer to the West End than Long Branch to the Battery,[21] and is accessible by boats and three lines of railway, running cheap excursion trains. It is an object not simply of town but of national pride. In its use and value as a public park, a thousand times more than anything else, lies the proper concern of government with it. Yet, as late as four years ago, the only allusion to it as a public park, in the stated report to Parliament of the commissioner in charge, was contained in two lines, in which the extent to which it is used for public recreation is mentioned as a reason why the commissioner cannot make a better return from the sale of timber and other forest products, the letting of pasturage, and so on.[22] It will be remembered, also, that yet every year a somewhat ridiculous public ceremony is performed in this park, called a hunt with the royal hounds, in which a venerable stag is turned out of a wagon and set after with great outcry, but with special precautions against his being seriously hurt when overtaken. These two facts suggest the degree in which the ancient theory of the use, value and economic management of this property has had influence with those in charge of it down to this very day.

Hyde Park, which may be considered as more particularly the progenitor of modern public parks, is now in the midst of London (the town having grown around it since the time of Mr. Pepys). But Hyde Park was classed with Windsor and under the same management when I first visited it, only thirty years ago.[23] I believe that it was transferred to a special commission, appointed, not by the local authorities, but by Parliament, at the time of the first International Exhibition,[24] but, though the deer and kennels have been removed, some of the rangers or gamekeepers are still living upon it and there is an attractive private residence in the middle of it, with stables and gardens, occupied by a gentleman who represents the office corresponding for this park to that held for Woodstock Chase by The Loyal Lee in the seventeenth century, as described by Scott.[25]

One of the two great parks of Paris was an imperial forest and hunting ground as late as 1850, the other still later.[26] The public park of Florence was the grand duke's private property until the last revolution.[27] The greater part of it is a dense wood, managed on the principles of economic forestry. The park of Munich, which people say was laid out by Rumford as a sanitary measure, is of the same character; it is still stocked with deer for the king's hunting, and its resident superintendent is a gamekeeper, as his father was before him. I saw him inspecting the repair of roads after a storm; he carried a gun in his hand, and was followed by aged hounds.[28]

The names of the parks of Berlin and Stockholm indicate what they have been; each, in a different language, meaning a place for keeping deer.[29]

I could show from facts of personal observation how, much more than it is easy to realize, the present condition of even the most changed of these old parks has thus been determined by motives as foreign to the forms of recreation in which their public value now lies, as the motives of a cotton mill are from those of a cathedral, and how the customs of management and of use now prevailing, have been *perforce*, largely fitted to these traditional motives. Also, how some of these customs, foreign in every sense to us, have lately emigrated and are crowding out that which is natural to us and belongs to our common sense.

I hope I have said enough to make it plain that during the long process through which the present ideas of the value of a park were gaining upon those which they have at last mainly superseded, the public demands, expectations and standards of value in respect to these grounds have been mixed, inconsistent and contradictory. This being realized, it will next be evident that the inherited and transmitted idea of a public park has been one of a body of land held for no clearly defined purposes, which is equivalent to saying, held for purposes always remaining to be determined. It also follows that the inherited and transmitted idea of the responsibilities of those in immediate direction of these parks has been a corresponding one, and that they have been little subject to popular criticism based on fixed, just and sound principles applicable to public recreation.

Lastly, it follows that the idea fitted to the word park in our minds, when, twenty-two years ago, we began, here in America, dealing with the subject, — having come to us much less from anything that we had seen, or from any dictionary, than through that marvelous process of race nutrition which gives every man his native tongue, — was an idea largely made up of irreconcilable impressions.

The fact remains to be more distinctly emphasized, that it is only through the use of this word of vague and inconstant significance that any limit has been placed upon the purposes to which public money, appropriated to parks, shall be applied. The simplest statement of purpose that courts would unhesitatingly accept or public opinion stand agreed upon, and, even then, not as a complete statement, but only as true so far as it goes, would be this: "A public park is a ground appropriated to public recreation."

Observe, then, that most of the public properties known as parks contain provisions for other purposes than recreation, and even opposed to recreation. Again, waiving the question how far these are legitimate parts of them, observe that recreation is so broad a term, and means so much more to some than to others, that to devote public funds to recreation is little less than to give a free rein to the personal tastes, whims and speculations of those entrusted with the administration of them.

We must fall back on usage. What, then, does usage prescribe?

In one European public park we find a race-course, with its grandstand, stables, pool-room and betting ring; in another, popular diversions of the class which we elsewhere look to Barnum to provide. In one there is a theatre with ballet-dancing; in another, soldiers firing field-pieces at a target, with a detail of cavalry to keep the public at a distance.

Attempts to introduce like provisions in several of our American parks have been resisted under the personal conviction that they would tend to subvert their more important purpose. In some of our parks, nevertheless, arrangements have been made for various games; concerts and shows have been admitted; there have been military parades; and it is impossible to find any line of principle between many favored and neglected propositions.

Usage, therefore, in this respect, decides nothing.

Asking what usage prescribes as to the simpler forms of recreation, we shall find that one ground, classed among public parks, consists of dense woods, with a few nearly straight roads through it, while others have open, pastoral landscapes, with circuitous drives, rides and walks; that the interest of one centres in an extremely artificial display of exotics and bedding plants, while another bids fair to be equally distinguished for its fountains, monuments, statues and other means of recreation in stone, concrete and bronze. Yet another is so natural and unsophisticated you can hardly use it in dry weather without choking with dust, or in wet weather without wading in mud.

Again, usage determines nothing.

What this laxity leaves us liable to, and how much may be safely presumed upon the public's confusion of mind, is shown by the fact that in one case, when local opposition was found to be inconveniently strong against the location of a small-pox hospital anywhere else, the difficulty was overcome by placing it in the midst of a park.[30]

I have known orders given in a park, and carried out at considerable expense, the motive and origin of which could be explained only by reference to an idiosyncracy of that class which, to some men, causes eggs or strawberries to be loathsome, and makes cats or curs objects of an irresistible, undefined terror.

The choice of site of most of our parks, and the definition of their boundaries, have been made without the slightest regard for any object of a park, except, possibly, that of securing an air space. Even as with a view to air spaces the locality, in some cases, is nearly the last that should have been selected, and the area taken much broader and greatly more costly than necessary to the purpose.

No one can for a moment suppose that the state of public opinion exemplified in the facts which have been stated, is one favorable to securing what the public wants most in a park, or, if at all, to its obtaining it at reasonable cost.

But the true state of the case will not be fully realized without taking into account certain elements of possible cost of a park which have hitherto had little general consideration.

A town is built to meet the demands of commerce — of commerce in a large sense. As these demands successively arise and their pressure is felt, street is added to street, building to building; railroads, canals and docks are introduced; sewers, water-pipes and gas-lights are pushed out here and there, and thus, not only the extent but the direction of the town's growth is in a large degree controlled by natural laws, the acts of government following much more than leading, directing, or resisting, the movements of supply and demand.

It will be evident that this element of security against injudicious municipal enterprise applies not at all to our great park trusts. A town does not grow into parks, as it does, by the law of its existence, into buildings and streets; on the contrary, when a great body of land is used as a park in the borders of a town, it will be a serious disturbance of what would otherwise be the natural development of the town.

See, for illustration, how Hyde Park has elbowed out the streets of London. See how the street system of Paris has been kept from its natural development because Catherine de Medici turned a tile-yard into a pleasaunce; or, to take the nearest example, see how the park of New York brings suddenly to a full stop more than ninety streets, which would otherwise constitute forty thoroughfares of commerce, at the very centre of an island which may yet be the most important point of commercial transfer in the world.

That when land is to be bought, or even accepted as a free gift, by a town for a park, its adaptation to the purpose of a park should first of all be considered, and that then none and no more should be taken than is necessary, or at least desirable, for that purpose, will be conceded.

A little consideration, then, will satisfy the Association that a large proportion of the objects which are more or less provided for in our parks might, at less cost and greater value, be provided for in a series of smaller grounds placed as nearly as practicable at regular distances through or around the town.

The argument is briefly this: That such scattered, smaller grounds would be more accessible; would less embarrass other interests of the town; would less interfere with its natural development; would involve less contention with local jealousies and consequent wasteful compromises; and would, on the whole, be less costly.

There is, however, an important element of value in most parks which could not be well provided for in such small local grounds. What is desirable in this respect is a long, unbroken, spacious drive, ride and walk, offering suitable conditions to a large number of people to obtain together moderate exercise in the open air, with such other conditions favorable to gayety as can be conveniently associated with them.

To a great many persons, perhaps the most of those who have much active influence upon the management of parks, the value of a park lies mainly, and to some it would seem exclusively, in the advantages it offers in this respect. Yet, as affecting these advantages, it will be obvious that the larger part of every park is waste land. Besides which, regarding this object from a point of view commonly taken by many intelligent people, and taking it up as a professional problem, it is little less than absurd to say that it might not be much better met, and at less cost, than it ever has been on any park, new or old. Indeed, from the accounts we have, it would seem that in some southern towns it has been so taken up, not in as clear-headed and bold a way as it might have been, but sufficiently to demonstrate that a result is easily attainable better adapted to the end in view than any we have hoped to attain in our parks.

An arrangement of the general type of the Spanish alamedas, developed with anything like the enterprise and outlay which we have been willing to put on our parks, would, for the purpose in question, be more commodious; its use simpler and more easily and efficiently regulated; there would be less liability to accidents upon it; it might be more effectively decorated, and thus in every way be made to present a gayer, more brilliant and festive scene.

Such an affair, without making half as great a break in our towns as, sooner or later, their parks will, would open a splendid field for the great and admirable enterprise, erudition and skill, which are now given to decorative gardening — a perfectly suitable field for it, which a park seldom offers. It would give fine show room for all the novelties on the market, and would allow a fine scenic arrangement to be made of the superb tropical and sub-tropical beauties which are just now in fashion, and the best use possible of floral ribbons, embroidery and gew-gaudry which, after doing their worst to degrade and destroy art in landscape gardening, are now, if not wholly going out of fashion, I am glad to say, tending to lapse more nearly to their proper places.

With these advantages, it would cost not nearly as much for land, for construction, for maintenance, or in readjustment of the natural plan of a town.

But, plainly, it is not for this that the "Genius of Civilization" has called for these broad spaces termed parks. In what, then, shall we find the originating impulse, aim and justification of the park-movement?

May we not, perhaps, wisely seek an answer to this question by con-sidering whether there are any other movements of our times with which the park-movement, as we know it, may seem to be related?

If I was right in saying that twenty-five years ago, when we began discussing parks as something to be made for us, the leading idea popularly attached to the word, throughout this country, was one of certain influences of scenery — soothing and reposeful influences — then it is reasonable to sup-pose that there was something in our motive very closely allied to a social force which, in this same quarter of a century, has had a very remarkable development — a force which has directed the investment of hundreds of mil-lions of private capital in travelling machinery, built up many towns, replen-ished many treasuries, enriched kingdoms, been a practical matter for states-manship, and swayed every commercial exchange in the world.

It is open to question whether we care much more than our ancestors did for all manner of beauty of nature; whether we appreciate leaf and flower form and flower color, for instance, more than they. We have a greater vari-ety of flowers; our curiosity about them is more stimulated, our science ad-vanced, we take more interest in them from the point of view of the collector and classifier; they are matters of fashion; we use them more profusely. But there is room for doubt if they act more powerfully upon our sensibilities, and if we make on the whole a more fitting use of them. There can be no like question as to our more general susceptibility to the beauty of clouds, snowy peaks, mountain gorges, forests, meadows and brooks, as we know them in *the broad combining way of scenery.* Even if this doubt should not have weight, it would be much easier to see something akin to regard for scenery in the demand which has led our cities to obtain possession of the broad bodies of land in our parks, than that of interest in the beauty of nature such as may be gratified in a conservatory, a garden, a flower-pot or a posey, saying nothing of natural beauty such as exists even in jewels, furs, fruits, or plumage, or in trees individually regarded and as they grow on the lawn of a cottage.

But now, if we call this force interest in the beauty of natural scenery (to distinguish it from interest in the beauty of nature) we shall find another form of its operation from that evinced by tourists and sojourning seekers of scenery in the more general development of talent in landscape-painting and in the demand for education in landscape-judgment, such as is met by works like those of Ruskin, Taine and Hamerton, of which more are now read by Americans in every year than were all works of similar aims by all the world in a hundred years before we began our first park.[31]

Why this great development of interest in natural landscape and all that pertains to it; to the art of it and the literature of it?

Considering that it has occurred simultaneously with a great enlargement of towns and development of urban habits, is it not reasonable to regard it as a self-preserving instinct of civilization?

Mr. Ruskin may be thought not only unpractical but fanatical, and many of his sayings may be regarded as wild, but that he is inspired by a great and good motive, few will doubt. What is the ruling conviction of his zeal? In his own bitter words, it is that "This is an age in which we grow more and more artificial day by day, and see less and less worthiness in those pleasures which bring with them no marked excitement; in knowledge which affords no opportunity of display."[32]

This is true, though a man ten times more unpractical and fanatical than Mr. Ruskin can be thought to be, had said it; and it is also true, that to all the economical advantages we have gained through modern discoveries and inventions, the great enlargement of the field of commerce, the growth of towns and the spread of town ways of living, there are some grave drawbacks. We may yet understand them so imperfectly that we but little more than veil our ignorance when we talk of what is lost and suffered under the name of "vital exhaustion," "nervous irritation" and "constitutional depression"; when we speak of tendencies, through excessive materialism, to loss of faith and lowness of spirit, by which life is made, to some, questionably worth the living. But that there are actual drawbacks which we thus vaguely indicate to the prosperity of large towns, and that they deduct much from the wealth-producing and tax-bearing capacity of their people, as well as from the wealth-enjoying capacity, there can be no doubt.

The question remains whether the contemplation of beauty in natural scenery is practically of much value in counteracting and alleviating these evils, and whether it is possible, at reasonable cost, to make such beauty available to the daily use of great numbers of townspeople? I do not propose to argue this question. I submit it to the Association as one needing discussion; for if the object of parks is not that thus suggested, I know of none which justifies their cost. On the other hand, if the object of parks is thus indicated, I know of no justification for a great deal that is done with them, and a great deal more that many men are bent on doing. That other objects than the cultivation of beauty of natural scenery may be associated with it economically, in a park, I am not disposed to deny; but that all such other objects should be held strictly subordinate to that, in order to justify the purchase and holding of these large properties, I am inclined to think, cannot be successfully disputed.

I will but add that the problem of a park, as it would appear, under the view which I have aimed to suggest, clear of unfortunate, temporary political necessities, is mainly the reconciliation of adequate beauty of nature in scenery with adequate means in artificial constructions of protecting the conditions of such beauty, and holding it available to the use, in a convenient and orderly way, of those needing it; and in the employment of such means for both purposes, as will make the park steadily gainful of that quality of beauty which comes only with age.

The text presented here was published as *A Consideration of the Justifying Value of a Public Park* (Boston, 1881). The original form of this material was a lecture that Olmsted delivered to a gathering of the American Social Science Association in Saratoga, New York, on September 10, 1880.

1. The American Social Science Association published Olmsted's lecture in its December issue of the *Journal of Social Science* (Frederick Law Olmsted, "The Justifying Value of a Public Park," *Journal of Social Science* 12 [December 1880]: 147–64).

2. Olmsted is referring to the use of Central Park as a site for the 1883 World's Fair. Details of this scheme are sketchy: however, in 1879 several leading citizens, including President Ulysses Grant, advocated using Central Park for the fair. Olmsted was a member of the Committee on Sites and the Executive Committee responsible for selecting a site. In January 1881 Olmsted wrote his friend and former partner Calvert Vaux regarding the possible selection of Central Park as a site for the World's Fair. He declared that such use of the park "would result in the planting of buildings on one or more of the central spaces of the park with approaches, &c utterly destroying the park as you and I regard it." After more than a year of considerable controversy the fair was postponed and eventually abandoned (Laura Wood Roper, *FLO: A Biography* [Baltimore, Md., 1973], p. 366; *Forty Years*, 2: 114–15; FLO to CV, Jan. 3 and 5, 1881; see also n. 3 below).

3. William Waldorf Astor (1848–1919), capitalist, journalist, and son of the wealthy John Jacob Astor. Astor was elected to the New York state senate in 1879, serving one term. On January 5, 1881, Astor introduced a bill entitled, "An act restricting the right to grant, use or occupy the Central park, in the city of New York, for the purposes of a public fair or exhibition." After receiving a copy of the bill, Olmsted wrote Astor on January 15, 1881, regarding its content. Olmsted noted that he hoped the bill would become law but suggested that Astor "consider whether a more comprehensive measure may not be desirable." Apparently, Astor took Olmsted's advice because on January 27, 1881, he introduced the bill to which Olmsted here refers. This second bill was sent to the Committee on Cities where it languished. Instead, on March 9 the Committee on Cities reported favorably on Astor's first bill, and on May 4, 1881, it became law (*DAB*; *Forty Years*, 2: 114–15; New York [State], *Journal of the Senate of*

the State of New York . . . [Albany, N.Y., 1881], pp. 21, 58, 196, 472; idem, *Laws of the State of New York, Passed at the One Hundred and Fourth Session of the Legislature* . . . [Albany, N.Y., 1881], chap. 208).

4. See FLO and CV, *General Plan for the Improvement of the Niagara Reservation* (1887) and note 7, below.

5. Samuel Pepys (1633–1703), British diarist. This excerpt is not from Pepys but rather from his contemporary John Evelyn. Evelyn noted in his diary on May 1, 1661, "I went to Hyde Park to take the air, where was his Majesty and an innumerable appearance of gallants and rich coaches, being now a time of universal festivity and joy" (*DNB*; William Bray, ed., *Diary and Correspondence of John Evelyn*, 4 vols. [London, 1872], 1: 371).

6. The Jardin des Tuileries, located between the Louvre and the Place de la Concorde in Paris, was first created in the late sixteenth century by Catherine de Medici. In the 1660s Louis XIV commissioned André Le Nôtre to redesign the gardens in the formal style. For a discussion of the Bois de Boulogne, see notes 14 and 15 below (Geoffrey Jellicoe et al., eds., *The Oxford Companion to Gardens* [Oxford, 1991], p. 565; *Papers of FLO*, 3: 342; see also, FLO, "Park," [1875], above).

7. That is, the Parc de la Colombière, located in Dijon, France. The design of the park has often been attributed to André Le Nôtre (1613–1700), French artist and gardener; however, except for one parterre plan signed by Le Nôtre, there is no evidence that he was the principal designer. Olmsted visited the park in 1878 when he traveled to Europe for his health (G. Jellicoe et al., eds., *Oxford Companion to Gardens*, p. 334; Helen M. Fox, *André Le Nôtre: Garden Architect to Kings* [New York, 1962], p. 167; F. Hamilton Hazlehurst, *Gardens of Illusion: The Genius of André Le Nostre* [Nashville, Tenn., 1980], p. 395; Jules Guiffrey, *André Le Nostre* [1913; rpt. ed., Lewes, Sussex, 1986], p. 40; FLO, travel notebook, March 3, 1878).

8. Possibly, Olmsted is referring to the great Roman villas that also included extensive gardens and grounds, called *horti* (house with a park). The grounds of Julius Caesar's villa in Trastevere were eventually granted as a public park. Augustus was able to construct a 50-acre artificial lake at his villa. Leading the way in extravagance, Nero's villa and grounds extended for over 125 acres and included a lake, vineyards, and forests. Eventually, these *horti* fashioned a "Green Belt" around the overbuilt, overcrowded section of the city (John P. V. D. Balsdon, *Life and Leisure in Ancient Rome* [New York, 1969], pp. 194–96).

9. The Mount of Olives is a ridge lying east of the city of Jerusalem. The "unpractical Jew" was Jesus Christ (*EB*).

10. John Evelyn (1620–1706), English author, diarist, and gardener. In 1662 the Commissioners of the British Navy, concerned about the increasing shortage of timber for shipbuilding, sought counsel from the Royal Society. That same year Evelyn addressed the Society on the subject of forest trees. His lecture was published in 1664 with the title *Sylva, or a Discourse of Forest Trees*. Evelyn spent the rest of his life encouraging English landowners to plant trees and was largely responsible for the reforestation of the royal hunting parks (*DNB*; Susan Lasdun, *The English Park: Royal, Private & Public* [1991; rpt. ed., New York, 1992], pp. 52–54).

11. Probably, St. James's Park, located in London's West End and laid out by John Nash in 1828 (George F. Chadwick, *The Park and the Town* [New York, 1966], pp. 33–34).

12. A reference to landscape gardener Andrew Jackson Downing's writings in the *Horticulturist* in 1848, 1849, and 1851 advocating the creation of public parks in the United States patterned after European models (see FLO, "The People's Park at Birkenhead, near Liverpool," [May 1851], unnumbered note, above).

13. See FLO, "Public Parks and the Enlargement of Towns," Feb. 25, 1870, note 33, above.

14. The Bois de Boulogne, located in the western part of Paris. Napoleon III granted the grounds to the city of Paris in 1852 to be developed as a public recreation area (G. F. Chadwick, *Park and the Town*, p. 153).

15. In 1852 Napoleon III gave Baron Georges-Eugène Haussmann, prefect of the Seine, the responsibility of laying out the Bois de Boulogne. Two years later Baron Haussmann appointed Jean-Charles-Adolphe Alphand, a French engineer and landscape architect, to supervise the construction of the park, and it was Alphand who was most responsible for the final design of the park (ibid., pp. 155–56; *Papers of FLO*, 3: 241; see also, FLO, "Park," [1875], above).

16. That is, Sir Joseph Paxton who designed Birkenhead Park in 1847. The other two parks may have been St. James's Park and Regent's Park, both in London (see FLO, "The People's Park at Birkenhead, near Liverpool," [May 1851], above).

17. Olmsted visited Germany, Italy, and Belgium and their parks in 1856 when he traveled to England and the Continent for eight months on business for the publishing firm of Dix, Edwards & Company, and again in 1859 when he visited Europe to study park administration and design at the behest of the Central Park commission (*Papers of FLO*, 3: 360; for a discussion of many of the parks that Olmsted visited, see FLO, "Park," [1875], above).

18. Epping Forest, located a few miles northeast of London and consisting of 5,347 acres of beautifully timbered land, was acquired for public use in 1878 by the Corporation of the City of London (*EB*; Sir Walter Besant, *London in the Nineteenth Century* [London, 1909], pp. 118–19).

19. The first park that Olmsted mentions here was presumably Central Park in New York City, with whose arrangement for direction of gardening he was most involved. The two periods when major alterations in design took place were during the time of the Tweed Ring in 1870–71 and the years following Olmsted's dismissal from the New York Department of Public Parks in December 1877 (see FLO and CV, "A Review of Recent Changes, and Changes which have been Projected, in the Plans of the Central Park," Jan. and Feb. 1872, above, and Frederick Law Olmsted, *The Spoils of the Park. With a Few Leaves from the Deep-Laden Note-Books of "A Wholly Unpractical Man"* [Boston, 1882], pp. 26–27, 44, 47–53).

20. That is, Windsor Great Park consisting of 4,800 acres and connected to Windsor Castle by the three-mile-long Great Walk. Here, Olmsted is referring to William Shakespeare's play *The Merry Wives of Windsor*, part of which takes place in Windsor Great Park. The ghost huntsman was Herne the Hunter, who in medieval times was supposedly the keeper of Windsor Forest and hanged himself from a great oak. Thereafter he haunted the forest. Herne the Hunter appears in *The Merry Wives of Windsor* in act 4, scene 4 (Donald Edgar, *The Royal Parks* [London, 1986], p. 196; Stanley Wells and Gary Taylor, eds., *William Shakespeare: The Complete Works* [Oxford, 1986], pp. 565–66; Margaret Drabble, ed., *The Oxford Companion to English Literature*, 5th ed. [Oxford, 1985], pp. 457, 642–43).

21. Windsor is approximately twenty-one miles east of London; Long Branch, New Jersey, a resort town, is approximately twenty-six miles south of the Battery at the southern tip of Manhattan Island.

22. In the report to which Olmsted here refers, the commissioner in charge of Windsor Great Park noted that

> The property . . . consists of more than 14,000 acres of land, maintained as part of the domain attached to Windsor Castle. The income arising from, and the expenditure upon the property which, like the Royal Parks in London, is largely used by the public for purposes of recreation, cannot be considered as a matter solely of profit and loss (Great Britain. Parliament, *The Fifty-fifth Report of*

the Commissioners of Her Majesty's Woods, Forests, and Land Revenues [London, 1877], p. 4).

23. Olmsted first visited Hyde Park in the summer of 1850 when he traveled to England with his brother John Hull Olmsted and his friend Charles Loring Brace (*Papers of FLO*, 1: 9–10).
24. That is, the International Exhibition held at Hyde Park in London in 1851.
25. A reference to Sir Walter Scott (1771–1832) and his novel *Woodstock* published in 1826. The "Loyal Lee" was Sir Henry Lee the ranger of Woodstock Chase (*DNB*; M. Drabble, ed., *Oxford Companion to English Literature*, pp. 1092–93).
26. That is, the Bois de Boulogne and the Bois de Vincennes. Work began on Vincennes, located in the eastern part of Paris, in 1858. It was ceded to the city in 1860 (see nn. 14 and 15 above; G. F. Chadwick, *Park and the Town*, p. 157).
27. That is, the Cascine, granted to the city of Florence after the war for Italian unification in the early 1860s (see FLO, "Park," [1875], above).
28. Benjamin Thompson, Count von Rumford (1753–1814), an American, born in Massachusetts, who went to England after the outbreak of the American Revolution. In 1784 he traveled to Bavaria where he was invited by the elector there to enter his service. In that same year he was knighted and made Count von Rumford. Rumford remained in Bavaria for eleven years acting as minister of war, minister of police, and grand chamberlain to the elector. He was also responsible for implementing several reforms in Munich, among them the laying out of the Englisher Garten (English Garden) with the German landscape architect Friedrich Ludwig Sckell. Olmsted saw the park when he traveled to Europe in 1859 and again in 1878. He was impressed with what he saw and noted in his travel diary that it was a "beautiful body of woodland scenery with large glades & some broad meadows" (*DNB*; G. Jellicoe et al., eds., *Oxford Companion to Gardens*, p. 176; *Papers of FLO*, 3: 231; FLO, travel notebook, Feb. 9, 1878).
29. That is, the Thiergarten in Berlin and the Djurgården in Stockholm (see FLO, "Park," [1875], above).
30. For a discussion of the placement of a small-pox hospital in Mount Royal Park, see FLO, *Notes on the Plan of Franklin Park and Related Matters* (1886), note 51, below.
31. That is, John Ruskin, Hippolyte-Adolphe Taine, and Philip Gilbert Hamerton. Among their many talents, all three were art critics and published their writings on the subject. Olmsted admired Ruskin greatly and often quoted from his multivolume *Modern Painters* (5 vols., 1843–60). Taine wrote *Philosophie de l'art* (1865), and Hamerton published *Etching & Etchers* in 1868 (for John Ruskin, see FLO and CV, "A Review of Recent Changes, and Changes which have been Projected, in the Plans of the Central Park," Jan. and Feb. 1872, n. 34, above; for Hippolyte-Adolphe Taine, see FLO, "Park," [1875], n. 1, above; for Philip Gilbert Hamerton, see FLO, *Notes on the Plan of Franklin Park and Related Matters*, [1886], n. 3, below).
32. A quotation from the appendix to the first volume of Ruskin's *Modern Painters* (E. T. Cook and Alexander Wedderburn, eds., *The Works of John Ruskin*, 27 vols. [London, 1903], 3: 650).

MOUNT ROYAL

Montreal

FREDERICK LAW OLMSTED

[1881]

"The tall rock,
    The mountain, and the deep and gloomy wood,
Their colors and their forms, were then to me
    An appetite; a feeling and a love,
That had no need of a remoter charm
    By thoughts supplied." — *Wordsworth.*[1]

"The groves were God's first temple." — *Bryant.*[2]

"Yet nature soothes and sympathises." — *Emerson.*[3]

"The landscape, forever consoling and kind, Pours her wine and her oil on the smarts of the mind." — *Lowell.*[4]

"No tears dim the sweet look that Nature wears." — *Longfellow.*[5]

"It is the greatest refreshment to the spirits of man, without which buildings and palaces are but gross handiworks." — *Bacon.*[6]

"Great Nature scorns control: she will not bear
    One beauty foreign to the spot or soil
She gives thee to adorn: 'T is thine alone
    To mend not change her features. Does her hand
Stretch forth a level lawn? Ah, hope not thou
    To lift the mountain there. Do mountains frown
Around? Oh, wish not there the level lawn.
    Yet she permits thy art, discreetly us'd,
To smooth the rugged and to swell the plain.
    But dare with caution!" — *Mason.*[7]

"The art itself is Nature." — *Shakespeare.*[8]

"For, and this is at the root of the matter, everything made by man's hands has a form which must be beautiful or ugly: beautiful, if it is in accord with Nature and helps her; ugly, if it is discordant with Nature and thwarts her." — *William Morris.*[9]

"Without principles, no true beauty can be attained."
"The first law of a good design is that it shall be a whole." — *André*.[10]

"The simple and uncombined landscape, if wrought out with due attention to the ideal beauty of the features it includes, will always be most powerful in its appeal to the heart." — Ruskin.[11]

PREFACE

Ideas like those expressed opposite have long had considerable currency. If they are of any practical value, the Mount Royal property gives a rare opportunity of turning them to business account in a special form of wealth for all of a large community. I have aimed to show in the following pages what has hitherto been in the way of it. When they were printed I had been in communication with no one in Montreal for upward of two years, and it is only since that I am informed of an entire change in the managing board of the property. I am yet ignorant of the motives of the change, and if what I have written touches any question of recent public discussion, or bears at all upon the present purposes or projects of any parties or persons, it is not of my intention.

I.

To the Owners of Mount Royal:[12]
In 1874 you had bought this property and were wishing to begin its improvement.[13] To do so prudently, you needed a fixed design and policy, and to forward this, I had the honor to be engaged to aid you, with the special duty of drafting a plan for laying out the ground.[14]

It was presumed that my draft would be matured, discussed, and, if necessary, revised in time to serve as the basis of operations to be prosecuted the following summer; and I have no reason to doubt that I could easily have supplied a drawing in a few months, which would have been accepted as the fulfillment of my duty.

The matter, however, gave me a great deal of labor, and was a source of constant and increasing anxiety for nearly three years, and when, at last, under repeated urgings, I reluctantly reported the result, it was with the conviction that my work had, with reference to its principal object, been vainly expended.[15]

Having a strong, abiding sense of its importance, I have not been able to acquit myself of accountability to you and your heirs, and have deferred a formal ending of my engagement, pending conditions less unfavorable than those of the late extreme hard times,[16] to solicit a consideration from you for views which it will be my aim in this writing to commend.

I cannot but think that a certain dead weight of passive public opinion, which, rather than an actively intelligent resistance, I have seen to stand in their way, is partly to be attributed to an overlooking of certain aspects of the business which I have had a special duty to keep before me.

For example, I just now referred to your heirs, which to some may have seemed superfluous; but with a little reflection it will be apparent that the property could not have been justly purchased with regard only for the profit to be got from it by a few thousands of the generation ordering it; and that I was bound, in suggesting a plan, to have in view the interests of those to inherit it as well as yours; and to bear in mind that, before the first planting of the plantations which I was to outline should reach their full growth, these inheritors would begin to be counted not by the thousand but by the million; and also to remember that, if civilization is not to move backward, they are to be much more alive than we are to certain qualities of value in the property which are to be saved or lost to them, as shall presently be determined.

And lest there should be the slightest doubt in any of your minds of the pertinence of my taking this way to draw your attention to this and some other considerations, I will submit a single illustration of many which might be offered of the teachings of history upon the point.

About the time that certain Frenchmen were laying out the first street of Montreal, a court comrade whom they had left behind, a distinguished man of my profession, André Le Notre by name, was laying out roads and walks, defining plantations, selecting trees, fixing the form and position of seats, and otherwise determining the character and quality of a park at Dijon, the capital of ancient Burgundy, and of the present Côte d'Or.[17]

Since I was last in Montreal[18] I have made a pilgrimage to this ground (long ago acquired by the town),[19] and found the superintendent of it still scrupulously following the plans prepared more than two hundred years ago by Le Notre, and the motives by which he was led, and the pictures which he had conceived, much better realized than they could have been while he was yet living. The roads, the walks, the verdant carpets, the leafy vistas — in none of these had the original work lost, or even ceased to gain, value; and I saw children of the seventh generation in direct descent from those whom Le Notre looked upon, carried by their mothers, and led by their teachers, as their kindred now are, to your mountain, to take their share of the value which had so long ago been prepared for them. It is not at all improbable that yet for hundreds of years to come every child of Dijon shall enjoy the same nurture.

To our nineteenth-century minds the design of the park might, for this end, have been better, but it was then the best attainable, and the good people of Dijon have shown the highest common-sense in resisting all passing fashions, fancies, and whims by which it might have been sophisticated; in religiously preserving its originating spirit and character; and in gaining for themselves, year by year, more and more of the incalculable advantage of learning, by communion with it, veneration for the past and duty to the future.

I have no reason to suppose that anyone in Montreal has been dissatisfied with my work. No one has spoken of it, as far as I know, but with praise. To understand why it seemed to me to have been futile, it must first by considered that the preparation of a plan means the invention of a process by which certain proposed ends may be brought about upon certain conditions. A plan serviceable for one scheme of ends will be worthless for another. A plan soundly based on one set of conditions will be good for nothing when these conditions are changed.

The reason for the prolonged labor, and the poor results of it, which were at the outset given to the study of a plan assigned, in your behalf, to me, was that, as to one point or another essential to the firm framing of a plan adapted to a fixed policy in this business, your appointed special agents, the commissioners,[20] could never be sure that their, or any attainable, conclusion was at all to be depended on; never sure of what might be determined over their heads; never of what, of their own judgment, upon the absolutely essential foundation-stones of a soundly-built plan, they might not feel it due, any coming day, to yield to what should appear to them to be a determined drift of public opinion.

More than once I had a design worked out upon grounds which I had been instructed to regard as fixed, or authorized to assume, at the least, as practicable, and upon which I had been urged to proceed; in which I had met, with a great deal of study, according to my ability, all the difficulties which I could foresee; each element devised, as far as controllable, to augment the value of all others and to be augmented in value by all devised of others; only to find that it must be thrown up and the work begun anew at the bottom, because of the ripening of some determination or the unsettlement of something previously regarded as determined.[21]

Not one of the changes to which I refer appeared to be the result of a more advanced deliberation upon the object which had led to the purchase of the property, or to have been made with a full realization of what was determined by it with respect to that object.

Nor, in the discussion of them, did I hear that what I believe and propose to argue should be the ruling motive of the undertaking had even been given the slightest weight. In the questions put to me it was not referred to; and the reason I suppose to be, not that those favoring the propositions in question really thought it of no consequence, but that they were not in the habit of looking at it in a practical way — of considering it from the point of view of business.

Even when, after three years, I had submitted my final draft and it had been favorably received by the commissioners,[22] I was told (as if it were a matter of little consequence and to have been more or less expected) that certain of the premises on which it had been based, and which had been as distinctly recognized in my instructions as any, would probably be withdrawn by the City Council, and others were referred as not unlikely to be. It did not appear to be supposed that the plan would be materially less adapted to its purpose in consequence, and yet I doubt if I had not had the particular premises in question in view, whether a line or a dot of my draft would have been in the same place or been made without a variation of motive.

Besides what occurred in the more conclusive official form, I was often asked to consider propositions urged upon the commissioners, which were based on ideas of the conditions of value in the property so different from those on which I was, with their concurrence, proceeding, and yet so urged, so received and labored with, as to show that no real anchorage in the matter was felt to be practicable.

In short, it was impossible to avoid a conviction that, whatever formality of adopting a plan might be ultimately come to, there could be no security against such subsequent interpolations and excisions as would make the result a burlesque of its leading motives.

Contending with easy, apparent success with the side-winds of doctrine (as to conditions of value of the property) to which I have referred, as far as the commissioners of the moment were concerned, the wish was often expressed that I would give you, directly, in the form of public discourse, the view which my study of the subject had led me to adopt, and upon which the plan was expected to be based, — upon which, indeed, important operations upon the ground had somewhat prematurely been begun, quite unjustifiably if that view was not to be sustained and borne out by those to direct the matter afterward.

And as, at last, it became more distinctly impressed upon me that the work I was doing, or the worthy work of any man at any time, was liable to be wasted or worse, because of the supposed impracticability of any fixed policy based on a deliberate study of principles, and as I saw no other way of putting myself face to face with this danger, I agreed that I would read before a public meeting to be called by the commissioners, two papers, one discussing general principles of design for works of the kind in hand, and showing the puerile, extravagant, and wasteful character of much that had been proposed in contravention of these principles; the other, their application to the particular conditions of the site to be dealt with, and the population to be served.[23]

I consented, however, only upon the promise of the commissioners that certain gentlemen should be specially invited by them to hear me, whose official positions and whose duty of influence on public opinion made it particularly to be wished that they should find some holding-ground in the matter; and as it had appeared to me that its educational, sanitary, and moral aspects particularly needed support against motives of comparatively trifling importance, I asked also that personal invitations should be given to the teachers, physicians, and clergymen of the city.[24]

I tell the result because of its bearing upon a point of direct pecuniary interest to you, which I shall more distinctly present later.

The result was that half an hour after the time appointed, of a fine autumnal afternoon, in a hall for a thousand, in the heart of the city, time and place being selected by your commissioners with a view to the convenience of those invited, less than thirty persons (ladies, gentlemen, and children) had come together. There was not, I believe, among them one teacher, one physician, or one clergyman; not one member of the City Council (the commissioners excepted) or of the executive departments of the city government. Nor was there one, as far as I have reason to suppose, of all those gentlemen as to whose propositions, demands, and questions my judgment had during the three previous years been asked, and whose power to embarrass the undertaking I had been led to regard with concern.[25]

At the end my little audience kindly thanked me and asked for the publication of the papers read.

This request, with some suggestions as to what might be omitted, the commissioners seconded. But it afterward became evident that they were not fully satisfied of its expediency, or that they questioned if it would be pleasing to the City Council. One of the commissioners acknowledged that he had not himself been able to follow my argument at all points, and that he doubted the results to the undertaking of its publication. I understood his doubt upon finding that another listener had been so well pleased with my efforts to set forth kindly and candidly certain common and conventional ideas of a park that he had failed to catch the argument by which I tried to show that they were not, as a matter of course, to be in all cases adopted; and would, in fact, be applied to the mountain most wastefully and extravagantly. I was even reported in a newspaper as urging a proposition which I had stated only that its unsuitability to the circumstances should be evident.

It must not be forgotten that the original suggestion that I should address you directly came from the commissioners, that the meeting was called by them, and invitations to it given by them. As I had been constantly assured of a great public interest in the work, not, it was to be presumed, the interest of indolent unqualified approval, but a critical interest, inciting to thorough study and cautious advance, review, and revision, the result was thought to require some explanation, and I was advised that it was not to be attributed, at least not wholly to be attributed, to the indifference of those invited, but to some extent, in some cases, to a disposition to repress any such excess of eagerness in the matter as might lead to hasty and excessive outlays during a period of extreme business gloom.[26] Expressions were quoted which seemed to imply that I had been regarded in the light of a paid counsel of a rash and extravagant policy, and that it was presumed that all I should have to say would be with the purpose of keeping alive what would now be termed a park "boom," or perhaps of aiding men who had been speculating in the effects upon the value of neighboring real estate of the city's expenditures upon the mountain to make better terms with their creditors; a purpose to be discountenanced by good citizens.

While these were to be considered as hasty expressions of the few thoughtless and uninformed individuals making them, they came into association in my mind with others which had proceeded from warm friends of the enterprise, much earlier in its history.

"We, who are to pay the bills, have an interest in economy, you know." Something of that kind had been said to me often, in a kindly, advisory, and even confiding way. (Yet one of those saying it, happening to be a lawyer, I should not like to think that a like implication advanced to him by a client would have been pleasing.)

Now, I profess, in what I am about to write, to wish to commend a policy of sound economy to you, and if there is the slightest disposition to suppose that as a stranger, from whose pockets nothing you expend on the property is to come, or from any supposed personal interests in the early accomplishment of sensational results, or lack of interest in what may follow, I am disqualified for advising you on questions of economy, or am insincere in my profession, I should like, not self-defensively, but in your defence against inconsiderateness, to tell you how the case really stands.

The management of properties of the class of that under consideration, it must be premised, is a branch of business unlike any in which you have hitherto been locally interested. Judicious courses in it are less matters of intuition than in building ships, locomotives, or sewers. A servile adoption in it, under any special circumstances, of methods in use elsewhere is seldom practicable; never profitable. And yet it is absurd to suppose that you can prudently strike out recklessly of the experience of others.

I have been thirty years engaged in the study of the experience of others; have four times visited, for the purpose, the principal examples of such properties in Europe; and have practically followed, with official opportunities for doing so, the management of nine in America, besides numerous smaller ones, some being for towns of much less wealth than Montreal.

I did not seek the engagement which your commissioners, after I had declined to come to Montreal for the purpose, came to New-York to make with me.[27] I was not eager to take it, partly, I admit, because of diffidence in my ability to do justice to so unusual a problem without living for years upon the ground, and personally watching the development of its singular opportunities.

I was finally induced to accept it by information and assurances which, given in good faith, were misleading.

But when I accepted it I did so with a sense of definite business responsibility, from which it resulted that if there has been one man among you who has at any time had a wish to secure a management for the property on a lower scale of outlay (for the long run), or in any way with a more economical motive, or one who has appreciated the continuous weight of taxation, and the difficulty of maintaining it, which any respectable management of the property would involve, more fully than I, or who has more habitually, studiously, and methodically sought to wisely limit its weight and secure adequate results from what would be continuously practicable, I have never been offered the benefit of his counsel, in the smallest particular, of a plan for the purpose, while I have been wearied with promptings, from comparatively short-sighted, time-serving, and improvident points of view.

Nor, if I can be regarded as your professional adviser and an honorable man, will it be thought in the least creditable to me, or reproachful to you or any among you, that this should be so.

Still, plainly, for sound counsel's sake, the fact needs to be better understood. Therefore, let me mention further that the first advice I gave in the matter was that parts of the land pointed out to me, in my preliminary visit to the property, as that to which it was desired that I should fit a plan, were of comparatively small value for the objects in view, and that large rebates of the purchase-money might be legally, honestly, and thriftily secured, and considerable subsequent expenditure avoided, by so managing the plan as to leave them out.[28]

Again, at the moment I first put foot on the ground, I pointed out the difficulty, danger, and extravagance which would result if certain suggested "improvements," common in parks elsewhere, but by no means essential to the more important purpose of them, should be attempted on the mountain; and the better to guard against the tendency to blindly follow expensive and inappropriate precedents in this respect I then urged, as I often did afterward, that the term park, as applied to the mountain, should be discarded, and its older, more dignified, and more wholesomely suggestive appellation preserved and emphasized.

I did not wait for the hard times to urge that all manner of superfluities, and all propositions based on a consideration of particular interests of portions of the community independently of all, should be left out of view. At no time did I advise the outlay of a dollar for a merely ornamental object; at no time any building which will not be indispensable for the convenient, orderly, and decent public use of the property or for keeping its operating expenses on an economical footing.

Finally, it is of record that much of the work done on the mountain during the period of my engagement would have been done more deliberately, savingly, and at a slower rate of expenditure had not my advice been overruled by what was supposed to be popular pressure upon the Council and the commissioners.[29] To make this the clearer to you, I refer below to letters not intended by me for publication, but given to the newspapers by the commissioners. Why given, if they were not at the time reluctantly yielding to the unstudied judgment of uninformed men against their own tendencies of conviction, I know not.

I do not mean to object to such a use of my letters. My opinions on the subject were at all times your property. I remind you of the fact only because it fixes the position in which I stood when not a man of you, as far as I had reason to suppose, stood with me, and thus makes manifestly absurd the apprehensions of any who may be disposed to regard my present essay as that of a Greek bringing gifts.

On the grounds thus sufficiently set forth, I ask a hearing for the counsel I am now to offer you, and I again remind you that it may have something of that claim upon your patience which any poor words may have, said in behalf of the absent, — in this case the children and the children's children of the present Montreal, over-busy with many things besides the shaping of a permanent policy of park-management.

Note. — June 10, 1876, a letter of mine to the commissioners was published (see *Star* of that date) protesting that the road on the mountain side had been so urged ahead as to waste much material and labor; that any beauty to be enjoyed in passing over it would exist in spite, not at all in consequence, of what had been done; that a valuable opportunity had been lost forever, and that such ill-considered work could never have been allowed under the supervision of a man "influenced in the least degree by a sense of professional responsibility." The copy of this letter in my hands is introduced by an editorial note that it "demands the earnest consideration of the taxpayers." It concludes with specific recommendations which were adopted at the time by the commissioners, *but were overruled within a year by the Council.*[30]

October 5, 1876, two letters were published from me (see *Gazette*); in the first "I strongly recommend a delay" in certain proposed operations, and advise instead "some slight and inexpensive improvements." The letter concludes: "I have not a doubt that any other course will require a large expenditure for a result less satisfactory." The second is a protest against intended operations, and contains the following warning: "The necessity of making the project temporarily popular is constantly urging a policy upon your Commission, which, if its results could be fully recognized, would be anything but popular. It is most unfortunate that any attempt should be made to improve such a noble property at all, while so many elements of uncertainty exist as to conditions by which its value must be affected, and with a policy toward it, on the part of the Council, so unfixed and uncertain from year to year."[31]

An illustration may be asked for of the manner in which disconcerting propositions were urged. I will tell of one, as my memory serves about it after six or seven years. A bridle-road was called for on a certain course. The only ground on which an outlay of public money for a bridle-road upon a park can be justified is that an important part of the population will want, and cannot otherwise obtain, a place in which horses may be ridden rapidly without excessive jar, and that it can be given them at reasonable cost, and without putting other people to loss or danger. The course, in this case, was through a very attractive part of the property, and on a line constantly crossed by those using it as a rambling and picnic ground, and it is much resorted to by children. It is rocky and wooded; and, as a horse, coming rapidly upon the soft surface of a properly-made riding-way, makes little noise, if the project had been carried out, lamentable accidents could have been avoided only by so restricting speed on the road as to make it useless for its purpose, or by depriving the public in general of the more natural, appropriate, and valuable use of an important part of the property. But, in any case, the necessary grade would have been so steep that no horseman would have wished to put his horse to speed upon it. Moreover, as the intention was to take out the natural, firm earth and rock, and substitute loose gravel to a certain depth in order to get a yielding surface, every great storm sweeping down the mountain side would have made the road a ditch or gully. To guard, as far as practicable, against this, to make necessary repairs and keep the road in tolerable condition, would have been a costly business, while its value to the community would have been very questionable. Nevertheless, when I first heard of the proposition (having been already at work upon the problem of introducing a bridle-road open to none of these objections), I was told that it was so strongly backed and peremptorily insisted on that it was feared that if the commissioners did not set about it before agreeing upon the general plan the City Council would compel them to do so, and one member of the Council was named as having avowed his intention of voting for nothing advised by the commissioners until this object was accomplished. The commissioners, however, fortunately proved to be too "unpractical."

II.

As in this affair you are taking up a line of business in which you have had no local experience, and as the special conditions, topographical and climatic, are so far out of common that judgments lightly formed upon superficial observation and partial information are to be trusted even less than in most business, it is best that you should see clearly that you are, in fact, systematically leaving more in this business than in any other that you have in common to just such judgments.

So far as you know that you are doing so, and are deliberately convinced that it is prudent because of the supposed trifling importance of anything at stake between cautious and incautious management, you and your heirs must take the consequences. So far as you do not know it I ask you to look at the facts.

No other branch of your city business is carried on without the constant aid of men who have made the ends to be accomplished through it, and the means of reaching them, a subject of systematic study under competent direction. The methods of your business, not only in courts, schools, and hospitals, for instance, but in pavements, gutters, and sewers, while determined, in part, by judgments based on scrutiny of local experience during long periods, are much more determined by what certain men have learned to be the conclusions of more thorough examinations of larger and wider ranges of experience. Even where these men stand out of sight in public discussions, they are not out of reach, and they are really your main security against falling into inadequate, uselessly experimental, theoretic, and impracticable courses.

In your business on the mountain you have no such precaution available against insufficiency and excess. The architects, engineers, and craftsmen whom you may at times employ in it, though they be of the highest standing, do not necessarily know more of what its distinctive value consists in, and in what way numerous parts and operations are to work together to secure it, than the surgeon and the purser, the engineer and the steward of a steamship know of what passes in the mind of the master navigator and seaman.

Some of you forgetting how much the value of a park must be the result of its *courses in growth*, as affected by seasons and the varying discipline of nature, may have supposed that I, living in New York, was to supply what was necessary in this respect. It might almost as well be supposed that a ship could be prudently sent to sea in charge of landsmen with the precaution only of giving them written sailing directions.

I advised your commissioners, when they first came to me in New York, that any "plan" I could furnish them would be "waste paper" if it were not to be followed up by a continuous work of design in detail by men imbued with its leading motives, trained and firmly required to steadily pursue them under contingent circumstances, and with reputations of value at stake in the permanent results of their work.

Note. — The site and the general purpose seemed to me to offer the best opportunity for the exercise of original judgment and of refined and delicate taste applied to novel conditions that had ever been presented to my profession. While other engagements would have prevented me, had I been asked, from undertaking a resident superintendence of the work, I thought, upon the assurances of the commissioners and the city engineer,[32] that it would be practicable to aid in its initiation in the manner that I understood I was asked to do; that is to say, to so far advance the scheme as to fix limits of economy to what should be attempted; establish its leading aims, and determine the general character of the results to be had in view, leaving yet open to the resident executive force a most attractive and worthy field for the exercise of a high order of designing judgment. My duty I conceive to have been to supply the main plot or arrangement — the theme of the work to be afterward composed. Shakespeare was not above giving his best powers to works thus laid out by inferior men — his predecessors.

III.

Seeing that you lack for this business an element of security against immature judgments, which you have in special professional servants for everything else of corresponding importance, consider next that what are called the commissioners in your case (the park commissioners of other cities are on a different footing) are simply three members of your elected Council asked, for the time being, to give more particular attention to this branch of its business.[33] There is no other of which, when appointed, they know as little. (My acquaintance with each of the three first commissioners began with his profession that his sole qualification was a good intention.) If they take hold as men do who are bent on mastering a new business, they have no assurance that they will not be superseded before they are grounded in its rudiments. (Two of the three first appointed were displaced while I was still in conference with them.)[34] They address the other members of the Council with no authority of their own in the matter, and with none such as a building committee derives from an architect; a committee on litigations from a barrister; quarantine from a physician; aqueducts from a hydraulic engineer; schools from a teacher; fire telegraphs from an electrician; matters of fine art from an artist; and public gardens, it is to be hoped, from a gardener.

Lastly, to fully understand the riskiness of the arrangement, it must be remembered that the actual directing power of these gentlemen is so limited and uncertain that they cannot feel any strong sense of responsibility in the business. They are constantly checked in any disposition to form cautious judgments upon the question, What would best serve the permanent interests of the city? by the intrusion of the question: What will suit the momentary disposition or fitful demand of more superficial observers and of the Council? Even if they enter upon courses marked out not only with a good intention, but with all the knowledge and judgment which they can, with their best efforts, bring to bear, they well know that they are liable at any moment to be ordered out of them through the influence of men less informed in the premises and acting on less mature reflection.

If I question whether the judgment required for the prudent management of the property is to be secured by such a method of direction, it is the *method* alone that I question. I write with respect for the members of the Council and the commissioners I have known. If they were the wisest and best men in the world, and had all given years to a study of the subject, steady, good management would only be possible by inducing some few men to act in the matter with a concentration of judgment as in private business, and, as in nearly all other important public business, through a more liberal delegation of responsibility and power.

But, of course, any improvement upon the present method would make those in immediate management of the property less directly amenable to the public will, and involve greater danger of an abuse of power for selfish, partisan, factional, or local ends, and the community of Montreal may as yet be so imperfectly communified (if the term may be allowed) that the difficulties of administration to which I have pointed must be accepted as a necessity. But in that case it is obvious that prudent dealing with the property can only be hoped for through strong convictions of the ends and limits of purpose for which it can profitably be used on the part of a sufficient number of the owners to lead the force to which the Council, Commission, engineer, superintendent, forester, and foremen will alike bend their personal wills — the force of public opinion.

So long and so far as such sound conviction and genuine concern fail to be evident, is it not certain that selfish, partisan, and speculative objects, and puerile, shallow, temporising, spendthrift interests will have undue weight and will overrule proper commercial prudence?

IV.

A Wall Street property was visited by a mining engineer who found capital pumping and hoisting works, efficiently operated; a shaft and gallery skilfully timbered; a busy tram, and, at the end of a long drift, miners hard at work. "But," said he, "I see no metal." "No, sir." "I see no vein." "No, sir." "I see no signs of a vein." "No, sir." "What are you working here for?" "Two dollars a day, sir." And his visit resulted in the abandonment of an enterprise lacking but one thing of perfect business management, — an adequate purpose.

Without constant reference to a fixed leading purpose, you cannot spend a dollar on the mountain with any assurance that it is not wasted. If your leading purpose is trivial, or of but temporary consequence, you have already spent more than you can afford upon it. It is childish to go further. Every dollar you appropriate will be a dollar more of inexcusable extravagance.

To open discussion upon the question, What purpose is adequate to justify your purchase of the property, the outlay you have made, and any fur-

362

ther outlay you may choose to make for better turning it to account? Suppose the following proposition offered for your consideration — a proposition I do not mean to sustain, but which, I doubt, will for a moment be very unsatisfactory to many of you to whom the business is new:

"The value of this city property is to depend on the degree in which it shall be adapted to attract citizens to obtain needful exercise and cheerful mental occupation in the open air, with the result of better health and fitness in all respects for the trials and duties of life; with the result also, necessarily, of greater earning and tax-paying capacities, so that in the end the investment will be, in this respect, a commercially profitable one to the city."

Taking this as a definition of your purpose, roads and walks will be so made to and on the mountain as to give the readiest access to its more important points of view and objects of interest, and to make exercise convenient and agreeable. Trees will be removed when of ugly forms, threatening to fall from decay, or when they too much interrupt distant prospects; trees planted where needed for shading and ornamenting the roads, walks, and points of view. Staircases, seats, shelters, and drinking-fountains will be provided to make the taking of air and exercise more convenient, and they will be so designed and placed as to form in themselves additional objects of attraction and agreeably hold the attention. If, through private liberality or by public subscription, as has occurred in most parks, statues, fountains, sculptural memorials of men or events, or other objects of art or scientific interest can be obtained, they will, as usual, be given such prominent position as will present them to the best advantage. So also as to buildings, such as museums, prospect-towers, club-houses, and fanciful houses of entertainment.

It will be obvious that with the general purpose thus stated, and the policy growing out of it, cheapness of management might easily be had. All required roads might be ordered, for example, almost as easily as so many miles of iron piping. The laying out and building of them is but a common engineering operation. In like manner, monuments and architectural works, as easily for the mountain as for a cemetery or a garden. Most of the work otherwise called for corresponds closely with that which can generally be got in private life out of any good hired man, well-directed, with an occasional lift from a jobbing gardener or florist. What more may be wanted at times in particular constructions is an every-day affair of architects, masons, carpenters, paviors, and painters.

To manage the mountain, with this theory of its value in view, would require more of a man's time and thought, because the operations would be larger and should, perhaps, be more substantial and more refined than those of an ordinary private lawn and door-yard, but only that; nothing essentially different from what hundreds of you are, every summer, doing for yourselves without any deep absorption of purpose; in fact, without interruption of your regular and more serious avocations, without special study, and rather in a recreative and care-free humor.

And the fact that such an estimate of what thought is wanted for the mountain slides easily into the ordinary courses of life, that it satisfies a common form of self-esteem, and suits established mental habits, makes it hard to lay aside even though it be seen to embody a fallacy.

That it does embody a fallacy will be clear to every man of you if he ask himself what would be the difference of attractive effect — literally speaking — if for that object which he has found most attractive, tree, flower-bed, or fountain, in the garden or fore-court, which is altogether the most attractive among all those which he is in the habit of passing, there should be substituted some fine morning a Punch and Judy show, or a hog with its face shaved, dressed in a woman's cap and cloak, seated in an arm-chair facing the street?

The truth is that with no shrewder purpose than the proposition I have stated represents, not half the dividends which the property may be profitably made to yield, will be attainable.

V.

The first step toward a safe conclusion as to the general purpose to be had in view will be, in this, as it would in any other business, to determine what the situation puts economically out of the question.

Suppose that the owners of a vacant lot with a narrow frontage on an important business street were about to determine what to build upon it. These stated conditions of space, frontage, and situation would at once rule out two large classes of buildings: first, such as would be inadequate to the value of the ground — a cottage, for example; second, such as the ground would be inadequate to sustain, as a hotel, an iron foundry, or a theatre.

So, as to the site for a park. If a city has a large area of level prairie it can, without excluding or cramping provisions for other park purposes, provide great breadths of tranquil scenery with parade, lacrosse, cricket, archery, tennis, and croquet grounds, all in excellent fashion at small cost, the landscape motives, and others in which the whole community has a direct interest, harmonizing with the special motives of recreation of particular classes.*

But any attempt to form picturesque scenery through abrupt variations of surface, not to be puerile in its results, will be costly and to aim at having an outlook comparable with that you have already obtained on the mountain will be, if not impossible, ridiculously extravagant.†

---

*In the New York park the number of people who come to it in summer for special forms of recreation is not one in several hundred of those who come for walking, riding, driving, and the enjoyment of the scenery in a broad way, and this, I believe, is true of all well-ordered parks.

†"Everyone knows how flat is the surface of Holland. Their parks may have plenty of still-water views, and grass, trees, and flowers all grow well there; but in Leyden they were determined to have a hill too. Great labor, no doubt, was spent, and enough

Having chosen ground everywhere broken and with but scanty breadths of thin soil at any point between its rocks your case is the reverse. Economy begins with fixing upon a plan and a permanent policy in the business which looks to nothing which could be better accomplished at much less cost on less rugged ground. True, this restricts the value of your park. But consider the compensation: for example, in this one respect.

In parks at Liverpool, London, Paris, Milan, Genoa, and other cities, there is a good deal of rock brought with cost from a distance, or of artificial rock made of materials brought from a distance, set as facings to mounds laboriously built up so as to obtain scraps and ravellings of scenery which will seem, under the circumstances, to have a flavor of this same quality of ruggedness. The rock, in itself, is generally ugly; the mounds are hills suitable for a doll's pleasure-ground, but, when aided by adequate vegetation skilfully selected and disposed, the comparatively insipid *picturesquishness* of the result is generally regarded by those who pay for the work as economically purchased.

Of raw material of this quality you have already on your ground a wealth beside which all that these older cities have accumulated is poverty. At slight cost you may soon obtain results of the same class beside which theirs will be backwoods makeshifts.

I know that there is a prevalent notion that you must make the best of such opportunities as you find upon your site for purposes to which it is not generally well adapted, but you cannot build a policy on this basis *without bringing aims in which success can never be satisfactory into conflict with aims through which any adequate return for your total outlay must mainly come.*

In short, the conclusive objection to the entire tendency of management with which I am now contending, and the drift to which may perhaps be deeper and stronger and more insidious than you can readily realize, is that it favors a constant waste of what, if preserved, will unquestionably be, in the long future of the city, the two most important elements of value in this property. For, if you think of it, the reasoning out of which it grows, while allowing some value to natural objects of beauty (trees, for example) with reference to the purpose of air and exercise, first, wholly disregards the pervading charm of natural scenery (scenery in distinction from scenes) with reference to this purpose, and the result of pursuing it would, by the interposition of a variety of objects appealing to a different exercise of taste, greatly restrict if not wholly pervert such charm; then, second, it wholly leaves out of account an element of value much more important to be borne in mind than inducements to take air and exercise — more important because much less available to the city by other means than the improvement of the mountain — the *intrinsic* value of charming natural scenery.

---

sticky clay has been scooped out of the neighboring canals and piled up in the centre of their park to make a mound, perhaps twenty feet high." — Professor S. E. Baldwin.[35]

That this last element of value in the mountain is one for practical consideration, that it is a matter of dollars and cents to you quite as much as air and exercise, I will show in the next chapter.

Here it remains to be affirmed that the opportunities and advantages for producing certain charms of natural scenery which you hold as yet *inert and unproductive* in the mountain, are such as are possessed by no other city in any ground held for a public park. To allow it to be so used and dealt with as that these elements of value shall be lost, will be a scandalous extravagance.

VI.

It is a great mistake to suppose that the value of charming natural scenery lies wholly in the inducement which the enjoyment of it presents to change of mental occupation, exercise, and air-taking. Beside and above this, it acts in a more directly remedial way to enable men to better resist the harmful influences of ordinary town life, and recover what they lose from them. It is thus, in medical phrase, a prophylactic and therapeutic agent of vital value; there is not one in the apothecaries' shops as important to the health and strength or to the earning and tax-paying capacities of a large city. And to the mass of the people it is practically available only through such means as are provided through parks.

This is simply a fact. If we want to go behind the fact—from the physician to the metaphysician—we must begin by reflecting that a charm is something that acts, we know not how, to make us in some way different from what we should otherwise be; that is, it acts otherwise than through our reason.

This is the primary superstitious idea of a charm—of what is charming. We can apply the term rationally to scenery only because of a common experience that certain scenery has a tendency to lift us out of our habitual condition into one which, were the influence upon us stronger and the moods and frames of mind toward which it carried us more distinctly defined, we should recognize as poetic. Let us say that for the time being the charm of natural scenery tends to make us poets. There is a sensibility to poetic inspiration in every man of us, and its utter suppression means a sadly morbid condition. Poets, we may not be, but a little lifted out of our ordinary prose we may be often to our advantage.

To compare our small measures with larger let us take a recorded experience of a full-grown poet.

Wordsworth (only greater in poetic sensibility than anyone of us, not differently organized, not differently affected by medicine) came home from a painful experience in France after its great revolution, sick, broken down, unfit for business. Everything was going wrong with him. His sister, Dorothy, of whom it has been well said that she was the greater poet of the two, only that she was *not a literary poet*, watched his symptoms, saw the nature of his trouble, and divined the cure. She persuaded him to let her guide him into the midst of charming scenery, and to subject himself for a time to its influence; "and thus," says Doctor Shairp, telling the story, "began that sanative process which restored him to his true self and made that blessing to the world he was destined to become."[36]

These terms (sanative, restoring) are not metaphorical. They testify precisely that the charm of natural scenery is an influence of the highest curative value; highest, if for no other reason, because it acts directly upon the highest functions of the system, and through them upon all below, tending, more than any single form of medication we can use, to establish sound minds in sound bodies — the foundation of all wealth.

For practical purposes, such as we are now discussing, it is not necessary to better understand how this influence works; it is not necessary that we should agree upon a theory of it, but some may like to feel their way toward an idea on the subject, with such aid as Doctor Shairp attempts to give in the following comments on the case of Wordsworth:

"Continuing that study of nature (not with the science of the botanist or the florist, but the poet) he at last came to hold with conscious conviction what he had at first felt, hardly knowing that he felt it, that Nature had a life of her own, which streamed through and stimulated his life; a spirit which, in itself invisible, spoke through visible things to his spirit.

"That the characteristics of this spirit were *calmness which stilled and refreshed man*.

"Sublimity which raised him to noble thoughts.

"Tenderness which, while stirring in the largest and loftiest things, condescends to the lowest; is with the humblest worm and weed as much as in the greatest movements of the elements and of the stars.

"Above all, nature he now saw to be the shape and image of right reason — reason in its highest sense, — embodied and made visible in order; stability; in conformity to eternal law. The perception of this satisfied his intellect, calmed and soothed his heart." — *The Poetic Interpretation of Nature*, p. 240.[37]

It may be added that this influence is such with reference to the highest form of the prosperity of a community that many divines have referred to it in terms commonly reserved for means of grace and religious nurture more distinctly canonical. Since the disciples were led out of the town to the mount (as to this day the children of Jerusalem are led to the same high olive groves), men have ever found "tongues in trees, books in running brooks, sermons in stones." Moreover, as George Herbert said of the work of the "literary poet," it may happen that the word thus preached shall sometimes

> " — find him who a sermon flies,
> And turn delight into a sacrifice."[38]

Another writer (J. A. Symonds, in *Fortnightly Review*) says:[39]

"What Science is not called on to supply, the fervor and the piety that humanize her truths, and bring them into harmony with permanent emotions of the soul, may be found in all that Wordsworth wrote: —

> 'For I have learned
>   To look on nature, not as in the hour
> Of thoughtless youth; but hearing oftentimes
>   The still, sad music of humanity,
> Nor harsh nor grating, though of ample power
>   To chasten and subdue. And I have felt
> A presence that disturbs me with the joy
>   Of elevated thoughts: a sense sublime
> Of something far more deeply interfused,
>   Whose dwelling is the light of setting suns,
> And the round ocean and the living air,
>   And the blue sky, and in the mind of man:
> A motion and a spirit, that impels
>   All thinking things, all objects of all thought,
> And rolls through all things.'"[40]

VII.

The possession of charming natural scenery is a form of wealth as practical as that of wholesome air, pure water, or sunlight unobstructed by smoke and fog; as practical, then, as that of sewers, aqueducts, and pavements. And whatever of sensible purpose there was in your selection of the mountain property for a park, was a purpose to increase your common wealth in that form.

If, therefore, in discussing questions of its management, or in urging what shall or what shall not be done with it on the ground of economy, you take, as you generally have done, no serious business-like account of what makes for or against poetic value, do you not stultify yourselves?

What I ask you to accept as the true key to economy on the mountain is the clear sense that by the degree in which people, while resorting to it, will be subject to the bracing, soothing, tranquilizing medication of poetical scenery, in that degree will it be valuable, and your investment in it profitable. In so far as the management fails to constantly serve that end; in so far, especially, as it runs counter to it, you must judge those responsible for it as you would judge those responsible for leaky sewers and wasting aqueducts.

Determine your attractions simply with reference to air and exercise instead of to this purpose, and your park will be like a school which provides instruction, but not education; a police which aims at the punishment, not the prevention of crime; a church aiming at a moral, but not a religious character.

Yet it may be as well to consider that if you secure this all else will be added. The air will not be fouled by that which gives poetic charm to the scenery, nor will exercise in it be enervating.

VIII.

Soon after you bought the property a friend of mine said to one of your citizens, whose experience should make his counsel valuable in your debates: "You are going to improve the mountain?" "No," was the reply; "we are going to spoil it." This gentleman may have had a greater degree of foresight in one respect than many of you. Possibly you would not have made your purchase if you had all as plainly seen that much of what made the property attractive to you depended upon the wildness and seclusion of its natural elements.

If it is to be cut up with roads and walks, spotted with shelters, and streaked with staircases; if it is to be strewn with lunch papers, beer bottles, sardine cans and paper collars; and if thousands of people are to seek their recreation upon it unrestrainedly, each according to his special tastes, it is likely to lose whatever of natural charm you first saw in it.

It is true, moreover, that when the mountain is suitably fitted for public use and traversed by gaily-dressed throngs of ladies and children, polished carriages, and highly groomed and caparisoned horses, that much of its original nature will appear comparatively rude, harsh, incongruous, and dreary.

What follows? Surely not that you should abandon your purpose; surely not that the more money you spend on improvements the less value for your purpose the mountain will have.

It follows only that all that you have seen and admired of the old work of nature must be considered as simply suggestive of what (that is practicable, suitable, and harmonious with your purposes of large popular use) nature, wisely entreated, will give you in place of what must be abandoned.

You need to have new mountain ideals in view; ideals with more not less, of poetic charm; and your roads and other artificial constructions must be made with studied regard to that which you thus have before you, not to what you are necessarily putting behind. To accomplish this transition skilfully and gracefully requires, it must be admitted, an exercise of judgment and taste in a direction not often followed with commercial purposes; and it must be further admitted that if you secure this and yet cannot, as a community, find satisfaction in anticipating, forecasting, and watching the development of the new charm, and in seeing it gradually emerge from and overgrow the ruin of the old, then the gentleman I have quoted was in the right, and the policy was sound which I presume him to have since followed, of opposing every measure of pretended improvements upon the mountain as, in truth, a measure for spoiling it. Indeed, no man should account himself a gentleman to whom any other course is not only repugnant, but in whom such measures do not stir up a disposition to something more than idle grumbling.

In short, it is not to be denied that you cheated yourselves when you bought the mountain for a park, unless you were prepared to have it managed on principles applicable to WORKS OF ART.

IX.

Before I go further it is perhaps but just that I should still more distinctly say that there was never a moment's difference between your first board of park commissioners[41] and myself as to the general soundness of the views I have been urging upon you. There were great departures from the course which I think those views would have prescribed, but they were always made on grounds of expediency — as a yielding to demands which it would be impolitic to further resist, and on the principle that half a loaf is better than no bread. But the fact is, if you could be convinced of it, the whole loaf would cost you less than the half.

X.

I have been urging you to regard the work to be done in your behalf on the mountain as primarily a work of art, and to insist that in this respect you shall have the fair value of what you pay for it.

I have used the term with some reluctance, because there is so much quacking and silly affectation afloat about art, that with many sensible people the simplest mention of it kindles prejudice. I know also that to speak of the work before you on the mountain as a work of art will again seem "unpractical," as looking to something above the heads of the people and opening channels of lavish expenditure.

I beg all who feel about it at all in this way to let me ask, first, are you sure that if you oppose art ever so much you are going to get on without it? Are you sure, that by a method which compels an offhand, slap-dash way of going to work you escape quackings and affectations? Is it not smart, shallow, Jack-of-all-trades art that is most of all contemptible to you? Can you despise or wish to put away art, of which the chief condition is a sincere, devoted, and devout application of judgment to the purpose upon which it is engaged?

Second, please reflect also whether it may not be a teaching of snobbishness and vulgarity against which every true man should rebel, that good art is above the heads of the common people. Those whom all accept as the highest authority regard the highest art to be that which was made for public places and for the use of all.

Psalms and hymns are works of art, and to this day, in the degree that they rank high or low in the scale of art, are they consoling and cheering to generation after generation of the poor and needy.

Among thousands of college-bred Scotchmen not one has shown as high poetic sensibility as the ploughboy Burns,[42] and this sensibility is strongly exhibited in respect to the charm of natural scenery formed largely by art.

This may seem a contradiction of terms. It is not. When an artist puts a stick in the ground, and nature in time makes it a tree, art and nature are not to be seen apart in the result. In verses called out by an enjoyment of a brawling stream under trees, the ploughboy begs for the planting of more trees, that the poetic charm by which he has been inspired may be deepened by art.*

But, third, as to the economy of art. You know that the market-value of a literary work of art (the psalms of David, the novels of Scott, the idylls of Tennyson) does not depend on the amount of paper and ink used in them; that a work of the painter's art is not valued by counting the cost of the canvas, pigments, and day's labor which has been spent on it, or a statue by the cost of the marble and its cutting. You know also that of the works of two men, given the same subject to draw, paint, or carve, one representing no more school-knowledge, industry, faithfulness, or hand-labor, only higher art, will sell at once for ten times as much as the other, and that this difference in market value instead of lessening will increase century after century.†

> * Last day I grat wi spite and teen,
>   As poet Burns came by,
> That to a Bard I should be seen
>   Wi half my channel dry:
> A panegyric rhyme, I ween,
>   Even as I was he shor'd me;
> But had I in my glory been,
>   He, kneeling, wud ador'd me.
>   *   *   *   *
> Would thou my noble master please
>   To grant my highest wishes,
> He'll shade my banks wi tow'ring trees,
>   And bonnie spreading bushes.
>   *   *   *   *
> Let lofty firs, and ashes cool,
>   My lowly banks o'erspread,
> And view, deep bending in the pool,
>   Their shadows' wat'ry bed!
> Let fragrant birks, in woodbines drest,
>   My craggy cliffs adorn;
> And, for the little songster's nest,
>   The close embowring thorn.[43]

† The city of Amsterdam possesses a little picture, and I have seen laboring men smiling before it, of which it has been lately written that "it was sold in 1766 for 8,000 francs, and in 1808, for 35,000, and that certainly a cypher added to the last sum would not be sufficient to buy it now." — Holland, by E. de Amicis. New York: Putnam's Sons.[44]

There is this, then, about good art; it is not, like bad art, to go out of fashion. Let your work upon the mountain be directed by sound art, and the older the results the more they will be valued; the oftener and more familiarly they are seen the more wholesome pleasure will be taken in them.

Again, then, in your choice of what to do, have some regard for your heirs.

XI.

An incident occurred in the early work upon the mountain which gave rise to some discussion in which a proposition was more or less definitely advanced or its soundness assumed, which may be thus stated:

"Suppose a road is to be made along a naturally wooded and otherwise attractive hillside, and it is an object to give those who pass over the road as much as practicable of the enjoyment of its natural scenery, then the simpler the means taken to obtain desirable courses and grades; the more strictly operations are confined to the space necessary to obtain them; and the less cutting and covering of the adjacent ground, the better. The highest art consists, under such circumstances, in making the least practicable disturbance of nature; the highest refinement in a refined abstinence of effort; in the least work, and the most simple and the least fussy and pottering."

To see the crudity of this dictum, consider first, what must necessarily result from proceeding upon it, and, to make the principle plainer, suppose that the hillside is a little steeper and a little more perfectly furnished with old wood than was the case on the mountain.

You lay out as an engineering affair what is the most direct, convenient, and economical route with reference to the purpose of transportation. You begin construction by removing the trees in the way of a road of the prescribed breadth. You then have two broken lines of spindling trunks supporting sprawling limbs, which sustain meagre tufts of feeble foliage, not at all natural, for if the opening had been a natural one, such as might have been caused, for example, by a watercourse, or a long narrow outcrop of rock, the trees would have grown beside it in a way much more effective for your purpose; a much more beautiful way.

Next, to obtain a plane surface for your road, you break into the slope of the mountain on one side, and bank out on the other. You then have two steep, formal, unnatural banks, one above your wheel-way, the other below it. Next, as you will have cut off a third of the roots of the trees growing above, and banked over a third of the roots of those growing immediately below, and established conditions favorable to a constant waste of the natural vegetable mould, the change from the circumstances to which the bordering trees are habituated in respect to moisture, food, frost, and light, will lessen their vitality.

It may happen that in process of time, by the death of some of them, the decay of their roots, and through the effect of freezing, thawing, washing, and vegetable growth and decay, your banks will take natural forms more or less agreeable. Of the trees that do not soon die, some will sprout out in an eccentric new growth; suckers will be thrown out from the roots of others; and, here and there, young trees and bushes will grow up from seed in front of the old ones.

In this way the first rude aspect of your work will be partly obliterated, partly obscured, and a degree of natural charm obtained; if the circumstances are favorable it may even be accounted a high degree of charm. And yet it will have been folly, worse than the folly of gambling, to take your chance in this way of the value of the results, for, even with the same inconsiderate grades and courses for your wheel-way, you can shape the banks at once in such desirable forms as frost, and rain, and root growths might chance to give them after many years. You can do more. You can, by a little forecast, make them at one point bolder and more picturesque in contour by a fitting buttress of rock than nature, working alone, would be able to do. By inserting little pockets of leaf-mould about this rock, and proper seeds or plants, you can then prevail upon nature to dress it with characteristic mountain forms of foliage and bloom, more interesting than nature would, in a century, otherwise provide. You can put in the way of immediate growth behind this rock a broad dark mass of low mountain pine, or a pensive, feathery and brooding hemlock, educated to a character which nature, left alone, gives to one of its species in a thousand, to supply the degree of canopy and shadow which will be most effective for your purpose. And, this being done, you are finally relieved of the nuisance and expense which the natural washing down of your abrupt bank would have otherwise entailed.

Then, at another point, you can cut back on the crest of your bank and make it gentle and graceful, with long double curves of the surface, dressed with low, soft verdure and decked with modest wild flowers.

You can cut out the feebler and uglier of the old trees (their ugliness is due in many cases to the falling of others upon them and other unhappy accidents); shorten in the tops of others more promising, but which have been strained upward in feeble forms to avoid suffocation in the crowd. You can enrich the soil and induce a lower growth upon them; and you can everywhere plant at once such trees, shrubs, and herbage as will best harmonize with what you select to stay of this old wood, and best carry out, grace, and enrich the necessary inanimate detail of the immediate road border.

Thus, you can rapidly establish a new face to the wood which will in truth be equally natural in aspect, and, whether regarded as the foreground of a distant view or looked at closely for its local beauty, far more charming than the best that nature, *unencouraged*, would much more slowly give you.

Why is it more irrational to thus sympathetically coöperate with nature for the end which you have in view in your use of this property, than for that of raising apples, corn, or buckwheat, where nature, left to herself, would not provide them?

373

And yet the process I have here imagined, of laying out a road, determining its courses and grades with no regard to scenery, and then adapting scenery to them, is by no means a completely rational or economical one.

Second, then, sound art, following sound sense and sound economy, will require, at the first step, and at every step afterward, a forecast of the best attainable ultimate results, and in view of them will waive a little of directness here, a little of grade there, so as to spare an interesting group of trees, or a bold rock, and place them at such a distance from, and in such relation of elevation to, the eye of those passing on the road, as to enhance their value. Sound sense and economy will make a similar concession in view of the poverty of some broad, flat, uninteresting body of rock; bending the road slightly from its direct course, or carrying it up a little more rapidly with a view either of putting the rock out of sight under the road, or of leaving sufficient beds of soil for the growth of plantations to cover it.

This, then, is the precept which a more mature study of art would have reached. A road must be located not alone with reference to economy of construction in respect to convenience of passage from one point to another, but with reference to *economy in the ultimate development of resources of poetic charm of scenery*; and these resources must be considered comprehensively and interactingly with reference to the entire property.

This is not simply a requirement of art over and above the requirements of mere engineering, but, as with reference to the manner in which the first road-making on the mountain was done differently from that I had provided for, is a requirement of sound in distinction from unsound art; of good art over bad. Those who urge the rejection of the good and the adoption of the bad, under the impression that something is to be thus gained in economy, are the real spendthrifts and prodigals. And the principle, thus illustrated, applies to every thing to be done — quite as much, for instance, to walks, staircases, seats, shelters, shades (and shade trees), to gutters, gratings, drinking-fountains, and horse-watering-places, as to wheel-ways; most of all to any necessary buildings.

XII.

There are, upon the mountain, spaces of raw, barren surface, possessing no element of natural beauty, and in no way agreeably interesting; simply blots. Indeed, it must be confessed that, in parts, most even of the trees are rather forlorn objects; forlorn both as individuals and in their grouping. Many on the heights are of kinds which, for anything like their full natural beauty, as they reach mature years, require a rich soil, genial climate, and freedom to stretch widely out in root and branch. In parts of the mountain they lack each one of these conditions, and, consequently, bear all the marks of severe exposure, of Arctic temperature, of having grown in shallow, rock-bottomed pockets of poor soil, alternately arid and water-soaked, and of barely surviving in a struggle for existence one with another, and all against those vermin which attack feeble vegetable life.

Many are decrepid with wounds and premature old age, and these, while they cannot possibly hold out many years, and are now falling, or casting their limbs with mortal injury to others in every storm, are yet cramping, starving, and suffocating the more promising.

The error in art, referred to in the last chapter, would preserve and maintain this aspect of mountain scenery, simply because it is a natural aspect, and *does not wholly exclude* the charm of nature. Would it not be as rational for a farmer to say that because his cows sometimes pick a little food out of boggy vegetation he will not drain the ground and get a field of rich, corn-producing soil?

By a little improvement of the elements of growth; removing unsuitable and hopelessly debilitated trees; heading down; healing the wounds; balancing and protecting the more sturdy; planting low and specially hardy conifers and underwood in the northern and western borders, and gradually developing wind-breaks; introducing in each available situation trees and shrubs distinctively adapted to the circumstances; protecting all from fire, vermin, and the violence of man, there is not the least ground for doubt that a great and happy change in the general aspect of even the most forlorn localities would be brought about; a change giving a large return for the necessary investment.

Nor is it to be apprehended that the new aspect would be less natural, or less mountain-like, or in any respect less valuable, than that which it would supersede. It would surely be much more so.

The most common trees on the more exposed, dry, barren parts of the mountain, are such oaks as under congenial circumstances are the stateliest of all northern trees. Examine them closely and (excepting the few white oaks, and these only where they have been a little favored in respect to room) you will hardly find one that does not appear out of place, deformed, mutilated in its trunks and limbs, scraggy, and, in the heat of summer, weak and sickly in foliage. These are not picturesque and interesting, as characteristic mountain trees often are, through their ingenious and successful efforts to adapt themselves to trying conditions, but have the fixed sad look of unacclimated emigrants, hopelessly depressed by conditions foreign to their inherited habits and instincts.

Yet, under the same, or even harder conditions, hanging where there seems to be no soil at all, you will find a few sumacs which are pictures of health and contentment; quite as much so as if the seed from which they sprang had happened to fall in a rich, sheltered meadow; more so than if they had been pampered in your lawns and gardens. Look, too, at some of the thorns; and, again, at the ironwood: where it has not been excessively crowded or crippled by fire or violence, you will almost always find it in good health. But here again you see the need of discrimination, for, if the mountain were covered with ironwood, you would lose a good month of summer beauty, its period of leafage being so unusually short.

But you need not lack all desirable variety.* If you do not find enough in the sound and healthy indigenous trees of the neighborhood, you can draw some beautiful species from Siberia and the high Alps of Europe, suitable for the most exposed situations, and if you go to work a-right they need cost you but a few cents a-piece.

A large proportion of all the trees on the mountain, not yet saplings, have suffered from the effects of ice storms or the falling of others. They have, in consequence, fractures and wounds which are the starting-points of processes of decay. Often this has already reached the heart of the tree, and is beyond remedy. These trees have little life left. Others not yet so badly affected are constitutionally injured and will not attain full growth. As they become weaker, their branches or trunks falling will again be destructive to others.

Trees should be planted with references to the vacancies which are to be anticipated, and a constant systematic pruning should be kept up. Thousands of trees could be preserved by good pruning to grow to twice the size, and ten times the age which they are otherwise likely to attain. The pruning required is not that of an orchard, or an avenue, or a forest, but it differs from that taught in scientific economical forestry only so far as the aim should be neither to induce individual symmetry of head, nor long, "clear" timber trunks, but rather a compact and sturdy growth, and heads formed not to stand independently, but picturesquely massing with others, the value of each tree being, as a rule, dependent on an interchange of influence with others grouping with it. Often it will be best to head off the natural leader; often to induce a strong low, lateral growth, such as in economic forestry is to be prevented. With this reservation, the best conveniently available instruction in the principles of good pruning for the mountain, for those who wish to intelligently watch its forestry, will be found in a recent publication for the Massachusetts Society for the Promotion of Agriculture, by Williams & Co., Boston: *A Treatise on Pruning Forest Trees, by A. des Cars. Translated from the Seventh French edition by C. S. Sargent, Professor of Arboriculture in Harvard College*.[45] One of the mottoes of this book is: "It is the duty of an enlightened

---

*There is a large park near St. Petersburg, in which trees of but three species have been used, and M. André, the author of "L'Art des Jardins," having examined it while travelling under a commission from the government of France, says that the result is impressive and agreeable. I advise no such simplicity, but it would be a great deal better than a meaningless medley of all available trees.[46]

community to plant trees, and to so take care of them *that posterity shall not suffer."* — Decaigne.[47]

XIII.

Necessarily, in a resort for thousands, there must be much that is not natural and not in itself poetic, but I fear that I have reason to more distinctly urge that this is no ground upon which to justify a neglect to secure the largest practicable measure of poetic charm. It simply requires that all available means shall be taken for making the necessary artificial things of the park as inconspicuous as is consistent with a frank avowal of their purpose, and for preventing incongruous things without the park from being forced on the attention of those needing to obtain relief from them.

Taking again for illustration, a road, (because it is the most unavoidably conspicuous artificial thing that you must have), you will have been compelled at various points by the topography to so lay it out that, though slightly curving, its course is open to view and excessively prominent far ahead, dissecting and distracting the landscape. Planting trees close upon the road, they must either be trimmed too high to serve as a screen to its course ahead, or their limbs will, in time, obstruct passage upon the road. Your resort, then, must be to bushes of species chosen with reference to the height and breadth of foliage they will ultimately develop, with a view to the range of vision of observers in carriages. If there is a walk following the road it should, in such cases, be so far divided from it as to give room for the required bank of low foliage between it and the wheel-way.[*]

A similar course will be taken where roads are approaching a junction, to prevent one from being unnecessarily conspicuous in looking from another.

Still more imperatively, with like motives, you will plant both trees and thickets of underwood wherever from within the property there is a liability that outside objects, of which the influence on the mind would be adverse to your ruling purpose, may, in the future, be forced on the attention.

For example, it cannot serve that purpose, it can serve no proper purpose for which you hold the property, that tombs, hearses, and groups of mourners shall be brought into view from it, or the backs and out-buildings of adjoining dwellings, or factory walls and chimneys, such as it may be some-one's interest, by and by, to build at any point on its borders. Consequently, the first thing to be done is the planting of outer screens of foliage that will guard against such waste of mountain value. These, on the northern

---

[*]These bushes, however large you may mean them finally to grow, will at first be mere whips, and of paltry and even disturbing effect, but you will thus, at a third of the expense of planting large ones, obtain in the end more valuable results.

side especially, will be mainly of sturdy conifers, as white and red pine, hemlock, and very hardy dwarf mountain-pines (lightened up a little with white birches, ironwood, and moose-maple), so that in time they will also provide wind-breaks and temperers by which the park will be made available to the recreation of delicate people one or two months longer than otherwise.

But besides the more direct economies, sufficiently suggested, of such low screen-plantings, they would, if wisely made, incidentally go far to secure qualities in the scenery of the mountain (generally referred to in books on the subject as intricacy, obscurity, and mystery, and through these affecting the apparent aerial-perspective) of which the result would be more than equivalent to doubling the extent and value, *for your purpose*, of the property. I have frequently known intelligent countrymen estimate an area of broken ground, through which they had been walked, actually of thirty acres, at from seventy-five to a hundred, and solely because of such treatment of it.

Such prescriptions as these, I hardly need say, are of the alphabet of the business. No man who has given the slightest study to it can be unfamiliar with them. Yet, as I regret to testify, propositions were at an early day urged upon your commissioners so confidently and from such influential quarters that they were forced, if not to yield to them, to give them grave and anxious consideration, in which principles of management directly the reverse were assumed as if their adoption were to be a matter of course, nor did your commissioners appear to have ground for confidence that in resisting them they would have any strong support in the public opinion of the present generation.

XIV.

In works of art which the experience of the world has stamped of a high grade of value, there is found a strong single purpose, with a variety of subordinate purposes so worked out and working together that the main purpose is the better served because of the diversity of these subordinate purposes. The first secures the quality of unity and harmony; the others, that of a controlled variety.

Sound business management will surely seek to gain value for your property by making use of the same double method. False economy will think it impracticable, or of no consequence, or that it will make too much trouble; failing to count the cost and losses of what it assumes to be of less trouble.

You have chosen to take a mountain for your park, but, in truth, a mountain barely worthy of the name. You would call it a hill if it stood a few miles further away from the broad, flat, river valley. Its scenery, that is to say, is but relatively mountainous. Yet, whatever of special adaptation it has to your purpose lies in that *relative* quality. It would be wasteful to try to make anything else than a mountain of it; equally wasteful to attempt anything which would involve a loss of such advantages as it has for this purpose. No condition of economical management, then, is more stringently binding than that of a steady resistance to all short-sighted aims which would result in such waste, or lead to conditions inconsistent with mountain dignity, serenity, and strength. Fancies, fashions, and affectations, for which room might be temporarily allowed on another site, should have no place. But this unity involves neither sameness nor sombreness. The queen is not less queenly for jewels on her head, ermine on her shoulders, and velvet in her skirts.

Small as your mountain is, it presents in different parts no little variety of mountain form and feature. A leading economy in its management will be found to lie in turning to still better account this consistent diversity, so that the visitor in passing out of one part into another, will receive a stronger impression and be more charmed than he would with greater sameness.

In a separate map appended to the general plan furnished you, I have designated eight topographical divisions of the mountain, each possessing natural characteristics distinguishing it from those adjoining. In the selection and development of the choicer distinctive peculiarities of these several divisions, the exhibition of them to the best advantage, and the merging of them harmoniously together in one consistent beautiful mountain, the highest economy will be found.*

I will presently point out the distinctive raw material of each, and give some indication of how its value is to be increased; but I wish first to suggest one other general motive of unity which should be kept in mind, in addition to that referred to in the last chapter of obscuring incongruities.

It is to so select the material of planting, or the native material to be left growing, that, within reasonable limits, the principle upon which Nature, unassisted, proceeds in her selections (though often very imperfectly) shall be emphasized, idealized, or made more apparent in landscape quality.

In the lower and less rugged parts, that is to say, the predominating trees should be such as attain their most perfect character only under conditions still lower, more fertile, and softer; the elms being the most characteristic of those available to you. These parts should also be planted (where screens or wind-breaks are not required) in more open groups, and every fair opportunity taken to leave clean, unbroken surfaces of turf between the groups.

On the other hand, in the most elevated, exposed, Arctic, and continuously rocky regions, the predominating trees should be those which are

---

* "The first law of a work of art, either on canvas or on the earth, is to be a whole." —*André, L'Art des Jardins*, p. 119.[48]

"Mount Royal

found to occur naturally in even more trying situations, certain scrubby pines, for instance (as *Banksiana*, which grows near Ottawa), and firs, with the lesser birches, hornbeams, and thorns. Yet, a little lower, the white and red pines and hemlock, the canoe and red birches, the rock, mountain, Norway, and moose maples, with underwood and thickets of rowans, wych-hazel, the native honeysuckles, wild currant, fragrant bramble, the Canadian redbud, sumacs, clethra, rhodora, and other thoroughly hardy and stronggrowing shrubs. Then, lower still, oaks, bass-wood, butternut, ash, cherry, red maple, and such variety of low trees, bushes, prostrate shrubs, and vines as will be found necessary to obscure all places where the soil is too thin and poor for turf and the rock flat, scaly and uninteresting.

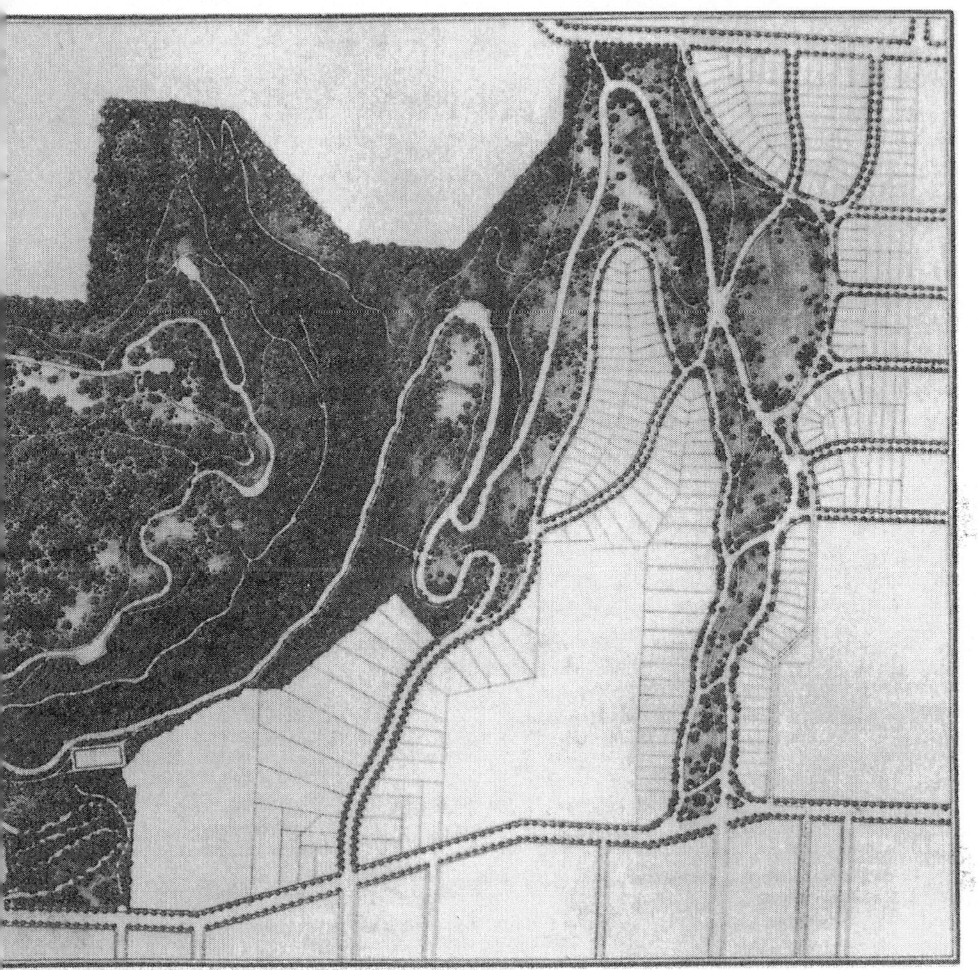

Design Map," 1877

Pursuing this hint skilfully, and not at all in a pedantic or exact spirit, you will cheaply give a stronger emphasis to the difference of elevation between your mountain top and base, making your mountain more mountainlike, gaining: withal, a natural and appropriate element of variety.*

I will now indicate the distinctive raw material of each of the topographical districts to which I have referred, and attempt to offer some slight indication of how its value is to be increased; the motive last explained being

* "Every herb. . . . has its peculiar habitation. . . . The highest art is that which. . . . assigns it its proper position. . . . and by means of it enhances and enforces the great impression." — Ruskin, *Preface, 2d ed. Mod. Painters.*[49]

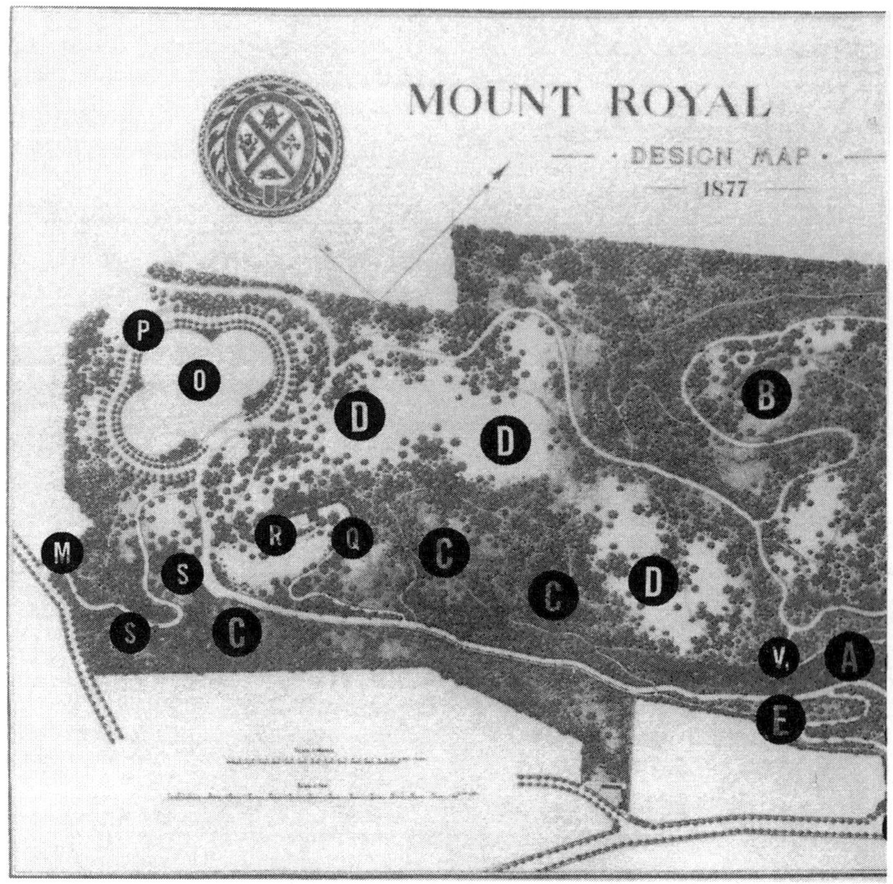

AA	The Crags	I	Entrance from Bleury Street Elevation above tide: 144 ft.
BB	The Upperfell		
CC	The Brackenfell	J	Entrance from Carlton Street Elevation above tide: 275 ft.
DD	The Glades		
EE	Cragsfoot	K	Entrance from Peel Street Elevation above tide: 284 ft.
FF	The Underfell		
GG	Piedmont	L	Entrance over end of Drummond Street Elevation above tide: 320 ft.
HH	Côte Placide		
		M	Entrance from Côtes–des–Neiges Road Elevation above tide: 440 ft.
		N	The little Reservoir Elevation above tide: 440 ft.

MAP OF MOUNT ROYAL KEYED

more or less "humored" to this of the development of local topographical conditions, as will be found easy, the requirements being nearly parallel.

(1.)   First, there is the broken, rocky declivity which, on the city side, stands between the upper and the lower parts, and which is designated

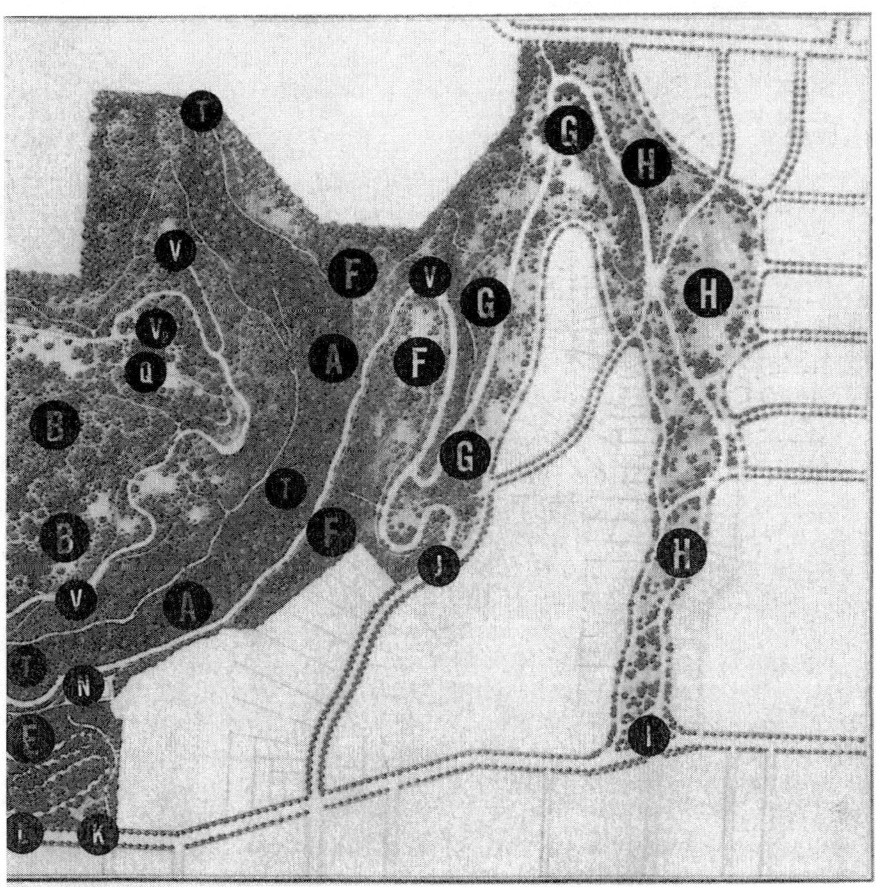

O	Côtes–des–Neiges Reservoir Elevation above tide: 522 ft.	V₁	Balcony Concourse Elevation above tide: 610 ft.
P	The Promenade Elevation above tide: 522 ft.	V₂	Crown of Mountain Elevation above tide: 735 ft. Elevation above Bleury St. Entrance: 591 ft.
Q	Inns		
R	Superintendency, Yards, Stables, &c.		
S	Deer Park and Stables		
T	Stairways		
V	Concourses, Resting Places and Points of View open to Carriages		

TO OLMSTED'S REPORT OF 1881

on my map THE CRAGS. Its special character and value as an element of scenery is so well known to you that it needs no description. I will refer at once to its defects.

In parts, the rock which is its distinguishing feature, is of a quality which rapidly decomposes under the influence of frost; consequently, its surface has a comparatively soft, weak appearance, and takes forms which are only half rocky. It results, also, that thin bodies of disintegrated rock and earth occur, the surface of which is more or less loose, so that no soil can be firmly bedded upon them. Large spaces have, therefore, the landscape quality simply of a steeply inclined plane with a scanty vegetation of coarse plants, chiefly annual, or of feeble seedlings of trees which are to be soon uprooted or slowly starved to death.

In a general view, these elements are not of sufficient consequence to prevent the Crags from having a most interesting character, but they detract materially from the value of what is most valuable in that character. (Really, pecuniary value.) Forty years ago, and more, their beauty was much greater than at present, because of a native forest growth chiefly of spruces, pines, and birches, which had the effect of checking the tendency of the softer surface to wash and slide, causing soil to accumulate, and support on the tamer parts a richer undergrowth both of shrubs and perennials, and partially veiling in shadow and obscurity that which was less bold, firm, and distinctive. The Crags, as a whole, appeared in consequence, larger, bolder, stronger, and approached more nearly to grandness and sublimity of effect; at the same time their general tone of color was more cheerful, and the impression of detail obtained under close observation more interesting and agreeable.

If you wish to realize the value of what you have paid for the property, as far as the Crags are concerned, what has thus been said indicates the general principles of design upon which you will proceed in dealing with them. You will by no means be content, however, with aiming to restore, as far as practicable, the old conditions. While trying to guard against landslides and destructive washing, and seeking to establish firmer and less barren surfaces, the growth of large trees will be prevented where they will have either of three results: first, to hide the bolder and more effective rocks in views from below; second, to interrupt, when of mature growth, the best distant views from above; third, where, from growing tall and spindling and unsupported by adjoining wood of the same character, they will be specially liable, when loaded with ice, to be broken or uprooted by high winds. (From the appearance of the stumps and wreckage which I found in 1874, I judged this to have been a chief cause of the destruction of the old forest.)[50]

Trees of a low and compact sort will be chosen; they will be planted while yet very small, their early growth nursed with care, and any tendency to shoot up in a thin and weakly way checked with the knife. The native growth of low shrubs, and particularly of vines, brambles, and bracken, will be generally encouraged, guarded from wash and fires, and supplemented by other like plantings. The different native sumacs will be specially propagated in the upper shelves of the ledges and in the gaps and wash-ways between the bolder rocks; because, with a little use of the knife, they will not, even when reaching within a few feet of the top, grow upward so much as to obstruct the view from the heights; because they supply the most beautiful of our northern foliage to be looked upon from above (being fountain-like in the disposition of spray spreading out under spray of foliage); and, lastly, because they maintain, as I have before observed, under the most unfavorable circumstances, cheerful qualities of color. Various diminutive spruces, firs, and pines may be used also to advantage where large trees will be undesirable; and in all the more moist, shady places the Canadian yew (an evergreen trailer with large bright berries) should be profusely planted. I would have it grown in seedbeds by thousands. I would make trial also of a Japanese yew (*Taxus adpressa*) which is hardier on the American Atlantic coast than the English churchyard yew, and much more bushy and graceful, falling very nicely over rocks.

(2.)   Immediately above the Crags there is a large district the surface of which lies at various inclinations and is much broken, though seldom abruptly, by comparatively small outcrops of rock, between which the soil is generally poor, thin, and arid. The trees upon it, when not standing singly, tend to grow in clusters and groups, and many are dwarfed, feeble, and sickly. A little yearly continuous planting will be needed to replace those falling out or intentionally removed. I have before indicated the principles which should govern its selection.

(3.)   Farther to the south, and extending from a little beyond the south end of the Crags to the Côte de Neige road is another district of similar character, with a little deeper and better soil between the rocks, and with finer trees (partly because of the better soil, and partly because less harshly treated by storm and frost.)

(4.)   Away to the north, and below the northern crags, there is another division of similar characteristics.

To all of this rugged and rocky land I apply the old English term FELL, and the three divisions of it indicated I distinguish respectively: the UPPERFELL being all that above the Crags, THE UNDERFELL being that below the Crags; and THE BRAKENFELL, which includes all the steep, broken ground, much overgrown with braken, south of the Crags.

The two latter districts should be treated as a forest with numerous ferny openings. The natural growth of the Brakenfell is largely of maples in the lower parts, of pines and birches above; none can be better. It simply needs to have the poorer trees taken out, to be broken a little into groups and groves, and to have younger low foliage added, on their skirts. This and careful pruning.

(5.)   Between the Upperfell and the Brakenfell there is a long, gentle depression of the surface, extending from the south end of the Crags westerly toward the Côte de Neige Cemetery. Here the ground is smooth, little wooded, and the soil generally alluvial and peaty; moister than any other on the mountain. It is, in fact, a mountain meadow of severe exposure. The old house, now occupied by the superintendent, stands in the midst of it (destroying its most marked natural quality, and interrupting lovely distant views). This district I call THE GLADES. It is important that its original, simple, attractive character should, as soon as you can afford it, be regained and made the most of. It needs no planting, except to restore a natural face to the bordering woods, where they have been ill-used. It can easily be made the finest spread of turf on the continent. But it will be best kept, when once well formed, with sheep and not with lawn-like smoothness.

(6.)   The small district below the Crags, between the Brackenfell and the Underfell, I have called THE CRAGSFOOT. It is that containing the little reservoir and the unfortunate zigzag road from Drummond Street, by which its natural character is destroyed. The native wood should be thickened, and the sides of the road planted densely and simply with thick bodies of ordinary underwood; the object being to make the artificial features unobtrusive, and induce a simple, calm, forest effect.

(7.)   On the slope below the Underfell, toward Saint Jean Baptiste, there is a district lying between two low but well-defined ledges of rock, being that in which the City Council has ordained a pest-house, and including a considerable smooth field of fair soil, on which is growing an orchard. This generally resembles the fell-land, but is less broken by lumpy rocks, and more amenable to cultivation. I designate it THE PIEDMONT. It should be planted, in addition to its present scattering growth (largely of basswood rapidly approaching decay), with groups of the lowland trees before mentioned (next above the lowest range), with underwood only to obscure the poorest rocky parts. The groups should be formed generally in connection with the rocks and ledges, leaving between them the broadest turfy openings practicable. In forming the groups, species should be associated which are inclined to form soft and harmonious outlines together, and most, if not all, the trees of each group should be of one kind, and the adjoining groups not of trees of strongly contrasting qualities, the object here being not local picturesqueness, but a softer charm enhancing the characteristic quality of the fells and crags.

(8.)   There remains the large district of gentle slopes below the last ledge, with still less of protruding rock, which, taking the way of your old Norman colonists, I call "CÔTE PLACIDE," a term to be liked none the less because it brings to mind that other branch from the same trunk, which formed the Parish Placide on the Red River of Louisiana, and poor Evangeline.[51] But it must be well understood that it is only by comparison with the adjoining mountain-land that it has the character indicated. Its value is great, if properly used; as, with reference to your possible scale of scenery, it will represent the opposite note to the necessary sternness of the Upperfells. Also, if properly used, it will add greatly to the effect of the views down the great valley from the northern heights, for, with lofty trees along its border, it will give greater distance and obscurity to the buildings in the adjoining quarter of the town, and form a rich and consistent foreground to a scene which, under certain atmospheric conditions, is hardly surpassed among all those of its class upon which the world has fixed the highest value.

By "properly used," I mean, however, not only so used that its present moderate contrast of character with the more rugged parts of your property should be increased, but that it shall also be adapted to provide a measurably complete sylvan experience in itself for visitors who have not time or, in the inclement part of the year, physical endurance for the ascent of the mountain.

What is first needed for these ends is additional soil. I consulted several of your city officers on the point of economy involved in this suggestion, and was assured by all that an abundant supply of street dirt and other wastes could be obtained, by an order of the Council, to more than double the present depth of soil wherever it is important, in two or three years' time, at a cost (in addition to what is now paid for disposing of the same material) that will make it inexpensive; some said it would even be at a saving.

Wherever there are rocks in this district, they should either be exposed as boldly as possible (other loose rocks being sometimes laid upon them, to make the incident more decided), and overgrown with vines, or they should be covered, at least two feet deep, with good loam and soil. Clusters, chiefly of elms, American white ash; and white oak may be planted as indicated on the design-map, and broken rows or narrow belts of the same along the exterior suburban roads.

XV.

One of the most inconsiderately wasteful ways of spending money on the mountain to which you are liable to be tempted, is that of the introduction upon it of flower-beds, clumps of flowering shrubs, cushions of rhododendrons or azaleas, schools of roses — possibly ribband-gardening, floral embroidery, sub-tropical borders, and whatever is commonly found on a polished lawn of the present fashion in lawns, in a place furnished with propagating houses and wintering pits, and given over to a fashionable gardener.

The delusion that these things may be of the required proper furniture of a public park, as they more or less may be of a luxurious private residence, of a botanic garden, or an urban promenade, is the more to be guarded against, because culpable neglect of the permanent and substantial business of the undertaking can be so readily glossed over by means of them, and the question will often be pressed, Why should the taste that they gratify not be catered to?

It should not, because the result would be an adulteration and counteraction of the wholesome influence of the appropriate scenery of the mountain, which alone supplies a sound justification for any of the outlay to be made on it, and the management which resorts to it will be tearing down with one hand what it builds up with the other.[*]

But does it follow that you can have none of the refinement of grace, delicacy, color, and incense which is supplied by flowering plants? By no means. There can be no greater mistake than to suppose either that dug beds or borders and garden primness are necessary to this end, or that it is inconsistent with mountain character.

I once stood at an elevation seventeen times higher than Mount Royal; great fields of snow below, and, in general view, nothing to be seen for hundreds of acres about me but shapeless fragments of rock; yet casting the eye downward, everywhere, even in the darkest shadows, there were gleams of color; and, upon looking closely, there was, in every slightest shelter, a most exquisite bloom and verdure.[52]

What, then, is not practicable that you can reasonably wish to have of floral wealth in your little mountain, clear of snow as it is for more than half the year, and with a climate which, on its sunny side at least, is not found inhospitable to more than one of the trees which grow naturally in association with the fig and the olive?

Let it be borne always in mind that your mountain of less than a thousand feet of elevation is royal only by courtesy, and that if you attempt to deal with it as if it had the impregnable majesty of an Alpine monarch, you only make it ridiculous.

Be assured that if you will keep but one good honest man intelligently at work for the purpose, you may in five years find upon it charming refinements of mountain beauty, refinements which will be thoroughly appropriate and add incalculably to its value.[†]

I will go further, and tell you that if you cannot afford to keep a single man so employed, there are hundreds of little places on the mountain within which, if you can but persuade yourselves to regard them as sacred places and save them from sacrilegious hands and feet, the original Gardener of Eden will delight your eyes with little pictures within greater pictures of indescribable loveliness. And remember that it is the lilies of the field, not the lilies of the garden we are bid to consider.

Such beauty as is thus available, will make no amends for rudeness, coarseness, and vulgarity in the borders of your roads and walks; it will but

---

[*] "Few human beings have contravened nature's laws more than our flower-gardeners." — *Robinson. The Sub-tropical Garden. London, Murray.*[53]

[†] Read upon this, I beg, simply as giving hints as to how much can be done with little effort, Mr. Robinson's two little books: one upon "Wild Gardening," the other upon "Alpine Flowers" (Murray, London, 1870).[54] The very best things for your purpose are such as, once established and a little guarded, will take care of themselves, propagate and spread, like our common American wild violets.

make what is crude and unnatural the more conspicuous, as a jewel set upon soiled linen makes it the more offensive. But when you have natural homes for it, especially with much and rapid inflections of surface, as in the little rocky notches and gaps, dinglets and runlets of the Brackenfell, you need not be afraid of too great a profusion nor too great a variety of perennial and annual plants; of too much color, nor of a growth too intricate and mazy.

This is not the most difficult form of refinement for you to gain; indeed, it is so easy, so cheap, that when I was last on the mountain I found many places where no small degree of it already existed, and places, too, which, when I had first studied them in 1874, appeared rude, raw, and barren. To what did you owe this improvement? To any digging and bedding; raking, sowing or weeding of a florist? Not at all, but simply and solely to the fact, as far as I could judge, that before that time cattle had been ranging over the ground, and afterward it had been protected from them.

But remember that there is nothing to prevent a hundred men from trampling over one of these spots to-morrow and making a complete wreck of it, destroying not only the plants but the conditions of their reproduction.

XVI.

If you attempt anywhere to have such refinements of detail as I have been last suggesting (I do not say they are essential), or even a fair quality of turf, trees, and shrubs, and yet shrink from attempting to control the movements of people on the ground, you will find the losses from filching and from injuries through carelessness, discouraging and disheartening. The natural flowering plants, except a few coarse weeds, will gradually disappear; choice trees will be sickened; often their bark will be cut or bruised, sometimes girdled and their limbs broken down in such a manner as to establish disease from which they never recover.[*]

The only way in which any town park can long be kept in a generally useful and improving condition, is by providing so well and amply for the uses which are designed to be made of it that the great body of decent, orderly, tidy, and respectable people will not be impelled to fall into practices inconvenient to others or unfavorable to the preservation and improvement of its natural beauty. This done, the silent influence of example and of an obvious custom, acting helpfully to the police regulations, will strongly persuade others to exercise due control upon perverse inclinations.

---

[*] "Even rain and air are denied them, because, as has been said, the soil gets hardened by constant trampling and baked by the hot sun." *Pall-Mall Gazette* on *"the miserable condition into which Kensington Gardens, the most characteristic and exceptional of all the London parks, has been allowed to sink." September, 1878.*[55]

I once examined 500 trees, in succession, upon a neglected public park, and found not one free from serious wounds due to careless or wanton violence. Two-thirds were so injured as not to be worth keeping.

389

Half the practical business of park management may, in fact, be referred to a lively sense of two traits of character of the average civilized man as we have to deal with him.

One is his disposition to adapt his conduct to the circumstances in which he finds himself, and especially to be neat, cleanly, and nice where the objects about him are neat, cleanly, and nice. I have repeatedly had occasion to observe that while any park work is in an incomplete condition, with materials in the rough, and litter of workmen lying about, no police, no fences, and guards are adequate to prevent the occurrence of wanton injuries and manifestations of rudeness, recklessness, and destructiveness. (How few boys can resist the temptation to throw stones at the windows of a vacant and dilapidated house?) Passing the finished point, the litter cleared up, the turf established and once smooth-mown, and everything in view having a complete and refined aspect, a change occurs, and fences and guards, before necessary, may be removed, and the police reduced without danger.

Again, if provisions for any purpose have an appearance of being well considered and liberal, there is a common disposition to be content with them; if they make no such impression, but on the contrary seem mean and makeshift, the sense of shame in what would otherwise be lawlessness cannot be counted on.

If in public places you have a walk of a certain capacity between borders of fine turf, people will submit to considerable crowding without going out of it; when the crowding passes a certain point a few will step on the turf, doing little harm, but when the walk is so crowded that the provision seems absurdly inadequate, of a sudden, the rule, by common assent, becomes a dead letter, and the most reserved and cautious take to the turf. Under corresponding influences seats will be used to stand upon, and may be broken or defiled without compunction.

So, if the necessities of the body cannot be accommodated decently within reasonable distance, there will soon grow up upon the park a common law by which they will be accommodated indecently. Your police will for a time contend with this in vain, and then will be sullenly blind to it.

At a small part of the study required for putting and keeping the mountain in a condition in which it will have a high degree of usefulness to the average citizen of Montreal, his wife and children, it can be kept in a condition in which a small proportion of your least valuable population, to whom any refinement of manners or check upon vulgar and brutal habits is irksome, will continue to resort to it with more or less of pleasure. This pleasure will consist not so much in positive enjoyment as in negative relief from what is elsewhere tiresome and dreary. And if nothing or but little more is done than is necessary to adapt the mountain to be satisfactory in this way, it will gradually come to be satisfactory in no other, and what money you spend on it will be mainly ill-spent.

On these grounds I advise you not to allow the mountain to be in all parts left open to be wandered over and used at will at all times by all comers.[55] You cannot afford the force of police which, if you do so, will be necessary to the protection of its finer elements of value. You cannot afford to waste these elements. As a measure of economy, therefore, I submit the following suggestions, to the adoption of which the roads and walks of the plan have been adjusted:

Open all of the Upperfell, to be used by all comers at all times, for rambling at will; for picnicing; for all boys' and childrens' games and plays that do not involve the use of missiles. Supply swings and other amusements for the little ones. Furnish abundance of comfortable seats, and do not forbid decent seating on the ground and rocks.

Have a well provided public house, with so much roofing that in case of sudden showers a large company may obtain shelter in it. Let a part of its rent be paid in providing, gratuitously, under constant supervision and in a cleanly and decent way, such accommodations as are necessary for women and children when absent some hours from home. Let it also provide gratuitously, or at a nominal price, hot water for those who want to make tea on the ground.*

Make it an easy custom to fall into for all classes of people, even your poorest workingman, to come here by families, once or twice a week, late in the day, during the hot season, to take their evening meal.

In short, let the district be used as, from the opening of the ground to the public, it has been used, with only the differences that would occur from additional conveniences and better provisions for the safety and comfort of women and children. Keep active and intelligent guardians *moving briskly* through it, so that the modest, timid, and nervous may have frequent assurance of protection against rudeness.

I was glad, in my last visit, to see clergymen leading large schools to the mountain for recreation. Offer every encouragement to the growth of the custom. The presence of these gentlemen will give countenance and confidence to mothers to come with their daughters and little ones.

When the ground shall be constantly and largely used in the domestic ways I have thus indicated, the danger of its misuse in any way will be slight, and your expense for police and for repairs may with safety be moderate. No men are reckless in their conduct in a place in which good women and children seem to be at home.

The district of which I here speak, the Upperfell, has an area of 50 acres, of very diversified surface; it includes the highest elevation of the

---

*The commissioners have plans for this house, prepared under my advice, by Mr. T. Wisedell, architect. The conspicuous parts are of axe-finished timber, not to be painted; it is fitted to sit on a saddle of rock, so surrounded by natural low wood, growing on ground declining from it, that while commanding from its upper parts a magnificent outlook the building will scarcely be seen except by those who have occasion to use it.[56]

mountain. It has little soil, and with a proper treatment will be occupied by low, sturdy wood and a few strong thorny thickets, the trees in groups and small groves with numerous mossy openings, with a great deal of natural rocky surface on which children can play and picnic parties sit, *harming nothing*. Many of these rocks command fine distant views, and it is the district now more resorted to by the public than any other.

This fifty acres of the Upperfell being at all times open to everybody, aim in other parts of the two fell-land districts to cultivate somewhat richer mountain character, and, in order to do so, restrict movement through them to the roads, walks, and prepared places, except upon holidays. Let there be, however, numerous places well adapted by the character of their ledges, open groves, and finely verdured dells for picnic parties. Provide springs or little natural rock fountains in connection with them. Hold each of these places open to be used at any time for picnic or festive parties, whether of friends or of schools, churches, societies, or any organizations either permanent or formed for the occasion.

Require only that each shall take the trouble to make application and have suitable grounds assigned for its use in advance, and that it shall give some reasonable assurance that the privilege will not be abused. All such places can then be decked about with shrubbery and suitable wild flowering plants, naturally disposed, and each have its own distinctive sylvan and idyllic attractions.

Again, at suitable houses, one in the Brackenfell and one in the Underfell, let desirable conveniences for such parties be supplied, and at the upper one let there be sheds so that some can come in vehicles and have their horses properly cared for.

The two districts being adequately provided in all respects for their designed use, in all the remainder of the park let visitors be restricted under ordinary circumstances to the roads, walks, and other accommodations specially prepared for them. On holidays, when (at special cost for the occasion) you throw all open, have much of the ordinary housekeeping work of the ground finished early in the morning or the night before, and let the more intelligent and trustworthy of the men ordinarily employed upon it act as assistant watchmen to the regular police, mainly with a view to check, by their presence and a polite cautionary word upon occasion, any tendency they may observe of visitors to fall into practices wasteful of the value of the property. It is wonderful how much may be accomplished in this way, especially when care has been once taken to establish good and prevent the forming of bad customs.

Such management of the property as I have thus advised may require some little self-restraint of you and some troublesome thoughtfulness of your servants. So does any soundly economical management of any of your business. So does every advantage which civilized men possess over barbarians.

XVII

Among properties of its class your mountain possesses one marked advantage over all others. I mean that of noble landscapes extending far beyond its borders. These are of such extent and so composed, and their foregrounds within the property are to be so easily adapted to increase their value; their interest is so varied according to the direction of the outlook and the passing effects of clouds and atmospheric conditions, that it is not only impossible to speak of them in adequate terms of admiration, but, trying to take a business estimate of them, and seeking standards of comparison for the purpose, it will be found that the best that other communities have been able to obtain by expenditures counting in millions of dollars, is really too insignificant to be available for the purpose.

And yet, trying still to take a business view of them, simply as an element in the general value of the mountain as a city property, it may possibly come about that you would be richer without them. I say this because among the currents of public opinion of which I had some experience with you, there was a certain spendthrift tendency to slight every element of value in the property except that of the great views. There were those who would have thought it a triumph of art to whisk people up to the highest eminence of the mountain, give them a big mouthful of landscape beauty, and slide them back to town in the shortest possible way; and there were, even before I was consulted, speculations afoot for doing something of the kind at so much a head.

It might be to some a question whether the most valuable influence of properties of this class is to be found in such distinct sensational features, even though provided by nature, as are commonly most consciously felt, talked about, and written about, or in more unobtrusive, pervading, home-like qualities of which the effects come to one less in a torrent-like way, than as the gentle, persuasive dew, falling so softly as to be imperceptible, and yet delightfully reinvigorating in its results. Even this might be to some a question; but let any man ask himself whether the value of such views as the grandest the mountain offers, is greater when they are made distinct spectacles or when they are enjoyed as successive incidents of a sustained landscape poem, to each of which the mind is gradually and sweetly led up, and from which it is gradually and sweetly led away, so that they become a part of a consistent experience, — let him ask this with reference to the soothing and refreshment of a town-strained human organization, and he will not need argument to lead him to a sound conclusion.

But as you have the one thing and as yet have not the other, except in a very crude and imperfect form, disturbed throughout with blotches, it may be worthwhile to try, if ever so poorly, to suggest what would rule a wise economy. (Would that a literary artist would undertake the duty.)

It is not the stronger but the weaker links of a chain that you must consider in determining what strain you will put upon it. Fit your work on the mountain to over-weighted nervous conditions and you may be sure that it will suit the robust and light-hearted.

On this principle it is better in dealing with it to cultivate the habit of thoughtful attention to the feebler sort of folk — of asking, for instance, can this or that be made easier and more grateful to an old woman or a sick child, without, on the whole, additional expense, except in thoughtfulness? If so, ten to one, the little improvement will simply be that refinement of judgment which is the larger part of the difference between good and poor art, and the enjoyment of every man will be increased by it, though he may not know just how.

With this idea in mind think over what you would like to be able to do if you were much concerned about the health of a father, brother, or son whose private business cares you saw to be wearing upon him to a point of danger; who was growing morbidly irritable and despondent, or, what is quite as bad, morbidly sanguine and reckless. Or again, take the case of a woman recovering with tedious slowness from a severe illness, still weak, low in spirits, and under obvious nervous prostration. Take cases such as these, that you never have to go far to find, and ask what of all practicable ways of turning the mountain to business account for their benefit a reasonably refined common-sense would lead you to adopt?

Would you, if you could take the man from his counting-room, the woman from her sick-room, and plant them both as quickly and abruptly as possible before the finest view on the mountain, keep them there till they tired of it, and then send them straightway back again?

Let us try to imagine a better way.

First, then, taking our friends in a carriage, we should find, under wise arrangements, that without going far we could turn into a road leading toward the mountain, by which noisy and jolting pavements would be escaped. In this road there would be no heavy grades to overcome; no street railways to be avoided; no funeral processions to be passed; but the carriage, moving at a steady pace, and with the least occasion to awaken sadness, irritation, anxiety, or impatience, would, in a few moments, have slipped easily out of town, and be passing along a shady, soft, and quiet suburban street, like a village highroad.

This would be lined on one side with cottages, before which trees would be rapidly falling out of lines into groups and spreading from groups into groves. The village would be divided by a pretty open green with a quietly undulating surface, skirting which our road would bend away to avoid too steep a course. Then, getting more and more out of town, it would wind along with gentle curves as the movement of the ground and the openings among the trees should invite. (This may be the Côte Placide of my plan.)

At a fork of the ways the last of the village houses would be passed, the surface grow more diversified, stretches of pasture land would open on both sides, and bits of stoney ground appear. Presently there would be a rocky bank in a dark shade of hemlocks, its base lost in a thicket of brambles, brake, golden-rod, Soloman's seal, and fringed gentian; preluding the mountain. Then moving along easily higher and higher, the ground would become more rocky, the herbage more tufty, till, at a turn in the road, views through the trees would open: on one side, of distant steeples over houses and gardens; on the other, of a stretch of woodland. (This from the Piedmont.)

Then, going on, the prospect on each side would be more confined, but by glimpses between the trees we should be aware that not far away to the left there was a great picturesque declivity shadowed by hanging woods. Before our attention had been fully fixed in the direction, it would be drawn off by a broad gap among the trees to the right, and we should find that we had already attained a sufficient elevation to command a far view to the north-west. The carriage would stop, and we should look upon a broad country-side with woods and fields, orchards and gardens, farm-houses and village spires, all sloping gently from distant blue hills down to a stream hidden among the trees of the intervening dale. (A peaceful, soothing prospect, this may be cheaply made, in which, though accessible in twenty minutes from the Post Office, and at a third the cost of a visit to the heights, the town may be left far out of sight and further out of mind.)

If it is the first airing of the convalescent here might well be the end of her day's journey. There would be a little inn near by at which she could rest, or from which she would perhaps be served with warm milk or tea; after which, varying the return road, within an hour from the time of starting, she would be back again in her armchair.

But going on after a few minutes' halt the scenery would become wilder and more forest-like, and as the road, winding where spurs of the ledge, and heaps of fallen rock, and old water-ways gave opportunity, led higher and higher, but always by easy grades, and, without apparent effort, following a course invited by nature, the trees would stand closer and the roadsides be crowded by underwood. Between and beneath overhanging foliage, glimpses would be caught, on the right, of the near crag-side decked with dark bushy evergreens and draped with creepers, mosses, and blooming Alpine plants; on the other hand, out of deep shade, through chance loopholes of the verdant screen, of a distant gleaming river and a sunny expanse beyond it. (From the Underfell.)

The crags passed, the underwood becoming more scattered, the wood more open, the road would now lead along a mountain slope of constantly gaining quietness, with gleams of sunlight falling upon ferny dells (the Brackenfell), until again, the tree tops opening to the right and left, the carriage would stop, and over a rapidly declining, bosky surface another outlook would be gained, revealing a lake-like expanse of water lying in a broad valley stretching far away to a faint horizon, beyond which the evening mists would be gathering to receive the declining sun.

After this, the road would presently lead out upon a broad highland valley, all its soft features bathed in sunshine unbroken by foliage (the Glades). From its wooded borders would rise rocky and fir-crested steeps, but crossing the space between them and following near the edge of the northern woods, we should be led, by quiet curves and with an easy ascent, to a position from which having now so long left the city, it would be looked down upon from the brink of a woody cliff. High above its roofs, beyond the harbor with its stately ships, a great champaign would open, broken by a few noble hills, and beyond all, the distant billows of the Adirondacks.

Turning back from this scene which, were it not familiar, might as yet be too strong for our purpose, it would be a relief to course along the edge of woods in which, while the surface is rough and the trees tell the story of much harder exposure than those we have seen below, there are pleasant sheltered and sunny openings in which groups of children will be at play. (The Upperfell.)

Still rising, the road will then lead with more rapid turns along the face of a steeper slope till, wheeling upon the depression of a narrow spur, a northern outlook is gained, with the lower valley of the great river spreading before the eye; that lovely view to which I have before referred.

At the next move, steeper and wilder declivities would be skirted, and the foreground show yet more evidence of elevation and the severity of its winter in the aspects of the rocks and the picturesque character of the vegetation, until with a final rapid turn the carriage would stop at the open porch of a timber-built hospice, so situated upon the highest rock of the mountain that from chairs on its wide galleries the nearest thing to be seen would, on all sides, be a broad mass of tree-top foliage, sloping quietly away in simple undulations of light and shade to a rounded edge distinctly defined against a much lower and more remote middle distance.

Looking over this deep foreground of forest, we should now have before us more extended views in all directions than we had had before in any. Did they offer nothing for our enjoyment but a rolling surface of grass or an endless prospect of desert sand, with only sky and clouds to relieve its monotony of color, the effect would be irresistible. As it is, what element of interest could be added without crowding? What new object of beauty without disturbance? Yet, gradually led up to it from the streets, as I have supposed our friends to be, so that it comes in natural and consistent sequence of the entire preceding experience, the impression could but carry to a still higher point the restful, soothing, and refreshing influence of the entire work.

I deplore my inability to present the purpose which good management of this property would have exclusively before it, in a manner more worthy than that of this scrappy memorandum of what might be offered even to a poor invalid taken up the mountain in a carriage. But in truth, the heart of the argument lies in something which it would be beyond the power of even a gifted writer to represent, and to which not the greatest of landscape painters could nearly do justice.

Yet if you have kindly let your imagination aid me you can hardly fail to see wherein the advantage of the property lies, not simply in the direction in which I have been pointing, as a sanitary influence, but also as an educative and civilizing agency, standing in winning competition against the sordid and corrupting temptations of the town. You can hardly fail to realize how much greater wealth it thus places within your reach than is to be found in the ordinary parks and gardens, not to say the museums and galleries, which are the pride of other cities, and which millions have been thriftily expended to obtain. Nor can you fail to recognize that what remains for your securing of this wealth is not any towering constructions, princely expenditure, or heavy addition to your taxation, but simply moderate ability, though of a special kind, continuously directed in a modest and frugal way by a suitable, sincere, consistent purpose. A purpose in which there shall be no mixture, for instance, of the motives proper to a circus or a variety show, to military parades or agricultural fairs, to race-courses or cemeteries. An intelligent purpose to bring out the latent loveliness of mountain beauty, which you have bought with the property, in such manner as shall make it of the highest distinctive value. Thinking over all that I have advised to be done as an affair of years, take the largest estimate of the cost and trouble of securing what is necessary to it that you can; all I ask is that you think out also what will become of the property, what will be spent and what will be lost, if it shall continue long to be managed with no more distinct purpose, upon no more firmly defined principles of economy, with no sharper limits to the enterprise of successive councils and commissioners (leaping from the ranks to the supreme command of it) than economy has thus far been held to require.

XVIII.

Wisely or unwisely you have bought the property, and must do something with it. You will probably take one of four courses:

1st.   Let it run to waste, in which case your purchase-money will have been misspent.

2d.   Make such ill-considered improvements upon it that your outlay for them will be an addition to that previously misspent.

3d.   Make extravagant improvements, misspending more.

4th. Make such substantial, well-devised, economical improvements that the result, as a whole, shall repay the original purchase-money, together with the cost of the improvements, and a fair percentage of profit.

I trust that you will choose to take the last, and that, choosing it, you will find the plan which I have prepared, adapted to aid you in doing so.

Do not think of it as if, by its adoption, you were binding yourselves to carry it out at once, or within any definite period, but as a plan, with reference to which you may, with advantage, organize, direct and restrict any expenditures which you shall hereafter, at any time, think well to make for the improvement of this property.

Do not, above all things, imagine that it can enable you to dispense with the constant exercise of refined discrimination in the determination of working details, any more than with technical skill, or with common administrative and executive ability.

It is no part of my duty to advise you how fast and how far to go on with the work of improvement, but I may suggest that a little desultory cobbling, a touch here and a touch there, and that what may pass for somewhat temporary improvements, are almost sure, not simply to be costly with reference to the value of their designed results, but to make obstructions and embarrassments to the essential permanent improvements that are desirable.

It will even now cost you more to carry out this or any other plan, you may adopt, looking to a permanently satisfactory improvement, and the result will be less valuable than would be the case if you had had the patience to do nothing until you could be sure that every stroke would tell toward a maturely studied comprehensive purpose.

You may, as a matter of convenience, or of necessity, put off for years entering upon well-organized, steady courses, but do not flatter yourselves that you can do so without paying a round penalty. You will find that this is, like any other important business, left at loose ends. The difficulty of getting it into an economical current increases the longer it is pottered with.

To proceed economically, you need to have a small staff of men who are, or who can be trained to be, experts in three or four main divisions of the required service, and, recollect that if these men are well chosen, their value is to increase with every year's additional special experience in the locality, and that their work is to be continuous work, the value of what they do in one year being relative to what, in doing it, they have intended to do and may do the following year.

These leading men of the work should be under such supervision and discipline as to insure the subordination of all they do to the general ends of the plan, but they should also be allowed, each man within his own field, that measure of discretion which is necessary to induce zealous, continuous effort, and pride and pleasure in its gradually accruing results.

Working with and under this staff, there should be a constant force — a very small force, if you please, at the outset, but a constant force — of men who can be trained and depended on for a variety of services, some of which will never fail to be in request. Such a minimum force, constantly employed, will, in time, accomplish much more than a much larger and costlier average force employed irregularly. Then, having such a constant force as a steady element, to maintain tone and method, you may, as from time to time you feel able and disposed, employ temporarily a much larger force, a great deal more economically than would be otherwise possible.

APPENDIX.
EXPLANATION OF THE PLAN.

(The drawing herein referred to was exhibited in November, 1877, and, to aid its public discussion, lithographed copies were furnished the commissioners for distribution. The following explanation is repeated from that then read and offered in manuscript to the press.)[57]

The surveyor's maps furnished me covered a little more ground than has at any time been expected to be included in the park, and some little of that which, at the time they were made, was supposed to be held by the city, has since, as I understand, been ruled out. The area which has been mapped and under definite consideration with reference to the plan has an extent of 550 acres. Of this, I have regarded 470 acres as already held by the city; out of which, 30 is to be set off for the reservoirs, and for streets outside the park proper. Border strips of the purchased land remaining, which (provided certain restrictions can be made as to the manner in which they shall be used) can be spared from the park, and which I recommend to be sold, will deduct an additional area of 60 acres. A rectification of boundaries of the remaining land, which is a part of my proposition, would require the city to obtain land which it does not now own to the extent of ten acres, and would allow an equal amount to be thrown out in addition to that before stated. This is arranged with reference to possible exchanges with private owners. That is to say, there are ten acres of land to be deducted in small bits, and ten acres in small bits to be added. (All these are estimates in round numbers.) With these deductions and adjustments, the area remaining for the park proper would be 380 acres.

Of the 80 acres of land you now hold, which it is proposed should be exchanged and sold, 56 are in that part of the property nearest the town, and in such relations to that reserved for public use, that any judicious step in the improvement of either will benefit the other. This (56 acres) you will see shown on the plan in building plots, suitable for villas and cottages fronting on the park, and laid open by winding roads of easy grade.

I suppose it is understood that the larger part of the land taken for the park is of such a character that it would be a misfortune to the city if it should be built upon, as its taxable value would not be equivalent to the cost of making and maintaining the highway improvements necessary to public health and convenience. The roads now proposed between the park and the land to be sold are, however, so adjusted to the topography, that this land may be opened for such private uses as will be consistent with the interests of the public, to the best advantage, at the least cost. The roadsides are intended, as you may observe, to be planted by the city, and the land to be sold under such reservations as will prevent buildings from being placed within 20 feet of the highway and encourage private planting.

I do not say that the arrangement as it would thus stand is precisely what I should advise if I had only the distant and permanent interests of the city in view, still less if I wished to make the finest thing of its kind possible of your park. There are three points at which I lament that more land should not have been bought, and at which, as you get to estimate the value and understand the conditions of the value of the park, I think it probable that you may wish hereafter to make annexations to it, but in the present condition of the city I think it better that the proposition should take the form given it in the drawing.

It may be observed that the Côte Placide district, north of the mountain proper (both sides of the line of Bleury Street), is, comparatively speaking, tame and featureless, and that it is tolerably well adapted to be built upon, and I may be asked what sufficient advantages are to be gained by including any portion of it in the park, or, at least, why, in the desire to reduce the area of the park to a minimum, more of it cannot be thrown out and a simpler street plan adopted? Why especially should the straight line of Bleury Street not be retained? The answer is:

1st.   That every curve of the roads here gives a course which is practically shorter than that of a straight line, because of the easier grade which is obtained, and that if the northern boundary of the park were pushed back, under no straight and rectangular street system in this district would it be possible to reach a park entrance in carriages, except at a slow pace and tediously.

2d.   It is desirable to interpose between the city and the ruggedness of the mountain an intermediate passage of scenery of a less picturesque, more beautiful, less wild and romantic, more comely and placid type, and the ground in question offers an opportunity which, properly improved, will answer that purpose.

3d.   Holding the land in question, you have the opportunity of stretching out the hand of welcome to that part of the city from which the park will otherwise be most distant. You may make a pleasure of what would otherwise be a toil in approaching the mountain from it.

4th.   Taking as much of this ground and improving it as I propose, you will offer to all those who cannot afford the time, exertion or expense of getting up the mountain, but who can spare a half hour for a stroll or drive, an agreeable and healthful resort. As the city grows, and is built out on the north and west, the number who will daily find this a privilege will be larger than the number of those who will be able to go upon the mountain proper. This I think a binding consideration.

5th.   In the early Spring and the late Autumn there will be many days when this lower park will be available for recreation, while the air of the upper would be found too harsh to be agreeable or useful, especially to delicate persons.

These advantages of retaining a considerable part of the lower ground seem to me so obvious and so conclusive, that I should not have thought it necessary to present them were I not informed that plans have been discussed and are now in suspense, by which they would be sacrificed.

You may, perhaps, find it more difficult to fully justify so great a reduction of the park area as is here proposed, and upon this point I can only suggest that in considering it you should not fail to foresee the effect of the proposed border plantations, and to recognize how the objection to the proposition in this respect will be lessened by the interposition of the anticipated skirting of gardens, cottages, and villas between the park and any possible tall, compactly associated buildings hereafter to come in beyond them.

Taking a large view of the interests of the city, I cannot say that I think the boundaries of the park entirely fortunate. It is much to be regretted that you should be so cramped between the Crags and the Allan[58] and Redpath[59] properties. A few yards greater breadth here would add more to the value of the park than you lose by throwing out double as many rods elsewhere. It is unfortunate also that the boundaries of the park do not fall so that a good broad road of easy grade can everywhere follow them.

I must make an unpleasant suggestion in recommending an early consideration of the question whether, if your city prospers, the time may not come when a thoroughfare from north to south will be required as near as practicable to the west boundary of the park. I am sorry that the topography forbids any arrangement for the purpose in connection with the park. The slight changes of the west line of the park which I recommend, in addition to those already arranged, are designed only to avoid waste from awkward corners and misfits.

The policy originally adopted of dovetailing the city into the park on the east, by a system of capes and bays, determined, I presume, simply by the accident of private occupation, will eventually cause a good deal of inconvenience. Following my own judgment, I should have planned to sweep it entirely away, west of the east line of Sir Hugh Allan's grounds, and obtained a more economical arrangement at any necessary cost. I feel sure that it could be at no cost that would not soon be outweighed by advantages gained both by the public and by the property owners.

East of Sir Hugh's, on the other hand, there is a body of land in the park, as represented in the maps given me, but which, since my plan has been formed with reference to it, I have been advised will have to be thrown out. This would be of great value to be retained. There is no other which could be sooner and at less cost made serviceable. I should not have laid out roads in other parts of the park as I have done, had I not counted on this land, and, much work having already been done, reckoning upon it, I consider a part of it indispensable. I have, therefore, adopted, in the last revision of my drawing, a compromise arrangement, which, when well considered, will, I sincerely trust, harmonize all interests.

I have to speak of but one more exterior question — that of the carriage approaches.

You have, unfortunately, used in Montreal the common frontier method of laying out streets, of which the only recommendation is that it requires no thought, and can be as well done by an infant after a month's schooling in a kindergarten as by the ablest engineer, and it happens, in consequence, that south of University Street there is no way of approaching the mountain at all suitable for general driving.

A pony, which would easily take a phæton with a lady and children to the top of the mountain, if driven around by the way of Bleury Street, would be entirely unequal to taking the same load up such grades as those of Peel Street (1 in 7), or McTavish (1 in 9). As to Drummond Street, your present arrangement, as I understand from the maps, makes it a cul-de-sac, always a very bad thing anywhere in a large town. This will, I presume, by and by, be remedied by ramp-ways, connecting it with Pine Avenue, but even then its grades will be worse than those of Peel Street.

Taking the best of these routes for approaching the park, two horses will be needed, on an average, to do, with some urging, strain, and risk, what one will do comfortably on the northern route.

The disadvantage of the southern part of the city, in this respect, is not generally recognized, because, as yet, a trip to the mountain is necessarily somewhat tedious, and so far a novel experience, that you have not begun to look after the small economies of pleasure in it; but it is one which will be felt more and more as the mountain comes into habitual use. The only remedy I am able to suggest is that of raising the grade of the lower part of McGill Street (above Sherbrooke), encroaching slightly on the college grounds below the corner of Carleton, and passing around to the east of the reservoir, with certain comparatively inexpensive changes in the course and grade of the existing road. It is practicable in this way to get a grade nowhere steeper than 1 in 15, which would be a gain of great value, and I recommend the suggestion to consideration as one of the first importance. It has been successively submitted to your former and present city surveyors, and received the hearty approval of each.

[Drawings exhibiting this proposition, with profiles showing the great advantages of grade to be gained by it, were prepared with the approval of the city engineer, and laid before the City Council. Lithographed copies of them were also prepared for distribution to those interested.]

We are now ready to pass within the boundaries of the park and consider the contemplated constructions in roads, walks, and other necessary matters. That what is designed in this respect may be intelligibly presented, it is shown on a map in which the natural conditions of the surface, in so far as it is essential that they should be taken into account in forming a judgment of the plan, are elaborately delineated.

Standing at a little distance, you may readily trace out the general features of the mountain with which you are familiar. Here you find the surface nearly flat; here moderately inclined; here is a steep declivity; here again it is smooth and meadow-like; here it is broken with small ledges; here with bolder masses of rock.

The strong bounding lines and distinctions of tint will enable you to readily distinguish the proposed roads, the walks and the buildings of various classes, and you will find little difficulty in understanding the position of each, and its relation, throughout its entire length, to the topography. This is the more important question to be discussed at this stage of your enterprise, and to avoid confusion in presenting my recommendations in respect to it, the design with regard to the improvement of the natural elements is developed only so far as to show by the pale green tint, which stands for turf, and by symbols, which indicate trees and bushes, the general disposition of foliage and open ground.

That the indications of the elevation and inclinations of surface, with reference to the discussion of the artificial features, may not be too much put out of sight, trees are not represented standing as closely or as much covering the ground as they are in reality expected to, especially in the lower parts of the declivities, and along the edges of the roads and walks near the base of the Crags.

From my saying this, please not to infer that any of the trees now standing should be left, or that others should, on any consideration, be planted upon any of the few comparatively broad openings. It is essential to the design that the surface should be of clear unbroken turf.

As a general rule, in laying out parks, the principal roads, walks, and other constructions should be so disposed as to leave the central parts unbroken, so that broad, quiet landscape effects may be had in looking across them; at the same time, they should be kept far enough from the boundaries to allow exterior objects which may not be consistent with the designed scenes, to be screened from view by border plantations, and to admit of such a free, natural, and interesting treatment of the intervening space as to avoid the suggestion of limit and confinement.

Petty sinuosities and all sharp turns or angles in the course of roads or walks are undesirable; and it should be possible to go from any point in the park to another distant point without excessive indirectness of course; certainly, without so doubling on a course as to produce an impression of a return to the starting-point. It is not desirable that visitors should be compelled to return for any considerable distance over the same ground, and get the same views twice.

You will observe that not one of the desiderata thus indicated is fully met in this design map, and if the plan were shown as a diagram and considered without a knowledge of the remarkable natural features to which the design is fitted, it might seem to defy sound principles.

A careful examination will, however, suggest, I believe, just occasion for all such apparent eccentricities. The topography will account for nearly every curve of road or walk. Here, for example, you observe that a slightly darker shade upon the surface indicates a little swell upon the gentle slope of the Côte Placide. The road approaching it, if it were carried straight on, would either be made of steeper grade than is desirable, or this would be avoided at the expense of a heavy cutting. The road, as you see, bends slightly away, therefore, and winds around the swell to the higher ground beyond it. Here, again, the road avoids a rocky ledge; here, approaching the borders of the property, it doubles around a knoll and turning into the Piedmont district, keeps steadily working at light grades up the hill; here it creeps diagonally through a depression of a wall of rock and doubles again so as to reach a point of view in the Underfell, commanding the western prospect, and so on.

I will call your attention to certain of the objects to which the course of the drive is adapted:

First, you will observe that it puts all parts of the property very closely under contribution to the driver's pleasure. Any point on the park, which you may wish to visit, can be driven to within about 200 yards, and there are but few points that cannot be approached by a carriage within half that distance. Next, it carries the visitor, not directly to every particularly interesting point of view — for it is desirable that there should be some such points held in reserve as an inducement to walking, — but to such a succession of points that each characteristic variety of scenery to which the property is adapted will be seen to advantage, and distant views obtained in every direction; so that, in fact, the horizon may be swept in the course of the drive. Third, it offers, though this may not at once be obvious, all practicable directness between different parts of the mountain, and especially between the lower and higher parts. The highest point of the mountain is near the present meteorological station. The central point is about a quarter of a mile to the south of it. The lowest point, and the most distant from the centre, is near the Hôtel Dieu.[60] If you wished to go from the latter point or from any other on the border of the park, on the town side, either to the central or to the highest point of the mountain, in the shortest time, with ease and pleasure, notwithstanding the great apparent tortuousness necessary in the drive in order to accomplish the two first of the above-stated objects, a better route for the third could hardly be taken than that laid down.

As to the object of securing interesting foreground conditions in the view from the drive, what I have before said will have sufficiently explained the motives of the design.

A few words as to the grades of the drive:

A pleasure-road, in passing over broken and undulating ground, should avoid a perfect monotony of grade as well as of course. Its inclination should be such that a good horse, with a fair load, can be kept moving at a trot without urging in going up hill, and without holding back in going down. Your main road, as laid out, is adapted to meet these requirements. Its average grade is 1 in 37, a grade upon which, in coaching days, the mail went up hill at the rate of ten miles an hour, and came down safely with equal speed. The maximum grade is 1 in 20, and occurs but twice, holding in neither case for more than a hundred yards. There are numerous nearly level, short stretches, and at a few points there is, for a few yards, a slight reverse of the inclination. The excavation or embankment required to obtain these grades rarely exceeds three feet upon the centre line of the road.

The surface of the drive is designed to be everywhere slightly below that of its immediate borders, and, in making it, it is intended that the borders shall be graded in connection with it in such manner that it shall seem to fit a course marked out and prepared centuries ago by nature. Any appearance of a retaining wall on one side, or of an embankment on the other; any plane glacis-like slopes, and any bald or lumpy surfaces are, of course, to be avoided. Whatever work is necessary to prevent them, and to make the borders what they should be, is to be regarded as one work with the grading of the drive.

The distance from Bleury Street entrance to the highest point of the mountain, by the main drive, will be a little over 4 miles. From Carleton Street entrance, 3¼ miles. From Drummond Street entrance 2¾ miles. The length of the main drive, with the link forming the circuit on the heights, will be 4¾ miles. The length of all pleasure-drives within the park, 7½ miles. (This includes the by-road to the superintendency and the two approaches at the Côtes des Neiges end, but not the roads along the boundary nor the short cross-roads for general use).

The public has been informed by a publication, for which I am not responsible, and which I regret, that the road now made fails to meet my instructions or intentions.

The building of this road, you will recollect, was set about precipitately, to meet an emergency of public charity. I was not informed that it had been undertaken until it was far advanced toward completion. It was prosecuted under circumstances which, had there been an intention to regard landscape details, would have made it very difficult to do so: The situation was bleak, the ground was deeply covered with snow, the mercury was often as low as 10° and sometimes 20° below zero, and the wind often by no means moderate. Nevertheless, had the road been made purely for an industrial purpose, or even as a means of access to, or of connection between, certain points of view upon the mountain, which was quite all that anyone concerned had in view, it could hardly have been made with better judgment or economy. On the other hand, it must be recognized that, had it been desirable to display barrenness on its borders, and to make the fact apparent that the road was a rude and hasty construction, made with no regard to those considerations for local and foreground scenery which I sought to explain in the early part of this discourse, the same amount of labor could hardly have been better applied to the object.

You must accept the result as a misfortune for your scheme, — a misfortune which it should be your aim to qualify as far as possible. The construction of the Côtes des Neiges reservoir will give you most valuable material for the purpose, and from the skill with which Mr. McGibbon[61] has used the small means at his command during the present year, I believe the qualifications may be greater than I at first thought practicable. In my detailed plans for the road (which were never seen by anyone engaged in its construction, and are lost), provision had been made against the danger, *and the appearance of danger*, of carriages running off the embankment, an object which remains very desirable.

One more consideration as to the drives.

As a general rule in laying out a park, a visitor should not be compelled to travel twice over the same ground, but should be free to go out upon one side and return upon another, as those on foot will be able to, for example, on Mount Royal, if this design is carried out. By large expense a return road from the heights could be brought down on the north side, but were expense at this time of less consideration, or if the necessary fund for the purpose, should, in the future, be offered the city as a gift, I would not advise such a road to be built, partly for the reason that it would necessarily greatly injure very interesting natural features, just as, in a much less degree, the road already made has done, but also because variety in this case is little needed. The aspects in which the scenery of the mountain side will be seen in coming down are highly interesting and very different from those which will have been enjoyed in going up, with the face in the reverse direction.

There is also, as I have before suggested, an advantage in holding something of a little importance in reserve from the drive. It is not to be desired that everything of interest on your park should be seen by a man lolling in his carriage for an hour. It is better that all should have some inducement to walk, and that those who cannot afford to drive should have something to themselves, as this design provides at the north end of the Crags for example. As for those who cannot toil up steep hillsides but must be carried wherever they go on the mountain, special provision is made for them as you will see presently.

I now ask attention to the system of foot communication. It traverses all parts of the park, you may observe, rather more completely than that of the drives, but offers more direct routes for all purposes of pleasure-seeking. This is feasible, partly because a man can walk without excessive exertion on a grade about twice as steep as that upon which a horse without excessive exertion can draw what would be an easy load for him on a level, and also because a footman can ascend declivities by stairs. Stairs, as you see, are introduced at several points, both upon the crags and upon the minor declivities. These stairs should be arranged and studied in detail with great care to make them easy of use for women and children, and pleasant to all. They should be divided by numerous landings, and some of them should have broad covered balconies furnished with low seats; they should be deftly fitted into, not made to bridge over the ground. The landings should be roofed for shelter in showers, and the stairs shaded by vines on trellises. The steps should not be less than fourteen inches in the tread, nor more than six inches on the rise.

Bear in mind that the stairs, like everything else on the park, should not be simply means of transit, but, as far as with reasonable expense they can be made, consistently with perfect adaptation to their special purposes, means by which a greater enjoyment of the beauty of nature will occur because of the art which they embody. They may be of wood with rough surface except on the seats and hand-rails, with many tool-marks of the axe and adze, yet should exhibit the talent of your best architects, for nothing is harder to get than good rude work fitted to nature.

But when the best has been done to make the stairs easy and agreeable, there will always be a large number of persons, to whom a daily walk of several miles upon paths of moderate grade, and to whom the ascent of the mountain by such paths, would be a great advantage, who could not mount some of these flights of stairs without injury or risk to which they should not be subjected. Persons with weak lungs, with disorders of the heart, with a tendency to apoplexy, or to congestion or hemorrhage at any point, and little children, should be kept away from them. Elderly, rheumatic, gouty, and all weakly people, and parents and nurses with baby-wagons, must avoid them.

Even when, however, you shall have made the lower part of the park as convenient and attractive as possible, it will still be hard to limit the movements of all these classes to that region or to compel them to take carriage to go higher.

For this reason and also because to the great body of all classes those forms of quiet and easy exercise which are favorable to contemplative enjoyment are the most valuable, two routes are arranged, by which the highest and most remote parts of the mountain can be reached without the use of stairs and without excessively steep grades. The two are so connected as to form a circuit walk within the park about three miles in length, and so also that by taking in a short piece of the sidewalk of Pine Avenue a round tour of four miles could be made by an invalid in a rolling-chair, exhibiting all the characteristic scenery of the mountain and the most extensive distant views, without twice crossing the same point.

(All that has been said as to the management of the skirting of the drives applies, of course, to the skirting of the walks.) The total length of walks laid down upon the map within the park, including the sidewalks of the cross-roads and the walk of the grand promenade, is a little less than 13 miles (12.9).

I will now refer to a few other constructions indicated on the map.

You may notice that, at various points on the drive, where there are particularly fine distant prospects to be had, rests or concourses are thrown out so that those halting may not block the way. At three points you will see houses indicated which are designed to have all the accommodations of inns on a moderately large scale, except sleeping rooms.

That in the Underfell is for the lower park, and as people here are not far from their homes, it is small, but should this ground become, in process of time, very popular, the situation admits of as much enlargement of the house as may be desirable.

At the highest point in the Upperfell — the crown of the mountain, — there is a larger establishment intended to have a deck and low tower from which visitors will overlook the trees on the adjoining slopes, and command a view all around the horizon. It should be no higher and in no way more conspicuous than is necessary to accomplish this object. This house is designed for summer use, and to supply only light refreshments.

Another house in a lower and more sheltered situation to the southward, on the edge of the Brackenfell, is to be kept open through the year. A range of shedding is connected with it, and it is designed to provide for man and beast, more particularly to meet all the requirements of pic-nic parties in the Brackenfell.

Adjoining it, is the establishment of the administration: barns, stabling, cart-sheds, storage-yards, tool-rooms, and the office and residence of the superintendent. The situation is chosen as that from which all parts of the park, on an average, will be most easily accessible to loaded teams, or, in other words, taking elevation into account, as substantially the most central for the work to be done. It is also screened by the adjoining high ground from that part of the park which will be the most frequented by the public, and *will be conspicuous from none of the main routes of passage.* It is well sheltered from the north, and, the back of the stables being set to the west, will have a favorable exposure.

A conspicuous feature of the map represents the proposed reservoir,

PLAN FOR MOUNT ROYAL WITHOUT CÔTES-DES-NEIGES RESERVOIR AND SHOWING
DRIVE, RIDE, AND WALK NEAR SUMMIT, 1876

with a broad, shaded drive; course for saddle horses, and a walk laid out about it. My first understanding with the commissioners was, that the park was to be extended in the direction of the Côtes des Neiges Cemetery, taking in thirty acres more of the dale-like alluvial district which I call the Glades. I thought this most desirable, because it afforded the opportunity of exhibiting here an exquisite landscape, which would have been the more charming from its contrast with the general character of the scenery of the mountain, and would have made that more striking and interesting.

Wishing to keep this as idyllic as possible, and knowing that in all much frequented public parks there comes a demand for a general rendez-vous or public promenade, and that, if it is not provided for, some stretch of road, often very poorly adapted to the purpose, is made to serve for it, I had laid out a drive, ride, and walk, in another part of the park, with this object in view, and had made a distinct short circuit here of a more retired character.

When the commissioners, last year, were driven to the conclusion that it was inexpedient to propose the acquisition of any more territory, even if a corresponding reduction of that originally in view was made, and when the Common Council determined that a reservoir was required at this point, I reversed, in my design, these features of the system of communication, and adopted a more picturesque method for the higher ground, with narrower, more winding, and somewhat steeper roads, and, after much debate, arranged with Mr. LeSage,[62] the engineer of the water-works, this outline for the reservoir, which allows a grand promenade, half a mile in length, upon a circuit of easy curves, to be placed much nearer the city.[63]

409

It is on the border of the park, and as no one is compelled to enter it in passing to the more sylvan and picturesque districts beyond, it is practically an affair by itself, not a part of the park proper.

The circuit of the promenade is, on an average, a little more than half a mile in length. The pad for saddle horses is represented as twenty feet wide, the carriage-way forty, and the walk fifteen, which dimensions can be enlarged if you prefer. It is a question of expense. All the divisions of the promenade are well shaded by trees symmetrically arranged.

There is a pavilion on the knoll to the eastward for overlooking the promenade, and there are gaps in the lines of shade trees, which leave the view open from this pavilion and from the promenade across the water in the direction of the Lake of the Two Mountains.

A road is indicated, leading out of the park in the same direction. This road should, for some distance, be a park-way with broad borders of turf and shrubbery, and building lines should be established, which would prevent the view from being obstructed or marred by incongruous objects on private property.

Seats and drinking-fountains are expected to be placed adjoining the walks at frequent intervals. Some of these seats should be covered by a tight roof so as to afford shelter in rain; others shaded, either by trees or trellis-work and vines, and some should be open above and screened about for old people, who, in the spring and autumn, enjoy to sit in the sun and out of the wind, but the precise position and character of these things is considered to be a question of detail not belonging to the general plan of so large a ground.

At each of the entrances on the town side of the park, shelters are indicated. These should be larger, and should have roofs and movable blinds or shutters, so they can be made tight on the windward side. They will be made use of, not only as shelters from rain, but as rendezvous for persons agreeing to meet to walk together in the park, or for parties which break up in the park and wish to unite before going home. There are so many other things of more importance to be secured, that these should not be expensive structures, but, eventually, lodges furnishing accommodations similar to those of small railway stations will be desirable in these positions. I would advise you also not to put your money, at present, into elaborate entrance ways.

As to an exterior fence, you can have none which will be more suitable for a long time to come, than one of the simplest form of split palings of wood, such as is commonly used for private parks in England.

I have thought that you might, by and by, wish to have a small herd of deer, and, the lower part of the Brackenfell being an excellent situation for the purpose, have indicated a line of fence, and position for sheds and stables for them, so placed as to be inconspicuous, and interrupt no communication. The arrangement admits of the maintenance of perfectly satisfactory and appropriate landscape effects, but is not at all essential to the general design.

I will say no more upon the distinctively artificial features of the design, only, I pray you, never for a moment to forget that they are not objects to be desired in themselves; that they are rather the impedimenta of the undertaking. Bear in mind that it is in the earth, the rocks, the soil, and what the soil, by the skilful adaptation of means to well-chosen ends, shall be made to produce and support, that the essential value of this property is to consist. These are the meat and drink of the entertainment, to which the roads and walks and buildings are as knives and forks.

The original was published as *Mount Royal, Montreal* (New York, 1881), pages 1–80.

1. This quotation is from William Wordsworth's poem "Lines Composed a Few Miles above Tintern Abbey, on Revisiting the Banks of the Wye during a Tour" written on July 13, 1798 (John O. Hayden, *William Wordsworth: The Poems*, 2 vols. [1977; New Haven, Conn., 1981], 1: 357–62).

2. Olmsted is quoting the first line of William Cullen Bryant's poem "A Forest Hymm" written in 1825 (Louis Untermeyer, ed., *The Poems of William Cullen Bryant* [New York, 1947], pp. 72–75).

3. This quotation is from Ralph Waldo Emerson's essay "Love" published in *Essays, First Series* (1844) (Ralph Waldo Emerson, *Essays, First Series* [1844; rpt. ed., Boston, 1903], p. 176).

4. This quotation is from James Russell Lowell's "Preliminary Note to the Second Edition" of *A Fable for Critics* published in 1848 ([James Russell Lowell,] *A Fable for Critics* . . ., 2d ed. [New York, 1848], p. 117).

5. Olmsted is quoting the last line of Henry Wadsworth Longfellow's poem "Sunrise on the Hills" written during his college years (Henry Wadsworth Longfellow, *Voices of the Night* [Boston, 1845], pp. 13, 15).

6. Olmsted is quoting from Francis Bacon's essay "Of Gardens" first published in 1625 (*Bacon's Essays and Wisdom of the Ancients* . . . [Boston, 1884], pp. xii, 249–58).

7. William Mason (1724–1797), British poet. Olmsted is quoting from Mason's "The English Garden. Book the First," published in 1772 (*DNB*; *The Works of William Mason, M.A.* . . ., 4 vols. [London, 1811], 1: 213–14).

8. A quotation from act 4, scene 3 of William Shakespeare's play *The Winter's Tale* written c. 1610 (Henry Norman Hudson, Israel Gollancz, and C. H. Herford, eds., *The Aldus Shakespeare* [New York, 1968], p. 88; Margaret Drabble, ed., *The Oxford Companion to English Literature*, 5th ed. [Oxford, 1985], pp. 1074–75).

9. William Morris (1834–1896), British poet and artist. This is a quotation from Morris's *The Decorative Arts* published in 1878 (*DNB*; William Morris, *The Decorative Arts: Their Relation to Modern Life and Progress* [London, 1878], p. 5).

10. Olmsted is quoting from Edouard André's *L'Art des Jardins* (Edouard André, *L'Art des Jardins* [Paris, 1879], p. 119).

11. A quotation from John Ruskin's preface to the second edition of *Modern Painters* (John Ruskin, *Modern Painters*, 5 vols. [New York, 1862], 1: xxxvii).

12. That is, the citizens of Montreal.

13. By 1874, 360 acres had been purchased for a park in Montreal at a cost of $550,900. An additional appropriation of $449,100 was made the following year for the purchase of another 125 acres (Kathleen Jenkins, *Montreal: Island City of the St. Lawrence* [Garden City, N.Y., 1966], p. 413).

14. In November 1874 Olmsted agreed to provide the Montreal park commissioners by

May of 1875 with a map showing recommendations for boundary changes, to be followed by a general report and plan for the park by May of 1876. In exchange Olmsted was to receive $5,000. In December the City Council agreed to Olmsted's proposals (FLO to the Mount Royal Park Commissioners, Nov. 23, 1874; Extract from the minutes of the City Council, Dec. 28, 1874).

15. Olmsted presented his plan for Mount Royal in two public addresses on September 28 and 29, 1877 (see nn. 23 and 25 below).

16. A reference to the financial panic of 1873 and subsequent depression. By 1876 the continuing depression in Montreal forced the city government to abandon work on Mount Royal Park for lack of funds (George D. Ansley to FLO, Dec. 13, 1876).

17. Although the Parc de la Colombière at Dijon has been attributed to André Le Nôtre, there is no evidence that he was the designer (see FLO, *A Consideration of the Justifying Value of a Public Park* [1881], n. 7, above; Derek Clifford, *A History of Garden Design* [London, 1962], p. 229).

18. Olmsted last visited Montreal on September 28 and 29, 1877, when he presented his two lectures regarding the park at Mount Royal (see nn. 23 and 25 below).

19. Olmsted visited the park at Dijon on March 3, 1878, when traveling in Europe for his health (FLO, travel notebook, March 3, 1878).

20. The three original members of the Mount Royal Park Commission were Horatio Admiral Nelson (1816–1882), chairman, Ferdinand-Conon David (1824–1883), and John W. McGauvran (d. 1877). All three were members of the Board of Aldermen of the City Council (Dossiers 016.658, 016.185, and 016.642, Archives Municipales de Montréal, Montreal, Quebec, Canada).

21. Among the difficulties Olmsted encountered while trying to create a plan for Mount Royal Park were boundaries that he thought were established but were not, land that he thought was purchased but was not, and the introduction of new elements to the park. From the beginning Olmsted had encouraged the city to purchase land for the park along its southwestern boundary toward the Côte des Neiges Cemetery. The city never purchased the property, and Olmsted was forced to alter his plans for roads in that part of the park. Moreover, when informed that he must plan a reservoir within the park boundaries he had to abandon his original plans and redesign the entire upper part of the mountain. Finally, after considerable time spent designing an approach road, he was informed that the Frothingham property, located along the northeastern boundary of the park, was not in the possession of the city and that the Council had decided not to buy it after all. An exasperated Olmsted wrote

> Had there been ever a doubt expressed as to the matter, I should not have advised the approach from Bleury Street which has been made but strongly against it, and had I received the information you now give me my whole design for laying out the mountain would have been very different from that upon which I have been working. At the first suggestion of a doubt therefore as to your ability to hold it I advised you that its possession had already become indispensable and I have never since admitted that a question about it was admissable.
>
> The Bleury Street approach having unfortunately been prematurely built, the upper part of the Frothingham property at least is now quite as necessary to you as any that you have below the base of the cliff and much more so than any of that lying to the north and east of it. It is an absolute necessity to your scheme as it now stands and as it has been partly carried out.

(FLO to W. J. Picton, Jan. 8 and March 18, 1876, Archives Municipales de Montréal, Montreal, Quebec, Canada; H. A. Nelson to FLO, June 19 and Nov. 1, 1876; FLO to H. A. Nelson, Nov. 3, 1876, Municipales de Montréal, Montreal, Quebec, Canada; for a discussion of the reservoir, see n. 63 below.)

22. See note 23 below.

23. Olmsted proposed that he present two papers on the topic of "Large Town Parks, Their Use and Abuse." The first paper was designed to be a discussion of the motivating factors behind the designing and creation of large parks in general and Mount Royal in particular. The second lecture was to exhibit and explain the Mount Royal plan itself. He delivered the lectures on September 28 and 29, 1877. Unfortunately, Olmsted's manuscript versions of these two papers have not survived (FLO to H. A. Nelson, Sept. 11, 1877; *Montreal Herald and Daily Commercial Gazette*, Sept. 27, 1877, p. 4).

24. In July 1877 Olmsted wrote two letters to H. A. Nelson in which he requested that members of the City Council as well as "those of your citizens who care most for the larger and more permanent interests of the city" be invited. In his second letter to Nelson, Olmsted noted

> I should prefer to address particularly the class of men indicated in the opening of my last letter to you, and those conservative citizens who while well disposed to philanthropic and educational interests look with some jealousy upon the park as an extravagent plaything by which the city is liable to be drawn into excessive expenditures.
>
> The success of the park scheme in Buffalo was largely influenced by getting a small hall full of such people together with the Common Council by special invitations, opportunity being given at the end of my lecture for questions and debate.

(FLO to H. A. Nelson, July 14 and 24, 1877.)

25. In a letter to his stepson John C. Olmsted, Olmsted clearly expressed his frustration over the reading of his two papers:

> My lectures were a farcical failure as far as reaching the people is concerned. The Commissioners thought apparently of nothing but how they could get out the business without incurring expense for which they had no funds. They took the hall at 3 P.M. because it could be had at half price; sent invitations only to the city officials, Common Council &c.; bid no advertizing but only requested editors to inform the public. The hall was a large & fine one with seating for 1200. When Norton & I went into it at the hour fixed, the floor had just been washed & it was dark, damp & cold. There were present 3 commissioners, Mrs Nelson & another lady; Ansley, the Engineer and four men whom I did not know; no other member of the city gov' nor did the mayor or commissioner of Health or any others come at all. In the course of half an hour the audience increased to 30 or 40. There were 5 reporters. I read my first paper. Of the reports, one had five lines saying that I thought the mountain an unfortunate site, another about the same with — different & equally absurd misstatement. Another had reserved a column for it & filled it up with very injudicious & misprinted selections from my MS. The next day I had a little better & a much more intelligent audience, including Principal Dawson of McGill College &c. & was thanked & complimented, but not one of the papers referred to the lecture or the plan. But it is to go to the City Hall & the lectures are to be printed (FLO to JCO, Oct. 7, 1877, John Charles Olmsted Papers, Loeb Library, Graduate School of Design, Harvard University, Cambridge, Mass.).

26. That is, the depression resulting from the 1873 financial panic.

27. The Mount Royal Park commissioners visited Olmsted in New York on October 20, 1874 (P. O'Meara to FLO, Oct. 16, 1874).

28. It is difficult to ascertain which parcels of land Olmsted determined the commission could dispense with. He did consistently maintain that the commission should try to acquire land in the southwest portion of the park or toward Côte des Neiges Cemetery

(FLO to Mount Royal Park Commissioners, Nov. 21 and 23, 1874; FLO to W. J. Picton, Jan. 8 and March 18, 1876, Archives Municipales de Montréal, Montreal, Quebec, Canada; FLO to H. A. Nelson, March 24, 1876).

29. Due to the depression and the lack of work in Montreal, Olmsted was constantly under pressure throughout 1875 to provide the Mount Royal plan "piecemeal" so that the city could keep men at work on a road to the top of the mountain. In addition, Olmsted received requests from the commission to provide plans for walks and bridle paths as well as advice concerning an inclined railway. In March 1876 the commission urged Olmsted to design or at least permit the construction of a restaurant on top of the mountain (H. A. Nelson to FLO, May 25, Sept. 13, and Dec. 17, 1875, and March 9, 1876).

30. Olmsted is referring to his letter of June 6, 1876, to H. A. Nelson (*Montreal Evening Star*, June 10, 1876, p. 2).

31. These two letters were dated September 25 and 28, 1876, respectively (*Gazette*, Montreal, Oct. 5, 1876, p. 4).

32. The city engineer was W. J. Picton.

33. The Montreal park commission was not independent or separate from the City Council. It served as little more than a committee of the council as a whole. The park commissioners themselves were members of the Board of Aldermen and were dependent on the city government and public opinion. The *Montreal Evening Star* referred to this situation as the "wheel-within-a-wheel." Park boards that were "on a different footing" and with which Olmsted had shared a good working relationship included the Buffalo park board, which was composed of citizens appointed by the mayor, receiving no salaries, and independent of the City Council. Olmsted tried to explain to Nelson the dangers of attempting to design and manage a public park under the auspices of a city council:

> Consequently when works of this kind have been managed by Committees dependent from season to season for their funds upon the satisfaction which is immediately felt by the public with what they appear to superficial observers to be doing, they have in every instance within my knowledge after a few years proved mortifying disappointments. On the other hand every one which is generally recognized as a great success, and in which there is general pride and satisfaction has been managed by a proper Commission specially constituted for the purpose in a large degree independent of the Common Council and employing funds, raised expressly with a view to carry out the whole of a particlar scheme, usually by a loan specially negociated for the purpose and secured by pledge of the property to be improved.

(*Montreal Evening Star*, July 3, 1876, p. 2; FLO to H. A. Nelson, Sept. 28, 1876.)

34. McGauvran served on the park commission until his death in June 1877. David resigned from the park commission in August 1877 (Dossier 016.642, Archives Municipales de Montréal, Montreal, Quebec, Canada; *Montreal Herald & Daily Commercial*, Aug. 14, 1877, p. 4).

35. Simeon Eben Baldwin (1840–1927), American jurist and governor of Connecticut from 1910 to 1914. He also was a member of several historical, scientific, and artistic societies. This quotation is from a lecture Baldwin gave at the Sheffield Scientific School of Yale University in 1881 (*DAB*; Simeon Eben Baldwin, *Public Parks: A Lecture, Delivered in the Mechanics' Course at the Sheffield Scientific School, March 17th, 1881* [New Haven, Conn., 1881], p. 21).

36. John Campbell Shairp (1819–1885), professor of poetry at Oxford and Wordsworth scholar. Olmsted's quotation and description of Dorothy Wordsworth (1771–1855), diarist, and her brother William is in Shairp's *On Poetic Interpretation of Nature*, pub-

lished in 1877. Shairp noted that "He expressed what he saw in verse, she in prose, and it is hard to say which is the more poetic" (*DNB*; John Campbell Shairp, *On Poetic Interpretation of Nature*, 2d ed. [Edinburgh, 1877], pp. 246–47; idem, *Studies in Poetry and Philosophy* [1868; rpt. ed., Port Washington, N.Y., 1970], p. 55).

37. Olmsted is paraphrasing passages found on pages 249 and 250 of the second Edinburgh edition of Shairp's *On Poetic Interpretation of Nature*.

38. George Herbert (1593–1633), British clergyman and poet. Olmsted is quoting from the first stanza of Herbert's poem "The Church-porch" published in 1633 (John W. Cousin and David Clayton Browning, comps., *Everyman's Dictionary of Literary Biography: English & American* [London, 1958], p. 316; F. E. Hutchinson, ed., *The Works of George Herbert* [Oxford, 1941], p. 6; A. G. Hyde, *George Herbert and His Times* [London, 1906], pp. 252, 259).

39. John Addington Symonds (1840–1893), British historian, biographer, and poet. This quotation is from Symonds's article, "Matthew Arnold's Selections from Wordsworth," published in *Fortnightly Review* in 1879 (Stanley J. Kunitz and Howard Haycraft, eds., *British Authors of the Nineteenth Century* [New York, 1936], pp. 601–2; *Fortnightly Review*, Nov. 1, 1879, p. 698).

40. See note 1 above.

41. See note 20 above.

42. Robert Burns (1759–1796), Scottish poet. Burns's ancestors had all been farmers, and much of his boyhood was spent working on his father's farm. Burns received little formal education, attending small parish schools irregularly or being taught at home by his father (*DNB*).

43. Olmsted is quoting from Burns's poem, "The Humble Petition of Bruar Water to the Noble Duke of Athole," written in 1787 (Allan Cunningham, *The Complete Works of Robert Burns* . . . [Boston, 1860], pp. 147–48).

44. Edmondo de Amicis (1846–1908), Italian traveler and writer. Olmsted is quoting from de Amicis's travelogue, *Holland*, published in 1874 (*EB*; Edmondo de Amicis, *Holland and Its People*, 5th ed. [New York, 1880], p. 268).

45. The edition that Olmsted is citing here was published in 1884 (A. Des Cars, *A Treatise on Pruning Forest and Ornamental Trees*, 2d ed. [1881; Boston, 1884]).

46. Edouard François André (1840–1911), preeminent French landscape architect, published *L'Art des Jardins* in 1879. André began his professional career as Principal Gardener to the city of Paris in 1860, a position he held for eight years. In 1869, while in Russia, André visited Tsarskoye Selo, located fifteen miles southeast of St. Petersburg. Tsarskoye Selo included two palaces, extensive formal gardens, and acres of parkland designed for Catherine the Great in the English landscape style by John Busch. Olmsted's statement here, however, best fits the description of Tsarskoye Selo by C. Piazzi Smyth in his book *Three Cities in Russia*, published in 1862. Smyth emphasized the predominance along the drives of the estate of three species of trees — birch, larch, and fir — and observed that "There was a sameness certainly as to species of tree, but never, never had we seen the peculiar class of beauty which by nature is implanted in those trees so admirably brought out before." André's description of the estate, in contrast, emphasized the variety of plant materials employed. In discussing the municipal parks of St. Petersburg, André did observe that the trees in them were limited to three species — elm, linden, and willow — but offered little praise of the effect achieved thereby (*Who Was Who in Literature, 1906–1934*, 2 vols. [Detroit, Mich., 1979], 1: 30; *The Gardeners' Chronicle*, Nov. 11, 1911, p. 338; Edouard André, *Un Mois en Russie* [Paris, 1870], p. 116; Geoffrey Jellicoe et al., eds., *Oxford Companion to Gardens* [Oxford, 1991], pp. 490, 564–65; C. Piazzi Smyth, *Three Cities in Russia* [London, 1862], p. 175).

47. Joseph Decaisne (1807–1882), French botanist and horticulturist. In 1834 Decaisne

became a director of the Annales des Sciences Naturelles and in 1851 he became head of the Jardin des Plantes in Paris. During his lifetime, Decaisne published several important works on botany and agricultural industry.

The motto to which Olmsted refers reads

... "If the forests should disappear, civilization would become extinguished on the earth. ...

"It is the duty of an enlightened community to plant trees, and to so care for them that posterity shall not suffer, — a duty unfortunately too little regarded in our day."

(*New-York Times*, Feb. 10, 1882, p. 5; A. Des Cars, A *Treatise on Pruning Forest and Ornamental Trees.*)

48. See note 10 above.

49. Ruskin's passage, which Olmsted excerpts here, reads

Every herb and flower of the field has its specific, distinct, and perfect beauty; it has its peculiar habitation, expression, and function. The highest art is that which seizes this specific character, which developes and illustrates it, which assigns to it its proper position in the landscape, and which, by means of it, enchances and enforces the great impression which the picture is intended to convey (J. Ruskin, *Modern Painters*, 1: xxxi).

50. In his letter of November 21, 1874, in which he provided the commissioners with his initial observations of the mountain, Olmsted noted that while improvements should be minimal they should first and foremost be intended "to relieve the surface of the mountain of the accidental and transient conditions through which it has at present an unnecessary desolate and melancholy aspect" (FLO to the Mount Royal Park Commissioners, Nov. 21, 1874).

51. A reference to the main character in Henry Wadsworth Longfellow's poem "Evangeline" published in 1847. The poem begins in Acadia (present-day Nova Scotia) where the lovers Evangeline and Gabriel are separated by the French and Indian War. Evangeline learns that Gabriel has gone to Louisiana and follows him there but cannot find him. The two lovers do not cross paths again until years later when Gabriel is dying. Evangeline dies shortly thereafter, and the two are buried together (Ian Ousby, *Cambridge Guide to Literature in English*, 2d ed. [Cambridge, 1993], s.v. "Evangeline").

52. A reference to Mount Gibbs, elevation 12,764 feet, in California. In September 1864 Olmsted, his stepson John, and the geologist William Brewer took a trip into the Sierra Nevada. They climbed an unnamed peak to the south of Mount Dana and named it Mount Gibbs after Oliver Wolcott Gibbs. Olmsted noted that "the surface of the mountain was composed of boulders and splinters of slate and quartz. . . . Growing on and among these stones even to the very top we found some beautiful Alpine flowers most of them I believe indistinguishable from those found in the Alps" (FLO to JO, Sept. 14, 1864 [*Papers of FLO*, 5: 252–53 and 257, n. 6]).

53. That is, William Robinson, the English landscape gardener. Olmsted and Robinson first met in 1870 in New York and quickly became friends. The two shared information about landscape design over the years and Olmsted drew much support from Robinson's writings for his own ideas concerning landscape design and parks. The entire sentence, which Olmsted excerpted here, reads "Nature *in puris naturalibus* we cannot have in our gardens, but Nature's laws should not be violated; and few human beings have contravened them more than our flower-gardeners during the past twenty years" (*Papers of FLO*, 6: 552; William Robinson, *The Subtropical Garden; or, Beauty or Form in the Flower Garden* [London, 1871], p. 5).

54. Olmsted is referring to William Robinson's *The Wild Garden* and *Alpine Flowers for English Gardens*, both published in 1870.
55. Olmsted is quoting from an article published in the *Pall Mall Gazette* in September 1878 ("Kensington Gardens," *Pall Mall Gazette*, Sept. 5, 1878, p. 9).
56. Thomas Wisedell (1846–1884), British-born architect. At Calvert Vaux's urging, Wisedell came to the United States in 1868. In England, Wisedell had studied under Robert Withers, brother of the architect Frederick C. Withers, who was Vaux's partner in the firm Vaux & Withers from 1853 to 1856 and later in the firm Vaux, Withers & Company from 1865 to 1872 as well as a member of the firm Olmsted, Vaux & Company. Wisedell worked with Olmsted and Vaux on Prospect Park in Brooklyn, assisting in the design of the Concert Grove buildings and some of the stonework. He also worked with Olmsted on designs of architectural features for the U.S. Capitol grounds in the 1870s and early 1880s. In 1879 Wisedell formed a partnership with Francis Hatch Kimball, and the two of them became known for their designs of theaters in New York and other cities.

   In response to an inquiry from H. A. Nelson regarding the construction of a temporary restaurant at the top of the mountain, Olmsted instead suggested building a permanent refectory. Olmsted engaged Wisedell to design the refectory and plans were prepared. The refectory would have cost $8,000 to build, but the City Council refused to vote for the needed appropriation and the building was never constructed. Wisedell's plans have not survived (*New-York Times*, Aug. 2, 1884, p. 4; *Papers of FLO*, 6: 69, 672; H. A. Nelson to FLO, March 9 and 21, 1876; FLO to H. A. Nelson, April 4, 1876, Archives Municipales de Montréal, Montreal, Quebec, Canada; FLO to H. A. Nelson, May 19, 1876; W. J. Picton to FLO, July 13, 1876; Thomas Wisedell to FLO, Aug. 31, 1876; *Montreal Evening Star*, July 3, 1876, p. 2; ibid., July 7, 1876, p. 3; ibid., July 11, 1876, p. 2).
57. Presumably Olmsted is referring to his second lecture on September 29, 1877, when he presented the plan for Mount Royal. Beginning in early October, a large lithograph of the plan was exhibited in the City Hall. It is unlikely that Olmsted offered his manuscript to the press for publication at the time of its presentation; subsequent correspondence indicates that he intended to have the park commission publish his lectures in pamphlet form after he made revisions. In October 1878 the commission requested Olmsted to forward his manuscripts to it but decided not to publish them, reserving the right to do so at some future time. Olmsted did not comply with the request (*Montreal Herald and Daily Commercial Gazette*, Oct. 5, 1877, p. 4; FLO to H. A. Nelson, Sept. 20, 1878; Extract from the Minutes of the Mount Royal Park Commission, ms, Oct. 17, 1878).
58. Hugh Allan (1810–1882) was born in Scotland and migrated to Montreal in 1826. He became a prominent Canadian businessman and founder of a steamship line, and he was knighted in 1871 in recognition of his service to his country. Hugh Allan's property was located just south of the Crags but the city refused to buy it (William Henry Atherton, *Montreal from 1535 to 1914*, 3 vols. [Montreal, 1914], 3: 635–37; A. L. Murray, "Frederick Law Olmsted and the Design of Mount Royal Park, Montreal," *Society of Architectural Historians* 26 [Oct. 1967], p. 170).
59. John Redpath (1796–1869), contractor and industrialist. Redpath was born in Scotland and migrated to Montreal in 1816. Redpath's property was located just south of the Crags; as with the Allan property, the city refused to purchase it for the park (*Dictionary of Canadian Biography*, 13 vols. [Toronto, 1966–94], 9: 654–55; A. L. Murray, "Frederick Law Olmsted and the Design of Mount Royal," pp. 170–71).
60. The Hotel-Dieu Hospital, originally built in 1644 near the shore of the St. Lawrence River, was moved in 1861 to its present location at the base of the mountain. At the time Olmsted prepared his plan for Mount Royal, the hospital grounds were bounded

by Bleury Street on the west and Upper St. Urbain Street on the east (Joseph Kearney Foran, *Jeanne Mance or "The Angel of the Colony"* . . . [Montreal, 1931], p. 57; F. N. Boxer, *Map of the City of Montreal Shewing the Victoria Bridge, Mountain & Proposed Boulevard, and the Different Dock Projects* [Montreal, 1859]; J. Johnson, *Map of the Island and City of Montreal* [Montreal, 1881]).

61. William McGibbon, Mount Royal's first park superintendent, was appointed in 1874 and continued in that position for twenty-two years (*Gazette, Montreal*, Feb. 28, 1970, p. 1).

62. Louis LeSage was the engineer in charge of Montreal's waterworks.

63. In April 1876 Olmsted was surprised to learn that he would need to allow for a twenty-acre reservoir within the boundaries of the park. While he had originally believed that a reservoir on the mountain was undesirable, he had relented due to the city's need for a water supply. In the previous month he had written to Picton describing a five-acre lake that he proposed be constructed near the southwestern park boundary, where it would least encroach upon the park. The reservoir issue continued to prove quite troubling for Olmsted for several months. In June and July he complained to Nelson and LeSage that the city's proposed reservoir would severely alter the plan of the park and that no work could be done until the issue was settled. The city finally agreed to a smaller reservoir than it had originally requested, but at the same time Olmsted was informed that the city would not purchase the Tompkins property, where he had intended to put the reservoir. He was forced to move it to the southeast, encroaching on the park in precisely the manner he had wished to avoid. On July 26 he wrote Nelson

> Having been advised by you that the project of a reservoir had been fully adopted, to be situated on the meadow of the Smith property, originally intended to be included in your park, I prepared a study of an outline to the same such as I thought would best suit its necessarily close relations with the park, while fully meeting the requirements of the Water Works. . . . Its adoption will involve a change in the general Theory of design for laying out all the upper part of the mountain. The element, which I have hitherto considered a very important one, of a piece of truly park-like ground, broad, simple, quiet and of a rich sylvan and pastoral character, forming a harmonious, natural foreground to the view over the Western valley and all in striking contrast to the ruggedness of the mountain proper, must be abandoned.

Olmsted did plan a reservoir of approximately seven acres to be located in the southwest corner of the park, but Nelson informed him in September 1876 that while the City Council had decided "to adopt your plan for it, and to allow you to make your plan accordingly, but it may be years before the reservoir is made, therefore it would not do to delay the park plan for the building of it, but I think the drives could be made, and the site of the reservoir turned into a Flower Garden in the meantime . . ." (FLO to H. A. Nelson, April 11, 1876; FLO to H. A. Nelson, July 26, 1876, Archives Municipales de Montréal, Montreal, Quebec, Canada; FLO to W. J. Picton, March 18, 1876, Archives Municipales de Montréal, Montreal, Quebec, Canada; Louis LeSage to FLO, April 15, 1876; H. A. Nelson to FLO, June 19 and Sept. 27, 1876; FLO to Louis LeSage, July 5, 1876).

BELLE ISLE: AFTER ONE YEAR.

BROOKLINE, June, 1884.

To the Citizens of Detroit, —

As an introduction to the present pamphlet, I would refer to advice offered in the same form a year and a half ago, and to the circumstances that prompted it.[1]

The city having, against the judgment of many, undertaken to make a park of Belle Isle, commissioners had been selected to start the work, who, it was supposed, would command public confidence in an unusual degree. The business being new to them, they had sought counsel of experience, and had been advised by the commissioners of parks of other cities to consult me. The grounds of this advice were, that I had been during thirty years a designer, superintendent, or commissioner of parks; had been practically engaged in their management in several cities, — some East, some West, — some larger, some smaller, than Detroit; and through this experience had become familiar with the public requirements gradually developed by their use.

An engagement with me followed, on the same terms that the commissioners were advised had been elsewhere found economical and satisfactory.[2] I refer to this action because it is said that the confidence of some citizens in the commissioners' fitness for their duties was shaken by it.

I soon learned that there was much anxiety — among those, especially, who had regarded Belle Isle as an extremely unsuitable site for a park — lest the city should be drawn into a course of extravagant and wasteful expenditure. It was obvious that this would, to a certain extent, depend upon the plan that should be adopted for the work; but it was known to me, that, in other cities, the chief difficulty of economy had not been in obtaining a plan satisfactory at the outset, but in subsequently pursuing any steady policy of working it out. Among the reasons for this may be mentioned the following: —

The site of an intended park is liable to be much resorted to by the public before it is half prepared for any suitable park-use, even when the operations are yet much more obstructive than aidful to all desirable forms of general recreation. Under these circumstances, work in progress upon it cannot but be seen disjointedly, and much of it appear discordant, confusing, pointless, and profitless. Thus, in parts at least, if offers a standing provocation to thoughtless expressions of impatience, leading on to surmises and guesses,

419

out of which grow rumors, running often, at last, to matter-of-fact statements, apparently showing that those in charge are proceeding ignorantly, recklessly, and extravagantly.

As an example of such reports, to which there has as yet been no parallel in Detroit, I will mention that it has repeatedly occurred that piles of soil laid up for temporary storage have been mistaken for permanent constructions, and as such have sustained a severe fire of public criticism; while, later, the removal of the soil to its original destination has been denounced as evidence that the work was being carried on without forecast, plan, or method. Charges of this character have repeatedly been made matters of bootless legislative investigation.

Such reports often prompt suggestions, and prepare the public to entertain suggestions for improvements in the general plan and organization of the work, and sometimes lead to the pushing of projects of supposed improvement, or for the arrest of what are thought wasteful operations, with the energy of an honestly heated antagonism.

As a park commission is a changeable body, and as city councils — more or less in control of park commissions — are still more changeable, there is a liability that such efforts may, because of hasty consideration in minds newly taking up the matter, have a degree of success of which the ultimate effect is very different from that contemplated. Nearly always it will follow that the object of various previous operations is thwarted, and the outlay that has been made for it in some degree wasted.

I thought it best to take advantage of the prevailing anxiety to avoid an extravagant plan, to call attention to dangers of this class, and to show how they might to a certain extent be guarded against in advance. For this purpose I printed a pamphlet, in which a scheme was sketched for the improvement of Belle Isle, giving reasons for its leading features, and explaining how they would hang together, and minor features grow logically and economically out of them. As a means to a soundly conservative public opinion, and of precaution against the hasty determination of the details of a plan in the future, I challenged and solicited immediate public discussion of this scheme.

The pamphlet being ready for issue, I called personally on the editor of each of the daily papers of the city, upon members of the council, officers of the city government, and other gentlemen of intelligence, stating its object, and asking their aid to secure the desired public discussion. Such aid was generally promised: the pamphlet was brought prominently to the attention of the public, it was gratuitously distributed in large numbers, and the substance of it widely disseminated by the newspaper press.[3]

In due time afterward, the intended draught of a plan upon the lines foreshadowed in the pamphlet was completed, and the commissioners caused it to be exhibited publicly. Lithographed copies were also freely distributed. The members of the city council, and others likely to be especially interested in the questions at issue, were, by special note to each, requested to give it their consideration. The commissioners brought in other citizens. Reporters of the press were daily present. That the essential characteristic features might be more plainly presented, and readily understood by all, the drawing was in black and white, and devoid of all ornamentation, pictorial quality, or taking detail. (A miniature of it is printed herewith). I stood before it for a week to answer inquiries, give explanations, and bring the whole scheme as far as possible into daylight.[4] As to many considerations affecting the plan, — such as the currents of the river, the action of ice, requirements of shipping, the costliness of various operations, — I had been necessarily dependent on information from residents more familiar than I could be with the local circumstance. I hoped, and aimed in this discussion before the drawing, to have this information enlarged, and, if need be, corrected. The plan was distinctly entitled a "preliminary plan," and held subject to immediate revision on any adequate ground for its reconsideration.

Could more have been done to secure general, intelligent examination, and a full understanding of what was proposed to be undertaken, before the work should begin? Could more have been done to guard against either hasty and inconsiderate, or insincere and specious, attempts to disintegrate the plan after the work should be fairly started?

At last, upon mature deliberation, the commissioners, with every assurance of public approval, agreed unanimously to adopt the draught thus exhibited, as the plan upon which Belle-Isle Park should be formed.

This having been publicly announced, can it be supposed that any citizens of Detroit having knowledge of serious objections to the plan, possibly overlooked by the commissioners, would have withheld it from the public or the city council? Can it be imagined that any good citizen should have wished the work to proceed for a year before showing that the plan of it rested, in certain respects, on mistaken grounds and erroneous calculations?

There was, in fact, no call at the time for a reconsideration of the plan in any respect, from any quarter. Neither through members of the council, nor the comments of the press, nor by private advice, did disapproval of the commissioners' conclusion appear.[5] The mayor gave official expression to his own and the general satisfaction with the plan, and congratulated the council on having obtained it;[6] and, the council having voted supplies, the work was duly entered upon without a whisper of protest.

This was one year ago. Already the composition of the city government has considerably changed. There are, probably, gentlemen now in it whose attention was not called at the time to the circumstances above stated, or who have since lost sight of them.[7] But half the commissioners remain, upon whose deliberations a determination of the plan last year depended.[8]

To understand the motives and expectations with which the expenditure of the year has been mainly directed, it will be best to consider that the foremost feature of the plan as shown in the exhibited drawing, and that feature of it to which attention was more given in the conferences before it than

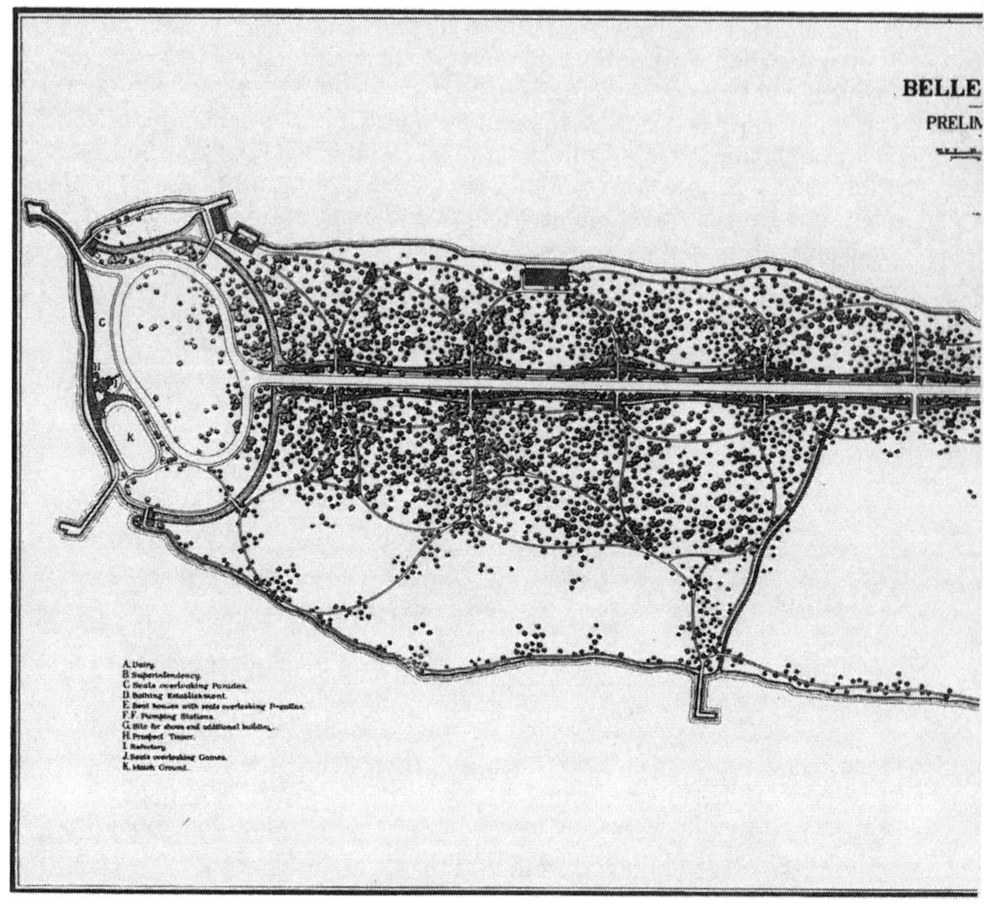

"Belle Isle Park

any other, is a structure, partly resting on a pier extending from the nearest land of the island toward the city, and partly carried from this point along the adjacent west shore. I wish now to hold the reader's attention, briefly, to one class of the motives determining this feature in the general design of the park. It is that which leads the structure in question to be styled the gallery. (A gallery in monumental architecture is a long, covered passage, in the sides of which are outlets to apartments for various purposes.) The central part of this so-called gallery had outlet on one side to a beach sloping from it into shallow water, upon which beach children could play, as children everywhere delight to do on a beach, while their parents could keep an eye upon them without leaving the seats in the shade of the frederick gallery-roof. On the land side of the gallery, a strip of ground was to be prepared, corresponding in length with the shore part of the gallery, and of a width and grade adapting it to be used

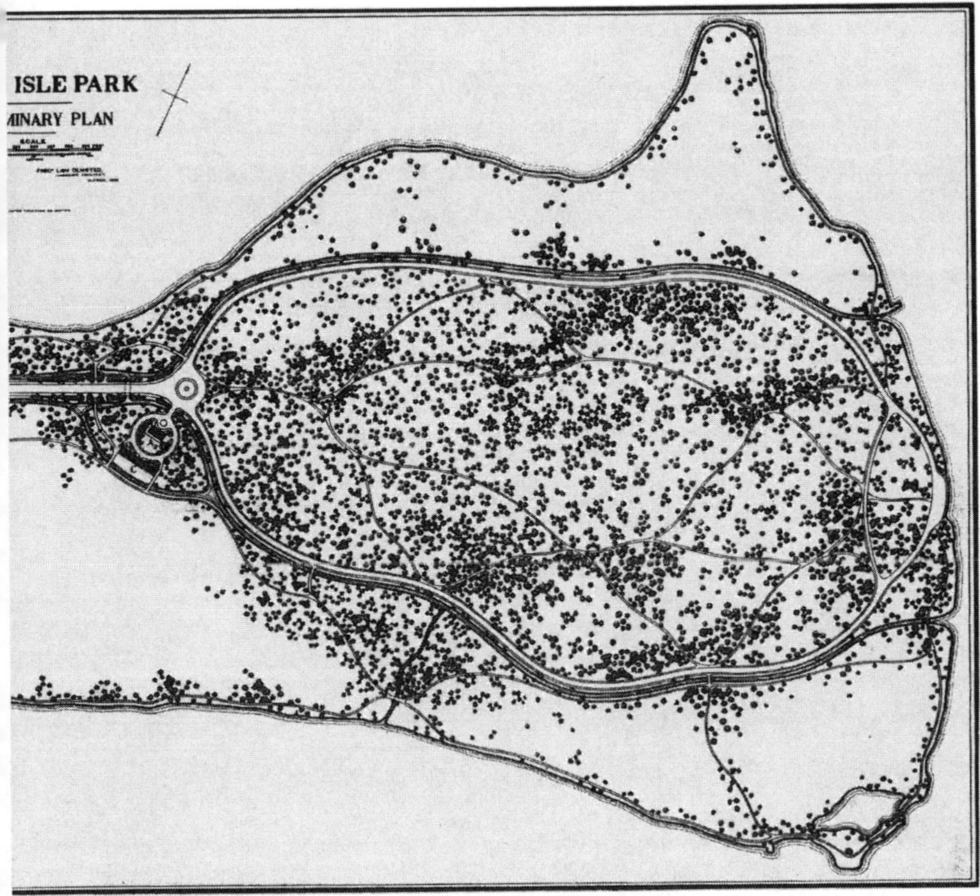

PRELIMINARY PLAN," 1883

as a site for a series of annexed apartments to be introduced, as they should from time to time be called for, upon the park, and which, as a matter of taste, it would be desirable to avoid scattering through its rural parts, and, as a matter of economy, to concentrate near the landing. The plan of the gallery was adapted to the ready fitting to it, at any time, of these annexes, which might be tents or buildings, and were to be entered from it at one end; while at the other they were to open upon a walk and road to be laid out parallel to, and at a suitable distance from, its landward side. Beyond the road, accessible from the gallery, either through the annexes or by the passages between them, was to be a space of greensward prepared suitably for lawn-games, and which, to indicate its distinctive character, might be called the ladies' ground. At the end was ground for match and exhibition games, and here the gallery merged into a stand for spectators of the games. Roads and walks were to be

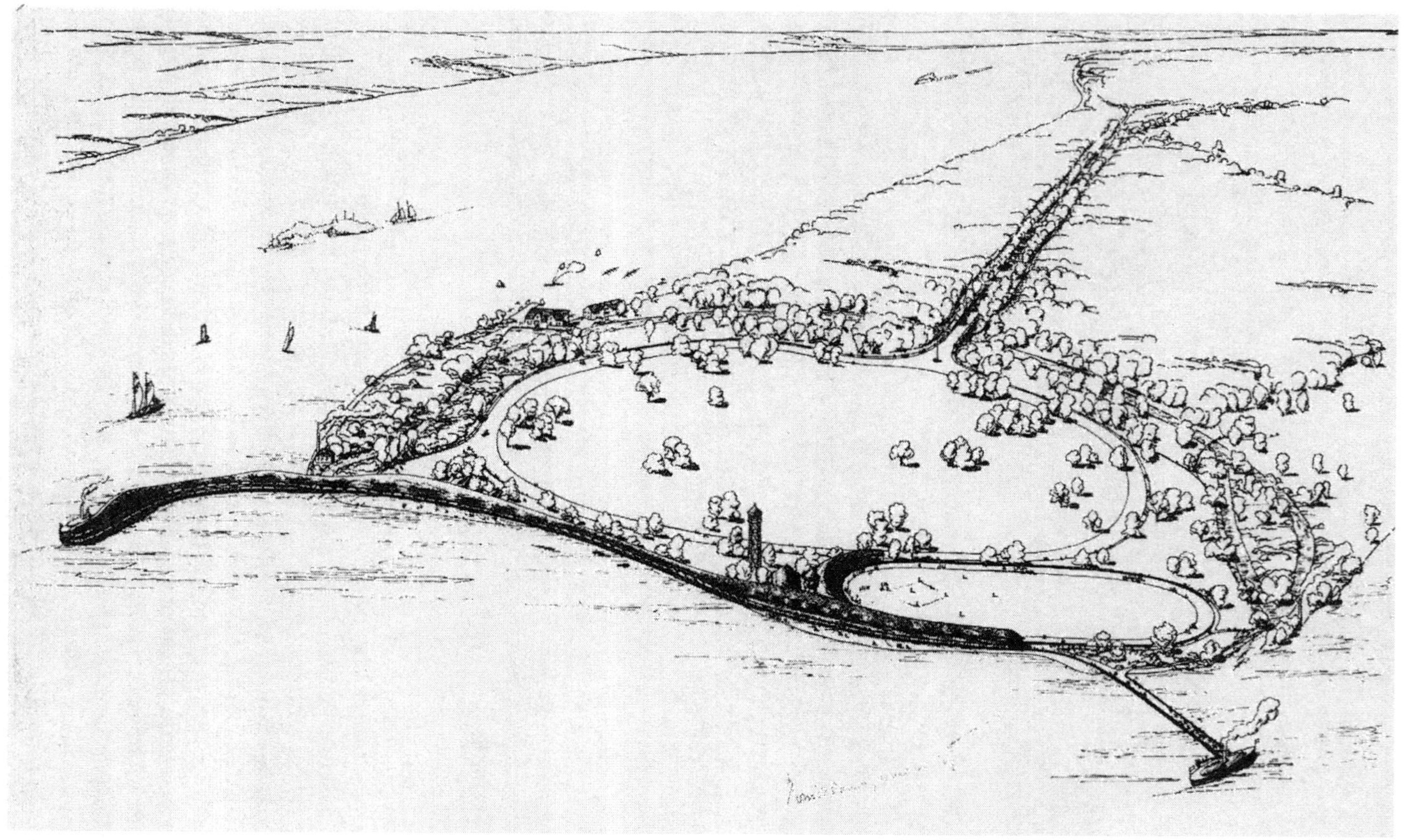

View of Proposed Gallery on Belle Isle, 1883

formed beyond the ladies' ground, and in adjustment to it; and a canal was to be dug, the extent and location of which had been determined in part with a view to enclosing the entire group of arrangements connecting with the pier and gallery, and to economy in obtaining the material required for grading the sites for them.

The larger part of the outlay made on the park the first year has been expended upon these arrangements. The site for the gallery has been, in one part, for some distance, cut down, and elsewhere filled up, to the intended grade of its floor. The beach before the gallery has been fully formed and gravelled. The sites severally of the annexes, of the road and walk, and of the ladies' ground, have been brought to sub-grades determined in adaptation to the grade of the gallery. The match-ground has been in large part graded; and the canal, by which all these features of the plan were detached from the main body of the wooded park, has been dug, and opened to boats; and the approaches to the principal bridge crossing it have been formed.

Here the work stood, when, in March, I visited the city to aid the commissioners in determining the plan of operations for the coming year.[9] It was an open question, whether the gallery should be included in it. It was determined that this should depend on the amount of the appropriation to be made by the council.[10] With the president, I went before the council to give reasons why the appropriation might desirably be made sufficient to this end.[11] I conversed with several members of the council individually about it. The question was discussed as a question of the rate of progress expedient to be provided for, and, slightly, of the order of advance, — not as a question of the merits of the plan, to which I did not then hear a word of objection.

I have but imperfect knowledge of what followed, until I was asked to consider what effect an abandonment of the pier and gallery would have upon the plan of other parts of the work.[12] But the reason for this inquiry I understand to be, that, after I left, representations came to members of the council, by which they were led to question, not only the expediency of providing for the pier and gallery immediately, but whether the notion of ever doing so should be entertained. In the end, the commissioners were advised that the opposition to this part of the scheme seemed so strong that it would probably be better to drop it, — drop it for good and all.[13]

To realize the position of the commissioners with reference to this suggestion, and especially of those of them who had not had part in the original discussion of the plan, it must be remembered that the more important work, other than that of the pier and gallery, which had been had in view for the coming year, was in continuation of work already done, the plan of which work done was largely dependent on the occupancy of the adjoining ground by the pier and gallery.

If, therefore, it was at all likely to appear necessary to the minds of new commissioners, or of the city council, at any time in the future, to compel a revision of the plan in respect to the pier and gallery, it was evident that the whole west-end plan would have to be reconsidered, and that probably much of the work to be done in the meantime could only be turned to account by some make-shift after-thought. It appeared prudent, therefore, at once to respectfully examine the objections made to the pier and gallery, and, pending the results, to hold parts of the work suspended, even if some advantages for economy of work were thereby lost.

The "pressure" against the pier and gallery having been informal, a precise responsible statement of the objections to it could not be obtained; but it was understood that that held most conclusive had been based on the alleged assurance of river-men, that the point in the river which would be the outer end of the pier would be accessible only to boats of light draught and small carrying capacity, and therefore of little public use. Before such large boats as those of the Windsor Ferry Company[14] could be brought to it, a long and costly channel would need to be made by dredging; and, the bottom being sandy, the process would need to be often repeated, at great expense to the city.[15]

To test the weight of this objection, a stake was set by the city engineer to mark the proposed point of the pier. The deepest of the Windsor ferry-boats was then run directly to this stake, and found to be lying in water of double the depth necessary to float her. She was then turned, and moved off abreast of the stake a distance of five hundred feet, finding no shallower water. The soundings indicated a bottom, not of sand, but of clay and small stones, corresponding with the subsoil of the island adjacent. It was apparent to the commissioners that the conditions were more favorable to the project than they had been supposed to be when it was first discussed.[16]

The great advantages to be gained by landing visitors, under ordinary circumstances, on the drier and better-wooded American side of the island, rather than at the old pier on the swampy Canadian side (a pier extending into a channel often crowded by long tows of shipping), has not, I believe, been questioned.

As to the other objections considered by the commissioners, they were such as would naturally occur to intelligent men looking at the proposition for the first time, and as would naturally lead to such questions as had been put to me by the commissioners and by others, and which, before the adoption of the plan, I had often answered much in the way I propose to answer them now. By this, I mean not at all in an authoritative, peremptory, or pedantic way, but chiefly by stating the grounds of experience that had led me to think the advantages to be gained, by the proposition traversed, outweighed or neutralized these objections.

The objection is made, that there can be no need of such an extent of shelter as the plan provides at the locality designated. To this I reply, that it nearly always occurs, when any considerable part of a new public park is well finished, that the public use of it greatly exceeds the estimates of its promoters. Because of this, I have repeatedly seen work ripped up and done over at excessive cost. They have, this year, been rebuilding the principal shelter of the Buffalo park, giving it double its original capacity.[17] They are enlarging their picnic-ground and conveniences to four times the capacity to which (against my advice) they were originally limited.[18] In New York, a part of the roads and bridges having, as a measure of economy, been laid out narrower than originally designed, in a few years it was found necessary to break them up, and rebuild them larger.[19] Many similar experiences could be referred to.

But Belle Isle must be regarded as combining, with the attractions of an ordinary urban park, not a little of those of such suburban water-side resorts as are approached by steam-ferries from Portland, Portsmouth, Boston, Providence, New London, New York, Newark, Baltimore, and other coast-towns. It cannot fail to be greatly used in this way if properly prepared. It will be ill used more or less in this way if not properly prepared. Having this consideration in view, before studying out the plan of Belle Isle I visited several resorts of this class, that I might consider more closely than I had before the manner of their use, and what was needed to make it satisfactory. At different times I have visited more than thirty of them, and have everywhere found the most popular, useful, and, relatively to cost, the most profitable feature of their outfit, to be one of a character corresponding to the proposed Belle-Isle gallery. It is generally placed, as it is planned to be placed on Belle Isle, parallel with the beach, and between it and a series of apartments for refreshment, recreation, and retirement. The arrangement to which the grading of last year at Belle Isle was adapted, differs from that which is thus common, in that the annexed rooms (not shown on the plan) for various purposes are designed to be in a series of structures, temporary or permanent (tents or buildings to be put up, if preferred, by lease-holders), so separated as to leave openings for the breeze, and for outlooks eastwardly. These structures may thus stand at different elevations, so as to avoid the reduction of the adjoining ground to a uniform level, and allow its surface to play out gracefully. The notion I had of the number of these structures, for which space, under such an arrangement, could be disposed of profitably by the city, was partly based upon the incessant demands that have been addressed to me when in charge of established parks, partly upon observation at the water-side resorts referred to, and partly upon knowledge of the eagerness with which privileges, not to be compared in value with those to be thus offered for supplying the wants of visitors, had already been sought upon Belle Isle. As to the breadth of the gallery, it is on an average less than that of galleries recently built at several public resorts. It will, judging from the experience of these, be found cramped and inconvenient if made narrower; and a necessity will probably be found, in a few years, for its reconstruction at an economical disadvantage.

Among the considerations that lead to this conclusion are these: As a rule, it may be said, that, if fifty thousand persons visit one of the shore-resorts in a day (as often occurs), not a dozen of such visitors fail to spend some time upon one of these galleries. It is a place of rest, and of cooling, after a ramble; it is occupied for the enjoyment of the view, and of the breeze from over the water; it is a rendezvous for meeting friends; and, when not too crowded, it is constantly used as a promenade. It is a place for all visitors to whom rest in the open air is more desirable than prolonged exercise. It is common to serve coffee, tea, and ices upon it. Even in a fair day, and with no unusual occasion for shelter, I have found, at more than one water-side resort, successive galleries (together many times as long as that proposed for Belle Isle), so densely occupied, that passage along them was much incommoded.

It may be said that these galleries are attached to hotels, and that they are used chiefly by lodgers in them. But I was advised in several cases by the proprietors that this was not the case, — often that not one visitor in a hundred spent the night at the establishment. Several of those built of late do not offer lodgings for visitors; and, where transit to the city approaches in convenience and frequency that from Belle Isle to Detroit, these are the more favored. They are the resort of townspeople who spend the night in their own homes, and of excursionists from a distance who come for a day's recreation. The use of these houses is in no way different from that to which the arrangement proposed on Belle Isle is adapted. The difference between the two lies chiefly in the circumstance, that, in the establishments referred to, there is one continuous structure opposite the water side; while, in the Belle-Isle arrangement, there will be openings between the annexes. The objection to the complete closing of the gallery on the land side is the shutting off of the views that way, and the obstruction to the breeze which sometimes makes the seashore galleries, as at Coney Island, harbors for mosquitoes. It will be found, I apprehend, that, when it is impossible to escape mosquitoes anywhere else on the island, the open water-side gallery will be completely free from them.

There is, I think, no reason to doubt, that, even looking only to such a use of the gallery as is constantly made of these to which I refer, it would be in the highest degree popular, and would prove none too large for the comfortable use of those who would resort to it.

But the gallery is intended to serve another purpose, as to which the experience of these water-side resorts is hardly more than suggestive. Whenever a shower occurs; or when, near the close of the day, friends who have been separated desire to return to the city together; and when (the boats being crowded) there is likely to be some delay in obtaining conveyance, — then these galleries become extended waiting-rooms, and are often suddenly filled to their capacity.

Now, Belle Isle is to be much more than a water-side resort. At times, when large numbers of people are widely scattered over the park engaged in various forms of recreation, there will be — because of a threat of rain, or a shift of wind, or the rapid approach of nightfall — a sudden impulse to move toward the boats. Then, for various reasons, many will be compelled, and others disposed (having arrived within sight of the boats), to linger a little before leaving the island. Large numbers of people cannot often be concentrated at any point on a park, without much discomfort to themselves, and destructive effects on trees and turf, unless special arrangements, not of a rural character, are provided for them. The gallery is intended to provide adequate and suitable arrangements for these contingencies; and it is not larger in plan than, after a close observation of experience elsewhere, must, I think, be concluded to be necessary. It should be remembered, that, on most parks, there are numerous places of outlet, and, generally, extensive railroad stations, to which resort can be quickly had when desired. There are, for instance, ten gates, widely distributed, in the New-York park, and seven in the Brooklyn park,[20] at which visitors leaving can step directly into steam or street cars. There are several others, from which railroad stations can be reached in a walk of two minutes. The case is still better at Philadelphia. There are three railway exits from Buffalo park. Public carriages ply through most parks at low rates of fare; and there are numerous structures (twenty in one case, over forty in another), at each of which from a hundred to a thousand people can obtain shelter. Nevertheless, I have seen crowds so pressing out from a park at times, that the roads and walks were inadequate for their passage; and great destruction resulted from the irresistible overflow upon the shrubberies. I have seen several thousand people soaked by a shower under these circumstances.

The number coming to Belle Isle may be comparatively small, but the rush will often be all toward one point.

It was observed in the preliminary pamphlet, that, following the completion of suitable park arrangements, customs before unknown are apt to grow up spontaneously.[21] Of the bearing of the anticipation to which this observation leads upon the question in hand, one or two illustrations may be given.

In Brooklyn park, there is what is called the May Festival.[22] I assisted at the modest beginning of it fourteen years ago. It has been growing since; and when last held, a month ago, it is reported that fifty thousand children were gathered at once upon the greensward near the principal entrance to the park, and a great concourse of people came to enjoy the sight of them.

Suppose, that, on some similar occasion, a quarter as many should be assembled on the green now preparing at the lower end of Belle Isle. Consider what, if a thunder-squall should suddenly come up, the rush toward the boats would be. Imagine excited parents seeking stampeded children. Think how easily some accident would precipitate a panic; and, if this could be avoided, how hard it would be to maintain such order as would be necessary to secure little ones from serious injury. The vague apprehension of what might occur until an apparently adequate place of temporary shelter had been provided, will prevent such a charming custom from growing up, and, by so much, limit the value receivable by the city from the park.

In New York, at the same season of the year, another custom has grown from a like impulse. It is that of independent Maying parties. They commonly consist of from ten to twenty children, wearing wreaths of flowers and gayly dressed. Each party asks a place to itself on the greensward, where it sets up its pole with garlands and ribbons, and crowns its May Queen. These parties come every fair day, but the larger number on Saturdays. I remember marshalling the first of them when the ground was in a condition of progress toward a park that Belle Isle is now. They have been increasing since; and it is said that one day this spring they came in five hundred distinct processions, — as pretty a sight as anyone could wish to see. No such custom can prudently be allowed to grow up on Belle Isle, unless you have, between your greensward and your boats, some sheltering place, much larger than would be imagined to be necessary, from any use that has yet been made of the island, or of any place of resort near Detroit.

Another objection to which I have been asked to reply takes form in questions.

Will not the gallery interrupt the view from the island down the river?

It will, to a considerable extent; but this view can be much more readily enjoyed when sitting in its shade, than from the open ground.

Will not the gallery screen the island from view, in approaching it from down the river?

From a distance nothing is seen of the island but a mass of foliage. The height of the gallery, on an average, is about a third the height of the trees forming this mass. It would obscure less than a quarter part of them. On nearing the island, from the upper deck of a steamboat a space of open ground is to be seen before the woods. It is true that the gallery will obscure the most of this space.

Might not trees be planted, by which in time the shore-walk would be shaded?

Yes: but these trees, when of serviceable size, would interrupt the view over the island from the river more than will the gallery, and would be useless as a shelter from rain. They would meet but imperfectly only one of the various purposes with reference to which the gallery is designed.

The question remains, —

Giving all the weight that may be desired to the objections thus recognized, do they outweigh the advantages to be secured by the gallery?

Upon this question of compensations, it is supposable that intelligent men might, after thorough discussion, be found to honestly differ for a hundred years to come; and, if it were a question to be settled by the votes of all concerned, the majority might be found on different sides every alternate year.

It is only to be said now, that those to whom the question was given for final decision, by the city, did not neglect a consideration of these objections. The question of injury to the view over the end of the island was first studied with the aid of photographs taken expressly for the purpose. The conclusion represented in the plan was by no means carelessly adopted. Is it not possible that those who have most objected to the pier and gallery have looked upon it as if it were an affair by itself? May they not have regarded the plan of the park as they properly might the plan of a city if they were considering a question of the removal or alteration of a particular store, shop, dwelling, or stable, which might be taken out, and replaced with a building of a different character and capacity, without in the least lessening the value of the adjoining buildings, still less of buildings more distant?

How much otherwise sound judgment must be used in discussing the several features of a park-plan, as far as the neighborhood of the pier and gallery are concerned, has been sufficiently suggested. There yet remains, however, to be considered, the more important relation of outgrowth and dependence of the whole group of arrangements devised in immediate connection with the pier and gallery with the central motive of the entire plan.

With a view to overcome as far as possible the peculiar difficulties of the site in respect of a water-soaked soil, of mosquitoes, and the danger of malaria, as well as to take advantage of its promising growth of wood, the leading idea of the plan of Belle-Isle Park is that of a large body of open forest, free from undergrowth, except of such close, fine herbage as is necessary to avoid a dusty surface; free to currents of air; and penetrable, in all its parts, by the rays of the sun through openings among the trees.

Starting from this central idea, it was shown in the preliminary pamphlet, that the plan must be further fitted to certain details of management, of which the most important, from its comprehensive bearings on the entire design of the park, may now be shown, through a single year's experience of practical management, better than it could be when the plan was first submitted to discussion.[23]

Let the ground be examined that was cleared of undergrowth in the first work done upon it, and it will be seen that a new undergrowth is springing up, which will soon be thicker, more obstructive to the breezes, more protective to mosquitoes, more prolonging of dampness, and more interruptive of passage, than that which has been taken off. How can this be avoided, without going every year to an excessive expense? Only by causing the young undergrowth to be closely browsed.

The plan of the park, then, and the scheme of management for it, must be devised throughout with a view to the necessity of keeping flocks and herds upon it, in a manner that will be profitable.

It follows, that the range of ground to be expensively worked over by the mower and roller, lawn-fashion, must be compact, of limited extent, and little open to inroads from the woods.

Tracts for this purpose, to be of the largest value to visitors using them, must be conveniently accessible from the boats, and in close connection with lavatories, shelters, and places of rest and refreshment. They must be better drainable than most of the island, and their preparation must not require the uprooting of many fine trees.

Better than anywhere else, these conditions may be combined upon the open ground at the west end, between the gallery and the canal.

An economical management of Belle Isle will never be possible if the necessity is forgotten, in discussions of its plan, of considering the relations of every feature to the purpose of maintaining the larger part of it, congruously, in the condition of a great, unencumbered, open-wooded, sun-penetrated, and breeze-swept pasture.

If more ambitious motives of design are entertained, or a more desultory, make-shift, scattering, and happy-go-lucky policy drifted into, the result will be a very unhappy one for the tax-payers.

I speak of more ambitious motives; but in truth, even from the artist's point of view, a motive of nobler ambition cannot be found than that of a forest, the elements of which shall be so ordered, that, through the silent persuasion of nature, it shall for centuries be growing, year after year, richer in sylvan picturesqueness and sylvan stateliness. It is a motive to command the devotion of a Salvator or a Turner.[24]

A noble effort is now being made to found a gallery of art in Detroit, and prominent among the motives urged in behalf of the enterprise is that of the educational advantages to grow out of it. It is probable, that, among the first fifty pictures that may be secured for it, there will be the work of an artist, who, going abroad to study his profession, has found his theme, and with it high means of cultivation, in the pastured suburban forest of Fontainebleau.[25] Hundreds of painters from all parts of the world resort to it. But their favorite scenes in Fontainebleau differ not in character from, and are in no respect more beautiful or fitting to the service of art than, such as may be easily offered to every citizen of Detroit by a suitable treatment of the woods of Belle Isle.

There are many who will say they care little for what may be accomplished by a prolonged course of treatment. They want results that they can themselves enjoy, and as soon as possible. Come, then, to the lower motive. Is there any course of management, other than that to which this higher ambition would lead, that, once economically set out upon, can be followed at as little cost? Is there any other that will quickly give more pleasing results?

Let anyone who carries well in the mind the general effect of the western woods of the island two years ago, walk through them now, and, considering the slight cost of the little that has been done, answer these questions.

Then, let those who are sensible of an added pleasure, through the results of the preliminary steps of improvement of the woods, reflect whether that particular kind of pleasure is likely to be augmented, or otherwise, by allowing what are called "decorative" structures, for all sorts of purposes, to be built here and there within the forest, as shall be thought, upon each occasion when permission for the purpose is sought, to be most fitting to the particular end at the time in view. An answer may be assisted by observing a few modest premonitions of such structures, now to be found along the southern skirt of the wood. Do they make the wood more stately, more impressive, more rurally recreative? The commissioners have often received applications for ground for others. They are to be found in every large public park, and at every water-side resort. They are a source of income; they are a source of pleasure of a different sort from, and incongruous with, that given by forest scenery; and it is not to be supposed or desired that Belle Isle shall be kept free from them. Where shall they be allowed? Under what rule or principle shall their sites be determined? Under what restrictions and regulations shall land be leased for them? How shall these restrictions and regulations be cheaply and effectually enforced? How shall needed supplies be brought to them, and their offal and wastage be removed without inconvenience, offence, or danger to the public?

Propositions to modify the plan of the park are to be often urged in the future, without the slightest regard to questions like these. Many times, the results of them will for a time seem to be cheap and satisfactory; yet, with gradually increasing use of the park, they may prove to have been most inconsiderately devised, costly, embarrassing, and burdensome.

In this, as in the former pamphlet on the same subject, I have had but one object. Having the honor to be called in counsel in behalf of the good people of Detroit, present and to come, I have wished to urge the importance of looking upon the propositions that will in the future successively be brought forward for tinkering the design of the park, from a more comprehensive point of view than I have elsewhere found apt to be taken. I would urge the importance to genuine economy, in the discussion of these propositions, of deliberation, candor, good nature, and a certain regard for the lessons of experience, even though, for a time, these need to be drawn from older and less thrifty cities.

Respectfully,

Frederick Law Olmsted.

The original was published as *Belle Isle: After One Year, June 1884* (Brookline, Mass., 1884).

1. In November 1882 Olmsted prepared a report for the park commissioners for the

design of Belle Isle. He presented his plan for the island in March 1883 (Frederick Law Olmsted, *The Park for Detroit* [Brookline, Mass., 1882]).

2. The Belle Isle park board hired Olmsted in April 1882 and agreed to pay him $7,000 to furnish a plan for the park and supervise its improvement for a term of three years beginning April 1, 1882, and to pay his travel expenses (City of Detroit, *Journal of the Common Council, from January 10, 1882, to January 9, 1883* [Detroit, Mich., 1883], p. 145).

3. The "pamphlet" to which Olmsted refers here was his first report for a park at Belle Isle, entitled *The Park for Detroit*. On December 26, 1882, the *Detroit Evening News* published a long summary of Olmsted's report for Belle Isle. On the following day it published an article applauding the park commission's hiring of him, concluding that

> There need be no further hesitation on the part of the city government. The distrust which the municipal legislature has heretofore shown can now be laid aside, and the most generous support given the commission in the immediate consummation of plans so happily conceived.

(*Detroit Evening News*, Dec. 26, 1882, p. 3; ibid., Dec. 27, 1882, p. 2.)

4. Olmsted's plan for Belle Isle was ready in March 1883, and he traveled to Detroit on March 16 to explain it to the city's councilmen, commissioners, and public. On March 22 he wrote to his stepson John that prior to that day no commissioner had come to see the plan. On March 22 he explained the plan to a special meeting of the board of commissioners and the press. The park commissioners asked Olmsted to stay in Detroit until after their next scheduled meeting on March 26. On March 23 he was scheduled to attend a meeting of the Common Council to explain the plan to the councilmen (FLO to CEN, March 11, 1883; FLO to JCO, March 22, 1883; *Detroit Evening News*, March 22, 1883, p. 1).

5. Indeed, on March 22 when the *Detroit Evening News* reported on Olmsted's plan for the park, it offered no negative comments (*Detroit Evening News*, March 22, 1883, p. 1).

6. William Gillon Thompson (1842–1904), mayor of Detroit from 1880 to 1884 (Silas Farmer, *History of Detroit and Wayne County*, 2 vols. [Detroit, Mich., 1890], 2: 1048; *Detroit Free Press*, July 21, 1904, p. 1).

7. Eighteen eighty-three was an election year in Detroit, which resulted in a turnover of ten of twenty-six seats on the Board of Aldermen and three of ten seats on the Board of Councilmen (City of Detroit, *Journal of the Board of Aldermen, from January 9, 1883, to January 8, 1884* [Detroit, Mich., 1884], p. 208; idem, *Journal of the Board of Aldermen, from January 8, 1884, to January 13, 1885* [Detroit, Mich., 1885], p. 450; idem, *Journal of the Board of Councilmen, from January 9, 1883, to January 8, 1884* [Detroit, Mich., 1884], p. 6; idem, *Journal of the Board of Councilmen, from January 8, 1884, to January 13, 1885* [Detroit, Mich., 1885], p. 38).

8. At the time Olmsted was hired by the park commission, its four members included Merrill I. Mills, August Marxhausen, William A. Moore, and James McMillan. On August 31, 1882, Mills's term expired and he was replaced by William B. Moran. In early February 1884 James McMillan resigned and was replaced by Dexter B. Ferry (City of Detroit, *Tenth Annual Report of the Commissioners of Parks and Boulevards* . . . [Detroit, Mich., 1899], p. 7).

9. As early as December 1883, probably at the request of the park board, Olmsted wrote to the board and suggested that it ask for a $60,000 appropriation for the next fiscal year. In Detroit all city commissions were required to submit financial estimates of their projected operating budget to the Common Council by April 1 of each year. The council then approved, disapproved, or adjusted the appropriation. Olmsted emphasized that that much money would be necessary to build the pier and gallery, and complete other work that had already been started on the island.

Olmsted traveled to Detroit the first week of March 1884, probably at the request of the park commission, and on March 7 met with numerous members of the Common Council to explain the work that needed to be done on the island for the coming year and the reason for the appropriation (FLO to John Stirling, Dec. 24, 1883, and Feb. 13, 1884; *Detroit Evening News*, March 8, 1884, p. 4).

10. On April 15, 1884, the Common Council recommended an appropriation of $32,000 for Belle Isle: $25,000 for improvements to the island, and $7,500 was reserved for building a pier at the location indicated on Olmsted's plan (City of Detroit, *Journal of the Board of the Councilmen, from January 8, 1884, to January 13, 1885*, pp. 39–40).

11. At the March 7 meeting Olmsted provided the council with an artist's rendition of what the pier and gallery would look like completed (*Detroit Evening News*, March 8, 1884, p. 4).

12. Apparently, John Stirling, secretary for the park board, wrote to Olmsted on May 5, 1884, asking him what impact dropping the gallery and the pier from the plan would have on the design as a whole (FLO to John Stirling, May 12, 1884).

13. As early as March 15, 1884, the *Detroit Evening News* published an editorial entitled, "The First Blunder at Belle Isle" denouncing Olmsted's plan for the pier and gallery as a "colossal folly." In condemning the plan the newspaper rhetorically asked, "Who can imagine . . . people in Detroit stupid enough to leave their homes and travel several miles, all for the purpose of walking up and down under a long shed in a sweating, crowding mob?" The *Evening News* continued the agitation throughout the rest of March with articles entitled, "A Very Stupid Scheme" and "Don't Want Any Sheds."

Probably more than anything else the *Evening News* contributed to the low appropriation granted the park board and the eventual failure to construct the gallery. Ironically, on May 1, 1884, the newspaper published an article complaining that "The fact that people will have to walk nearly a quarter of a mile in a blazing sun before they can reach a point where anything in the way of recreation can be enjoyed makes it somewhat doubtful if the number of pleasure seekers will be any larger this year than it was last summer" (*Detroit Evening News*, March 15, 1884, p. 2; ibid., March 18, 1884, p. 2; ibid., March 19, 1884, p. 4; ibid., May 1, 1884, p. 4).

14. The Detroit, Belle Isle and Windsor Ferry Company, established in 1881 (*Detroit City Directory for 1884* [Detroit, Mich., 1884], p. 44).

15. Apparently not only did the *Detroit Evening News* start the agitation over building the gallery, but it also started a discussion of whether there was sufficient deep water where Olmsted wanted to build the pier. On March 20 the paper included an article noting that Olmsted's sketch of Belle Isle included a ship drawing at least twelve or fourteen feet of water where the river was only six feet deep. It continued to warn against the new pier and on April 8 accused Olmsted of neither sounding the water himself nor examining U.S. Coastal Surveys. It stated that

> When the commissioners have built their dock . . ., their dock may be ornamental, but will not be useful to any sort of craft except row boats, and pleasure yachts, unless they expend about $100,000 more in digging a good sized hole around it.

(*Detroit Evening News*, March 20, 1884, p. 2; ibid., April 8, 1884, p. 2.)

16. Olmsted traveled to Detroit in late May at the request of the park board, and on May 30 wrote to his stepson John

> I was ill-treated yesterday. The Ferry Company gave me their heaviest & deepest & most unwieldy boat and neither Captn Sullivan nor any of the pilots I know was allowed to go. It turned out that the pilot they sent never had been in our channel, did not know there was a channel there, was very timorous and after we had started at 9 A.M. advised that we should put back and take a lighter boat.

We had no lead line aboard & I made one of spun yarn and some scrap iron. There was a strong N.W. wind & the danger signal was flying. I felt so sure of my ground however that I insisted on going on and finally brought the boat alongside the buoy I had had Ludden place the day before showing the end of our wharf. I found 3 fathom water within ten feet of it and 6 fathom within 30 ft. so that the pilot said that no dredging at all would be required to land at a wharf so placed. Then I turned the boat round, with some difficulty because of the high wind but she came and the Commissioners were fully satisfied that the project was perfectly feasible.

(*Detroit Evening News*, May 15, 1884, p. 1; FLO to JCO, Decoration Day [May 30], 1884.)

17. In 1883 the Buffalo park commission determined to remodel and enlarge the boat house at Delaware Park. The work was started in September 1883 and completed in April 1884. Most of the remodeling consisted of building a two-story addition to the boat house with verandas and restaurants on each level. The addition was constructed in such a way that the upper story was nearly level to the picnic grove and provided easy access (City of Buffalo. Park Commission, *Fourteenth Annual Report of the Buffalo Park Commissioners. January, 1884* [Buffalo, N.Y., 1884], pp. 8–9, 27–28; idem, *Fifteenth Annual Report of the Buffalo Park Commissioners. January, 1885* [Buffalo, N.Y., 1885], p. 10).

18. In April 1884 the New York state legislature passed an act enabling the Buffalo park board to purchase an additional twelve acres of land to expand the picnic grove in Delaware Park. Olmsted had included that same property in the original site for the park, but the 1869 park act's requirement that at least one-fifth of the land purchased for park purposes be located east of Jefferson Street forced the park board to exclude that area from the park (ibid., pp. 10, 15–16; see also F. L. & J. C. Olmsted, "Plan for a Public Park on the Flats South of Buffalo," Oct. 1, 1888, nn. 3 and 4, below).

19. Possibly a reference to the widening of the East and West drives between 79th and 104th streets on Central Park (see FLO and CV, "A Review of Recent Changes, and Changes which have been Projected, in the Plans of the Central Park," Jan. and Feb. 1872, n. 58, above).

20. That is, Central Park in New York and Prospect Park in Brooklyn.

21. In his preface to *The Park for Detroit*, Olmsted discussed these issues (F. L. Olmsted, *Park for Detroit*, p. 4).

22. See FLO, *Notes on the Plan of Franklin Park and Related Matters* (1886), note 31, below.

23. In sections 1 and 4 of the second part of *The Park for Detroit*, entitled "The Key to all Improvements of Belle Isle must be found in the Character of the Existing Wood," and "Opening the Woods," Olmsted discussed the management and grazing of the woods on Belle Isle (F. L. Olmsted, *Park for Detroit*, pp. 33–38, 42).

24. That is, Salvator Rosa (1615–1673), Italian landscape painter, and Joseph Mallord William Turner, English landscape painter (*EB*).

25. The forest at Fontainebleau, almost fifty-six miles in circumference and located on uneven and picturesque ground. It contains groves of oaks, birches, pines, and beeches and has unusual sandstone formations, the remnants of old sandstone quarries. For centuries it has been a favorite subject for French landscape painters (see OVC, "Report Accompanying Plan for Laying Out the South Park," March 1871, n. 5, above; *EB*; A. Vincent, *Fontainebleau: The Palace, the Town, the Forest* [Paris, 192–?], pp. 90–91).

Paper on the {Back Bay} Problem and its Solution
Read Before the Boston Society of Architects[1]

[April 2, 1886]

I have been asked to give you some account of the public work at
the outlet of Back Bay.[2]

The central purpose of this work is simply that of a basin for holding
water, as an adjunct of the general drainage system of the city. With this basin
a variety of arrangments have been planned to lessen the unseemliness and
inconvenience of an affair for such a purpose in the midst of a residential
quarter, the more important of these being expedients for controlling the
movements of water in the basin and to it and from it.

How it happens that it is universally called a park, criticised as a park
and the beauty and usefulness of a park anticipated for it I will explain presently.[3] It might as well be called a dry dock or rural cemetery or a cathedral
close, and discussed from a corresponding point of view, and the persistance
with which it is thus held to be what it is not, never was and never can be, is
an interesting illustration of the absurd difficulty that a professional man must
be prepared to find sometimes standing in his way of getting a fair hearing
from the public.

It occurs to me that the most instructive aspect in which this work
can be presented to you as architects, is that in which it will appear as an
illustration of the advantages that may be had from professional combination.

The professional fields respectively of the Architect, the Engineer,
the Sanitary Engineer and the Landscape Gardener or Landscape Architect
are in the main well-defined. Yet, at certain points, one merges into the other
in such a manner that they may be regarded as so many convenient subdivisions of one field and each profession as a branch of one trunk profession. You
see engineering journals giving plans of buildings, and architectural journals
discussing plans of drainage of bridges and of parks. But as yet there is much
{less}[4] disposition to ready and cordial cooperation between these branch pro-
fessions than is desirable for the public interests.

At a very late stage in the construction of the Brooklyn Bridge, the
trustees of that work concluded to employ a board of architects in consultation with their engineer. The result is to be seen by walking through some of
the narrow streets that pass under the inclined approaches to the bridge
proper, and it is a very interesting result. By and by, when the granite gains
the tints of age, the painters and etchers will find it out and instruct the public
about it. As yet it is almost unknown.[5] Suppose that the great engineer who

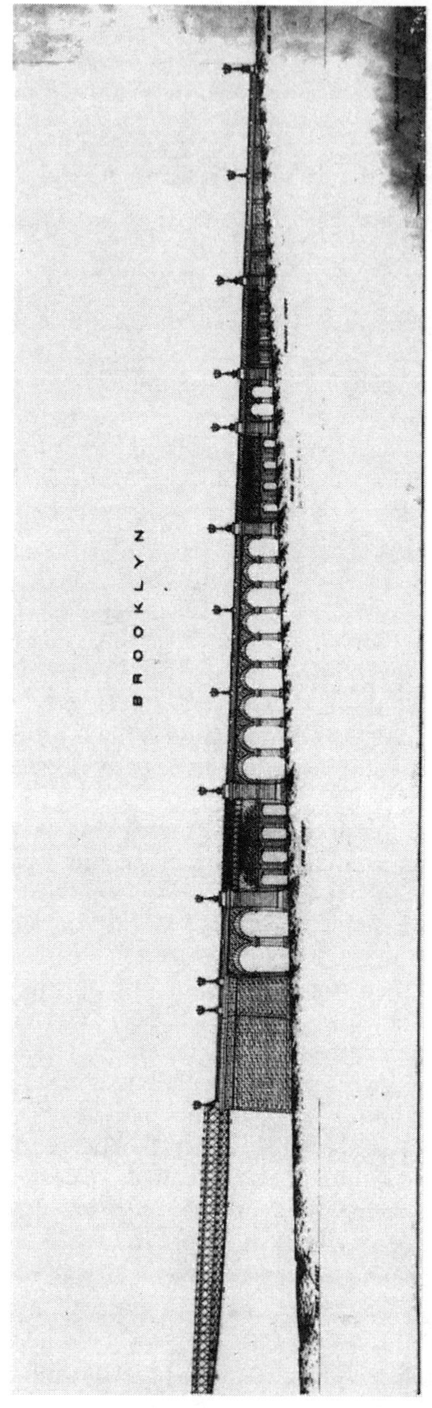

Wilhelm Hildenbrand, Elevation of Brooklyn Approach to Brooklyn Bridge, c. 1877

438

Wire Bridge over the Schuylkill River, 1843

planned the main structure had been led to seek the cooperation of the same architects in planning the towers of that edifice and all other parts of the structure, how much the public would have gained.

There is a bridge over the Schuylkill planned by another eminent engineer, in which, as it is really a part of the great park of Philadelphia, much effort for magnificent effect is evident.[6] There is not a member of this Association who if he had been consulted by the engineer before the plan was fully conceived would not have shown him in a moment how much a greater degree, of the effect he desired, could be obtained, with no addition to the cost of the bridge.

As an illustration of the reverse practice, the employment of Mr Hunt at the suggestion of General Stone, the engineer of the base work of the Bartholdi statue may be referred to.[7]

This work of Back Bay is instructive of the advantage of inter-professional cooperation in another way. That a landscape artist should have been associated with a sewer engineer in the planning and superintendence of a public work, and of the two should rather have been given the first place is certainly remarkable. Supposing it to be a wise arrangment you may be curious to know how it could have been brought about through the working of our present methods of city government. The best way to explain it will be by a narrative which would be unduly personal, egotistical and confidential if you had not done me the honor to make me an honorary comrad,[8] and I were talking to you at any other time than after dinner.

In 1876, three gentlemen of notable position and character, of great commercial ability, liberal & public spirited were appointed Park Commissioners of the city of Boston with the duty of considering a variety of projects for the advancement of which there had been more or less public demand.[9] As is apt to be the case in the early days of any such undertaking there was a disposition with these gentlemen to enter as soon as possible upon some scheme, the practical results of which would not be very remote. The scheme that first engaged their attention, and with reference to which there seemed to them to be the most immediately pressing demand, was the project of a pleasure ground within or adjoining that quarter of the city toward which fashion was setting, and in which there was the most activity of trade or specu-lation in real estate.[10] Anything else the Commission could have in contem-plation seemed by comparison, distant and obscure.

They therefore soon advised the City Council to authorize the pur-chase of 100 acres of land for a park on Back Bay. The City Council was not disposed to comply but under various influences, an order was at length adopted which permitted the Park Commissioners to buy, if they could, not less than 100 acres of land within certain defined limits, provided the whole could be obtained at a sum not exceeding \$450.000, or at a rate of 10 cts a foot. This success was not brought about without some log-rolling and com-promising among the members of the Council, and the order would not have been passed, it is said, and I have no doubt truly, had not some of those who voted for it felt quite sure that it would be impossible to buy the required amount of land at the price fixed.[11]

After a great deal of skillful bargaining, however, the result was accomplished, a little being picked up here and a little there, until finally an area was obtained of 106 acres of the singular shape that you see.[12]

If you ask how it came to take such a shape, the answer is to be found in the circumstance that the principal part of the ground the Commissioners were able to purchase at the fixed price, was a gulf of mud and water of such depth that the cost of filling it up and preparing it to be built upon would be so great that it offered no prospect of a return for the needed investment. The substance of the locality was not like that found in those parts of the Back Bay that have been built upon, but was a flowing mud. Its surface was in considerable parts 20 feet below the grade of Commonwealth Ave[13] and at one point soundings could be taken in it twenty feet deeper so that the solid ground was 40 feet below street grade.

Another circumstance was that the owners of the property wanted as large a frontage of lots as possible, consequently the more extended the outline of the park in proportion to its area, the better for any sellers who could retain a portion of their land.

By the way, you will here please reflect that the disadvantages which these circumstances established with reference to building purposes, applied almost equally to what are ordinarily and rightly understood to be the purposes of a park. In my opinion the whole scheme of a park at this point was an illconsidered one. As Mr Davis the City Engineer afterwards told the Commissioners: If the state of Massachusetts had been hunted over, a space combining more disadvantages for a park could not have been found.[14]

Having obtained the land, or rather the space of marsh, mud and water, they had sought, the Commissioners went through the usual form of conciliating an ignorant public opinion, which is called a Competition for plans.[15] They did so I have no doubt in perfect good faith, more or less sharing the delusion of the public with respect to this expedient.

Now I come to my personal narrative. I was in Europe at the time this competition was entered upon.[16] I returned about the time it ended, and immediately received an invitation to assist the Commissioners in selecting the prize plan.[17] I declined to do so and when pressed, told the Commissioners that I considered that the terms of the competition were thoroughly unfair and the result could not but be most unsatisfactory and prejudicial to their undertaking. I predicted certain misfortunes which, do the best they could, must result from it. Misfortunes for which I was unwilling to bear any responsibility.

Several months afterwards the Commissioners sought me again, and said: — "It is turning out just as you said that it would. We realize that the Competition was unfortunate. Not one of the twenty odd plans comes near to suiting our views. We have only raised a swarm of hornets to plague us. Now we want to see what you can do. Will you make us a plan?"

"I will not," I first answered. "The only possible justification that can be made for your inducing a score of educated men to direct their ambition and spend their brains for some months in preparing plans for you for which they would receive no compensation, is that by such a course you might be helped to pick out from among them the man best fitted to advise you in the matter. If you don't like your prize plan, nevertheless you have found the man who comes most nearly among twenty to meeting your ideas. Take him into council, and you will soon obtain what you want. That is due to him.

They answered, "That we shall never do. The man would not suit us. We have paid him $500, and he is perfectly satisfied. He wanted nothing more."[18]

After turning the matter over for a week I saw the Commissioners again and said, "I will not make you a plan to be accepted or rejected as you may be disposed, but for certain considerations I offer to become your professional counsel in this matter for a period of not less than three years. I will discuss the subject of a plan with you and will aid you to advance such discussion to profitable conclusions by means of drawings, until a plan is attained that shall be satisfactory to you."

An engagment was made on those terms, my office being entitled that of Advisory Landscape Architect.[19]

Three successive studies were made and finally a plan was reached acceptable to the Commissioners.[20] I had before, more than once, suggested that it would be a good plan to call the City Engineer in consultation with regard to the project, and I now advised that the plan should not be formally adopted without a conference with that officer, and this was assented to and a meeting arranged for the purpose.

At this meeting the City Engineer said, "I never have seen how it was practicable to have a park in the locality that you have chosen, and if you had given me an opportunity I should long ago have pointed out what I think to be insuperable difficulties in the way of it. But the question is one in which the Superintendant of Sewers[21] is better prepared in some respects to advise you than I am. You had better send for him."

This was done and there followed a discussion of four hours at the end of which the Engineers retired, leaving the Commissioners fully convinced that all their movements in the matter had been precipitate and that all the labor given to a park on Back Bay had been wasted.

The fact to be faced was this: —

Within the territory of which they had obtained possession, there was an estuary formed by the coming together of two streams, one being the Muddy River which flows through Brookline; the other Stony Brook flowing through Roxbury, and of which you have some knowledge from the full accounts of it given in the Press during the Freshet of last February.[22] At the ebb of the tide the water of both these streams moved steadily into Charles River under a bridge upon the mill dam road.[23] But as the tide rose there was a back set, the banks of the estuary were overflowed, forming mud flats. Beyond these there were plateaus of sedge and salt grass, over which the tide occasionally flowed, and in time of freshet, especially if at the same time there was a spring tide and an Easterly wind, a district about 300 acres in extent was flooded. There was thus a natural tidal basin of this extent.

For some time before and after full flood of the tide, the body of water set back in this natural basin was at rest and under these conditions it became a settling basin. Both the streams flowing into it had long served the purpose of main sewers for the people of a large territory, and the matter brought down by them, being constantly precipitated, had been incorporated with the mud of the estuary. The water moving over it became exceedingly filthy so that even eels could not live in it. Then, as the water went out with the tide the mud was exposed to the sun, and a stench arose that became an insufferable nuisance to people living half a mile away.

These conditions you will consider existed at a point toward which population was moving more rapidly than any other and close about which there was soon to be an irresistable demand for building ground as soon as the nuisance could be abated.

What could be done? The tide could be shut out by a dam. But the dam that would bar the tide at high water would also bar the outflow of the streams at low water; and at such junctures as have been referred to, of which the freshet of last winter affords an example, a great accumulation would occur before the tide would fall so low that it could be let out through a gate in the dam.

A basin to hold it, then, was a necessity, and if there was to be a reasonable development of the neighborhood as a residence quarter, it was necessary that it should be one of much less extent than the natural basin and one of much less disagreeable aspect.

The regular thing to do under these circumstances would, I suppose, be to form a basin like that at Providence[24] — a basin in which the water would be allowed to rise to a height of perhaps 15 ft above low water, and its extent made sufficient to hold all the water likely to accumulate while the tide was too high for an outflow. It would be formed by a retaining wall of stone and the city could be built up closely about it. Such an arrangment would be very costly and would be far from an attractive circumstance in the Back Bay quarter of the city. Its character being realized, the prospect of it would not advance the value of neighboring real estate or enlarge the basis of taxation.

But being the simplest thing to be done and, so to say, the normal engineering idea of a basin, it was the natural starting point for the discussion that now ensued between the City Engineer and the Landscape Architect, and which proceeded from step to step, somewhat in this way.

"Can sewage matter be kept out of the basin?"

Answer, "yes, by intercepting sewers."

"But the ordinary flow of the streams will yet be often foul; can this flow, except in the emergencies for which the basin is needed, be kept out of it?"

Answer, "Yes, by conduits of moderate dimensions laid outside the basin."

"That being the case, can the basin when not required for its main purpose be kept clean and sweet?"

Answer, "yes, by flooding it as far as necessary for the purpose with salt water, letting this move in and out enough to avoid stagnation."

"But suppose we go to the very expensive expedient of high retaining walls, will not the deposit that will occasionally be made above these, when the water subsides after a flood, leave a slime upon them offensive both to the eye and the nose, and would not their aspect be in all respects unpleasant?"

Answer, "It could not be otherwise."

"Sloping earthen banks instead of masonry would answer the purpose of holding the water, what would be the objection to them."

Ans. "The slope would need to be as nearly level as that of a sea beach, or, to be pitched with stone in all that part liable to be flooded and for some feet above it. Otherwise it would be undermined and washed out by waves beating against it. Such a slope for the necessary depth would require a great space of ground and it would not have a pleasing appearance. Moreover such a lining of stone would be open to the same objections as a vertical wall of stone."

"Suppose the wash of waves could be avoided, the lining of stone dispensed with, the margin of the water be made inoffensive, could a basin of sufficient extent be formed within the area now under control of the Park Department?"

By calculation it was found that it could.

"By taking care that there shall nowhere be any great breadth of water for the wind to act upon, we may avoid the liability to waves of destructive force. By taking care that the slope of the bank between high and low water level, shall be at an inclination of about 1 to 6; by making the breadth of ground to be flooded during freshets so great that the difference between high and low water need not exceed four feet and by providing for a growth of foliage on the banks, not liable to be flooded with salt water, that will obscure the margin, should we not have a result that would serve all the engineering requirements as well as they would be served in a basin of masonry and be much less objectionable on the score of taste?"

Ans. "We should."

"And would not a basin of this character cost much less than a basin of masonry?"

Ans. "It would."

Thus we came to the problem of which the plan now being carried out was finally accepted as a tolerably satisfactory solution.

I will give you a description of the apparatus for controlling the movements of the water, reading most of it from a paper prepared for the Boston Society of Civil Engineers by Mr Howe, the Assistant Engineer in Superintendence of the work, and printed by the Society.[25] This was written five years ago, and as you will see under the influence of the habit and the popular understanding which still with the public generally leads the locality to be called a park and any water in it a lake. He is describing the intentions which have since been carried out.

> Muddy River is to be taken to Charles River by an independent conduit. A conduit is to {be} made for carrying the ordinary flow of Stony Brook also to Charles River, but as the water in Charles River would be liable to rise at times so as to back up the water in this conduit about the street level in parts of Roxbury, a lower outlet for such occasions must be provided.
>
> The ordinary area of water within the basin will be 30 acres with its surface at 8 feet above city datum. In times of freshet the water of Stony Brook will be turned by an automatic arrangment into this basin, and the water as it rises will spread over an area of fifty acres — p. 130

So much for the appliances for regulating the flow of the water.

Now as to the design of the basin; this is the drawing of the plan originally presented to the Commissioners.[26] You will see that a public street is carried all around the territory and at several points across it. This was required by the City Council and the space needed for the streets was to be taken, as you see that it has been, out of the 100 acres to be purchased.[27] These streets are broader than ordinary city streets; they have very broad side walks and between the walks and the wheelway, planting spaces. On one side of the basin provision is made for a riding pad in addition to the wheelway, and half a mile of this is guarded from being crossed either by carriages or by people on foot so that a gallop can be safely taken upon it.

The basin lies within these circumferential highways. The water within the basin at its ordinary height is ten feet below the level of the highways, and the distance between the edge of the highways and the high-water line is about seventy feet on an average but constantly varying in most parts from forty to a hundred feet. Where it is ordinarily liable to be flooded, the surface of the bank has an inclination of about one vertical in six horizontal. Above that it has an ogee section until a swell is formed generally a foot or two above the surface of the highways to the border of which it is brought with another ogee.[28]

Such a section constantly varying in its curvature, corresponds with that naturally formed on the banks of streams, where the soil is moderately friable but somewhat variable in density.

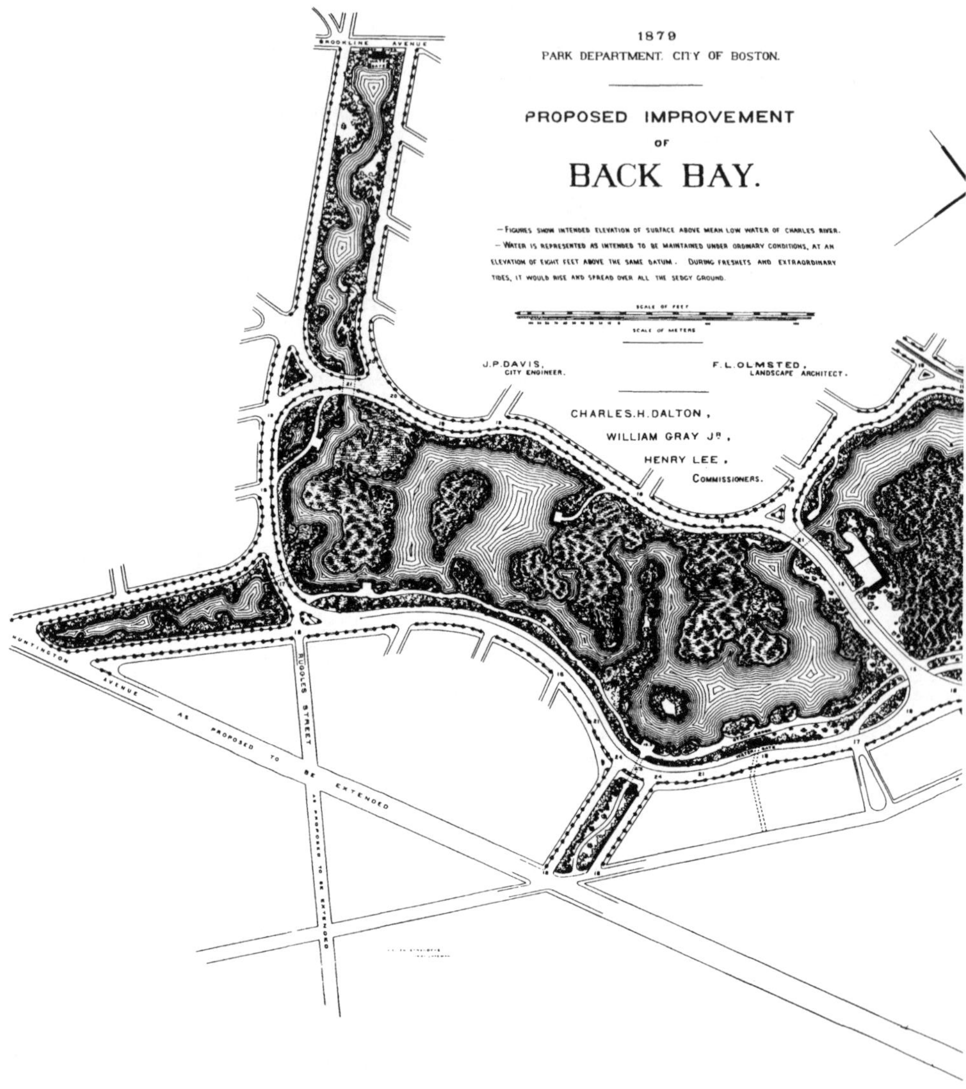

"Proposed Improvement

The visible bottom of the basin is to have the character of a salt marsh, through, and on the border of which, a tidal creek flows in rapidly winding courses, there being nowhere any straight reach. The object of this crookedness is to prevent the surface of the water from being raked by the wind for any considerable distance and consequently to prevent a swell from

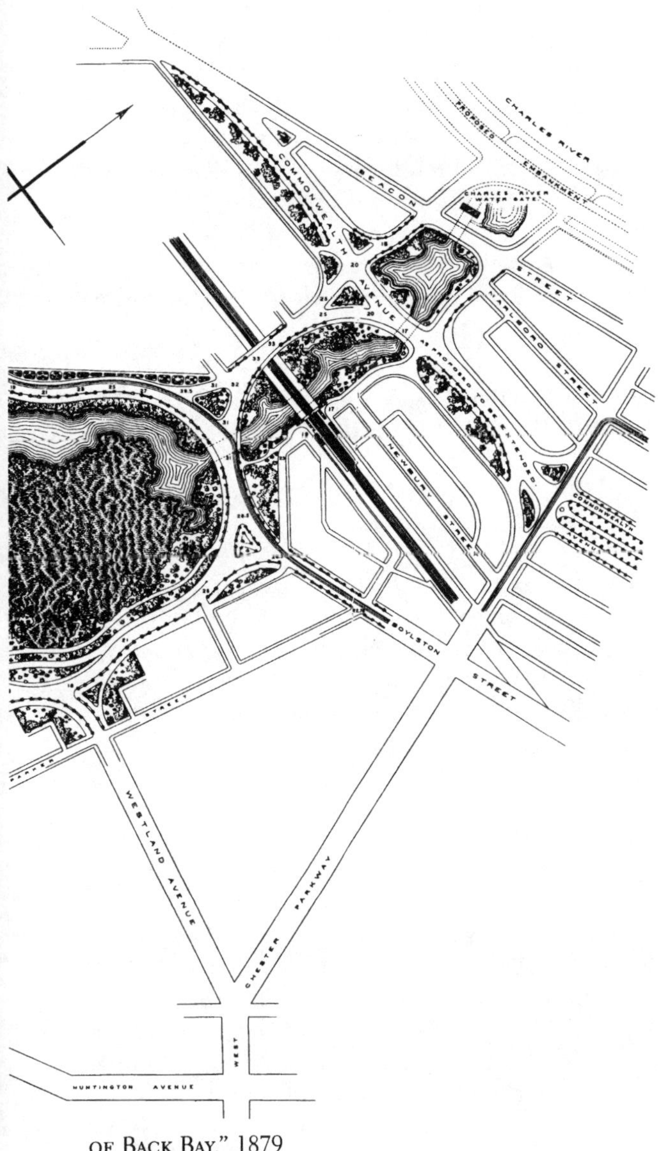

OF BACK BAY," 1879

forming. The ordinary level of the water will be from three inches to a foot below the level of the salt marsh but, it can be readily raised when necessary to keep the sedge and salt grass in flourishing condition.

When floods come and the tide is up so that there can be no outflow from the basin, the water will rise rapidly until it reaches the salt marsh level,

447

then, having double the area to spread over, more slowly. Very rarely, according to the calculations of the engineers, will it rise more than a foot above the surface of the roots. The sedge tops will generally be more than that height above the roots, and with the obstacle they will provide, it will remain impossible for the wind to raise a destructive swell over the enlarged water surface. If the water ever rises still higher, which it may do once only in several years, the space of time before the tide outside will have fallen so that an outflow can again be had will be short, the swell raised above the sedge cannot be heavy and the damage to the banks is likely to be slight and readily repaired. With these conditions in view the engineer yielded the point of a formal zone of stone for the protection of the bank, which would have destroyed all possibility of giving the basin a picturesque or natural aspect.

The further treatment of the banks became then an ordinary question of landscape gardening under certain motives that need not be here particularly explained.

The best result that can be hoped for is that after trees have grown and nature has in various ways not to be minutely anticipated come to our aid, and in effect adopted and given a truly natural character to the details of the salt creek and salt marsh elements, it will appear that there is nothing artificial about the affair except the roads and bridges required for convenience, but that the city has grown up about the locality leaving all within its boundaries in an undisturbed natural state.

For convenience, I have confined my account thus far exclusively to the Basin proper. What will have been more conspicuous to any of you passing near the locality is the outlet or passage between the basin and Charles River. There are special local features in this part of the work of which the more important, being that of the causeway and arch, will not need description.[29] The outline of these having been established, I requested the Commissioners to employ an architect for designing them and they engaged Mr H. H. Richardson for the duty.[30] My intention had been that the causeway if built at all of stone, should be of field stone so laid with pockets and with a heavy batter in the manner of the wall built in Franklin Park that it would be much overgrown with foliage and its artificial character except at the parapet be unobservable.[31] Mr Richardson fell in with this idea, and his first plans for the Boylston Street arch were for a very picturesque structure of field stone, harmonizing in character with the proposed plan of {the} causeway.[32] The cost of the work on the whole would have been much less if this had been adopted but the Commissioners were afraid to undertake anything so out of common, and so we had to come to what you now see.[33] It is very agreeable as a matter of general outlines and of color, but I think it would have suited the circumstances better if it had not been quite so nice.

View of Back Bay Fens with Boylston Street Bridge and Causeway

As to the treatment of this outlet district in other respects I will read from my published report for 1884. (page 14)[34]

The work is now so far advanced and in respect to its hydraulic apparatus so far in operation as to have already been fairly tested with respect to its main purposes. The flood of last winter was an extraordinary one and all the conditions were as unfavorable as they are ever likely to be. The great destruction of property which it caused in the valley of Stoney Brook is evidence of this.[35] But within the field of our operations not the slightest disturbance occurred. The whole selfacting apparatus did its work smoothly and continuously. The water in the basin rose at no time while the tide was too high for an outflow as much as four feet above its ordinary level. There was no wash of consequence.

There has been some question whether we could succeed in making an artificial salt grass or sedge meadow marsh. If you look over the Western parapet of Mr Richardson's bridge, you will see that we have done so on a space of several acres, quite sufficient to show that our plans for the purpose are practical. We have tried two methods, one by sodding and one by sowing; both are successful.

Where we are not successful as yet is in establishing any satisfactory vegetation between salt sedge and a line about three feet above it, within which salt appears to be deposited probably by evaporation of salt water, carried up by capillary attraction, but until last year we had no proper organization for planting, being dependent on a contractor,[36] and I am confident that we shall yet succeed. Even if we fail, it is but a question of time when this zone will be obscured by overhanging foliage from the trees and bushes growing above it.

It has been thought that the place would be a breeding ground for muskitoes. No evidence that it was so appeared last summer.

It was thought that our plan would not overcome the filthiness of the locality, that the stench would not be relieved and that the water in the basin would be always disgustingly foul. The air was perfectly sweet all of last summer, and notwithstanding the fact that steam dredgers were at work in the upper part of the basin and a steamboat with scows loaded with mud was often moving in the lower part, the water was generally fairly clean. I have no doubt that it will be perfectly so when the work ends.

The plans for the Basin having been adopted, I asked the City Engineer, "what are your plans for dealing with the Muddy River above the Basin?"

"We have none."

"What are you likely to have there eventually — a big conduit of masonry to carry the flood, several miles in length, and intercepting pipes for the sewerage from both sides?"

"That is not unlikely."

"Such arrangment will be very costly and will be delayed many years

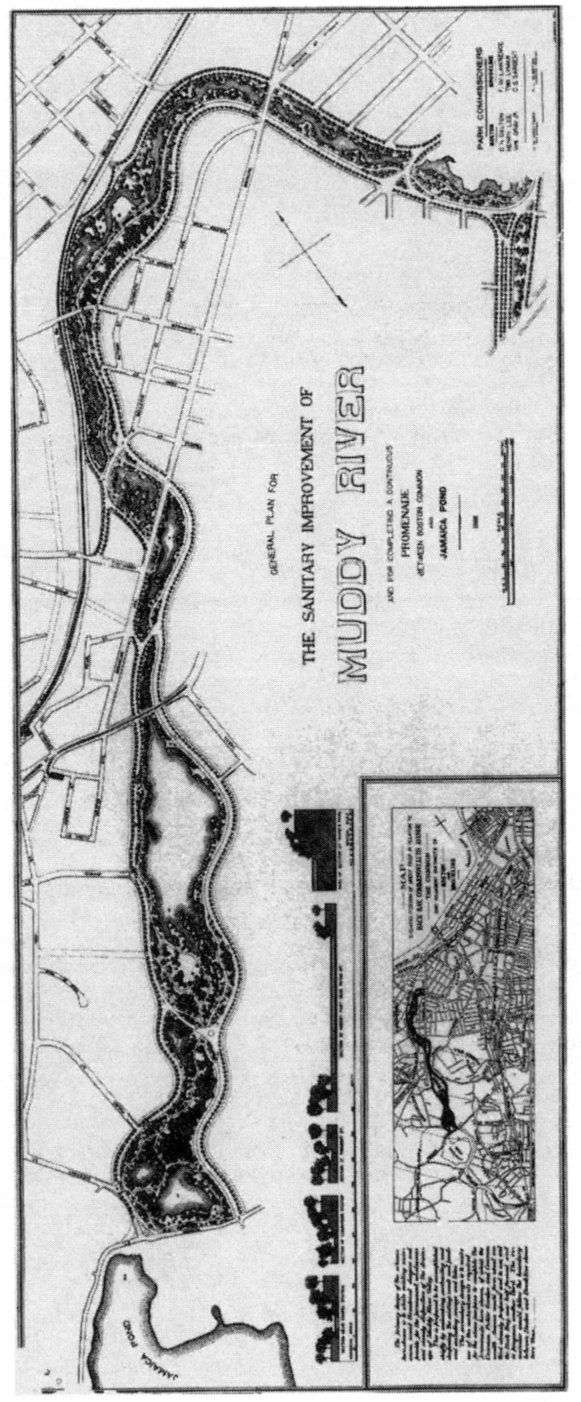

"General Plan for the Sanitary Improvement of Muddy River," 1881

because of its cost. Meantime and before many years the Muddy River valley will be very dirty, unhealthy, squalid. No one will want to live in the neighborhood of it. Property will have little value and there will grow up near the best residence district of the city an unhealthy and pestilential neighborhood."

"All that is not improbable."

"Why not make an open channel there and treat the banks of it as we are going to treat the banks of the Basin. Would not that be an economical move?"

"I don't see but it would."

"Then the roads leading up that valley to Jamaica Pond would be the beginning of a Park-way leading from the Back Bay to the Arboretum and West Roxbury Park."[37]

"They might be."

"Suppose then that we put our two professional heads together again and see if we can't make a practicable plan for that purpose and get the city to adopt it."

"Agreed."

And from that conference came this plan which you will see is essentially an extension of the Back Bay Plan, and has been fully adopted by {. . .}[38] Brookline and Boston.[39]

The text presented here is from a draft in the Olmsted Papers of a paper that Olmsted read before the Boston Society of Architects on April 2, 1886 (manuscript minutes, April 2, 1886, Boston Society of Architects *Records*, Boston Society of Architects Archives, Boston, Massachusetts).

1. The Boston Society of Architects was founded in 1867. Its dual purpose was to improve the standing of architecture as a profession and to standardize fees, rules for advertising, and the relationship of architect to client. In 1870 the society became a chapter of the American Institute of Architects. During the latter part of the nineteenth century, the society took on a more scholarly tone and devoted several meetings to the presentation of papers on historical subjects (Bainbridge Bunting, *Houses of Boston's Back Bay* [Cambridge, Mass., 1967], pp. 163, 355; Boston Society of Architects, *The Year-Book of the Boston Society of Architects for 1901* [Boston, 1901], p. 2).

2. Back Bay was bounded by Beacon Street on the north, Parker Street on the east, Longwood Avenue on the south, and Western Avenue on the west. Originally Back Bay had consisted of 300 acres: 160 acres of flats called the "Full Basin" and 140 acres of marsh lands called the "Empty Basin." Between 1850 and 1870 the "Empty Basin," east of Parker Street, had been filled in and had become home to some of Boston's wealthiest citizens. The flats of Back Bay, however, had become home to the runoff of Muddy River and Stony Brook including the sewage of all the territory drained by the two streams. The sewage settled on the flats and at low tide especially in summertime created an unbearable nuisance (*Map of Boston, 1875* [Boston, 1875]; Edward Willard Howe, "The Back Bay Park, Boston," in *Proceedings of the Boston Society of Civil Engineers* [Boston, 1881], pp. 127–28; Matthew Edel, Elliott D. Sclar, and Daniel Luria, *Shaky Palaces: Homeownership and Social Mobility in Boston's Suburbanization* [New York, 1984], p. 50).

3. One critic asserted that Back Bay would accumulate deposits "of more or less filthy silt at the bottom, which will require frequent removal at a formidable cost, and of which the portions on the shores left bare at low tide will not fail to make themselves emphatically conspicuous to at least one of the senses of neighboring citizens." Another critic believed that "the thirty acres of marsh will furnish such clouds of mosquitoes, of the peculiarly malignant type generated in such places, as will make the surrounding neighborhood a very uncomfortable place of residence during the better part of the year." Most of the criticism surrounding Back Bay, however, centered around the misnomer "park." Edward W. Howe, an engineer on the Back Bay project, put it most succinctly when he wrote,

> the name given to this improvement is, I think, an unfortunate one, though perhaps no better could be suggested; but the title of "park" arouses in the citizen unfamiliar with the locality and its surroundings an expectation which I fear he will fall far short of realizing, and already we have heard condemnations, loud and severe, of the city authorities for choosing such a low-lying, level, foul mud-hole as this, for the location of a public park.

(E. W. Howe, "Back Bay Park," p. 126; *American Architect and Building News*, March 20, 1880, p. 118; ibid., April 3, 1880, p. 145; for Edward Willard Howe, see n. 25 below.)

4. The manuscript page is torn here.

5. The Brooklyn Bridge, a suspension bridge spanning the East River in New York, was designed in 1867 by John A. Roebling (1806–1869), a German-born civil engineer. After Roebling's death in 1869, his son, Washington A. Roebling (1837–1926), oversaw the completion of the building of the bridge from 1870 to 1883. Roebling envisioned the approaches as buildings that would house stores and warehouses and prepared rudimentary sketches for their design. After his father's death, Washington Roebling, who believed the approaches should be even grander than his father intended, employed Wilhelm Hildenbrand, a young German-born architect, to design them. In 1877 Roebling and the New York Bridge Company board of trustees invited a panel of three well-known professional architects to give their evaluation of Hildenbrand's design. The panel, consisting of George B. Post (1837–1913), Joseph M. Wilson (1838–1902), and Napoleon LeBrun (1821–1901), quickly gave its approval. The approaches, from both the Brooklyn side and the New York side of the river, are nearly one-half mile in length and include arches built of brick and faced in granite (Robert M. Vogel, *Building Brooklyn Bridge* [Washington, D.C., 1983], pp. 4, 11, 14, 26; David McCullough, *The Great Bridge* [New York, 1972], pp. 145–46, 331–32; Albert Fein, "Urban Design: The Bridge and Prospect Park," in *The Great East River Bridge, 1983* [Brooklyn, N.Y., 1983], p. 151; Adolf K. Placzek, ed., *Macmillan Encyclopedia of Architects*, 4 vols. [New York, 1982], 3: 460; Henry F. Withey and Elsie Rathburn Withey, *Biographical Dictionary of American Architects [Deceased]* [Los Angeles, 1956], p. 664; Sandra L. Tatman and Roger W. Moss, *Biographical Dictionary of Philadelphia Architects: 1700–1930* [Boston, 1985], p. 469; E. F. Farrington, *Concise Description of the East River Bridge . . .* [New York, 1881], p. 59).

6. The Wire Bridge, designed and built in 1841 by Charles Ellet, Jr. (1810–1862), a civil engineer. The bridge was the first permanent wire suspension bridge built in the United States and spanned the Schuylkill River just south of the Fairmount reservoirs at the bottom of Callowhill Street in Philadelphia's Fairmount Park (*Appletons' Cyc. Am. Biog.*; Donald Sayenga, *Ellet and Roebling* [York, Pa., 1983], pp. 17, 23; *Papers of FLO*, 6: 244, n. 11).

7. Charles Pomeroy Stone (1824–1887), soldier and engineer, rose to the rank of brigadier general during the Civil War. In 1883 he accepted the position of chief engineer in charge of constructing the pedestal for the Statue of Liberty on Bedloe's Island in

New York Harbor. In 1881 the American Committee of the Franco-American Union, responsible for raising funds for the pedestal, invited architect Richard Morris Hunt (1827–1895) to design a pedestal for the statue. As early as 1874, the French commissioned Frédéric Auguste Bartholdi (1834–1904), an Alsatian-born sculptor, to design and build the statue.

By early 1883, Stone and his engineers determined that Fort Wood, an eleven-point, star-shaped structure on Bedloe's Island, would serve as the foundation for the statue's pedestal. The entire interior of the fort was filled in and built up as a hollow pyramid almost sixty-six feet high. Hunt's task was to design a pedestal that would harmonize with the base as well as with the statue, which by this time was largely completed. By August 1885, the pedestal was finished. It was constructed of concrete and granite and measured eighty-nine feet in height. Hunt's design proved highly successful. He subordinated the decorative detail of the pedestal so as not to detract from the statue, and he emphasized vertical thrust and solidity to give the image of a statue securely anchored to the ground. Engineers tied the statue's supporting frame to the pedestal, and the pieces of the statue, made from thin sheets of copper, were then placed on the frame. The completed Statue of Liberty was unveiled on October 28, 1886 (*NCAB*, s.v. "Stone, Charles Pomeroy"; Paul R. Baker, *Richard Morris Hunt* [Cambridge, Mass., 1980], pp. 314–19; A. K. Placzek, ed., *Macmillan Encyclopedia of Architects*, 2: 436, 440).

8. Olmsted is probably referring to his induction as an honorary member of the American Institute of Architects in 1867 (*Papers of FLO*, 6: 677).

9. On July 6, 1875, Mayor Samuel Cobb appointed Charles Henry Dalton, William Gray, Jr., and Thomas Jefferson Coolidge to the first Boston park commission. Charles H. Dalton (1826– 1908), a Boston businessman, was a member of the commission until 1884, and for eight of those nine years, he served as its chairman. Of the three park commissioners, Dalton was the most actively involved in establishing a park system for Boston. In 1875, after Dalton became a Boston park commissioner, he asked Olmsted to aid the commission in selecting possible park sites for the city, and thereafter the two worked together closely on Boston park projects. William Gray, Jr. (c. 1831–1886), a prominent businessman from a wealthy Boston family, served on the park board until 1884. He was keenly interested in horticulture, and his estate in Roxbury became a showplace of beautiful gardens and extensive lawns. He was a member of the Massachusetts Horticultural Society and in 1878 became its president. Thomas Jefferson Coolidge (1831–1920), a Boston businessman and financier, served on the park board for less than two years before resigning ("City Document No. 12," in City of Boston, *First Report of the Board of Commissioners of the Department of Parks for the City of Boston* [Boston, 1876], p. 1; Roger Bigelow Merriman, "Memoir of Charles Henry Dalton," in Massachusetts Historical Society, *Proceedings* 42 [April 1909]: 287–312; *Boston Evening Transcript*, Aug. 17, 1886, p. 1; *DAB*, s.v. "Coolidge, Thomas Jefferson").

10. That is, Back Bay.

11. In May of 1877 Alderman Hugh O'Brien delivered a report recommending that $1,000,000 be appropriated for parks. For the next two months the Board of Aldermen debated the merits of appropriating so large a sum for parks in Back Bay, South Bay, and West Roxbury. On July 2 the board agreed by a vote of eight to four to an amendment reducing the appropriation to $450,000 for Back Bay stipulating that the "land or flats so to be purchased shall be located with special reference to the improvements of the sewerage of the City" and that the price to be paid for the land not "exceed ten cents per superficial foot." The Common Council concurred on July 19 by a vote of fifty-seven to ten. While some members of the Common Council may have voted for the reasons asserted by Olmsted, the prospect of securing the land at ten cents per

foot was an argument put forward by supporters of the project in the Board of Aldermen (City of Boston, *Reports of Proceedings of the City Council of Boston, for the Municipal Year 1877* [Boston, 1878], pp. 301, 474, 477, 530).

12. As originally proposed in their 1876 report, the park commissioners noted that Back Bay would contain about 102½ acres. In its order of July 23, 1877, the city council authorized the expenditure of $450,000 for 103³⁄₁₀ acres. When the park board made its final surveys it found that the land needed for the park totaled slightly over 106 acres and requested additional appropriations for the purchase of the land. The city council acceded to this request the following year and appropriated an additional $16,000 for the purchase of the remaining 2⅘ acres.

    Purchasing the land for Back Bay, however, proved a slow and tedious process for the park board, because the site was composed of small parcels with multiple owners. In an effort to help facilitate the park board's work, the city council revised the July 23 order and permitted the board to purchase tracts as they became available rather than purchasing all of the land simultaneously ("City Document No. 42," in City of Boston, *Second Report of the Board of Commissioners of the Department of Parks* [Boston, 1876], p. 19; "City Document No. 16," in idem, *Third Annual Report of the Board of Commissioners of the Department of Parks* [Boston, 1878], pp. 1–2; "City Document No. 15," in idem, *Fourth Annual Report of the Board of Commissioners of the Department of Parks* [Boston, 1879], p. 1; "City Document No. 104," in idem, *Sixth Annual Report of the Board of Commissioners of the Department of Parks* [Boston, 1881], p. 5).

13. Commonwealth Avenue extended from the Public Garden to West Chester Park (now Massachusetts Avenue) on the edge of Back Bay. This original segment of Commonwealth Avenue was laid out in the 1860s as part of the residential plan of Back Bay (Cynthia Zaitzevsky, *Frederick Law Olmsted and the Boston Park System* [Cambridge, Mass., 1982], p. 110).

14. In 1871 Joseph Phineas Davis became the Boston city engineer and worked closely with Olmsted on the construction of the Back Bay Fens (NCAB; see OVC, "Report to the Brooklyn Park Commission," Jan. 1, 1868, n. 2, above).

15. On March 1, 1878, the Boston park commissioners voted to hold a competition and award a $500 prize for the best plan for laying out Back Bay Park. By May 1, twenty-three plans had been submitted and placed on public display in City Hall (City of Boston, Parks and Recreation Commission Minutes, March 1, 1878, p. 84; *Boston Post*, May 17, 1878, p. 3).

16. In poor health, Olmsted traveled to Europe in January 1878 and returned home in late April.

17. On May 6, 1878, Charles Dalton wrote to Olmsted requesting that he come to Boston and assist the board in deciding which design for Back Bay should receive the $500 prize. On May 8 Olmsted declined Dalton's request, stating that he believed it inappropriate for him to participate in the selection process because of his relationship to the board. In an additional letter on May 13 Olmsted elaborated on his dislike of design competitions writing, "I do not know one of the usual kind, . . . which has not had unpleasant and reprehensible results" (Charles H. Dalton to FLO, May 6, 1878; FLO to Charles H. Dalton, May 8 and 13, 1878).

18. In late May the Boston park commission awarded Hermann Grundel, a Boston florist, the $500 prize for his design for Back Bay (*Boston Evening Transcript*, May 31, 1878, p. 4; "Document No. 15," in City of Boston, *Fourth Annual Report*, p. 6; *Boston Directory* . . . [Boston, 1878], p. 395).

19. In December 1878 Olmsted and the Boston park commission signed an agreement whereby Olmsted would prepare a plan for Back Bay and supervise its execution. The board would pay Olmsted $2,000 per year for three years. Olmsted requested that his

title be "Landscape Architect Advisory" and the board agreed (Charles H. Dalton to FLO, Oct. 21, 1878, B69: #916, OAR/LC; "Articles of Agreement," in City of Boston, Parks and Recreation Commission Minutes, Dec. 10, 1878, pp. 115–17; FLO to Charles H. Dalton, Dec. 14, 1878).

20. During the summer and fall of 1878 Olmsted prepared, and the park board rejected, two studies for Back Bay. The board accepted Olmsted's third proposal dated October 24, 1878 (for a comparison of Olmsted's first three studies for Back Bay, see C. Zaitzevsky, *Frederick Law Olmsted and the Boston Park System*, pp. 139–40).

21. William Hammatt Bradley (b. 1835), a civil engineer, was educated at the Lawrence Scientific School in Cambridge, Massachusetts. In 1863 he became Superintendent of Sewers for the city of Boston, a position he retained until his retirement in 1883 (Charles Edwin Hurd, ed., *Representative Citizens of the Commonwealth of Massachusetts* [Boston, 1902], pp. 194, 196).

22. On February 11 and 12, 1886, heavy rains combined with melting snow caused the Stony Brook conduit to fill and overflow its banks, submerging a two-square-mile section of Roxbury known as the "lowlands" (*Boston Daily Advertiser*, Feb. 13, 1886, p. 1; ibid., Feb. 15, 1886, p. 1).

23. From 1814 to 1821 an earthen dam designed to hold the waters of Back Bay was built from Beacon Street in Boston to Gravelly Point in Brookline. It was called the Mill Dam and eventually the road along the top of it became a toll road (B. Bunting, *Houses of Boston's Back Bay*, p. 33).

24. Olmsted is referring to the Cove basin in Providence, Rhode Island. This tidewater cove was formed by the waters of the Moshassuck River from the north and the Woonasquatucket River from the west. In 1846 the Providence and Worcester Railroad Company proposed to build a stone retaining wall around the easterly side of the basin, providing openings to control the discharge of the Moshassuck River into the basin and the discharge of basin waters into the Providence River. In addition, an eighty-foot-wide promenade was constructed just outside the retaining wall. In 1852 the City Council gave the Hartford, Providence and Fishkill Railroad permission to complete the westerly side of the retaining wall around the basin, leaving a bridged opening for the flow of the Woonasquatucket River into the basin. The railroads filled the areas outside the retaining wall and used the filled land for yards and other buildings, eventually extending their tracks and constructing freight and passenger depots around the basin.

    Unfortunately, during low tides mud flats were exposed within the basin. In 1850 the city built a dam that eliminated the problem of exposed mud at low tides but did not prevent flooding during the time of extremely high tides or freshets. The dam was removed in 1878 (John Hutchins Cady, *The Civic and Architectural Development of Providence, 1636–1950* [Providence, R.I., 1957], pp. 3, 115–19).

25. Edward Willard Howe (1846–1931), a civil engineer, graduated from Middlebury College in 1869. In 1874 Howe was appointed assistant civil engineer for the city of Boston and held that position until 1914. From 1883 until 1898, Howe was in charge of the engineering work for most of the park projects in Boston, including Back Bay, Franklin Park, Marine Park, and Wood Island Park. In 1898 park construction was taken out of the city engineer's office, and Howe was placed in charge of building several of the city's bridges. He became a member of the Boston Society of Civil Engineers in 1874 and maintained an active role in the organization throughout his life.

    The publication to which Olmsted here refers was entitled "The Back Bay Park, Boston" and was published in the Boston Society of Civil Engineers *Proceedings* ("Edward Willard Howe," *Journal of the Boston Society of Civil Engineers* 19 [June 1932]: 362–64; E. W. Howe, "Back Bay Park, Boston," pp. 126–33; see n. 3 above).

26. That is, the 1879 plan entitled "Proposed Improvement of Back Bay" included in the 1880 annual report of the Boston park commission. Olmsted notes that the 1879 plan was the one "originally" shown to the commissioners, because at the time he presented this paper he was at work on substantial alterations of the plan. These changes appear on the December 30, 1887, plan entitled, "Park Department — City of Boston. Map of the Back Bay Fens, Showing the public ways bordering and crossing them and the neighboring newly laid out parts of Commonwealth Avenue, Beacon Street and Audubon Road by which will be made available a circuit drive of the district, tree-lined throughout and passing above railroads" ("City Document No. 15," in City of Boston, *Fifth Annual Report of the Board of Commissioners of the Department of Parks* [Boston, 1880], between pp. 16 and 17; City of Boston. Department of Parks, *Thirteenth Annual Report of the Board of Commissioners for the Year 1887* [Boston, 1888], between pp. 64 and 65).

27. On July 23, 1877, the city council ordered that Back Bay be bounded on all sides by public roads, and that the land taken for the streets come from the land purchased for the park ("City Document No. 16," in City of Boston, *Third Annual Report*, p. 2).

28. An ogee is a continuous double curve, turning from concave to convex. Olmsted made constant use of the ogee curve, as indicated by his instructions for constructing roads and walks in Genesee Valley Park in Rochester:

> In forming side slopes of drives and walks on steep hillsides or in deep cuts or hills, there should be allowed a level or nearly level border of five feet and the slopes from this border to the natural surface should be formed to *varying ogee* curved cross-sections no part of which should be steeper than one vertical to two horizontal.
>
> On level or nearly level ground the differences in grade between the natural surface and that of the drives and walks should be overcome by nearly level borders two feet wide and slopes having long, varying ogee curved cross-sections not steeper than one in ten.
>
> In both cases particular care should always be taken to join the new slope to the natural surface so gradually and gently that no one can tell where the junction has been made (FLO, "Suggestions for Treatment of Slopes of Road and Walks," c. 1890).

29. That is, the causeway and arch of the Boylston Street bridge.

30. Henry Hobson Richardson (1838–1886), architect. Richardson was born in Louisiana, graduated from Harvard in 1859, and traveled to Paris to study at the Ecole des Beaux-Arts. After his return to the United States, he entered into partnership with another architect, Charles D. Gambrill. The partnership lasted from 1867 to 1878. In the early 1870s Richardson's designs for Boston churches earned him a national reputation as an architect.

> In 1870 Olmsted requested that Richardson design the memorial for the grave of his friend Alexander Dallas Bache. After that Olmsted and Richardson developed a friendship and collaboration that lasted until the latter's death. They worked together on a number of projects including the redesign of the New York State Capitol, the Boston park system, and several projects for the Ames family in North Easton, Massachusetts (*DAB; Papers of FLO*, 6: 391).

31. Olmsted proposed in the 1886 Franklin Park report that the wall enclosing the Country Park be made of field stone, covered with vines, and built no more than four feet high (FLO, *Notes on the Plan of Franklin Park and Related Matters*, 1886, below).

32. In a letter to Joseph Davis, Olmsted noted that

> the Boylston bridge will be the most conspicuous object in all the scheme. It will be forced on the attention above and below and on each side. It will dominate

everything & be seen from Charles River to Parker Hill. People will rest & lounge upon it & look at it more closely than anything else on the Bay. A natty, formal elegant structure would put all rural elements of the Bay out of countenance. It would be a discord. The bridge must, if possible, have a rustic quality and be picturesque *in material* as well as in outlines & shadows. . . . I would like an arch of Roxbury pudding-stone; or an arch of boulders, or of rough field stone, with voussoirs &c of cut stone or brick; or an arch wholly of cheap rough brick. I would much prefer wood to iron. I would not at all object to a timber bridge of almost the simplest and cheapest possible construction.

Olmsted enclosed a copy of the letter containing this quote with one he sent Dalton on the same day requesting Richardson's assistance in designing and constructing the bridge (FLO to Joseph P. Davis, Jan. 24, 1880; FLO to Charles H. Dalton, Jan. 24, 1880).

33. The Boylston Street bridge as completed did not employ the rough stone or boulders that Olmsted had wanted but was instead constructed of Cape Ann granite (C. Zaitzevsky, *Frederick Law Olmsted and the Boston Park System*, pp. 165–66).

34. Olmsted probably read the following paragraphs:

> In that part of the work now more nearly completed, being the outlet part, north of Boylston Bridge, there are special local features, some reasons for which may be stated.
>
> The circumstances allow a contrast of character to be sought between the banks of this short narrow passage and the miles of banks to be found about the broad basins on the south side of the bridge and the parkway beyond them; and, to make the most of the opportunity, it is desirable here to aim at a degree of variety of form and slope that would otherwise be excessive.
>
> *The outflow channel is required by the plans of the Street Department to be carried between two straight lines of bridge abutments at five different points within a distance of less than 600 yards.* The intermediate reaches of the channel are too short for expanded pools or a quiet character in the shores and what would otherwise be an excessively wriggling disposition of the banks has the advantage of avoiding a sewer or canal-like directness of channel. Much would have been gained if all the bridges had been of masonry; but the conditions would have made them excessively costly.
>
> It is necessary to use a certain amount of stone at points in the facing of the banks to guard against drifting ice. This gives reason for a buttress-like abruptness of bank at these points. Such abruptness being accepted, it is better to make a decided feature of it, and let it control the character of the scenery of the outlet in contrast with that of the basins above where there can be no headlands. Large field-stones, have, therefore, been procured from the waste of the city's gravel banks and piled together to obtain boldness of projection. At present the stones, somewhat unhappy in color, are offensively conspicuous, and the several points have too much repetition of character. They will not only in time, lose their present rawness of color, but will all, in a great measure, soon disappear under leafage, while, through the difference in the forms of vegetation growing out from between the stones and upon their flanks, their similarity of aspect will be lost ("City Document No. 7," in City of Boston, *Tenth Annual Report of the Board of Commissioners of the Department of Parks* [Boston, 1885], pp. 14–15).

35. The flood caused almost $300,000 in damage to homes and businesses and displaced several families (*Boston Daily Advertiser*, Feb. 17, 1886, p. 1; see n. 22 above).

36. The contractor was F. L. Temple, a Cambridge, Massachusetts, nurseryman, who had contracted with the Boston park commission to provide plants for Back Bay's Beacon

Street entrance in 1883. Between 1883 and 1886 Temple planted over 100,000 plants near the entrance, but the plants did poorly and in 1885 Olmsted discovered most to be dead or dying. In March 1886 Olmsted wrote Temple expressing his disappointment with the plantings and stated that the

> mere loss of so many plants is the smallest part of the disaster. The whole design is a wreck. Of what remains of your planting that which should be most prominent and characteristic is least so, that which was desired to be an inconspicuous element merging in a mass of a certain quality, stands out exclusively; that which was to be subordinate, predominates.

Olmsted also commented to Temple that when he pointed out the extreme condition of the plants to the foreman of the work, "he showed such extreme disappointment and mortification that when I heard of his suicide I suspected it to be due to the depression thus caused" (C. Zaitzevsky, *Frederick Law Olmsted and the Boston Park System*, pp. 188–89; FLO to F. L. Temple, March 15, 1886).

37. That is, Olmsted proposed a series of parkways that would eventually connect Back Bay with the Arnold Arboretum and West Roxbury Park (Franklin Park) by way of Jamaica Pond (and Park).
38. The manuscript page is torn here.
39. That is, the Muddy River Improvement for which Olmsted had written a report in 1880. Olmsted proposed to extend the Back Bay design west and south along Muddy River, the boundary between Brookline and Boston. Muddy River, a small tidal creek, had become a nuisance in itself, carrying filthy water and creating a fetid swamp. Due to difficulties in acquiring the land for the project, however, improvements did not begin until the 1890s (Frederick Law Olmsted, "Suggestions for the Improvement of Muddy River," in *Brookline Town Reports* [Brookline, Mass., 1881], pp. 170–75; C. Zaitzevsky, *Frederick Law Olmsted and the Boston Park System*, pp. 82–83).

NOTES ON THE PLAN OF
FRANKLIN PARK
AND RELATED MATTERS.

1886.

CONTENTS.

INTRODUCTION.

PUBLIC OPINION COMPARATIVELY ILL-PREPARED TO SUSTAIN AN ECONOMICAL MANAGEMENT OF A LARGE PARK WORK

PART FIRST.

THE CONDITION OF BOSTON IN REGARD TO PROVISIONS FOR VENTILATION AND URBAN RECREATION

PART SECOND.

THE PLAN OF FRANKLIN PARK

Part Third.

THE KEY OF A CONSERVATIVE PARK POLICY, AND THE COST OF CARRYING OUT THE PLAN UNDER SUCH A POLICY

A Brief History of the Rural Park of Buffalo, with Reference to its Management, Cost, and Value
The Maintenance Cost of Parks

Part Fourth.

OF THE DIFFICULTIES OF PURSUING A SOUND POLICY, AND THE MEANS BY WHICH THEY ARE TO BE OVERCOME

I. Of the Supreme Importance that a Large Park may come to have in the History of a City
II. The Element of Lastingness as affecting the Importance of what is to be Determined in the Early Work of a Park
III. The Earnings of a Park to a City accrue largely through the Less Conspicuous Use of it, and through the Use of the Less Conspicuous Parts of it
IV. The Adaptation of the Park to the Use of Invalids
V. The Value of a Rural Park to the Parts of a City more distant from it
VI. The Bearing of the Difficulties that have been reviewed upon the Main End of these Notes

Part Fifth.

THE PARK AS A DEPARTMENT OF EDUCATION

INTRODUCTION.

In the course of the series of notes to follow, reasons will be given for thinking that what shall occur in the history of Franklin Park during the next few years, whether the undertaking be much advanced or little, will determine results of greater lasting consequence to the city than those of any other of its public works of the present time. Therefore, in connection with an exposition of the plan for the park, various facts and considerations are to be presented, bearing upon the policy of the city in dealing with it.

An addition to the numerous, extensive, and varied public grounds now available to the people of Boston, of a body of land in one block of the extent, situation, and topographical characteristics of that to be reviewed, would have been a proceeding of great extravagance and folly, unless made with regard to a purpose for which no provision existed or could be made upon those grounds.

It may be held also that to justify the undertaking, this distinctive purpose should have been one through success in which the city's rate of taxation might be expected to be reduced, and this in a manner to benefit all its people of whatever condition and in whatever parts of it domiciled.

It is believed that such a purpose may be defined, and that the land taken for Franklin Park may be shown to be neither of greater extent than is needed, nor in any essential respect unsuitable to the pursuit of it. It is believed to be perfectly practicable, as the business now stands, to secure results more valuable and less costly than the most sanguine promoters of the scheme have heretofore been authorized to promise.

It must nevertheless be recognized that there has been much in the experience of other cities to justify fear that the work will grow to be a very costly one.

How is this danger to be met?

What is first of all necessary is that those who are alive to it should not be content to remain under a mere blind apprehension, moving to a distrustful, hesitating attitude, favoring a desultory, devious and intermittent advance of the work. They must seek to clearly understand, through a closer study than is often made of the history of the large park works of other cities, in what the danger of extravagance consists.

Reasons will be given for believing that such a study will result in a conviction that it consists mainly in the prevalence, during the earlier years of such undertakings, of vague, immature, conflicting, and muddled ideas of their purpose, and a consequent tendency to fritter away the advantages of the ground upon results that pass for collateral, but are really, for the most part, counteractive of their main design. These ideas lead to expectations, disappointments, customs, demands, that become important factors in determining the character of the park. If a notable number of the people, though a minority of all, come to suppose that it is not being prepared to meet expectations they may have happened, even though inconsiderately, to have formed, it is quite possible that their influence will compel the work to proceed upon a fluctuating plan to a degree that would be generally recognized to be scandalously wasteful in any other important class of public works.

What has been done thus far in the undertaking of Franklin Park, encourages a belief that the danger is less in Boston than it has been found to be in other communities. But if anyone doubts that it exists and is to-day the chief difficulty in the way of a successful prosecution of the enterprise, let him first consider that the proposition to form a large rural park for the people of Boston has already been before them at least twenty years, that it has been annually debated in the City Council seventeen years, and in the form of a distinct project has been ten years before an executive department of the government expressly formed to advance it; that from year to year it has been brought up freshly in the Mayors' messages, in reports of Commissioners and Committees, and in proceedings of public meetings reported and discussed by the press. A site for it has been obtained and preliminary work for its improvement has been two years in progress.

These circumstances borne in mind, let a judgment be formed of the standing which this park project has at the present moment in the minds of any considerable number of citizens to whom it is not in some way a matter of special personal interest, in comparison with the standing had in the minds of a similar body, of projects of other sorts of public works at corresponding periods.

Let those projects be taken, for example, by the successive carrying out of which the present complex system of waterworks for the city has come to be what it is. Of the uses and consequently of the practical value of water, everyone knows something experimentally. Everyone knows that water may be held in a vessel or reservoir, and that through an outlet at its bottom it will run from this vessel downward wherever a way is opened. With this knowledge, the conditions of efficiency of various proposed new works for supplying water have been easily comprehended, and the value of what has been aimed to be accomplished has been generally appreciated.

So it has been with all other important public works of the city. The benefits to be gained by the people, for example, through various important steps in the improvement of the sewer system have been matters of clear-headed popular discussion. Even the questions at issue between the engineers in this respect have been generally fairly well understood. It was the same as to the advantages to be gained by the substitution of steam for hand fire-engines, and of horse power for man power in moving them, and many other modern improvements. The same as to the Public Library and as to the Court House. By comparison it will be seen that such notions as prevail of the benefits to be realized through outlays to be made by the city on the body of land of five hundred acres bought for a purpose defined as that of "a park," are not only varied and conflicting between different men, but in each man's mind are apt to be wanting in practically serviceable clearness and definiteness.

That this is the case even with many who suppose themselves better informed than most, may appear a more reasonable assumption if the fact can be established that while the business of forming a large park and bringing it into suitable use is one in which the government and people of the city have no local experience, it is also one of which less is to be learned by casual observation than of most others in which cities commonly engage.

Let it be considered, then, that the persons who manifest the highest sense of the value to themselves individually of a park, in all large cities, are not those who in the aggregate resort most to it, and, as a body, benefit most by it. They are those to whom time, because of the weight of affairs resting upon them, is most valuable, and to whom an alert working condition of mind and body is worth the most money. In Paris and London, New York and Chicago, many of this class may be found for a certain time daily in a park. It is almost as fixed a habit with them to go there at a certain hour, as at certain other hours to go to their meals or to repose. It is not a matter of fashion or social custom, for their manner of using the park varies: some of them walking, others driving, others riding; some pursue their course alone, others seek company, some keep to the main thoroughfares, others seek the secluded parts. With some men of much public importance now in New York, their present habit of using the park, began when the first section of it was opened to public use, seven-and-twenty years ago.

It will be obvious that the manner in which such men, making such use of a park, find it of value is not that in which a stranger or an occasional visitor finds it interesting; and, looking further, it may be recognized that the benefits of a park to the people of a city, of all classes and conditions, come chiefly in a gradual way, through a more or less habitual use of what it provides, and that such benefits are neither experienced nor are the conditions on which they depend apt to be dwelt upon by an occasional observer, to whom the interest of a visit unavoidably lies largely in the comparative novelty to him of what he sees. Neither do the gains in value of the park in this more important respect often engage the attention of the press. Columns will necessarily be given to the introduction of a statue, or a new piece of masonry, or a novelty in horticulture, for every line to the development of the essential constituents of the park, or the eradication of obstructive conditions. The eyes of a frequenter of a park rarely rest for a moment on objects before which strangers generally halt. A park may affect a man at the first visit exhilaratingly, which, when he is accustomed to the use of it, will have a reverse, that is to say, a soothing and tranquillizing effect. Thus, that only is of much solid and permanent value to a city in a park which increases in value as it becomes less strikingly interesting, and of that which has value in this way, an occasional visitor is apt to be in a great degree oblivious. No guide book calls his attention to it. No friend can bring it home to him.

As an illustration of the wrong impressions that are naturally propagated in the manner thus suggested, it may be said that the costliness of certain parks is habitually assumed by many intelligent men to have been chiefly in outlays for what is called "decoration." This term is not thus applied to trees, plants, and turf; to the plain work, however good, of substantial structures, nor to gracefulness or picturesqueness of modelling in graded surfaces, but first to objects which are merely decorative, such as fountains, vases, artificial rockwork, pagodas, temples, kiosks, obelisks, or other independent structures; and, second, to works of decoration superadded to structures for use, such as crestings, carvings, mosaics, mouldings, flutings, panellings, and the like. The fact is that no large part of the cost of any great park has been for these purposes. Of upwards of ten millions of dollars paid by cities upon the certificate of the writer, it is believed that less than four per cent has been for such decorative work. On the Buffalo Park, than which none is more satisfactory to the people, the outlay for decorative work is reckoned not to have exceeded one half of one per cent.[1] And it may be added, with respect to another form of this error, having its origin probably in early impressions from superficial and incomprehensive observation, that the value of no rural park to the people who habitually use it would be seriously impaired if every scrap of ornament to be found upon it should fall to decay or be effaced, except as the spaces left unfurnished would appear shabby and incongruous with the general character of the place. Beyond question, the value of many large parks would be increased by the removal of a variety of objects which, when introduced, were thought to be desirable acquisitions.*

In one of the notes to follow it will be shown that the confusion of the popular mind in the early years of a large park work which has been described gradually passes off with an experience of the benefits resulting from an habitual use of the finished ground. The chief peril from it occurs during the period of constructive operations, and before any important results of growth have been attained. For this reason, it is important that those who may be able to aid in moulding a sound public opinion should see how the difficulty of working out of the confusion is increased by a common equivocal use of certain terms applicable to park work.

There is a space in Boston called Park Square, and in it there has lately been a sign with the inscription, "Park Square Garden."[2] There is neither a park nor a square nor a garden in the vicinity, nor has there been. The word park is applied in a similar loose way to various comparatively small public spaces which are otherwise more discriminatingly called Greens, Commons, Squares, Gardens, and Places. In most considerable cities there is now to be found a ground called a park to which none of these names are applied. It is a ground more or less well adapted to serve a purpose that cannot be served on the smaller class of grounds. Such a ground is therefore a park distinctively, — a park proper. But it thus occurs that when a large space of

---

* Consistently with this view is Hamerton's observation that "very much of the impressiveness of natural scenery depends on the degree in which mass predominates over details."[3] The chief advantage of the "new" (of the last century) over the old gardening was found in the fact that while works of the latter might be striking and impressive as they were to be seen for a moment from particular points of view, and might have an endless number of interesting points of detail, these advantages were greatly outweighed by the more sustained, comprehensive, and pervading pleasantness of the simpler, unostentatious, and uneventful work of the "new gardening." This advantage is easily dissipated on a public park. Where it is to be largely so by the introduction of numerous objects of special admiration, it would be better to adopt thoroughly the old architectural motive. F.L.O.

ground is taken by a city for the purpose of a park proper, there is a tendency to regard it simply as a larger provision for the same ends with those which Commons, Greens, Squares, and Gardens are adapted to serve, and the real park is looked forward to not a little as it might be if it were in effect an aggregation or a combination and improved form of various smaller public grounds.

Even though, when ground is taken for a park proper, it may be understood that a purpose distinct from any or all of the purposes of these smaller grounds is had in view, this tendency leads propositions to be urged as to the uses to which it shall be put, and the way in which it shall be fitted and furnished, that common sense would otherwise recognize as propositions to set aside the distinctive purpose of the park.

Such confusion as may naturally occur in the way that has been thus explained is apt to be aggravated by the additional circumstance that the word landscape is constantly used, is used even by eminent writers, confoundingly, with reference to two essentially distinct arts. One of these arts is inapplicable to the smaller grounds of a city, but fully applicable to a large ground; the other is a decorative art, applicable to all forms and conditions of ground in which vegetation is possible, available for the smallest city grounds, and often, as for years past in Boston, practised upon small grounds with results most gratifying to the public. With such results, that to be wisely had in view in the undertaking of a rural park is scarcely more to be brought in comparison than the results proper to a Public Library building with those proper to a Court House, those of a church with those of a theatre.

The object of these notes is to give reasons for the convictions that have been thus expressed, and, in a measure, to meet in advance the dangers that have been indicated. This object obliges an exposition of the subject, under various heads, from many points of view. It is not to be expected, with the present slight public interest in the scheme of the park, that such an exposition will have many readers; but should it have none, proper respect for the future interest of the public in the matter requires a somewhat detailed record of the groundwork of the plan, of the expectations with which the work is entered upon, and of the foreseen conditions of its successful prosecution.

For those who may wish to obtain in the briefest possible way a slight general knowledge of what is intended, the drawing illustrative of the plan hereto attached, with which a concise statement is printed explanatory of the design, will be independently distributed in the form of a broadsheet, and it is hoped that with such aid as the public journals may see fit to give the purpose, an understanding of what is to be reasonably expected of the park may become common before customs in the use of it, growing out of different expectations, can be established.

FIRST.
A CONSIDERATION OF PUBLIC PROPERTIES IN OR NEAR BOSTON AVAILABLE FOR OCCUPATION OTHERWISE THAN BY BUILDINGS OR FOR THOROUGHFARES.

AMONG habits of thought that we have by inheritance there is one which is evinced in the custom of speaking of public grounds comprehensively and indiscriminatingly as "the lungs" of a city, "ventilating-places," "breathing-holes," and "airing-grounds."

This habit originated in walled towns, with extremely narrow, crooked streets, half built over, in which all the filth and garbage of dwellings was deposited, and often remained until flushed out by heavy rains. In such cities of fifty thousand inhabitants, the deaths due to foul air were larger than they now need be in cities of five hundred thousand.

With it has come down to us a subtile disposition, — the ghost of a serious, solid, and firm-footed ancestral conviction, — by which we are often influenced in dealing with questions of public grounds more than we are aware. It is a disposition to assume that the chief value of such grounds is that of outlets for foul air and inlets for pure air, and to regard whatever else our taxes are required to provide upon them in the character of a comparatively trifling luxury, adding something to the pleasure of life, no doubt, like sweet things after dinner, or buttons on the back of a man's coat, or the "gingerbread work" of a ship, but supplying almost nothing of solid sustenance and strength.

A wholly different understanding of the use of public grounds has long since begun to prevail; yet we are so much haunted by the old idea that we are rarely able to take clear, business-like views of the conditions of value in their equipment.

Even those who have been advocating the great addition lately made to the ground reserved from building within the city of Boston, have frequently made the sanitary requirement of airing-spaces in the midst of a city, and the need of providing them well in advance of the line of compact building, their main argument. Let it be supposed that the term "airing-place," as now used, means a little more than it once did; that it means a place to which people shall be drawn by various attractions, and having been drawn shall be induced to exercise in such a manner as to quicken their circulation and give their lungs a good cleansing of fresh air; it is yet an error fruitful of bad management and of waste to suppose that such an undertaking as this of Franklin Park is to be justified on that ground.

This will be better seen and several other considerations affecting the problem of the plan, will be made plainer if the advantages which the people of the city now hold with respect to airing-grounds are passed in review.

To aid a cursory examination of them the accompanying map has been prepared,[4] showing the city and so much of its outskirts as can conveniently be brought within the limits of the sheet, and indicating one hundred and eighty-six localities, in each of which there is now a body of land, great or small, serving, or available to serve, at least a ventilating purpose. Of these, seventy-one have been already "improved," are now in process of improvement, or are held with a definite intention of improvement, with a view to recreative qualities, as for example, by being turfed and planted. Fifty-six of these are public squares, commons, or gardens, of the city of Boston proper, the number of these much exceeding that of the same class of grounds of the united cities of New York and Brooklyn. Thirty-nine are burial grounds, most of them small, ancient, and disused. These are not likely to be built upon, and should the course now being pursued in London and other old cities be followed, as in time it probably will be, most of them will eventually be made public groves and gardens. At least they will be verdurous breathing-places. Forty-seven are lands which in various ways have come into the possession of the city, and may at any time be sold when the government thinks it wise to part with them. Their bearing on the present subject is this, that when it shall be thought that additional urban grounds are needed in any part of the city, it will not always be necessary to make a special purchase of land to supply sites for them. Many of these properties, for instance, are well situated for playgrounds for school children, and could be adapted to that use at moderate expense. Others, smaller, are available for open-air gymnasiums.

Within the city of Boston, or close upon its border, there are nearly two hundred public properties which are not held with a view to building over them, and most of which are secured by legal enactments from ever being built over. Omitting the larger spaces recently acquired and held by the Department of Parks, these grounds are on an average thirteen acres each in area. Omitting the islands, the burial grounds, the larger grounds of the Department, and all that would not ordinarily be classed with "city squares and gardens," the latter have an average area of about four acres each.

The area of the entire number of public properties numbered on the map, and of which a classified list follows showing the situation and area of each, is 3356.63 acres, or over five square miles. Of those likely to be permanent green oases among the buildings of the city, the area is about four square miles, or nearly as much as the entire building space within the walls of some cities that had great importance in the world when the building of Boston was begun.[5]

Before taking up the question of the proposed large park, it may be desirable to form some idea of the present standard for the equipment of cities in respect to public grounds other than large parks, and consider how Boston's possessions, as they have been set out, may be rated by it. Of course this can be done but loosely, but the purpose may be carried far enough to answer with assurance the question, How are the people of Boston faring and likely to fare in this particular in comparison with civilized townspeople generally?

For this purpose it must be kept in mind that the public grounds of most cities have come to be what they are and where they are by various detached and desultory proceedings, of which the result, as a whole, illustrates penny-wise-pound-foolish wisdom quite as much as the result of laying out streets with reference to immediate local and personal interests, regardless of burdens loading up to be carried by an entire city ever after.

Of late, however, ideas of systematization, with a view to comprehensive and long-sighted public economy, have taken root, and in a few instances are growing to profitable results.

These ideas move in two directions; and as confusion between them can only lead to blunders, it is well to see where the parting occurs.

If a large town were about to be built on a previously determined plan, a series of public grounds might be contemplated, to be situated at regular distances apart, all of the same extent, and all looking to a similarity and an equality of provisions for the use of those who would resort to them, the aim being to distribute the value of whatever should be done for the purpose of public recreation, as nearly as possible equitably among the several corresponding districts of the city. A type of grounds would result, an inclination to approach which is here and there evident.

Certain advantages follow, but they are obtained at a cost that would be unreasonable in any city, the site of which was not generally flat, rockless, and treeless, or in any the natural growth, expansion on all sides and prosperity of which were not singularly assured. Nor are the advantages aimed at in such a system, so far as attainable, of controlling importance.

As cities grow in a manner not to be accurately foreseen, as centres of business and centres of residence sometimes shift, and in the course of years become interchanged, and *as some parts of the site or the neighborhood of a city will nearly always be specially favorable to provisions of recreation of one class, other parts to provisions of another class,* it is generally better to have in view the development of some peculiar excellence in each of several grounds. And this may be considered the central idea of the alternative system, only that in proceeding with reference to it, it is to be remembered that cities are built compactly because of the economy of placing many varied facilities of exchange of service in close and direct intercommunication. Any large area within a city, not occupied by buildings, and not available as a means of communication between them, lessens this advantage, compelling circuitous routes to be taken and increasing the cost of the exchanges of service, upon the facilities offered for which the prosperity of the city depends.

It follows that so far as any purpose of public grounds can be well provided for on a small ground, it is better to so provide for it, rather than to multiply and complicate the purposes to be provided for on a larger ground. In a system determined with unqualified regard to this principle no ground would be used for any purpose of recreation which purpose could as well be served by itself elsewhere, on a small ground.

It follows, also, that the larger the ground needed for any special purpose, the more desirable it is (other things being equal) that the ground should be at a distance from the centres of exchange, which will be the denser parts of the city, and out of the main lines of the compact outward growth of the city.

The smaller grounds of the class designed for general use (being such as are commonly called squares and places) may with advantage, as far as practicable, be evenly distributed, with a view to local convenience, throughout a city. Yet, with regard to these, there are at least three circumstances which should make numerous deviations from such equalizing distribution: First, topographical circumstances may compel spaces unsuitable for building to be left between streets, which it will be economical to use for such grounds; many such are found in and about Boston. Second, spaces should be left about public buildings, in order to give them better light, remove them from the noise of the streets, protect them from conflagrations, and make the value of their architecture available. Such spaces will economically become small public grounds.

Lastly, it is most desirable to make use of any local circumstance of the slightest dignity of character to supply a centre of interest for such grounds. Such a circumstance may be found, for instance, in a natural feature, as a notable rock, or in a historical feature, as the site of an old fort, or in the birthplace of a great man, or simply in a point of vantage for a view, as a prospect down the harbor. There is no better example of a very small public ground than one in Paris, where a beautiful church tower, decorated by centuries of superficial decay and mossy incrustations, has been taken as the centre of the work, the body of the church being removed and its place occupied by seats and gardenry.[6]

Usually, however, there is nothing better for the purpose of this class of grounds than a simple open grove, or, on the smaller spaces, a group of forest trees (selected with regard for probable vigor and permanent health under the circumstances) with a walk through or around it, proper provisions against injury and unseemly use, a drinking fountain, and convenient seats out of the lines of passage, of which type there are good illustrations in Boston.

Playgrounds for children need not be so large as to interfere with direct, short communication, and should be evenly distributed in the residential part of the town, except as special localities are to be preferred on account of unusual topographical fitness.

If it is thought desirable to make any special provision for carriage and saddle exercise without going far from the central parts of the town, the most convenient and economical plan is that of a passage having the character of a street of extraordinary width, strung with verdant features and other objects of interest, so laid out as not to seriously interfere with the primary business of the city; that is to say, with convenience of exchange. Such passages are found between the principal palaces and better-built parts and the more frequented parks in Paris, Berlin, Brussels, Dijon, and other European cities, and are there more commonly classed as boulevards; in America they are to be found notably in Buffalo and Chicago, and are there called parkways.[7]

To further develop a system of public grounds, areas will be selected as far as practicable in parts of the city where they will least interrupt desirable general communication, the topographical conditions of each of which adapt it to a special purpose, and each of these will be fitted for public use upon a plan intended to make the most of its special advantages for its special purposes.

These observations may be considered to suggest the present standard of civilization in respect to the urban grounds of a city situated as Boston is. Looking with reference to this standard to Boston possessions and Boston's opportunities held in reserve to be used as her borders extend, hardly another city will be found in an equally satisfactory condition.

In the Boston provisions for urban public grounds there are:

(1) Two extensive parkway systems, one formed by Massachusetts Avenue, expanding into the broad, shady drives and walks that pass around and divide Chestnut Hill Reservoir; the other formed by the Muddy River (Riverdale) roads, spreading into the Promenade now forming about the Back Bay Drainage Basins, and with Commonwealth Avenue connecting the Common and Public Garden with Jamaica Pond, the Arboretum, and the site of Franklin Park.

(2) There are numerous local grounds so small in extent as not to interfere with desirable lines of street communication.

(3) There are a few grounds adapted to serve a similar purpose of a brief recreation for the people of their several neighborhoods, which are larger than the first, but so situated that they will interrupt street communication only where natural obstacles occur (such as the deep slough of Back Bay).

(4) There is one ground which, though centrally situated, is fully large enough for the purpose, wherein the enjoyment of floral beauty and plant beauty of a specific character is liberally provided for.

(5) In another, much larger and of strikingly diversified surface, on the outskirts of the city, provision is made for the greatest possible variety of hardy trees in a manner to show their specific qualities, and to combine opportunity for scientific research and popular instruction with the enjoyment of the forms of individual sylvan beauty to be thus presented.

(6) In another, marine landscapes are offered and special provisions made for various aquatic recreations under particularly favorable natural conditions for their enjoyment.

(7)   In another, a natural lake with beautifully wooded borders is to be availed of, which, besides its value in other respects, has this, that it will serve as a general skating-place and a safe still-water boating-place.

Looking for deficiencies in this system of non-rural grounds, the chief will be found to be the want of sufficient local and suitable general grounds for active exercises. It would be a good thing for the city to have a large, plain, flat, undecorated ground, not far away, easily accessible, if practicable, both by rail and boat, adapted to military and athletic exercises.

Considering the advantage which pertains to the subdivision of the city by bays and rivers, and the constant movement through and around it of strong tidal currents, and the advantages thus offered for boating and bathing, as well as for obtaining unstagnant air, it is believed that this exhibit of Boston's Breathing-Places will be found gratifying. Few cities have a larger number of small urban grounds proportionately to their population; and, while some of Boston's grounds are of a nondescript character, serving no particular purpose very well, others are models of their class, and in no Northern city is the average usefulness of such grounds greater. As to reservations for the future, in respect to this class of grounds, no city is more forehanded.

Finally, it will be plain that with such advantages as Boston has been shown to have within reach for a great variety of purposes to be served upon public grounds, it would have been a wholly irrational thing for the city to have purchased five hundred acres more of land, all in one body, except for a purpose to which so large a space was more essential than it is to the purpose of making a place attractive and suitable for those needing air and exercise.

As to the idea that the main object of making a park beautiful is to make it attractive, argument is hardly needed by anyone giving the slightest reflection to the question. Much more efficient means than can be found in any public ground could be easily and cheaply adopted for the purpose.

"Tell them, dear, that if eyes are made for seeing,
Then beauty is its own excuse for being."[8]

PART SECOND.
THE PLAN OF FRANKLIN PARK.
I.
OF CERTAIN CONDITIONS OF THE SITE OF
FRANKLIN PARK.

THAT the site for Franklin Park could have been rationally bought only with a view to a purpose previously not at all provided for, and that no use of the ground should now be permitted likely to lessen its value for this distinctive purpose, will yet more clearly appear if the topography of the ground and the manner of its selection are considered.

The scheme of Franklin Park, as it now stands, is a contraction of a much larger scheme outlined to the city government in 1869.[9] This larger scheme included bodies of comparatively rich, humid, flat land, much better adapted to provide many forms of public ground than any within the field of the present scheme; a parade ground, for instance, and ball grounds; much better adapted, also, to the beauty to be obtained through refined horticulture, floral displays, and other decorations. It included streams of water and areas in which lakes with provisions for boating, skating, and bathing, as well as water-side beauty, could have been readily provided. All such ground has, long since, upon mature consideration by the city government, been thrown out of the scheme.

The ground finally selected has in its larger part the usual characteristics of the stony upland pasture, and the rocky divides between streams commonly found in New England, covered by what are called "second growth" woods, the trees slow growing from the stumps of previous woods, crowded, somewhat stunted, spindling; not beautiful individually, but, in combination forming impressive masses of foliage. It not only contains no lake, permanent pool or stream of water, but it commands no distant water view. It includes no single natural feature of distinguished beauty or popular interest. It is in all parts underlaid by ledges which break out at some points in a bold and picturesque way, at others in such a manner only as to make barren patches, with scanty vegetation that wilts and becomes shabby in dry, hot weather. It is thickly strewn with boulders; even in parts where the surface appears smooth and clear, their presence just below it generally becomes obvious in dry weather, and they are turned out by the plough in great numbers. Any fine cultivation of the ground will be comparatively costly. It is not generally adaptable at moderate expense for lawn-like treatment, nor to the development of what are commonly, though perhaps not accurately, regarded as the beauties of landscape gardening. As a whole, it is rugged, intractable, and as little suitable to be worked to conditions harmonious with urban elegance as the site of the Back Bay Drainage Basins, Mount Royal Park at Montreal, East Rock Park at New Haven, or Arthur's Seat at Edinburgh.[10]

It is on the borders of the city, remote from its more populous quarters, remote, also, from any of its excellent water highways, and out of the line of its leading land thoroughfares.

What can be said for the property as a whole is this: That there is not within or near the city any other equal extent of ground of as simple, and pleasingly simple, rural aspect. It has been at various points harshly gashed by rudely engineered roads, scarred by quarries and gravel-pits, and disrural-ized by artificially disposed trees and pseudo-rustic structures, but, consider-ing its proximity to the compact town, it has remarkably escaped disturbances of this character.

II.
THE PURPOSE OF THE PLAN.

UNDER this head a distinction is to be made which is of critical im-portance. It is a distinction so rarely regarded in gardening works, or in engi-neering or architectural works nominally subsidiary to gardening works, that a strong prejudice of mental habit will be found to be working against a com-plete entertainment of it. It will be necessary, therefore, to set it forth pain-stakingly and to justify insistence upon it. An indolent indisposition to be bothered with it has added greatly to the taxes of several cities.

What is the special purpose of a large park in distinction from the various purposes that may be served by such smaller grounds as Boston is provided with?

In the first division of these pages reference has been made to the manner in which various evils of town life, by the introduction of one special expedient after another, have been gradually so well contended with, that in cities that at present have several times the population they had in the last century, much less time is now lost than then to productive industry; the average length of life much advanced, and the value of life augmented. The evils in question have been for the most part intangible, and to those who were not close students of them have been considered inscrutable; not to be measured and reckoned up like the evils of fire and flood, famine, war, and lawlessness. Consequently plans for overcoming them have always been re-garded for a time as fanciful, and those urging them as theorists and enthusi-asts. For a time, no city outlays have been so grudgingly made or given so much dissatisfaction to taxpayers as those required to advance measures of this class. Looking back upon their results, after a few years, it is admitted that no other money has been so profitably expended. No one thinks that they were untimely or were advanced too rapidly.

Of this class of evils there is one rapidly growing in Boston, in con-tention with which nothing has yet been accomplished. It is an evil depen-dent on a condition involved in the purpose of placing many stacks of artifi-cial conveniences for the interchange of services closely together. It may be suggested if not explained (for evils of this class are seldom fully explainable) in this way.

A man's eyes cannot be as much occupied as they are in large cities by artificial things, or by natural things seen under obviously artificial conditions, without a harmful effect, first on his mental and nervous system and ultimately on his entire constitutional organization.

That relief from this evil is to be obtained through recreation is often said, without sufficient discrimination as to the nature of the recreation required. The several varieties of recreation to be obtained in churches, newspapers, theatres, picture galleries, billiard rooms, baseball grounds, trotting courses, and flower gardens, may each serve to supply a mitigating influence. An influence is desirable, however, that, acting through the eye, shall be more than mitigative, that shall be antithetical, reversive, and antidotal. Such an influence is found in what, in notes to follow, will be called the enjoyment of pleasing rural scenery.

But to understand what will be meant by this term as here to be used, two ideas must not be allowed to run together, that few minds are trained to keep apart. To separate them let it be reflected, first, that the word beauty is commonly used with respect to two quite distinct aspects of the things that enter visibly into the composition of parks and gardens. A little violet or a great magnolia blossom, the frond of a fern, a carpet of fine turf of the form and size of a prayer rug, a block of carved and polished marble, a vase or a jet of water, — in the beauty of all these things unalloyed pleasure may be taken in the heart of a city. And pleasure in their beauty may be enhanced by aggregations and combinations of them, as it is in arrangement of bouquets and head-dresses, the decoration of the dinner-tables, window-sills and door-yards, or, in a more complex and largely effective way, in such elaborate exhibitions of high horticultural art as the city maintains in the Public Garden.[11]

But there is a pleasure-bringing beauty in the same class of objects — foliage, flowers, verdure, rocks, and water — not to be enjoyed under the same circumstances or under similar combinations; a beauty which appeals to *a different class of human sensibilities*, a beauty the art of securing which is hardly more akin with the art of securing beauty on a dinner-table, a window-sill, a dooryard, or an urban garden, than the work of the sculptor is akin with the work of the painter.

Let beauty of the first kind be called here urban beauty, not because it cannot be had elsewhere than in a city, but because the distinction may thus, for the sake of argument in this particular case, be kept in mind between it and that beauty of the same things which can only be had clear of the confinement of a city, and which it is convenient therefore to refer to as the beauty of rural scenery.

Now as to this term scenery, it is to be borne in mind that we do not speak of what may be observed in the flower and foliage decorations of a dinner-table, window-sill, or dooryard, scarcely of what may be seen in even a large urban garden, as scenery. Scenery is more than an object or a series of objects; more than a spectacle, more than a scene or a series of scenes, more than a landscape, and other than a series of landscapes. Moreover, there may be beautiful scenery in which not a beautiful blossom or leaf or rock, bush or tree, not a gleam of water or of turf shall be visible. But there is no beautiful scenery that does not give the mind an emotional impulse different from that resulting from whatever beauty may be found in a room, courtyard, or garden, within which vision is obviously confined by walls or other surrounding artificial constructions.

It is necessary to be thus and even more particular in defining the term used to denote the paramount purpose embodied in the plan of Franklin Park, because many men, having a keen enjoyment of certain forms of beauty in vegetation, and even of things found only in the country, habitually class much as rural that is not only not rural, but is even the reverse of rural as that term is to be here used.

For example: in a region of undulating surface with a meandering stream and winding valleys, with much naturally disposed wood, there is a house with outbuildings and enclosures, roads, walks, trees, bushes, and flowering plants. If the constructions are of the natural materials of the locality and not fashioned expressly to manifest the wealth or art of the builders, if they are of the texture and the grain and the hues that such materials will naturally become if no effort to hide or disguise them is made, if the lines of the roads and walks are adapted to curves of the natural surface, and if the trees and plants are of a natural character naturally disposed, the result will be congruous with the general natural rural scenery of the locality, its rural quality being, perhaps, enhanced by these unobtrusive artificial elements. But in such a situation it oftener than otherwise occurs that customs will be followed which had their origin in a desire to obtain results that should be pleasing, not through congruity with pleasing natural rural circumstances, but through incongruity with them. Why? Simply because those designing them had been oppressed by a monotony of rural scenery, and desired to find relief from it, and because also they desired to manifest the triumph of civilized forces over nature. And on account of the general association with rural scenery of things determined by fashions originating in these desires, they are carelessly thought of as rural things, and the pleasure to be derived from them is esteemed a part of the pleasure taken in rural scenery.

It thus happens that things come to be regarded as elements of rural scenery which are simply cheap and fragmentary efforts to realize something of the pleasingness which the countryman finds in the artificialness of the city. This is why, to cite a few examples familiar to everyone, wooden houses are fashioned in forms and with decorations copied from houses of masonry, and why the wood of them is not left of its natural color, or given a tint harmonious with natural objects, but for distinction's sake smeared over with glistening white lead. This is the reason why trees are transplanted from natural to unnatural situations about houses so treated, why they are formally disposed, why forms are preferred for them to be obtained only by artificial processes, as grafting, pruning, and shearing; why shrubs are worked into fantastic shapes that cannot possibly be mistaken for natural growths; why groups are made studiously formal, why the trunks of trees are sometimes whitewashed; why rocks too heavy to be put out of sight are cleared of their natural beauty, and even sometimes also whitewashed; why flowering plants are often arranged as artificially as the stones of a mosaic pavement; why pools are furnished with clean and rigid stone margins and jets of water thrown from them; why specimens of rustic work and of rock work are displayed conspicuously that have been plainly designed to signalize, not to subordinate or soften, the artificialness of artificial conveniences.

Defining the purpose of the plan of Franklin Park to be that of placing within the easy reach of the people of the city the enjoyment of such a measure as is practicable of rural scenery, all such misunderstanding of the term as has thus been explained must be guarded against.

That rural scenery has the effect alleged, of counteracting a certain oppression of town life, is too well established to need argument, but as the manner of its action will have a practical bearing on the purpose of the plan, the circumstances may be recalled that the evil to be met is most apt to appear in excessive nervous tension, over-anxiety, hasteful disposition, impatience, irritability, and that the grateful effect of a contemplation of pleasing rural scenery is proverbially regarded as the reverse of this. It is, for example, of the enjoyment of this pleasure, and not simply of air and exercise, that Emerson says, "It soothes and sympathizes,"[12] that Lowell says, "It pours oil and wine on the smarts of the mind,"[13] and which Ruskin describes as "absolute peace."[14]

It is not an easy matter, in the immediate outskirts of a great city, to make a provision of scenery which shall be so far rural in character and pleasing in effect as to have a high degree of the influence desired.

Some wise men are accustomed to ridicule the earlier result of efforts to that end by comparing it with scenery remote from cities the rurality of which owes nothing to human care. But these higher examples not being available for the frequent use of the mass of the people of a city, it is only a question whether a result is to be gained under such conditions as are offered in the site of Franklin Park which shall be of so much value in this respect that it will be worth more than it will cost. And, in considering this question, it is to be borne in mind that the purpose requires no elements of scenery of a class that would induce sensational effects. It will be answered in a measure — it is a question whether it may not even be better answered — by scenery that may be comparatively characterized as tame and homely. It is almost certainly better that the aim in overcoming the difficulties of securing such scenery should be modest, provided a modest aim can be sustained, and the temptation to put it out of countenance by bits of irrelevant finery resisted. Given sufficient space, scenery of much simpler elements than are found in the site of Franklin Park may possess the soothing charm which lies in the qualities of breadth, distance, depth, intricacy, atmospheric perspective, and mystery. It may have picturesque passages (that is to say, more than picturesque objects or picturesque "bits"). It may have passages, indeed, of an aspect approaching grandeur and sublimity.

It is to be feared that there are some who may be inclined to question if a considerable degree of refined culture, such as is common only to the more worldly fortunate, is not necessary to enable one to enjoy the charm of rural scenery sympathetically with Wordsworth, Emerson, Ruskin, and Lowell. To enjoy it intellectually, yes; to be affected by it, made healthier, better, happier by it, no. The men who have done the most to draw the world to the poetic enjoyment of nature have, in large part, come from lowly homes, and been educated in inexpensive schools. Burns, the ploughboy, was one such, known to all.[15] Millet, whose works are honored in the stateliest houses, was a peasant in habit, manner, and associations all his life long.[16] Léon Bonvin, whose pathetic love of the most modest natural scenery was illustrated in Harper's Magazine of last December, was by vocation the bar-keeper of a wayside tavern.[17] And in thinking of this question, especially with reference to a majority of the people of Boston, it is well to remember a phrase used by Dr. Shairp in his treatise on the Poetic Interpretation of Nature.[18] Speaking of Wordsworth and his sister, he says that the woman was the greater poet of the two, "only not a literary poet."[19] Poetic sensibility is one thing; inclination and capacity to give coherent form to poetic sentiment another.

The following is an account by Mrs. Gaskell[20] of the poorer sort of the humblest work-people of Manchester, England, and is drawn from life, as anyone chancing to be in that town on a fine summer holiday may test. Abating something from the grandeur of the trees, similar scenes have been witnessed during the past summer in the new Brooklyn, Buffalo, and Philadelphia parks, and in the yet hardly begun Beardsley Park of Bridgeport.[21] It is a question of time and of a wholesomely restrained ambition when they shall be seen in Franklin Park.

"He was on the verge of a green area, shut in by magnificent trees in all the glory of their early foliage, before the summer heat had deepened their verdure into one rich monotonous tint. And hither came party after party — old men and maidens, young men and children. Whole families trooped along after the guiding fathers, who bore the youngest in their arms or astride upon their backs, while they turned round occasionally to the wives, with whom they shared some fond local remembrance. For years has Dunham Park[22] been the favorite resort of the Manchester work-people. Its scenery presents such a complete contrast to the whirl and turmoil of Manchester. . . . Depend upon it, this sylvan repose, this *accessible quiet*, this lapping the soul in green images of the country, forms the most complete contrast to a town's person, and consequently has *over such the greatest power of charm.* . . . Far away in the distance, now sinking, now falling, now swelling and clear came a ringing peal of children's voices, blended together in one of those psalm tunes which we are all of us familiar with, and which bring to mind the old, old days when we, as wondering children, were first led to worship 'Our Father' by those beloved ones who have since gone to the more perfect worship.

"Holy was that distant choral praise, even to the most thoughtless; and when it, in fact, was ended, in the instant's pause during which the ear awaits the repetition of the air, they caught the noontide hum and buzz of the myriads of insects who danced away their lives in the glorious day; they heard the swaying of the mighty woods in the soft but resistless breeze, and then once more burst forth the merry jests and the shouts of childhood, and again the elder ones resumed their happy talk as they lay or sat 'under the greenwood tree.'

"But the day drew to an end; the heat declined, the birds once more began their warblings, the fresh scents hung about plant and tree and grass, betokening the fragrant presence of the reviving dew. . . . As they trod the meadow path once more, they were joined by many a party they had encountered during the day, all abounding in happiness, all full of the day's adventures.

"Long cherished quarrels had been forgotten, new friendships formed. Fresh tastes and higher delights had been imparted that day. We have all of us our look now and then, called up by some noble or loving thought (our highest on earth) which will be our likeness in heaven. I can catch the glance on many a face, the glancing light of the cloud of glory from heaven, which is our home. That look was present on many a hard-worked, wrinkled countenance as they turned backwards to catch a longing, lingering look at Dunham Woods, fast deepening into blackness of night, but whose memory was to haunt in greenness and freshness many a loom and workshop and factory with images of peace and beauty."[23]

III.
A REVIEW OF THE PLAN BY DIVISIONS.

As to Local Names to be used in the following Review. — For convenience of reference, names have been given on the drawing to various localities. Some of these have been found in use, as ABBOTSWOOD, GLEN ROAD, and ROCK HILL. In most of the others, old homestead names of the neighborhood are recalled, a choice among them having been made of such as would couple not too roughly with appropriate terminals. SCARBORO HILL, HAGBORNE HILL, WAITTWOOD, ROCK MORTON, and ELLICOTTDALE are examples.[24] Some of this class were suggested by the late Francis D. Drake, author of a History of Roxbury,[25] shortly before his lamented death; others have been obtained from Colonial records of the park property, found at the Registrar's office of Norfolk County. NAZINGDALE is from the birthplace of the first settlers. LONG CROUCH was the Colonial name of the road now known as Seaver Street, adjoining the woods to which it is given in the drawing. OLD TRAIL ROAD is nearly on the line of the Indian footpath used in the earlier communications between Boston and Plymouth. The name RESTING PLACE marks a shady knoll upon which the first military company formed in the Colonies with the purpose of armed resistance to British authority rested on its march home after the fight at Lexington. The captain and lieutenant of the company were both of families that at one time had homes on the park lands, and from them the names HEATHFIELD and PIERREPONT ROAD are taken.[26]

The region named THE WILDERNESS is referred to in records of the early part of the last century as "the Rocky Wilderness Land." PLAYSTEAD is an old designation of a rural playground, STEADING of the offices of a rural estate. GREETING refers to the purpose of a promenade. COUNTRY PARK is a term used to mark the intended distinction of character between Franklin Park and other public grounds of the city in a report made by Alderman, now Mayor, O'Brien in 1877.[27] SCHOOLMASTER HILL is so named in allusion to the circumstance that William Emerson and his brother, Ralph Waldo, while keeping school in Roxbury, lived in a house on the east side of this hill.[28] Private letters of Emerson are preserved in which he refers fondly to the wildness and rurality of the neighborhood.[29]

As to the map. — The broad sheet that has been spoken of in the Introduction can be folded and carried in the pocket, and it is intended that copies of it shall be exhibited at different favorable points on the park site, with indices to the position on the ground of the more salient features of the plan. The drawing will best meet the intention with which it is prepared if it is examined on the ground with some exercise of the imagination, being considered as a map of what may be expected should the plan be carried out, the usual limitations of a map being had in mind.

In the review of the plan by divisions presently to be made, the verbal observations upon the broad sheet will be repeated, but in a slightly extended form, with a statement of some additional particulars, and with special reference to readers intending to look over the ground as just suggested.

The "limitations of a map" advised to be had in mind will be understood if it is reflected that a map of Boston would give a stranger but little idea of what he would see if he were walking the streets of the city; still less of that more important part that exists under its roofs.

Seen from above, the trees of even a half-grown park would hide the outlines of the principal part of its roads, walks, and other surface constructions. Hence in a map designed to exhibit the general plan of a park, the woods, which will be the most important element of its scenery, can be but vaguely and incompletely represented; and bushes beneath trees, not at all.

Again, if it were attempted to show by the ordinary method of map-makers those variations of the surface which, next to the woods, are the most important features of the design, the drawing would be too complicated to fairly exhibit the plan of the work to be done. To avoid the obscurity which would thus occur, figures are given on the drawing, by which the relative elevation of the ground at various points may be determined. The more important swellings and depressions are also indicated by names ending in "hill" or "dale."

If the drawing is taken on the ground where the existing hills and valleys can be seen, and if these and the principal existing masses of foliage are regarded as fixed features, the observer may with little personal trouble readily form a good general idea of what is projected. The conventional signs for foliage show, according as they are closely clustered, scattered, or wanting, the intended division into wooded, semi-wooded, and open turf-land; the positions of the principal outcrops of rock are indicated; the various routes for opening the scenery of the park to exhibition, in carriage, saddle, horse, and foot travel, are conspicuously lined out, and sites for the few structures necessary to public convenience are plainly shown.

It is to be considered in observing the position of these structures on the ground, that they are designed, as are all the artificial objects of the park, to be kept as low as will be consistent with their several purposes of utility, that their walls are to be of the stones of the locality, with weather stained and lichen mottled faces, and that they are to be so set in among rocks and foliage that, with a single not very marked exception, they will be seen only on near approach by those wishing to use them, and not at all by visitors following the walks, drives, and rides of the main circuit. The bolder ledges, on the other hand, will be rather more open to view than they now are. The woods, again, as they generally occupy the more elevated ground, will be relatively more prominent than they appear in the drawing.

It has been considered necessary to public convenience that the park should be divided by a road crossing it from Blue Hill Avenue to Forest Hill Street, and that this should be open night and day for all ordinary street uses as the park roads will not be. Also that a considerable space of ground should be open for pleasure use after daylight; that this space should be lightable in such a manner that no part of it will be in dark shadow, and to this end that it should be free from underwood, low-headed trees or other conditions offering facilities for concealment. (To keep all of the park open at night, making it a safe and decorous place of resort, would greatly augment its running expenses without securing an adequate return.)

The only favorable line for the cross-road is one corresponding nearly with the present Glen Road. (The following diagram represents the outline of the park property. Glen Road passes from A to B.) Such a road will divide the park into two parts, as Charles Street divides the Common from the Public Garden. The division on the side furthest from the compact part of the city will contain two-thirds of the ground, and this being enclosed by itself may be considered as the main park.

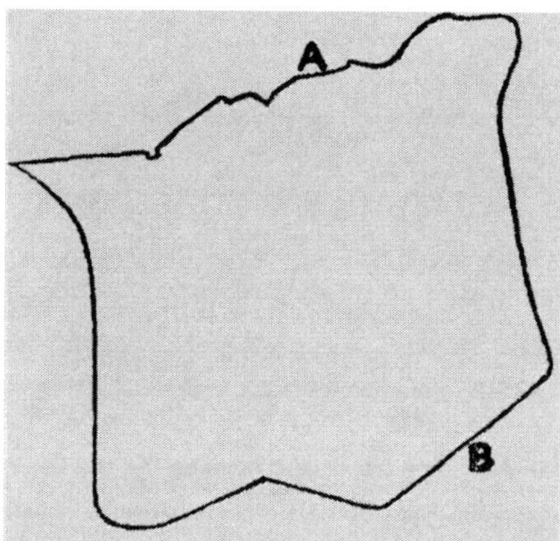

The ground on the other side is designed to answer purposes relatively to the main park analogous to those of a fore-court, portico, and reception room, with minor apartments opening from them for various special uses, and to which it is desirable access should be had at all times without entering the main park. It may be called the ante-park. From the ante-park there are to be two general entrances to the main park and an additional entrance for foot visitors.

For convenience in explaining the plan, the park must be considered as further subdivided as indicated by the black lines of the diagram below, but it must not be imagined that these lines will be obvious in looking over the ground. They are in part imaginary, and where not so will have the effect of barring the view or creating disunity of scenery less than an ordinary country road would do. Corresponding to letters on the diagram, names will be used to designate the several divisions as follows:

The distinctive purpose to which each of these divisions is to be fitted

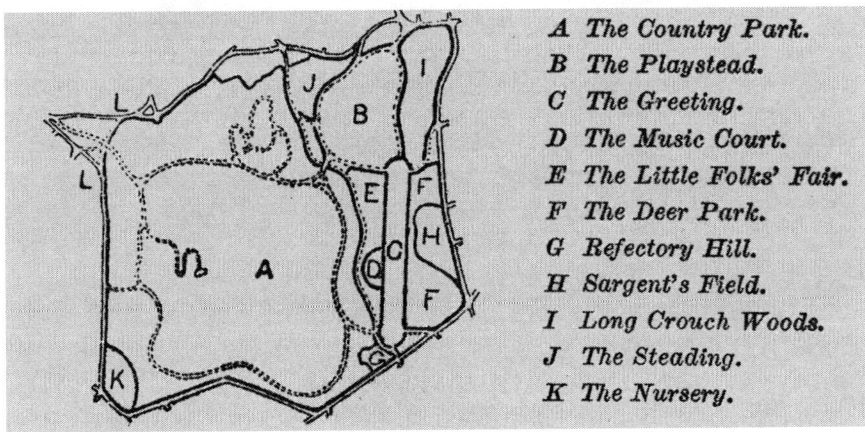

will now be stated, the more comprehensive landscape design which includes them all being afterwards described.

A. *The Country Park* (before referred to as the main park) is designed to be prepared and taken care of exclusively with reference to the
enjoyment of rural scenery, that is to say, if it is to be used for any other
purpose, it is meant that its advantages for that other purpose shall have accrued at no appreciable sacrifice of advantages for this primary and domi-
nating purpose.

The division will be a mile long and three quarters of a mile wide.
Natural scenery of much value for the purpose in view cannot be permanently secured in a tract of land of diversified surface of these limits with a
great city growing about it, if the essential elements of such scenery are to be
divided, adulterated, or put out of countenance by artificial objects, at all
more than is necessary to its protection and to the reasonable convenience of
those seeking the special benefits offered. The plan proposes, therefore, that
in the Country Park nothing shall be built, nothing set up, nothing planted,
as a decorative feature; nothing for the gratification of curiosity, nothing for
the advancement or popularization of science. These objects are provided for
suitably in the Public Garden, the Arboretum, and other grounds of the city.
No other city in America has as good arrangements for them.

To sustain the designed character of the Country Park, the urban
elegance generally desired in a small public or private pleasure ground is to
be methodically guarded against. Turf, for example, is to be in most parts
preferred as kept short by sheep, rather than by lawn mowers; well known and
long tried trees and bushes to rare ones; natives to exotics; humble field flowers to high-bred marvels; plain green leaves to the blotched, spotted, and fret-
ted leaves, for which, in decorative gardening, there is now a passing fashion.
Above all, cheap, tawdry, cockneyfied garden toys, such as are sometimes

placed in parks incongruously with all their rural character, are to be es-chewed. But a poor, shabby, worn, patchy, or in any way untidy ruralty is equally to be avoided with fragments of urban and suburban finery. In this respect the park is designed to be an example of thoroughly nice, though modest and somewhat homespun housekeeping.

The site of the Country Park is in most parts rugged, everywhere undulating. Where there are no outcropping ledges, solid rock is often close under the surface, and where it is not, there is in many places almost a pave-ment of boulders. Compared with that of most public parks, the surface soil is poor, while the subsoil is stony and hard. For these reasons, when the natu-ral surface is much trampled and worn it becomes an inert dust, pernicious to vegetation. It cannot, therefore, be prepared to resist the wear of athletic sports without undue expense.

Under wise regulations and with considerate customs of use, for the establishment of which the good will of the people must be engaged, the site of the Country Park will be found happily adapted to its special distinctive purpose. But it can be wisely used for no recreations which would tend to the destruction of its verdant elements; for none not of the class of those in which women and children may not and do not customarily take part. The plan looks to its being maintained in quietness; quietness both to the eye and the ear. A grateful serenity may be enjoyed in it by many thousand people at a time, if they are not drawn into throngs by spectacular attractions, but allowed to distribute themselves as they are otherwise likely to do.

As will soon be shown, the intention of the plan of the park, as a whole, is that from no part of this Country Park division of it shall anything in any other of its divisions be visible, or, at most, be noticeable, except rock, turf, and trees, and these only in harmonious composition with the natural scenery of the Country Park. A large part of the Country Park is to be wooded, and adapted to the use of picnic and basket parties, especially small family parties. Various conveniences for these are to be prepared. Tennis courts, cro-quet grounds, archery ranges, and small lawns for children's festivities, are provided for in connection with suitable picnic grounds in the several dis-tricts which are named on the Commissioners' map — *The Wilderness, Juni-per Hill, Waittwood, Heathfield, Rock Milton, Rock Morton*; on the western slopes of *Scarboro Hill* and in *Abbotswood*.

Near the picturesque declivity and hanging wood of Schoolmaster's Hill, several small level places are designed to be formed by rough terracing on the hillside. Each of these is to be covered by vines on trellises, and fur-nished with tables and seats. Most of the arbors so formed look, at consider-able elevation and advantageously, upon the broadest and quietest purely pas-toral scene that the park can offer. These arbors are intended especially for the use of family basket parties. A small house is placed among them, to con-tain an office for the superintendence of the district, a parcel room and clos-ets, and at which hot water for making tea can be had without charge. The

SCHOOLMASTER HILL, FRANKLIN PARK, WITH SHELTER AND PICNIC TERRACES

house is to be placed and the other conveniences are to be so sheltered by existing trees and vines to be grown upon the trellises that they will be invisible except to those seeking them.

At a point central to all the picnic and basket party grounds that have been named, Abbotswood excepted, the map shows a space of unbroken turf, about eight acres in extent, named Ellicottdale, with a winding margin, which is generally rocky and shady. This ground is now for the most part boggy, and its surface strewn with boulders. The design is to convert it into a meadow adapted to be used (in the manner of the Long Meadow of the Brooklyn Park) for lawn games, such as tennis and croquet. On the north side of it another small house is provided, at which parties wishing to play will obtain assignments of ground, and can leave outer garments and store or hire needed implements. The position of this house is in a recess of the margin, near a great knuckle of rock and a large oak tree on the east side.[*30]

---

[*] In Brooklyn nearly every religious organization of the city, Catholic and Protestant, has an annual picnic in the Park. During the last year permits were given to seven hundred and fifty parties to occupy ground for the purpose. Of these parties, three hundred numbered above one hundred and fifty persons each, and one twenty-five hundred persons. On the 24th of May last, twelve thousand children paraded on the Meadow under the observation of forty thousand spectators.[31] Seven hundred small parties of children applied for and obtained the use of swings under special superintendence. The Commissioners in their Annual Report say that the custom of taking children to a distance for picnics has been generally given up in Brooklyn, the use of the Park being found more

485

LAWN TENNIS IN ELLICOTTDALE, FRANKLIN PARK

The district last described and the circumjacent picnic groves may be approached by a walk coming from William Street. The entrance at this point is arranged with a view to a terminus and turning place of a street railroad; and to avoid compelling women and children to pass through a throng of carriages, the walk from it to Ellicottdale passes the circuit drive of the Park by a subway.

South of the Meadow last described a walk and a narrow branch of the main drive will be seen on the map winding up the steep and rocky woodside of Scarboro Hill to a resting-place upon the summit, where a temporary shelter for visitors now stands. Half-way up the hill, where a level shelf may be found under a steep ledge, buildings are shown marked "DAIRY." The Refectory, on the opposite side of the Park, being intended to supply more substantial refreshments, and to accommodate considerable numbers, the Dairy is designed, first, to provide the necessities of picnic parties in this part of the

---

convenient, cheaper, and safer.[32] The Park keepers, during the last year, returned to their parents fifty little children who had strayed away while playing in the Park. Permits were given to more than four hundred lawn tennis clubs, with an average membership of ten persons each, half of whom were young women, to occupy courts on the Park, and to many others for archery and croquet. These items show to some extent what an excellent, popular, innocent, and wholesome use is made of the Park during the hot months.

PLAYSTEAD AND PLAYSTEAD OVERLOOK SHELTER, FRANKLIN PARK

Park; second, to supply to all a few simple refreshments, such as are to be recommended for children and invalids, more especially fresh dairy products of the best quality. Cows are to be kept in an apartment separated from the main room by a glass partition, as in the famous exquisite dairies of Holland and Belgium;[33] and those who desire it are to be furnished with milk warm from the cow, as in St. James's Park, London.[34] Fowls are also to be kept and new-laid eggs supplied. Immediately east of the grove in which this house will stand lies the principal expanse of turf of the Country Park. This is intended to be cropped with sheep, and a court with sheds south of the dairy and connecting with its cow-house is for the folding of the flock at night. The district of which this establishment is the centre slopes toward the prevailing summer breeze; is sheltered on the north; is already agreeably wooded, and will be a place at which invalids and mothers with little children may be advised to pass the best part of the day.

B. *The Playstead.* This is a field of turf, thirty acres in extent (the most nearly flat ground on the property, little broken by rock), designed to be used for the athletic recreation and education of the city's schoolboys, for occasional civic ceremonies and exhibitions, and for any purpose likely to draw spectators in crowds. The ground about Ellicottdale not being adapted to accommodate many spectators, for example, and a crowd being undesirable at any point in the Country Park, if a parade of school children, such as occurs in the Brooklyn Park every year, were to be made, this would be the place for it. "The Overlook," on its left, is an elevated platform for spectators. It is eight hundred feet long, covering a barren ledge which would otherwise be disagreeably prominent. It is built of boulders obtained in clearing the Playstead, which are to be mainly overgrown with vegetation befitting the form and material of the structure, adapted to harmonize it with the natural scenery, and make it unobtrusive. The Overlook will be in the shade of existing trees during the afternoon, and spectators will look away from the sun. Among these trees, in a depression of the rocks, a rectangular block appears on the map. This stands for a structure which will supply a platform, to be covered by a roof, to serve as a retreat for visitors during summer showers, and in the basement a station for park keepers, with a lock-up, a woman's retiring-room, a coat-room, lavatory for players, and closets. An arched passage through the wall of the Overlook gives admission to it from the Playstead.

C. *The Greeting.* This division is to be wholly occupied by a series of parallel and contiguous drives, rides and walks, a double length of each, under rows of trees forming a Promenade, or Meeting Ground, of the Alameda type,[35] half a mile in length. Monumental, architectural, and various decorative adjuncts are here admissible, but not essential. There are suitable positions for statues, water-jets, "baskets" of flowers, bird-cages, etc. The Playstead and the Greeting are to be without underwood, and adapted with electric lighting for night as well as day use. Together they will form an unenclosed ground, reaching across the Park, nearly a mile in length.

D. *The Music Court.* A sylvan ampitheatre adapted to concerts.

E. *The Little Folks' Fair.* A division for childish entertainments, to be furnished with Swings, Scups, See-saws, Sand Courts, Flying Horses, Toy Booths, Marionettes, Goat Carriages, Donkey Courses, Bear Pits, and other amusing exercises and exhibitions, mostly to be provided by lessees and purveyors, to be licensed for the purpose.

F. *The Deer Park.* This will supply a range for a small herd to be seen from the Greeting. Most of the ground, owing to the thinness of the soil over a flattish ledge, cannot be adapted to occupation by the public, or to be planted, except at excessive expense.

G. *Refectory Hill.* A place for refreshments, to be principally served from the house shown, out of doors, under a large pergola, or vine-clad trellis, upon a terrace formed in the manner of the Playstead Overlook. From this terrace extensive sylvan prospects open, one of which will be later referred to. In the rear of the Refectory building, across a carriage-court, there is a circular range of horse-sheds for the use of visitors.

H. *Sargent's Field.* This ground being comparatively free from rock, and to be easily brought to a nearly level surface of good turf, tennis courts and a small ball ground may be provided in it; the object being to save players coming from the east from walking further to reach a playing ground, and to provide a place for players in general to go to, when on holidays the Playstead shall be reserved for other uses. Until found to be needed, it may with advantage be made a part of the Deer Park.

I. *Long Crouch Woods.* A rambling ground, with sheltered southwestern slopes, to be held subject to lease to a suitable organization for a Zoölogical Garden.

J.   *The Steading.*   A rocky, sterile knoll, reserved for the Commissioners' offices, within a screen of woods.

K.   *The Nursery.*   Depressed ground, to be used, when adequate drainage outlets for this part of the city shall have been provided, for a service garden.

Border Ground.   The streets by which the property taken for the park is bounded, are generally laid down on this plan as if moderately enlarged from the present thoroughfares (which at various points are but narrow lanes) and with a sidewalk on the park side, at such varying distances from the wheelway as may be necessary to avoid, in forming them, the destruction of fine trees and the cost of excessive grading. This arrangement is made practicable by setting back park fences and other obstructions fifty to eighty feet from the wheelways. In this way, also, a much larger widening of the wheelways than is suggested by the drawing can be made whenever public convenience will be served by it, without inordinate cost. In a few cases, for short distances, streets are shown as they may be improved by a slight taking of private land. This is to avoid heavy outlay for grading and the destruction of fine natural features on the park side of the present roads—as where, for example, rocky eminences of the park have their bases in the street. It is suggested that Canterbury Street should be widened ten feet opposite the park in order to avoid injury to the fine trees now growing in the park close to the street.

It is suggested on the drawing, also, that at the Williams Street entrance to the park the course of Forest Hills Street should be made more direct, and the grade improved by throwing it entirely into the park; and that some other variations from the present arrangements should be effected with a view to greater public convenience. To avoid interruption of pleasure travel by funeral processions, and to improve passage around the park, a short cross-road is planned opposite Forest Hills Cemetery, passing the park drive by a subway (LL in the index map). A short new street in extension of Sigourney Street is suggested to facilitate passage around the park. A small piece of land is proposed to be taken into the park at the corner of Sigourney Street to avoid awkward complications. The land proposed to be thrown out of the park property for all these purposes of street improvement is much larger than that to be taken in.

A direct approach to the park from Boylston Station of the Providence Railroad, is suggested by an extension of the present Boylston Street to the Playstead entrance. By this route a thousand men could, in half an hour, be transferred in a body from the Common to the Playstead.

IV.
A REVIEW OF THE GENERAL LANDSCAPE DESIGN.

SUITABLE provision has not commonly been made in the first laying out of a large city park for the purposes of the Greeting and the Music Court. Wherever it has not, ground that could only be poorly adapted to these purposes, and this at heavy cost, has generally come, in after years, to be used for them. It is best to avoid this danger. The best arrangements will be of a formal character, and these can be best provided on the site of Franklin Park, in the locality indicated, near the east corner. This not only has topographical advantages for the ends in view, but it is at such a distance from, and stands so related to, the Country Park, that great throngs upon it will in no wise disturb the desired serenity of the latter. The formal arrangement of trees within this division, and the small structures that will be required in the adjoining Little Folks' Fair Ground, will not be observable except upon close approach, the rows of trees being so flanked by the outer, naturally disposed trees that, seen at a short distance in connection with the latter, they will have the effect of a forest growth.

Setting aside these two features, which stand to the rest of the park somewhat in the relation of the dwelling-house to a private park, except that care is taken to place them in landscape obscurity, the landscape design may be understood by considering that the intention is to make no change in any of the present leading features of the ground except with the purpose of giving a fuller development, aggrandizement, and emphasis to what are regarded as the more interesting and effective existing elements of their scenery, and of taking out or subordinating elements that neutralize or conflict with those chosen to be made more of. This first, and second, the sequestration, as far as possible, of the scenery of the park so that the outer scenery, to be formed by the gradual growing of the city about it, and which will necessarily be conflicting in expression, sentiment, and association with it, may be kept out of sight.

The latter purpose accounts more particularly for the woods which, it will be seen, are intended to be formed where no woods now are, along the borders of the Country Park; and the further to promote seclusion, these and other border trees are to be imagined as furnished with underwood.

The woods of the Wilderness, after having been much thinned and trimmed with a view to the growth of the best of them in sturdier and more umbrageous forms, and to some degree of grouping and more harmonious companionship, are also to be interspersed with scattered, irregular thickets of low, sturdy bushes, not only for picturesqueness, but to keep the ground, in the more arid parts, better shaded and moister, hide its barrenness, check rushing movements of visitors, and prevent the trampling of the drier ground to dust.

Trees in the Greeting and Playstead are to be all of large growth, and

SCENE THE WILDERNESS, FRANKLIN PARK

high stemmed (like those now growing spontaneously upon the Playstead), leaving room for light and vision to range under their branches.

The slope west of Glen Lane where, near the entrance to the Country Park, drives, rides, and walks come together, is designed to be closely planted with low bushes (shown on the Commissioners' map, but not on the reduced reproductions), the object being to obscure the artificial features without making a screen between the natural features of the Playstead and Nazingdale. Looking in this direction from nearly all of the Playstead quarter there will be an open prospect extending to the Blue Hills of Milton, five miles away, the first mile within the park. The proposed plantation along the line of Canterbury Street will hide ordinary buildings that may hereafter be erected between the Park and the Blue Hills, leaving this permanently a broad, extended, purely rural prospect. The outlook westwardly from the hillside ending at the Refectory terrace will also extend permanently to a distant wooded horizon formed in part by the tree tops of Forest Hills Cemetery and in part by those of the Arboretum, two miles away, both these properties, though out of the Park, being preserved from building by legal enactments, and the objects to which they are devoted requiring that they should be always overgrown with trees.

NAZINGDALE IN THE COUNTRY PARK SECTION OF FRANKLIN PARK

The centre lines of the two broad fields of extended vision that have been pointed out, cross nearly at right angles, the point of their crossing being where the Ellicott and Nazing dales run together, nearly midway between the two hanging woods of Schoolmaster Hill and Abbotswood crags. This locality, being at the centre of the property, may be considered the pivot of the general landscape design. Looking in the general direction of the lines that have been defined as crossing it from either of four quarters of the Park, a moderately broad, open view will be had between simple bodies of forest, the foliage growing upon ground higher than that on and near the centre lines. From wherever these larger prospects open, the middle distances will be quiet, slightly hollowed surfaces of turf or buskets, bracken, sweet-fern, or mosses, the backgrounds formed by woodsides of a soft, even, subdued tone, with long, graceful, undulating sky lines, which, according to the point of view of the observer on the Park, will be from one to five miles away. Causeways, trees, rocks, and knolls interrupting or disturbing the unity, breadth, quiet, and harmony of these broader open passages of the Park scenery are to come away. There are none of importance that are not of artificial origin and easily removable. Trees wanting to the results proposed are to be planted and suitably developed by timely thinning.

A contrast to the fair open part of the Park which has been thus described will be found in following the circuit road where it is carried between Scarboro Hill and Rock Morton, Rock Milton, Waittwood, and Juniper Hill, through a part of the Wilderness, and between Hagborne and Schoolmaster

Hill, all of the localities named being rugged, rocky, and designed to be for the most part somewhat closely planted. A narrow road is thrown out from and brought back to the circuit drive, passing by winding courses among the rocks of the upper part of the Wilderness, by which a higher degree of this character of scenery (serving as a foil to that of the open dales) may be enjoyed than it would be practicable to offer in a broad and much used thoroughfare. The branch drive to the summit of Scarboro Hill, before described, will serve a similar episodical purpose.

Comparatively speaking, this western region is picturesque and romantic; and the design is to remove what is inconsistent with this character, and to add, develop, and expose elements favorable to it.

Drives and Walks. — The roads and walks of the park have been designed less with a purpose of bringing the visitor to points of view at which he will enjoy set scenes or landscapes than to provide for a constant mild enjoyment of simply pleasing rural scenery while in easy movement, and this by curves and grades avoiding unnecessary violence to nature. There is not a curve in the roads introduced simply for the sake of gracefulness. Every turn is suggested by natural circumstances. Notwithstanding the rugged surface of the larger part of the site, the circuit drive is at no point steeper than Bromfield Street between Washington and Tremont, its heaviest grade being one in twenty-five; nor are the branch drives at any point steeper than Brattle Street near Court, the steepest pitch being one in sixteen. The Greeting is an inclined plane with a fall from south to north of four feet in half a mile, which is about the same with that of State Street, or essentially level. These grades are obtained without much disturbance of natural features; the heaviest cutting is in continuance of an excavation already made for the quarrying of building stone, the heaviest filling through an adjoining rocky depression. As a general rule, the surface of the roads is to coincide closely with the natural surface, where the natural surface has been hitherto undisturbed. As far as practicable, it is designed to be slightly below it, so that the road may be less observable from a distance.

Riding Pad. — From Boylston Bridge, Back Bay Basin, there will be a shaded pad extending to the Park and through it from Forest Hills to the main entrance from the Playstead. It will be six miles long and from twenty-four to thirty feet wide. There is a double riding course in the Greeting, one division in the central alley, adjoining the carriage promenade, forty feet wide; the other in a side alley thirty feet wide.

Enclosures. — The Country Park is designed to be enclosed with a wall formed of the field stone drawn from its surface, the wall to be four feet high and similar to that first built for the New York Central Park. It is to be draped with vines, and, though not costly, will be perfectly suitable for a rural park. If, as the city is built about the park, a wall of more urban elegance is thought to be required, the stone of the original wall will be used for its foundation. The present enclosing wall of the Central Park, which is but a neat,

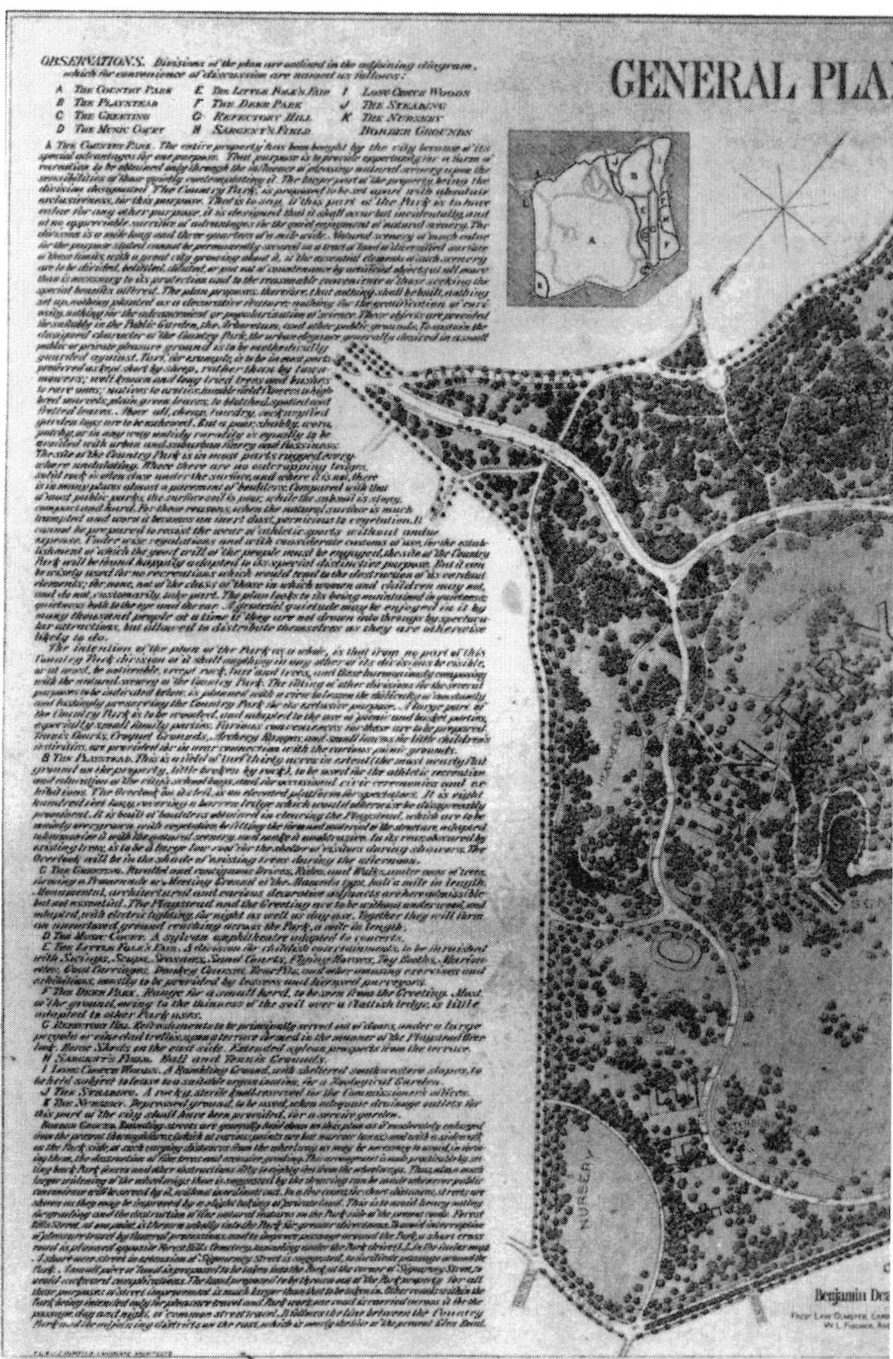

"GENERAL PLAN OF

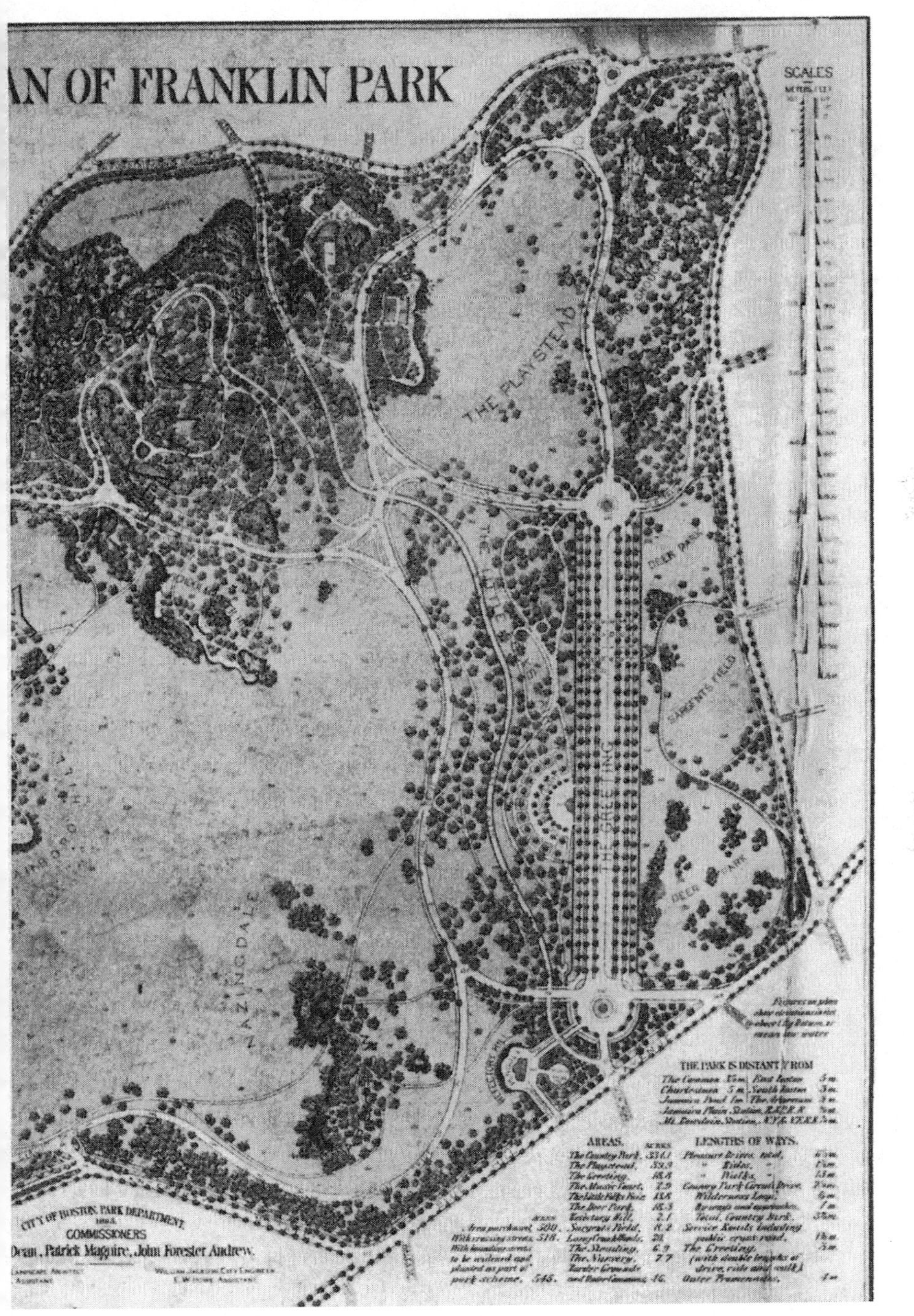

Franklin Park," 1885

unobtrusive piece of masonry four feet high on the street side, has probably cost half a million dollars, and is yet incomplete.[36]

Entrances. — Much pressure is generally brought to bear on those controlling a park to establish entrances with a view to neighborhood convenience and favorably to local real estate speculations. Every entrance is costly in various ways, and there should be none that can be avoided without incommoding the general public. The plan provides ten carriage and foot entrances and eight additional special foot entrances to the park as a whole, and five carriage entrances and two special foot entrances to the Country Park, all at points offering natural facilities of entrance and on easy grades. The average space between entrances is a little more than in the New York park, a little less than in most other large parks.

The drives within the park will be about 6 miles in length; bridle-roads, 2 miles; walks, 13 miles.

The Country Park will contain about 334 acres; Playstead, 40 (of playing ground about 30); Greeting, 19; Music Court, 3; Little Folks' Fair, 14; Deer Park, 18; Sargent's Field, 8; Long Crouch Woods, 20. (Boston Common is 48 acres in area; the Public Garden, 22. The "Green" of the New York Central Park is 16 acres in area; the "Ball Ground," 10; the "North Meadows," 19. The Central Park Mall is half the length of the Greeting.)

The area prepared for public recreation of Franklin Park will be 500 acres; (of the Central Park, 680; Brooklyn Park, 540. The drives of Central Park are 9 miles in length; riding pads, 5; walks, 28).

PART THIRD.
THE KEY OF A CONSERVATIVE PARK POLICY AND THE COST OF CARRYING OUT THE PLAN UNDER SUCH A POLICY.

THE project of a rural park for Boston has been more than twenty years under consideration. It has been advanced always deliberately and cautiously. The earlier leaders of the movement in its favor, most of whom have now retired from active interest in local public affairs, and many passed away, were, as a rule, no more anxious to press argument for a rural park than to press the importance of proceeding toward it by slow, frugal, and conservative methods. And this disposition has not only been constant, but has been growing in the community. There has hardly been a public utterance on the subject for several years past in which it has not been manifest. To carry out the scheme that was most prominently before the public fifteen years ago, would have cost more than double as much as to carry out that now in view. There is no party, faction, division, or class of citizens pressing the matter. There are no strong private interests engaged to force it.

The reasons why Boston should proceed in such an undertaking with exceptional caution are fully realized; yet, under the circumstances that have been stated, there can be little danger in pointing out the possibilities of an extravagant holding back.

Twenty years ago — even ten years ago — Boston was not conspicuously behind other cities in providing for the rural recreation of her citizens, but there was an apprehension that she might come to be, and a livelier conviction than at present that it would be a calamity. In 1869, Mr. Wilder, addressing a meeting called by the City Council, pointed out that Boston to sustain her reputation must not only have a park, but the first park in the country;[37] and seven years later Mr. Collins, at a meeting in Fanueil Hall, called to discuss the park question, asked, "Can Boston afford to be *less* comfortable to dwell in, *less* attractive, *less* healthy than her sister cities?"[38]

If such a question was then at all timely, it is now a great deal more so. There were then but two well advanced rural parks in America. There are now more than twenty. Every city that was then at a parallel stage in the discussion of a park project with Boston, now has that project in a large degree realized, and is enjoying the profits of it. There is not one city of America or of Northern Europe distantly approaching to rank with Boston in population, wealth, and reputation for refinement which, before unprovided with a park, has not gone further and moved more positively than Boston to make good the deficiency. London and Paris, Brussels and Liverpool have each within a generation twice doubled the area of their rural recreation grounds. All the cities of the British Islands thirty years ago possessed but four parks adapted to rural recreation; they now hold thirty, as large, on an average, as Franklin Park is intended to be.

There is an impression with some that the civilized world has been swept by a ruinous rage for parks. Not an instance is known of a park adapted to provide rural recreation that is not regarded by those who are paying for it as well worth all it has cost. No city possessed of a rural park regrets its purchase. During the last year New York City, which has had the largest and costliest experience of park-making of any in the world, has been purchasing land for six additional parks averaging six hundred acres each in area.[39] This after long and heated debate as to questions of extent and location, but upon the undisputed ground, so far as known, that the city's outlay for parks hitherto has had the effect of reducing rather than increasing taxation. Philadelphia has a park nearly six times as large as Franklin Park will be.[40] Chicago has six rural parks, in each of which large works of construction have been completed, and are found valuable beyond expectation.[41] Even smaller cities than Boston (as New Haven, Bridgeport, Albany, Buffalo, Montreal) have provided themselves with rural parks.[42]

It cannot be questioned that a rural park is rapidly coming to be ranked among the necessities of satisfactory city life, or that a city that offers simply promises or prospects in this respect stands at a certain commercial and financial disadvantage — a more decided disadvantage to-day, very much, than it did when Mr. Wilder or even when Mr. Collins advised attention to the danger.

At the present stage of the Franklin Park undertaking another consideration enforcing a like caution presents itself.

Land having been acquired, a plan for forming a park upon it adopted, operations of construction begun, and considerable resort being had to the ground, the affair is bound to grow in some fashion. And if the work is to be pursued in a desultory, intermittent, and unimpressive way, that fashion will not be altogether the fashion of a desirable rural park. The ground will be much disordered by the work, it will be streaked and scarred, dusty and muddy. There will be an increasing public use of it; the process of determining the customs of its use and the manner in which it is to be regarded by the people will be continuous, and every year something will be done toward an irretrievable settlement of its character.

In their examination of parks last summer, the Commissioners were struck with the different standard of keeping and of manners that had evidently become established on different parks. The keeping in one case was of a sort which in housekeeping might be described as squalid, and the manners largely loaferish. In another the keeping was comparatively neat and efficient, the manners decorous and civil. No matter what may be ultimately expended for a park, its value cannot fail to be largely determined by the expectations and usage of it into which the public is led in the early years of their resort to it.

Boston should continue to practice conservatism with respect to the park, but there cannot be a greater mistake than to suppose that conservatism will be concerned only to keep down the current cost of the work, and to this end will be engaged to impose checks on its progress at every opportunity. Conservatism cannot be concerned to have a state of things under which the leading aim of those in direction of the work is forced to be that of enlisting public support from year to year, by producing results from year to year that shall be immediately pleasing to superficial observation. It cannot fail to be concerned that the work shall be directed with a wise regard to what experience may have taught as to conditions of lasting, growing, and substantial value in works elsewhere of the same leading purpose.

The cardinal requirement of economy in obtaining such conditions has never yet been realized by the public in the early stages of a park work, but it is perfectly plain to anyone who has so closely followed the history of a number of parks as to be able to compare marked differences in methods of management and the respective results obtained. It would take too much space to present an extended comparative statement of this kind, but the lesson it would present may be indicated by reference to a few typical facts.

To realize the full bearing of those that will be cited, it must be kept freshly in mind, first, that the only justification of the cost of a large park near a growing city is the necessity of spaciousness to the production of rural scenery.

Second, it must be remembered that the choicest rural park scenery is that which, other things being equal, has been longest growing, and which has the least of the rawness and smartness of new constructions, and the weak puerilities of new plantations.

Third, it is to be kept in mind that the oldest part of the oldest rural park in the country is not yet half grown, and the primary construction of some of its parts is not even yet begun.

Take, then, this oldest park and see by what courses it has come to be what it is, and has been made to cost what it has.

Its site was determined almost by accident; no one, when it was first defined in the bill which became the act establishing it, giving the least thought to the question whether it was well adapted to the purpose of a large park; no one concerned having any clear notion what that purpose might be. In fact the idea in mind was simply this: "The great cities of the old world have large areas called parks, and they are popular. Let us have a great area to be called a park. To neutralize conflicting local jealousies let us have it as nearly as possible in the centre of the city's territory." That was thought to be the common sense of the matter. Not the slightest inquiry was made as to what sort of land there might be at this central point, and so thoughtlessly were the boundaries determined that upwards of a million dollars were judiciously spent after a few years, to secure an economical modification of them.[43] Even since this modification a great sum has been expended in retaining walls and other adjustments between the park and its bounding streets. A few pages further on, official statistics will be quoted, further illustrating the costliness of this common sense proceeding, about which it may be as well to mention that there was nothing peculiarly American or democratic. The Emperor of France began the Bois de Boulogne in the same spirit, trusting to common sense in a matter which was not one for common sense but for careful study and foresighted regulation; fell into blunderings even more humiliating than those of New York, and was obliged to make an abrupt change of plan after his work had been put well under way.[44]

There is no important general public purpose now served, or likely to be served in the future, by the New York Park, for which if ground had been well selected, and if every step in the subsequent operations had been well devised with reference to it, and pursued without unnecessary complexity or confusion, provisions of equal value might not have been made at half the cost of those now possessed by the city.

The degree of public unpreparedness at the outset to sustain such a course, however, may be inferred from the fact that one of the leading newspapers at that time treated the undertaking as an affair for the benefit of rich men — an affair of fashionable luxury — while another thought that any park in New York would be so entirely taken possession of by the low, rowdy, and ruffianly element of the population, that respectable people would avoid it, and that a woman would not be able to enter it without compromising her reputation.[45] Each of these views turns out to have been as wrong as possible. There is not a church in the city in which rich and poor come together as satisfactorily to both. And for years after it came into use there was not a public street of the city in which a woman or girl was as secure from rudeness.

The next most instructive circumstance in its history, as far as it concerns Boston at this time, is the gradual advance of public opinion toward a correct understanding of the conditions of the park's value. Such an understanding has not yet, after twenty-nine years, been universally attained. The papers of the city are at this moment denouncing a proposition, made in good faith and urged with elaborate arguments, for introducing an important new feature into the plan of the park.[46] An interview is publicly reported (in the Sun, January 15) with a prominent citizen, who urges in counter-argument not the waste that would be involved in the value of the park as a place prepared at great expense for the ready enjoyment of rural scenery, but what is assumed to be the more practical objection of the contraction of areas available for games, a use of the park in which with the present area available for it when the park is in largest use, but one in several hundred of its visitors takes part.*[47]

*The New York _Tribune_, in a leading article of the 10th January, commenting on the proposition, classes it with a thousand others that one after another have been urged upon the Park Commissioners, some of which it recalls as follows: "Persons of quality who delight in steeple-chasing, and those who pursue the fleet anise-seed bag to its lair, have had an eye upon the rolling meadows and dense coppices of the Park as an inviting field for manly sport. Commissioners have been petitioned to throw open the Park as a parade ground for our citizen soldiery, and space has been asked for tents and enclosures for popular exhibitions, circuses, shooting-matches, and trials of strength and skill. Eminent educators have urged that the Park should be planned on the model of a map of our native land, with miniature states, lakes, and rivers, with every physical and geological feature complete, so that the children of the public schools could be turned loose thereon to study geography in its most attractive form. It has been proposed that each religious sect should be invited to build places of worship there; that one section should be set apart for a World's Fair, and another section as a den for wild beasts, and again that a vast building should be erected there as a sample-room and advertisement for all the wares the merchants of the city have to sell; that the lakes should be enlarged so as to float a full-rigged ship where the great maritime city of the continent could train sailors for our merchant marine; that it should be transmuted into a burial-place for the country's distinguished dead, an experimental form in the interest of scientific agriculture, and a permanent Metropolitan Fair Ground.

"Now, if the Park is only a big scope of unimproved ground, it is natural that

Twice in the history of this park, after enormous expenditures had been made upon it with the stated purpose of excluding urban and securing rural scenery, this purpose has been distinctly and publicly repudiated; in one case, the Superintendent for the time being, explaining to a reporter of the press that his leading object was a display of architectural and urban elegance, and that he had removed certain trees because they prevented visitors passing through the park from seeing the stately buildings growing up outside of it.

But although these incidents may seem to argue otherwise, no one can have long been a reader of New York newspapers without knowing that the public opinion of the city has of late years been often aroused to prevent various proceedings upon the park, running counter to the purpose of rural recreation, that earlier would have been permitted to pass without objection. For example, when the trees of the park were yet saplings, and its designed rural scenery wholly undeveloped, the suggestion that the most central and important position upon it should be given to a public building was received with no apparent disfavor, and one of the Commissioners of the park declared that any ground the promoters of the undertaking might desire would be gladly assigned to it. Fortunately, because of hard times, the scheme fell through. Ten years later, a monumental building was actually given a site upon the park, but it was one in which the structure would not interfere with any extended view, or be seen from a distance, and even this concession did not pass without much remonstrance.[48] When the next scheme of the class was disclosed, though coupled with many most attractive incidental propositions, skillfully presented, and supported by eminent citizens, so much popular indignation was soon manifested that in response to petitions a bill was rapidly advanced in the legislature to make it illegal for the Commissioners to entertain the proposition, and would have passed had not the head of the movement publicly and apologetically announced the abandonment of the idea.[49] At the present time, a proposition similar to that once similarly accepted in the case of the Museum of Art, no matter how highly its objects were valued, and no matter how worthy a body of public-spirited citizens were backing it, would be less agreeable to the public opinion of New York than would be a proposition to build a public hospital in the middle of the Common to that of Boston.

In the early days of one American park a proposed ordinance to establish a Small-Pox Hospital in its midst was gravely debated in the City

---

people of different tastes should desire to pre-empt a quarter section here and there for the particular business or pleasure in which they are chiefly interested. For this reason, the people who drive their own carriages, or are able to hire one occasionally, have clamored for widening the wheelways, to give them ample space to roll around and be seen. Other citizens, in less fortunate circumstances, have asked that a street railroad be run up through the centre of the Park, so that they might view it from the economical and democratic horse-car."[50]

Council, being advocated on the ground that there was plenty of unoccupied room there, that no private interest would suffer from it, and that nobody wanted it anywhere else.[51] Many occurrences showing similar public indifference, in the early work of a park, to the essential conditions of its ultimate value, might be cited. At least four times in the history of one park obstructive disturbances of natural scenery have been established, and afterwards, in respect to a rising public sentiment, have been removed. Twice these have been works of alleged art presented to the city and received and set up with acclamation.

Is Boston quite safe from falling into similar costly courses? Has she been so in the past? Let the history of the little but important ground called the Public Garden be considered.

The design first made public for this ground, prepared by an eminent and popular architect, had in view a highly decorative garden, with many beds of flowers and ornamental foliage, architectural basins of water, jets, fountains, and other richly artificial embellishments.[52] The weight of influence in the matter, however, tended toward a parklet in the natural style, simple, quiet, and in a degree sequestered. The plan at length adopted was devised mainly with reference to such a ground, with a slight compromise manifested in a few scattered features which would have been more congruous with a decorative garden. But the work had not gone far before objections were urged to its more important naturalistic features, and several of these, one after another, were modified or radically changed. Large mounds of earth at first formed in accordance with the design were afterwards removed. What was intended to be a rural lakelet with natural borders was changed to a basin with formally curving outlines and a rigid edging of stone. After many years and large outlays made with a plan thus fluctuating in the spirit of its details, the purpose, originally rejected, of a splendid urban garden, with all practicable display of art, was fully revived, and has been gradually carried out as far as it could be without a complete structural transformation of the site, but necessarily under great disadvantages from the necessity of working upon the timbers of a wreck originally modelled with a wholly different ideal. It cannot be doubted that, had all the work from the beginning been undeviatingly directed with reference to the essence of the present leading motives in the management of the ground, more valuable results would have been attained, at much less cost.

Whatever the difficulties may be of avoiding another experience of the same kind, but on a much larger scale, it is best to look them fairly in the face. It is best to beat them, and beat them now, at the start. That it is practicable to do so, and at moderate cost, may be established, if a single instance can be shown in which a city has been able to secure a steady, straightforward, business-like pursuit of the proper purpose of such a park.

Testimony of such an instance that cannot be gainsaid has been furnished the Commissioners from Buffalo, a city that has not earned a reputation for honesty and efficiency of administration exceeding that of Boston.

It is believed that the difficulties of securing a sound public opinion were at the outset much greater in Buffalo than they are in Boston. There was a more general and a more heated apprehension among the tax-payers that the undertaking of a "big park" would be excessively costly. More ignorance and confusion of mind prevailed as to its proper purposes. The history of what has since occurred is summarized in the statement below. Of the gentlemen signing this statement, five have been Mayors of Buffalo during the period in which the park work has been in progress, three Judges of its Courts, three presidents of the Board of Aldermen, five members of Congress, several members of the State Legislature, Commissioners of the Park, leading editors, bankers, and merchants, and heads of the working organization of each party, and of each faction of party of any importance in local politics, a fact in itself evincing the remarkable popularity earned by the management to be described.

A BRIEF HISTORY OF THE RURAL PARK OF BUFFALO, WITH REFERENCE TO ITS MANAGEMENT, COST, AND VALUE.

"There were at the outset many grounds of objection to the site selected for the main Park of Buffalo. Parts of it were rocky and bare of vegetation; other parts swampy and most unattractive. It was at the opposite end of the city from its populous quarter, and more than three miles from its centre. Hence the project had to encounter a strong sectional jealousy, and for this and other reasons met with determined opposition, which succeeded in reducing the area originally intended to be taken—a misfortune since deeply regretted even by those to whom it was due. After the work of construction was entered upon, repeated efforts were made to arrest it; to alter the plans; to introduce new features, and to compel the adoption of different methods of operation.

"In full view of the acknowledged objections to the site, it was selected as, on the whole, the best that could be found for the purpose exclusively had in view. This was to provide recreation for the people of the city through the enjoyment of simple, rural, park-like scenery. The ground was laid out upon a plan that made everything subordinate to this purpose.

"The work was organized with exclusive reference to the steady and methodical carrying out of the plan. The heads of the organization were drawn from a similar work in another city, and were at once familiar with their duties, disciplined and co-operative. No change in the staff of the superintendence has since been made, except as the work has advanced to points where permanent reduction could be afforded. The present General Superintendent has been Superintendent from the start.[53] In the city reform movement that first brought Grover Cleveland as mayor of the city prominently before the public, no occasion for reform or improvement was found in the park work.[54] No change of men or methods was made or suggested to be desirable. The work has been pursued steadily and without the slightest deviation from the plan upon which it was started. As it advanced and the intentions of the plan approached realization, the park grew in favor. Opposition to it gradually died out. It is now universally popular, and with no class more so than the frugal, small house owning tax-payers, who constitute an unusual proportion of the population of the city.

"The cost of the work has been much less than was predicted by the opponents of the undertaking, and even less than its promoters expected it to be. It is regarded as moderate relatively to the return already realized. It is believed that through the increased attractiveness of the city as a place of residence, the rise in the value of property adjacent to the park and its approaches, and the additional taxable capital invested in land and buildings in the vicinity of these improvements, the outlay for the park has lightened the burden of the tax-payers. The city has recently obtained an act of the legislature authorizing a portion of the land originally thrown out to be purchased and added to the park.[55] Its market value is now estimated to be from four to five times as much as when thrown out. Broad avenues from different directions have been opened, and a street railroad constructed expressly for the use of visitors to the park. Its value is largely increasing every year. The city is now proud of it and grateful for it.

"But its promoters had ultimate results in view, which cannot be fully realized during the lifetime of the present generation or of the next. As the growth of its plantations develops, as the city extends to its borders and becomes densely settled at the centre, the attractions, the accessibility, and the benefits to the community to be derived from the park, will correspondingly increase. Its chief value lies in its ever-growing capabilities of usefulness in the future, as the city grows in wealth and population.

(Signed)

"PASCAL P. PRATT.　　　　　　　S. S. JEWETT.
SOLOMON SCHEW.　　　　　　　EDWARD BENNETT.
J. MOTHAN SCOVILLE.　　　　　JOHN M. FARQUHAR.
JAS. SHELDON.　　　　　　　　EDGAR B. JEWETT.
W. S. BISSELL.　　　　　　　　FRANCIS H. ROOT.
ALEX. BRUSH.　　　　　　　　GIBSON I. WILLIAMS.
JAMES D. WARREN.　　　　　　R. R. HEFFORD.
HENRY A. RICHMOND.　　　　　CHAS. BECKWITH.
SHERMAN S. ROGERS.　　　　　WM. F. ROGERS.
PHILIP BECKER.　　　　　　　JOHN B. SACKETT.
DANIEL N. LOCKWOOD.　　　　L. P. DAYTON.

JAMES M. SMITH.
JNO. B. WEBER.

JAMES MOONEY.
WM. FRANKLIN."[*][56]

The estimate to be presented of the cost of preparing Franklin Park for public use, will be so much less than has been generally anticipated by those familiar with the cost of parks elsewhere, that it will be received with incredulity. Something, therefore, should be said in explanation of it.

First, it may be observed that more than two-thirds of the cost is calculated to be for the construction of roads, walks, concourses and other structures, for the estimates of which the City Engineer is responsible, and that the entire estimate is made in the same manner as that, of about the same amount, prepared for the Department with respect to the work of the Back Bay Basins, which work after a progress of seven years is likely to be completed within the estimate.[57]

That it is possible to meet Mr. Wilder's[58] demand that the Boston park should be the first park in the country, meaning the first in respect to adaptation to provide city people with rural recreation, is largely to be accounted for by the fact that the site was selected discriminatingly for that purpose.

The advantage gained by this circumstance has already been partly suggested in the statement that the cost of piecing out the New York park has been considerably more than a million dollars. It may be added that the annexations to the primary scheme in the case of the Brooklyn and the Philadelphia parks, made in each case with a view to rural advantages, have been much larger though less costly. In Brooklyn the original site was greatly modified by a process of exchange.[59]

But a more important part of Boston's economical advantage may be inferred from the statement made in the Third Annual Report of the New York Department of Parks that the modifications of the surface of the site of the Central Park had involved the lifting and readjustment of its entire surface to an average depth of nearly four feet, and of the material moved that nearly half a million cubic yards had been originally in the form of solid ledge rock, twenty thousand barrels of gunpowder having been used for breaking it

---

[*] Since the above paper was signed, a change has occurred in the city government of Buffalo, and the new Mayor,[60] addressing the new Council, has said: "We have a park system of which we may be justly proud, and there will be very little complaint of the cost so long as the parks are kept in order and made accessible." In a later document, signed by the Mayor and the Park Commissioners, the following congratulatory statement appears: "In looking back over the period since the establishment of the park scheme, the retrospect cannot fail to be exceedingly gratifying. The cost of the parks has been in a large measure compensated by taxes receivable from increased valuation of adjacent property, to say nothing of the health-giving recreation and pleasure the parks afford to thousands who visit them during the summer months. With the rapid increase of our city in wealth and in density of population, have grown up both the need for such recreation *and the taste to enjoy it.*"[61]

out.[62] More than two hundred thousand cubic yards of first-class solid mason work have been laid on the Central Park, a large part under ground and most of it in retaining walls that would have been unnecessary to the proper purposes of a park in a situation as well adapted to those purposes as is that of Franklin Park.

A considerable part of the outlay for most parks has been made for materials which the site for Franklin Park supplies. The stone and gravel of the Chicago parks, for example, is brought to them from distant quarries and pits, and the cost of transportation is not a small matter. The same is the case at Detroit. The gravel used in the New York and Brooklyn parks has cost twice as much per yard as that to be used in Franklin Park. (It must be said that it is a better sort of gravel.) In Franklin Park there are no difficulties of drainage to be overcome by costly expedients (there are thirty-three miles of sewers in the Central Park). No costly works of damming and puddling or concreting will be required as has been the case elsewhere. And as an illustration of the advantages of its site in these particulars (the plan being adjusted to it) it may be said that the conditions in question of the five hundred acres of Franklin Park are directly the reverse of those which the city has for seven years past been gradually and slowly and at great cost overcoming in the one hundred acres of the Back Bay Basin.

The work required to carry out the plan of Franklin Park can nearly all be done, after practicable training, by a force recruited from the class of working-men who command but the lowest wages, and who are most liable to fall into a condition requiring charitable assistance from the city. More than nine-tenths of the needed outlay would be in wages to citizens. The few manufactured articles necessary would nearly all be manufactured in the city. Not one per cent. of the entire expenditure contemplated would be required for what are commonly called park and garden decorations. The larger part would be for substantial matters, to endure, and generally to gain, in value, for centuries.

Estimates of cost, to have any value, must be based on some definite understanding as to the manner in which the work is to be conducted, the adequacy and what in military operations is called the solidity of the organization, the thoroughness of the discipline, the time within which the work is to be completed, and, above all, the degree in which steady, orderly progress, smoothly interlocking in all parts, can be calculated on.

The work will proceed much more economically with a moderately large force, if kept "well in hand," than with a small one. The reason can easily be seen. It is to be mainly a transfer of material, — stone, sand, gravel, earth, soil, peat. To proceed with the work at one point certain materials are to be sent away that are wanted for the work at another point, and certain materials are required that are to be taken out at yet another. Unless a force large enough to keep a considerable system of exchanges in operation is employed, the same materials will need to be rehandled, perhaps repeatedly.

It is to be assumed that the work of construction will be completed within a period of six years; that it will be carried on with as large a force as may be best; that advantage may be taken of favorable seasons and favorable markets, and that it will be placed and maintained from the start in all respects upon a soundly economical basis.

The work to be done during the period stated is not to include the public roads and their borders outside the park, as this would extend it beyond the territory under the Commissioners' control. It does not include fountains, sculptural or other purely decorative works that may be thought desirable later, upon the Greeting, or in connection with the gateways, nor does it include movable furniture. But it includes all that is necessary to the making of the park in substantial accordance with its general plan as it has been set forth.

As thus proposed, the work may be expected to cost not exceeding fifteen hundred thousand dollars.*

Maintenance Cost. — The question of the economy of what is proposed in the plan for a park is less a question of what the work of construction will cost than of what ever afterwards will be required for reconstructions, repairs, and for pursuing a system of maintenance adapted to secure its intended qualities of beauty, and keep it in suitable order for its intended uses. An explanation of the character of the plan in this respect will therefore be offered.

Rural parks may be excessively costly of maintenance, either by setting the standard so low that visitors gain but little rural refreshment from them, or by setting it so high that it cannot be lived up to, and they become forlorn through shabby gentility. In some parks both errors are illustrated, high keeping being apparently attempted at some points as a compensation for general gracelessness and dowdiness, with a result like that from putting a few bits of bravery upon a meanly dressed and dirty person. Nearly all American Park Commissioners apologize for the condition of some parts of their work, stating that they are not allowed funds enough to keep them in good order throughout.

In a considerable part of one park examined by the Boston Commissioners last summer, they found roads in very rough condition and dusty gravel walks in such bad repair that they had actually gone out of use, and

---

* The following is a comparative approximate statement of the cost of preparing several large public grounds: —

Central Park	per acre,	$14,000
Brooklyn Park	" "	9,000
Buffalo Park	" "	1,400
Back Bay Basin and Promenade, as estimated, and in large part realized	" "	14,000
Franklin Park, estimated	" "	2,900[63]

visitors were trying to walk in lines parallel with them, some making a crooked way among trees and bushes, or over what had once been turfed ground, some turning out upon the wheelway. A family party was seen moving along the ruts of the dusty road, the father dragging a baby wagon, the mother in trepidation lest they should be run over, and the entire party evincing anything but the quieting and restful pleasure that they would have had in a park suitably fitted and kept. Elsewhere they saw lawns from which the turf had wholly disappeared, dry brooks and fountains, green stagnant waters, dilapidated and rotting rustic structures, trees with dead branches, flower-beds gray with dust, set in coarse seedy grass half trodden out, opposite a sign, "Keep off the Grass." They saw a large and substantially fine house, of which the details and furniture were so out of repair that the public had been for some time excluded from it, and its windows appeared to be targets for ambushed boys. The explanation in every case was that the city was unwilling to suitably carry out and sustain what had been undertaken.

It is difficult to make comparative statements of the cost of maintenance of different classes of public grounds. In most cases it is found to vary widely from year to year, and this capriciously, accordingly as successive city councils are disposed. The appropriation for one year has in several cases been but half that for others. Accounts are kept upon different bases.

But omitting police, museum and menagerie expenses it may, be roughly reckoned that the annual running expenses of a park of the extent of Franklin Park, if laid out, stocked, and maintained in the manner of the Public Garden of Boston, or of any much decorated, garden-like ground, would be about $500,000; of the Central Park, New York, $160,000; Brooklyn Park, $80,000; Buffalo Park, $40,000.

The plan adopted by the Commissioners for Franklin Park is one that, when the designed plantings have been well established, will require comparatively little fine garden work, no exotic or fine decorative gardening, no glass, no structures of an unsubstantial class, and few of any kind subject to fall into serious disrepair, except roads and walks. All walls and roofs are to be of stone, tile, or slate; all guard rails and seat supports of stone or wrought iron. The economy of substantial work in all such matters may be seen in the fact that of upwards of forty arches and bridges on the Central Park built more than twenty years ago, all but three were structures of stone, brick, or iron. As a matter of alleged economy, three were built with timber superstructures. Each one of these three has been at times closed for use because of disrepair, each has been entirely rebuilt, and one twice rebuilt; each has already cost more than a substantial structure would have cost, and no one of them is now in a satisfactory condition. The others remain perfectly sound, and with but one important exception have been in continuous service. The exception is an iron bridge with a wood flooring.[64] This has been several times closed for painting and the relaying of the wood-work. A similar story could be told of other structures; and the moral could be enforced by reference to every class of work done on the park. Its entire history is an indication of the economy of using as sterling masonry and thorough, exacting professional superintendence in park work, as in water-works, sewers, and monumental buildings. If the Commissioners could have taken a different view of their duty, which for the moment would possibly be a more popular view, the estimate they have presented might have been reduced.

To restate briefly the lesson in conservatism most important for Boston to learn from the experience of other cities in park-making, it is this: —

That those in charge of a park work may proceed economically and with profit they must be able to proceed with confidence, method and system, steadily, step after step, to carry to completion a well-matured design. Until the point of completion is reached the work of each year must be the carrying out of work prepared for in the previous year, and the preparation of work to be done the following year. Plans laid with an economical purpose in this respect must not be held subject at any moment to be nullified, or hastily and radically modified, even under worthy impulses of economy.

PART FOURTH.
OF THE DIFFICULTIES OF PURSUING A SOUND POLICY, AND THE MEANS BY WHICH THEY ARE TO BE OVERCOME.

THE difficulties in question are difficulties of securing a sound controlling public opinion and of avoiding a costly accommodation to demands based on mistaken or inadequate impressions of what is desirable in the business of a rural park.

As the notes to follow will be somewhat discursive, and the facts to be stated will have bearings other than those indicated by the headings under which they will be arranged, several master difficulties may be here mentioned to which it is believed that all will relate.

First, the difficulty of realizing the importance of a park work, from which follows the danger that details of serious consequence to the community may be settled too lightly.

Second, the difficulty of understanding the essential economies of so intangible a commodity as that of rural scenery.

Third, the difficulty of realizing how largely the interest of the community as a whole lies in parts and elements of a park that are of little direct personal interest to those who make the largest figure in it, and who have the most direct influence upon the conduct of the work.

Fourth, the difficulty, no matter how important the results of the work to be soon obtained may be, of realizing how immeasurably more important are those to come later.

Fifth, the difficulty to most men of realizing how greatly the cost of suitably preparing a park is to be increased by frequent shifts of responsibility, unsteady courses, breaks of system and of routine methods.

I.
OF THE SUPREME IMPORTANCE THAT A LARGE PARK MAY COME TO HAVE IN THE HISTORY OF A CITY.

IT is contrary to habitual modes of thought to take due account of the comparative economico-political importance of what is at stake in a large park undertaking — to recognize how costly a park may be, otherwise than through the taxation which it directly calls for; how useful it may be in wholly different ways from those most readily and customarily thought about. How it has come to be so will be partly explained later. The purpose of what is immediately to follow is to give a single reason for soliciting a more thorough consideration of various aspects of the subject than the occasion will be generally thought to require.

It is to be considered, to begin with, how much less likely than we are apt to suppose, the larger fortune of a city is, in these days, to turn controllingly and lastingly upon the local legislation that from year to year is led up to and brought about through an activity of local public opinion favorable to its object: how much more the historic course of the city is commonly determined by a discovery or an invention, for example, made by someone having no personal interest or direct part in it, as of a cotton-gin, a steel process, or of gold in a river-bed.

When currents of such exterior sources have been established, the local defects of a city, with reference to them, are apt sooner or later, at more or less cost, to be remedied. The methods by which needed means for this purpose shall ultimately be reached, may vary radically, as, with reference to the currents of modern oceanic commerce, in the landing and loading facilities of the ports, respectively, of Liverpool, New York, and New Orleans. But the tendency to come nearer to a common standard of utility in essential results is so strong that if at one time a mistake of dealing inadequately with a problem is made, while the blunder will be costly, it is but a question of time when a sufficiently courageous and well-considered effort is to follow and sweep it away and build anew on firmer ground.

It may be considered, also, how much more cities gain on an average in all that makes them converging points of the growth of nations in population, wealth, and refinement, from general currents of scientific progress by which all the world benefits, than from political proceedings of local origin and special local application.

It is, for instance, through falling into such a current that the ancient city of Cairo has come to be so relieved from its former annual devastations by the Plague, that the life of its people has come to be twice as long as it was in the first half of the century, and the value of life in it has been more than doubled through avoidance of pain, anxiety, and sadness, and the steadier profits of all industry.[65] It is by falling into such a current that most of our southern cities have come to keep at home and in active employment during the entire summer a large part of the population, that would otherwise go out from them at the cost of a general suspension of many profitable branches of their trade, and nearly all important productive industry.[66]

Through the tendency thus illustrated, to work up to standards mainly provided by agencies acting on public opinion from without, and established no one quite knows how, it occurs, notwithstanding the great differences of origin and historical development, of early social circumstances, of climate, of back-country conditions, and of resources of wealth and products to be dealt with, that schools, churches, hospitals, courts, police, jails, methods of fire protection, methods in politics, in benevolence and almsgiving, in journalism, in banking and exchange, are rapidly growing to be closely alike in San Francisco and in Boston.

The change by which this similitude comes about, goes on about as rapidly in the older as in the younger city. In many small ways Boston is taking up customs originating on the Pacific. In dealing with its sewerage problem, Boston availed itself of Mr. Chesborough's experience in Chicago,[67] as well as of Mr. Bazalgette's in London;[68] and the Boston Police Commissioners are this winter seeking to engraft on their system, which is of direct descent from Peel's system for London, a scion grown in Chicago.[69] In Europe there is quite as evident a gravitation to American methods as in America to European methods. Paris is just now looking to gain something from observation of the Boston Fire Department, and something from the experience of Memphis in sewerage. One European government has within five years sent expeditions of experts in three different branches of science applicable to the administration of cities, to see by what, in the recent experience of Boston, its people might profit. At least two other European governments have sent skilled agencies here for the same purpose.

Looking for important advantages which one city may possess permanently over another in respect to the constant value of life of those who are to dwell in it, in scarcely anything, perhaps in nothing, will the estate of cities, as it may be affected by local wisdom, effort, and timely legislation, be found to vary more and more lastingly than in the matter of public grounds. In scarcely anything is the general drift of civilized progress to be less depended on to set right the results of crude and shortsighted measures. In scarcely anything, therefore, to be determined by local public opinion acting influentially upon local legislation and administration, is a city as likely to be so much made or marred for all its future as in proceedings in prosecution of a park project.

To many who have not been closely following the history of park enterprises, and tracing cause and effect in connection with them, this will seem to be the assertion of a man with a hobby. But let what has been occurring at the port of New York, in a large degree under the direct observation of thousands of the more active-minded business men of Boston, be thoroughly reviewed, and it will not be found unreasonable.

First, let it be reflected how little of permanent consequence in the history of New York has come about through the spontaneous movements of local public opinion as reflected in legislation during the last thirty years, of which the broad, essential results were not almost a matter of course. It has been little more than a question of time, for instance, when and how the port should be provided with docks, basins, elevators, and better general water-side facilities for commerce; when certain streets should be widened; when rapid transit for long, and street cars for short, transportation, a civilized cab system, telegraphs, telephones, and electric lights should be introduced, better conveyances across the rivers gained, better accommodations for courts provided, the aqueduct enlarged, public schools multiplied, graded, and made more educational, industrial and night schools started, public museums of art and natural history founded, the militia made more serviceable, the volunteer fire department superseded, and a strong police force organized.

There is nothing of general and permanent consequence in all that has been gained in these particulars that could have been more than delayed and made foolishly costly by careless, capricious, or perverse local public opinion and corresponding legislation. The same general currents of civilization that have brought what has been gained to New York in these respects have brought results answering the same general purposes to Philadelphia and Boston, to Cincinnati and to Montreal. Or, if not fully so in each case, every live man in those cities looks to see like results reached in a few years, — makes his business plans, builds his house, orders his investments, educates his children, with reference to them. The general plan of the combined city of New York harbor, the position severally, for example, of its domestic, its manufacturing, and its trade quarters, has been very little determined as the result of local legislation or of a settled purpose of public opinion. Such changes of domestic and social habits as have occurred are much less to be attributed to any of these improvements than to circumstances governing the general increase and distribution of wealth throughout the world, to the general advances of science, and to fashions originating in Europe.

But now let it be considered how it has been with regard to what has occurred through the park enterprises. Each of the two large parks that during the same period have been set a-growing through local agitation and the care-less legislation it has obtained, has had more such effect than all the other measures of that class together. The Central Park blocks fifty streets that, had it not been formed, would now be direct channels of commerce and of domestic movement from river to river. It takes out of the heart of the city two square miles of building-space, as completely and as permanently as a gulf formed by an earthquake could do, and for several square miles about this place it determines an occupation of land and a use of real estate very different from what would have been otherwise possible. Its effect on social customs may be illustrated by the statement that to enjoy the use of the park, within a few years after it became available, the dinner hour of thousands of families was permanently changed, the number of private carriages kept in the city was increased tenfold, the number of saddle horses a hundredfold, the business of livery stables more than doubled, the investment of many millions of private capital in public conveyances made profitable.

It is often asked, How could New York have got on without the park? Twelve million visits are made to it every year. The poor and the rich come together in it in larger numbers than anywhere else, and enjoy what they find in it in more complete sympathy than they enjoy anything else together. The movement to and from it is enormous. If there were no park, with what different results in habit and fashions, customs and manners, would the time spent in it be occupied. It is often said that the park has made New York a different city. If it has not done so already, it surely will soon have made New York a city differing more from what it would have been but for the park than Boston differs either from San Francisco or from Liverpool.

And the park of Brooklyn, while it has not as yet equally changed the destiny of this branch of the town, is sure, as the city grows, to be a matter of the most important moulding consequence, — more so than the great bridge; more so than any single affair with which the local government has had to do in the entire history of the city.

Similar results may be seen, or surely foreseen, from the new parks in each case of Philadelphia, of Chicago, of Buffalo, of St. Louis, of San Francisco.

Not less significant illustrations of the general fact may be found abroad, in Paris and Liverpool, for instance and in Melbourne, Australia.

But, it may be asked, if the Central Park had not been formed as it was, would not another park have been formed before this time? No doubt; but if so, the results of a different park would have been more importantly different from those that have followed the Central Park than the results of any determination of the city's fortune equally open to be made thirty years ago, through the action of its local government, in any matter of architecture, of engineering, of jurisprudence, or of popular education.

But before the comparative importance of what is to be determined by a park work in the history of a city can be at all realized, a very different view must be taken from that which is common of the irretrievableness of any blundering in its direction.

II.
THE ELEMENT OF LASTINGNESS AS AFFECTING THE IMPORTANCE OF WHAT IS TO BE DETERMINED IN THE EARLY WORK OF A PARK.

It needs to be emphatically urged (for a reverse impression is often apparent) that the plans of no other class of the public works of a city are to be rightly devised with reference to as prolonged and unchanging methods of usefulness as those of parks.

That the fact of the matter in this respect may be understood, let it be first reflected that the value of a large park does not lie, as is apt to be thoughtlessly taken for granted, in those elements which cost and manifest the most labor and the largest absorption of taxes; that is to say, in the roads, walks, bridges, buildings, and other obviously constructed features. These have value as conveniences for making the larger elements of a park available for the enjoyment of the public. If these larger elements are destroyed, the value of the artificial elements is lost. In the degree that they are ill-treated the value of the artificial elements depreciates. A park road is pleasant by reason of that which adjoins it, or is open to contemplation from it, not because it favors speed. Mainly the value of a park depends on the disposition and the quality of its woods, and the relation of its woods to other natural features; ledges, boulders, declivities, swells, dimples, and to qualities of surface, as verdure and tuftiness. Under good management these things do not, like roads and walks, wear out or in any way lose value with age. Individual trees must from time to time be removed to avoid crowding, or because of decay; but, as a rule, the older the wood, and the less of newness and rawness there is to be seen in all the elements of a park, the better it serves its purpose. This rule holds for centuries—without limit.

It is very different with nearly every other material thing—material in distinction from moral or educational—to which a city may directly outlay from its treasury. The highest value, for example, of civic buildings, of pavements, aqueducts, sewers, bridges, is realized while they are yet new; afterwards a continual deterioration must be expected. As to a park, when the principal outlay has been made, the result may, and under good management must, for many years afterwards, be *increasing in value at a constantly advancing rate of increase, and never cease to increase as long as the city endures.*

This (with an explanation presently to be made in a footnote) will be obviously true as to the principal element of a park—its plantations. But whatever value a park may reach simply through the age of its well ordered plantations, something of that value will be lost wherever repairs, additions, or restorations are made by which the dignity of age in its general aspect (or what the ancients called the local genius) is impaired. Looking at the artificial elements of parks in Europe — the seats, bridges, terraces, staircases, or any substantial furniture of them, supposing that they are not ruinous — it cannot be questioned that they are pleasing in the degree that they are old and bear evidence of long action of natural influences upon them — the most pleasing being those which nature seems to have adopted for her own, so that only by critical inspection is human workmanship to be recognized. Hence, not only should park things be built for permanence, but ingeniously with a view to ready adoption and adornment of them by nature, so that they may come rapidly and without weakness to gain the charm characteristic of old things. For every thousand dollars judiciously invested in a park the dividends to the second generation of the citizens possessing it will be much larger than to the first; the dividends to the third generation much larger than to the second.

The better to bring this class of considerations home, it may be suggested that had five hundred acres of land been set apart as a park for Boston, and trees planted, natural plantations thinned, opened, preserved, renewed, and other natural features protected and judiciously treated for two centuries past, instead of deteriorating as most other public works would have done, the park would have been all the time advancing with a constantly accelerating rate of advance in value. But had the artificial features been originally made *in adaptation solely to the wants of the people of the day* or their immediate successors, an enlargement and re-adjustment of them suitably to a convenient use of the park by the present population of Boston could only be effected by much destruction of the natural features; by the rooting out of great and venerable trees, the blasting of ledges rich in picturesque, time-worn crannies and weather stains, the breaking up of graceful slopes, and the interpolation of much that could be comparatively crude, raw, incongruous, and forlorn. Rather than make radical changes with these results, much inconvenience would long be endured. For two hundred years, conditions of public inconvenience and of peril and of uncouthness, have rightly been submitted to, for this reason, in Hyde Park, which would not be endured for a year in any new work.

In no other public work of a city, then, is it of as much importance as in a park to determine courses to be pursued with regard to growing results, and in a great degree distant ends rather than ends close at hand and soon to be fully realizable.*

---

* It is the consideration that the value of a *rural* park grows with its age, and that the value of the immediate result of principal expenditures for construction must be slight compared with those to accrue in after years, added to the consideration that it is a political impracticability to steadily pursue any fixed, definite and limited purposes in park work while those conducting it are dependent for the means of carrying it on upon their ability to immediately satisfy tax-payers of the value of what they are doing, that has elsewhere

III.

THE EARNINGS OF A PARK TO A CITY ACCRUE LARGELY THROUGH THE LESS CONSPICUOUS USE OF IT, AND, IF IT IS SUITABLY PLANNED AND MANAGED, THROUGH THE USE OF THE LESS CONSPICUOUS PARTS OF IT.

THERE are two ways of estimating the earnings of a park. There is no doubt that the sixteen millions of dollars which Central Park has cost New York have been returned through the profit that has accrued from the attrac-

---

than in Boston been generally thought to require that the cost of the primary work of a park should be provided for by long loans, even exceptionally to a general administrative policy. Where this course has not been taken, the results have been such as to establish beyond question the extreme importance — the vital necessity to anything like economy — of securing a sound and controlling public opinion at the outset. The park of Detroit (seven hundred acres in extent) is a case of this kind. During all of last summer, work upon it was wholly suspended because a majority of the City Council, and a majority of the Park Commissioners whom a previous City Council appointed, were not quite of one mind on a question of police regulations, which might have been decided either way without the slightest effect upon any permanent interest of the city in the park. The Council refused to make any appropriation without a pledge from the Commissioners that they would take action contrary to the judgment of a majority of their Board. Consequently the plant of the work lies idle for an entire year, the organization and discipline of the force is lost, the constructions that were in progress are wasting, and the ground is used by the public in a way sure to breed customs and expectations much to be regretted. That a similar catastrophe is not impossible in Boston is fairly to be inferred from an occurrence of the last summer. The Park Commissioners prepared a drawing and numerous cross-sections showing the necessity before any other work could be proceeded with at all economically upon the site for Wood Island Park, of building a bridge by which it would be made accessible, and of doing a large amount of rough grading. For this preliminary work they advised that an outlay should be authorized, to be made during the present fiscal year, of $25,000. The result was an appropriation of $5,000, with the condition that it should all be applied to planting. As no planting was practicable without an abandonment of the plan, the appropriation was unavailable.[70]

A liability to such occurrences is oppressively costly in its effects on the management of the work, even when it does not actually result, as it sometimes does, in compelling purposes to be adopted of weak, narrow, trivial, short-sighted, and time-serving character for those of more important lasting consequence.

F.L.O.

As the value of everything else to be contemplated in the plan of a park must be forever dependent on the condition of its trees, and as, while every tree of a park may go on improving for a certain period, it must also in time fall into decay and eventually disappear, it may be questioned if a limit is not thus fixed to the alleged advancing value of a well-directed park work.

The answer is that the trees of a park must be expected to decay and disappear

tiveness of the city as a place of residence for men of means. All classes of the people benefit by the wealth thus brought to and held in the city, and it is generally considered by its financiers that simply through the increased value of real estate which has thus occurred, taxes are lighter than they would have been but for the park.

This is one way in which the value of the park is seen. The other is that which has been already indicated in pointing out the use of it that the leading capitalists of the city have been taught by experience to make, as a means of preserving their faculties in high working condition, — the value in health, vigor, and earning capacity, and in capacity to enjoy results of earnings, which is gained through the use of it. This value is not traceable in such form that it can be entered on the ledger and totalled up in annual statements. In estimating it, every man is, almost irresistibly, over much affected by his personal experiences. In ordinary social conference about what is desirable in a park, such a personal point of view sometimes becomes ludicrously apparent.

A gentleman much before the public, and who had taken an active part in urging publicly and privately certain measures of alleged improvement in a park, but who probably had never entered it on foot or seen any part of it not visible from the drives and rides, once asked in passing through it, "What is this pleasant odor?" "It is from the bloom of the locust; we are passing between two groups of it." "I see. Beautiful bloom! beautiful foliage! Why should not that tree be planted more? Why not everywhere? Why should not the park roads be lined with it? Then this delightful scent would be constant, and the beauty also. Why not have the best everywhere?" The answer was, "The tree is not long in bloom, and after midsummer droughts we have few trees less beautiful; where its foliage predominates, as in some parts of New Jersey, it makes the landscape really sad." "That's of no consequence," was the rejoinder, "for nobody wants to see the park in midsummer."

This, while said thoughtlessly, manifested an habitual mode of thought. The man was neither thoughtless nor heartless. Yet the truth is, that the most important purpose of a park, and that through its adaptation to which its largest earnings should be expected, is at the season of the year when the fewest visitors come to it in carriages, when all citizens who can, have gone to the country, and that it lies in conditions, qualities, appliances,

---

one by one, and never, under decently economical management, in such numbers at any time as to materially affect the general aspect of the park, a main condition of good management being that it shall secure the little care necessary to provide a sufficient succession of nurslings (generally through a selection of those self-sown) and thinnings for the purpose. The plan of many parks in Europe, originally private, has remained unchanged for centuries, and they have never hitherto been more finely timbered, never as useful as they are now.

F.L.O.

and modes of superintendence of which many citizens and most strangers know hardly anything.

To understand this, let the imagination be gradually brought from the consideration of the general, mixed body of park visitors to the particular point of view of a distinct type. For this purpose let that part of the people be thought of, first, who are able to save enough from daily wages to be distinctly removed from penury, but whose accumulation is too small to relieve them from an anxious and narrowly dogged habit of mind and a strong incitement to persistent toilsome industry. Let it be considered that, setting aside the more floating and transient, and the useless and harmful sections, men of this class, and those who are dependent upon them, form much the larger part in numbers of a city's population. For every storekeeper or head of a shop there are several clerks and workmen. Let it be considered also that those who shortly in the future are to lead in the affairs of the city, are to-day of this class, and are acquiring the aptitudes which are chiefly to determine the strength and character of the city in the early future. Then let it be further considered that more than half the battle for the city's future prosperity lies, in fact, with the matronly element — the housekeeping women — of this class. Let the plan of the park then be regarded, for a moment, from the point of view of this subdivision of those who are to be its owners.

As a rule such women are compelled to live closely, in confined spaces, with a more monotonous round of occupations and more subject to an unpleasant clatter than is wholesome for them or for those whom they are bringing into the world and training. Many are constrained to give themselves up so to live even more confinedly than is necessary, from having a morbid sense of housekeeping necessities, bred by their confined life. In the nervous fatigue that comes upon them, it is easier to go with the current of habit than to make the exertion necessary to find and secure opportunities of relief and refreshment. The misfortune of the housekeeper in this respect, tells day by day, as long as she lives, upon every member of the family, from the master to the infant; its most important result being, perhaps, that of a disliberal educative tendency, a narrowing, stinting, materialistic, and over-prosaic educative tendency, affecting so many of the city's heirs as may be subject to it.

Suppose that women of this condition could be largely induced to so far break out of their confining habits as, during the season when the schools are closed, to frequently spend part of a day with their children in a place secluded from all the ordinary conditions of the town; a place of simple, tranquillizing, rural scenery, taking their needle-work, and the principal means of a simple out-of-doors repast. Suppose that after work-hours the master of the family and the older daughters, who have been all day in a shop, should join the party, and all should have their supper in the open air, under a canopy of foliage. Suppose that once a week, during the hot weather, a half-holiday should be taken, to provide for which in the regulation of shops is a rapidly growing custom; that parties of friends should be made up to visit and picnic together in the park; what is likely to be the value in the long run of provisions adapted to encourage such practices? The possibility of a general custom of this sort, and the value of it, is a question of how the park is laid out, how it is nursed to grow, and of how it is superintended, and by suitable service made convenient and attractive to such use. The character and habits, then, of these women may with profit be a little further considered.

Not uncommonly those the confinement and monotony and clatter and petty detailed worry of whose lives it would be most profitable for the city to have somewhat broken up are modest, retiring, often shy, of timid disposition, and of nervous temperament, a little thing leading them to painful and wearing excitement and loss of presence of mind.

The idea which many would thoughtlessly be satisfied to see realized in a public park would make it a place to which, coming by street-cars with a number of children, some of them marriageable girls, the mother's day would be one of greater toil, anxiety, irritation, and worry than she would have had at home.

It is an important test of the value of a park that it should be found of such a character, so finished and provided with such service, that a woman under these circumstances would always find a visit to it economical, restful, tranquillizing, and refreshing for herself and her household.

Such a preparation and management of a park as will make it tolerably satisfactory with reference to this standard will only make it more than tolerably satisfactory to the more robust and less burdened part of the population.

But even a little greater refinement than is thus called for may profitably be aimed at, as will now be shown.

IV.

THE ADAPTATION OF THE PARK TO THE USE OF INVALIDS.

A HIGHLY important part of the business of a park is that of arresting the progress of disease, hastening recovery, and conservating the strength of the weak and the infirm of a city.

It is a common practice with physicians to order patients to be sent to the country. The necessity for doing so is commonly called a necessity for change of air and scene. The importance of the practice is indicated by the fact that the Massachusetts General Hospital Corporation maintains an establishment in the midst of rural scenery, near the Waverly Oaks, expressly for the purpose of hastening and confirming the convalescence of patients first cared for at its general city establishment.[71] It is economical to do so. But it is impracticable to send the vast majority of those who in private practice come under the care of physicians, to be domiciled out of town; nor, in the

519

majority of cases, were it practicable, would it be best to remove them wholly from the comforts of home and the attentions of friends.

There are two conditions on which a visit under favorable circumstances to a suitably equipped park may be very useful. One is where it is a question whether a person is going to be able to throw off a little depression, or must let it be the beginning of a serious illness; the other, at a stage of convalescence when a brief change from the air and scene of a sick-room, a little easy exercise and a little variation from home diet may greatly hasten a return to a healthy working condition. To make such use of the park as is desirable in either of these cases, a visit to it should not be costly or troublesome or attended with needless worry or apprehension of rude encounters. In several cities what is thus desirable is now in a good degree realized. A weary woman, broken down by watching and anxiety, with a weakly child recovering from the debilitation of summer complaint, may be put by friends on a streetcar in a distant part of the city, and be taken to the gate of the park for five cents; may then be assisted by a person appointed for the duty into a low-hung, topped carriage and be driven two or three miles through rural scenery at a cost of ten cents; may be set down to rest and saunter at a pleasant rambling place with seats and drinking fountains scattered along its walks; may find, near by, a house with a woman whose business it is to meet the common necessities of an invalid, without charge, and at which a glass of milk, a cup of tea, or of hot beef broth, or a boiled egg may be had at a cost of five cents, the wholesome quality of these things being assured. She may then return by the carriage and a street-car, at a further cost of fifteen cents. The entire outlay of the day thirty-five cents. The city supplies the buildings and the roads and walks and rural scenery, and bargains with contractors for the rest, and contractors finding a profit on the whole transaction.

Let not this statement pass for a romantic fancy. Just that thing has been done many thousand times, and year after year, and in several cities. Charitable societies make contracts under which carriages take poor invalids from and return them to their own doors without charge, but this is another matter. What has been described is no more a matter of charity than the bringing of water and the carrying away of garbage by the city for the same people. Every man whose wife or mother or daughter benefits by it, has the satisfaction of knowing that he is one of the owners of the park, and that he pays from his earnings the full commercial value for the service of the street-car, the carriage, the gardener, the keeper, and the purveyor.

A park on a suitable site, discreetly prepared, and arranged with reference to the class of considerations that have been suggested, will, simply through the increased savings and increased earning capacity of the industrial masses of a city, make a profitable return for its cost. Yet, in the progress of every large park undertaking, much public discussion occurs with reference to it, in which this element of value and that of the domestic use of it by people of small means are entirely overlooked.

V.
THE VALUE OF A RURAL PARK TO THE PARTS OF A CITY MORE DISTANT FROM IT.

THAT a well prepared and arranged rural park adds greatly to the value of real estate in its neighborhood is well known. It may be questioned if the gain at one point is not balanced by loss at another. But in all growing towns which have a rural park evidence appears that, on the whole, it is not. With a good route of approach, such as was provided by the Champs Elysées and the Avenue de Bois de Boulogne in Paris, Unter den Linden in Berlin, the Parkways in Chicago, and such as will be supplied by Columbia Street, Humboldt Avenue, and the Riverdale Parkway from Back Bay, in Boston, people who ride or drive do not object to a lengthened passage between their residences and a park. As to others, the mass, even of habitual users, do not use a rural park daily, but at intervals, mostly on holidays and Saturdays, birthdays, and other special occasions. How much less than is apt to be considered, in the early stages of a park undertaking, such use of a park is affected by its being at the far side of a town, has been shown in Brooklyn.

When the rural park of Brooklyn was determined on, the people of a part of that city, the most remote from the site taken, pleading their distance from it and the difficulties of communication with it, were able to obtain a special exemption from the taxation that it would enforce.[72] They had local advantages for recreation, and would never, it was thought, want to cross the town to be better provided in that respect at its opposite side. Nevertheless, long before the plan of the park had been fully carried out, the people of this very district began to resort to it in such numbers that two lines of street cars were established, and on holidays these are now found insufficient, to meet their demand.

There is no doubt that the health, strength, and earning capacity of these people is increased by the park; that the value of life in their quarter of the town is increased; that the intrinsic value, as well as the market rating, of its real estate is increased.

The larger part of the people to whom the Brooklyn Park has thus proved unexpectedly helpful are the very best sort of frugal and thrifty working-men, their wives, and their children.

Every successful park (for there are rural parks so badly managed that they cannot be called successful) draws visitors from a distance much greater than its projectors had supposed that it would. It is common for people living out of New York, anywhere within a hundred miles, to visit its park in pleasure parties on all manner of festive occasions. In Paris, the celebration of weddings by the excursion of an invited party to a park and an entertainment in it, is so common with people of moderate means that the writer has seen ten companies of marriage guests in the Bois de Boulogne in a single day.

VI.
THE BEARING OF THE DIFFICULTIES THAT HAVE BEEN REVIEWED UPON THE MAIN END OF THESE NOTES.

FIRST, the chief end of a large park is an effect on the human organism by an action of what it presents to view, which action, like that of music, is of a kind that goes back of thought, and cannot be fully given the form of words.*

Excellence in the elaboration and carrying out of a plan of work of this kind will be largely dependent on the degree in which those having to do with it are impressed with the importance of the intangible end of providing the refreshment of rural scenery, believe in it, and are sympathetic with the spirit of the design for attaining it. Now, it has happened that Mayors, Members of City Councils, Commissioners, Superintendents, Gardeners, Architects, and Engineers, having to do with a park work, have not only been wanting in this respect, but have been known to imagine that it would be pleasing to the public that they should hold up to ridicule any purpose in a park work not of a class to be popularly defined as strictly and definitely utilitarian and "practical," and should seek to eliminate from it all refinement of motive as childish, unbusinesslike, pottering, and wasteful. In the history of the park of New York, three gentlemen of wealth, education, and of eminent political position, two of them Commissioners of the park, have used the word landscape to define that which they desired should be avoided and overcome on the park. One of them, and a man of good social position, a patron of landscape arts for the walls of private houses, said in a debate in regard to the removal of certain trees: "The park is no place for art, no place for landscape effects; it is a place in which to get exercise, and take the air. Trees are wanted to shade the roads and walks, and turf is wanted because without it the ground would be glaring and fatiguing to the eye; nothing more, nothing else." He believed that in saying this he was expressing the public opinion of the city, and at the time it was not as certain as it has since come to be that he was not.

Second, spaciousness is of the essence of a park. Franklin Park is to take the best part of a mile square of land out of the space otherwise available for the further building of the city of Boston. There are countless things to be desired for the people of a city, an important element of the cost of providing which is ground space. It is the consequent crowded condition of a city that makes the sight of merely uncrowded ground in a park the relief and refresh-

---

* "It gives an appetite, a feeling, and a love that have no need of a remoter charm by thought supplied." — Wordsworth, with reference to rural scenery. "It would be difficult to conceive a scene less dependent on any other interest than that of its own secluded and serious beauty. . . . *the first utterance of those mighty mountain symphonies.*" — RUSKIN.[73]

ment to the mind that it is. The first condition of a good park, therefore, is that from the start a limited number of leading ends shall be fixed upon, to serve which as well as possible *will compel opportunity for serving others on the space allotted to it to be excluded.* The desirability of opportunity for using it for some of the ends thus set aside will be constant, and in a great city there will always be not only thousands in whose minds some one of them will be of more distinct and realizable importance than those that will have been provided for in the plan of the ground, and who will be moved to undervalue, relatively to them, that which has been done and reserved for the accepted purposes; but many thousands more who will fail to see that the introduction of appliances for promoting new purposes is going to lessen the value of the ground for its primary purposes. Where a strong and definite personal interest is taken, even by a few persons, in any purpose that is indirectly and furtively at issue with a purpose of comparatively indefinite general interest to a community, the only permanent security for the efficient sustenance of the larger purpose lies in a strong conviction of its importance pervading the community.

Such a conviction cannot be expected to develop intuitively or spontaneously, at an early period of a large park undertaking, because the work will as yet be supplying little of immediate and direct pleasing interest to the public. On the contrary, the earlier work on a park site is apt to destroy, for the time being, much of whatever rural beauty it may possess. Such is the first result of operations in drainage, in road-grading, and in tillage, for example: — such the result of all operations for the improvement of woodlands. Even a new plantation, if well designed for future beauty, is apt at first to make an unpleasant impression; and, while the heavy work of park construction is going on, with much blasting of rocks, loaded carts occupying the roads and crossing the ground in all directions, and squads of workmen everywhere, the experience of visitors can hardly fail to be adverse to a right understanding of the aims of the work.

In the management of a large park it is then of the first importance that the people to whom its managers are responsible should be asked and aided to acquaint themselves, otherwise than by observation on the ground, with the general plan upon which it is to be formed, to understand the leading ends and motives of this plan, the dependence of one part upon another, the subordination of the minor to the major motives, and to take an intelligent and liberal interest, and a well-grounded satisfaction, in its development through growth, as well as through the advance of constructive operations the results of which are to be of value only as they are fitted to serve as implements by which to obtain enjoyment of the results of growth.

"And this the more, because it is one of the appointed conditions of the labor of men, that, in proportion to the time between the seed-sowing and the harvest is the fullness of the fruit."

"Let it not be for present delight, nor for present use alone; let it be such work as our descendants will thank us for, and let us think . . . that a time is to come when . . . men will say, '*See! this our fathers did for us.*'" — SEVEN LAMPS.[74]

<hr>

PART FIFTH.
THE PARK AS A DEPARTMENT OF EDUCATION.

THERE is yet one aspect of the scheme too important to be left wholly unconsidered in a review of the design. As a seat of learning and an "Academy," Boston is yet the most metropolitan of American cities. Others are gaining at many points with gratifying rapidity; but, on the whole, Boston is moving in a more simply evolutional and democratic way, taking ground less by forced marches and at isolated points in advance of her main line, consequently with a firmer footing. Her advantage in this respect is a good form of civic wealth. Any sterling addition to it is worth more to the reputation and commercial "good-will" of the city than an addition of the same cost to its shops, banks, hotels, street railroads, or newspapers. The Arboretum,[75] with the library, cabinets, laboratory, correspondence, and records, of which it will be the nucleus, will not simply bring a certain excellent accession to the population of Boston; it will extend her fame, and will make in a measure tributary to her every man on the continent who wishes to pursue certain lines of study, and lines rapidly coming to be known as of great economic national importance.

The Park, if designed, formed, and conducted discreetly to that end, will be an important addition to the advantages possessed by the city in the Athenæum, in the Museum of Art, in the examples of art presented in some recent structures and their embellishments, and in the societies and clubs through which students are brought into community with men of knowledge, broad views, and sound sentiment in art.

To see something of its value in this respect, imagine a ground as near the centre of exchange of the city as the Agassiz Museum or the Cambridge Observatory, in which, for years, care has been taken to cherish broad passages of scenery, formed by hills, dales, rocks, woods, and humbler growths natural to the circumstances, without effort to obtain effects in the least of a *"bric-à-brac,"* "Jappy," or in any way exotic or highly seasoned quality.

What would be the value of such a piece of property as an adjunct of a school of art? The words of a great literary artist may suggest the answer: —

"You will never love art till you love what she mirrors better."[76]

If we would cultivate art we must begin by cultivating a love of nature, and of nature not as seen in "collections" or in mantel-piece and flower-garden ornaments.

As to the value that a park may have in this respect, the use may be recalled that is made by the art students of Paris, with the doors of the Louvre always open to them, of the out-of-door gallery of Fontainebleau, thirty miles away. There are no rocks at Fontainebleau more instructive than those to be had in Franklin Park. The woods of Fontainebleau that have been models of a thousand painted landscapes, being mostly of artificially planted trees, grown stiffly for the timber market, and not for natural beauty, are no more art-educative than woods that may be had on Franklin Park. And though the region to which the name Fontainebleau is applied is so much larger, it offers the student no better examples of landscape distance, intricacy, obscurity, and mystery than may be had in Franklin Park.

But the art aspect of the scheme cannot be fairly seen from the point of view of the school of the artist. The value of an artist in the economy of a city, is as one of many agencies for the exchange of services. The artist dies when the love of art and of what art mirrors is dead.

Would you have an art-loving people? Take them to nature, and to nature not as it is to be enjoyed in glass cabinets, or in rows of specimens, or in barbered and millinered displays, or as wrought into mosaics, embroideries and garden ribbons. Let them enjoy nature, rather, with as much of the atmosphere of scenery and on as large a scale as the walls of your school will allow.

The main difficulty of gaining such an addition to the Boston Academy is that which lies in the momentary impatient misunderstanding of the public, or of those who speak for the public, of a policy that does not propose to make a great show from year to year for the public money from year to year expended, and that does not look to making a splendid show at any time.

Such misunderstanding and such impatience is not likely to have a permanently and gravely disturbing effect on such a work as that of Back Bay, where the justifying end is to be reached wholly by engineering skill, and into which art enters only as a process of dressing, but it may easily be absolutely disastrous where this condition is reversed, as to any success in its justifying purpose it must be, in the undertaking of Franklin Park.

The text presented here was published as City of Boston. Park Department, *Notes on the Plan of Franklin Park and Related Matters* (Boston, 1886), pages 7–115.

1. That is, the Park (renamed Delaware Park) (see Olmsted, Vaux & Co. to William Dorsheimer, Oct. 1, 1868, above).
2. Park Square was located in the intersection of Columbus Avenue, Boylston Street, and Charles Street at the southwest corner of Boston Common (M. F. Sweetser, *New Map of Boston* [Boston, 1880]).

3. Philip Gilbert Hamerton (1834–1894), writer and art critic. Olmsted is paraphrasing a statement from *Etching & Etchers* in which Hamerton writes, "The leading ideas of good etching are the interpretation of nature by the selection of the most important lines and the separation of the most important masses, with a suggestion of the most characteristic details" (Stanley J. Kunitz and Howard Haycraft, eds., *British Authors of the Nineteenth Century* [New York, 1936], p. 273; Philip Gilbert Hamerton, *Etching & Etchers*, 3d ed. [London, 1880], p. 345).

4. Olmsted is referring to an oversized map included in his published report entitled "City of Boston — Park Department. Map of Boston and of a Part of its Suburbs Showing Public Recreation Grounds, Burial Grounds and Certain Other Public Properties Generally Free from Buildings. 1886."

5. At this point Olmsted included a detailed seven-page description of the public spaces located on the map noted above. Olmsted divided these "airing places" into seven classes: Class I included public recreation grounds; Class II included burial grounds; Class III included public water works; Class IV included grounds of public institutions; Class V included miscellaneous properties all within the Boston city limits; Class VI included public properties on the islands in Boston Harbor; and Class VII included U.S. government properties on the mainland but in part open and planted. Of the total acreage of these properties (3356.63 acres), only 659 acres were not within Boston's city limits (*Boston Daily Advertiser*, Feb. 18, 1886, p. 5).

6. Olmsted is referring to the Tour St. Jacques la Boucherie, built in 1508, in Paris. In 1856 the grounds about the tower were planted, and Olmsted may have seen the work in progress when he visited Paris that year (William Robinson, *The Parks, Promenades & Gardens of Paris* . . . [London, 1869], pp. 84–85; *Papers of FLO*, 2: 484).

7. In Buffalo, Olmsted and Calvert Vaux had designed four parkways providing connection to the principal park, Delaware Park. Humboldt Parkway connected the Parade with the eastern end of the park, while three short parkways, Chapin, Bidwell, and Lincoln provided connection to streets leading to the Front and the center of the city. In Chicago, Olmsted and Vaux designed a parkway in 1869 to link their suburb of Riverside with the city. In their plan for the Chicago South Park of 1871 they proposed construction of three parkways leading to the Upper Division (later named Washington Park): Southgrove Parkway, Southopen Parkway, and Pavilion Parkway (*Papers of FLO*, 6: 345, 348; see OVC, "Report Accompanying Plan for Laying Out the South Park," March 1871, nn. 19 and 20, above).

8. A quotation from Ralph Waldo Emerson's poem "The Rhodora: on Being Asked Whence is the Flower?" (Stuart P. Sherman, *Essays and Poems of Emerson* [New York, 1921], p. 46.)

9. In November 1869 the city held two public hearings encouraging Bostonians to express their views on the creation of a public park or parks for the city. Olmsted is probably referring to Edward Crane's proposal made at the first public hearing on November 5, 1869. Crane, a prominent railroad contractor, suggested that the city build a park two-and-one-half miles long by one mile in width "with country surrounding it capable of being made into ponds, skating places, boating places, with one hundred acres that you can make as level as a floor for military parades and encampments" ("City Document No. 123," in City of Boston, *Documents of the City of Boston, for the Year 1869*, 3 vols. [Boston, 1870], 3: 21; *Boston Evening Transcript*, June 5, 1889, p. 9).

10. The area selected for East Rock Park in New Haven, Connecticut, included the jagged cliffs of Indian Head, East Rock, and Whitney Peak. Most of the ground was covered with forest, rocks, and underbrush, conveying a rough and wild appearance. Arthur's Seat forms the summit of Holyrood Park in Edinburgh, Scotland. It is a fragment of a long-extinct volcano and is bounded on two sides by steep crags, making it inaccessible from the south or west (Edward E. Atwater, ed., *History of the City of*

New Haven to the Present Time [New York, 1887], p. 403; George P. Black, *Arthur's Seat: A History of Edinburgh's Volcano* [Edinburgh, 1966], pp. 18–19).

11. By the 1880s, under the superintendency of William Doogue, an Irish-born florist and horticulturist, the Boston Public Garden became a major showplace of the "gardenesque" style of planting. Doogue included carpet and ribbon bedding of multicolored floral displays, and by 1888, 90,000 plants had been set out in 150 beds. He also used exotic plants such as yucca and cactus and displayed throughout the year many tropical varieties in huge pots and planters (Friends of the Public Garden and Common, Inc., *The Public Garden: Boston* [Boston, 1988], pp. 10–11, 28, 30; see also n. 52 below).

12. For this Ralph Waldo Emerson quotation, see FLO, *Mount Royal, Montreal*, (1881), note 3, above.

13. For source of this quotation by James Russell Lowell, see ibid., note 4, above.

14. The editors have been unable to locate this John Ruskin quotation.

15. Robert Burns, Scottish poet (see FLO, *Mount Royal, Montreal* [1881], n. 42, above).

16. Jean François Millet (1814–1875), a French artist, born of peasant stock. Millet lived in poverty most of his life, and the subjects of his paintings were peasants and members of the working class (*EB*).

17. Léon Bonvin (1834–1866), a French watercolorist, emphasized wild flowers and landscapes in his work. Bonvin was forced to operate a tavern by day to support himself and paint in the early morning hours or late at night. By 1866, unable to sell his paintings for a fair price and falling increasingly into debt, Bonvin committed suicide (Philippe Burty, "Léon Bonvin," *Harper's New Monthly Magazine* [December, 1885], pp. 37–48).

18. John Campbell Shairp published *On Poetic Interpretation of Nature* in 1877 (*DNB*).

19. That is, William Wordsworth and his sister Dorothy (see FLO, *Mount Royal. Montreal*, [1881], n. 36, above).

20. Elizabeth Cleghorn Gaskell (1810–1865), novelist, born in Chelsea, England (*DNB*).

21. That is, Prospect Park in Brooklyn, the Park (later Delaware Park) in Buffalo, and Fairmount Park in Philadelphia. In 1881 the city of Bridgeport, Connecticut, hired Olmsted to lay out Beardsley Park. The land for the park was a bequest from James Walker Beardsley and was located in the northwestern part of the city on the Pequonnock River and Lake. Olmsted and his stepson John provided the park commissioners with a report and a plan in 1884 (City of Bridgeport. Park Commission, *Beardsley Park. Landscape Architects' Preliminary Report. September, 1884* [Boston, 1884], pp. 3–14).

22. Dunham Park refers to the grounds of Dunham Massey Hall, which was the seat of the Earls of Stamford and Warrington in southwest Manchester. The family spent most of its time at another home in Staffordshire, which is probably why the Manchester working class was allowed to use the grounds of Dunham Massey as a park (Suzanne Lewis, ed., *Elizabeth Gaskell: A Dark Night's Work and Other Stories* [Oxford, 1992], p. 314, n. 176).

23. The excerpt Olmsted includes here is from Elizabeth Gaskell's short story "Life in Manchester: Libbie Marsh's Three Eras" published in *Howitt's Journal* in 1847 under the pseudonym Cotton Mather Mills (Cotton Mather Mills, "Life in Manchester: Libby Marsh's Three Eras," *Howitt's Journal* 1 [June 1847]: 335–36; Robert L. Selig, *Elizabeth Gaskell: A Reference Guide* [Boston, 1977], p. xvii).

24. Abbotswood was the site of the Abbott family homestead. Land located on Canterbury Street was purchased from William E. Abbott for Franklin Park. Glen Road and Rock Hill were the original names of these sites. Scarboro Hill was named for the Scarborough family, of which the last of the Roxbury line died in 1789. Hagborne Hill was named for Samuel Hagborne. Hagborne, a wealthy first settler of Roxbury, owned

several acres of property and founded the first free school in the town in 1642. Waitt-wood was named for the Waitt family. Samuel Waitt, a mill owner, purchased the last of the town's common land in 1812, and his brother, Benjamin, was a local grocer. Samuel owned considerable property at the time of his death including two mills and the old Scarborough estate. Rock Morton was probably named for the Morton family. In 1879 the heirs of Joseph Morton sold property located on Morton Street for Franklin Park. Ellicottdale was probably named for Joseph Ellicott who purchased the Scarborough estate after the death of Samuel Waitt. Joseph P. Ellicott sold property located along Walnut Street for Franklin Park (Francis Samuel Drake, *The Town of Roxbury* . . . [1878; rpt. ed., Boston, 1905], pp. 139, 229, 230, 317, 319, 320; "Document No. 123," in City of Boston, *Documents*, 3: 3).

25. Francis Samuel Drake (1828–1885), historian. Drake wrote several historical works, among them the book Olmsted mentions here, *The Town of Roxbury*, originally published in 1878 (*DAB*).

26. Nazing was a village on the River Lee in Essex County about twenty miles east of London. Between 1631 and 1640 most of the Nazing pilgrims settled in Roxbury. The "Long Crouch" was renamed Seaver Street after Ebenezer Seaver (c. 1763–1844) who was popularly known as "Squire" and "Father of the Town." Seaver Street extends between Blue Hill Avenue and Walnut Avenue and is the northeastern boundary of Franklin Park. The Resting Place or Ground was located on the Scarborough homestead. Heathfield was named for the family of William Heath who came to Roxbury from Nazing in 1632. Here, Olmsted is referring to Captain Joseph Heath, a descendent of the original Roxbury settler. Pierrepont Road was named for the family of John Pierpont who settled in Roxbury in 1640. Robert Pierpont, a descendent of John's, is the lieutenant to whom Olmsted is referring here (F. S. Drake, *Town of Roxbury*, pp. 10, 28, 29, 223–24, 229, 387; *Vital Records of Roxbury, Massachusetts, to the End of the Year 1849*, 2 vols. [Salem, Mass., 1926], 2: 633; *Glimpses of Early Roxbury* [Boston, 1905], pp. 15–16; R. Burnham Moffat, *Pierrepont Genealogies* . . . [New York, 1913], p. 132).

27. Hugh O'Brien (1827–1895), city politician, was born in Ireland. At age five his family immigrated to the United States and settled in Boston. O'Brien attended public school and as a youth began working for the *Boston Courier*. Later he founded and was the editor and publisher of the *Shipping and Commercial List*. O'Brien was elected to the Board of Aldermen in 1875 and served almost continuously until 1883. In 1884 he was elected mayor of Boston and served four years in that position. Throughout his tenure as alderman and mayor, O'Brien was a strong supporter of the working classes and an advocate of public parks in Boston.

In the 1877 report to which Olmsted here refers, O'Brien stated that

> The Charles River embankment, for instance, on account of its connecting the poorest and most crowded part of the city and drive, and the great additional facilities for using the river for boating and pleasure purposes which it affords, is, perhaps, the park of greatest local value; but, as a part of the system of parks, its chief value is as the great avenue through which Charlestown and the North and West Ends find ready and pleasant access through the Back Bay park to the country parks in West Roxbury and to Brighton.

(John C. Rand, ed., *One of a Thousand* . . . [Boston, 1890], pp. 446–47; Albert P. Langtry, ed., *Metropolitan Boston: A Modern History* [New York, 1929], p. 235; "City Document No. 44," in City of Boston, *Documents of the City of Boston, for the Year 1877*, 3 vols. [Boston, 1878], 1: 2.)

28. In 1820 William Emerson (1801–1868) began a school for young ladies in Boston. A year later, his younger brother, Ralph Waldo Emerson, joined him. In 1823 Ruth Emerson, their mother, moved the entire family to Canterbury Lane in Roxbury, and

it was here that the Emerson brothers lived while continuing to teach school in Boston. In 1824 William left teaching to continue his education in Germany, and in 1825 Ralph closed the school to begin his studies at the Divinity School at Harvard.

Olmsted knew William Emerson when they were neighbors on Staten Island in the late 1840s and early 1850s. In October 1857 Olmsted retained Emerson, a lawyer and judge, to represent him after the bankruptcy of the publishing company Dix, Edwards & Company in which Olmsted was a partner (John McAleer, *Ralph Waldo Emerson: Days of Encounter* [Boston, 1984], pp. 66–69; Richard Garnett, *Life of Ralph Waldo Emerson* [London, 1888], pp. 32–35; *Papers of FLO*, 2: 334; FLO to JO, Oct. 9, 1857 [*Papers of FLO*, 3: 103]).

29. In one such letter Emerson wrote to a Harvard friend, John Boynton Hill, "my brother, & I teach, aye teach teach in the morning, & then scamper out as fast as our cosset horse will bring us to snuff the winds & cross the wild blossoms & branches— of the green fields" (Ralph Waldo Emerson to John Boynton Hill, June 19, 1823, in *The Letters of Ralph Waldo Emerson*, ed. Ralph L. Rusk, 6 vols. [New York, 1939], 1: 133).

30. This house, known as Ellicott House, was built in the early 1890s and used as a place for tennis players to change clothes. The building itself, designed by Rotch and Tilden, was built with boulder walls (Cynthia Zaitzevsky, *Frederick Law Olmsted and the Boston Park System* [Cambridge, Mass., 1982], p. 177).

31. Olmsted is referring to the Brooklyn Sunday-school Union parade. The parade, held annually in late May, consisted of Sunday school children from various divisions, one being the Prospect Park division (*Brooklyn Eagle*, May 27, 1885, p. 4).

32. In the annual report for 1884 Superintendent John Y. Culyer noted

> During the past year the school and church organizations, without regard to sect, have found congenial and acceptable facilities at the Park; it having acquired a deserved repute for comfort, variety of entertainment, and freedom from annoyance and danger. These attractions, together with the accessibility of the grounds, have established for them a permanent reputation in almost every way as a desirable resort (BPC, *Twenty-Fourth Annual Report* [1885], p. 6).

33. For centuries Dutch and Belgian farmers had protected their cattle during the harsh winter months by sheltering them under the roofs of their farmhouses. The cattle were fed and watered without being turned outside. Often only a partition separated the cattle from the farmhouse kitchen, but everything was kept clean and orderly (Frederick L. Houghton, *Holstein-Friesian Cattle* . . . [Brattleboro, Vt., 1897], pp. 10–11).

34. See OVC, "Report Accompanying Plan for Laying Out the South Park," March 1871, note 21, above.

35. Spanish for a public walk or promenade with a row of trees on each side. Olmsted also discussed the use of the alameda in his 1873 report for Riverside Park in New York (*OED*, Frederick Law Olmsted, "Report of the Landscape Architect on Riverside Park and Avenue," March 29, 1873 [*Papers of FLO*, 6: 598, 599]).

36. Very early in Central Park's construction it was determined that some sort of boundary enclosure would be necessary in order to protect the park from inappropriate entrance or exit as well as to close the park at night. In 1861 Olmsted provided suggestions for constructing a barrier between the park and the street, and the park commissioners finally decided to build a wall of Dorchester stone. At the time Olmsted was writing this report those sections of the boundary wall on the Fifth Avenue side of the park at 60th and 74th streets were still incomplete (*Forty Years*, 2: 391, 396; FLO to the Board of Commissioners of the Central Park, April 1861 [*Papers of FLO*, 3: 338–41]; DPP, *Minutes*, Jan. 27, 1886, p. 531).

37. Marshall Pinckney Wilder (1798–1886), merchant and horticulturist. At the first pub-

lic hearing on November 5, 1869, to which Olmsted here refers, Wilder stated that "The advance of art, science, and high civilization requires, as I think any gentleman who has taken cognizance of the progress of the last forty years will say, that Boston should have a park. Not only she should have a park, but she should have had the first park in our country" (*DAB*; *Boston Daily Evening Transcript*, Nov. 6, 1869, p. 1; "City Document No. 123," in City of Boston, *Documents*, 3: 7).

38. Patrick Andrew Collins (1844–1905), mayor of Boston from 1902 until 1905, was born in Ireland. He came to the United States with his family in 1848. Largely self-taught, Collins entered Harvard law school in 1868 and was admitted to the bar in 1871. Collins entered politics in 1868 and served four years in the Massachusetts state legislature and six years in the U.S. House of Representatives. On June 7, 1876, Collins attended a meeting of public park advocates held at Faneuil Hall. Among those attending the meeting were Oliver Wendell Holmes and Richard Henry Dana, Jr. Collins was the last to speak, and in his speech delivered the words Olmsted quotes here (J. C. Rand, *One of a Thousand*, p. 138; A. P. Langtry, *Metropolitan Boston*, p. 237; *Boston Daily Globe*, June 7, 1876, p. 4; *Boston Morning Journal*, June 8, 1876, p. 2).

39. In June 1884 the New York state legislature passed a law authorizing the laying out of parks and parkways in the Twenty-third and Twenty-fourth wards of New York City. The six parks for which the park commission selected sites were Van Cortlandt Park (1,069 acres), Bronx Park (653 acres), Pelham Bay Park (1,700 acres), Crotona Park (135 acres), St. Mary's Park (25 acres), and Claremont Park (38 acres). The average for the total acreage of these six parks is 603 acres (New York [State], *Laws of the State of New York, Passed at the One Hundred and Seventh Session of the Legislature . . .* [Albany, N.Y., 1884], chap. 522; John Mullaly, *The New Parks beyond the Harlem . . .* [New York, 1887], map).

40. Fairmount Park in Philadelphia consisted of 2,648 acres (*Boston Daily Globe*, Oct. 8, 1880, p. 4).

41. The six parks in Chicago to which Olmsted here refers were Washington and Jackson parks, located on the southside of the city near Lake Michigan (for a description of these parks see OVC, "Report Accompanying Plan for Laying Out the South Park," March 1871, above); Lincoln Park, located on the northside of the city along Lake Michigan; and Humboldt, Garfield, and Douglas parks, located on the westside of Chicago.

42. That is, East Rock Park in New Haven, Connecticut; Beardsley Park in Bridgeport, Connecticut; Washington Park in Albany, New York, designed in 1869 by John Bogart and John Y. Culyer, Olmsted and Vaux's associates on Prospect Park; the Park (Delaware Park) in Buffalo, New York; and Mount Royal Park in Montreal (see nn. 10 and 21, above; H. P. Phelps, comp., *The Albany Hand-Book* [Albany, N.Y., 1884], pp. 159–61; *Papers of FLO*, 6: 300; see also OVC to William Dorsheimer, Oct. 1, 1868, and FLO, *Mount Royal. Montreal* [1881], both above).

43. Olmsted is probably referring to the extension of Central Park from 106th Street to 110th Street. Enabling legislation to extend the park was not passed until April 1859, and at that time it appeared the cost of the land would be prohibitive. Finally, in 1863 the additional sixty-five acres was purchased but at a cost exceeding $1.1 million (*Forty Years*, 2: 52–54; *Papers of FLO*, 3: 289).

44. In his enthusiasm to begin work on the Bois de Boulogne, Napoleon III brought in a gardener with no experience for the task that lay ahead of him. By the time Baron Georges Eugène Haussmann took charge of the project in the summer of 1853, the gardener was already excavating the site for a lake that would be similar to the Serpentine in Hyde Park. Haussmann realized that the bed of the lake was so uneven that when filled with water it would be dry at one end and overflow at the other. He solved the problem by creating two lakes on different levels and having the overflow of the

higher lake feed the lower one by a waterfall. Napoleon, however, was disappointed with the solution, because he had his heart set on a waterway similar to that in Hyde Park (J. M. and Brian Chapman, *The Life and Times of Baron Haussmann: Paris in the Second Empire* [London, 1957], pp. 86–87; David H. Pinkney, *Napoleon III and the Rebuilding of Paris* [Princeton, N.J., 1958], p. 95).

45. On September 6, 1857, the *New York Herald* reported that the "great Central Park . . . will be nothing but a huge bear garden for the lowest denizens of the city of which we shall yet pray litanies to be delivered" (*New York Herald*, Sept. 6, 1857).

46. On January 10, 1886, the *New-York Daily Tribune* reported that a proposal had been made to lay out a race track for trotting horses in Central Park. The *Tribune* denounced the idea and stated that the original intent of the park was to provide rural views and refreshment for those wearied by the confines of the city. The author of the article stated that "it is melancholy enough that such a statement as this needs to be made after the Park has existed for thirty years and that there are people of fair intelligence in the city to-day who do not realize that this is the only justifying reason for the existence of so large a pleasure ground in the heart of a busy city" (*New-York Daily Tribune*, Jan. 10, 1886, p. 4).

47. In the New York *Sun* article to which Olmsted refers, Central Park commissioner John D. Crimmins (1844–1917) did not object to the race track on the basis that it would destroy the design and purpose of the park but rather that it would infringe on grounds already used for "lawn tennis courts, football and cricket" (*Sun*, Jan. 15, 1886, p. 2; *New York Times*, Nov. 10, 1917, p. 13).

48. In March 1862 the state legislature granted the New-York Historical Society permission to use the old State Arsenal, located in the southeastern corner of the park, and adjacent property for a museum. However, the Historical Society requested higher ground for its museum, and in 1868 the state legislature passed an act granting the area of the park located adjacent to Fifth Avenue and between 81st to 84th streets to the society for a museum of "history, antiquities, and art." Between 1868 and 1870 the Historical Society attempted to raise the necessary funds for its museum but finally was forced to abandon its scheme because of the enormous costs of building construction.

 Meanwhile, early in 1870 the Metropolitan Museum of Art was incorporated, and in 1871 the state legislature passed an act authorizing the erection of a building for the museum either within Central Park or on some other city public space. In March 1872 the park commissioners determined to place the museum in the same location that the Historical Society had attempted to build its museum, on the eastern side of the park between 79th and 84th streets. Calvert Vaux, Olmsted's former partner in designing the park, received the commission to design the building and the Metropolitan Museum of Art was opened to the public on March 30, 1880 (Winifred E. Howe, *A History of the Metropolitan Museum of Art* [New York, 1913], pp. 41–43, 138–39, 189; Jay E. Cantor, "The Museum in the Park," *Metropolitan Museum of Art Bulletin* 26 [April 1968]: 337–40).

49. The "next scheme" may well have been the debate over using the Central Park as the site for a World's Fair in 1883 (see FLO, *A Consideration of the Justifying Value of a Public Park*, Jan. 28, 1881, nn. 3 and 4, above).

50. See note 46 above.

51. In March 1877 Montreal's park commissioners discussed with Olmsted the possibility of putting a small-pox hospital in Mount Royal Park. It was necessary to move the hospital from its original site, and H. A. Nelson, chairman of the Mount Royal Park Commission, suggested as a possible site land behind the Hotel Dieu that had been purchased for the park and was just north of the city boundary. Olmsted argued against the proposal stating that "of course the park is the last place in all of the unoccupied suburbs of the city where it can stand appropriately and there is no position

in the park where it can go without being an offence to good taste" (FLO to H. A. Nelson, March 19 and 26, 1877; H. A. Nelson to FLO, March 15 and 21, 1877).

52. The designer of the Boston Public Garden was a young Boston architect, George F. Meacham. Meacham's plan for the twenty-four-acre Public Garden, adopted in 1859, called for elements of formal flower beds combined with winding paths and an irregularly shaped pond. It also included a site for a new city hall, a playground, and a greenhouse. While much of Meacham's plan was carried out including the pond and paths, James Slade, city engineer, was able to soften the original design by eliminating the geometrical flower beds and shaping the land to look less man-made. The city hall was built on a different site and the greenhouse was constructed on Charles Street (C. Zaitzevsky, *Frederick Law Olmsted and the Boston Park System*, pp. 33–34; Friends of the Public Garden and Common, Inc., *Public Garden*, pp. 9–10).

53. That is, William McMillan (see F. L. & J. C. Olmsted, "Plan for a Public Park on the Flats South of Buffalo," Oct. 1, 1888, n. 24, below).

54. Stephen Grover Cleveland (1837–1908), president of the United States. In 1881 the Democratic party nominated Cleveland, a lawyer of modest means, for mayor of Buffalo on a reform ticket. Cleveland was elected and was so successful at cleaning up Buffalo's city government that the state Democratic party took notice and nominated him for governor. Cleveland was elected in 1882 and two years later was nominated for the presidency. Cleveland was elected president in 1884 and again in 1892 (*DAB*).

55. The act was passed April 21, 1884, and provided for the acquisition of twelve acres of land adjacent to Delaware Park (see F. L. & J. C. Olmsted, "Plan for a Public Park on the Flats South of Buffalo," Oct. 1, 1888, n. 4, below).

56. Olmsted wrote this document in 1885 intending to include it with a report to the Boston park commission as part of a protest against economic retrenchment on the parks. He asked William McMillan, superintendent of the Buffalo parks, to secure the signatures (FLO, typescript [c. 1885], B65: #700, OAR/LC; FLO to [William] McMillan, March 16, 1885).

57. In 1877 the city engineer of Boston estimated that it would cost $1,625,800 to construct Back Bay park. At the time Olmsted wrote this report $1,108,500 had already been spent on construction ("City Document No. 44," in City of Boston, *Documents*, 1: 6; City of Boston. Department of Parks, *Twelfth Annual Report of the Board of Commissioners for the Year 1886* [Boston, 1887], p. 11).

58. See note 37 above.

59. Before the Civil War, Philadelphia's Fairmount Park lay entirely east of the Schuylkill River, but in the decade following the war the city purchased over two thousand acres, primarily west of the river.

   In 1861 Egbert L. Viele prepared a plan for Prospect Park in Brooklyn, New York. By 1865 the park commission had become dissatisfied with Viele's plan and asked Calvert Vaux to examine the site. Vaux wrote a report entitled "Preliminary Report on Boundaries" in which he recommended that the commission discard the land east of Flatbush Avenue since the street divided the park site. He also recommended that the commission purchase property south and west of the original park site (Olmsted, Vaux & Co. to the Chairman of the Committee on Plans of the Park Commission of Philadelphia, Dec. 4, 1867 [*Papers of FLO*, 6: 231–45]; *Papers of FLO*, 6: 19–20; see also OVC, "Preliminary Report to the Commissioners for Laying Out a Park in Brooklyn, New York, Jan. 24, 1866, above).

60. Jonathan Scoville (1830–1891), an iron manufacturer, was elected mayor of Buffalo in 1884 and served only one term (Melvin G. Holli and Peter d'A. Jones, eds., *Biographical Dictionary of American Mayors, 1820–1980* [Westport, Ct., 1981], p. 322).

61. An altered version of this document was reprinted in the park commission's annual report for 1886 (City of Buffalo. Park Commission, *Sixteenth Annual Report of the Buffalo Park Commissioners. January, 1886* [Buffalo, N.Y., 1886], p. 17).

62. In addition to the figures Olmsted cites here, the report noted that 4,825,000 cubic yards of material, most of which was original to the site, was handled in grading, fertilizing, and building the park (New York [City], Department of Public Parks, *Third General Report of the Board of Commissioners of the Department of Public Parks . . . from May 1st, 1872, to December 31st, 1873* [New York, 1875], pp. 350–51).

63. Olmsted's calculations are probably based on computing the total amount expended for land purchases, construction, and maintenance through 1885 divided by the number of acres in each park.

64. The iron bridge with the wooden floor is Bow Bridge in Central Park.

65. In 1882 the British occupied the city of Cairo, Egypt, and in doing so rectified many of the unsanitary aspects of the city by improving the water supply and the drainage system (*EB*).

66. Prior to the Civil War, it was customary for planter families to leave their coastal homes in summer to avoid diseases such as malaria and yellow fever. After the war and the abolition of slavery, both blacks and whites began moving into the cities. As populations increased, diseases and epidemics became even more prevalant particularly in the summer months. After the yellow fever epidemic of 1878 in New Orleans, southern businessmen recognized the economic costs of disease in their cities and began to call for measures to improve sanitary conditions. Southern city officials began ordering the installation of sewers, the improvement of water supplies, and the creation of boards of health with the power to enforce laws governing sanitary improvements. Cities in the forefront of this movement were Atlanta, Georgia, and Memphis, Tennessee (Howard N. Rabinowitz, "Continuity and Change: Southern Urban Development, 1860–1900," in *The City in Southern History: The Growth of Urban Civilization in the South*, eds. Blaine A. Brownell and David R. Goldfield [Port Washington, N.Y., 1977], pp. 103, 111).

67. Ellis Sylvester Chesbrough (1813–1886), railroad and civil engineer. In 1855, after having served as engineer of the Boston waterworks for nine years, Chesbrough accepted the position of engineer to the Chicago board of sewerage commission. In that capacity he designed the sewerage system of the city. In 1879 Chesbrough resigned as Chicago's commissioner of public works, but he continued to consult with officials from other cities including New York, Boston, Toronto, Detroit, and Milwaukee on water-supply and sewerage problems (*Appleton's Cyc. Am. Biog.*).

68. Sir Joseph William Bazalgette (1819–1891), civil engineer. Between 1855 and 1889, Bazalgette was chief engineer to London's metropolitan board of works, and from 1858 to 1875 he was in charge of the construction of London's drainage system and the Thames embankment (*DNB*).

69. Sir Robert Peel (1788–1850), prime minister of Great Britain from 1834–35 and 1841–46. He became a member of the House of Commons in 1809 and served several years. Peel instituted several legal reforms in Great Britain, and in 1829 he created the Metropolitan Police Force. While the police force would be supervised by two commissioners responsible for recruitment, discipline, and training, it fell under the aegis of the British Home Office, and the Home Secretary confirmed the appointment of the commissioners, thus removing the police from local authority and placing it under national control.

    This same pattern was repeated in American cities in the nineteenth century, removing control of city police departments from the hands of city politicians and placing them under the control of state-appointed boards of police. In 1859 the Illinois legislature passed a law creating a three-member board of police commissioners appointed by the governor for the city of Chicago, and in 1885 the Massachusetts legislature did the same thing in Boston.

    The "scion grown in Chicago" that was grafted onto the Boston police system may well have been a signal system created in Chicago in 1880. The system enabled patrolmen to communicate with the police station at any time through a call box. By 1887 the Boston police department had a call-box system in place (*DNB*; Norman Gash, *Mr. Secretary Peel: the Life of Sir Robert Peel* [1961; rpt. ed., New York, 1985], pp. 496–98; John J. Flinn, *History of the Chicago Police* [1887; rpt. ed., Montclair, N.J., 1973], pp. 93–94, 398–99; Leonard Vance Harrison, *Police Administration in Boston* [1934; rpt. ed., New York, 1971], pp. 21–22; Roger Lane, *Policing the City: Boston, 1822–1885* [New York, 1971], p. 287; City of Boston, *Third Annual Report of the Board of Police for the City of Boston* [Boston, 1888], pp. 19–20).

70. Wood Island Park, located at Boston Harbor, was first proposed in 1876 as a small neighborhood park. In 1884 Olmsted prepared a preliminary report and plan for the park, but by 1891 additional land had been acquired for the site and he prepared a revised plan at that time. The incident to which Olmsted here refers occurred in 1885 and 1886. The annual reports of the Boston park commission indicate that in 1885 the park received an appropriation for $5,000. That parsimonious amount was spent filling Neptune Road, which according to the design would be the principal parkway leading into the park. The commissioners indicated, however, that a much larger appropriation was needed to construct a bridge over the Boston, Revere Beach, and Lynn Railroad and without it no approach was possible to the park since the railroad's tracks were a barrier to the park itself. Apparently this request went unheeded by the legislature, and the 1886 annual report indicated no appropriation for Wood Island Park but included a cursory note that no work was done on the park that year (C. Zaitzevsky, *Frederick Law Olmsted*, pp. 99–100; City of Boston, *Tenth Annual Report of the Board of Commissioners of the Department of Parks for the City of Boston, for the Year 1884* [Boston, 1885], pp. 20–22; idem, *Eleventh Annual Report of the Board of Commissioners of the Department of Parks for the Year 1885* [Boston, 1886], pp. 7, 21; idem, *Twelfth Annual Report*, pp. 8, 30).

71. A reference to McLean Hospital in Belmont, Massachusetts, for which Olmsted provided advice in the selection of the site in 1872 and the laying out of the grounds, buildings, and drives in 1875 (FLO to Henry Bromfield Rogers, Dec. 13, 1872 [*Papers of FLO*, 6: 584–88]).

72. In 1861 the New York state legislature passed an amendment to the original law that created Prospect Park. The new law stated that only the first twelve wards would be taxed for park purposes. The Thirteenth through the Nineteenth wards, exempt from taxation, lay farthest from the park in the areas of Williamsburgh, Green Point, and Bushwick (New York [State], *Laws of the State of New York, Passed at the Eighty-Fourth Session of the Legislature* . . . [Albany, N.Y., 1861], chap. 340; *Map of the Consolidated City of Brooklyn. 1861* [New York, 1861]).

73. Olmsted is quoting from William Wordsworth's poem, "Lines Composed a Few Miles above Tintern Abbey, on Revisiting the Banks of the Wye during a Tour," written on July 13, 1798. The second quotation is from chapter six entitled "The Lamp of Memory" in John Ruskin's *The Seven Lamps of Architecture* (John O. Hayden, *William Wordsworth: The Poems*, 2 vols. [1977; rpt. ed., New Haven, Conn., 1981], 1: 357–62; E. T. Cook and Alexander Wedderburn, eds., *The Works of John Ruskin*, 39 vols. [London, 1903–12], 8: 221).

74. Another quotation from the sixth chapter of Ruskin's *Seven Lamps of Architecture* (E. T. Cook and A. Wedderburn, eds., *Works of John Ruskin*, 8: 233).

75. That is, the Arnold Arboretum in Boston for which Olmsted prepared a plan in 1879.

76. This quotation is from John Ruskin's lecture entitled, "The Relation of Wise Art to Wise Science" delivered at Oxford University in 1872. The exact quotation reads, "There is nothing that I tell you with more eager desire that you should believe — nothing with wider ground in my experience for requiring you to believe, than this, that you never will love art well, till you love what she mirrors better" (E. T. Cook and A. Wedderburn, eds., *Works of John Ruskin*, 22: 152 – 53).

General Plan for the Improvement
of the Niagara Reservation.

[1887]

THE HONORABLE WILLIAM DORSHEIMER,[1]
President of the Board of Commissioners of the State Reservation at Niagara.

SIR —

In the work to be undertaken by the State upon the Niagara Reservation, it is to be hoped that whatever is done shall tell toward a general result that shall be lastingly satisfactory, nothing being wasted on matters of temporary expediency.

To this end, it is chiefly important that everything shall be done in pursuance of a general plan, in the preparation of which a judicious view has been taken of the ultimate scope of the undertaking.

Before asking attention, therefore, to specific features of the plan that we have the honor now to submit, we shall present a few statements as to its aspect in this respect.

Of all the territory of the Reservation, about a seventh part has at present an objectionable artificial character, most of it, for example, having been heaped up or dug out in connection with road or building operations.[2]

Upon this seventh part the plan looks to operations the aim of which is to re-establish a permanently agreeable natural character, harmonious with that of the undisturbed parts.

The plan aims at nothing else, anywhere upon the Reservation, but to make a suitable provision of roads and walks, of platforms and seats, at the more important points of view, and of other accommodations, such as experience has shown to be necessary to decency and good order when large numbers of people come together.

It looks to such operations as will be required to prevent these provisions from appearing harshly intrusive upon the natural scenery, and to guard the elements of natural scenery from injury and secure their healthy development.

The above is a round statement of all that the plan has in view.

As to the extent and quality of the provisions for use that the plan contemplates, they are in that degree of a substantial character that experience in all much frequented grounds has proved to be soundly economical. That is to say, if less capacious, substantial and well ordered than the plan contemplates that they shall be, there is reason to think that the expense of care-taking, repairs and renewals would more than compensate the saving in construction.

The question, then, whether the scope of the plan might providently be less than it is, must be a question chiefly of the numbers of people who in the future will be drawn to the Reservation.

Intending later to present some facts as to the increasing visitation of the place, we wish here to bring to mind a consideration, the bearing of which upon the question, in a study of the policy of the State in the premises, should not be overlooked.

People have been heretofore influenced by two motives to wish to see Niagara, one is that they may be astonished. People in whose minds this motive has been largely predominant have generally been disappointed in what they found. The removal that your Board has made of various structures and ornaments that had been placed near the Falls has not lessened the disappointment of this class of visitors, and it may be safely assumed that no improvement that the State can make will increase the astonishing qualities of Niagara.[3]

The other motive with which people come to the place is that of the enjoyment to be obtained through the pensive contemplation of distinctive qualities of beauty in happily associated passages of natural scenery.

It is in this respect that Niagara deserves to rank among the great treasures of the world. What your Board has done in the removal of circumstances by which its distinctive natural scenery has been divided, belittled and put out of countenance, has made it much more enjoyable in this respect, and it is with reference to further gains of the same kind that the value of all operations of improvement is to be determined.

If they are well devised with reference to it, then, for this reason alone, the number of visitors to be attracted to the place in the future might be expected to increase more rapidly than the population from which they are to be drawn.

But there is reason to expect a much larger increase than would thus be accounted for.

There are many passages of natural scenery which, from the effect they produce, may be classed with Niagara among the world's treasures; yet none of them have long been highly valued by anyone. A few centuries ago, that is to say, people, even in the advanced lines of civilized progress, seem to have taken no pleasure in them.

But a change has since been gradually occurring. It was already well marked among the educated classes of the last century. In the present it has advanced rapidly with the main body of the people of all advancing countries.

As far as our own is concerned, no better evidence could be wanted of such an advance than is to be had by considering the legislation that has established the duties of your commission, and the manner in which this legislation was brought about, in connection with the fact that when in 1806 the State sold the property which it has lately re-acquired at Niagara, it is not known that a single one of all its people thought of it as having even a prospective value otherwise than as a mill-power.[4]

There is not the least reason for assuming that this movement has run its course. There is every reason to suppose that if improvements should now be made upon the Reservation, suited only to the present obvious demands of the public, they would before many years have to be destroyed to make way for others more sagaciously adjusted to the tendency of civilized progress in this respect.

Suppose that this should occur. It is to be borne in mind that the wasteful result would not be, simply, that occurring through the demolition of the constructed improvements, but in the loss of much that would, in the meantime, have been gained by growth, and in the necessity for opening a new, raw and gaunt face to the forest in order to accomplish the enlargement of the constructions adjoining it.

We have no doubt that, in the final judgment of the Commissioners, and of all who will thoroughly study the question with a desire to avoid such waste and destruction, that more anxiety will be felt lest the plan shall prove inadequate than that it should prove superserviceable.

As to the question thus suggested, namely, whether the accommodations proposed by the plan may not be insufficient, two considerations are to be weighed.

First, that the more artificial features fill the eye the less will be the effect of the natural features.

Second, that when the improvements proposed in the plan shall have been fully carried out, and when, to these, the improvements to be made on the Canadian Reservation shall have been added,[5] the number of persons at any time visiting Niagara, will be much more extensively distributed, and will be much more in circulation, than might be supposed from any experience hitherto had.

For the reasons given, it is, we think, little to be feared that serious waste will result, either because the plan has been conceived with too broad or with too narrow a view of the number of guests which the State will be obliged to entertain upon it.

It is more to be apprehended that waste will come because the main object of the State in making the Reservation shall be lost sight of or become confused in the minds of those engaged in its direction with objects that are wholly foreign to it.

All the original designers can do to prevent this confusion is to point out the distinction between the organic purpose with which the plan has been formed, and the purpose of the class of improvements of which bits and scraps are most likely, as the work advances, to be interpolated upon it. The effect of such interpolations would be that, to the extent to which they shall be admitted, neither the older nor the later motives of design could be followed to fully excellent conclusions, the pursuit of the earlier having established bars against the introduction of the later, and the pursuit of the later interrupting and wastefully frustrating the fruition of the earlier.

The danger lies chiefly in the circumstance that the plan looks for none of the beauty which is commonly the chief object of gardening improvements, and in the probability that it will be assumed that the pleasure of visitors is to be increased by the introduction, here and there, of beautiful incidents of that character.

It thus lies largely in the difficulty that may be experienced in distinguishing between the ultimate object of the designed operations and the object in view in the operations of common garden works. Take for instance the operations of road and walk making, the grading of slopes, the dressing of ground surfaces and their clothing with herbage, the planting and nursing of trees, the building of foot-bridges and other constructed objects. The direct local result of all such operations as are intended on the reservation will be precisely the same that it is in ordinary gardening works. And to those who do not see the very different way in which they are intended ultimately to give pleasure, it will always be thought that the introduction of decorative detail would be an improvement. Once the reason for excluding decorative detail is lost sight of, there is nothing to hinder the introduction of any amount of it, and thus bringing about the gradual transformation of the Reservation into an affair of the sumptuous park and flower-garden order, than which nothing would be more deplorable.

The danger is the greater because, when such results as the plan has in view, have at last come from operations of improvement, they are generally supposed to have been much easier of attainment than those seen to come from similar operations in sumptuous gardening. Probably no one who has not taken to himself a task of each kind and pursued it to its proper end can imagine how far the contrary is the fact. At no time, therefore, in the progress of a work such as that of the Reservation is meant by the plan to be, is the relation plainly obvious of that which comes before the eye of the casual observer to the operations from which it has resulted. And, in the end, hardly ever is that which is most valuable in it recognized to be what it is—the ripened fruit of long preceding forethought and of patient persistence in carrying out the organic purpose of a plan. It is looked upon rather as a wild fruit. It follows that the motives of a plan, in the pursuit of which designed results of this character have been partly attained, are little apt to be searchingly inquired after, and, consequently, in all the progress of the work, are much apt to be misapprehended in details, and overridden with a wasteful sacrifice of the partly attained results. The necessity, to the full attainment of designed results, for excluding from such a plan various features that may from time to time come into the minds of impulsive persons as desirable to have been included — the motives, that is to say, of *reservation,* in its design — are particularly liable to be thus misapprehended, and attempts to afterwards make good mistakenly supposed omissions of inadvertence are thus particularly apt to lead to waste of value already gained.

There being this difficulty in the way of carrying out the strict intention of the plan, why should that strict intention be entertained?

Why should it not be intended to give visitors the pleasure that results from the more usual methods of improving places of public resort?

A sufficient answer to this point, is that the purpose for which the Reservation has been established leaves no room for choice in this respect.

It is true that no fixed limits, by which all manner of floral and exotic objects of interest would be excluded from the Reservation, have been prescribed by statute law nor by any form of legislative record. None have been laid down for us in the instructions of your Board.[6] Nevertheless, such limits have been fixed in a perfectly binding way, and in order to guard as far as possible against any misapprehension, at any time hereafter, as to the organic purpose of the plan, we propose to show how this has occurred.

The question of the Reservation had been under active discussion six years before a decision in regard to it was reached. The debate on it had been opened by a communication of the Governor of the State to the Legislature; many leading men took part in it, and it engaged, at last, a great deal of popular interest.[7] It has been well set forth by a member of your Board that the result marked the potency of a sentiment closely allied to that of patriotism and of that form of self-respect that moves men to the greatest acts of heroism.[8]

It needs to be pointed out, however, that, while this is true, it is also true that the heartiest, if not the most loudly pronounced, opposition to the measure had its root in the same sentiment.

The apparent paradox is to be explained in this way. The result of the larger part of all operations, with which the public has for many years past been familiar, that have passed under the name of improvements, and especially of "landscape" or of "park" improvements, has been that of presenting objects for admiration calculated to draw off and dissipate regard for natural scenery. Examples of such a result may be found in the suburbs of most of our cities, where, for example, roads attractive because of certain picturesque natural elements in their borders have been made by improvements to take the character of straight, broad, formal streets, avenues or "boulevards." They may be found also in many costly private villa grounds where the most complete antithesis possible to charming natural conditions has been obtained through lavish displays of horticultural art as artificial as Japanese embroidery or Florentine mosaics. They may be found again in operations of improvement at many places of public resort, one of which, as it passes for an eminent success, may be particularly referred to. It is that of a place on the sea coast originally attractive not at all above thousands of others except because of the movement of advancing and retiring waters, as seen from the sands at the head of a superb beach. The result of improvements at this place has been the supersedure of this beach by an extensive embankment, formed of logs and stones, supporting a plateau where visitors are invited to enjoy, from plank walks, an exhibition of garden finery conceivably pleasing in some other situation, but as far from helpful to an enjoyment of the ocean scenery as anything that can be thought of.

A common association of ideas growing out of such improvements will explain how a strong prejudice was established in the minds of many against the project of the Reservation, upon reading a brief statement that it had been proposed that the State should form a public park at Niagara. Any such prejudice could hardly fail to be nourished in the minds of all who visited the Falls on the American side by the fact that a considerable body of land previously known as The Grove had, a few years before, been made the subject of works of improvement, the character of which had led to its being called a park ("Prospect Park").[9] This ground had originally been truly park-like, that is to say, not inconveniently wild or rugged nor densely wooded, but of a large and simple natural topography, and, in a degree, of a secluded sylvan aspect. Its moderate undulations of surface had a general slope toward the verge of natural crags of some grandeur, and an outlook across a great chasm upon the face of others unsurpassed in beauty of varied vegetation naturally growing from crannies and crevices; it looked, also, upon one of the most impressive water scenes in all the world. The improvements made included specimens of ordinary garden rock-work, a wall-sided stream of water, with a decorative bridge and an island having constructions upon it designed to resemble mossy ruins, specimens of pseudo-rustic work and of pseudo wild gardening, terraced slopes, flowerbeds, "ornamental trees," a monument, a cast-iron fountain, several pavilions, an "archaeological collection," a "Gallery of Fine Arts," a variety theatre and a quantity of theatrical machinery for decorating the great Fall with red, white and blue lights.[10]

What was the organic purpose of these improvements? It was to draw visitors by any means to a particular piece of ground where money could be made out of them, and to so occupy them when there that they should not wish to go elsewhere. In this respect the improvements were so far a success that it was boasted that many persons coming from a distance, and for the first time in their lives, to see Niagara, have been known to go away having seen no more of it than could be obtained from the midst of this "park," and that some of them left without having looked for a single moment at anything beyond the field of its artificial improvements.

Of similar significance is the fact that the largest number of visitors ever drawn to Niagara had been upon occasions when, to such attractions as have been described, there were added grotesque performances by mounte-banks, with fireworks and music.

The discussion of the Reservation project disclosed the fact that great numbers of people had an uneasy sense of humiliation, which needed but a proper occasion for activity to develop into a form of righteous indignation against these proceedings; and it occurred, in consequence, that the most determined, if not the most loudly expressed opposition that the project of the Reservation at any time received, came from a heated apprehension that it would open the way to other so-called improvements, of which the effect would be to yet further divert attention from the distinctive natural scenery of the place.

From the first, the scheme had been presented with a studied pur-pose to guard against such a misapprehension; nevertheless, so commonly have the minds of intelligent men been impressed by the fact that the result of what are called works of improvement is generally the injury of natural scenery, and more so where they are called works of landscape improvement or of park improvement, than in any other case, that it was at length found necessary to organize and for two years maintain a systematic effort by tract distribution, colporterage and elaborate newspaper publication, to root out the honest opposition thus arising to the measure.[11] Nor would these means have been successful at the time but for another circumstance that remains to be stated.

It is this: that while the agitation of the matter was in progress a legal proceeding occurred that made an early sale of Goat Island probable.[12] To those in whose minds regard for the preservation of natural scenery would otherwise have remained a ground of prejudice against the Reservation proj-ect, nothing seemed more likely than that any change in the ownership of Goat Island would be the occasion of a speculation looking to money-making on the principles that had ruled in the improvements that passed under the name of "Prospect Park," and those carried out at the seashore resort that has been described. The probability of such result made it possible to obtain a better hearing than could otherwise have been gained for the assertion that the leading purpose to be accomplished by the proposed act providing for the Reservation was the defense of the scenery natural to the place, and its de-fense, more than anything else, from a class of improvements embodying such objectionable principles. When conviction on this point had thus at last been gained, what had before been the most formidable opposition to the measure became its most effective support.

The history thus summarized is the justification of a view of the proper organic purpose of the Reservation that, without doubt, will be often regarded by those urging interpolations upon the plan as meanly restrictive and prosaically illiberal.

In providing for the removal from the Reservation not only of mills and other constructions for industrial purposes, but of many things originally regarded as luxuries for the entertainment of visitors, especially of the great illuminating apparatus; in preventing the approach of a railway for the accommodation of visitors, because of the injury to the scenery that it would entail, and in forbidding exhibitions in or over the waters of the Reservation, the effect of which would be to attract a larger number of visitors to it for other reasons than those presented in its natural scenery, your Board has taken what we have assumed to be the only admissible view of the proper purpose of the proposed improvement.

There can be no doubt of the general satisfaction of the sober-minded citizens of the State in all these proceedings. But when works of more positive improvement shall have been undertaken it will be found that great differences of opinion will prevail as to the line to be followed in carrying out the accepted principle. And some of the warmest supporters of the measure will prove to be on one side, some on the other, of the line contemplated in the plan that we suggest. It is our duty, therefore, to more exactly define our views.

First, then, we are far from thinking that all that is required to accomplish the designed end is to "let Nature alone."

Incongruities, discordancies, disunities and consequent weaknesses of natural scenery may result, even at Niagara, from natural causes which, though not as unpleasing to an observer of fine sensibilities as those from the so-called park improvements that have been mentioned, are yet decidedly regrettable. Of this character, for instance, are the immediate results of landslides, where otherwise quiet river banks have been undermined by eddies caused by a temporary snagging near them of drifting stuff. Of this character trees, the branches of which have been broken down by ice or stripped of foliage by vermin, or the roots of which have been made inert by an accidental puddling of the clayey surface above them, or by torrents washing the soil from them, and much else, of which examples may be found in the Reservation.

Not only are systematic measures for the remedy and prevention of such unfortunate natural occurrences to be reckoned upon in devising a plan for the lasting improvement of the Reservation, but systematic arrangements, also, looking to better fortune for many elements of its scenery than could be expected everywhere to occur through unassisted processes of nature, as, for instance, in the planting of spots that have accidentally become bare of vegetation, and in securing nourishment and protection for young growths.

On the other hand, it would equally be a mistake to assume, as many are ready to do, that it will be consistent with the leading purpose of the undertaking and will add to the interest of the public in the premises, to introduce into its scenery many forms of vegetation which undeniably possess beautiful qualities and which, if introduced, might not be unlikely to flourish. Some such would, in our opinion, be as undesirable as the ornaments of stained glass, cut stone, plaster, paint and fountains that your Board has been removing. They would be undesirable because, though natural objects somewhere else, perhaps, they would have an alien individuality and an irrelevant, diverting and disturbing effect if seen among the elements of the natural scenery of Niagara.

The conservation of the natural scenery at Niagara, in the sense of the term that has been indicated in the foregoing observations, being accepted as the primary purpose of the undertaking, it must next be considered that all that may be done for this purpose will be futile, except as the enjoyment of the result is to be made available by means of such artificial appliances as walks, roads, bridges, stairways, seats and standing places, and that, as all such furniture of convenience will lessen the visual space to be occupied by elements of natural scenery, the smaller and the less showy or in any way obtrusive upon the attention such furniture is, the better the primary purpose will be realized. But this principle being recognized, it is not to be overlooked that, unless such furniture is much larger, more substantial and obtrusive than might otherwise be thought desirable, not only will visitors be put to a degree of toil and discomfort interfering with their enjoyment of the scenery, but they will be led to movements of more injury to the scenery than that directly caused even by furniture otherwise undesirably large. Examples of such injury are already to be found on the Reservation and, as it is not to be doubted that, in the exercise of a common false sentiment, measures rightly to be taken for guarding against such injury will from time to time be vehemently objected to, we will ask attention to one of them, to be found on the Sister Islands.

Till lately the Sister Islands could only be visited by those who had paid the admission fee to Goat Island;[13] the approach to them is off the short routes to and from the more celebrated sights of Goat Island; to go to them it is necessary to leave a carriage and pass over a foot bridge. They have thus been much protected hitherto from the hurried and thronging movements of visitors. The admission fee being now abolished, and it having become the custom for all visitors to go to Goat Island, this protection can no longer be counted on; and when the regular low-priced omnibus system shall have been perfected, with a station for setting down and taking up visitors at the foot bridge to the Sisters, it is to be expected that they will be much oftener and more densely occupied than they yet have been.[14] Yet, even before the entrance charge had been done away with, the movement of visitors upon them had already been sufficient to cause a perceptible and unhappy modification of their original natural character.

A large part of the old ground verdure, for instance, had been killed out, and mud or dust was often found in its place.

A large part of the rocks no longer had their former interesting surface character, all their distinctive qualities having been ground out by the heels of visitors. Not many years before there were to be enjoyed here remark-

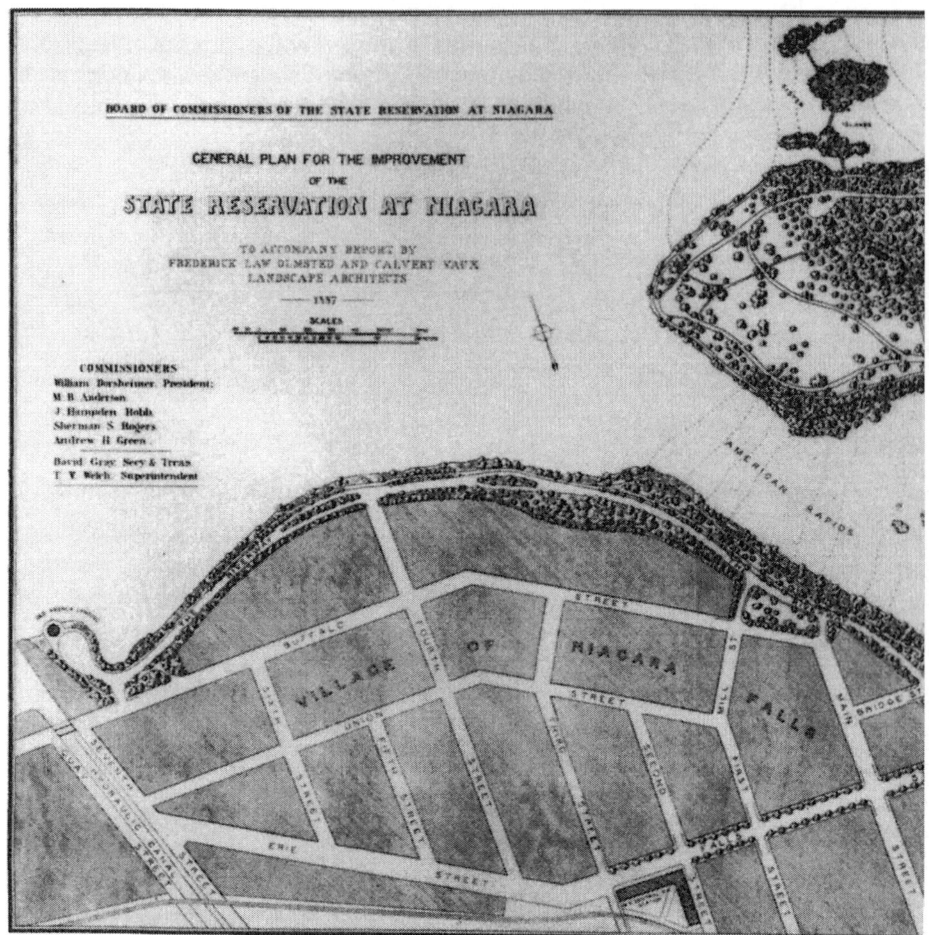

"General Plan for the Improvement of

ably luxuriant, low massive bodies of a description of foliage rare even to most horticultural visitors, and when in perfection not less beautiful, as a constituent of landscape composition, than that of the most valued acquisitions our gardens have ever received from distant lands — our native yew, a shrub supplying the darkest green and the brightest red of our forest. Because of the unrestricted movements of visitors, some of whom have been crowded by others out of the more beaten paths, these plants had already lost not a little of their characteristic beauty and were in a fair way to be gradually worried to death. Elsewhere on the islands numerous roots of trees were to be seen exposed through the wearing off of the surface soil, bruised and rendered incapable of supplying the nourishment they formerly had to the foliage above,

THE STATE RESERVATION AT NIAGARA," 1887

which was, consequently, beginning to lose its vigor, grace and density; and though your superintendent[15] has taken some precautions to lessen the evil, what has been said can yet be readily verified by a visit to the islands.

The lesson is the more strenuously taught by the present condition of Luna Island, because, relatively to its area, its surface has been more generally worn by the feet of visitors. Half the dense foliage, originally growing wherever the rock gave it a foothold, has disappeared, and much of that which remains is feeble and shabby. Unless stringent measures are used to prevent it, Luna Island will, in a few years, inevitably become a barren rock.

That many parts of the Reservation shall be prevented from being gradually made desolate by like process, an extent of artificial accommodation, and of artificial expedients for protecting nature, must be provided that would otherwise deserve condemnation.

But it is not simply to enforce this consideration that the above facts have been referred to; there is a principle affecting the plan to be based upon them of much greater importance and which, experience in nearly every public ground wherein the enjoyment of Nature has been an object has shown to be most difficult to be fully and continuously kept prominently in view. It is this:

Having regard to the enjoyment by visitors of natural scenery, and considering that the means of making this enjoyment available to large numbers of them will unavoidably lessen the extent and value of the primary elements of natural scenery, nothing of an artificial character should be allowed a place on the property, no matter how valuable it might be under other circumstances and no matter at how little cost it may be had, the presence of which can be avoided consistently with the provision of necessary conditions for making the enjoyment of the natural scenery available.

Suppose, for instance, that a costly object of art, like that of the Statue of Liberty, should be tendered to the State on the condition that it should be set up on Goat Island, the precept to which our argument has tended would oblige a declension of the gift as surely as it would the refusal of an offer to stock the Island with poison ivy or with wolves or bears.

This conclusion will be found to dispose of many suggestions of alleged improvement that have already been urged, and the like of which will probably never, for many years at a time, cease to be urged, and urged earnestly, by good men, on grounds superficially plausible.

It has been supposed, for example, that one of the first improvements to be made after throwing open Goat Island would be to replace the little old eating-house upon it by a much finer and larger establishment. If it were a commercial undertaking into which the State was entering, in competition with the people of the village of Niagara, it cannot be questioned that the restaurant could be made a profitable branch of it. But adopting the view upon which the plan of improvement now submitted is based, it is to be considered that no house can be built upon the island that will not in some degree dispossess, obscure and disturb elements of its distinctive natural scenery. The question, then, is, will the absence of places of refreshment cause such hardship to visitors, reasonably provident for themselves, as to seriously interfere with the general enjoyment by the public of the scenery? It is a sufficient answer to say that there is no point in the Reservation at which a house can be placed that is more than ten minutes' walk or five minutes' drive from hotels and restaurants standing on land of private ownership.

Similar reasoning will apply to a variety of projects that it can have been supposed that your Board would entertain only through a failure to understand that it is precisely against obtrusions of essentially the same character on the natural scenery as they would involve that the State has placed the premises in reserve. The project of a camera obscura is one such; that of prospect towers another, that of a militia parade ground another.

But of suggestions that have been publicly made for using the Niagara Reservation for purposes other than that of conservation and protection for its natural scenery and the facilitation of the public enjoyment of it, that which calls for the gravest consideration is one for the establishment upon it, in a suitable building, of a collection of objects helpful to a study of the geology of the region and of the interesting history of the border lands of the St. Lawrence, the Niagara and the lakes. A museum and library for these purposes being desirable, there would be obvious advantages in placing them near the Falls; but the advantage of placing them within the Reservation, rather than at some other point within the village of Niagara Falls, cannot outweigh the objections that we have aimed to present to complicating in any manner the purpose which the State has primarily in view in forming the Reservation. This is no more a scientific or a scholarly or an educational purpose than it is a commercial purpose.

A venerable and public-spirited citizen of the village, of a family to which the State already owes much, has offered to present, for the purposes named, a building site, now his private property, bordering upon the Reservation, on condition that the building and necessary support of the institution shall be otherwise provided.[16] The situation offered is a commanding one; it is in the most attractive quarter of the village; the ground is higher than any on the Reservation; the body of land is larger than would be strictly necessary; it would have a direct entrance from the Reservation, and it is in all respects a better site than any that could be proposed on the Reservation.

If the State should think it expedient to take action favorably to a museum, it would be much better that it should be in a form thus suggested than in that of reappropriating to the purpose ground that it has reserved for the enjoyment of natural scenery.

In arguing against the proposition to provide refreshment places on the Reservation, we have taken the position that it could be approved only on the ground that otherwise visitors might suffer hardship preventing enjoyment of the scenery. It is necessary, however, to maintain that some visitors must even be condemned to what they will think something of a hardship at certain points in order that the organic purpose of the Reservation may be carried out as fully as the plan contemplates that it shall be.

In the cases to which we thus refer the question to be considered is this:

What is to be the effect of certain proposed arrangements in respect to the enjoyment of the scenery, not by a few visitors of a particular condition, at certain times, but, in the long run, by the great body of visitors? And this question is to be discussed not without regard for those who, from natural endowments or the results of training, are susceptible to a higher enjoyment than most. It is a question, we are bound to consider, of the highest average enjoyment.

We will direct attention at once to the point where the judgment on a question of this kind that is represented in the plan is most likely to be differed with by an important element of public opinion. It is for your Board to say whether it is sound.

To see the Canadian Fall from the height called on the drawing Porter's Bluff,[17] visitors approaching in carriages will be obliged, by the arrangement proposed in the plan, to leave them and walk, or be moved in wheel chairs, a distance of thirty paces. Why should they be subjected to this inconvenience?

The following statement is our answer:

The view of the vortex of the Fall which makes the locality especially attractive can only be obtained from a space of ground so limited in extent that it does not offer standing room for the numbers who, at times even at present, wish to occupy it. It is certain that in the near future newcomers will, for short periods, in many days, be obliged to wait for those to move on who have come to this point of view before them. The space in question having this exceptional value, and being so limited in extent, it is to be considered whether it would be judicious to attempt to provide accommodations for people in carriages in any part of it? After careful study of the circumstances, we have concluded that it would not. Our reasons will be better understood after an actual trial of the present arrangements on any day next summer, when visitors are unusually numerous, but they may be simply presented as follows:

1.   A considerable part of those coming in carriages usually leave them at this point in order to descend to the brink of the Fall, which is inaccessible by carriages, and those who know the ground often send their carriages forward in order to enjoy the short walk to a point beyond, where the Canadian Rapids are best seen. It is those who will not choose to take either of these courses whose case is to be considered.

2.   As to these, it is to be remembered that where carriages are brought, one after another, into a group, in which as they successively arrive and depart some margin for movement is necessary, each carriage takes up a space of ground, on an average, upon which at least fifty men can comfortably stand.

3.   People of an artistic and poetic turn of mind, and all to whom Niagara is naturally most enjoyable, are more given than others to wander from point to point of it on foot. The highest enjoyment of it is unquestionably to be obtained in that way. It is not to be supposed that visitors coming on foot shall be forbidden under all circumstances to stand upon any part of the small piece of ground in question when it is not occupied by a carriage. It is not to be supposed that a passage for people coming on foot to this ground

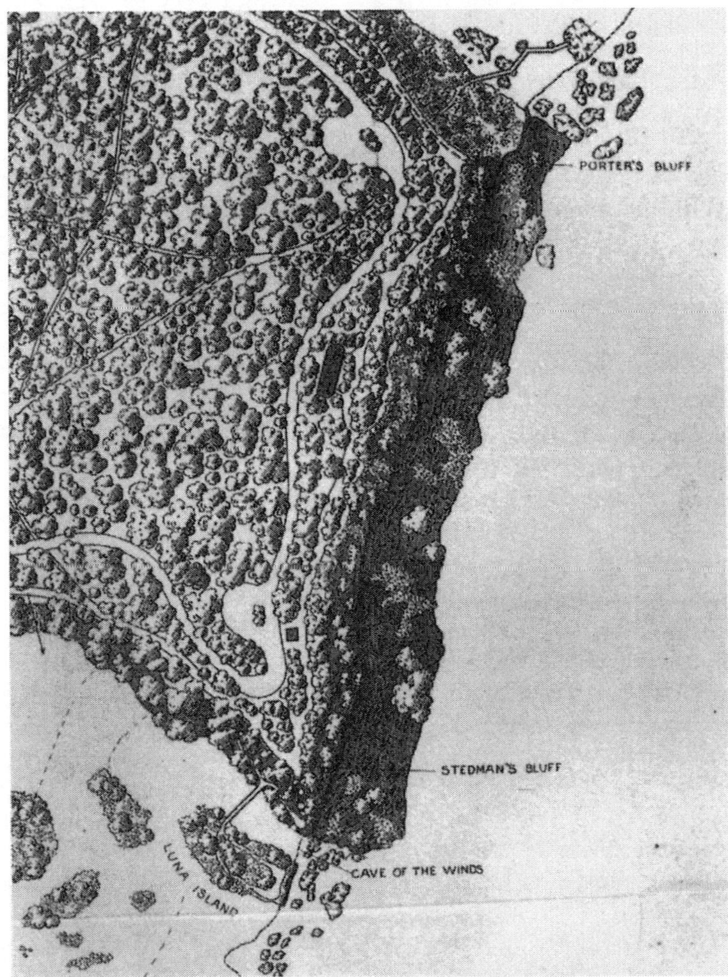

DETAIL OF 1887 NIAGARA RESERVATION PLAN, SHOWING CONCOURSES AT PORTER'S BLUFF AND STEDMAN'S BLUFF ON GOAT ISLAND

is not to be kept open from end to end of it, or that such foot people are not to be allowed a standing-place, where, as on the ordinary sidewalk of a curbed street, they may be protected from being driven over by carriages. As the edge of the bank toward the point of interest of such a standing-place is likely to be often crowded, those waiting until opportunity offers to take their places along the edge should be provided with seats, and when there is no crowd, as will most of the time be the case, these seats will be taken by visitors on foot wishing to contemplate the Fall. There will, then, be a strip of ground following the edge of the bank from which carriages are to be kept off, and this space, making allowance for the people standing, passing and sitting upon it, cannot be less than ten feet wide. To a man in a carriage wishing to look, as in this case, at an object considerably below the level of the eye, a line of men standing parallel to and nearly on a level with the side of his carriage, at a distance of ten feet, would be as effective an obstruction as a high stone wall. Even if we think of the place when it is not to be crowded, we shall see that it would not often occur that so few people would be found standing, sitting and passing upon it, that the view across it would fail to be so much interrupted and disturbed, that it would be better for the occupants of carriages caring to enjoy it to get out of them and step to the edge of the bank.

Taking all these considerations into account, it will be seen that the number of those who will choose, being informed of the conditions, if they are allowed, to take such views as they can, from a carriage, in the line of view of greatest interest, is likely to be extremely small relatively to the number of those who will come to the ground on foot, together with those who will, in any case, leave their carriages when they have reached the place. It is also further to be considered that, to persons disposed to look at the Falls from near the edge of the bank in an absorbed and contemplative way, carriages standing and moving close behind them, and all that is apt to occur in connection with numbers of waiting horses and drivers, may be seriously discomposing.

But we may be asked if it is not practicable, by a resort to such means as are used for placing spectators one above another in theatres, for example, to supply standing-room for even a larger number of visitors on foot than the plan provides for, and at the same time to give a place to a certain number of carriages from which a moderately good view toward the Fall could be had. This is possible, but the number of carriages that could at any time be so accommodated would be small, and, the space prepared for them being occupied, there would often be a larger number of those impatiently waiting their turn to be admitted to it than of those holding it. This objection being duly weighed, it is then to be considered that any tolerable arrangement of the kind thus suggested, by which a tier of carriages could be so placed that their occupants could overlook a tier of people on foot, would destroy naturalness of character in the locality, involve the loss of trees that are an important element of the local scenery, prevent any subsequent sylvan occupation of the ground, and interpose an urban, artificial element plainly in conflict with the purpose for which the Reservation has been made. Would the advantage to be gained outweigh this objection to the arrangement? It is assumed on the plan that it would not, and for like reasons, and, more particularly, to avoid the destruction at important points along the shore of existing trees or of opportunities to grow trees in a manner consistent with, and to the improvement of, existing natural scenery, no carriage road is, as a general rule, proposed by the plan to be brought within fifty feet of the river banks. In short, carriages when used on Goat Island are regarded simply as convenient means of locomotion from point to point, and at all points where visitors are likely to come together in large numbers because of views of special general interest to be had from them, provisions are proposed to be made for stopping carriages a few yards back from the river banks within the edge of the woods, and for having them turned out of the road to wait in convenient shady harbors, partially veiled by foliage, while those coming in them are, with others who have arrived on foot, enjoying the outlooks from the best point of view.

We have thus shown certain limits upon the scope of the undertaking, fixed by the conditions necessary to the successful accomplishment of the central organic purpose of the State in making the Reservation. We wish next to call attention to a series of circumstances by which the range of design in preparing the plan submitted has been more rigidly controlled than, without some special consideration of them is likely to be supposed.

The first is this:

The scheme of the Reservation of the State of New York is but a part of a larger scheme. On a review of the whole scheme it will be found that in certain respects the scheme of the Reservation of New York has advantages over the Reservation of the Province of Ontario.[18] It has incomparably greater beauty of a kind depending on refinement and delicacy, and subtle qualities of natural elements of scenery, and these largely apart from the actual cataract — incomparably greater beauty of a kind in which the nearness to the eye of illumined spray and mist and fleeting waters, and of the intricate disposition of leaves, with infinitely varied play of light and shadow, refractions and reflections, and much else that is undefinable in conditions of water, air and foliage, are important parts.

But there is no place within the New York Reservation from which, as from that of Ontario, a view of the entire face of the Falls, or a near view of the face of either division of the Falls, can be had. To obtain even a quartering view of the American Fall, it is necessary to leave the American shore.

Again, the topography of the Ontario Reservation is so large in scale, and the interest of what is to be seen from it is so independent of all such details as contribute to make the charm of the New York part of the scheme, that even the broad military road that follows the brink of the Canadian cliff strikes the eye only as an insignificant circumstance.[19] In respect to grandeur of scenery, nothing can be offered on the New York side to compare with what is now, even before any improvements are made, to be had at any point upon a line nearly a mile in length on the heights of Ontario.

To what, as a definite requirement of design for the improvement of the American Reservation, does this consideration lead?

To this: that as it would be impossible to provide satisfactorily for extensive pleasure-driving on Goat Island, without destroying its sequestered woodland beauty, and that as a direct view of the Cataract could be had by a thousand people at a time while seated in carriages, without similar destruction on the Canadian bank, the plan of improvement for Goat Island, without excluding carriages as a means of transportation, should make provisions for them with solicitous care to avoid unnecessary injury to its forest, and especially to its forest borders, and should in all parts be devised with painstaking regard for enjoyments only to be had in perfection by those willing to seek them at the expense of some little movement on foot.

The second of this series of considerations to which we would ask attention is this: that at the point where the Falls occur the Niagara river makes an abrupt turn, the reach above being exactly at right angles to the reach below the Cataract. From this results not only the circumstances just referred to, that a full view of the Falls can only be enjoyed from the Ontario side, but this other, that at no point within the New York Reservation can any but a distant view be had of either one of the Falls except upon a line nearly raking its line of fall. The space that can be occupied by visitors is thus, in each case, rigidly limited, and but a very small number of persons can ever, at the same moment, be provided with a favorable opportunity of looking at the Falls. Hence it will be seen that improvements in these places, if planned on a very large scale, will be grandiose, useless and wasteful.

Third: Niagara Falls has been the most celebrated place of resort on the Continent, perhaps the most celebrated in the world. It has had a reputation, however, that has prevented it from being popular. During the last two years, under the direction of your Board, many of the circumstances out of which this reputation has slowly been bred have been removed or mitigated, and, as your superintendent has reported, a notable increase has followed in the number of visitors, a perceptible increase in the length of their visits, and a marked increase in their enjoyment of that which is distinctively enjoyable at Niagara.[20]

In view of what has thus already come about, let it be considered what is likely to be the effect on the reputation of Niagara and its popularity as a place of resort of further improvements to be made; what the effect of a growing better understanding by the people of Niagara, of their interest in protecting visitors from the annoyances to which, though much has been gained, they are still subject in approaching the Reservation; what the effect of the further development in all parts of the country with large classes of hitherto home-keeping people, of the growing custom of annual vacation journeys and the tendency of the great railroad corporations to encourage the growth of this custom by offering tourist and excursion special cheap rates of fare for long journeys, as to which last point some information may be found in a note below.*

---

* Not looking beyond Pennsylvania, Kentucky, Illinois, Wisconsin and Michigan, visitors are found to have been brought to the Falls and returned last summer at one-fifth the expense that the journey would have cost them (taking the regular passenger trains) ten years ago.[21]

What, at last, is to be expected as to the number of visitors for whose movements the Reservation must be prepared?

Already upwards of ten thousand people are known by the record of the railroads to have arrived in a single day in which no unusual attraction was offered, having come by night trains, with an intention of leaving on the evening of the same day, consequently with an impulse to crowd all at once upon the more celebrated points of attraction.[22]

Of this ten thousand it is thought by the superintendent that full half sought within a single hour to come to the nearest point on the Reservation at which a view of the Falls is to be obtained. But, because of the circumstance last described, of the narrowness of the ground from which the view alone is to be had, not more than twenty of the five thousand could have been at any moment of this hour in a position to see the Falls from top to bottom; not more than two hundred could have had so much as a glimpse of the upper half of it. The condition thus illustrated is one of great gravity.

Fourth: Each of the better known points of attraction on the New York Reservation is close upon a danger line, established by the circumstance that the position of the Falls and that of the shelf over part of which they pour is constantly subject to recession. The upper part of this shelf is of a stone much firmer than that of the lower part on which it rests. Through the action of the air, of dampness, frost and thaw, and of the jar from the concussion of the falling water, the weaker supporting stone is cracked and thrown out much faster than that above it. Recesses are thus formed of varying depth and breadth. At intervals they become so deep that the upper stratum fails to be supported and falls, sometimes suddenly in large masses, more commonly by bits and bits, the result being that along the upper edge, both where it is covered with water and where, as on the flanks of the Cataract, it is not, there is a degree of instability not to be exactly defined, but of which an illustration is presented in the sudden fall this present winter, without the slightest previous warning, of a large block of rock that was last summer daily crowded with visitors, the iron railing fixed for them to rest against having gone down with the rock. This was on the Canadian bank.[23]

The recession at the head of the Canadian Fall has been upwards of a hundred feet in thirty-three years, and Professor Gilbert, of the U.S. Geological Survey, points out that, as the head of the Fall wears back, the sides of necessity fall in, whether the water falls over them or not, so that the gorge is really extending as fast as the head of the Fall recedes.[24]

The recession of the American Fall has, for years past, been much less rapid; not perhaps exceeding a foot a year, while on the dry land it may have been even a little less. Yet the process described is constant. Every year several tons of fallen rock are removed from the public foot-path at the foot of the cliff by which visitors approach the Cave of the Winds.[25] During the last year a mass has fallen at a point directly under the wooden balcony of

Hennepin's View,[26] a point much frequented by visitors. Twenty years ago the carriageway between Stedman's Bluff[27] and Porter's Bluff ran upon ground much of which has since been undermined and fallen.

All of the more widely celebrated points of view of the New York Reservation are close upon the edge of the cliff, and are subject to the insecurity here explained.

When in the midst of a dense throng, men generally fail to realize the danger of its moving upon insecure ground, and often with no bad intention aid to communicate an impetus to it that suddenly brings great peril to those on its margin. This being considered, reason for prudence will be found in the fact that last summer your police were often obliged to forcibly draw men, women and children back from positions in which a light push would have compelled them to step on crumbling, half detached rock, below which there was empty space for a hundred feet.

It will be seen that the circumstance thus illustrated makes many propositions that might otherwise be thought desirable for the better accommodation of visitors at the points of chief attraction impossible to be entertained. It also condemns suggestions that might otherwise be approved looking to the use of more substantial and expensive expedients of accommodation than the plan we submit has in view, because they would not be sufficiently lasting to justify their cost.

We do not wish to close this division of our report without observing that great throngs of visitors are to be anticipated only during a short period of the year, and then only during certain hours of the day. During these few hours those composing them will rarely scatter far from certain well defined localities and the routes of movement between them. They will but little occupy parts of the Reservation most delightful to ramblers. This because few visitors, coming in any large company for a day's refreshment or even for two days', will wish to leave without having seen the more celebrated spectacles of the place, or will have time, beyond what will be needed for seeing them, for the quiet strolling and resting, through which alone the more secluded beauty of the Reservation is to be contemplatively enjoyed.

A word may also be said here as to the quality of the visitors to whom, by the low rate of fare offered by the railroads, Niagara is now becoming available as never before. They are thus far, as a rule, of the most orderly class of people in the country — of disciplined habits and good-natured if not courteous disposition. Eighty of the companies, coming at excursion rates the last year, were religious, benevolent and scientific associations. All such bodies are under leadership of such a character that they can be depended on to conform to reasonable rules, provided the motive at the bottom of these rules is understood; and, on this point, what is mainly important is that the one purpose for which the State invites the Reservation to be visited — namely, the enjoyment of certain passages of natural scenery of a distinctive character — shall plainly control all the arrangements it makes, and that this purpose shall not be found so complicated with purposes common to any other places of resort as to confuse the sense of propriety of its guests.

The leading general principle of the plan having been so far set forth, what is intended in various particulars will be explained under several heads to follow.

The Upper Grove.
Reception House, Public Lavatory, Bureau of Advice for Excursionists, Arrangements for Picnics, Offices of Administration.

The State has undertaken to provide for an enjoyment by all comers of that which is distinctively valuable within its Reservation. No plan should be adopted for the improvement of the Reservation under which any number of well disposed and decently well-bred visitors shall find it difficult to avoid a serious interference with the requirements of this enjoyment on the part of others.

What will be the extremest trial in this respect to which the proposed improvements will be subject?

It will occur when several trains are arriving nearly together loaded principally with people who are not accustomed to travelling, who are ill-provided with means for lessening the discomforts of travel, who have passed a hot night with little sleep in rattling cars, from which, loaded with dust and cinders, carrying baskets of provisions, and some of them little children, they come in troops upon the Reservation, "to see Niagara."

We are assured by the experience of many other places of resort that, unless extraordinary precautions are taken to prevent it, results will follow of a most unseemly character, destructive of the pleasantness of the place in all respects, and this not only for the time being but permanently, the most secluded and otherwise delightful parts of the grounds gradually acquiring a disorderly and squalid character, the reverse of that natural sylvan freshness which it is the principal aim of the undertaking to conserve. How can such a result be guarded against?

The answer of the plan is this:

The Reservation on the shore of the mainland is limited, except for a short distance at one point, to a strip intended to be barely broad enough to sustain a belt of woods by which the buildings of the village will be screened from other parts of the New York, and from the Ontario, Reservations. At the excepted points its breadth is doubled, and the ground in this broader part is already wooded. This additional breadth was advised to be taken with a view to the arrangement to be described below. It includes the district before referred to, formerly known as the Grove, later as Prospect Park, and is to be considered here in two divisions, to be called respectively, the Upper Grove and the Lower Grove.

The point in the Reservation that will be first reached by visitors coming directly towards the Falls from the railroad stations is in the Upper Grove. The Upper Grove commands no view of the Falls and is separated from them by the Lower Grove.

The plan proposes, first, that at the point of entrance to the Upper Grove for visitors coming from the railroad stations, a large building shall be open to them in which there shall be an office of advice and guidance, a check-room, and large lavatory, toilet and other conveniences, of the general character of those to be found in a few of our best railway stations.

Second, that outside of this house, but within the Upper Grove, conveniences shall be supplied for those who wish to eat provisions that they have brought with them. Among these conveniences there are to be large shelters, partly open and partly inclosed, that may be used in rainy weather. The entire series of arrangements is to have in view economy and efficiency in keeping the premises neat and tidy.

Third, that the taking of provisions of any kind on any other part of the Reservation shall be forbidden by ordinance and really prevented as a cardinal necessity of the success of the plan.

It is expected to result from these measures that, however large the number of people arriving at any time may be, they will tarry a varying period of time in the Upper Grove, according to the varying use they will have occasion to make of what it offers them, and then will leave it for the most part singly, or in small parties, and will gradually scatter, some moving away in carriages, some on foot, some taking the Inclined Way[28] to the foot of the Falls, some going to Goat Island, some to Canada, some lingering much longer than others at the nearer points of interest — all having been refreshed and brought to a state of body and mind more favorable to their enjoyment of the scenery and to the exercise of good nature in the pursuit of that enjoyment than would be possible except through the use of arrangements of the nature thus indicated.

There will need to be a superintendent's office, with, near by it, storage rooms, tool rooms and workshops for repairs. These should be accessible by carts without entering the roads of the Reservation and should not attract the attention of visitors within the Reservation. The plan proposes that they should be under the same roof with the reception-rooms for excursionists, with entrances both from the boundary street and from within the Reservation, the length of the building being increased from time to time as convenience shall be found to require. The exterior walls of this building are intended to be of stone taken from the walls of the buildings to be moved. It is to be one story in height, with a basement.

The Lower Grove.

This section of the Reservation is likely to be more frequented and to be oftener inconveniently crowded with people than any other. This is because it is the nearest point to the village and to the railway stations, at which a view of the Falls and of the great Chasm can be had, and because the place of descent to the ground below the Falls and to the steamboat and ferry landing,[29] by the Inclined Railway, is within it.

Near the parts where crowds are most likely to gather the trees are dilapidated through the effects of the freezing of the spray from the Falls upon them. They are more or less rotten-hearted and not to be depended upon; nor can any trees be expected to be grown with lasting good effect in the locality. For these reasons, and also because of the insecure character of the rock on which the place rests, as before explained, it cannot be hoped that a pleasing natural character can be fully attained throughout the district. This makes it particularly important to do away with its present artificial elements as much as possible, and to make those that are necessary, in the greatest degree practicable, unobtrusive.

The removal is advised of all the yet remaining structures intended for ornament or amusement, and of all the buildings except the little cottage in the border of the Reservation near the Suspension Bridge,[30] and the ferry-house which is low and the stone walls of which, being under a roof, may be covered by creepers to be easily protected in winter from being dragged down by ice.

Eventually, when the Inclined Railway shall require extensive repairs, it will be wise to substitute for it an arrangement such as will be advised for another locality in which there are essentially similar requirements to be met. This could be placed at a point less subject to be crowded and where it would be more unobtrusive than the present structure. But considerations of economy will postpone this improvement for many years, and the existing arrangement will be here considered as permanent.

Little explanation of the plan of roads, walks, standing and sitting places, beyond that which can be obtained from the drawing will be required. Along the edge of the crags a space is to be prepared for people to stand upon, from twenty to thirty feet wide and extending from the brink of the fall to the high ground back of the present wooden balcony, from all of which a fine view will be had of the nearer Fall and the river above it, a view of the islands, of the Canadian Falls and of the verdurous declivity of the Ontario Reservation. The present surface of this standing space is intended to be reduced to a slope with an inclination towards the Falls of about one in sixteen, which is not too steep for convenience in walking, while it will allow visitors at a distance to look over the heads of those nearer the most attractive point. The present stone parapet is obtrusively artificial in its rigid lines and angles, and is a needless obstruction where every inch of foreground view of the Falls is of great value. Its removal is advised. As to what should be substituted for it, choice lies between a wall of field stone varying little in character from a natural foreground object and of the same tone of color and texture of surface with that of the adjoining ledge, and an iron railing. If a railing can be made offering equal security without holding the eye, so valuable is space at this point, that we think it is to be preferred.

We have designed a railing that we would recommend for experimental consideration, and as its advantages cannot be otherwise explained a model of it is submitted.[31]

The aim of the entire plan for the improvement of this critical point of the Reservation is, while providing much larger and simpler accommodations for visitors, to restore, as nearly as it is now practicable, the original aspect of the brink of the Fall and the verge of the Chasm.

There are two points on the edge of the crag from which fine near views of the face of the American Fall are to be had. One is from a projection of rock south of the wall of the Inclined Railway. It is advised that the available space for visitors at this point shall be enlarged by a balcony extending from the projecting rock mentioned to another less prominent on the other side of the railway wall. It would be supported by brackets built into the face of the wall, an existing and for the present indispensable piece of construction. While hiding nothing natural, throwing a shadow on that which is artificial in the existing arrangement, and in itself unnoticeable, it would add not a little to the pleasure of the public.

The other point is that of Hennepin's View, now occupied by a wooden balcony, a few rods further from the Fall. It commands the best general view of the Falls to be had from the Reservation. It is also, from the condition of the rock below, the most hazardous point to which visitors are invited, and cannot long be safely left in its present condition. It is proposed that a better and less conspicuous balcony of iron shall take its place, and that it shall be made secure either by a construction to support the rock below it, or that it shall be sustained in the rear in such manner that it will remain when the rock falls out.

A striking and impressive view of the Fall from a point just within the ordinary drift of its spray, and midway between its crest and its foot, is to be had with perfect safety by removing the house built for the apparatus for illuminating the Fall and replacing it with a convenient covered balcony. The whole affair should be exteriorly of rough unpainted wood, and as much as possible obscured. Skilfully managed, it would scarcely be seen from any point. It does not appear on the drawing, its place being under the rock shown. It would be accessible by the existing stairs alongside the railway.

The great iron structure housing the railway is excessively conspicuous from Stedman's Bluff, and is a very awkward circumstance. So long as it must be retained, there should be large openings in its sides, to be closed in winter by shutters, and it should be made less obtrusive by painting it more nearly the color of the rocks behind it.

The Mainland Above the Groves.

Except in the groves at the north and upon a few rods of ground at one or two points elsewhere, the present surface of the mainland within the Reservation is of artificial, and most of it of markedly unnatural and infelicitous form. Little material has been brought upon it, and little taken away, but in the grading of roads, canals and embankments, cellar digging and the depositing of rubbish, nearly the whole has been shifted or buried.

For half a mile above the Fall the present shore is in part a substantial wall of stone, in part a crib-work construction of stone and logs, and is everywhere built out from ten to thirty feet beyond the old natural shore. Originally, all of the ground inclined with gentle undulations toward the river, the immediate margin of which was in some cases flat and boggy, but generally sloping, with a surface partly strewn with boulders and overgrown with bushes and grass.

An exact restoration of the old shore is not to be attempted, but its original character is intended in the plan to be regained, the original causeways, embankments, ridges and mounds being mostly reduced, the canals and excavations filled, all the waterside crib-work and walls removed, and the surface brought to flowing lines of varying inclination toward the river.

Some have been of the opinion that the removal of the walls would lead to violent inroads upon the land because of the intensity of the current of the river close against the present shore.

After examining, at various points, the condition of the shore where it is in its natural state and washed by a similar current, it is our judgment that no serious incursion of the river would result, and that little more earth would wash away than would give a new natural shore of the most desirable form and outline. If, at points, a continuous and increasing wear should appear to be threatened, it is proposed to use the stone of the removed constructions to form provisional rip-rap walls, afterwards to be made firm against ice where required, by such expedients, neither conspicuous nor costly, as may be necessary to answer the purpose.

The short walls would need generally to be not more than three feet in height above the ordinary surface of the water; they would have pockets and crevices running through them, and would serve as revetments for banks of soil in which the dwarf willows, rushes, ferns, irises, flags and other waterside plants of the region would be planted so as to partly grow through and partly over them, with a result in view that would differ but little in character from that of the natural, low, rocky shores of the neighboring islands.

DRIVE ON THE MAINLAND.

It will be seen from the drawing that a carriage-road called the Riverway is intended to be made from end to end of the Reservation. This is a necessity and will stand in stead of the old village street from which it varies in course only through the motive of keeping it, as a broad artificial object, and those moving upon it, as far from the shore and as much out of sight from Goat Island as possible, and in the substitution of continuous, long, curving outlines for the present discontinuous straight outlines with angular changes of direction. At points it is divided in order to avoid injury to a few promising trees of spontaneous growth.

WALKS ON THE MAINLAND.

A broad walk is planned to follow near and on the river side of the carriage-road, but at a slightly varying distance from it, in order that trees may be planted near the road, not in rows but naturally disposed.

Narrow branch walks are thrown out from the main walk, and generally upon sub-branches of these, and in positions where they may be partially screened from view from the drive and main walk, seats facing interesting points in the Rapids are provided for.

These and other seats in the Reservation may generally be formed with a substantial structure of the stone from the old buildings of the locality, the actual seats being of slat-work, darkly stained and at points fortified with metal, the object being to reduce to a minimum the opportunities for pencilling and cutting them so irresistible to a certain class. Some are to have simple trellises over them upon which canopies of vines and creepers, natural to the region are to be trained.

The Reservation includes a part of a bluff by which the Riverway abreast the upper rapids is bent toward the river. Upon the face of this bluff there are some good trees and from the upper part of it there is a fine view of and over the placid water of the river above the Rapids. A walk by which this point of view can be gained is shown on the drawing, and at the best point of view a sheltered seat.

Where the present street has been formed by cutting into the bluff, and the bluff side is sustained by a retaining wall, it is proposed to use the same expedient, but to reconstruct the wall with a sloping face and in such a manner as to subdue its artificial character and partially cover it with fitting vegetation.

CONCOURSES ON THE MAINLAND.

At the upper end of the Riverway at the point known as the Old French Landing,[32] which is of historical importance and from which views open of much interest in different ways, a space for the turning and resting of carriages is planned.

In connection with it a summer-house is proposed, to which visitors may resort in case of showers, and in which walkers may rest in seats convenient for the enjoyment of the views.

Where, near the opposite end of the Reservation, the Riverway and the broad village street between the railroad stations and the Reservation come together, another turnway and resting place is required. At this point is the terminus of a street railway and the Soldiers' Monument,[33] of the town of Niagara, and from it the greater number of visitors will first come upon the Reservation and first see the river and the Rapids. It will be a vestibule to the reception-house, the Upper Grove and the Superintendency, and the principal point for taking hired carriages.

For all these reasons, the turning place should have considerable amplitude, and as it must, for convenient use, be of nearly level surface, and as the present surface of the ground has a rapid slope, a retaining wall will be economically used to sustain it on the sides toward the river, giving the concourse the character of a terrace. This wall is intended to be formed of rock-faced stone, to be taken from the retaining wall of a disused canal near by.[34]

PLANTATIONS.

The Mainland division is designed to be planted with a view to its being ultimately covered with forest trees, growing to as great a height as they can be brought while retaining umbrageousness and enjoying conditions in respect to abundant nourishment, air and light likely to give them long life. To this end, such trees of the different species now growing on Goat Island as attain to the first magnitude are to be planted thickly. They are to be thinned out gradually as they come to interlock, until at length not more than one-fourth of the original number will remain, and these, because the less promising will have constantly been selected for removal with little regard to evenness of spacing, will be those of the most vigorous constitution, those with the greatest capabilities of growth, and those with the greatest power of resistance to attacks of storms, ice, disease and vermin. Individual tree beauty is to be little regarded, but all consideration given to beauty and effectiveness of groups, passages and masses of foliage. Except willows for some damp places along the shore in front of the high ground, quick-growing, fragile and short-lived trees are to be excluded. Of others, a considerable variety of species is to be used, and those of each species are to be well distributed throughout the plantation in order that if any one of the species becomes specially subject to destructive influences, as is liable to be the case, the body of foliage, as it will be seen from the bridge, from Goat Island and from the Ontario shore, may not be greatly injured, and may not fail to screen the village houses from view.

The trees are to be planted with the intention, while avoiding formality, to leave frequent clear spaces between their trunks, the centre lines of which spaces will be diagonal to the shore line, in the direction that will leave the Rapids open to view from the drive, and opposite to that of the line of view from Goat Island toward the buildings on the inland side of the Reservation.

The native underwood of the neighborhood is to be planted in thickets and allowed to grow in natural forms, at frequent intervals along the shore, and in occasional groups on the upland, enough of it being introduced to prevent, in connection with the grouping of trees and interspaces of groups to be formed by the process of thinning the tree plantations, a grove or orchard-like monotony of trunks.

GOAT ISLAND.
TREATMENT OF THE ARTIFICIALLY CLEARED GROUND.

Early in the century the upper part of the forest of Goat Island was cleared and the ground cultivated. A few small clearings have been made at other points, in some of which a thick young growth has sprung up. By thinning and planting it is intended that all these spaces shall be refurnished with trees in the manner proposed for the mainland but less closely, as the foliage is not intended as a screen, and some variety in its disposition, as shown on the drawing, will be pleasing.

WEST BANK OF GOAT ISLAND.

The steep river bank between Porter's Bluff and the Sisters has at times been slightly undermined by the river, and thus made a graceless inclined plane, with a raw surface and an angular crest. Deflecting piers of logs and stones, so slight as to be unnoticeable, placed at the water's edge by the former owners, have proved adequate to prevent the undermining process from going further. It may be desirable after a few years to replace these with something of the same character equally unobtrusive, but more substantial. It will also be desirable to hasten the process already begun by which nature would in time substitute outward curves for the angle at the top of the bank and inward curves nearer the base, and to fully reclothe the whole with foliage and verdure. Except a few trees in the upper part to cast shade upon the adjoining walk, the planting for this purpose would be of such bushes and plants as would not grow above the line of sight, toward the Rapids, of visitors standing on the walk that is laid out along the top of the bank. None such can be found anywhere in the world more beautiful than those indigenous to the island.

No other improvements are contemplated on Goat Island, except in connection with the means of communication to be spoken of elsewhere, and except those which will gradually result from continuous proper care of

562

the forest, the particular methods of which involve too much of expert detail to be profitably considered in this report.

BATH ISLAND.

The same course suggested for the shore of the Mainland is proposed to be taken in dealing with the present artificial shores of Bath Island, the old dams and crib-work being wholly removed and the river allowed to take its course. The result will probably be the washing away of nearly all of the made land, leaving a new shore varying little from the outline shown in the drawing. A considerable improvement of the scenery will thus be gained, and it need not be feared that more of the island will go than is desirable. When the intended result shall have been accomplished, a most attractive view will be had of the Rapids and the shore of Goat Island — dark and exceedingly beautiful, under overhanging foliage, from the point where, on the drawing, seats are indicated which are to be approached by a branch from the main walk across the island.

THE BRIDGES.

The bridges by which Goat Island is reached from the Mainland are proposed to be retained, superfluities of ornament only being removed. After a few years the walks on them may, if found necessary, be widened by outriggers, and slightly projecting balconies added at the piers in order that visitors wishing to look from them upon the Rapids may do so without impeding those moving by on the sidewalks. They are so shown on the drawing.

With these improvements the bridges will not be as spacious as could be desired and will be inelegant, but they are unpretending, and to remove them and substitute anything much better would be a more costly piece of work than we can recommend to be soon undertaken. We think that, with watchful care of the piers and prompt strengthening of them at any point where they may seem to be at all falling into disrepair, they are likely to hold good, barring extraordinary lunges of ice or floating timber, for many years.

We have been asked to consider whether, when a new bridge shall be wanted, it might not be better placed at a point some distance up the stream where a bridge had stood for a time before the present one was built. The view from the Mainland near the present bridgehead toward the islands, with the cross currents setting between them, has great interest and would be more pleasing if the bridges were removed. But the view from the same quarter in the direction of the middle of the Rapids is still more interesting — there is, indeed, nothing to compare with it in all the world, and no possible form of bridge could be placed in the position suggested that would not greatly injure it. In our judgment less will be lost by keeping the bridge where it is.

We propose no change in the foot-bridges of the Sister Islands so long as they may continue safe without extensive repairs. There is a little scroll work upon them which may with advantage be removed.

The foot-bridges by which passage is had with what is now called Terrapin Rock are suitably simple, rude structures, but from their position disagreeably hold the attention of visitors looking from Porter's Bluff upon the Canadian Fall and mar the scene. It is proposed that they shall be shifted to the lines shown in the drawing, where they would be less conspicuous, and the rocks which serve for abutments and piers for them would be more prominent. We also propose that they should be set somewhat lower.

The foot-bridge to Luna Island is a disagreeable artificial object, so placed as to mar a scene that in certain conditions of light and atmosphere is the most gorgeous of any of the Falls. We propose that it shall be shifted a short distance up-stream, where it will be much covered by trees, will be out of the direct line of view of the American Fall from Stedman's Bluff, and much less obtrusive. There are rocks projecting on each side from the shore on the line suggested, making the position constructively satisfactory.

Bridges to other of the islands in the Rapids have been suggested. Nothing would be gained by making these islands accessible that would compensate the injury which the bridges and the people who would be seen upon them and upon the islands would bring to the scenery.

The Drive on Goat Island.

Nothing has done so much to deter people from making good use of Niagara Falls as the bad character of the carriage service of the village. This has, till lately, been ill-organized and unregulated, and has so fully represented penny wisdom pound folly as to give rise to a general belief that strangers could not avoid taking carriages without being subject to such persecution wherever they went as destroyed their peace of mind, and, when they had taken them, could not escape swindles, impositions and incivilities, to many, more vexatious than downright robbery. The evil has, during the last two years, been much lessened, but it has not been removed, and until a much greater improvement can be secured the bad reputation of the Falls will not be wholly overcome.

The best means to get the better of it that your Board can use lies, probably, in the direction of a further development and improvement of the route-carriage system, in which a beginning has been made, the methods of use and manner of payments of which vary not essentially from those of the omnibus and street-car system of large cities.

By such improvement of the roads as is practicable, and by a finely economical adjustment of horses, vehicles, movements and stoppages to the peculiarities of the service, the cost rate per passenger can be even yet further reduced, while the convenience, comfort and care-freeness which can be offered at a fixed low price will be much greater than could heretofore be secured at any price. It may be fairly reckoned, therefore, that after a few years but a small proportion of the visitors to Goat Island will use any other form of wheel conveyance, and the road system of the plan has been devised accordingly.

The drive shown, by which a circuit of the island may be made in a carriage, at a distance usually from fifty to a hundred feet from the bank, is generally intended to be twenty feet wide, varying slightly in accommodation to the trees between which it is to pass. This is less than many would have it. We feel, however, that the road should be as narrow as it can be and tolerably answer its purpose, because at best many trees must be destroyed to make way for it, and the wider the opening the more havoc will storms make with trees left standing near by.

The intention is that carriages shall be allowed to pass through the road moving only in one direction. At all points where there will often be occasion for carriages to stop, the road is to be broadened, and, as before explained and as will be seen from the drawing, harbors are to be opened for carriages that are to stand in waiting. With these precautions a given number of carriages proceeding between the harbor points at a not very greatly varying rate of speed will be less crowded on a road of twenty feet than on one of forty feet, as roads are ordinarily used; less than on a city street of sixty feet if slow freighting wagons are admitted and stoppages are frequent at houses on either side.

It will be seen that two cross roads are provided by which visitors in carriages who may wish to return to the main land without completing the circuit of the island can do so.

WALKS ON GOAT ISLAND.

A circuit walk of the island, in the more frequented parts, fifteen feet wide but intended to vary slightly in adjustment to the trees, will be seen on the drawing. It mainly follows as close to the steep bank as will be safe and convenient, and to a great extent takes the place that had been cleared of trees for the old carriage road.

Where it would be imprudent to lead a throng, and at a few points, where, if carried close upon the bank, the walk would be inconveniently indirect or would oblige the removal of trees of special importance, it is kept back, and usually in these cases there are loop walks running nearer the bank upon which are shaded seats commanding specially interesting views. The circuitousness of these minor walks will prevent them from being used by hurried crowds and they will bring no danger to those moving deliberately.

Numerous trails through the thick woods will provide for moderately direct passage between all distant points. They are designed to be little more than trodden foot-paths and will give forest seclusion to those using them.

We believe that with rare exception (as of invalids), a much greater degree of the distinctively characteristic enjoyment of Niagara is to be had by those who go on foot than by those who take carriages. Carriages may be often seen driving past the most charming passages of the scenery, their occupants not having had their attention called to them. Last year we saw several carriage loads of visitors within an hour pass Porter's Bluff at a trot, without having their eyes turned toward the Fall. Had they been on foot and following the circuit walk of the plan such a loss would have been impossible to them. What has hitherto led the greater number of visitors to take carriages has been a supposition, assiduously nursed by those interested, that they would need a guide, and that, except by the aid of the only guide offering, in the person of an irresponsible brawler on the box of a shabby vehicle, they would not know where to go or what to see.

Simple instructions posted at the railroad stations, the hotels and the entrances of the Reservation, with modest guide-boards at all points where strangers might be at fault as to their best course, would, with the system of walks proposed in the plan, remove the difficulty and greatly advance the popularity of the place.

Reckoning upon a turn of custom in this direction the plan of walks is more spacious and extended than it would otherwise have been.

At points of special attraction, provisions are made for seats out of the line of movement upon the main walks. At two points on Goat Island large shelters, also, are suggested to which resort would be had by walkers in case of sudden showers. Both are in the midst of the woods; they are intended to be simply large roofs supported upon piers of rough masonry, without walls, except that at opposite ends of each there should be inclosures for water-closets, and the keeping of police conveniences. They are to be the only things on the island of the character of buildings except the covering of a piece of machinery next to be described.

APPROACH TO THE CAVE OF THE WINDS.

The wooden staircase by which visitors descend to the Cave of the Winds has been represented to be much dilapidated and inadequate to present demands, and a number of propositions have been before your Board to put in its place a structure several times as large to contain a passenger elevator as well as a staircase.

All these propositions are open to the objection that the structure proposed would present prominently to view, from widely different points both on the Ontario and the New York shores, and from the bridge and the boats, a large artificial object, crossing from top to bottom one of the grandest features of the natural scenery of the Falls. Also to the objection that as the face of the Cliff recedes a readjustment of the affair would soon be necessary.

It is our opinion that any structure at this point would be contrary to the fundamental principles of the undertaking. Assuming that access to the Cave of the Winds is desirable, if it can be had without injury to the scenery, we should propose, as an alternative, that the descent should be made through a shaft and tunnel; the head of the shaft to be about fifty feet from the edge of the bank, with an elevator moving in it of the form of an ordinary hotel elevator, to be operated by concealed water-power. This would cost less than a structure of the same capacity built out from the cliff.

There is nothing at all unusual in any of the required operations, and no difficulty in the combination.

Near the bottom of the elevator a small cabin is proposed to be built of logs, and made as unnoticeable as shall be practicable, which will be used as a dressing-room for those who wish to enter the Cave. From this cabin a steep penthouse roof, supported by strong framework of timber is advised to be constructed over the path leading to the Cave, in order that visitors may be protected from falling stone. These structures would come where the sloping mass of debris meets the vertical face of the cliff, and being formed of timber left unpainted, and partially covered by the trees and bushes that have sprung up just outside of the position, would in a few years be scarcely visible.

We should, perhaps, add that we do not think that there is an immediately pressing necessity for the construction proposed. The present structure can be put in good repair at a trifling outlay, and it answers its purpose fairly well. The improvement of roads and walks is a matter of much more importance to the great body of visitors.

STEDMAN'S BLUFF.

On the arrival at Stedman's Bluff of visitors coming from the bridge, the interest of the scenery culminates in the view of the American Fall from that height. The present stairway leading down the bank to the brink of the Falls is on the line of this view, and it is proposed to reconstruct it as shown on the drawing, so as to afford a series of opportunities for outlook to be reached by steps that will be used by the visitor only in descending, another path with steps for ascent being provided a little to the eastward where there will be no outlook of special interest.

LUNA ISLAND.

The intention of the plan is, that the walk from the footbridge to this island shall be carried, as at present, to the verge of the Fall at its west end, but that visitors shall be prevented from crowding upon the side of the island toward the bluff, and that bodies of foliage shall here be grown sufficient to secure the larger part of the ground on which visitors will be allowed to occupy from the sight of those looking from the superior point of view on Stedman's Bluff.

Porter's Bluff.

At this point is to be found the most impressive view upon the Reservation, being that looking into what, because of the former shape of the Canadian Fall, is called "The Horseshoe." The nearer the spectator stands to the precipice on the north, looking westwardly, the better the view. It is fine, however, all along the edge of the bluff for about fifty yards, beyond which point considerable bodies of foliage interpose that cannot be removed without detriment to the scenery. This space of fifty yards, therefore, is invaluable.

At present the enjoyment to be obtained from what is otherwise the best point of it is much less than it might be because it is at the head of a flight of wooden stairs that lead to the ground at the foot of the bluff, people passing upon which break the view, and because, also, horses, carriages and people on foot, seeking this best point, are often crowded together in a way most unfavorable to quiet contemplation.

At a point about a hundred feet southward a wall of stone was built many years ago to sustain a made bank of earth where, before, there must have been a recess in the face of the bluff and probably a gully extending a short distance back. The plan proposes to take down this wall, open and enlarge the gully in such a manner as to form an inclined path, to be used instead of the present stairway, a part of it being bridged over so that the line desirable to be occupied by visitors looking from the height toward the Horseshoe may not be interrupted. At the point now occupied by the upper steps of the staircase the general level would be preserved, and a small projection made which would still further improve the best point of view.

As an additional facility for reaching the ground under the bluff opposite this point a foot-path with steps at intervals is planned at a short distance to the southward.

Check Upon Throngs at Certain Points.

There are two duties of the State to the people in regard to which there should be no doubt of the Commission's responsibility or of its powers to meet it efficiently.

One is to make sure that visitors, in the orderly and reasonably prudent use of the means provided them for the enjoyment of the scenery of the Reservation shall not be placed in conditions of peril from sources that the Commission can guard against by such police regulations as have been approved in the experience of other places of large public resort. The other is to make sure that visitors, not actively disposed to disorder, shall not be constrained to courses through which any important elements of scenery or any property of the State shall unduly come to injury.

Having in view a much larger number of visitors than has heretofore been known, there are places on the Reservation where we must question whether due precautions for the safety of visitors and the preservation of the property of the State can be maintained if access to them and occupation of them is absolutely unrestricted.

It is advised that in every such situation the Superintendent shall be authorized to regulate by means of a gate and turnstile the number of visitors to be at any time in occupation of the ground. Under ordinary circumstances the gate would be open and passage to the place unobstructed, but, upon needful occasions, the gate would be closed and visitors let in and let out by turnstiles at each end of the gate, the turnstiles for admission not opening after a certain number had entered except as room was made by those leaving, their outgoing serving mechanically to give the proper number admission by an action communicated through the turning of the outlet turnstile.

CONCLUDING OBSERVATIONS.

In the general design thus submitted we have endeavored to foreshadow and fairly meet all the requirements that can be legitimately conceived as having a just claim to your consideration.

We believe that none of the improvements suggested can be left out of any comprehensive scheme undertaken by the State for a judicious development of the Reservation over which it has assumed control.

Each work of construction will at some time, in our judgment, require to be executed in a conscientiously complete way, but when all that is proposed is fairly done there will be no need for any fresh appropriations for construction. The work henceforth will be, strictly, a work of maintenance. It is for your Board to determine what recommendations should be made to the State in regard to appropriations for improvement, what works should be first undertaken and what should be postponed. Although not asked to advise at this time as to the relative importance of the various features of this necessarily large and complex undertaking, we may be permitted to close our report with the expression of a hope that you may decide to take up first the proposed carriage drives on Goat Island; not only because it is desirable to meet an obvious public demand in this respect for additional accommodations, but because it is expedient, as soon as practicable, to take advantage of the healing processes of natural restoration by fresh growth, which will commence as soon as the openings required for the new roads are cut through the existing woods.

Respectfully,

FRED'K LAW OLMSTED
and CALVERT VAUX,
Landscape Architects.

The text presented here was published as *General Plan for the Improvement of the Niagara Reservation* (New York, 1887), pages 1–45.

1. William Dorsheimer became president of the board of commissioners for the Niagara reservation in 1883 (Thomas V. Welch, "How Niagara Was Made Free," in *Publications of the Buffalo Historical Society*, vol. 5 [Buffalo, N.Y., 1902], p. 327; for William Dorsheimer see OVC to William Edward Dorsheimer, Oct. 1, 1868, n. 1, above).
2. James T. Gardner, director of the New York State Survey in 1879, best described the scarring of the Niagara's banks along the American Rapids in his report

   > In place of the pebbly shore, the graceful ferns and trailing vines of former days, one now sees a blank stone wall with sewer-like openings through which tail races discharge; some timber crib work bearing in capitals a foot high the inscription, "Parker's Hair Balsam;" then further upstream, more walls and wing dams. Overlooking this disfigured river brink stands an unsightly rank of buildings in all stages of preservation and decay; small "hotels," mills, carpenter shops, stables, "bazaars," ice-houses, laundries with clothes hanging out to dry, bath houses, large, glaring white hotels, and an indescribable assortment of miscellaneous rookeries, fences, and patent medicine signs, which add an element of ruin and confusion to the impression of solid ugliness given by the better class of buildings (James T. Gardner, "Report of the Director on the Plan for a Proposed State Reservation at Niagara," in New York [State], *Special Report of New York State Survey on the Preservation of the Scenery of Niagara Falls . . . for the Year 1879* [Albany, N.Y., 1880], pp. 20–21).

3. During the year 1886 the commission ordered the removal of paper-mill buildings, a brick shop, a stone shop, the Rapids house, the Bath Island store, and several unsightly fences, sheds, flumes, and piers (New York [State], *Third Annual Report of the Commissioners of the State Reservation at Niagara, for the Year 1886* [Albany, N.Y., 1887], p. 4).
4. In 1805 the State of New York sold at auction lots within a one-mile strip along the Niagara River both above and below the falls that included the present site of the village of Niagara Falls. The Porter brothers, Augustus and Peter B., were among the first to purchase land there. Augustus Porter built a grist mill and a saw mill on the river bank to take advantage of the water power provided there and was also instrumental in laying out the town of Niagara Falls, originally called Manchester after the English industrial city (Theodora Vinal, *Niagara Portage: From Past to Present* [Buffalo, N.Y., 1949], p. 16; George Washington Holley, *Niagara: Its History and Geology* [New York, 1872], p. 77).
5. In 1880 the Canadian government passed an act providing for cooperation between the governments of New York State and Canada in restoring the scenery about Niagara Falls. Nothing came of this law, however, and the Canadians for the most part ignored Niagara until 1885. In 1885 the legislature of Ontario Province passed a law establishing a commission authorized to select lands to be taken for the protection of the Niagara scenery on the Canadian side of the river. The law also provided for the restoration of "the scenery around the Falls of Niagara to its natural condition, and to preserve the same from further deterioration." It was not until 1887, however, that Ontario Province passed the "Queen Victoria Niagara Falls Park Act" that provided for the permanent establishment of a Canadian reservation (Ronald L. Way, *Ontario's Niagara Parks: A History* [Niagara Falls, N.Y., 1946], pp. 23, 29–30, 37–38).
6. The board of commissioners's written instructions simply indicated that Olmsted and Calvert Vaux were "to prepare a plan for the improvement of the State Reservation at Niagara to be the basis of the future operation of the Commissioners." The commis-

sioners' verbal instructions, however, no doubt paralleled the following statement from their fifth annual report

> The Commissioners are unanimously of the opinion that nothing in the direction of restoration or improvement on the reservation should be tolerated that would in the slightest degree tend to divert the attention of visitors from the river and the Falls. Rather should all efforts be directed towards making them the chief objects of popular interest and observation. No garish or glaring structures are to be erected; no pretentious exhibitions of statuary or architecture are to be permitted; the simplicity of nature should at all times be preserved. The contemplation of natural scenery unquestionably tends to refine the sentiments and elevate the mind, and it is entirely unnecessary to descant upon the important educating and moral influence of so majestic and marvelous a natural object as Niagara Falls.

(Copy of Resolution adopted at Board of Commissioners meeting, Oct. 6, 1886, Olmsted Papers; New York [State], *Fifth Annual Report of the Commissioners of the State Reservation at Niagara, for the Year 1888* [Albany, N.Y., 1889], pp. 10–11.)

7. Lucius Robinson (1810–1891), governor of New York from 1877 to 1880. On January 9, 1879, Robinson addressed the New York state legislature expressing his concern over the harassment of visitors to Niagara Falls. He noted that it was "a matter of universal complaint, that the most favorable points of observation around the falls are appropriated for purposes of private profit, while the shores swarm with sharpers, hucksters and peddlers, who perpetually harass all visitors." He also discussed a meeting he had had in the summer of 1878 with Lord Dufferin, Governor-General of Canada. Dufferin was also troubled by the abuses existing on both sides of the falls. He suggested that the State of New York and the Province of Ontario form an "international park" whereby the falls and the area surrounding them might be protected from encroachment and misuse. Robinson concluded his comments by recommending that the state legislature appoint a commission to act in concert with a Canadian commission, should it be appointed, to consider the possibility of providing for such a park (Robert Sobel and John Raimo, eds., *Biographical Directory of the Governors of the United States, 1789–1978*, 4 vols. [Westport, Conn., 1978], 3: 1088; New York [State], *Journal of the Senate of the State of New York, at their One Hundred and Second Session* [Albany, N.Y., 1879], pp. 26–27).

8. Probably William Dorsheimer or James Hampden Robb (1846–1911), a banker and state senator who had been highly instrumental in securing the Niagara reservation (*Appleton's Cyc. Am. Biog.*; *New York Times*, Jan. 22, 1911, p. 11).

9. In 1872 the Prospect Park Company purchased eleven acres of land around Prospect Point, the bluff overlooking the falls. The area became known as Prospect Park, and the company "improved" the area by surrounding it with a high picket fence and establishing the numerous amusements and bazaars to attract tourists that Olmsted describes here (T. Vinal, *Niagara Portage*, p. 92; T. V. Welch, "How Niagara Was Made Free," p. 350).

10. At Prospect Point there was an electric light that at night illuminated part of the American Fall. Rotating colored glass plates were put in front of the light and caused the falls and rapids to change colors. One visitor noted that as she looked upon the water "rays of rosy light which melted into amber, then into emerald" could be seen (John F. Sears, "Doing Niagara Falls in the Nineteenth Century," in *Niagara: Two Centuries of Changing Attitudes, 1697–1901*, Jeremy Elwell Adamson [Washington, D.C., 1985], p. 114; Alice [Hyneman] Sotheran, ed., *Niagara Park Illustrated* [1885; rpt. ed., New York, 1888], p. 68).

11. This letter-writing campaign to save Niagara began after Governor Alonzo Cornell vetoed the Niagara bill of 1881. Olmsted and Charles Eliot Norton raised the funds to

pay Jonathan B. Harrison and Henry Norman to write letters and tracts for newspaper publication stressing the need to preserve Niagara. This campaign continued until the 1883 act was passed that provided for the reservation (Alfred Runte, "The Niagara Falls Preservation Campaign," *The New-York Historical Society Quarterly* 57 [January 1973], pp. 45–46; Jonathan Baxter Harrison, *The Condition of Niagara Falls, and the Measures Needed to Preserve Them* [New York, 1882], passim).

12. The Porter family had owned Goat Island since 1816 when Augustus Porter purchased a "float," a document entitling the bearer to 200 acres of unsold state land, from Samuel Sherwood. Porter attached his "float" to Goat Island and the adjacent smaller islands. In 1817 Porter built a bridge connecting Goat Island to the mainland. Visitors gladly paid the fifty-cent toll to cross the bridge, and Goat Island immediately became a tourist attraction. Porter added roads and paths to the island as well as additional bridges and a tower at Terrapin rock for viewing Horseshoe Falls.

    During the almost seventy years of the Porters' stewardship the island's natural state had been fairly well protected. However, in 1879 Gardner reported in his Survey report that the Porters might lose Goat Island due to a pending partition suit and that proposals for the use of the island by new owners included a huge summer hotel, a rifle range, and a race track. Moreover, in 1882 J. B. Harrison wrote that the Porters were about to sell the island and that it would probably fall into the hands of an industrial developer if the state did not buy it first (G. W. Holley, *Niagara*, pp. 77, 81; T. Vinal, *Niagara Portage*, pp. 39, 43; J. T. Gardner, "Report of the Director," pp. 21–22; J. B. Harrison, *Condition of Niagara Falls*, pp. 24–25).

13. Admission to Goat Island was fifty cents per person. This also gave visitors access to the three Sister Islands in the Canadian Rapids, which were accessible from Goat Island by foot-bridges (David Young, *The Humbugs of Niagara Falls Exposed* . . . [Suspension Bridge, N.Y., 1884], pp. 25–26).

14. A possible reference to the establishment during the summer of 1886 of a carriage service operated by the Niagara Reservation Carriage Service Company. Seven stops were established within the reservation, and carriages were provided to convey passengers to and from those locales. Visitors purchased coupon tickets at a nominal cost allowing them to disembark at one location and later be picked up by the next carriage or any carriage during the same day. The carriages proved successful and provided inexpensive, reliable service (New York [State], *Third Annual Report of the Commissioners of the State Reservation at Niagara*, pp. 4, 11–12; idem, *Fifth Annual Report of the Commissioners of the State Reservation at Niagara*, p. 22).

15. Thomas Vincent Welch (1850–1903) was appointed superintendent of the Niagara reservation in 1885 and served in that position until his death. Welch was born in Camillus, New York, but moved to Niagara Falls in 1857. Welch was long an advocate for the government ownership and protection of Niagara. He was a member of the New York Assembly from 1882 to 1884 and had charge of the bill for the establishment of the Niagara reservation (New York [State], *Second Annual Report of the Commissioners of the State Reservation at Niagara, for the Year 1885* [Albany, N.Y., 1886], p. 3; Charles M. Dow, *The State Reservation at Niagara: A History* [Albany, N.Y., 1914], p. 180; *New York Times*, Oct. 21, 1903, p. 9).

16. In January 1888 Albert H. Porter, a member of the Porter family, offered to donate land located in the town of Niagara Falls between the Niagara reservation and Buffalo Street for the purposes of building a Museum of Natural Sciences and History of Niagara. He stipulated that the State of New York would have to provide the funds for a suitable structure or he would rescind his offer. The museum was never built. In their annual report the following year, however, the commissioners suggested that a building in the Upper Grove that once housed an art gallery could be used for a museum and library (New York [State], *Fourth Annual Report of the Commissioners*

of the State Reservation at Niagara, for the Year 1887 [Albany, N.Y., 1888], pp. 13, 65–66; idem, *Fifth Annual Report of the Commissioners of the State Reservation at Niagara*, pp. 14–15).

17. Porter's Bluff, located on Goat Island, was named for the Porter family who had owned the island for nearly seventy years (see n. 12 above).

18. The Canadian reservation, or Queen Victoria Niagara Falls Park, was opened to visitors on May 24, 1888. The park extended upstream from the Suspension Bridge for nearly two miles along the Niagara River. It was three hundred acres in extent and contained sweeping lawns and well-kept roads (New York [State], *Fifth Annual Report of the Commissioners of the State Reservation at Niagara*, p. 8).

19. Possibly a sixty-six-foot-wide road (or chain reserve) provided for by the government in early surveys along the rivers to allow for direct communication between military posts constructed at the time (*Niagara Falls, Canada: A History of the City and the World Famous Beauty Spot, An Anthology* [Niagara Falls, Ontario, 1967], pp. 17, 291).

20. In his 1886 report, Welch stated that

> The number of visitors has been greater than during the first season of the management of the reservation, and their stay longer than in former years. The public enjoyment has been greatly increased by facilities which have been provided for cheap, pleasant and reliable transportation to the places of interest. Better order has been observed, owing in part to the increased efficiency of the village government (New York [State], *Third Annual Report of the Commissioners of the State Reservation at Niagara*, p. 1).

21. Olmsted's statement here is misleading. Excursion fares to Niagara had not changed in several years, but because admission to most of the points of interest within the reservation was now free, the actual cost of visiting Niagara Falls was four to five times cheaper than it had been previously (C. E. Healy to Thomas V. Welch, Jan. 18, 1887).

22. Welch noted that on August 19, 1885, fourteen excursion trains containing over 10,000 tourists arrived at the reservation (New York [State], *Third Annual Report of the Commissioners of the State Reservation at Niagara*, p. 13).

23. A portion of Upper Table Rock, a popular tourist site and located between Prospect House and Horseshoe Falls, fell on January 12, 1887. The *Buffalo Express* reported that thousands of tons of rock and ice fell into the gorge. The rock gave way without warning, but fortunately the incident occurred at night and no lives were lost (*Buffalo Express*, Jan. 14, 1887, p. 5).

24. Grove Karl Gilbert (1843–1918), geologist. Having assisted on previous surveys, Gilbert joined John Wesley Powell's geological survey team in 1874. Five years later it became the U.S. Geological Survey. Gilbert continued to work for the Survey eventually serving as chief geologist from 1889 to 1892.

    In August 1886 Gilbert and Robert Woodward, also of the U.S. Geological Survey, conducted a survey of Niagara Falls and Woodward wrote the report, entitled "On the Rate of Recession of Niagara Falls as shown by the Results of a Recent Survey," explaining their findings concerning the rate of recession of Horseshoe and American falls. They concluded that American Fall had receded only slightly but that between 1842 and 1875 the recession of Horseshoe Falls was 100 feet and that between 1875 and 1886 in the center of the channel, where the greatest volume of water passed over the fall, it was over 200 feet. They calculated that on average the fall was receding approximately 2⁴/₁₀ feet per year (*DAB*; Charles Coulston Gillispie, ed., *Dictionary of Scientific Biography*, 16 vols. [New York, 1970–80], 5: 395–96; Robert Simpson Woodward, "On the Rate of Recession of Niagara Falls as Shown by the Results of a Recent Survey," *American Journal of Science* 28 [Aug. 1886]: 383–84;

New York [State], *Third Annual Report of the Commissioners of the State Reservation at Niagara*, p. 14).

25. The Cave of the Winds is located behind the American Fall near Goat Island. It was first entered in 1834 and became a popular attraction in the Niagara Falls tours. Originally known as Aeolus' Cave or Ingraham's Cave it eventually took on the current name Cave of the Winds (T. Vinal, *Niagara Portage*, p. 43).

26. Named for Father Louis Hennepin (1640–c. 1701), Flemish-born Catholic friar who traveled to Canada as a missionary in 1675 and accompanied Robert de La Salle in 1678 in his explorations of the upper Mississippi region (*DAB*; New York [State], *Second Annual Report of the Commissioners of the State Reservation at Niagara*, p. 13; see n. 32 below).

27. Stedman's Bluff, located on Goat Island and overlooking the American Fall, was named for John Stedman who in 1770 pastured goats on the island (hence its name). Stedman was one of the first settlers in the area, building his home at Schlosser's Landing on the banks of the Niagara just above the rapids in 1761. The carriageway to which Olmsted refers would have run close to the edge of the Niagara River gorge between the two bluffs that he mentions (W. T. Horner, *Horner's Buffalo and Niagara Falls Guide . . .* [Buffalo, N.Y., 1874], p. 73; New York [State], *Second Annual Report of the Commissioners of the State Reservation at Niagara*, p. 13; G. W. Holley, *Falls of Niagara*, pp. 77–78).

28. The inclined railway, its terminus located at the ferry landing, carried people from the top of the American Fall at Prospect Point down to the water's edge. The track for the railway was completed in 1845. The apparatus for moving the cars was water-driven and housed in a deep pit, giving the appearance that the railway was self-operated. Originally the fare for the railway was twenty-five cents one way, but after the establishment of the reservation the price was reduced to five cents one way (G. W. Holley, *Falls of Niagara*, pp. 125–26; New York [State], *Second Annual Report of the Commissioners of the State Reservation at Niagara*, p. 3).

29. The ferry landing and service located at the base of the American side of the falls transported tourists to the Canadian side for twenty-five cents. The ferry had been established in the 1820s and by the 1860s had forty boats in service (W. T. Horner, *Horner's Buffalo and Niagara Falls Guide*, p. 69; T. Vinal, *Niagara Portage*, p. 92).

30. The Suspension Bridge, which crossed the Niagara River gorge just below the reservation, was built in 1868 replacing a previous structure destroyed in the fall of 1867. The new suspension bridge was designed for carriage and pedestrian traffic (G. W. Holley, *Falls of Niagara*, p. 143).

31. This iron railing, designed by Vaux, consisted of a simple curved vertical post with three cross bars. At first the commissioners authorized the use of about 50 feet of the railing, but in his annual report for 1887, Welch noted that 100 feet of it had been installed along the western shore of Goat Island near the Cave of the Winds building. Photographic evidence indicates that the railing was eventually used throughout the reservation (CV to FLO, April 5, 1887; New York [State], *Fourth Annual Report of the Commissioners of the State Reservation at Niagara*, p. 23).

32. The Old French Landing located at the top of the reservation just above the rapids was a natural landing site because of the calm water there. It was used for many years by French settlers and traders. Legend maintains that La Salle and Hennepin departed on their voyage from the this site (New York [State], *Second Annual Report of the Commissioners of the State Reservation at Niagara*, p. 13; see nn. 26 and 28 above).

33. The Soldiers' Monument, located at the intersection of Falls and Canal streets at the entrance to Prospect Park, was dedicated on August 22, 1876, to the memory of the Niagara County soldiers who had fought in the Civil War (William Pool, ed., *Landmarks of Niagara County, New York* [Syracuse, N.Y., 1897], p. 89).

34. Probably the canal or raceway built adjacent to River Street to provide water power for the mills that lined the Niagara River's edge along the American Rapids. Olmsted's plan called for eliminating the buildings and the canal for the creation of the Riverway; however, the commissioners chose not to remove the canal entirely (Beers, Upton & Co., comp., *Atlas of Niagara and Orleans Counties, New York* [Philadelphia, 1875], map; John J. MacIntire, *Map of Niagara Falls, New York* [Buffalo, N.Y., 1890]).

Plan for a Public Park on the
Flats South of Buffalo.

BROOKLINE, Mass.,
1st October, 1888.

TO THE PARK COMMISSIONERS:

Sirs, —

We have the honor to submit drawings showing a plan for a park adapted to a site on the shore of Lake Erie, south of the city, as contemplated in a resolution of the Common Council of February, 1887, and in subsequent action of your Commission, recorded in its last Annual Report.[1] For distinction's sake, we shall refer to the proposed park as the South Park, and to your present park as the North Park.[2]

It is believed that many citizens of Buffalo are of the opinion that discussion of the subject of this report might better be deferred until it has been more maturely considered whether the city just now wants to engage in another park enterprise, and whether if it does so, the required park had better be in a place naturally so unattractive within itself as that which you have had in view. Mature consideration can be given to neither of these questions, without a much more definite statement of the project than has hitherto been possible, and a better knowledge than has hitherto been had by the public, of what could be made of the conditions of the locality. What is thus wanting to open a profitable discussion, it is hoped that this report may supply.

Nevertheless a conviction that the project is, at least, premature, must stand much in the way of the patient and candid study necessary to a just estimation of a plan of character so unusual and so little to be judged by ordinary standards, as that to which your attention will be asked. For this reason we wish, as a preface, to recall certain facts of the recent history of your city.

When, twenty years ago, the bill providing for the North Park was before the State Legislature, an amendment was introduced with an intention of keeping down its cost. Its immediate effect was to compel a few acres of ground to be thrown out, which had before been included in the scheme.[3] Had this not been done, the plan afterwards adopted for laying out the park might have been bettered at nearly all points, but particularly so at one. As soon as the park began to be a place of much popular resort, the need of greater spaciousness at the point referred to became so evident, that at length the City Council united with the Park Commission in asking the Legislature to authorize a portion of the land thrown out under its first action to be annexed to the park. This has since been done, but the cost of taking the annexed land has been about ten times as much as it would have been, but for the delay; the cost of its improvement will be much greater, and the value of the result will be less.[4]

A similar experience, as you are aware, has been had at the Front, proceedings yet being in progress for obtaining additions to the area of your property there, which could have been acquired, at the time of the city's original purchase, at a tenth of what it will cost now.[5]

With these incidents as a guide, it is to be considered what would have occurred if the park movement of twenty years ago had been much delayed.

It is likely that if the site of the North Park had not been secured about the time it was, it never would have been. The cemetery might have been extended over a part of it[6] or a new cemetery laid out upon it. The State Insane Hospital, afterwards built on its border, might have been placed upon it, or might have been placed where the buildings and grounds of the institution would have blocked approaches to it from the city.[7] Various structures since erected in the vicinity of it would have been built upon it; the Belt Railroad, shortly afterwards laid out a few hundred feet away, might have been carried through it.[8]

But it is unlikely that the city would have gone without a park to this time. It is almost certain that it would have acquired somewhere else, a much inferior site for it at greater cost for the real estate, and have made a much inferior park upon the site, at much greater cost for the making.

What now is to be anticipated of Buffalo in the next twenty years? Twenty years hence Buffalo will be not only a city of much larger trade, much larger wealth and much larger population, but it will be a city of much more metropolitan character, than, notwithstanding its recent rapid advance in this respect, it has yet come to be. The currents of civilization, which in all metro-

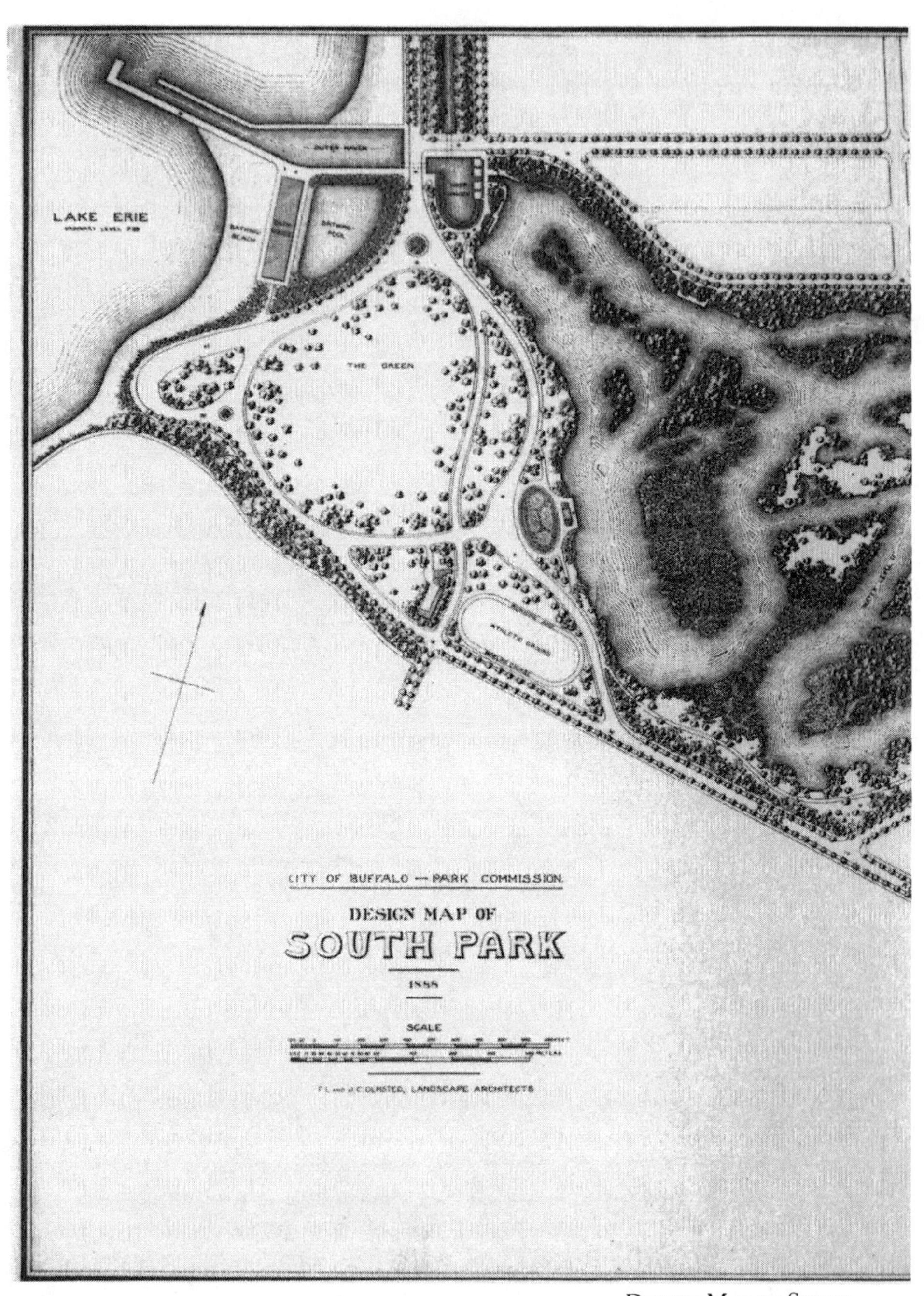

Design Map of South

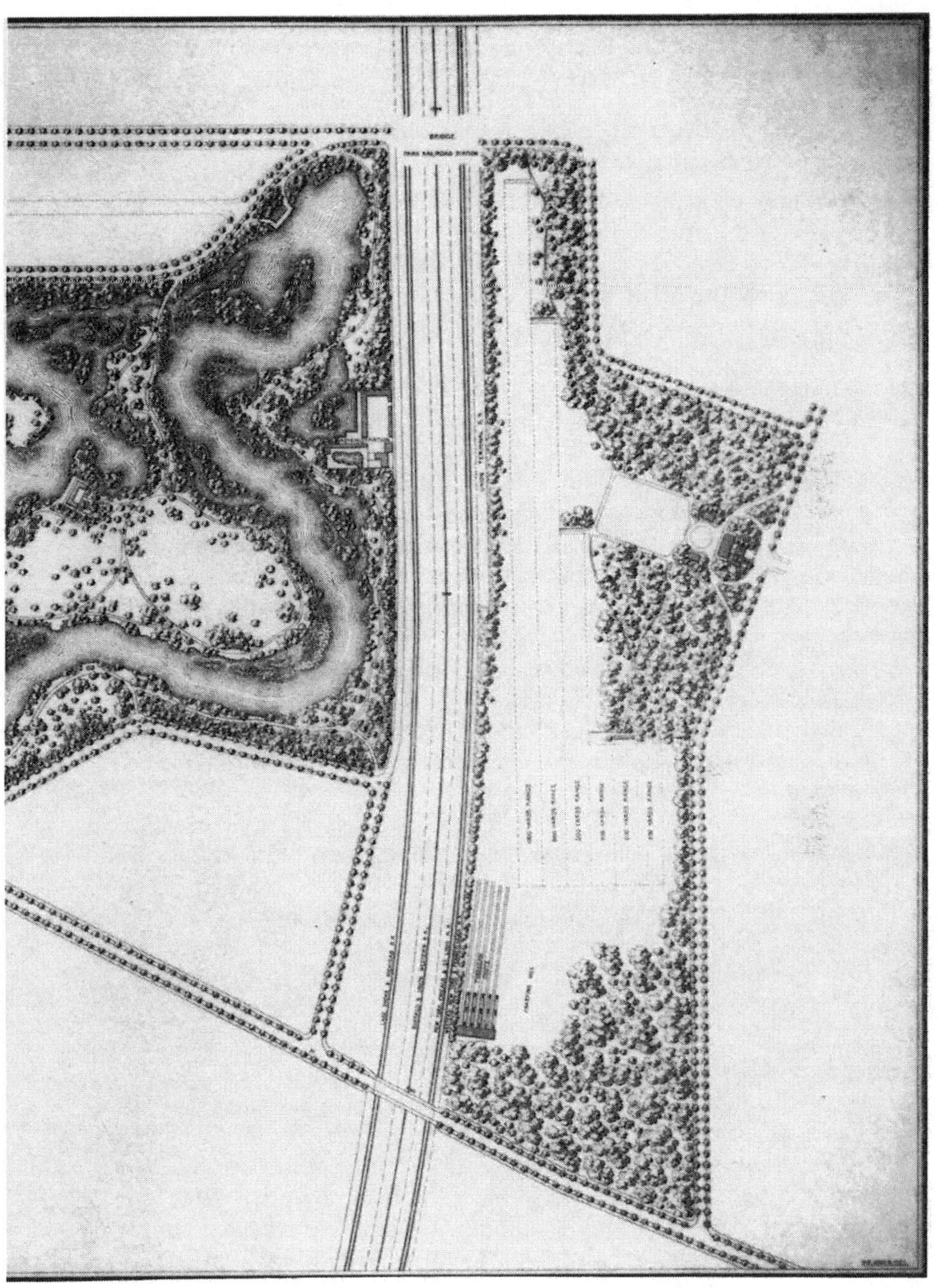

PARK, BUFFALO, 1888

politan centres have, in modern times, been increasingly manifest, will have been growing correspondingly stronger. The drift of these currents in relation to parks is indicated by the fact that eleven cities of Europe and America have, during the last thirty years, added twenty thousand acres of land to their park properties, and that towns which a few years ago were thought to be particularly well provided, have been recently adding largely to what they had; as London, 6000 acres, New York, 3000, Boston, 700.

The drift being as thus indicated, the question upon which this report bears, is not whether the people of Buffalo require just now more and other park provisions than they have, but whether the people of Buffalo twenty years hence will have required no more and no other? It is wholly probable that in less time than that a considerable additional park will have been required and will have been provided for. If so, it is not to be questioned that going about the business now in a deliberate way, pursuing the same steady, methodical, frugal but efficient methods that have distinguished the proceedings of your Commission from its origin, such additional park provision as will be required may be obtained of a much more valuable character and at much less outlay than it will be, if all effective action toward the result is now staved off indefinitely. This consideration, rather than a conviction of any immediate urgent necessity for an additional park, accounts for such favor as the project has hitherto received from conservative citizens.

There is another consideration, however, that should be allowed a bearing in the same direction, the weight of which is likely to have been duly appreciated only by those who have closely followed the history of older parks in other cities. It may be presented in this way: —

Your present North Park is rarely well adapted to certain quiet forms of recreation, favoring a contemplative or musing turn of mind and restful refreshment. It is not in the least larger than it should be for a park designed to that end, and in a single park of its size, provision for no other end is more desirable for a city. But it is not always that merely soothing, out-of-door refreshment is wanted. Occasionally by all, but oftenest by those who pass most of their time in monotonous occupations and amid sombre surroundings, tranquilizing natural scenes are less demanded than those by which gayety, liveliness, and a slight spirit of adventure are stimulated. This being the case, it is inevitable that an inclination will arise, and year by year increase, to have better provision made for the purpose on the North Park. It will follow that unless comprehensive provision for it is soon undertaken elsewhere, you will be constrained to meet the requirement by a succession of small, feeble, imperfect and desultory interpolations upon the design of the North Park. An unconsciously indulged tendency in that direction has, we think, already been manifest in the minds of some of your number. If it should continue and spread, the North Park will come in time to lose the character in which otherwise it will, year after year, be gaining, and by which it would take a more and more distinguished position among the parks of the world, while, because not having been broadly designed for anything else, it can be made respectable in no other character. Thus the question now to be decided may be this:

Twenty years hence shall Buffalo have one park, of a poor, confused character, or two, each of a good, distinct character?

Assuming that it is wise that the City should soon enter upon proceedings looking to the acquisition, in good time, of another park, and of a park which shall have a character essentially different from that of the park which it set about obtaining twenty years ago, argument will hardly be needed to make the following conclusions acceptable: —

1st.   Buffalo owes its importance as a city to its position on Lake Erie. It has in Lake Erie really great natural scenery. It has no other, and can have no other to be compared with it in value. It has no work of art and can have no work of art that will compare with it in value. Having made no use of its good fortune in this particular for the aggrandizement of its first large park, it ought not, except for absolutely conclusive reasons, to fail of making use of it in its second. The new park should be in a position to annex to itself the grandeur of Lake Erie.

2d.   The situation of the first park having secured much greater advantages of access and use to those who would visit it in carriages upon common roads, than those who could come to it only by other means of transit, it will be better, in fixing the place and determining the plan of the second park, that special regard should be given to the point of providing inexpensive, convenient and agreeable means of access to it and conveyance within it, independently of ordinary road vehicles.

The site which we were specially invited by your Board to consider,[9] has the following obvious advantages: —

1st.   It looks upon the Lake.
2d.   There is navigable water and there are four lines of railway already in operation, and others contemplated, between the place and the heart of the city.
3d.   To acquire the site, nothing of importance would have to be paid for buildings or other improvements. The land as a whole has little productive value, and probably none as near the heart of the city has had as little commercial or speculative value.*

* It has another grand advantage which will be better stated in our report on the parkway question.[10]

There are, however, serious objections to the locality, — serious difficulties to be overcome before a park can be made of it. They may be indicated as follows: —

Of the area proposed to be taken, the surface of nine-tenths is almost perfectly flat. Upon this larger part there are no trees growing, no rocks, no natural features of value for a park. Its surface is but a little above the ordinary surface of the water in Lake Erie. It is below the level to which the Lake occasionally rises. It is consequently imperfectly drained and not only half swampy at all times, but liable at intervals to be completely submerged. The difficulties growing out of these circumstances are aggravated by the fact, that below the gravel beach and the low shifting sand dunes that form the apparent lake shore, there is a stratum two feet thick or more of rotten vegetation in the form of black muck, which is easily washed out, undermining the beach. On this account the shore is rapidly wasting and the lake encroaching upon the land. Finally, there is no natural protection or facility of any kind for landing from boats on the Lake.

The weight of these objections to the site being realized, it will be seen that the first question in a discussion of a plan must be this: — By what devices, if any, can the objections to the site be so far overruled that a result of any attempted improvement of it can be looked for, that shall not have cost more than it will be worth?

This was found to be so difficult a question, that we were for a period in doubt whether we ought not to advise you to give up the idea of a Lake shore site, and we accordingly took upon ourselves the duty of examining all the southerly borders of the City in search of a site that we might recommend you to consider in place of it.

Our conclusion, however, at last came to be, that unless an excessive price would have to be paid for the site on the Lake shore, it would be wise to adopt it, and undertake to overcome its disadvantages by means, the general nature of which will presently be indicated. We believe that a park can be made upon this site which, for all time, will be of greater value to the city than any park possible to be made in any other situation as near to the city's centre.

We must now ask your attention to the drawing with the title of "Design-Map," which represents what a map of the park would be, should the plan be carried out. On the left is Lake Erie; at the bottom the "Ridge Road" as proposed to be widened and improved; near the right hand border appear a series of parallel railroad lines.

For the present, only that part between the railroads and the lake is to be considered. The extent of this part is about 240 acres, and about nine-tenths of it lies below the surface of the lake at high stages. There is, however, a narrow strip of ground on the south side, and a larger space on the west side, where the surface is several feet higher, and these elevations, with the embankment already constructed for the railroads on the east, leave the tract subject to flooding from without only on the north and a short distance on the west side. A levee four and a half feet high along this unprotected line will, therefore, shut the lake water out of the entire area. Suitable material for its construction is found in a stratum of clay two feet below the surface, on and adjoining the line of required protection. Looking at the map it is to be supposed that the planted sidewalk of the street adjoining the northern border of the park, is made upon such a levee.

With reference to the difficulty of landing from boats on the lake, adequate provision for very large boats is not important; frequent trips of numerous boats of a smaller class being more desirable than trips of large boats at longer intervals. This for the reason not only that less time will be wasted by visitors at the starting point, but that a large throng thrown all at once from a boat into a pleasure ground, is a dangerous and inconvenient occurrence. For boats of the length of those now mostly used for public pleasure excursions from Buffalo, an artificial haven is proposed to be formed; entrance to it being between two parallel piers extending to a point on the lake, where at low stages, there can be had without dredging, a depth of water of seven feet. Such a structure, to be thoroughly secure, will be costly but well worth its cost.

With regard to inroads of the lake, a firm sand bank may be expected to form on the south side of the piers, which, so far as it extends, will protect the wasting shore. How far such a bank will extend cannot be accurately determined in advance. If it is inadequate for the protection of the entire shore of the park, it may be supplemented by a riprap wall, the boulders for the construction of which can be gathered near by. If this is insufficient the method can be adopted which has been successfully used for the protection of the property of the Lehigh Valley Railway Company nearer the city.[11]

We shall now describe other parts of the plan.

As before stated, there is a body of land in the southwest part of the tract, the surface of which is several feet above high-water level of the lake. The old Hamburg turnpike passes through it;[12] there are several dwellings upon it, the soil is good and much of it is cultivated as a market garden. It is proposed to make as much of this ground as practicable, into a single park-like body of turf, with scattered trees upon its margin. It is designated The Green, will be about twenty acres in area, and is expected to be commonly used as a general playground. Upon occasions it will be a good place for parades, exhibitions, balloon ascensions, and public ceremonies. Near it, where the upland is narrower, there is to be an Athletic ground, with a running and bicycling track and an out-of-door Gymnasium, three acres in extent.

Between the Athletic Ground and the Green there is a pleasant dwelling house, the old Crocker Mansion,[13] which it is proposed to retain and improve. In this would be rooms for the deposit of dressing and playing gear and other conveniences, for those using the Athletic Ground and the Green. Near the house the map shows, also, a range of public horse-sheds.

A road for general traffic across the park, is shown on the eastern limit of the Green. It will take the place of the Hamburg turnpike, the line of which it nearly follows.

A proper pleasure road, with broad bordering walks mainly in the shade of trees, will be seen making a circuit of the Green, with liberal curves and liberal turning places. On one side of the circuit this road will command a broad view up Lake Erie, on the other a broad view over the park water. Where these views will be seen to the best advantage, there are expansions of the drives, and places arranged for people both in carriages and on foot to congregate. On the west side of the Green a minor circuit road is introduced, and the junctions are made so large that there can be a circulation of carriages about the point where the lake and the breeze from over the lake can be best enjoyed. On the east side, where the best lines of view over the park water are to be had, there is a standing place for carriages, and near it a large aquatic garden, for growing choice water-plants.

Where the lake beach is likely to be finest, owing to the packing of sand to the windward of the Pier, a bathing establishment is provided for. From its dressing rooms, bathers would pass on one side to the surf beach of the lake; as at the Newport and Long Branch bathing places, or that of Rochester on Lake Ontario, and Detroit on Belle Isle;[14] on the other side they would pass to the beach of a still-water bathing pool. In the latter, the water being shallow and brought from the shallow waters of the park, although constantly flowing, would be heated above the temperature of the lake, by the sun, and it is intended for the use of delicate persons and children, and as a swimming school. But about this feature of the plan, until the effect of building the pier is determined, there must be some doubt. At present the material of the peaty stratum before referred to, washing out from the shore makes the beach unattractive for bathing. It is confidently hoped that the defect may be remedied. If it cannot, surf-bathing as a feature of the park must be abandoned, but a still-water bathing place can, by a slight modification of the plan, be provided in the interior park waters.

All the arrangements of the plan thus far considered are situated at the west end of the site and either upon the naturally high ground, or upon ground in connection with the beach which is to be protected and kept above the lake level by the pier.

There remains to be laid out about 180 acres of the low, flat, more or less swampy land to be protected by embankment from being occasionally submerged by the lake. What we propose for this is that it shall, in the first place, be thrown into ridges and furrows, mounds and hollows, the material taken from the depressions forming the elevations, being heaped for the purpose upon intervals of flat land left between them. The ridges being often discontinued, so that the furrows will wind round the ends of them, and water being then let in to a suitable height, the result will be a body of water nearly a mile in length and a third in breadth, within which the elevations will form islands, savannas, capes and peninsulas.

The required water is expected to be drawn from Cazenovia Creek[15] by gravity, either through the canal which has been projected for the relief of the Thirteenth ward from floods,[16] or if that and all similar schemes should be abandoned, by two miles of tile pipe laid for the purpose. The water thus brought would flow first through the park, then into the still-water bathing pool, and thence between the piers into the Lake. The islands of the park water are to be of varied form and extent, and it has been a principal part of our study to so contrive them, that when overgrown by suitably designed verdure and foliage, they will, with the waters upon their borders, form pleasing landscape compositions of a natural character.

The half-decayed vegetable matter which forms the surface of the ground, having been thrown up, exposed to frost and aerated, will make the principal part of a deep, rich mould on the surface of the islands. This mould kept moist by the adjoining water, and the water shallow and heated by the sun, the conditions will be favorable to types of vegetation, such as it is rare to see profusely displayed in nature except at much inconvenience to the observer and in close association with disagreeable elements, and which it is still rarer to see exhibited in a large and intricate way in works of gardening.

By varying the conditions, so that the water will at points be comparatively shallow and at others deep, and the land at points low and at others high, the shores here abrupt, there gently inclined; giving them, sometimes the form of beaches, at others of banks, and the banks being at some places shaded by trees, at some overgrown by bushes, at some dressed with turf, at some hidden by rushes, flags, irises and other waterside plants, an extended series of interesting passages of scenery will result. At intervals there will open long vistas over water under broad leafy canopies; there will be coves completely overarched with foliage, forming verdant grottoes; some of the islands will be large enough to have within them spacious forest glades; some will be low and densely wooded, their shores so shallow that boats cannot land upon them, and their skirts so hedged with thickets as to be impenetrable. These will be nurseries for song birds, where their nestlings will have protection from natural enemies. The waters will everywhere abound with water-fowl, for the breeding of which other islands, unapproachable by visitors, will be set apart.[17] They will be navigated largely by a special class of boats gaily painted and gilded, decorated by day with bright awnings and bunting, and at night with colored lights. Small electric lights will also at night mark out the shores, the electricity to be supplied from storage batteries charged by dynamos to be run by windmills, for the use of which the locality has special advantages.

The largest of the islands shown on the drawing is to be reached in a two minutes' walk from the entrance of the park, over a short foot bridge. It will be twenty acres in area, or more than twice as large as that portion of the North Park hitherto used for picnics, and is intended to be used in a similar manner. Its surface is to be mainly four or five feet above the level of the water; it is to be planted with large-growing umbrageous trees, chiefly near the shores, and its central parts are to be open spaces of turf. There is to be a refectory upon it with the usual conveniences for picnic parties. There are to be swings and other resources of recreation; sand parks and means of amusement for infants and little children. There is to be a landing for boats bringing passengers entering the park from the land side.

The three islands near the centre of the map, being the largest of all except that last described, are to be of the same general character. Each is to have a landing, and to be entered upon only at the landing, bars below the surface preventing boats from coming elsewhere to the shores. The landings are also to be barred at will. These three islands vary from one and a half to two and a half acres in area, and are to be assigned as there may be occasion, on application in advance, each for the exclusive use for a day, or part of a day, of picnic parties that may prefer to be secured from intruders. Thus family and club entertainments may be given upon them, or a charitable society may take one as a place for a day's outing of a body of children or the conva-

lescents of a hospital. They may be used, as parts of the parks of Paris are much used, for wedding parties, or for the anniversary festivals of all manner of associations. The outlooks from these picnic islands will be particularly attractive, and quite unlike anything to be had from the places which have usually to be accepted for such occasions.

But it is impossible to convey much idea of what it would be sensible to expect in respect to the local scenery to be enjoyed from them, or in any part of the park waters or their shores. No example of a realized design of such a character can be pointed to. Growing largely out of the peculiar conditions of the locality and the distinctive requirements upon the designers, the result would be a park of unique character. To judge the plan in this respect, free play must therefore be given the imagination. The bird's-eye view and the sketches we set before you, are designed to give a general direction to the imagination, but even in this respect they must be regarded as but crudely and distantly suggestive.

Looking upon the ground as it now appears, there may be a doubt whether what we have said does not represent a day-dream of impracticably romantic character? As to this we may reasonably take it upon ourselves to say, that if twenty years ago, one standing at a certain great piggery, slaughter and pork packing house, and looking over a nauseous and dismal swamp on the northern outskirts of your city, had read a description of what was actually to be seen from the same place ten years afterwards, such a doubt would have been much more reasonable. In truth, the processes to be used for realizing the design which we are now trying to suggest, so far as the production of effects of natural scenery is concerned, will be simpler and surer, and, in this sense, of a more practical character, than those used to bring about the existing water-side scenery of the North Park.

Your attention is now asked to that part of the tract represented by the map, which lies east of the railroad embankment and six to eight hundred feet from the park water. It is suggested that on this ground a Rifle Range should be established, not necessarily as an integral part of the park, but as a public institution which may be, to the extent indicated, advantageously associated with the Park. At present the Rifle Range for the militia of Western New York is a leased ground ten miles from Buffalo.[18] The lease of it is soon to expire, and officers have been looking for a ground elsewhere, less open to certain objections than the present ground has been found to be.

The proposition to use this ground adjoining the park has been submitted to some of these officers and received their warm approval. In their opinion there would be no danger of bullets straying from it; the conditions would be more favorable for accurate shooting than they are at the present ground, and the multiplied means of transportation between the locality and the city, with the saving of time, expense and inconvenience that they would secure, would make the arrangement a desirable one.

As the adoption of this division of the plan must be contingent upon action of the State authorities, and as details of the military part of it must be approved by a military board, we shall not here dwell upon them. The breadth of the range, as shown on the plan, is greater than that of the present range, partly with a view to the larger numbers of the military forces that may be expected to resort to it in the future; partly that there may be accommodations upon it for sharp-shooting by civilians. There is a pleasant grove upon the ground under which there may be tables for refreshments; there is room for a small camp-ground, and positions for a mess-house, officers', armorer's and sutler's quarters are indicated.

Our suggestion is that the Range should be owned by the city, and such use of it as may be required leased to the State. If this is approved, it would be used as a range only in summer, and we propose that in winter the larger part of the ground shall be flooded, forming a skating pond, and that upon the southern hill-side toboggan and coasting courses shall be formed leading to lanes upon the ice, guarded from the incursion of skaters. Skating and sledding on the waters of the park proper are to be avoided, because of the destruction involved to the shrubbery and plants along the shores.

One advantage of placing the Rifle Range in the vicinity of the park, is that those visiting it, added to those visiting the park, would give reason for better railroad service than there might otherwise be between the locality and the city. There are four railroads passing from the city to a point between the northeast corner of the park and the northwest corner of the Range, and from this point passengers may be conveyed to the central station of the railroads in the city in ten minutes.

A bridge for general street business over the railroads will eventually be necessary at this point, and in connection with it a passenger station common to all the railroads is assumed. From this station to a boat on the park on the one side, and to the Range on the other, will be but a minute's walk.

We shall make a separate report to you on the question of approaches to the Park. For the purpose of this report it is only necessary to say, that besides the approaches by rail and carriage to the northeast corner just referred to, the plan takes into account probable approaches in the future by inside and outside boats, carriage-road and street railroad at the northwest corner. It is presumed that many people will come to one of these entrances, pass through the park by boat and return to the city from the other; also that many will come by one of them, make the tour of the park by boat and return from the same entrance at which they arrived. In either case, their chief enjoyment of the park would be while afloat, and the designed boating arrangements of the park are of critical importance.

Before describing them, it may be observed that wherever any considerable advantages for boating are offered in a park, the use of them has proved to be exceedingly popular. The principal park of Stockholm is accessible only by boats,[19] and besides those used by the public in general, many citizens have private boats which are used by their families, as private carriages in parks elsewhere. The park at Detroit is accessible only by boats, and it is noticed that many visitors never land from them.[20] In the Philadelphia park several small steamboats are in use, besides a large fleet of row boats.[21] In Boston harbor there are six hundred pleasure boats in use, not including row boats or a large fleet of small fishing craft often used for pleasure. The city is now building an iron pier at a cost of two hundred thousand dollars as a single feature of a haven, to be exclusively used as a mooring place for pleasure boats.[22]

It has been a surprise to us that Lake Erie is no more used than it is by Buffalonians for this manly and wholesome form of recreation; we believe that the reason must be the lack of places pleasant to visit by boat within convenient distance of the creek. The use of the row boats on the North

Park, shows that under favorable circumstances there is as much fondness for boating in Buffalo as in any city.

In the South Park plan, land, water and plantations have been disposed not only with regard to landscape beauty to be best enjoyed from boats, but with a view to prevent any swell from occurring, so that boats can never run out of still water. The islands are so disposed that, without much appearance of it to those in boats, they will practically be kept to water-roads, a hundred and fifty feet wide, and in navigating them the ordinary rule of land roads, "keep to the right," will apply. For an additional precaution against collisions, care is taken in the plan that where bends of the channel occur between one reach of water and another, the point of land to be turned will bear no foliage that will prevent the boatmen from seeing over it. The water is expected to be nowhere beyond a man's depth. The course of the channels is such, that while a direct line from the northeast to the southwest landing would measure but 1000 yards, the route to be taken by a boat would be 4000 yards. The length of the round trip would be nearly four miles. Rapid movement of the boats would not be desirable; the time occupied in a round trip of a steam launch, including stoppages at five landings, might be three-quarters of an hour.

Row boats, canoes and small steam yachts for private parties are expected to be used. For the conveyance of the public in general, however, regular lines of packet boats are had in view. For the propulsion of these, the circumstances are particularly favorable to the use either of electric or of compressed air engines, but steam or naphtha engines will be available.

The packet boats would be broader, roomier and stiffer than ordinary steam launches. Making but short trips they would carry little fuel. Never running out of still water they would need no decks. Boats of twenty-five feet length accordingly, would be spacious for the conveyance each of sixteen passengers under an awning. Each boat would be well managed by one man, who would have police authority, and the boat police thus provided, constantly reviewing as it would, all the waters, would see that suitable regulations were observed in other boats as well as in the packets.[23]

The cost of a water carriage of the class proposed, with efficient machinery, will be less than that of any style of land carriage fitted to convey the same number of passengers with anything like equal comfort and luxury; it would be half the cost of a good hackney coach that would carry a fourth part of the number. Its ordinary running expenses would be but a trifle more than the pay of the boatman. Plying in the manner of omnibuses or street cars, with five-cent fares, a numerous fleet of such water carriages would be profitably employed.

The most weighty objection to the scheme as it has been thus presented will doubtless be its costliness, and its costliness will be felt chiefly through comparison with that of the North Park. Therefore it should not be forgotten that the North Park has been obtained at exceptionally low cost. We know of no other park with which comparison could be at all fairly made that has not cost twice as much.

There have been two reasons for this:

First, a smaller number of requirements were sought to be provided for in the North Park than there usually have been in others, and it was practicable to adjust to the natural topography a simple plan for securing what was attempted, so that the item of grading has been comparatively insignificant. In the New York, Brooklyn, Philadelphia, Boston, Montreal, Albany and Bridgeport parks, for example, the grading of walks and roads with their immediate borders, has probably cost, on an average, more than twenty times as much as it has in your North Park.

Second, the greater part of the work on the North Park has been done under circumstances unusually favorable to economy, steadily; with freedom from political embarrassments; mainly by unskilled labor, at comparatively low wages, and under the unbroken direct superintendence of one man of unusual zeal, industry and competency for his duty, enjoying your confidence in such degree that he could plan his operations well in advance and carry them on with decision, discipline and method, such as is rarely practicable on our public works.[24]

The Rifle Range is not an essential part of the plan for the park, and as your action upon the proposition for it will necessarily wait on action of the military representatives of the State, we shall not regard it in what we have to say of the cost of the park.

As to the market value of the site for the park, we find men who should be well-informed varying in their estimates by more than a hundred per cent., and we need only repeat what we said at the beginning of this report, that if the city is ever going to want another park, there is no other body of land which can be taken for it that will not probably be more costly than this. Certainly there is none on the Lake shore. It is of much less intrinsic value than the land of the North Park. Very little of it is fit for cultivation or for a dwelling place, while that at the North Park was the choicest near the city either for agriculture or for healthful residence. Had the North Park not been made, and it was now a question of the choice of sites for a park, the North Park site would undoubtedly be much the more costly.

Assuming that the wages of labor and the prices of materials are to remain as at present, and that work is to proceed about as rapidly and as steadily as it did on the North Park, we calculate that to complete the South Park as planned, an average outlay for ten years will be needed of sixty-two thousand dollars a year, or about thirty per cent. more than the outlay made during the same period upon the North Park.

591

A more important question than that of the cost of construction is that of the constant cost to keep the park when made in good order. In all the principal items of maintenance, the work required for this purpose would be considerably less than that required for corresponding items in the North Park. The North Park is about a third larger in area than the South Park is proposed to be, and of its area more than twice as much will be occupied by water. Water-space costs less than any other in a park to take care of. The extent of road and walk space will be less in the South than in the North Park. The distances to which materials, such as gravel and sand, must be carried will be less. On the whole, the cost of maintaining the South Park would probably be less by about a quarter than that of the North Park.

We have thus indicated what we believe the undertaking would cost the city. You will consider whether the result would justify the cost. In our opinion there is better reason to think that it would, than there was twenty years ago that the undertaking of the North Park would be so generally conceded as it now is, to have been entered upon discreetly and providently.

Respectfully,

F. L. & J. C. OLMSTED,
Landscape Architects.

The original was published in City of Buffalo. Park Commission, *The Projected Park and Parkways on the South Side of Buffalo. Two Reports by the Landscape Architects. 1888* (Buffalo, N.Y., 1888), pages 3–26.

1. On February 28, 1887, citizens living in the Thirteenth Ward, located in the southeastern portion of the city, petitioned the Common Council for an extension of the park system through their ward to the shore of Lake Erie. On the same day the council adopted a resolution providing for the extension of the park system to the lake shore and referred it to the park board. The park board in turn requested Olmsted to visit the site of a possible park and also to determine the possibilities of extending Fillmore Avenue south and using it as a parkway to the new park. Olmsted visited the site on March 22 and 23, 1887, and on March 31 submitted a letter to the park board advocating a lake-shore park but cautioning the board against premature decisions regarding a parkway (*Buffalo Express*, March 1, 1887, p. 6; ibid, March 24, 1887, p. 5; "Park Commissioners' Report," in City of Buffalo. Park Commission, *Eighteenth Annual Report of the Buffalo Park Commissioners. January, 1888* [Buffalo, N.Y., 1888], pp. 8–9; "Proposed Extension of the Park System," in ibid, pp. 32–39).

2. That is, the Park (Delaware Park) for which Olmsted and Calvert Vaux prepared plans in 1870. The first published plan for the Park appeared in the Buffalo park commissioners *First Annual Report* (1871) (see OVC to William Edward Dorsheimer, Oct. 1, 1868, above).

3. While the bill authorizing creation of a park system in Buffalo was before the New York state legislature in early 1869, a provision was added to it requiring that one-fifth of the land acquired for the system be east of Jefferson Street. That street had marked the eastern boundary of the system as proposed by Olmsted and Vaux in 1868. To

comply with the law as passed, they had to reduce the area of Delaware Park west of Jefferson Street (City of Buffalo. Common Council, *Minutes*, Feb. 8, 1869, p. 81; *Buffalo Express*, Feb. 11, 1869, p. 20; New York [State], *Laws of the State of New York, Passed at the Ninety-Second Session of the Legislature . . .* [Albany, N.Y., 1869], chap. 165; City of Buffalo. Park Commission, *Sixteenth Annual Report of the Buffalo Park Commissioners. January, 1886* [Buffalo, N.Y., 1886], p. 18; see OVC to William Edward Dorsheimer, Oct. 1, 1868, above).

4. In 1874 Olmsted sent a communication to the park board entreating it to purchase approximately ten acres of land on the southern border of the park that had been discarded when the park act was passed. Olmsted wrote,

> Your Commission was advised at the time that this reduction was a very unfortunate one, chiefly because, after pinching the ground on the north side of the water as much as possible without abandoning the design, it was still necessary, in order to conform to the law, to throw out some ten acres of land on the south side of the water previously intended to be included in the Park and which for many years to come would be more valuable than any other.
>
> I have several times since suggested to the Commission that application should be made to the Legislature for an Act providing a remedy for this misfortune, and in the light of the experience of the year now closing, I beg to renew that advice with earnestness. The ground in question is a part of a grove of well-grown beeches and maples, upon a nearly level surface, and there is no other ground in or near any of your parks or places which for twenty years to come will be equally well adapted for large picnic parties.

Not until 1883 did the park board request an appropriation to purchase the land in question. The following year the state legislature passed an act for the purchase of twelve acres adjacent to the park and bounded by Lincoln Parkway, Delaware Avenue, and Forest Avenue. In 1887 the land was appraised at $50,000, which was $20,000 above the purchase price authorized by the law. The landowners, however, agreed to accept $30,000, providing the city would repay them for the taxes that they had paid on the land during the previous two years while the proceedings had been pending, as well as the interest on the amount for the same time period, the total amounting to $4,204.68. The original park land when purchased in 1870 cost the city approximately $657 an acre, and the additional twelve acres purchased in 1887 cost $2,833 per acre (City of Buffalo. Park Commission, *First Annual Report of the Buffalo Park Commissioners. January, 1871* [Buffalo, N.Y., 1871], p. 7; idem, *Fifth Annual Report of the Buffalo Park Commissioners. January, 1875* [Buffalo, N.Y., 1875], pp. 11–12; idem, *Fourteenth Annual Report of the Buffalo Park Commissioners. January, 1884* [Buffalo, N.Y., 1884], pp. 9–10; idem, *Fifteenth Annual Report of the Buffalo Park Commissioners. January, 1885* [Buffalo, N.Y., 1885], pp. 15–16; idem, *Seventeenth Annual Report of the Buffalo Park Commissioners. January, 1887* [Buffalo, N.Y., 1887], pp. 10–11).

5. The same year that the state legislature passed a law providing for the purchase of additional land for Delaware Park, it also passed a law for the purchase of twenty additional acres for the Front. In that case, however, years of litigation prevented the city from acquiring all of the land until 1890. It cost the city $109,479 for twenty acres or $5,474 an acre compared to $657 per acre in 1870 (idem, *Fifteenth Annual Report of the Buffalo Park Commissioners*, pp. 14–15; idem, *Twenty-first Annual Report of the Buffalo Park Commissioners. January, 1891* [Buffalo, N.Y., 1891], p. 13; for a description of the Front, see OVC to William Edward Dorsheimer, Oct. 1, 1868, and n. 11, above).

6. That is, Forest Lawn Cemetery, which adjoins Delaware Park on the south (see OVC to William Edward Dorsheimer, Oct. 1, 1868, n. 12, above).

7. The site for the Buffalo State Hospital for the Insane was approved by the city's Common Council on November 1, 1869, the same day it approved the selection of land for the Park. In fact, the asylum did take up an area south of the western end of Delaware Park where Olmsted in his report of 1868 intended to build a parkway that would connect with streets leading to the Front. Olmsted and Calvert Vaux designed a plan for the asylum in July 1871. In the mid-1870s Olmsted provided plans and planting lists for the grounds (City of Buffalo. Common Council, *Minutes*, Nov. 1, 1869, pp. 715–16, 725–29; "Preliminary Suggestions for the Grounds of the Buffalo State Hospital for the Insane," [July 7, 1871] [*Papers of FLO*, 6: 452–56]).

8. The Belt Line, built in 1883, was Buffalo's first mass-transportation system and consisted of a fifteen-mile railroad loop designed to transport passengers around the outskirts of the city. The line was a branch of the New York Central Railroad and provided service of two trains an hour in each direction (Richard C. Brown and Bob Watson, *Buffalo: Lake City in Niagara Land* [Buffalo, N.Y., 1981], pp. 10–11, 150–51).

9. The site of the proposed park was an area located on the shore of Lake Erie on the southern border of Buffalo. The site included part of Buffalo's Thirteenth Ward and part of the town of West Seneca (Frederick Law Olmsted, "Proposed Extension of the Park System," April 11, 1887, in City of Buffalo. Park Commission, *Eighteenth Annual Report of the Buffalo Park Commissioners*, p. 32).

10. Published with the South Park report was a companion document entitled "Report on the South Parkway Question." In this document Olmsted noted that the South Park site had distinct advantages in that it could be easily approached by water.

> Plantations having been grown on the borders of the canal, there would, by this process, have been prepared a pleasant water-avenue, providing a direct inside passage for boats between the park and the lower wharves of Buffalo Creek. The western slope of the levee would be everywhere washed by the waters of the lake, and in passing along the parkway upon it, the full expanse of the lake, clear to the horizon, would be open to view. It would thus form a superb promenade, and as it would be crossed by no streets, but be bordered by a belt of wood on one side and by the lake on the other, it would in effect bring the park a mile and a half nearer the city; that is to say, within two miles of the City Hall (F. L. & J. C. Olmsted, "Report on the South Parkway Question," in *Projected Park and Parkways on the South Side of Buffalo*, pp. 18–19).

11. The Lehigh Valley Railway Company's property was located just north of the proposed site for South Park. The company had purchased the 320-acre Tifft farm in 1880. The property provided the company additional room to construct a system of slips connected to the City Ship Canal as well as wharves and storage yards. The company had constructed a levee to protect its holdings from high water (Henry Wayland Hill, ed., *Municipality of Buffalo, New York: A History, 1720–1923*, 4 vols. [New York, 1923], 2: 775; see also F. L. & J. C. Olmsted, "Report on the South Parkway Question," in *Projected Park and Parkways on the South Side of Buffalo*, pp. 17–18).

12. The old Hamburg turnpike followed a north-south route along the shore of Lake Erie between Hamburgh, New York, and Buffalo. The turnpike became Ohio Street north of Buffalo Creek in Buffalo's Thirteenth Ward (Matthews, Northrup & Co., *New Map of the City of Buffalo & Erie County* [Buffalo, N.Y., 1886]).

13. A house belonging to "L. Crocker" at the western end of Ridge Road in West Seneca, probably the property of Lemuel L. Crocker (c. 1830–1885), a Buffalo businessman (*Buffalo Commercial Advertiser*, March 28, 1885, p. 3; F. W. Beers & Co., *Illustrated Historical Atlas of Erie Co., New York* [New York, 1880]; *Buffalo Express*, Feb. 1, 1887, p. 6).

14. Newport, Rhode Island, and Long Branch, New Jersey, were two popular sea-side

resort communities that provided ample bathing facilities for their visitors. The bath houses were separate accommodations from the hotels and boarding houses and were located along the beach. Guests entered from the landward side, changed into appropriate bathing costumes, and exited onto the beach. By the mid-1880s Rochester, New York, could boast of several resorts with bathing facilities along Lake Ontario including Summerville, White City, and Charlotte Beach. At Detroit's Belle Isle, Olmsted proposed a similar arrangement to that of Buffalo with a bathing establishment being constructed on the north side of the island and east of the "City Fair" section (A *Guide to Narragansett Bay* . . . [Providence, R.I., 1878], p. 67; Blake McKelvey, *Rochester: The Flower City, 1855–1890* [Cambridge, Mass., 1949], p. 353; Frederick Law Olmsted, *The Park for Detroit* [Brookline, Mass., 1882], p. 55).

15. Cazenovia Creek was located west of the proposed site of South Park. It flowed in a northwesterly direction and entered Buffalo Creek in the city's Thirteenth Ward at White Corners Plank Road (*New Map of the City of Buffalo*).

16. In an effort to reduce the damage done to property in the Thirteenth Ward from constant flooding, the Common Council passed a resolution on February 28, 1887, to appropriate a strip of land 200 feet wide from Cazenovia Creek at the junction of Potters Corners and Abbotts Corners plank roads to Lake Erie for the purposes of building a canal. Surveys estimated that the canal would be about 2½ miles long and cost $185,000 to build. The project was never carried out (*Buffalo Express*, March 1, 1887, p. 6; ibid., March 10, 1887, p. 5).

17. Other of Olmsted's designs provided for the creation of islands unapproachable by visitors but to be used by birds for nesting. Chicago's South Park and Boston's Back Bay were two such examples. Olmsted also intended that these locations be well stocked with waterfowl, taken from the region's lakes and rivers, if possible, and domesticated for the purpose (OVC, "Report Accompanying Plan for Laying Out the South Park," March 1871, pp. 227–28, above; "City Document No. 15," in City of Boston. Department of Parks, *Fifth Report of the Board of Commissioners of the Department of Parks for the City of Boston* [Boston, 1881], p. 13).

18. The rifle range was situated in Bay View, on the shore of Lake Erie eight miles south of Buffalo. The range was owned by the Bay View Rifle Association and used by both the 65th and 74th New York militia regiments (*Pauls' Dictionary of Buffalo* . . . [Buffalo, N.Y., 1896], p. 13).

19. That is, the Djurgården (deer park) (see FLO, *A Consideration of the Justifying Value of a Public Park*, [1881], n. 29, above).

20. That is, Belle Isle in Detroit (see FLO, *Belle Isle: One Year After*, June 1884, above).

21. Ample facilities were provided for pleasure boating in Philadelphia's Fairmount Park. Steamboat landings as well as rowboats for hire were stationed along the Schuylkill River and provided access to and boating on the park (*Visitors' Guide to the Centennial Exhibition and Philadelphia* [Philadelphia, 1876], p. 46).

22. Olmsted had provided the city of Boston with a plan for Pleasure Bay (Marine Park) in 1883. The park was to be laid out at City Point in South Boston and would incorporate Castle Island by a causeway on the northeast. On the southeast a long pier was planned for promenading. A wooden pier was first constructed and immediately became popular with Boston residents. Later an iron pier was built as an extension of the wooden one, making the pier 1,300 feet in length. Work on the iron pier was underway at the time Olmsted wrote this report, but it was not completed until the 1890s (Cynthia Zaitzevsky, *Frederick Law Olmsted and the Boston Park System* [Cambridge, Mass., 1982], pp. 91–93; Rand, McNally & Co.'s, *Handy Guide to Boston and Environs* [Chicago, 1898], p. 50; City of Boston. Department of Parks, *Sixteenth Annual Report of the Board of Commissioners for the Year 1890* [Boston, 1891], p. 20).

23. On the lagoons and canals at the 1893 World's Columbian Exposition in Chicago, Olmsted realized his vision of awning-covered electric launches. He sailed to En-

gland in the summer of 1892, traveling up and down the Thames trying several different types of launches and all the while studying them to determine the best design for use at the fair (Laura Wood Roper, *FLO: A Biography of Frederick Law Olmsted* [Baltimore, Md., 1973], pp. 432–33, 440; FLO to Partners, July 17, 1892; FLO to Daniel H. Burnham, June 20, 1893).

24. That is, William McMillan (1830–1899), horticulturist, landscape architect, and superintendent of the Buffalo parks from 1871 until 1898. Olmsted had long valued McMillan's work on the Buffalo parks, and in October 1893 he stated that "on none of the public grounds that I visit do I find a superintendent who performs his duties as industriously, economically and intelligently as Mr. McMillan" (*Buffalo Courier Express*, Aug. 3, 1899, p. 8; *Buffalo Illustrated Express*, Oct. 1, 1893, p. 2).

OLMSTED, OLMSTED & ELIOT, LANDSCAPE ARCHITECTS.

BROOKLINE, MASS.

EDWARD D. BOLTON,[1]
SUPERINTENDENT OF CONSTRUCTION.
WARREN H. MANNING,[2]
SUPERINTENDENT OF PLANTING.

30th January, 1894

The Honorable J. T. Carew, President of the
Park Commission of Cincinnati, Ohio[3]
Dear Sir: —
    Under your instructions we came to Cincinnati early in January.[4] The next day we were taken by your Commission[5] on a tour of observation of the works of which it is in charge. Afterwards, we made other visits to these works under the guidance of your Superintendent,[6] and were furnished with a number of documents relating to their history.

    By your invitation, several representatives of the Press were with us on our introductory tour,[7] and many questions were asked of us, some of which could not be answered satisfactorily upon a cursory, superficial examination of the ground, in the dead of Winter, without reference to maps or plans. Others referred to such details that they could not be wisely answered without better knowledge than we then had of the leading motives of design of works of which these details were minor incorporate parts. Others were of such a class that before answering them we should have wished to consult an engineer who had had opportunities of observing the results of operations carried on under the conditions involved. It is not surprising that some of our impromptu answers, made conversationally, to questions partly of a technical character, were a little misunderstood, and, as reported, were liable to make wrong impressions.

Having regard to the probable object with which it had been provided that what we might off-handedly say under the circumstances, should be made public, we have since obtained through a commercial agency a collection of reports and comments upon the park affairs of the city which have appeared in your public journals. From these and other sources of information, we infer that there has been for sometime past a questioning attitude of public opinion as to the policy and methods under which conditions have been brought about that your Board has inherited.

No general report of the results of our visit has been formally asked of us. But such a report appeared to be expected by members of your Board, who, referring to doubts that had been prevailing in the public mind, expressed the hope that we should not be reluctant to state what we thought of the past dealings of the city with park affairs, nor to state wherein its policy seemed to us open to improvement.

We think that we can serve you best by adopting the view of our duty thus suggested, and, as the value of what we may say is to be largely estimated by regard for the opportunities we have had for comparing the operation of different policies and methods of administration for the public parks, we will here briefly indicate what these have been.

We have examined and, several times at intervals of years, have re-examined, a large number of European public grounds, and have conferred and compared experience with those in charge of them. We have, in like manner, visited most of the public grounds of this continent and, with regard to seventy of them, divided among twenty different cities, we have had professional and official responsibilities giving us an intimate knowledge of their modes of management. We have attended several hundred meetings of different park commissions, and have had part in their debates. We have devised the plans for several local series of parks connected by parkways; have watched the carrying out of them, and have studied the results comparatively. We have prepared regulations afterwards adopted by park commissions for the public use of several such series of parks and parkways, and have watched the manner in which they have operated in practice.

As bearing, in a preliminary way, on the question of sound policy and methods in the park department of city business, we submit the following considerations to which, however simple and primary they may seem to be, we have not found that due regard is apt to be given.

No man can be expected to contrive a good method of accomplishing a result who does not set about the contriving of that method with a fairly clear idea of the result required. If two men or ten men are to do the contriving, it is a necessity of their working efficiently together, that all shall have in mind the same idea of the result to be reached. It is equally necessary that all shall steadily keep this idea in view. Inefficiency and extravagance must grow from a difference of understanding in this respect, or from any understanding held weakly and vacillatingly. It follows that if some of those engaged in advancing such a work retire and others take their places, waste is liable to occur if the new men proceed upon a different view of the result to be accomplished from that which has been taken by their predecessors. We have known several hundred thousand dollars of public money wasted because of the prevalence of different ideas of their duty with successive honest members of a park commission.

Suppose that the result of the co-operation of several men is meant to be an apparatus of many parts; then each of these parts needs to be contrived to serve, in some subordinate way, the general purpose of the required apparatus as a whole. If, in the contrivance of these contributive parts, a wrong idea is had of the main purpose, then the work of contriving them is likely to be wasted, or worse. A bolt, for example, may be a good piece of workmanship in itself, but if it has been made too large or too small for the part it is to play in the work of the whole apparatus, or if it is made of too brittle or too flexible material for that part, not only will the labor which has been spent upon this bolt have been badly spent, but all the labor which has been applied to the whole apparatus will have been spent to less advantage than it otherwise would have been. The waste thus occurring through bad dealings with details may be very great.

The larger the number of those who are at any time to be engaged in the preparation of the apparatus, the greater is the necessity of a clear, common understanding among them as to the purpose which the apparatus as a whole is wanted to serve.

All that has thus been said as to providing an apparatus for any purpose applies to an arrangement for providing the people of a city with parks. To a useful inquiry, then, whether the park arrangements of a city have been well contrived, it is first of all necessary to ask with reference to what purpose these arrangements have been contrived, and how steadily, closely and shrewdly this purpose has been kept in view.

A sound understanding of the purpose that should be kept in view by a park commission is not always to be obtained by consulting the statute under which it has been formed. Such statutes are generally extremely vague in their statement of purpose.

When a statute provides for a commission to look after the building of a Court House, a School House or a Poor House, if anything results unsuited to the purpose intended, the commissioners can be held accountable for this unsuitableness. But when a statute provides for a commission to look after the forming of that which is called a park, there is commonly thought to be room for a wide difference of opinion as to the purpose with reference to which the Commission is entitled to use public property. Within places which are called public parks, the land of which belongs to the public and which are kept in order and guarded at public expense, there are to be found a theatre, a church, an arsenal, a grave-yard, a race-track, a dance house, a menagerie, a flower garden, a picture gallery, beer houses, club houses, and private homes in houses with gardens about them, leased to the occupants.

The legal definition of a park according to Blackstone is "an enclosed chase extending over a man's own ground."[8] Dr. Johnson defines a park as a body of land enclosed and stored with wild beasts.[9] Dr. Crosby Brown adds that when the beasts are destroyed the land is no longer to be legally known as a park.[10] In the laws of Colorado a park means a body of treeless prairie-like ground, the ownership of which may be divided among a hundred private citizens.[11] There is an Act of Congress,[12] and there are Acts of State Legislatures in which it is explained that by the word park is meant a place of public recreation, and much that has been written assumes that, to define the business of a park commission, it is sufficient to say that it is to prepare places suitable for public recreation, no definite limitation being provided in respect to the character of the recreation to be had in view. A large part of all that has been written for the public about the parks of the United States has been written with an equally inexact understanding of the end for which park commissions exist. Yet, with a moment's reflection, the practical inadequacy of such an idea of a park commission's duties should be evident.

Suppose that the building committee of a Normal School, or of a singing school, a dancing, a riding or a fencing, school should go to work with no more specific object than is to be expressed by the word education. Suppose that it should spend large sums for costly pictures and statuary, and meet criticism by asking—Are these things not educative? Obviously, the question the building committee should answer is, not whether they are educative, but whether they are educative in the specific manner to provide for which the committee, in this particular case, has been given other people's money to spend?

There have been men; in some parts of the world there are yet men; who regard it as a recreation to see criminals hanged. Public money is expended in Spain for the recreation of the people by means of bull fights. A cock-pit is often built and maintained with public money for public recreation in the principal public grounds of a Mexican town.

No one, so far as we know, has yet distinctly advocated such a view of the duty of a park commission, but a great deal of the criticism of the doings of park commissions, and a large proportion of the propositions urged upon park commissions, and of the arguments used in favor of these propositions, betray confusion of mind between the proper purpose of public parks and a view of that purpose that must be essentially the same, not only with that upon which it is thought best for the public authorities to provide for popular recreation by means of bull fights and cock fights, but with that under which, in the days that went before the downfall of the Roman Empire, men were paid from the public funds to take the risk of being slaughtered in the amphitheatre for the recreation of the populace.

There is no duty resting on any intelligent citizen of our republic more imperative than that of resisting all tendency of public opinion to drift toward such a confusion. If parks are to promote such confusion it would be better to have no parks.

A search for a sounder idea of the duty of a park commission; for an idea that can be followed without peril to the republic, may begin with the consideration that park commissions are departments of city government of comparatively recent origin, the larger number of all in the United States having set about their work within the last eighteen years, while the pioneer of all of them began its work but thirty-four years ago.[13] It is to be inferred that park commissions began to be established in order to meet a public want which in most communities has only of late been recognized to be of pressing importance. That this want has, nevertheless, been widely felt and that no adequate means of meeting it has been found except through some such machinery of government as has with us been provided in park commissions is evident, not only from the number of park commissions for which American cities have obtained legislation, but from the fact that within forty years nearly every growing city in Europe, not before provided with parks, has taken measures to acquire them, and those cities which had before happened to possess any, have been securing land for more and larger parks. London and Paris, for example, have each added several thousand acres to the park areas they formerly possessed. The amount of land now held by European cities with a view to its use for public recreation is, in many cases, several times larger than it was twenty years ago. There has been nothing like a corresponding increase in the number of play-houses, billiard rooms, picture galleries, race-tracks and provisions for bull fights, cock fights and other means of recreation.

So large, so costly, so continuous has been this public park movement that it cannot wisely be regarded merely as the transit of a fashion; of an epidemic of vague, romantic sentiment, or as the result of a passing phase of popular taste.

To get nearer to a rational explanation of the movement, it is to be considered, first, that it began, and has been growing in all parts of the civilized world, only since another yet more notable movement became manifest, namely, the movement of which the present result is seen in a great recent enlargement of the population of many of the oldest large towns of the civilized world, and in the growing up of many entirely new large towns.

Cincinnati presents an example of what had thus been everywhere occurring shortly before the park movement set in; her population having advanced from 31,000 to 145,000 in the period of fifteen years before the first move occurred in the proceedings which ended in the formation of the first American Park commission.[14] Within this period large public parks were begun to be formed in London, Liverpool and Paris, each of which towns had for some time previously been greatly gaining in population. So, also, within this same period, more was done for the multiplication, enlargement and improvement of places of popular open air recreation in several other European cities than had been done in centuries of their previous history.

The space occupied by the population of the principal towns of the world has been enlarging more than correspondingly with the enlargement of the population; the effect of street railways, telephones, telegraphs and other apparatus of modern introduction, having been to cause towns to spread over their old suburbs, even faster than their population has increased. Yet fewer people than formerly, relatively to the whole population of a large town, now attend evening church meetings, theatres and other entertainments in it, because so many more of its people live at a distance from the central parts of the town, and the increase of means of transportation within the town has not been proportionate to the increasing popular need for transportation.

With enlarging populations, notwithstanding the fact that towns are now built less compactly than they formerly were, and for this reason and others are much cleaner and better ventilated, evils of a particular class are apt to increasingly prevail in them; evils by which the vigor, sound-mindedness, earning capacity and tax-paying capacity of their people is made seriously less than it otherwise would be.

Increase in this particular class of evils is not due, as is often assumed in the advocacy of parks, to the increasing impurity of air attending the enlargement of towns. As a rule, in modern built towns, people have much better air than the people of much smaller towns formerly had. Then, it is a fact that the evils in question have been increasing in quarters of these enlarging towns, in which the buildings are upon heights looking seaward and with air pressing into them which has come over the sea, or in other cases, which has come over great rivers and forests; quarters in which not the slightest taint of foul air can be detected; quarters in which a change of air is constantly occurring.

In all aggravated individual cases in which this particular class of evils appear, there is one means of relief which, when it is possible to be used, good physicians seldom fail to advise. It is that of a holiday or vacation to be taken largely with a view to the usual result of what is called a change of scene; more accurately to be specified as a change of scenery.

To what kind of scenery is it most desirable for the purpose that a man should escape from the scenery of a city? Broadly speaking, it is to that kind which will supply the strongest contrast that can be had to city scenery.

There should not be a doubt in any man's mind; there cannot be a lingering doubt, after he has taken the trouble to investigate the facts, or has sought the advice of those who have investigated them, that what is here said is wholly free from false sentiment or romance. It is plain, prosaic, matter-of-fact of which our knowledge is derived from the practical experience of many thousand over-worked men and women; men and women many of whom have had less admiring interest than the average man and woman, in beautiful trees and plants and flowers. There is no room for doubt that it pays exceedingly well; pays in the form, among others, of increased money-making capacity, and in the form of increased tax-paying capacity, for such men and women, living in towns, to take from time to time, doses of rural scenery; the more completely rural the better, provided the taking of doses of it does not involve too much inconvenience, fatigue, hardship and resulting nervous depression.

In every large city in the civilized world there are men distinguished for their devotion to pursuits which can only be followed to advantage in large cities; men of wealth, who under the advice of the ablest physicians that their wealth can obtain, are in the habit, much against their inclinations, of using this remedy. Such men have experimental knowledge that the time they lose from their pursuits for the purpose of using this remedy is profitably spent; is profitably spent with reference to commercial profits in those pursuits. Many a man has come to bankruptcy, even many a man to premature death, because he would not soon enough accept his physician's advice to use this remedy. And the experience applies to poor working men and women as much as to those upon whom the cares of large commercial enterprises are weighing.

If relief from the evils in question is to be obtained by occasional change from town scenery to suitable country scenery, what means are people to use to guard against the coming on of that sapping of health, strength and means of usefulness and earning capacity, to which, when engaged in town pursuits, they are peculiarly and increasingly liable?

The sound answer seems to be that they must look to such measure of change of scenery as it is practicable for them to systematically secure in frequent doses.

It is a plain fact that the troubles in question can be thus guarded against; a fact as well established as any other in sanitary and medical science; and it is only a matter of common sense to recognize, as the people of large cities have lately come to recognize, that the man who cannot act upon this fact; the inhabitants of a city who cannot act upon this fact, are only less unfortunate than they would be if they could not act upon the fact that food and drink are necessary for the maintenance of their strength.

By what physiological process this remedy operates, it is unnecessary here to attempt an elaborate, scientific explanation. It is enough to say that it plainly operates in the main by inducing a change of mental bents or moods;

that the inducement of such change comes primarily through a subtle action of the remedy which sets a movement going of a man's imagination and that the resulting changes of mood are more or less in a direction from a materialistic toward a poetic mood. Through these changes of mood the whole human system is affected healthfully.

The only way in which it is possible that provision for the object thus explained can be made available for the mass of the people of a large and growing town is by preparing places for the purpose at public expense. The places now called parks in our laws are places intended to be adapted to this purpose. The ultimate value of what parks in preparation are to be depends, first, on the adaptation of the design with regard to which they are to be prepared to the purpose which has been stated; second, on the adaptation of the work to be done upon them to a realization of that design; third, on the manner in which use shall be made of them, this last being chiefly a matter of suitable rules for visitors and inducements to them to comply with those rules.

Now it has to be considered that the time required for the realization of the design for a public park does not depend on the force employed, the money spent or the energy or skill of the management, in anything like the degree that is required for the realization of the design of a public building or the pavement of a street, or any other ordinary piece of corporation work. After all advantage has been gained that it is practicable to gain through the energy and skill of those in charge of the work, the realization of the design must be more or less dependent on progress by natural growth. In many cases it is so largely a question of the advance by natural growth that it may be estimated that such value as the parks shall have at the end of twenty years will, under good management, be doubled at forty; doubled again at sixty, and will thereafter be advancing continuously. The older the park, provided it is conservatively managed, the more valuable it will be relatively to the only purpose for which public money should have been spent upon it. Park works, it will be seen, differ in this respect from building works and from almost all other public works.

It is for this reason right that public parks should be largely paid for, as they commonly are, by the proceeds of loans, maturing as the value of the parks increases and comes more and more to be realized.

The first time that provisions adapted to the purpose which has thus been explained were made in the United States, they were made with reference to the wants of the future people of that one of the cities of the country which had already become the largest and most crowded of all, and in which strains upon health of the class that have been explained, were already most marked and were already obviously detracting from the prosperity of the city. And it was with reference to this undertaking that the first of the present forty or more park commissions of American cities was constituted and the first park loan authorized.

We do not say that in the case of that park; we do not say that in any existing case, the purpose explained was clearly and precisely defined and limited in the minds of those who prepared the statutes under which park commissions have been constituted. What we urge is that the powers given to park commissions, and the use of borrowed money which has been allowed them, can only be reasonably accounted for and justified through reference to such a purpose, and that often blunderingly in particulars, sometimes with great departures in particulars, from this purpose, the work that has been done by park commissions has, in a large view of it, been done as it would have been if regard for such a purpose had been enjoined upon them by the law.

Nor is there a single case within our knowledge in which this idea of the distinctive function of this new department in city governments, called the park commission, has been accepted, and at all intelligently acted upon for a sufficient time to allow the designed results to be fairly tested, that it has not been found that the people are obtaining a degree of benefit to health through their use of the park that far more than compensates for the outlay by which it has been obtained for them.

This conclusion is sustained by the general testimony of physicians, even in cases where the outlay has been extravagant. Such testimony only fails where this idea of the distinctive function of a park commission has been wholly lost sight of or been largely eclipsed by the rising, during the work, of other motives wholly inconsistent with it.

Reviewing the experience as a whole, that has been gained in such public parks of this country as have been established within the last five and thirty years, the following conclusions may be considered as established.

First, that people living in large towns are liable to be acted upon by the class of subtle influences to the more aggravated results of which the terms nervous exhaustion and nervous irritation have come to be commonly applied.

Second, that when thus acted upon, people are more liable than they otherwise would be to suffer from various more distinct forms of ill health, and in all cases, to lose strength, vigor and ability to bear well their part in the general business of the city.

Third, that this liability may be materially lessened, and the bad effect of the class of influences in question counteracted by certain means.

Fourth, that the most efficacious of such means, so far, at least, as they can be provided for by legislation, is that by which the people of a town are, at frequent intervals, brought under the counter influence of natural scenery.

Fifth, that forms of natural scenery the most efficacious that can be secured for the purpose under local circumstances must be so presented that they will be generally available and will not be materially lessened in value by such means, in the form of roads and walks, seats and shelters, as will be necessary for the immediate comfort of those to be benefitted.

Sixth, that works of this class are likely to be well designed only by designers who have been qualified for the duty by much industry and discipline in the pursuit of special professional studies and through courses of special professional training.

Seventh, that when men who are without the results of such special study, training and discipline attempt to direct such works, the result is apt to compare with that of the work of trained designers as the work of amateurs on the stage or in architecture, or any other of the Fine Arts, is apt to compare with that of suitably trained and disciplined artists.

Park commissioners are not intended by the law to be selected for their duties, nor, in practice, have they ever been selected for their duties, because of any special training that they have had in the exercise of judgment in determining the adaptation of lands to the purpose of parks, or in determining by what series of operations such lands may be well prepared for parks. They have generally been selected and it is the intention of the laws that they shall be selected, on the same grounds that are commonly regarded in the choice of men to serve as trustees of funds provided for the buildings of hospitals, churches, bridges, railroads or for obtaining statues or historical paintings for a public place or building.

Taking this view, what is the first duty of a board of trustees for a public park? Plainly, it is the same with the duty of a board of trustees of a building fund for any public purpose. It is to select and employ men who are specially and technically trained for the designing and management of park undertakings; and to deal with their undertaking through them as do the directors of a bank, or a factory, or a railroad, or a line of steam boats, through the skilled men whom they employ.

When the trustees of a hospital undertake to prescribe the medicines and the diet of patients; to personally regulate the means of ventilation of the wards, or to determine the qualifications of the nurses and stewards, it is time for the surgeons to resign. Nor can we see how any man competent for the duty of our profession, can rightly hold a position in which a board of trustees as a body, much more in which trustees individually, feel themselves at liberty to give orders whereby his professional responsibility for the value of the results of the work upon a public park may be made questionable. The case, in our opinion, is precisely the same with any in which the professional responsibility of an architect, a sculptor, a painter, a lawyer, or a physician is involved. Nor, when we have been employed have we, in thirty years ever failed to offer our resignation when it had become demonstrable that the trustees or commissioners of a park on which we were engaged took a different view in this respect from that which we have thus presented. We have four times resigned our position under such circumstances, and if we have earned a reputation for a successful performance of our professional duties, as your call upon us may be thought to indicate that you believe, it is largely because we have thus refused to allow ourselves to be made responsible before the public for work the character of which was to be determined by men not professionally qualified to determine it.[15]

If the people of Cincinnati are dissatisfied with the result of the money spent in their behalf by your predecessors, the reason they are so may be that a view of the duties of those who have been trustees for them has been taken as differing from that usually taken in business affairs of a corresponding character in commercial life. It seems to us not improbable that this is the case from evidence which the public grounds of the city present that they have been operated upon with inconstant, incoherent, inharmonious and disunited motives; with motives, also, to some extent, such as no honest man of our profession would have entertained. There are many fine things in your parks. There are many examples of good work, but, from our professional point of view, these fine things do not appear to have been designed, or where they are natural, to have been made use of, as parts contributive to the working out of a fixed and legitimate common comprehensive purpose.

Why have they not?

That we may answer this question we review, with such means as we have, the history of the proceedings of which the parks of Cincinnati as we find them, are the result. At the outset of such a review, three notable circumstances are to be recognized.

First, In the near borders of Cincinnati there were, thirty years ago, more of certain natural and unsophisticated elements of beautiful sylvan scenery than in the borders of any equally large town in the country.

Second, Numbers of the citizens of Cincinnati at that time were keenly appreciative of this fact; keenly interested in the pursuit of methods whereby the value of such elements of scenery might be combined, preserved and developed. There was but one town in all the country, if there was even one, in which, more than in Cincinnati, intelligent interest in horticulture was then manifest.

Third, Twenty-two years ago, Adolph Strauch was employed to devise and supervise the carrying out of a plan for providing the future people of Cincinnati with means of counteracting the special dangers to health which attend the collection of people in large towns.[16]

For the duty to which he was called, we suppose that Mr. Strauch was better qualified by nature, by special education in the art required, and by the results of close observation of the local conditions to be dealt with than any other man in the world. As the professional advisor and chief executive agent of a corporation not of a political character, he had already produced a work which, not having the same class of ends in view, yet required the same class of materials to be dealt with, the same art to be used and the same class of processes to be followed. The result has been what was to be expected of such a man when rightly dealt with, the very finest thing of its kind in the world. It has become celebrated as such. It has been often referred to as an example and illustration as to what should be done for other communities.[17]

Birdseye View of Spring Grove Cemetery, Cincinnati, Designed by Adolph Strauch

The work is to-day being maintained, and is being carried forward and enlarged by another artist, with reverent respect for the special purposes, principles and motives of design originating with its first master, and the carrying out of which was studiously superintended by him until the day of his death.[18] To illustrate the success attained in the carrying out of Strauch's design as it has been carried out, we will mention certain circumstances. Several works have since been begun in places distant from Cincinnati with the purpose of accomplishing similar results; results that Strauch was the first man to think of attempting to attain. Again, similar works have since been entered upon in Europe. Again, views of passages of this work have been engraved, published and extensively circulated and favorably reviewed in Europe. Again, we have several times traveled a hundred miles out of our way to benefit by such means of education in our art as were to be obtained by an examination of the gradual unfolding on the ground of Strauch's design. We have repeatedly conducted students of our art to Cincinnati that they might study it. Again, when our services have been sought for designing a work with the same purpose, while Strauch lived, we have told those coming to us that they had much better take counsel with him, to whom we should be but disciples.[19]

This was the master of our art who was employed to contrive the plan of the required park system of Cincinnati.

Lately, visiting one of your public grounds, the plan of which was said to have been devised by Strauch, pains were taken by the Superintendent of the work to explain to us what ideals of scenery he supposed that Strauch, in making this plan, had had before him, and he pointed out how various things had been done with the ground and had been put upon it by which it had now become impossible to return to any such ideals. We may indicate the impression in this respect which was made upon us by saying that we suppose that now, after twenty years work and twenty years growth, it would cost more to realize what all the work of Strauch and all the work that was done in accordance with his wishes, was intended to bring about, than if not one dollar had in the meantime been spent upon the ground.

What did Strauch himself think about it? It so happens that we are able to give some slight testimony on this point from personal knowledge. On one of our visits for instruction in our art to Spring Grove, having expressed a wish to look also at Strauch's public park work, he made a reply which, while we will not attempt to quote the words of it, we well remember to have been strikingly expressive of impatient repudiation of responsibility for what was to be seen in the park properties of Cincinnati.[20]

Suppose Strauch had been treated by the Trustees of the park undertaking as he was by the Trustees of the Spring Grove undertaking? Suppose that the same respect had been paid to his special professional knowledge and rare special talent in one case that was paid in the other? Suppose the same business methods had been followed in carrying out his design in one case as in the other? Suppose, in short, that Strauch had been given such professional control of the work as was necessary to make him professionally responsible for the results to be attained, as the architect of a bank is made so responsible by its Directors, do the people of Cincinnati doubt that they would now already be getting much greater dividends from their investments in parks than, as things are, there is any prospect will ever be realized?

It is our opinion that had Strauch been given the problem of a park as we have been stating it, and had he selected what he thought the best ground near Cincinnati with a view to the solution of that problem, and had he been allowed to direct the work with the same freedom to follow his own judgment in details, under the general control of a committee with a single eye to the proper end of the enterprise, Cincinnati would be provided with the best public park system in America, and the cost of it would have been less than has been the cost of the parks as they now are.

As to what should be done with your parks as they now are, you need no advice from us other than that which we have in effect thus given. It is hardly possible that good work in park making can be done prudently, at reasonable cost, or with respectable results even at extravagant cost, upon plans that are held easily subject to adjustments, amendments and interpolations from year to year. It would be much more feasible to build a good courthouse or prison economically under such conditions than to form good parks. This for the reason that the value of parks depends mainly on the relations of every other element of value in them to conditions of natural growth. Plans in the carrying out of which progress has once been made cannot be changed; processes of growth cannot be interrupted, without a spendthrift waste of results previously gained.

The first requirement of sound park administration, then, is a fixed design; the second is a steady pursuance of that design with a well-organized and well-trained working force, efficiently commanded and disciplined. Payment for such work as you have now going on should plainly be charged in large part to the charities of the city. Not much of it can justly be regarded as a part of the cost of your park system.

We recognize that the counsel which we have thus offered is little more than that the real object for which a park commission exists should be more clearly recognized than it seems to have been by some of your predecessors, and that ordinary business principles should be applied to the pursuit of this object. If such counsel seems superfluous, we can only apologize for giving it by saying that what is faulty in your park system has seemed to us to be the result of failures to apply common sense in this respect, rather than to lack of sound professional advise such as you may have expected to obtain from us.

If your present Superintendent is competent for the duties you are putting upon him, and we have no reason to doubt that he is; if your engineer is a competent advisor in respect to the strictly engineering problems that are presented in your park works, and we have no reason to doubt that he is; common business sagacity will lead you to trust much to the discretion of these gentlemen, as the Trustees of Spring Grove at a corresponding stage of their enterprise trusted much to the discretion of Strauch. If they fail to bring about good results, you should dismiss them and look for others, but while they remain, you should take care that their proper professional and official responsibilities are clearly established and that they have no excuse for not meeting them, especially no excuse of that class of excuses commonly referred to in political affairs as "influences," of which the effect always is a practical dissipation of official responsibility.

On our arrival in Cincinnati, we were led to suppose that our advice would be asked with reference to the selection of a site for a park of a more suburban character than any you are now preparing. Afterwards, any intention there had been to consult us in this respect seemed to be abandoned. It may, nevertheless, be within our duty to say that, judging from general experience elsewhere, regard for public health in the future of your city and for its attractiveness as a place of residence, will soon lead a park to be desired of a different scope and character from any of those you are now preparing; that within moderate distance of your present center of population there are yet sites unoccupied by expensive improvements, or cut up by public roads, which are adapted to provide a degree of sequestered rural and sylvan scenery of very much greater value with reference to the essential purposes of a park than any which you now possess. We should not think it our duty to make even this suggestion were it not for the fact that we have never been asked to advise as to the selection of a site for a public suburban ground for the healthful recreation of the people of a city, without hearing that if this duty had been set about a few years sooner, a much better place for the purpose could have been obtained than any that remained available; and that such a place could then have been obtained at comparatively small cost. It is a prudent custom to obtain and hold in reserve such bodies of land in the outer suburbs of a city with reference to its future needs. London has lately acquired 6000 acres of land for this purpose; New York 4000; Boston is now acquiring 10,000. Neither city is spending anything for permanent improvements upon these reservations. They are held simply in order that their value for future use may not be destroyed, and that the cost of obtaining them may not be excessively increased.

Respectfully,

Olmsted, Olmsted & Eliot
Landscape Architects.

The original of this report is a typed draft signed by Olmsted for the firm in the Olmsted Papers. Heavily edited excerpts from the report were published in the *Annual Report of the Park Department of the City of Cincinnati. 1894* (Cincinnati, Ohio, 1895), pages 14–16.

In December 1893 the Cincinnati park board invited Olmsted to Cincinnati to inspect its parks and give advice on the improvement and possible expansion of the city's parks. Olmsted and an assistant, Edward Sturgis, arrived on January 1, 1894, and visited the parks on January 2 and 3. Olmsted met with the park board on the afternoon of January 2 and requested clarification of the reason he had been invited to Cincinnati. The board answered that it originally had wanted him to lay out some new parks for the city; but after meeting with a group of leading citizens who believed that it would be unwise for the city to go further into debt to buy park lands, the board instead requested him to provide advice on improving the existing parks.

On January 17, 1894, Senator Frank Kirchner, a Cincinnati contractor and owner of a steam roller company, presented a bill before the Ohio state legislature to abolish the park board. Newspaper accounts cited irregularities with contracts, noting that the park board had authorized the purchase of pipe and a steam roller without funds being available at the time the contracts were signed to pay for the items. Kirchner's bill passed and became law on January 30 (the same day as Olmsted's report), abolishing the park board and placing the park department under control of the city's Board of Administration, a four-member, non-partisan panel appointed by the mayor and responsible for the improvement of city streets and public places. The *Cincinnati Enquirer* condemned the passage of the bill and claimed that "the abolishment of the Park Board gives the politicians who rule the city additional patronage over about 100 men."

Unfolding events in Cincinnati must have stung Olmsted. He had spent much of his professional career contending with politicians and the influence of patronage in cities for which he had designed parks. On January 25 Olmsted wrote his partner and stepson John requesting that he and Charles Eliot, the other partner in the firm, carefully read the draft of this report. Olmsted observed that it provided "a rare opportunity to say something for our faith & we should use it. If we are going to do so we should hit the enemy of our profession as hard as we know how. . . ." Olmsted also believed that this was a particularly opportune time to present such a report, because it would follow soon after a "National Conference for Good City Government," promoting the cause of city government reform, that was just ending in Philadelphia.

Upon learning that the park board had been abolished, Olmsted offered the report to Reuben H. Warder, superintendent of the city's parks, for publication. He explained that "what we want is to do the best thing we can under the circumstances for the public interests, for the spread of sound ideas, and for the good standing of our art and profession, of which we regard you as representative in the premises." There is no evidence, however, that the report was ever published in the Cincinnati newspapers as Olmsted wished (Cincinnati Park Department, *Annual Report of the Board of Park Commissioners for the Year ending December 31, 1893* [Cincinnati, Ohio], p. 19; Report of Visits, Jan. 1, 1894, E4: #212, OAR/LC; *Cincinnati Commercial Gazette*, Jan. 3, 1894, p. 8; ibid., Jan. 30, 1894, p. 8; Ohio [State], *Journal of the Senate of the State of Ohio, for the Regular Session of the Seventy-First General Assembly Commencing on Monday, January 1, 1894* [Norwalk, Ohio, 1894], p. 69; *Williams' Cincinnati Directory . . .* [Cincinnati, Ohio, 1894], p. 837; Ohio [State], *General and Local Acts Passed and Joint Resolutions Adopted by the Seventy-First General Assembly, . . . 1894* [Norwalk, Ohio, 1894], pp. 7–8; Charles Theodore Greve, *Centennial History of Cincinnati and Representative Citizens*, 2 vols. [Chicago, Ill., 1904], 1: 961; *Cincinnati Enquirer*, Jan. 30, 1894, p. 8; FLO to JCO, Jan. 25, 1894; FLO to Reuben H. Warder, Jan. 30 and Feb. 3, 1894).

1. Edward D. Bolton, a draughtsman employed by the Olmsted firm (Cynthia Zaitzevsky, *Frederick Law Olmsted and the Boston Park System* [Cambridge, Mass., 1982], p. 134; *Spencer's Brookline Directory for 1894* . . . [Brookline, Mass., 1894], p. 49).
2. Warren Henry Manning (1860–1938), horticulturist and landscape architect. Manning learned his craft working with his father, Jacob Manning, in the senior Manning's nursery in Reading, Massachusetts. He began working for the Olmsted firm in 1888. In his capacity as superintendent of planting for the firm, he oversaw the planting plans and selection of plants for over 100 of the firm's designs including the World's Columbian Exposition in Chicago and Biltmore in North Carolina. In 1896 Manning started his own practice in Cambridge, Massachusetts, completing over 1,500 designs before his death (Robin Karson, "Manning, Warren Henry," in *Pioneers of American Landscape Design*, eds. Charles A. Birnbaum and Lisa E. Crowder [Washington, D.C., 1993], pp. 82–83; William Grundmann, "Warren H. Manning," in *American Landscape Architecture: Designers and Places*, ed. William H. Tishler [Washington, DC., 1989], pp. 56–59).
3. Joseph Thomas Carew (b. 1848), businessman born in Canada and elected president of the park board on January 15, 1894 (George Mortimer Roe, *Cincinnati: The Queen City of the West* [Cincinnati, Ohio], p. 202; Report of Visits, Jan. 1, 1894, E4: #212, OAR/LC).
4. In December 1893 the Cincinnati park board invited Olmsted to visit its city parks. Olmsted and his assistant, Edward Sturgis, arrived on January 1, 1894, and visited the parks over the course of the next two days (Cincinnati Park Department, *Annual Report of the Board of Park Commissioners*, p. 19; Report of Visits, Jan. 1, 1894, E4: #212, OAR/LC).
5. At the time Olmsted wrote this report the Cincinnati park board included Joseph T. Carew, Joseph P. Carbery, C. C. Cook, H. L. Sunderbruch, and W. J. Breed (Cincinnati Park Department, *Annual Report of the Board of Park Commissioners*, p. 23).
6. Reuben Haines Warder (1843–1907), horticulturist and superintendent of the Cincinnati parks from 1893 to 1900. Warder studied and worked with his father, Dr. John Aston Warder (1812–1883), a physician turned horticulturist, at their farm in North Bend, Ohio. From 1900 until his death, Warder was superintendent of Lincoln Park in Chicago. He also served as horticultural director of the World's Columbian Exposition in 1893. Olmsted maintained a high opinion of Warder and sent him extra copies of this report, requesting that he publish it in the local newspapers. Warder probably felt that as park superintendent it would be imprudent for him to provide the local press with copies of Olmsted's report, and it was never published (Eslie Asbury, "Reuben H. Warder," unpublished paper in City of Cincinnati, Board of Park Commissioners Library, Cincinnati, Ohio, courtesy of Kurtzie Gonzales; Sherda K. Williams, "Warder, John Aston," in *Pioneers of American Landscape Design*, eds. C. A. Birnbaum and L. E. Crowder, pp. 125–26; FLO to JCO, Jan. 25, 1894; FLO to Reuben H. Warder, Feb. 3, 1894).
7. The press entourage probably included reporters from the *Cincinnati Enquirer* and the *Cincinnati Commercial Gazette*.
8. Sir William Blackstone (1723–1780), British legal authority and judge. Blackstone provided this definition of a park in his *Commentaries* on British law (*DNB*; William Blackstone, *Commentaries on the Laws of England* . . ., 4 vols. [1765–69; rpt. ed., New York, 1847], 2: 38).
9. Samuel Johnson (1709–1784), British writer and lexicographer. Johnson's complete definition of a park was "a piece of ground enclosed and stored with wild beasts of chase, which a man may have by prescription, or the king's grant" (*DNB*; Samuel Johnson, *Johnson's English Dictionary* . . . [Philadelphia, 1841], s.v. "park").

10. John Croumbie Brown (1805–1895) Scottish writer and traveler, not John Crosby
Brown (1838–1909), the New York financier. (Olmsted had provided John Crosby
Brown with plans for the grounds of his home at Orange Mountain, New Jersey, in
1873–74.) John Croumbie Brown wrote that three things were required to constitute
a park:

> 1, A grant thereof; 2, Enclosures by pale, wall, or hedge; 3, Beasts of a park, such
> as the buck, doe, &c.; and it is declared that when all the deer are destroyed, it
> shall no more be accounted a park: for a park is determined by vert, venison, and
> enclosure, and if it is determined in any of them it is a total disparking.

(John Crosby Brown to FLO, Oct. 13, 1873, and Jan. 7 and 30, 1874; *New York Times*,
June 26, 1909, p. 7; Robert Mackenzie, *John Brown of Haddington* [London, 1918],
p. 190; John Croumbie Brown, *The Forests of England and the Management of Them
in Bye-Gone Times* [Edinburgh, 1883], p. 15.)

11. Olmsted may have been referring to the "chain of parks" that ran from north to south
through the middle of Colorado. These parks were large grassy basins partially surrounded by trees and ideal for grazing and farming. Between 1889 and 1894, Olmsted
prepared plans for a subdivision, Lake Wauconda, in Perry Park, Colorado. The site of
the subdivision was similar to the "park" that Olmsted describes here (Works Progress
Administration, *Colorado: A Guide to the Highest State* [New York, 1941], p. 6; *Web-
ster's New International Dictionary of the English Language*, 2d ed. [Springfield,
Mass., 1959], s.v. "park").

12. Olmsted is possibly referring to the act that granted the Yosemite Valley and Mariposa
Big Tree Grove to the state of California in 1864. The act stipulated that "the premises
shall be held for public use, resort, and recreation." Olmsted was appointed one of
the eight commissioners to manage the land grant as provided for in the act (George
P. Sanger, ed., *Statutes at Large, Treaties, and Proclamations, of the United States of
America, from December 1863, to December 1865 . . .*, vol. 13 [Boston, 1866], chap.
184; *Papers of FLO*, 5: 512–13).

13. That is, the Board of Commissioners of the Central Park created in 1857.

14. That is, Ambrose Kingsland's promise in the 1850 mayoral campaign calling for a
New York City park. Legislation for the creation of the park was passed by the New
York state legislature in the spring of 1851 (*Papers of FLO*, 3: 91).

15. Olmsted submitted his resignation three times during the years he was employed by
commissioners of the New York City parks: January 22, 1861; May 12, 1863; and
September 17, 1873. He also resigned from work on the grounds of Stanford University in 1890 or 1891 (*Papers of FLO*, 3: 35; FLO to the Board of Commissioners of
the Central Park, Jan. 22, 1861 [*Papers of FLO*, 3: 297–319]; FLO to JO, May 22,
1863 [*Papers of FLO*, 4: 623–24]; *Papers of FLO*, 6: 45; Laura Wood Roper, *FLO: A
Biography of Frederick Law Olmsted* [Baltimore, Md., 1973], p. 414; FLO to FLO,
Jr., Aug. 1, 1894).

16. Adolph Strauch (1822–1883), landscape architect born in Prussia. Strauch traveled
to the United States in 1851. He arrived in Galveston, Texas, in November of that
year, eventually making his way north to Cincinnati in the spring of 1852. When his
steamer was delayed, forcing him to stay over, Strauch went to the home of Robert A.
Bowler, a wealthy Cincinnati businessman, whom he had met at the London Exhibition in 1851. Bowler persuaded Strauch to stay in Cincinnati and offered him a commission to design the grounds of a new home he had purchased in Clifton, an exclusive suburb of Cincinnati. For the next two years Strauch laid out the grounds of
Bowler's estate, "Mount Storm." That commission led to several others for Clifton
estates. The reputation that Strauch built for himself laying out the estates of Cincinnati's wealthy led to his being consulted regarding Spring Grove Cemetery in 1854.
The idea for a rural cemetery in Cincinnati had been started in 1844, and a plan had

been designed as early as 1848. Strauch found much that was wrong with the cemetery and the cemetery directors hired him in 1854 as a landscape gardener. In 1859 he became Spring Grove's superintendent, serving in that capacity until his death.

In 1872 due largely to the work he had done on the cemetery grounds, the Cincinnati park commission hired Strauch as superintendent of the Cincinnati parks. Strauch served in this capacity through 1875, when he resigned his position citing a lack of funds to continue planned improvements on the parks (*Cincinnati Enquirer*, April 26, 1883, p. 4; Ernest Stevens Leland, *The Pioneers of Cemetery Administration in America* [Barre, Vt., 1941], s.v. "Strauch, Adolph"; David Charles Sloane, *The Last Great Necessity: Cemeteries in American History* [Baltimore, Md., 1991], p. 100; Geoffrey J. Giglierano and Deborah A. Overmyer, *The Bicentennial Guide to Greater Cincinnati* [Cincinnati, Ohio, 1988], pp. 214, 227, 440; Adolph Strauch to the Board of Park Commissioners, Jan. 1, 1873; ibid., Jan. 1, 1876 [typed copies of the reports are in the Olmsted Papers]).

17. Adolph Strauch is considered by some to be the founder of the modern cemetery. At Spring Grove, he found the cemetery to be overly crowded with enclosures, multiple and gaudy monuments, excessive plantings, and crisscrossed with numerous avenues and pathways. In an effort to open up the grounds and provide for enhanced vistas, better light, and a more pastoral effect, he introduced what became known as the "lawn system" to Spring Grove Cemetery. With the full support of the cemetery's board of directors, Strauch was able to remove fences, hedges, and other enclosures and eliminate several drives. In addition, he urged lot owners to limit monuments to one monument for each family. By 1875 he noted that "the Lawn system is beginning to grow in favor with the people altho' they do make considerable opposition at first." Strauch's intent was to take control of the cemetery away from individual lot holders and place it in the hands of the cemetery staff. He wanted a more uniform appearance and one that was based on a coherent design. Over time, Strauch's ideas were accepted and adopted in other cemeteries in the United States (Adolph Strauch, *Spring Grove Cemetery: Its History and Improvements* ... [Cincinnati, Ohio, 1869], pp. 12, 14, 66; D. C. Sloane, *Last Great Necessity*, pp. 100–9; Adolph Strauch to FLO, March 17, 1875).

18. William Salway (1841–1925), English horticulturist and engineer. Salway came to the United States in 1867 at the behest of Charles Butler, a New York merchant, who wanted Salway to do some special work on the grounds of his estate. Salway began to make a reputation for himself, and within two years he was invited to become superintendent of Cedar Hill Cemetery in Hartford, Connecticut. He served as superintendent of Cedar Hill until May of 1883, when he was invited by the Spring Grove Cemetery board of directors to replace the recently deceased Adolph Strauch. Salway remained as superintendent of Spring Grove until his death (E. S. Leland, *Pioneers of Cemetery Administration*, s.v. "Salway, William").

19. In February 1875 William Robinson, the English landscape artist, wrote to Olmsted requesting photographs or illustrations of American cemeteries. He mentioned Spring Grove specifically and stated that he understood the cemetery was "very well arranged." Olmsted in turn wrote to Strauch requesting photographs and reports regarding Spring Grove. He noted that "I know of no cemetery in the country in which there are any material effects of landscape gardening, properly so called, except at Spring Grove ..." Strauch sent the material and Olmsted forwarded it to Robinson, who used the photographs in a book entitled, *God's Acre Beautiful; or, The Cemeteries of the Future*, published in 1880 (William Robinson to FLO, Feb. 21, 1875; FLO to Adolph Strauch, March 12, 1875; Adolph Strauch to FLO, March 17, 1875; FLO to William Robinson, March 20–30, 1875; William Robinson, *God's Acre Beautiful; or, The Cemeteries of the Future* [London, 1880], pp. 62–65).

20. The editors can find no surviving evidence of an Olmsted meeting with Adolph

Strauch. Strauch's annual reports to the park commissioners do indicate his unhappiness with the board's lack of coherent plans for park improvements. Strauch noted its lack of foresight in purchasing additional lands for some of the parks as well as its insistence on subordinating the parkland's natural beauty by introducing artificial improvements and "fanciful ornamentations" (Adolph Strauch to the Board of Park Commissioners, Jan. 1, 1873; ibid., Jan. 1, 1874; ibid., Jan. 1, 1875; ibid., Jan. 1, 1876 [typed copies of the reports are in the Olmsted Papers]).

LIST OF TEXTUAL
ALTERATIONS

Each entry in the list gives the page and line number of the altered text, followed by the original form of the text. For documents beginning after the first line of a page, lines are counted from the addressee line or from the first line of the title of the document. Alterations of text in the endnotes of a document are identified by page, note, and line number.

PRELIMINARY REPORT TO THE COMMISSIONERS FOR LAYING OUT A PARK IN BROOKLYN, NEW YORK, JANUARY 24, 1866

87: 30	result that	103: 20	necessary, for
89: 25–26	misapprehension in	103: 41	payers through
89: 26	judgment generally		

REPORT TO THE BROOKLYN PARK COMMISSION, JANUARY 1, 1868

114: 17	condition it	123: 17	puddle through
114: 27	offers this	124: 30	although of
115: 9	sanitary recreative	124: 30	years experts
115: 21–22	public they	129: 12	men while
115: 27	line, and	129: 13	disease are
118: 9	others who	129: 14	happiness and
122: 11	them: the	129: 32	comfort-pleasure,
122: 34	London and	130: 39	introduction but
122: 36	entertained it	138: 27	increase he
123: 7	towns and	138: 28	calibre ultimately
123: 8	established it	138: 32	it he
123: 10	requirement we	140: 37	"It

ADDRESS TO THE PROSPECT PARK SCIENTIFIC ASSOCIATION, MAY 1868

147: 3   treatᵗ
147: 4   refce
147: 4   pk
147: 4   ppss
147: 7   espclly
147: 8   chfly
147: 27   business There
147: 36   slow perhaps
148: 3–4   water-works bridges
148: 6   insufficᵗ
148: 6   recreation so
148: 7   betwn
148: 8   recn
148: 15   consolidated The
148: 16   recreation certainly
148: 42   wh.
149: 42   prefᵈ
151: 13   pleast
151: 13   pleast

151: 24   sun easy
151: 35   parks this
152: 12   appld
152: 13   apᵈ
152: 14   grace
152: 24   us we
152: 31   simplest purest
153: 31   which using
153: 32   noun is
153: 36   park are
154: 1   and
154: 25   over Among
154: 25   such, conditions
154: 33   landscape the
154: 34   express the
154: 41–42   obscurity that
155: 14   nothing, — not
156: n. 5, l. 6   difft
157: n. 10, l. 6 noun. that

TO WILLIAM EDWARD DORSHEIMER, OCTOBER 1, 1868

158: 28   judment
160: 15   an
160: 32   In as-much

160: 35   in-as-much
161: 35   enevitably
162: 43   might be here

"REPORT ACCOMPANYING PLAN FOR LAYING OUT THE SOUTH PARK," MARCH 1871

208: 39   entire
216: 27   so, mere

222: 43   streets.)
230: 5   made though

"GENERAL ORDER FOR THE ORGANIZATION AND ROUTINE OF DUTY OF THE KEEPERS' SERVICE OF THE CENTRAL PARK," MARCH 31, 1873

285: 34   2:5

300: 15   crowded the

"PARK," FROM THE AMERICAN CYCLOPEDIA, 1875

311: 11   opened the

"MOUNT ROYAL. MONTREAL," JUNE 1881

369: 27   what that
369: 28   use, nature

413: n. 25, l. 7 &c. bid

"PAPER ON THE BACK BAY PROBLEM AND ITS SOLUTION," APRIL 2, 1886

440: 21   personal egotistical
440: 30   scheme the
440: 31   attention and
440: 32   demand was
441: 7   shape the
441: 18   possible consequently
441: 26   Commissioners If
441: 26   over a
441: 29   sought the

441: 36   pressed told
442: 3   I
442: 3   not,
442: 3   answered, the
442: 10–11   him. They
442: 11   answered. "That
442: 15   said "I
442: 17   years, I
442: 29   said. "I

442: 30   chosen and
442: 34–35   him." This
442: 40   possession there
443: 5   flowed and
443: 6   wind a
443: 8   tide the
443: 11   territory and
443: 23   to of
443: 27   necessity and
443: 28   quarter it
443: 38   realized the
443: 41   and so
444: 1   Can
444: 1–2   basin? Answer,
444: 2   yes,
444: 2   sewers.
444: 3   But
444: 5–6   it? Answer,
444: 6   Yes
444: 7   basin.
444: 8   That
444: 8   case can
444: 9–10   sweet? Answer,
444: 10   yes,
444: 11   stagnation.
444: 12   But
444: 13   walls will
444: 15–16   unpleasant? Answer,
444: 16   It
444: 16   otherwise.
444: 17   Sloping
444: 18–19   them. Ans.
444: 19   The
444: 25   stone.
444: 26   Suppose
444: 27   with the
444: 27   inoffensive could
444: 29–30   Department? By
444: 31   By
444: 40   taste?
444: 41   We
444: 41   should.
444: 42   And
444: 43   masonry?

445: 1   It would.
445: 15   Roxbury a
445: 19   basin and
445: 26   taken as
445: 26   been out
445: 28   wheelway planting
445: 33–34   highways and
445: 36   flooded the
447: 2   but it
448: 1–2   rarely according
448: 2   engineers will
448: 4   provide it
448: 27   arch will
448: 28   established I
448: 31   stone should
448: 34   idea and
448: 40   color but
450: 15   bridge you
450: 22   attraction but
450: 31–32   summer and
450: 37   what
450: 38   Basin?
450: 39   We
450: 39   none.
450: 40   What
450: 41   length and
450: 42   sides?
450: 43   That
450: 43   unlikely.
450: 44   Such
452: 4   neighborhood.
452: 5   All
452: 5   improbable.
452: 6   Why
452: 8   move?
452: 9   I
452: 9   would.
452: 10   Then
452: 12   Park.
452: 13   They
452: 13   be.
452: 14   Suppose
452: 16   it.
452: 17   Agreed.

"NOTES ON THE PLAN OF FRANKLIN PARK AND RELATED MATTERS," 1886
473: 7   not all

"GENERAL PLAN FOR THE IMPROVEMENT OF THE NIAGARA RESERVATION," 1887
543: 22   that in   543: 22   sentiment measures

TO JOSEPH THOMAS CAREW, JANUARY 30, 1894
607: 6   taken differing

INDEX OF
PLANT MATERIALS

Current Latin names are given in brackets. The correct spelling of plant names misspelled by Olmsted is given in parentheses. Names of varieties and cultivars are given between single quotation marks.

Alpine plants, 224, 388, 395, 416, 417
Andromeda [*Pieris japonica*], 96
Aquatic plants, 97, 584
Arborvitae, 335
Ash [*Fraxinus*], 380
Ash, white, American [*Fraxinus americana*], 387
Aster, 268
Azalea, 96, 268, 387

Bamboo, 213
Basswood [*Tilia*], 380, 386
Birch [*Betula*], 380, 384, 385, 415
Birch, canoe [*Betula papyrifera*], 380
Birch, red [*Betula nigra*], 380
Birch, white [*Betula populifolia?*], 378
Bittersweet [*Celastrus*], 242
Bracken [*Pteridium*], 384, 492
Brake [*Pteridium, Pteris*], 395
Bramble [*Rubus*], 371, 384, 395
Bramble, fragrant [*Rubus odoratus*, flowering raspberry], 380
Broad-leaved plants, 91
Bulrush [*Scirpus*], 97

Bushes, 97, 260, 377, 476, 483, 491, 562, 567, 585. *See also* Shrubs
Butternut [*Juglans cinerea*], 380

Cat-tail [*Typha*], 97
Cedars, 156
Cephalanthus [buttonbush], 268
Cherry, 380
Clethra [white alder], 268, 380
Conifers, 267, 314, 375, 378
Coppice-wood, 98
Creepers, 91, 268, 395, 557, 560
Currant, wild, 380

Dogwood [*Cornus*], 76, 242

Elm [*Ulmus*], 184, 267, 326, 379, 387, 415
Evergreens, 96, 395

Ferns, 73, 91, 97, 224, 251, 268, 300, 475, 559
Fir [*Abies*], 380, 385, 396, 415
Flags [*Acorus, Iris*], 97, 559, 585

GENERAL INDEX

Italic numbers indicate illustrations.

Baltimore, Md., 230, 427

Barillet-Deschamps, Jean-Pierre, 204

Barnum, P. T., 169

Bartholdi, Frédéric Auguste, 454; designs
Statue of Liberty, 440

Baxter, Sylvester, 45

Bay View, N.Y.: rifle range at, 588, 595

Bazalgette, Sir Joseph William, 511, 533

Beach, Alfred E., 203

Beddoe, John: "On the Physical Degeneration of Town Population," 202

Belgium, 487, 529

Belle Isle (Detroit, Mich.), 37–40, 41,
584; accessible only by water, 589; appropriations for, 425, 434, 435; bridge
for, 425; and criticism of pier and gallery for, 426, 435; construction of, 39;
FLO explains plan for, 421, 434; landscape features of, 38; plan for, 38,
420–21, 422–23, 431; and policy for,
516; "prairie" section of, 61; site of,
419; visitors to, 426; as waterside resort, 428, 595
——architectural structures in: gallery, 4,
38, 39, 40, 422–23, 424, 425–30, 432,
434, 435; pier, 4, 38, 39, 40, 422–26,
434, 435
——areas in: City Fair, 38, 39, 595; ladies'
ground, 425; match-ground, 425;
meadow, 38
——board of commissioners for, 39, 425,
434; adopt plan for park, 421; engage
FLO to lay out park, 419, 434; and
objections to park plan, 426; relations
of, with Common Council, 38, 40; relations of, with FLO, 37, 425
——circulation system of: avenue, 38, 40;
drive, 425; walk, 425
——water features of: canal, 38, 39, 40,
425, 432

Bennett, James Gordon, 26

Bentham, Jeremy, 198, 205

Berkeley, Calif., 8–9

Berlin, Germany, 13, 134, 173, 258; boulevards in, 471

Birkenhead, England, 6–7, 70, 74, 75, 76;
Abbey in, 69, 76; docks in, 74, 77;
Hamilton Square in, 76; parks and
public spaces in, 321; as a suburb of
Liverpool, 69; and Woodside ferry,
76

Birkenhead Park (Birkenhead, England),
3, 6–7, 30, 61, 62, 348; description of,

71, 73; entrance to, 70; plan of, 72;
and residential lots for, 73

Blackstone, Sir William, 600, 613

Blandford, Mass., 201–2

Board of Commissioners of the Central
Park (N.Y.C.) (1857–1870), 18–19,
239, 273, 336, 501, 522; appointed by
the governor, 195; and construction
of boulevards, 105, 111; and construction of the park, 278; creation of, 205,
601, 614; and development of Manhattan streets, 12–13, 140, 145–46,
200, 205; elimination of, 273; policies of, 264, 265, 277; relations of,
with city government, 196; relations
of, with FLO, 50

Board of Commissioners of the Department of Public Parks (N.Y.C.)
(1870–), 24; and the clearing of
undergrowth on Central Park, 268,
278–79; creation of, 239, 273; dis-
misses FLO, 348; and erection of
structures on Central Park, 266; and
newly conceived projects for Central
Park, 246, 274; policies of, during
Tweed Ring, 24, 25, 26, 27, 263; relations of, with FLO, 28; and removal
of screening woods on Central Park,
266, 278; terminates relationship
with FLO and CV, 275

Board of Commissioners of Prospect Park
(Brooklyn, N.Y.) (1860–), 106; and
laying out of Kings County streets,
142; and maintaining possession of
property east of Flatbush Avenue,
103, 105; and park keepers, 114; and
zoological garden, 109

Bogart, John, 113, 143, 530

Bolton, Edward D., 597, 613

Bonvin, Léon, 478, 527

Boston, Mass., 14, 181–82, 427, 503, 524;
advantages of, for residences, 472;
Boston Athenaeum, 524; Boston
Academy, 525; Chestnut Hill Reservoir, 471; Charles River dam, 43; disadvantages of, 474–75; Faneuil Hall,
530; fire department in, 511; flood in,
450, 458; movement for public parks
in, 17, 18, 19, 463, 467, 497, 526,
529, 530; and Muddy River, 43, 471;
Museum of Art, 524; police commission in, 511; police force in, 533–34;
politics in, 44; and Stony Brook, 450